About the cover image

Vue de San-Francisco Vista de San-Francisco

Lithographer Isador Laurent Deroy (1797–1886), working in Paris, produced many images of the United States for French audiences. They included scenes of the White House and other government buildings in Washington, D.C.; Wall Street in New York City; and natural wonders such as Niagara Falls. This lithograph shows early San Francisco on the eve of the Civil War. As a boomtown created in the chaos of the California gold rush, San Francisco was probably less tidy than it appears here. Its inhabitants were certainly more racially diverse, including Mexicans, African Americans, Hawaiians, Chileans, and other gold seekers from around the world.

Vue de San-Francisco Vista de San-Francisco. Drawing and lithography by Deroy, c. 1860. Library of Congress.

AMERICA'S HISTORY

VOLUME 1: TO 1877

AMERICA'S HISTORY

NINTH EDITION

VOLUME 1: TO 1877

Rebecca Edwards
Vassar College

Eric Hinderaker
University of Utah

Robert O. Self
Brown University

James A. Henretta
University of Maryland

bedford/st.martin's
Macmillan Learning

Boston | New York

For Bedford/St. Martin's

Vice President, Editorial, Macmillan Learning Humanities: *Edwin Hill*
Program Director for History: *Michael Rosenberg*
Senior Program Manager for History: *William J. Lombardo*
History Marketing Manager: *Melissa Rodriguez*
Director of Content Development: *Jane Knetzger*
Senior Developmental Editor: *Leah Strauss*
Senior Content Project Manager: *Gregory Erb*
Senior Workflow Project Manager: *Lisa McDowell*
Production Supervisor: *Robert Cherry*
Media Project Manager: *Tess Fletcher*
Composition: *Jouve*
Cartographer: *Mapping Specialists, Ltd.*
Photo Editor: *Sheena Goldstein*
Photo Researcher: *Naomi Kornhauser*
Permissions Editor: *Kalina Ingham*
Permissions Researcher: *Eve Lehmann*
Senior Art Director: *Anna Palchik*
Text Design: *Maureen McCutcheon*
Cover Design: *William Boardman*
Cover Art: *Vue de San-Francisco Vista de San-Francisco.* Drawing and lithography by Deroy, c. 1860.
   Library of Congress.
Printing and Binding: *LSC Communications*

Manufactured in the United States of America.

2   1   0   9   8   7
f   e   d   c   b   a

For information, write: Bedford / St. Martin's, 75 Arlington Street, Boston, MA 02116

ISBN: 978-1-319-06060-2

Acknowledgments

Acknowledgments and copyrights appear on the same page as the text and art selections they cover; these acknowledgments and copyrights constitute an extension of the copyright page.

Preface
Why This Book This Way

History classrooms present a unique dilemma. How do we offer our students a basic understanding of key events and facts while inviting them to see the past not as a rote list of names and dates but as the fascinating, conflicted prelude to their lives today? How do we teach our students to think like historians? As scholars and teachers who go into the classroom every day, the authors of *America's History* know these challenges well. We have composed the ninth edition to help instructors meet them. *America's History* has long been known for its breadth, balance, and ability to explain to students not just what happened, but *why*. The latest edition preserves and builds on those strengths.

The foundation of our approach lies in a commitment to an integrated history. *America's History* combines traditional "top down" narratives of political and economic history with "bottom up" narratives of the lived experiences of ordinary people. Our goal is to help students achieve a richer understanding of politics, diplomacy, war, economics, intellectual and cultural life, and gender, class, and race relations by exploring how developments in all these areas were interconnected. Our analysis is fueled by a passion for exploring big, consequential questions. How did a colonial slave society settled by people from four continents become a pluralist democracy? How have struggles for liberty, equality, and justice informed the American experience? To whom has the "American Dream" appealed — and who has achieved it, or experienced disillusionment or exclusion? How has the experience of war shaped American politics, society, and culture? Questions like these help students understand what's at stake as we study the past. In *America's History*, we provide an integrated historical approach and bring a dedication to *why history matters* to bear on the full sweep of America's past.

One of the most exciting developments in this edition is the attention we have devoted to fresh interpretations of the colonial, early national, and antebellum periods. Since his arrival as a new author on the eighth edition, Eric Hinderaker, an expert in Native American and early American history, has invigorated the chapters on Native, colonial European, and African societies and the revolutionary Atlantic world of the eighteenth century, bringing them in line with the most current historical scholarship. Rebecca Edwards, an expert in women's and gender history and nineteenth-century electoral politics, has done the same for the chapters covering the antebellum decades and the "long Progressive Era" of the late nineteenth and early twentieth centuries. These authors have integrated coverage of slavery and the South's economy and society into all the pre–Civil War chapters. They have also consolidated antebellum coverage, enabling teachers to move more efficiently through this material, and have updated coverage of the Civil War. Robert Self, whose work explores the relationship between urban and suburban politics, social movements, and the state, has updated the twentieth- and twenty-first-century chapters, with special attention to Chapter 30, which chronicles the extraordinary events of the most recent decades. Together, we strive to ensure that energy and creativity, as well as our wide experience in the study of history, infuse every page that follows.

In this edition, we bid a fond and deeply appreciative adieu to James Henretta, one of the original authors of *America's History* and its ballast and intellectual leader for eight editions. Professor Emeritus at the University of Maryland, and soon to be an emeritus author, James will use his retirement to pursue a variety of personal and scholarly endeavors. His influence on this book, and his name on the title page, will continue for some time, but he will no longer participate in our cycles of revision. We wish him the best and thank him for sustaining *America's History* for so many years and for his commitment to the highest standards of scholarship and prose.

In our contemporary digital world, facts and data are everywhere. What students crave is analysis. As it has since its inception, *America's History* provides students with a comprehensive explanation and interpretation of events, a guide to why history unfolded as it did and a road map for understanding the world in which we live. The core of a textbook is its narrative, and we have endeavored to make ours clear, accessible, and lively. In it, we focus not only on the marvelous diversity of peoples who came to call themselves Americans but also on the institutions that have forged a common national identity. More than ever, we daily confront the collision of our past with the demands of the future and the shrinking distance between Americans and others around the globe. To help students meet these challenges, we call attention to connections with the histories of Canada, Latin America, Europe, Africa, and Asia, drawing links between events in the United States and those elsewhere.

Of course, the contents of this book are only helpful if students read and assimilate the material before coming to class. So that students will come to class prepared, they can receive access to **LearningCurve** — an adaptive, online learning tool that helps them master content — when they purchase the **LaunchPad e-Book** (which is free when bundled with the print book). To learn more about the benefits of LearningCurve and LaunchPad, see the "Versions and Supplements" section on page xvi.

A Nine-Part Framework Highlights Key Developments

One of the greatest strengths of *America's History* is its part structure, which helps students identify the key forces and major developments that shaped each era. A four-page part opener introduces each of the nine parts, using analysis, striking images, and a detailed **thematic timeline** to orient students to major developments and themes of the period. **Thematic Understanding** questions ask students to consider periodization and make connections among chapters. By organizing U.S. history into nine distinct periods, rather than just thirty successive chapters, we encourage students to trace changes and continuities over time and to grasp connections between political, economic, social, and cultural events.

In this edition, as in earlier ones, we have refined the part structure to reflect the most up-to-date scholarship. Part 4 now focuses more tightly on the history of the emerging republic, ending with the U.S.-Mexico War rather than in 1860. Part 5 offers expanded coverage of immigration, while Part 6 gives more emphasis to economic and intellectual debates during the era of industrialization. Part 9 extends to the end of Obama's presidency and the emergence of Donald Trump, linking political upheavals in this era to earlier events and themes.

Part 1, "Transformations of North America, 1491–1700," highlights the diversity and complexity of Native Americans prior to European contact, examines the transformative impact of European intrusions and the Columbian Exchange, and emphasizes the experimental quality of colonial ventures. **Part 2, "British North America and the Atlantic World, 1607–1763,"** explains the diversification of British North America and the rise of the British Atlantic world and emphasizes the importance of contact between colonists and Native Americans and imperial rivalries among European powers. **Part 3, "Revolution and Republican Culture, 1754–1800,"** traces the rise of colonial protest against British imperial reform, outlines the ways that the American Revolution challenged the social order, and explores the processes of conquest, competition, and consolidation that followed it.

Part 4, "Overlapping Revolutions, 1800–1848," traces the transformation of the economy, society, and culture of the new nation; the creation of a democratic polity; and growing sectional divisions. **Part 5, "Consolidating a Continental Union, 1844–1877,"** covers the conflicts generated by America's empire building in the West, including sectional political struggles that led to the Civil War and national consolidation of power during and after Reconstruction. **Part 6, "Industrializing America: Upheavals and Experiments, 1877–1917,"** examines the transformations brought about by the rise of corporations and a powerhouse industrial economy; immigration and a diverse, urbanizing society; and movements for progressive reform.

Part 7, "Domestic and Global Challenges, 1890–1945," explores America's rise to world power, the cultural transformations and political conflicts of the 1920s, the Great Depression, and the creation of the New Deal welfare state. **Part 8, "The Modern State and the Age of Liberalism, 1945–1980,"** addresses the postwar period, including America's new global leadership role during the Cold War; the expansion of federal responsibility during a new "age of liberalism"; and the growth of mass consumption and the middle class. Finally, **Part 9, "Globalization and the End of the American Century, 1980 to the Present,"** discusses the conservative political ascendancy of the 1980s; the end of the Cold War and rising conflict in the Middle East; and globalization and increasing social inequality.

Helping Students Work with Primary and Secondary Sources

America's History has long emphasized primary sources. In addition to weaving lively quotations throughout the narrative, we offer students substantial excerpts from historical documents — letters, diaries, autobiographies, public testimony, and more — and numerous figures that give students practice working with data. These documents allow students to experience the past through the words and perspectives of those who lived it, to understand how historians make sense of the past using data, and to gain skill in interpreting historical evidence.

To sharpen the ability of students to think historically, and to expose them to diverse historical views, we have added a new feature in this edition, called **Interpretations**. The new **Interpretations** feature brings historical argumentation directly into each chapter. Students read short, accessible passages from two scholarly works of history that offer different interpretations of the same event or period. By examining the passages side by side, and responding to the questions we pose, students learn how historians interpret evidence, weigh facts, and arrive at their conclusions. This feature highlights how *history* is a way of thinking and analyzing, rather than an inert set of facts.

Each of the thirty chapters of *America's History* contains an **Interpretations** feature in addition to three primary source–based features, continued from the eighth edition.

Analyzing Voices, a two-page feature in each chapter, helps students learn to think critically by comparing primary source texts written or spoken from two or more perspectives. New topics include "Susanna Martin, Accused Witch," "Native Americans and European Empires," "To Secede or Not to Secede?" "The Omaha Platform, 1892," "Race and Geography in the Civil Rights Era," and "The Toll of War," about the Vietnam War.

The **America in Global Context** feature, developed for the previous edition, uses primary sources and data to situate U.S. history in a global context while giving students practice in comparison and data analysis. These features appear in every chapter on topics as diverse as the fight for women's rights in France and the United States, an examination of labor laws after emancipation in Haiti and the United States, the loss of human life in World War I, the global protests of 1968, and an analysis of the worldwide economic malaise of the 1970s.

Finally, we are excited to retain and reinvigorate a dynamic feature to aid you in teaching historical thinking skills that we developed for the eighth edition. A **Thinking Like a Historian** feature in every chapter includes five to eight brief primary sources organized around a central theme, such as "Beyond the Proclamation Line," "Making Modern Presidents," and "The Suburban Landscape of Cold War America." Students are asked to analyze the documents and complete a Putting It All Together assignment that asks them to synthesize and use the evidence to create an argument. Because we understand how important primary sources are to the study of history, we are also pleased to offer for **free**, when packaged, the companion reader, *Sources for America's History*, featuring a wealth of additional documents.

As in past editions, an outstanding **visual program** engages students' attention and gives them practice in working with visual sources. The ninth edition features over four hundred paintings, cartoons, illustrations, photographs, and charts, most of them in full color and more than a quarter new to this edition. Informative captions set the illustrations in context and provide students with background for making their own analysis of the images in the book. Keenly aware that students lack geographic literacy, we have included dozens of **maps** that show major developments in the narrative, each with a caption to help students interpret what they see.

Taken together, these documents, figures, maps, and illustrations provide instructors with a trove of teaching materials, so that *America's History* offers not only a compelling narrative, but also — right in the text — the

rich documentary materials that instructors need to bring the past alive and introduce students to historical analysis.

Helping Students Understand the Narrative

The study aids in the ninth edition have been strengthened to support students in their understanding of the material and in their development of historical thinking skills. **Identify the Big Idea** questions at the start of every chapter guide student reading and focus their attention on identifying not just what happened, but why. Chapter chronologies have been moved from the last page of the chapter to the third, to enable students to more readily grasp the major events and developments as they begin to read. A variety of learning tools from the beginning to the end of each chapter support this big idea focus. As they read, students will gain proficiency in historical thinking skills via **marginal review questions** that ask students to "Identify Causes," "Trace Change over Time," and "Understand Points of View," among other skills. New **Section Review Questions** help students articulate the main points of each section of a chapter. Where students are likely to stumble over a key concept, we boldface it in the text where it is first mentioned and provide a **glossary** that defines each term.

The Chapter Review section provides a set of **Review Questions** that restate the individual section review questions, a **Thematic Understanding** question, and **Making Connections** questions that ask students to consider broader historical issues, developments, and continuities and changes over time. **Terms to Know** provides a list of **Key Concepts and Events** and **Key People** students should know. Lastly, a **Key Turning Points** question reminds students of important events and asks them to consider periodization.

Helping Instructors Teach with Digital Resources

As noted, *America's History* is offered in Macmillan's premier learning platform, **LaunchPad**, an intuitive, interactive e-Book and course space. Free when packaged with the print text or available at a low price when used alone, LaunchPad grants students and teachers access to a wealth of online tools and resources built specifically for our text to enhance reading comprehension and promote in-depth study.

Developed with extensive feedback from history instructors and students, *LaunchPad for America's History* includes the complete narrative of the print book, the companion reader, *Sources for America's History*, and **LearningCurve**, an adaptive learning tool that is designed to get students to read before they come to class. With **new source-based questions in the test bank and in LearningCurve** and the ability to **sort test bank questions by chapter learning objectives,** instructors now have more ways to test students on their understanding of sources and narrative in the book.

This edition also includes **Guided Reading Exercises** that prompt students to be active readers of the chapter narrative and auto-graded **primary source quizzes** to test comprehension of written and visual sources. These features, plus **additional primary source documents, video sources and tools for making video assignments, map activities, flash cards,** and **customizable test banks,** make LaunchPad a great asset for any instructor who wants to enliven American history for students.

New Updates to the Narrative

In the new edition, we continue to offer instructors a bold account of U.S. history that reflects the latest, most exciting scholarship in the field. Throughout the book, we have given increased attention to political culture and political economy, including the history of capitalism, using this analysis to help students understand how society, culture, politics, and the economy informed one another.

The opening chapters incisively analyze the processes by which European colonization transformed the Western Hemisphere. They emphasize the way Native Americans shaped, and were shaped by, the contact experience — a focus that carries through the ninth edition in a continental perspective and sustained coverage of Native Americans, the environment, and the West in every era. These chapters highlight the varied and tenuous nature of experiments in colonization; in doing so, they stress the opportunity, as well as the instability and violence, inherent in the colonial enterprise. And they trace the rise of British North America, the Atlantic world, and the many revolutions — in print, consumption, and politics — that transformed the eighteenth century.

In the early-nineteenth-century chapters, coverage of the South and slavery has been integrated throughout, to give more emphasis to the economic and political clout of the "Cotton Kingdom" and its "peculiar institution." Antebellum urban culture and Irish and German immigration also get more attention. The 1850s and the secession crisis receive more extended treatment, showing students that there was no direct or inevitable path from the Kansas-Nebraska Act to war. The Civil War chapter has been extensively revised to reflect recent scholarship, balancing military and technological history with crucial diplomatic and political events, while conveying the experiences of civilians, self-liberated former slaves, refugees, and soldiers.

In the post–Civil War chapters, enhanced coverage of gender, ethnicity, and race includes greater emphasis on gay and lesbian history and Asian and Latino immigration, alongside the entire chapter devoted to the civil rights movement, a major addition to the last edition. Finally, we have kept up with recent developments with an expanded section on the Obama presidency and the election of 2016. Students keen to understand contemporary political developments will find in the post–World War II chapters a strong political and economic narrative that helps them contextualize the very recent past.

Acknowledgments

We are grateful to the following scholars and teachers who reported on their experiences with the eighth edition or reviewed features of the new edition. Their comments often challenged us to rethink or justify our interpretations and always provided a check on accuracy down to the smallest detail.

Roger Carpenter, *University of Louisiana at Monroe*
Petra DeWitt, *Missouri University of Science and Technology*
Blake Ellis, *Lone Star College–CyFair*
Roger Greenland, *Mineral Area College*
Daniel Haworth, *University of Houston–Clear Lake*
Alan Lehmann, *Blinn College*
Philbert Martin, *San Jacinto College*
Suzanne McCormack, *Community College of Rhode Island*
William Morgan, *Lone Star College–Montgomery*
Daniel Murphree, *University of Central Florida*
Manfred Silva, *El Paso Community College*
Andrew Slap, *East Tennessee State University*
Whitney Snow, *Midwestern State University*
Michael Wise, *University of North Texas*

As the authors of *America's History*, we know better than anyone else how much this book is the work of other hands and minds. We are especially grateful to Kevin B. Sheets of the State University of New York at Cortland for his peerless help in assembling the material for the new Interpretations feature. We are indebted to the team at Bedford/St. Martin's: Michael Rosenberg, William J. Lombardo, Jane Knetzger, Laura Arcari, Nathan Odell, Blythe Robbins, Leah Strauss, and Kathryn Abbott, who asked the right questions and suggested a multitude of improvements. Greg Erb did a masterful job consulting with the authors and seeing the book through the production process. Melissa Rodriguez and Janie Pierce-Bratcher in the marketing department understood how to communicate our vision to teachers; they and the members of college and high school sales forces did wonderful work in helping this edition reach the classroom. We also thank the rest of our editorial and production team for their dedicated efforts: Media Editor Tess Fletcher; Editorial Assistant Lexi DeConti; copyeditor Susan Zorn; proofreaders Deborah Heimann and Diana George; indexer Rebecca McCorkle; art researchers Naomi Kornhauser and Sheena Goldstein; and text permissions researchers Eve Lehmann and Kalina Ingham. Finally, we want to express our appreciation for the assistance of Michelle Whalen and the U.S. historians at Vassar College—Robert Brigham, Miriam Cohen, James Merrell, and Quincy Mills—for their invaluable help and advice. Many thanks to all of you for your contributions to this new edition of *America's History*.

Rebecca Edwards
Eric Hinderaker
Robert O. Self

Versions and Supplements

Adopters of *America's History* and their students have access to abundant print and digital resources and tools, the acclaimed Bedford Series in History and Culture volumes, and much more. The LaunchPad course space for *America's History* provides access to the narrative as well as a wealth of primary sources and other features, along with assignment and assessment opportunities at the ready. See below for more information, visit the book's catalog site at **macmillanlearning.com**, or contact your local Bedford/St. Martin's sales representative.

Get the Right Version for Your Class

To accommodate different course lengths and course budgets, *America's History* is available in several different versions and formats to best suit your course needs. The comprehensive *America's History* includes a full-color art program and a robust set of features. The Concise Edition also provides the full narrative, with a streamlined art and feature program, at a lower price. The Value Edition offers a trade-sized two-color option with the full narrative and selected art and maps at a steeper discount. The Value Edition is also offered at the lowest price point in loose-leaf, and all versions are available as e-Books. For the best value of all, package a new print book with LaunchPad at no additional charge to get the best each format offers — a print version for easy portability with a LaunchPad interactive e-Book and course space with LearningCurve and loads of additional assignment and assessment options.

- **Combined Volume** (Chapters 1–30): available in paperback, Concise, Value, and e-Book formats and in LaunchPad
- **Volume 1: To 1877** (Chapters 1–15): available in paperback, Concise, Value, loose-leaf, and e-Book formats and in LaunchPad
- **Volume 2: Since 1865** (Chapters 14–30): available in paperback, Concise, Value, loose-leaf, and e-Book formats and in LaunchPad

As noted below, any of these volumes can be packaged with additional titles for a discount. To get ISBNs for discount packages, visit **macmillanlearning.com** for the comprehensive version or Value Edition or contact your Bedford/St. Martin's representative.

LaunchPad Assign LaunchPad — an Assessment-Ready Interactive e-Book and Course Space

Available for discount purchase on its own or for packaging with new books at no additional charge, LaunchPad is a breakthrough solution for history courses. Intuitive and easy to use for students and instructors alike, LaunchPad is ready to use as is and can be edited, customized with your own material, and assigned quickly. *LaunchPad for America's History* includes Bedford/St. Martin's high-quality content all in one place, including the full interactive e-Book and the companion reader *Sources for America's History*, plus LearningCurve formative quizzing, guided reading activities designed to help students read actively for key concepts, autograded quizzes for each primary source, and chapter summative quizzes. Through a wealth of formative and summative assessments, including the adaptive learning program of LearningCurve (see the full description below), students gain confidence and get into their reading before class. These features, plus additional primary source documents, video sources and tools for making video assignments, map activities, flash cards, and customizable test banks, make LaunchPad an invaluable asset for any instructor.

LaunchPad easily integrates with course management systems, and with fast ways to build assignments, rearrange chapters, and add new pages, sections, or links, it lets teachers build the courses they want to teach and hold students accountable. For more information, visit **launchpadworks.com**, or to arrange a demo, contact us at **history@macmillan.com**.

Assign LearningCurve So Your Students Come to Class Prepared

Students using LaunchPad receive access to Learning-Curve for *America's History*. Assigning LearningCurve in place of reading quizzes is easy for instructors, and the reporting features help instructors track overall class trends and spot topics that are giving students trouble so they can adjust their lectures and class activities. This online learning tool is popular with students because it was designed to help them rehearse content at their own pace in a nonthreatening, gamelike environment. The feedback for wrong answers provides instructional coaching and sends students back to the book for review. Students answer as many questions as necessary to reach a target score, with repeated chances to revisit material they haven't mastered. When LearningCurve is assigned, students come to class better prepared.

iClicker, Active Learning Simplified

iClicker offers simple, flexible tools to help you give students a voice and facilitate active learning in the classroom. Students can participate with the devices they already bring to class using our iClicker Reef mobile apps (which work with smart phones, tablets, or laptops) or iClicker remotes. We've now integrated iClicker with Macmillan's LaunchPad to make it easier than ever to synchronize grades and promote engagement—both in and out of class. iClicker Reef access cards can also be packaged with LaunchPad or your textbook at a significant savings for your students. To learn more, talk to your Macmillan Learning representative or visit us at **www.iclicker.com**.

Take Advantage of Instructor Resources

Bedford/St. Martin's has developed a rich array of teaching resources for this book and for this course. They range from lecture and presentation materials and assessment tools to course management options. Most can be found in LaunchPad or can be downloaded or ordered at **macmillanlearning.com**.

Bedford Coursepack for Blackboard, Canvas, Brightspace by D2L, or Moodle. We can help you integrate our rich content into your course management system. Registered instructors can download coursepacks that include our popular free resources and book-specific content for America's History. Visit **macmillanlearning .com** to find your version or download your coursepack.

Instructor's Resource Manual. The instructor's manual offers both experienced and first-time instructors tools for presenting textbook material in engaging ways. It includes content learning objectives, annotated chapter outlines, and strategies for teaching with the textbook, plus suggestions on how to get the most out of LearningCurve and a survival guide for first-time teaching assistants.

Guide to Changing Editions. Designed to facilitate an instructor's transition from the previous edition of America's History to this edition, this guide presents an overview of major changes and revisions in each chapter.

Online Test Bank. The test bank includes a mix of fresh, carefully crafted multiple-choice, matching, short-answer, and essay questions for each chapter. Many of the multiple-choice questions feature a map, an image, or a primary source excerpt as the prompt. All questions appear in Microsoft Word format and in easy-to-use test bank software that allows instructors to add, edit, re-sequence, filter by question type or learning objective, and print questions and answers. Instructors can also export questions into a variety of course management systems. This test bank is tagged to book-specific learning outcomes and to the Texas Higher Education Coordinating Board's Student Learning Outcomes for History 1301 (U.S. History to 1877) and History 1302 (U.S. History Since 1865).

The Bedford Lecture Kit: **Lecture Outlines, Maps, and Images.** Look good and save time with *The Bedford Lecture Kit*. These presentation materials include fully customizable multimedia presentations built around chapter outlines that are embedded with maps, figures, and images from the textbook and are supplemented by detailed instructor notes on key points and concepts.

America in Motion: Video Clips for U.S. History. Set history in motion with *America in Motion*, an instructor DVD containing dozens of short digital movie files of events in twentieth-century American history. From the wreckage of the battleship *Maine* to FDR's fireside chats, to Ronald Reagan speaking before the Brandenburg Gate, *America in Motion* engages students with dynamic scenes from key events and challenges them to think critically. All files are classroom-ready, edited for brevity, and easily integrated with presentation slides or other software for electronic lectures or assignments. An accompanying guide provides each clip's historical context, ideas for use, and suggested questions.

Print, Digital, and Custom Options for More Choice and Value

For information on free packages and discounts up to 50%, visit **macmillanlearning.com**, or contact your local Bedford/St. Martin's sales representative.

NEW *Sources for America's History*, **Ninth Edition.** This primary source collection provides a revised and expanded selection of sources to accompany *America's History*, Ninth Edition. *Sources for America's History* provides a broad selection of over 225 primary source documents as well as editorial apparatus to help students understand the sources. *To support the structure of the parent text, unique document sets at the end of each part present sources that illustrate the major themes of each section.* This companion reader is an exceptional value for students and offers plenty of assignment options for instructors. Available free when packaged with the print text and included in the LaunchPad e-Book. Also available on its own as a downloadable PDF e-Book.

NEW Bedford Tutorials for History. Designed to customize textbooks with resources relevant to individual courses, this collection of brief units, each 16 pages long and loaded with examples, guides students through basic skills such as using historical evidence effectively, working with primary sources, taking effective notes, avoiding plagiarism and citing sources, and more. Up to two tutorials can be added to a Bedford/St. Martin's history survey title at no additional charge, freeing you to spend your class time focusing on content and interpretation. For more information, visit **macmillanlearning.com/historytutorials**.

NEW Bedford Document Collections for U.S. History. This source collection provides a flexible and affordable online repository of discovery-oriented primary source projects ready to assign. Each curated project — written by a historian about a favorite topic — poses a historical question and guides students step by step through analysis of primary sources. Examples include What Caused the Civil War?; The California Gold Rush: A Trans-Pacific Phenomenon; and War Stories: Black Soldiers and the Long Civil Rights Movement. For more information, visit **macmillanlearning.com**. Available free when packaged.

NEW Bedford Document Collections Custom Print Modules. Choose one or two document projects from the collection (see above) and add them in print to a Bedford/St. Martin's title, or select several to be bound together in a custom reader created specifically for your course. Either way, the modules are affordably priced. For more information, contact your Bedford/St. Martin's representative.

The Bedford Series in History and Culture. More than one hundred titles in this highly praised series combine first-rate scholarship, historical narrative, and important primary documents for undergraduate courses. Each book is brief, inexpensive, and focused on a specific topic or period. Revisions of several best-selling titles, such as *The Cherokee Removal: A Brief History with Documents* by Theda Perdue; *Narrative of the Life of Frederick Douglass*, edited by David Blight; and *The Triangle Fire: A Brief History with Documents* by Jo Ann Argersinger, are now available. For a complete list of titles, visit **macmillanlearning.com**. Package discounts are available.

Rand McNally Atlas of American History. This collection of more than eighty full-color maps illustrates key events and eras from early exploration, settlement, expansion, and immigration to U.S. involvement in wars abroad and on U.S. soil. Introductory pages for each section include a brief overview, timelines, graphs, and photos to quickly establish a historical context. Free when packaged.

The Bedford Glossary for U.S. History. This handy supplement for the survey course gives students historically contextualized definitions for hundreds of terms — from *abolitionism* to *zoot suit* — that they will encounter in lectures, reading, and exams. Free when packaged.

Trade Books. Titles published by sister companies Hill and Wang; Farrar, Straus and Giroux; Henry Holt and Company; St. Martin's Press; Picador; and Palgrave Macmillan are available at a 50% discount when packaged with Bedford/St. Martin's textbooks. For more information, visit **macmillanlearning.com/tradeup**.

A Pocket Guide to Writing in History. Updated to reflect changes made in the 2017 *Chicago Manual of Style* revision, this portable and affordable reference tool by Mary Lynn Rampolla provides reading, writing, and research advice useful to students in all history courses. Concise yet comprehensive advice on approaching typical history assignments, developing critical reading skills, writing effective history papers, conducting research, using and documenting sources, and avoiding plagiarism — enhanced with practical tips and examples throughout — has made this slim reference a best-seller. Package discounts are available.

A Student's Guide to History. This complete guide to success in any history course provides the practical help students need to be successful. In addition to introducing students to the nature of the discipline, author Jules Benjamin teaches a wide range of skills, from preparing for exams to approaching common writing assignments, and explains the research and documentation process with plentiful examples. Package discounts are available.

Going to the Source: The Bedford Reader in American History. Developed by Victoria Bissell Brown and Timothy J. Shannon, this reader combines a rich diversity of primary and secondary sources with in-depth instructions for how to use each type of source. Mirroring the chronology of the U.S. history survey, each of the main chapters familiarizes students with a single type of source — from personal letters to political cartoons — while focusing on an important historical episode such as the Cherokee Removal or the 1894 Pullman Strike. The reader's wide variety of chapter topics and sources provokes students' interest as it teaches them the skills they need to successfully interrogate historical sources. Package discounts are available.

America Firsthand. With its distinctive focus on first-person accounts from ordinary people, this primary documents reader by Anthony Marcus, John M. Giggie, and David Burner offers a remarkable range of perspectives on America's history from those who lived it. Popular Points of View sections expose students to different perspectives on a specific event or topic. Package discounts are available.

Brief Contents

Contents

PART 1 Transformations of North America, 1491–1700   2

CHAPTER 1
Colliding Worlds, 1491–1600   6

How did the political, economic, and religious systems of Native Americans, Europeans, and Africans compare, and how did things change as a result of contacts among them?

Private Collection/Bridgeman Images.

CHAPTER 2
American Experiments, 1521–1700   38

In what ways did European migrants transfer familiar patterns and institutions to their colonies in the Americas, and in what ways did they create new American worlds? How did Native Americans adapt to the growing presence of Europeans among them?

Private Collection/Peter Newark American Pictures/Bridgeman Images.

CHAPTER 7
Hammering Out a Federal Republic,
1787–1820 *202*

What was required to make the United States a viable independent republic, and how did debates over the Constitution shape relations between the national government and the states?

Courtesy of the John Carter Brown Library at Brown University.

Maps, Figures, and Tables

Special Features

AMERICA'S HISTORY

Transformations of North America
1491–1700

Each of the nine parts in *America's History* covers a particular period of time. The choice of beginning and ending dates is called *periodization*: the process of deciding how to break down history into pieces with coherent themes. Throughout this book, each choice of periodization represents a form of historical argument, and we'll explain and explore each periodization choice as we go.

Part 1 of *America's History* is about collisions and experiments. Our choice to begin in 1491 is symbolic: it represents the moment before Columbus's first voyage in 1492 bridged the Atlantic Ocean. At this time North America, Europe, and Africa were home to complex societies with distinctive cultures. But their histories were about to collide, bringing vast changes to all three continents. Sustained contact among Native Americans, Europeans, and Africans was one of the most momentous developments in world history.

No one knew what European colonies in the Americas would be like. Only by experimenting did new societies gradually emerge. These experiments were neither easy nor peaceful. Warfare, mass enslavement, death, and destruction lay at the heart of colonial enterprise. Native Americans, Europeans, and Africans often clashed violently as they struggled to control their fates.

But colonies also created opportunities for new societies to flourish. Across two centuries, five European nations undertook colonial experiments in dozens of places. Some failed miserably; some prospered beyond anyone's imagining. We bring Part 1 to a close in 1700, when the first fruits of these experiments were clear, though colonial societies remained insecure and unstable. Would other concluding dates be possible for this part — for example, 1607? Yes, but to our minds, it's best to consider the early decades of British and French colonization — 1607 to 1700 — in tandem with a deep exploration of precontact Native American and African societies. Chapters 1 and 2 address three main developments that are central to this period: ▶

Native American Diversity and Complexity

Native American societies ranged from vast, complex imperial states to small kin-based bands of hunters and gatherers: a spectrum much too broad for the familiar term *tribe* to cover. Native Americans' economic and social systems were adapted to the ecosystems they inhabited. Many were productive farmers, and some hunted bison and deer, while others were expert salmon fishermen who plied coastal waters in large oceangoing boats. Native American religions and cultures also differed, though many had broad characteristics in common.

These variations in Native American societies shaped colonial enterprise. Europeans conquered and co-opted the Native American empires in Mexico and the Andes with relative ease, but smaller societies were harder to exploit. Mobile hunter-gatherers were especially formidable opponents of colonial expansion.

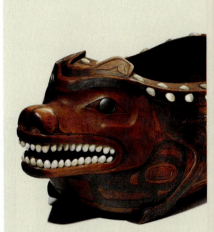

National Museum of the American Indian, Smithsonian Institution 9/7990.

The Columbian Exchange

European colonization triggered a series of sweeping changes that historians have labeled the Columbian Exchange. Plants, animals, and germs crossed the Atlantic as well as people. European grains and weeds were carried westward, while American foods like potatoes and maize (corn) transformed diets in Europe and Asia. Native Americans had domesticated very few animals; the Columbian Exchange introduced many new creatures to the American landscape. Germs also made the voyage, especially deadly pathogens like smallpox, influenza, and bubonic plague, which took an enormous toll. Having lost on average 90 percent of their populations from disease over the first century of contact, Native American societies were forced to cope with European and African newcomers in a weakened and vulnerable state.

Inanimate materials crossed oceans as well: enough gold and silver traveled from the Americas to Europe and Asia to transform the world's economies, intensifying competition and empire building in Europe.

Sarin Images/Granger, NYC.

Experimentation and Transformation

The collisions of American, European, and African worlds challenged the beliefs and practices of all three groups. Colonization was, above all, a long and tortured process of experimentation. Over time, Europeans carved out three distinct types of colonies in the Americas. Where Native American societies were organized into densely settled empires, Europeans conquered the ruling class and established tribute-based empires of their own. In tropical and subtropical settings, colonizers created plantation societies that demanded large, imported labor forces — a need that was met through the African slave trade. And in temperate regions, colonists came in large numbers hoping to create societies similar to the ones they knew in Europe.

Everywhere, core beliefs were shaken by contact with radically unfamiliar peoples. Native Americans and Africans struggled to maintain autonomy, while Europeans labored to understand — and profit from — their relations with nonwhite peoples. These transformations are the subject of Part 1.

Library of Congress.

Transformations of North America 1491–1700

Thematic Understanding

This timeline arranges some of the important events of this period into themes. Look at the entries for "Culture and Society" from 1450 to 1700. How did the Protestant Reformation and the response of the Catholic Church influence the colonization of the Americas in these years? In the realm of "Work, Exchange, and Technology," how did colonial economies evolve, and what roles did Native American and African labor play in them? ▶

	AMERICAN AND NATIONAL IDENTITY	POLITICS AND POWER	WORK, EXCHANGE, AND TECHNOLOGY	
1450	• Castile and Aragon join to create Spain; the Inquisition helps create a sense of a Spanish identity • John Calvin establishes a Protestant commonwealth in Geneva, Switzerland	• Rise of monarchical nation-states in Europe • Aztecs and Incas consolidate their empires • Probable founding of the Iroquois Confederacy • Rise of the Songhai Empire in Africa	• Diversified economies of Native America • Rise of the Ottoman Empire blocks Asian trading routes of the Italian city-states • Europeans fish off North American coast • Portuguese traders explore African coast	
1550	• English conquest and persecution of native Irish • Growing Protestant movement in England	• Elizabeth's "sea dogs" plague Spanish shipping • English monarchs adopt mercantilist policies • Defeat of the Spanish Armada (1588)	• Growth of the outwork system in English textile industry • Spanish *encomienda* system organizes native labor in Mexico • Inca *mita* system is co-opted by the Spanish in the Andes	
1600	• Pilgrims and Puritans seek to create godly commonwealths • Powhatan and Virginia Company representatives attempt to extract tribute from each other	• James I claims divine right to rule England • Virginia's House of Burgesses (1619) • English Puritan Revolution • Native Americans rise up against English colonists in Virginia (1620s and 1640s) and New England (1630s) • Restoration of the English crown (1660) • English conquer New Netherland (1664) • Native American revolts against colonial authority in New England (1670s) and New Mexico (1680s) • Bacon's Rebellion in Virginia (1675–1676)	• First staple exports from the English mainland colonies: furs and tobacco • Subsistence farms in New England • Transition to sugar plantation system in the Caribbean islands	
1700	• Social mobility for Africans ends with collapse of tobacco trade and increased power of gentry		• Tobacco trade stagnates • Maturing yeoman economy and emerging Atlantic trade in New England	

CULTURE AND SOCIETY	MIGRATION AND SETTLEMENT	GEOGRAPHY AND THE ENVIRONMENT	AMERICA IN THE WORLD	
• Protestant Reformation (1517) sparks century of religious warfare • Henry VIII creates Church of England (1534) • Founding of Jesuit order (1540)	• Christopher Columbus explores the Bahamas and West Indies (1492–1504) • Pedro Alvares Cabral makes landfall in Brazil (1500) • Spanish conquest of Mexico and Peru (1519–1535)	• Native American burning practices alter North American landscapes • Martellus map underestimates distance from Europe to Asia (1489) • Yellow fever, malaria, and dysentery help keep European traders from African interior • Columbian Exchange begins to transform global ecology	• Amerigo Vespucci gives America its name • Spain and Portugal begin to tap American resources	**1450**
• Philip II defends the Roman Catholic Church against Protestantism • Elizabeth I adopts Protestant Book of Common Prayer (1559)	• Castilians and Africans arrive in Spanish America in large numbers • English colonies in Newfoundland, Maine, and Roanoke fail	• Plantation complex brings sugarcane agriculture to the Americas • Steep Native American population decline in Hispaniola, Mesoamerica, and the Andes	• Protestant nations challenge Catholic control of the Americas • American gold and silver flow to Europe and Asia	**1550**
• Persecuted English Puritans and Catholics migrate to America • Established churches set up in Puritan New England and Anglican Virginia • Dissenters settle in Rhode Island • Metacom's War in New England (1675–1676) • Bacon's Rebellion calls for removal of Indians and end of elite rule • Salem witchcraft crisis (1692)	• First set of Anglo-Indian wars • African servitude begins in Virginia (1619) • Caribbean islands move from servitude to slavery • Growing gentry immigration to Virginia • White indentured servitude shapes Chesapeake society • Africans defined as property rather than people in the Chesapeake	• Chesapeake colonists suffer from unbalanced sex ratios and subtropical illnesses • New England colonists benefit from balanced sex ratios and healthy climate • Native American burning practices decline in the eastern woodlands	• Opportunities for trade and settlement in America attract European investment • American colonies become a prime destination for bound labor • England's American colonies become a destination for free migrants	**1600**
	• Three types of colonies formed in America: tribute, plantation, and neo-European	• French merchants found New Orleans		**1700**

1

Colliding Worlds
1491–1600

In April 1493, a Genoese sailor of humble origins appeared at the court of Queen Isabella of Castile and King Ferdinand of Aragon along with six Caribbean natives, numerous colorful parrots, and "samples of finest gold, and many other things never before seen or heard tell of in Spain." The sailor was Christopher Columbus, just returned from his first voyage into the Atlantic. He and his party entered Barcelona's fortress in a solemn procession. The monarchs stood to greet Columbus; he knelt to kiss their hands. They talked for an hour and then adjourned to the royal chapel for a ceremony of thanksgiving. Columbus, now bearing the official title *Admiral of the Ocean Sea*, remained at court for more than a month. The highlight of his stay was the baptism of the six natives, whom Columbus called Indians because he mistakenly believed he had sailed westward all the way to Asia.

•

In the spring of 1540, the Spanish explorer Hernando de Soto met the Lady of Cofachiqui, ruler of a large Native American province in present-day South Carolina. Though an epidemic had carried away many of her people, the lady of the province offered the Spanish expedition as much corn, and as many pearls, as it could carry. As she spoke to de Soto, she unwound "a great rope of pearls as large as hazelnuts" and handed them to the Spaniard; in return he gave her a gold ring set with a ruby. De Soto and his men then visited the temples of Cofachiqui, which were guarded by carved statues and held storehouses of weapons and chest upon chest of pearls. After loading their horses with corn and pearls, they continued on their way.

•

A Portuguese traveler named Duarte Lopez visited the African kingdom of Kongo in 1578. "The men and women are black," he reported, "some approaching olive colour, with black curly hair, and others with red. The men are of middle height, and, excepting the black skin, are like the Portuguese." The royal city of Kongo sat on a high plain that was "entirely cultivated," with a population of more than 100,000. The city included a separate commercial district, a mile around, where Portuguese traders acquired ivory, wax, honey, palm oil, and slaves from the Kongolese.

•

Three glimpses of three lost worlds. Soon these peoples would be transforming one another's societies, often through conflict and exploitation. But at the moment they first met, Europeans, Native Americans, and Africans stood on roughly equal terms. Even a hundred years after Columbus's discovery of the Americas, no one could have foreseen the shape that their interactions would take in the generations to come. To begin, we need to understand the three worlds as distinct places, each home to unique societies and cultures.

IDENTIFY THE BIG IDEA

How did the political, economic, and religious systems of Native Americans, Europeans, and Africans compare, and how did things change as a result of contacts among them?

Their greene corne

Corne newly sprong.

Their sitting at meate

The place of solemne prayer

...horse wherin the Tombe of their Herounds standeth.

SECOTON.

A Ceremony in their prayers strange iestures and songs dansing about posts carued on the topps lyke mens faces.

Village of Secoton, 1585 English colonist John White painted this view of an Algonquian village on the outer banks of present-day North Carolina. Its cluster of houses surrounded by fields of crops closely resembled European farming communities of the same era. White captured everyday details of the town's social life, including food preparation and a ceremony or celebration in progress (lower right). Private Collection/Bridgeman Images.

CHAPTER CHRONOLOGY

As you read, ask yourself why this chapter begins and ends with these dates and then identify the links among related events.

c. 13,000–3000 B.C.	▶ Asian migrants reach North America	c. 1350	▶ The Black Death sweeps Europe; Cahokia goes into rapid decline
c. 6000 B.C.	▶ Domestication of maize begins in Mesoamerica	c. 1400	▶ Songhai Empire emerges
312	▶ Roman emperor Constantine converts to Christianity	1435	▶ Portuguese trade begins along West and Central African coasts
c. 600	▶ Pueblo cultures emerge	c. 1450	▶ Founding of the Iroquois Confederacy
632	▶ Death of Muhammad	1492	▶ Christopher Columbus makes first voyage to America
632–1100	▶ Arab people adopt Islam and spread its influence	1497–1498	▶ Portugal's Vasco da Gama reaches East Africa and India
c. 800	▶ Ghana Empire emerges	1500	▶ Pedro Alvares Cabral encounters Brazil
c. 1000	▶ Irrigation developed by Hohokam, Mogollon, and Anasazi peoples	1513	▶ Juan Ponce de León explores Florida
c. 1000–1350	▶ Development of Mississippian culture	1517	▶ Martin Luther sparks Protestant Reformation
c. 1050	▶ Founding of Cahokia	1519–1521	▶ Hernán Cortés conquers Aztec Empire
1096–1291	▶ Crusades link Europe with Arab trade routes	1532–1535	▶ Francisco Pizarro vanquishes Incas
c. 1150	▶ Chaco Canyon abandoned	1536	▶ John Calvin publishes *Institutes of the Christian Religion*
c. 1200	▶ Mali Empire emerges	1540	▶ De Soto meets the Lady of Cofachiqui; founding of the Jesuit order
c. 1300–1450	▶ The Renaissance in Italy		
c. 1325	▶ Aztecs establish capital at Tenochtitlán		
1326	▶ Mansa Musa's pilgrimage to Mecca	1578	▶ Duarte Lopez visits the Kongo capital

The Native American Experience

When Europeans arrived, perhaps 60 million people occupied the Americas, 7 million of whom lived north of Mexico. In Mesoamerica (present-day Mexico and Guatemala) and the Andes, empires that rivaled the greatest civilizations in world history ruled over millions of people. At the other end of the political spectrum, **hunters and gatherers** were organized into kin-based bands. Between these extremes, **semisedentary societies** planted and tended crops in the spring and summer, fished and hunted, made war, and conducted trade. Though we often see this spectrum as a hierarchy in which the empires are most impressive and important while hunter-gatherers deserve scarcely a mention, this bias toward civilizations that left behind monumental architecture and spawned powerful ruling classes is misplaced. To be fully understood, the Americas must be treated in all their complexity, with an appreciation for their diverse societies and cultures.

The First Americans

Archaeologists believe that migrants from Asia crossed a 100-mile-wide land bridge connecting Siberia and Alaska during the last Ice Age sometime between 13,000 and 3000 B.C. and thus became the first Americans. The first wave of this migratory stream from Asia lasted from about fifteen thousand to eleven thousand years ago. Then the glaciers melted, and the rising ocean submerged the land bridge beneath the Bering Strait (Map 1.1). Around eight thousand years ago, a second movement of peoples, traveling by water across the same narrow strait, brought the ancestors of the Navajos and the Apaches to North America. The forebears of the Aleut and Inuit peoples, the "Eskimos," came in a third wave around five thousand years ago. Then, for three hundred generations, the peoples of the Western Hemisphere were largely cut off from the rest of the world.

MAP 1.1 The Ice Age and the Settling of the Americas
Some sixteen thousand years ago, a sheet of ice covered much of Europe and North America. As the ice lowered the level of the world's oceans, a broad bridge of land was created between Siberia and Alaska. Using that land bridge, hunting peoples from Asia migrated to North America as they pursued woolly mammoths and other large game animals and sought ice-free habitats. By 10,000 B.C., the descendants of these migrant peoples had moved south to present-day Florida and central Mexico. In time, they would settle as far south as the tip of South America and as far east as the Atlantic coast of North America.

Migrants moved across the continents as they hunted and gathered available resources. Most flowed southward, and the densest populations developed in central Mexico — home to some 20 million people at the time of first contact with Europeans — and the Andes Mountains, with a population of perhaps 12 million. In North America, a secondary trickle pushed to the east, across the Rockies and into the Mississippi Valley and the eastern woodlands.

Around 6000 B.C., Native peoples in present-day Mexico and Peru began raising domesticated crops. Mesoamericans cultivated maize (corn) into a nutritious plant

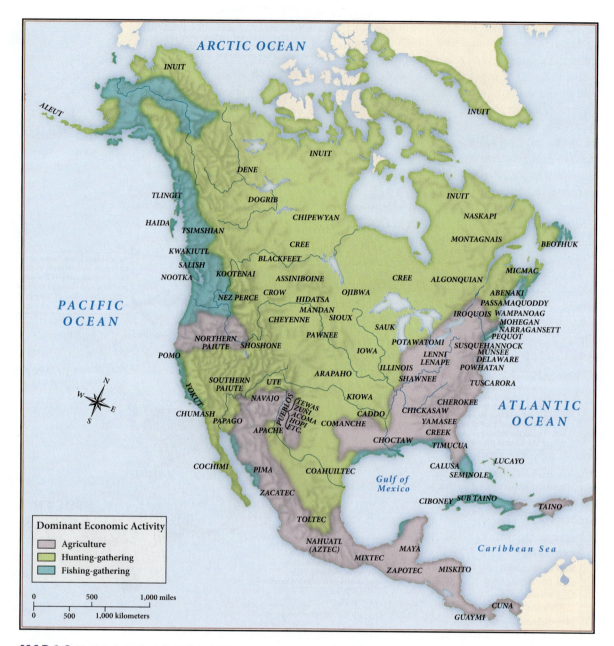

MAP 1.2 Native American Peoples, 1492
Having learned to live in many environments, Native Americans populated the entire Western Hemisphere. They created cultures that ranged from centralized empires (the Incas and Aztecs), to societies that combined farming with hunting, fishing, and gathering (the Iroquois and Algonquians), to nomadic tribes of hunter-gatherers (the Micmacs and Shoshones). The great diversity of Native American peoples — in language, tribal identity, and ways of life — and the long-standing rivalries among neighboring peoples usually prevented them from uniting to resist the European invaders.

IDENTIFY CAUSES

What factors allowed for the development of empires in central Mexico and the Andes?

with a higher yield per acre than wheat, barley, or rye, the staple cereals of Europe. In Peru they also bred the potato, a root crop of unsurpassed nutritional value. The resulting agricultural surpluses encouraged population growth and laid the foundation for wealthy, urban societies in Mexico and Peru, and later in the Mississippi Valley and the southeastern woodlands of North America (Map 1.2).

American Empires

In Mesoamerica and the Andes, the two great empires of the Americas — the Aztecs and Incas — dominated the landscape. Dense populations, productive agriculture, and an aggressive bureaucratic state were the keys to their power. Each had an impressive capital city. Tenochtitlán, established in 1325 at the center of the Aztec Empire, had at its height around 1500 a population of about 250,000, at a time when the European cities of London and Seville each had perhaps 50,000. The Aztec state controlled the fertile valleys in the highlands of Mexico, and Aztec merchants forged trading routes that crisscrossed the empire. Trade, along with tribute demanded from subject peoples (comparable to taxes in Europe), brought gold, textiles, turquoise, obsidian, tropical bird feathers, and cacao to Tenochtitlán. The Europeans who first encountered this city in 1519 marveled at its wealth and beauty. "Some of the soldiers among us who had been in many parts of the world," wrote Spanish conquistador Bernal Díaz del Castillo, "in Constantinople, and all over Italy, and in Rome, said that [they had never seen] so large a market place and so full of people, and so well regulated and arranged."

Ruled by priests and warrior-nobles, the Aztecs subjugated most of central Mexico. Captured enemies were brought to the capital, where Aztec priests brutally sacrificed thousands of them. The Aztecs believed that these ritual murders sustained the cosmos, ensuring fertile fields and the daily return of the sun.

Cuzco, the Inca capital located more than 11,000 feet above sea level, had perhaps 60,000 residents. A dense network of roads, storehouses, and administrative centers stitched together this improbable high-altitude empire, which ran down the 2,000-mile-long spine of the Andes Mountains. A king claiming divine status ruled the empire through a bureaucracy of nobles. As with the Aztecs, the empire consisted of subordinate kingdoms that had been conquered by the Incas, and tribute flowed from local centers of power to the imperial core.

Chiefdoms and Confederacies

Nothing on the scale of the Aztec and Inca empires ever developed north of Mexico, but maize agriculture spread from Mesoamerica across much of North America beginning around A.D. 800, laying a foundation for new ways of life there as well.

The Mississippi Valley   The spread of maize to the Mississippi River Valley and the Southeast around A.D. 800 led to the development of a large-scale northern Native American culture. The older Adena and Hopewell cultures had already introduced moundbuilding and distinctive pottery styles to the region. Now residents of the Mississippi River Valley experienced the greater urban density and more complex social organization that agriculture encouraged.

The city of Cahokia, in the fertile bottomlands along the Mississippi River, emerged around A.D. 1000 as the foremost center of the new **Mississippian culture**. At its peak, Cahokia had about 10,000 residents; including satellite communities, the region's population was 20,000 to 30,000. In an area of 6 square miles, archaeologists have found 120 mounds of varying size, shape, and function. Some contain extensive burials; others, known as platform mounds, were used as bases for ceremonial buildings or rulers' homes. Cahokia had a powerful ruling class and a priesthood that worshipped the sun. After peaking in size around 1350, it declined rapidly. Scholars speculate that its decline was caused by a period of ruinous warfare, made worse by environmental changes that made the site less habitable. It had been abandoned by the time Europeans arrived in the area.

Mississippian culture endured, however, and was still in evidence throughout much of the Southeast at the time of first contact with Europeans. The Lady of Cofachiqui encountered by Hernando de Soto in 1540 ruled over a Mississippian community, and others dotted the landscape between the Carolinas and the lower Mississippi River. In Florida, sixteenth-century Spanish explorers encountered the Apalachee Indians, who occupied a network of towns built around mounds and fields of maize.

Eastern Woodlands   In the **eastern woodlands**, the Mississippian-influenced peoples of the Southeast interacted with other groups, many of whom adopted maize agriculture but did not otherwise display Mississippian characteristics. **Algonquian** and **Iroquoian** speakers shared related languages and lifeways but were divided into

The Great Serpent Mound   Scholars long believed that this mound was the work of the Adena peoples (500 B.C.–A.D. 200) because of its proximity to an Adena burial site in present-day southern Ohio. Recent research places the mound at a much later date (A.D. 950–1200) and, because of the serpent imagery, ties it to the Fort Ancient culture, which is closely related to the Mississippian complex. The head of the serpent is aligned with the sunset of the summer solstice (June 20 or 21 in the Northern Hemisphere), an event of great religious significance to a sun-worshipping culture.   Richard A. Cooke/Corbis Documentary/Getty Images.

dozens of distinct societies. Most occupied villages built around fields of maize, beans, and squash during the summer months; at other times of the year, they dispersed in smaller groups to hunt, fish, and gather. Throughout the eastern woodlands, as in most of North America, women tended crops, gathered plants, and oversaw affairs within the community, while men were responsible for activities beyond it, especially hunting, fishing, and warfare.

In this densely forested region, Indians regularly set fires — in New England, twice a year, in spring and fall — to clear away underbrush, open fields, and make it easier to hunt big game. The catastrophic population decline accompanying European colonization quickly put an end to seasonal burning, but in the years before Europeans arrived in North America, bison roamed east as far as modern-day New York and Georgia. Early European colonists remarked upon landscapes that "resemble[d] a stately Parke," where men could ride among widely spaced trees on horseback and even a "large army" could pass unimpeded (America in Global Context).

Algonquian and Iroquoian peoples had no single style of political organization. Many were chiefdoms, with one individual claiming authority. Some were paramount chiefdoms, in which numerous communities with their own local chiefs banded together under a single, more powerful ruler. For example, the Powhatan Chiefdom, which dominated the Chesapeake Bay region, was made up of more than thirty subordinate chiefdoms, and some 20,000 people, when Englishmen established the colony of Virginia. Powhatan himself, according to the English colonist John Smith, was attended by "a guard of 40 or 50 of the tallest men his Country affords."

The Kincaid Site Located on the north bank of the Ohio River 140 miles from Cahokia, the Kincaid site was a Mississippian town from c. A.D. 1050 to 1450. It contains at least nineteen mounds topped by large buildings thought to have been temples or council houses. Now a state historic site in Illinois, it has been studied by anthropologists and archaeologists since the 1930s. Artist Herb Roe depicts the town as it may have looked at its peak. Herb Roe, Chromesun Productions.

Elsewhere, especially in the Mid-Atlantic region, the power of chiefs was strictly local. Along the Delaware and Hudson rivers, Lenni Lenape (or Delaware) and Munsee Indians lived in small, independent communities without overarching political organizations. Early European maps of this region show a landscape dotted with a bewildering profusion of Indian names. Colonization would soon drive many of these groups into oblivion and force survivors to coalesce into larger groups.

Some Native American groups were not chiefdoms at all but instead granted political authority to councils of sachems, or leaders. This was the case with the **Iroquois Confederacy**. Sometime shortly before the arrival of Europeans, probably around 1500, five nations occupying the region between the Hudson River and Lake Erie — the Mohawks, Oneidas, Onondagas, Cayugas, and Senecas — banded together to form the Iroquois.

These nations had been fighting among themselves for years. Then, according to Iroquois legend, a Mohawk man named Hiawatha lost his family in one of these wars. Stricken by grief, he met a spirit who taught him a series of condolence rituals. He returned to his people preaching a new gospel of peace and power, and the condolence rituals he taught became the foundation for the Iroquois Confederacy. Once bound by these rituals, the Five Nations began acting together as a political confederacy. They

Altered Landscapes

In the eastern woodlands, Native Americans set fires once or twice a year to clear underbrush and open up landscapes that would otherwise have been densely wooded. The burnings made it easier to plant corn, beans, and squash and drew big game animals into the clearings, where hunters could fell them. As European colonization displaced Indian populations, this practice ended. Some scholars have even suggested that the decline in burning caused a drop of carbon in the atmosphere large enough to account for the Little Ice Age, an episode of global cooling that lasted from about 1550 to 1850, though the claim is controversial.

THOMAS MORTON, OF THE CUSTOME IN BURNING THE COUNTRY, AND THE REASON THEREOF (1637)

The Savages are accustomed to set fire of the Country in all places where they come, and to burne it twize a yeare, viz: at the Spring, and the fall of the leafe. The reason that mooves them to doe so, is because it would other wise be so over-growne with underweedes that it would be all a coppice wood, and the people would not be able in any wise to passe through the Country out of a beaten path.

The meanes that they do it with, is with certaine minerall stones, that they carry about them in baggs made for that purpose of the skinnes of little beastes, which they convert into good lether, carrying in the same a peece of touch wood, very excellent for that purpose, of their owne making. These minerall stones they have from the Piquenteenes, (which is to the Southward of all the plantations in New England,) by trade and trafficke with those people.

The burning of the grasse destroyes the underwoods, and so scorcheth the elder trees that it shrinkes them, and hinders their grouth very much: so that hee that will looke to finde large trees and good tymber, must not depend upon the help of a woodden prospect to finde them on the upland-ground; but must seeke for them, (as I and others have done,) in the lower grounds, where the grounds are wett, when the Country is fired, by reason of the snow water that remaines there for a time, untill the Sunne by continuance of that hath exhaled the vapoures of the earth, and dried up those places where the fire, (by reason of the moisture,) can have no power to doe them any hurt: and if he would ende-voure to finde out any goodly Cedars, hee must not seeke for them on the higher grounds, but make his inquest for them in the vallies, for the Savages, by this custome of theirs, have spoiled all the rest: for this custome hath bin continued from the beginninge.

And least their firing of the Country in this manner should be an occasion of damnifying us, and indaingering our habitations, wee our selves have used carefully about the same times to observe the winds, and fire the grounds about our owne habitations; to prevent the Dammage that might happen by any neglect thereof, if the fire should come neere those howses in our absence.

For, when the fire is once kindled, it dilates and spreads it selfe as well against, as with the winde; burning continually night and day, untill a shower of raine falls to quench it.

And this custome of firing the Country is the meanes to make it passable; and by that meanes the trees growe here and there as in our parks: and makes the Country very beautifull and commodious.

SOURCE: Thomas Morton, *The New English Canaan* (Boston: John Wilson and Son, 1883 [orig. pub. 1637]), 172–173.

QUESTIONS FOR ANALYSIS

1. What benefits and dangers does Morton attribute to the practice of Indian burning? How did he and his fellow colonists respond to the practice?
2. Since Europeans did not practice widespread burning in the Indian manner, they achieved deforestation only slowly, through many years of backbreaking labor. Thinking comparatively about European and Native American approaches to landscape management, how would you assess the benefits and challenges of each approach?

made peace among themselves and became one of the most powerful Native American groups in the Northeast.

The Iroquois did not recognize chiefs; instead, councils of sachems made decisions. These were matriarchal societies, with power inherited through female lines of authority. Women were influential in local councils, though men served as sachems, made war, and conducted diplomacy.

Along the southern coast of the region that would soon be called New England, a dense network of powerful chiefdoms—including the Narragansetts, Wampanoags,

Mohegans, Pequots, and others — competed for resources and dominance. When the Dutch and English arrived, they were able to exploit these rivalries and pit Indian groups against one another. Farther north, in northern New England and much of present-day Canada, the short growing season and thin, rocky soil were inhospitable to maize agriculture. Here the Native peoples were hunters and gatherers and therefore had smaller and more mobile communities.

The Great Lakes   To the west, Algonquian-speaking peoples dominated the **Great Lakes**. The tribal groups recognized by Europeans in this region included the Ottawas, Ojibwas, and Potawatomis. But collectively they thought of themselves as a single people: the Anishinaabe. Clan identities — beaver, otter, sturgeon, deer, and others — crosscut tribal affiliations and were in some ways more fundamental. The result was a social landscape that could be bewildering to outsiders. Here lived, one French official remarked, "an infinity of undiscovered nations."

The extensive network of lakes and rivers, and the use of birchbark canoes, made Great Lakes peoples especially mobile. "They seem to have as many abodes as the year has seasons," wrote one observer. They traveled long distances to hunt and fish, to trade, or to join in important ceremonies or military alliances. Groups negotiated access to resources and travel routes. Instead of an area with clearly delineated tribal territories, it is best to imagine the Great Lakes as a porous region, where "political power and social identity took on multiple forms," as one scholar has written.

The Great Plains and Rockies   Farther west lies the vast, arid steppe region known as the **Great Plains**, which was dominated by small, dispersed groups of hunter-gatherers. The world of these Plains Indians was transformed by a European import — the horse — long before Europeans themselves arrived on the plains. Horses were introduced in the Spanish colony of New Mexico in the late sixteenth century and gradually dispersed across the plains. Bison hunters who had previously relied on stealth became much more successful on horseback.

Indians on horseback were also more formidable opponents in war than their counterparts on foot, and some Plains peoples leveraged their control of horses to gain power over their neighbors. The Comanches were a small Shoshonean band on the northern plains that migrated south in pursuit of horses. They became expert raiders, capturing people and horses alike and trading them for weapons, food, clothing, and other necessities. Eventually they controlled a vast territory. Their skill in making war on horseback transformed the Comanches from a small group to one of the region's most formidable peoples.

Similarly, horses allowed the Sioux, a confederation of seven distinct peoples who originated in present-day Minnesota, to move west and dominate a vast territory ranging from the Mississippi River to the Black Hills. The Crow Indians moved from the Missouri River to the eastern slope of the **Rocky Mountains**, where they became nomadic bison hunters. Beginning in the mid-eighteenth century, they became horse breeders and traders as well.

In some places, farming communities were embedded within the much wider territories of hunter-gatherers. The Hidatsa and Mandan Indians, for example, maintained settled agricultural villages along the Missouri River, while the more mobile Sioux dominated the region around them. Similarly, the Caddos, who lived on the edge of the southern plains, inhabited farming communities that were like islands in a sea of more mobile peoples.

Three broad swaths of Numic-speaking peoples occupied the **Great Basin** that separated the Rockies from the Sierra Mountains: Bannocks and Northern Paiutes in the north, Shoshones in the central basin, and Utes and Southern Paiutes in the south. Resources were varied and spread thin on the land. Kin-based bands traveled great distances to hunt bison along the Yellowstone River (where they shared territory with the Crows) and bighorn sheep in high altitudes, to fish for salmon, and to gather pine

Anasazi Ladle Crafted between A.D. 1300 and 1600 and found in a site in central Arizona, this Anasazi dipper was coiled and molded by hand and painted with a geometric motif. Anasazi pottery is abundant in archaeological sites, thanks in part to the Southwest's dry climate. Clay vessels and ladles helped Anasazi peoples handle water — one of their most precious resources — with care. National Museum of the American Indian, Smithsonian Institution 21/5025.

nuts when they were in season. Throughout the Great Basin, some groups adopted horses and became relatively powerful, while others remained foot-borne and impoverished in comparison with their more mobile neighbors.

The Arid Southwest In the part of North America that appears to be most hostile to agriculture — the canyon-laced country of the arid Southwest — surprisingly large farming settlements developed. Anasazi peoples were growing maize by the first century A.D., earlier than anywhere else north of Mexico, and Pueblo cultures emerged around A.D. 600. By A.D. 1000, the Hohokams, Mogollons, and Anasazis (all Pueblo peoples) had developed irrigation systems to manage scarce water, enabling them to build sizable villages and towns of adobe and rock that were often molded to sheer canyon walls. Chaco Canyon, in modern New Mexico, supported a dozen large Anasazi towns, while beyond the canyon a network of roads tied these settlements together with hundreds of small Anasazi villages.

Extended droughts and soil exhaustion caused the abandonment of Chaco Canyon and other large settlements in the Southwest after 1150, but smaller communities still dotted the landscape when the first Europeans arrived. It was the Spanish who called these groups Pueblos: *pueblo* means "town" in Spanish, and the name refers to their distinctive building style. When Europeans arrived, Pueblo peoples, including the Acomas, Zuñis, Tewas, and Hopis, were found throughout much of modern New Mexico, Arizona, and western Texas.

The Pacific Coast Hunter-gatherers inhabited the Pacific coast. Before the Spanish arrived, California was home to more than 300,000 people, subdivided into dozens of small, localized groups and speaking at least a hundred distinct languages. This diversity of languages and cultures discouraged intermarriage and kept these societies independent. Despite their differences, many groups did share common characteristics, including clearly defined social hierarchies separating elites from commoners. They gathered acorns and other nuts and seeds, caught fish and shellfish, and hunted game.

The Pacific Northwest also supported a dense population that was divided into many distinct groups who controlled small territories — both on land and on the sea — and spoke different languages. Their stratified societies were ruled by wealthy families. To maintain control of their territories, the more powerful nations, including the Chinooks, Coast Salishes, Haidas, and Tlingits, nurtured strong warrior traditions. They developed sophisticated fishing technologies and crafted oceangoing dugout canoes, made from enormous cedar trees, that ranged up to 60 feet in length. Their distinctive material culture included large longhouses that were home to dozens of people and totem poles representing clan lineages or local legends.

Chilkat Tlingit Bowl This bowl in the form of a brown bear, which dates to the mid-nineteenth century, is made of alder wood and inlaid with snail shells. The brown bear is a Tlingit clan totem. Animal-form bowls like this one, which express an affinity with nonhuman creatures, are a common feature of Tlingit culture. National Museum of the American Indian, Smithsonian Institution 9/7990.

Patterns of Trade

Expansive trade networks tied together regions and carried valuable goods hundreds and even thousands of miles. Trade goods included food and raw materials, tools, ritual artifacts, and decorative goods. Trade enriched diets, enhanced economies, and allowed the powerful to set themselves apart with luxury items.

In areas where Indians specialized in a particular economic activity, regional trade networks allowed them to share resources. Thus nomadic hunters of the southern plains, including the Navajos and Apaches, conducted annual trade fairs with Pueblo farmers, exchanging hides and meat for maize, pottery, and cotton blankets. Similar patterns of exchange occurred throughout the Great Plains, wherever hunters and farmers coexisted. In some parts of North America, a regional trade in war captives who were offered as slaves helped to sustain friendly relations among neighboring groups. One such network developed in the Upper Mississippi River basin, where Plains Indian captives were traded, or given as diplomatic gifts, to Ottawas and other Great Lakes and eastern woodlands peoples.

Rare and valuable objects traveled longer distances. Great Lakes copper, Rocky Mountain mica, jasper from Pennsylvania, obsidian from New Mexico and Wyoming, and pipestone from the Midwest have all been found in archaeological sites hundreds of miles from their points of origin. Seashells — often shaped and polished into beads and other artifacts — were highly prized and widely distributed. Grizzly bear claws and eagle feathers were valuable, high-status objects. After European contact, Indian hunters often traveled long distances to trade for cloth, iron tools, and weapons. Historians debate the extent to which such long-distance connections helped to create deeper cultural ties (Interpretations).

Powerful leaders controlled much of a community's wealth and redistributed it to prove their generosity and strengthen their authority. In small, kin-based bands, the strongest hunters possessed the most food, and sharing it was essential. In chiefdoms, rulers filled the same role, often collecting the wealth of a community and then redistributing it to their followers. Powhatan, the powerful Chesapeake Bay chief, reportedly collected nine-tenths of the produce of the communities he oversaw — "skins, beads, copper, pearls, deer, turkeys, wild beasts, and corn" — and then gave much of it back to his subordinates. His generosity was considered a mark of good leadership. In the Pacific Northwest, the Chinook word *potlatch* refers to periodic festivals in which wealthy residents gave away belongings to friends, family, and followers.

Sacred Power

Most Native North Americans were animists who believed that the natural world was suffused with spiritual power. They interpreted dreams and visions to understand the world, and their rituals appeased guardian spirits to ensure successful hunts and other forms of good fortune. Although their views were subject to countless local variations, certain patterns were widespread.

Women and men interacted differently with these spiritual forces. In farming communities, women grew crops and maintained hearth, home, and village. Native American ideas about female power linked their bodies' generative functions with the earth's fertility, and rituals like the Green Corn Ceremony — a summer ritual of purification and renewal — helped to sustain the life-giving properties of the world around them.

For men, spiritual power was invoked in hunting and war. To ensure success in hunting, men took care not to offend the spirits of the animals they killed. They performed rituals before, during, and after a hunt to acknowledge the power of those guardian spirits, and they believed that, when an animal had been killed properly, its spirit would rise from the earth unharmed. Success in hunting and prowess in war were both interpreted as signs of sacred protection and power.

Ideas about war varied widely. War could be fought for geopolitical reasons — to gain ground against an enemy — but for many groups, warfare was a crucial rite of passage for young men, and raids were conducted to allow warriors to prove themselves in battle. Motives for war could be highly personal; war was often more like a blood feud

EXPLAIN CONSEQUENCES
How did landscape, climate, and resources influence the development of Native American societies?

CONSIDER POINTS OF VIEW
How did Native Americans' conceptions of the spiritual world influence their daily lives?

How Connected Were Native American Communities Before 1492?

For a long time, American history textbooks largely ignored the thousands of years of history lived by North America's Native peoples before the arrival of Europeans. The focus of U.S. history was on the planting of European ideas and institutions in the "new world." More recently, some historians have explored the long history of the Americas that stretches back more than fifteen thousand years. Peopled by diverse groups with distinctive customs and unique cultures, America's early history defies easy categorization. In the following excerpts, historians Robert F. Berkhofer Jr. and Neal Salisbury reach different conclusions regarding the extent to which Native North American peoples interacted with each other prior to European contact.

ROBERT F. BERKHOFER JR.

SOURCE: Robert F. Berkhofer Jr., *The White Man's Indian: Images of the American Indian from Columbus to the Present* (New York: Knopf, 1978), 3.

The first residents of the Americas were by modern estimates divided into at least two thousand cultures and more societies, practiced a multiplicity of customs and lifestyles, held an enormous variety of values and beliefs, spoke numerous languages mutually unintelligible to the many speakers, and did not conceive of themselves as a single people — if they knew about each other at all.

NEAL SALISBURY

SOURCE: Neal Salisbury, "The Indians' Old World: Native Americans and the Coming of Europeans," *William and Mary Quarterly* 53 (July 1996): 444.

Given the archaeological record, North American "prehistory" can hardly be characterized as a multiplicity of discrete microhistories. Fundamental to the social and economic patterns . . . were exchanges that linked peoples across geographic, cultural, and linguistic boundaries. The effects of these links are apparent in the spread of raw materials and finished goods, of beliefs and ceremonies, and of techniques for food production and for manufacturing. . . . Exchange constitutes an important key to conceptualizing American history before Columbus.

QUESTIONS FOR ANALYSIS

1. Describe one way in which these historians disagree in their understanding of early Native American history.

2. How does each of these historians explain the diversity among Native American peoples?

3. Identify a specific passage or section from the textbook chapter that supports or challenges the arguments presented by each of these two historians.

---

between families than a contest between nations. If a community lost warriors in battle, it might retaliate by capturing or killing a like number of warriors in response — a so-called mourning war. Some captives were adopted into new communities, while others were enslaved or tortured.

> **IN YOUR OWN WORDS** What factors might best explain the variations among Native American societies and cultures?

Western Europe: The Edge of the Old World

In 1491, Western Europe lay at the far edge of the Eurasian and African continents. It had neither the powerful centralized empires nor the hunter-gatherer bands and semi-sedentary societies of the Americas. Western Europe was, instead, a patchwork of roughly equivalent kingdoms, duchies, and republics vying with one another and struggling to reach out effectively to the rest of the world. No one would have predicted that Europeans would soon become overlords of the Western Hemisphere. A thousand years after the fall of the Roman Empire, Europe's populations still relied on subsistence agriculture and were never far from the specter of famine. Moreover, around 1350, a deadly plague was introduced from Central Asia—the Black Death—that killed one-third of Europe's people. The lives of ordinary people were afflicted by poverty, disease, and uncertainty, and the future looked as difficult and dark as the past.

Hierarchy and Authority

In traditional hierarchical societies—American or European—authority came from above. In Europe, kings and princes owned vast tracts of land, forcibly conscripted men for military service, and lived off the peasantry's labor. Yet monarchs were far from supreme: local nobles also owned large estates and controlled hundreds of peasant families. Collectively, these nobles challenged royal authority with both their military power and their legislative institutions, such as the French *parlements* and the English House of Lords.

Just as kings and nobles ruled society, men governed families. These were patriarchies, in which property and social identity descended in male family lines. Rich or poor, the man was the head of the house, his power justified by the teachings of the Christian Church. As one English clergyman put it, "The woman is a weak creature not embued with like strength and constancy of mind"; law and custom "subjected her to the power of man." Once married, an Englishwoman assumed her husband's surname, submitted to his orders, and surrendered the right to her property.

Men also controlled the lives of their children, who usually worked for their father into their middle or late twenties. Then landowning peasants would give land to their sons and dowries (property or money given by a bride's family to her husband) to their daughters and choose marriage partners of appropriate wealth and status. In many regions, fathers bestowed all their land on their eldest son—a practice known as primogeniture—forcing many younger children to join the ranks of the roaming poor. Few men and even fewer women had much personal freedom.

Powerful institutions—nobility, church, and village—enforced hierarchy and offered ordinary people a measure of security in a violent and unpredictable world. Carried by migrants to America, these security-conscious institutions would shape the character of family and society well into the eighteenth century.

Peasant Society

Most Europeans were **peasants**, farmworkers who lived in small villages surrounded by fields farmed cooperatively by different families. On manorial lands, farming rights were given in exchange for labor on the lord's estate, an arrangement that turned peasants into serfs. Gradually, obligatory manorial services gave way to paying rent or, as in France, landownership. Once freed from the obligation to labor for their farming rights, European farmers began to produce surpluses and created local market economies.

As with Native Americans, the rhythm of life followed the seasons. In March, villagers began the exhausting work of plowing and then planting wheat, rye, and oats. During the spring, the men sheared wool, which the women washed and spun into yarn. In June, peasants cut hay and stored it as winter fodder for their livestock. During the summer, life was more relaxed, and families repaired their houses and barns. Fall brought the harvest, followed by solemn feasts of thanksgiving and riotous bouts of merrymaking. As winter approached, peasants slaughtered excess livestock and salted or smoked the meat. During the cold months, they threshed grain and wove textiles, visited friends and relatives, and celebrated the winter solstice or the birth of Christ. Just before the cycle began again in the spring, they held carnivals, celebrating with drink and dance the end of the long winter.

For most peasants, survival meant constant labor, and poverty corroded family relationships. Malnourished mothers fed their babies sparingly, calling them "greedy and gluttonous," and many newborn girls were "helped to die" so that their brothers would

COMPARE AND CONTRAST
In what ways were the lives of Europeans similar to and different from those of Native Americans?

have enough to eat. Half of all peasant children died before the age of twenty-one, victims of malnourishment and disease. Many peasants drew on strong religious beliefs, "counting blessings" and accepting their harsh existence. Others hoped for a better life. It was the peasants of Spain, Germany, and Britain who would supply the majority of white migrants to the Western Hemisphere.

Expanding Trade Networks

In the millennium before contact with the Americas, Western Europe was the barbarian fringe of the civilized world. In the Mediterranean basin, Arab scholars carried on the legacy of Byzantine civilization, which had preserved the achievements of the Greeks and Romans in medicine, philosophy, mathematics, astronomy, and geography, while Arab merchants controlled trade in the Mediterranean, Africa, and the Near East. This control gave them access to spices from India and silks, magnetic compasses, water-powered mills, and mechanical clocks from China.

In the twelfth century, merchants from the Italian city-states of Genoa, Florence, Pisa, and especially Venice began to push their way into the Arab-dominated trade routes of the Mediterranean. Trading in Alexandria, Beirut, and other eastern Mediterranean ports, they carried the luxuries of Asia into European markets. At its peak, Venice had a merchant fleet of more than three thousand ships. This enormously profitable commerce created wealthy merchants, bankers, and textile manufacturers who expanded trade, lent vast sums of money, and spurred technological innovation in silk and wool production.

Italian moneyed elites ruled their city-states as **republics**, states that had no prince or king but instead were governed by merchant coalitions. They celebrated civic humanism, an ideology that praised public virtue and service to the state; over time, this tradition profoundly influenced European and American conceptions of government. They sponsored great artists — Michelangelo, Leonardo da Vinci, and others — who produced an unprecedented flowering of genius. Historians have labeled the arts

Procession in St. Mark's Square in Venice, 1496 Venice was one of the world's great trading centers in the fifteenth century. Its merchant houses connected Europe to Asia and the Middle East, while its complex republican government aroused both admiration and mistrust. Here, Venetian painter Gentile Bellini (c. 1429–1507) depicts a diplomatic procession celebrating the League of Venice, a union of European states opposed to French expansion into Italy. Galleria dell 'Accademia, Venice, Italy/Giraudon/The Bridgeman Art Library.

and learning associated with this cultural transformation from 1300 to 1450 the Renaissance.

The economic revolution that began in Italy spread slowly to northern and western Europe. England's principal export was woolen cloth, which was prized in the colder parts of the continent but had less appeal in southern Europe and beyond. Northern Europe had its own trade system, controlled by an alliance of merchant communities called the Hanseatic League. Centered on the Baltic and North seas, it dealt in timber, furs, wheat and rye, honey, wax, and amber.

As trade picked up in Europe, merchants and artisans came to dominate its growing cities and towns. While the Italian city-states ruled themselves without a powerful monarch, in much of Europe the power of merchants stood in tension with that of kings and nobles. In general, the rise of commerce favored the power of kings at the expense of the landed nobility. The kings of Western Europe established royal law courts that gradually eclipsed the manorial courts controlled by nobles; they also built bureaucracies that helped them centralize power while they forged alliances with merchants and urban artisans. Monarchs allowed merchants to trade throughout their realms; granted privileges to guilds, or artisan organizations that regulated trades; and safeguarded commercial transactions, thereby encouraging domestic manufacturing and foreign trade. In return, they extracted taxes from towns and loans from merchants to support their armies and officials.

> **TRACE CHANGE OVER TIME**
> How did the growth of commerce shift the structure of power in European societies?

Myths, Religions, and Holy Warriors

The oldest European religious beliefs drew on a form of animism similar to that of Native Americans, which held that the natural world — the sun, wind, stones, animals — was animated by spiritual forces. As in North America, such beliefs led ancient European peoples to develop localized cults of knowledge and spiritual practice. Wise men and women created rituals to protect their communities, ensure abundant harvests, heal illnesses, and bring misfortunes to their enemies.

The pagan traditions of Greece and Rome overlaid animism with elaborate myths about gods interacting directly with the affairs of human beings. As the Roman Empire expanded, it built temples to its gods wherever it planted new settlements. Thus peoples throughout Europe, North Africa, and the Near East were exposed to the Roman pantheon. Soon the teachings of Christianity began to flow in these same channels.

The Rise of Christianity Christianity, which grew out of Jewish monotheism (the belief in one god), held that Jesus Christ was himself divine. As an institution, Christianity benefitted enormously from the conversion of the Roman emperor Constantine in A.D. 312. Prior to that time, Christians were an underground sect at odds with the Roman Empire. After Constantine's conversion, Christianity became Rome's official religion, temples were abandoned or remade into churches, and noblemen who hoped to retain their influence converted to the new state religion.

For centuries, the Roman Catholic Church was the great unifying institution in Western Europe. The pope in Rome headed a vast hierarchy of cardinals, bishops, and priests. Catholic theologians preserved Latin, the language of classical scholarship, and imbued kingship with divine power. Christian dogma provided a common understanding of God and human history, and the authority of the Church buttressed state institutions. Every village had a church, and holy shrines served as points of contact with the sacred world. Often those shrines had their origins in older, animist practices, now largely forgotten and replaced with Christian ritual.

Christian doctrine penetrated deeply into the everyday lives of peasants. While animist traditions held that spiritual forces were alive in the natural world, Christian priests taught that the natural world was flawed and fallen. Spiritual power came from outside nature, from a supernatural God who had sent his divine son, Jesus Christ, into the world to save humanity from its sins. The Christian Church devised a religious

The Beaune Altarpiece, c. 1445–1450 Fifteenth-century Christians understood their lives to be part of a cosmic drama. Death — and their fate in the afterlife — loomed large in their imaginations, and artists depicted their hopes and fears in vividly rendered scenes. In this massive altarpiece by Dutch painter Rogier van der Weyden, Christ sits in judgment as the world ends and the dead rise from their graves. The archangel Michael weighs the souls of the dead in a balance to determine their final fate: either eternal life with God in heaven or everlasting punishment in hell. Erich Lessing/Art Resource, NY.

calendar that transformed animist festivals into holy days. The winter solstice, which had for millennia marked the return of the sun, became the feast of Christmas.

The Church also taught that Satan, a wicked supernatural being, was constantly challenging God by tempting people to sin. People who spread heresies — doctrines that were inconsistent with the teachings of the Church — were seen as the tools of Satan, and suppressing false doctrines became an obligation of Christian rulers.

The Crusades In their work suppressing false doctrines, Christian rulers were also obliged to combat **Islam**, the religion whose followers considered Muhammad to be God's last prophet. Islam's reach expanded until it threatened European Christendom. Following the death of Muhammad in A.D. 632, the newly converted Arab peoples of North Africa used force and fervor to spread the Muslim faith into sub-Saharan Africa, India, and Indonesia, as well as deep into Spain and the Balkan regions of Europe. Between A.D. 1096 and 1291, Christian armies undertook a series of **Crusades** to reverse the Muslim advance in Europe and win back the holy lands where Christ had lived. Under the banner of the pope and led by Europe's Christian monarchs, crusading armies aroused great waves of popular piety as they marched off to combat. New orders of knights, like the Knights Templar and the Teutonic Knights, were created to support them.

The crusaders had some military successes, but their most profound impact was on European society. Religious warfare intensified Europe's Christian identity and prompted the persecution of Jews and their expulsion from many European countries. The Crusades also introduced Western European merchants to the trade routes that stretched from Constantinople to China along the Silk Road and from the Mediterranean Sea through the Persian Gulf to the Indian Ocean. And crusaders encountered sugar for the first time. Returning soldiers brought it back from the Middle East, and as Europeans began to conquer territory in the eastern Mediterranean, they experimented with raising it themselves. These early experiments with sugar would have a profound impact on European enterprise in the Americas — and European involvement with the African slave trade — in the centuries to come. Although Western Europe in 1491 remained relatively isolated from the centers of civilization in Eurasia and Africa, the Crusades and the rise of Italian merchant houses had introduced it to a wider world.

The Reformation In 1517, Martin Luther, a German monk and professor at the university in Wittenberg, took up the cause of reform in the Catholic Church. Luther's *Ninety-five Theses* condemned the Church for many corrupt practices. More radically, Luther downplayed the role of the clergy as mediators between God and believers and said that Christians must look to the Bible, not to the Church, as the ultimate authority in matters of faith. So that every literate German could read the Bible, previously available only in Latin, Luther translated it into German.

Meanwhile, in Geneva, Switzerland, French theologian John Calvin established a rigorous Protestant regime. Even more than Luther, Calvin stressed human weakness and God's omnipotence. His *Institutes of the Christian Religion* (1536) depicted God as an absolute ruler. Calvin preached the doctrine of predestination, the idea that God chooses certain people for salvation before they are born and condemns the rest to eternal damnation. In Geneva, he set up a model Christian community ruled by ministers who prohibited frivolity and luxury. "We know," wrote Calvin, "that man is of so perverse and crooked a nature, that everyone would scratch out his neighbor's eyes if there were no bridle to hold them in." Calvin's authoritarian doctrine won converts all over Europe, including the Puritans in Scotland and England.

Luther's criticisms triggered a war between the Holy Roman Empire and the northern principalities in Germany, and soon the controversy between the Roman Catholic Church and radical reformers like Luther and Calvin spread throughout much of Western Europe. The **Protestant Reformation**, as this movement came to be called, triggered a **Counter-Reformation** in the Catholic Church that sought change from within and created new monastic and missionary orders, including the Jesuits (founded in 1540), who saw themselves as soldiers of Christ. The competition between these divergent Christian traditions did much to shape European colonization of the Americas. Roman Catholic powers — Spain, Portugal, and France — sought to win souls in the Americas for the Church, while Protestant nations — England and the Netherlands — viewed the Catholic Church as corrupt and exploitative and hoped instead to create godly communities attuned to the true gospel of Christianity.

> **IN YOUR OWN WORDS** How had recent developments changed Western Europe by 1491?

TRACE CHANGE OVER TIME
How did the growing influence of the Christian Church affect events in Europe?

West and Central Africa: Origins of the Atlantic Slave Trade

Homo sapiens originated in Africa. Numerous civilizations had already risen and fallen there, and contacts with the Near East and the Mediterranean were millennia old, when Western Europeans began sailing down its Atlantic coast. Home to perhaps 100 million in 1400, Africa was divided by the vast expanse of the Sahara Desert. North Africa bordered on the Mediterranean, and its peoples fell under the domination of Christian Byzantium until the seventh century, when Muslim conquests brought the region under Islamic influence. In its coastal seaports, the merchandise of Asia, the Near East, Africa, and Europe converged. South of the Sahara, by contrast, the societies of West and Central Africa bordering on the Atlantic were relatively isolated. After 1400, that would quickly change.

Empires, Kingdoms, and Ministates

West Africa — the part of the continent that bulges into the Atlantic — can be visualized as a broad horizontal swath divided into three climatic zones. The Sahel is the mostly flat, semiarid zone immediately south of the Sahara. Below it lies the savanna, a grassland region dotted with trees and shrubs. South of the savanna, in a band 200 to 300 miles wide along the West African coast, lies a tropical rain forest. A series of four major watersheds — the Senegal, Gambia, Volta, and Niger — dominate West Africa (Map 1.3).

Sudanic civilization took root at the eastern end of West Africa beginning around 9000 B.C. and traveled westward. Sudanic peoples domesticated cattle (8500–7500 B.C.) and cultivated sorghum and millet (7500–7000 B.C.). Over several thousand years, these peoples developed a distinctive style of pottery, began to grow and weave cotton (6500–3500 B.C.), and invented techniques for working copper and iron (2500–1000 B.C.). Sudanic civilization had its own tradition of monotheism distinct from that of Christians, Muslims, and Jews. Most Sudanic peoples in West Africa lived in stratified states ruled by kings and princes who were regarded as divine.

MAP 1.3 West Africa and the Mediterranean in the Fifteenth Century
Trade routes across the Sahara had long connected West Africa with the Mediterranean region. Gold, ivory, and slaves moved north and east; fine textiles, spices, and the Muslim faith traveled south. Beginning in the 1430s, the Portuguese opened up maritime trade with the coastal regions of West Africa, which were home to many peoples and dozens of large and small states. Over the next century, the movement of gold and slaves into the Atlantic would surpass that across the Sahara.

From these cultural origins, three great empires arose in succession in the northern savanna. The first, the Ghana Empire, appeared sometime around A.D. 800. Ghana capitalized on the recently domesticated camel to pioneer trade routes across the Sahara to North Africa, where Ghana traders carried the wealth of West Africa. The Ghana Empire gave way to the Mali Empire in the thirteenth century, which was eclipsed in turn by the Songhai Empire in the fifteenth century. All three empires were composed of smaller vassal kingdoms, not unlike the Aztec and Inca empires, and relied on military might to control their valuable trade routes.

Gold, abundant in West Africa, was the cornerstone of power and an indispensable medium of international trade. By 1450, West African traders had carried so much of it across the Sahara that it constituted one-half to two-thirds of all the gold in circulation in Europe, North Africa, and Asia. Mansa Musa, the tenth emperor of Mali, was a devout Muslim famed for his construction projects and his support of mosques and schools. In 1326, he went on a pilgrimage to Mecca with a vast retinue that crossed the Sahara and passed through Egypt. They spent so much gold along the way that the region's money supply was devalued for more than a decade after their visit.

To the south of these empires, the lower savanna and tropical rain forest of West Africa were home to a complex mosaic of kingdoms that traded among themselves and with the empires to the north. In such a densely populated, resource-rich region, they also fought frequently in a competition for local power. A few of these coastal kingdoms were quite large in size, but most were small enough that they have been termed ministates by historians. Comparable to the city-states of Italy, they were often about the size of a modern-day county in the United States. The tropical ecosystem prevented them from raising livestock, since the tsetse fly (which carries a parasite deadly to livestock) was endemic to the region, as was malaria. In place of the grain crops of the savanna, these peoples pioneered the cultivation of yams; they also gathered resources from the rivers and seacoast.

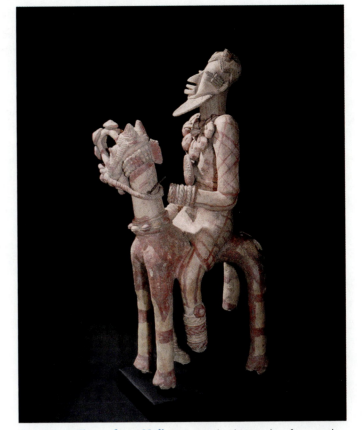

Terracotta Figure from Mali Dating to the thirteenth or fourteenth century, this terracotta figure came from an archaeological site near Djenné. The rider wears a large, ornate necklace, while the horse has a decorative covering on its head. The Mali Empire relied on a large cavalry to expand and defend its borders, and the horse was an important symbol of Mali's wealth and power. Werner Forman/Art Resource, NY.

COMPARE AND CONTRAST
How do the states of the savanna compare to those of the Americas and Europe?

Trans-Saharan and Coastal Trade

For centuries, the primary avenue of trade for West Africans passed through the Ghana, Mali, and Songhai empires, whose power was based on the monopoly they enjoyed over the trans-Saharan trade. Their caravans carried West African goods — including gold, copper, salt, and slaves — from the south to the north across the Sahara, then returned with textiles and other products. For the smaller states clustered along the West African coast, merchandise originating in the world beyond the Sahara was scarce and expensive, while markets for their own products were limited.

Beginning in the mid-fifteenth century, a new coastal trade with Europeans offered many West African peoples a welcome alternative. As European sailors made their way along the coast of West and then Central Africa, they encountered a bewilderingly complicated political landscape. Around the mouths of the Senegal and Gambia rivers, numerous Mande-speaking states controlled access to the trade routes into the interior. Proceeding farther along the coast, they encountered the Akan states, a region of several dozen independent but culturally linked peoples. The Akan states had goldfields of their own, and this region soon became known to Europeans as the Gold Coast. East of

Colliding Cultures

Carefully consider each of the objects or texts below. What meanings might you — thinking like a historian — impart to them?

1. **Mississippian warrior gorget (neck guard),** A.D. **1250–1350.**

SOURCE: National Museum of the American Indian, Smithsonian Institution 15/853.

2. **Portuguese officer's account of de Soto's expedition, 1557.** *This excerpt describes Indian resistance in the face of de Soto's campaign of conquest against Indians in the southeastern United States.*

[Spanish soldiers] went over a swampy land where the horsemen could not go. A half league from camp they came upon some Indian huts near the river; [but] the people who were inside them plunged into the river. They captured four Indian women, and twenty Indians came at us and attacked us so stoutly that we had to retreat to the camp, because of their being (as they are) so skillful with their weapons. Those people are so warlike and so quick that they make no account of foot soldiers; for if these go for them, they flee, and when their adversaries turn their backs they are immediately on them. The farthest they flee is the distance of an arrow shot. They are never quiet but always running and crossing from one side to another so that the crossbows or the arquebuses can not be aimed at them; and before a crossbowman can fire a shot, an Indian can shoot three or four arrows, and very seldom does he miss what he shoots at. If the arrow does not find armor, it penetrates as deeply as a crossbow. The bows are very long and the arrows are made of certain reeds like canes, very heavy and so tough that a sharpened cane passes through a shield. Some are pointed with a fish bone, as sharp as an awl, and others with a certain stone like a diamond point.

3. **Duarte Lopez,** *A Report on the Kingdom of Kongo,* **1591.** *A Portuguese explorer's account of his travels in southern Africa in the sixteenth century.*

[T]he Kingdom of Sofala lies between the two rivers, Magnice and Cuama, on the sea-coast. It is small in size, and has but few villages and towns. . . . It is peopled by Mohammedans, and the king himself belongs to the same sect. He pays allegiance to the crown of Portugal, in order not to be subject to the government of Monomotapa [Mutapa]. On this account the Portuguese have a fortress at the mouth of the River Cuama, trading with those countries in gold, amber, and ivory, all found on that coast, as well as in slaves, and giving in exchange silk stuffs and taffetas. . . . It is said, that from these regions the gold was brought by sea which served for Solomon's Temple at Jerusalem, a fact by no means improbable, for in these countries of Monomotapa are found several ancient buildings of stone, brick, and wood, and of such wonderful workmanship, and architecture, as is nowhere seen in the surrounding provinces.

The Kingdom of Monomotapa is extensive, and has a large population of Pagan heathens, who are black, of middle stature, swift of foot, and in battle fight with great bravery, their weapons being bows and arrows, and light darts. There are numerous kings tributary to Monomotapa, who constantly rebel and wage war against it. The Emperor maintains large armies, which in the provinces are divided into legions, after the manner of the Romans, for, being a great ruler, he must be at constant warfare in order to maintain his dominion. Amongst his warriors, those most renowned for bravery, are the female legions, greatly valued by the Emperor, being the sinews of his military strength.

4. **Benin figurine of a Portuguese soldier from the seventeenth century.** *This brass figure would have been kept on an altar or on the roof of the royal palace of Benin.*

5. **Sixteenth-century Portuguese coin made from African gold.** *Before the discovery of the Americas, half of the Old World's gold came from sub-Saharan Africa.*

6. **Sixteenth- or seventeenth-century Spanish silver real.** *Spain minted enormous quantities of American silver; much of it was shipped to Manila, where it was exchanged for Asian luxury goods.*

Sources: (2) John E. Worth, "Account of the Northern Conquest and Discovery of Hernando de Soto by Rodrigo Rangel," trans. John E. Worth, in Lawrence A. Clayton et al., eds., *The De Soto Chronicles: The Expedition of Hernando de Soto to North America in 1539–1543* (University of Alabama Press, 1993), 59; (3) Filippo Pigafetta, *A Report of the Kingdom of Congo*, trans. Margarite Hutchinson (London: John Murray, 1881), 117–119.

ANALYZING THE EVIDENCE

1. What can you infer about cultural values among Mississippian peoples from source 1? About the cultural values of the Spanish and Portuguese from sources 5 and 6? What *can't* you infer from these objects?

2. How does de Soto describe the Native peoples he encounters in Florida (source 2)? How does that compare to the traits of the African kingdoms that Lopez comments upon in source 3? Why might the king of Sofala prefer a Portuguese alliance to subjection to Monomotapa?

3. What does source 4 suggest about Benin relations with the Portuguese?

PUTTING IT ALL TOGETHER

What do these sources tell us about the ways Native Americans, Europeans, and Africans thought about themselves, perceived one another, and capitalized on cross-cultural exchanges as they came into sustained contact? Write a short essay that considers the connection between the impulses of warfare and commerce, which appear again and again in contact settings.

the Akan states lay the Bight of Benin, which became an early center of the slave trade and thus came to be called the Slave Coast. Bending south, fifteenth-century sailors encountered the Kingdom of Kongo in Central Africa, the largest state on the Atlantic seaboard, with a coastline that ran for some 250 miles. It was here in 1578 that Duarte Lopez visited the capital city of more than 100,000 residents. Wherever they went ashore along this route, European traders had to negotiate contacts on local terms (Thinking Like a Historian).

PLACE EVENTS IN CONTEXT
Why were West African leaders eager to engage in trade with Europeans?

The Spirit World

Some West Africans who lived immediately south of the Sahara—the Fulanis in Senegal, the Mande-speakers in Mali, and the Hausas in northern Nigeria—learned about Islam from Arab merchants and Muslim leaders called imams. Converts to Islam knew the Koran and worshipped only a single God. Some of their cities, like Timbuktu, the legendary commercial center on the Niger River, became centers of Islamic learning and instruction. But most West Africans acknowledged multiple gods, as well as spirits that lived in the earth, animals, and plants.

Like animists in the Americas and Europe, African communities had wise men and women adept at manipulating these forces for good or ill. The Sudanic tradition of divine kingship persisted, and many people believed that their kings could contact the spirit world. West Africans treated their ancestors with great respect, believing that the dead resided in a nearby spiritual realm and interceded in their lives. Most West African peoples had secret societies, such as the Poro for men and the Sande for women, that united people from different lineages and clans. These societies conducted rituals that celebrated male virility and female fertility. "Without children you are naked," said a Yoruba proverb. Happy was the man with a big household, many wives, many children, and many relatives—and, in a not very different vein, many slaves.

> **IN YOUR OWN WORDS**   How was sub-Saharan Africa affected by the arrival of European traders?

Exploration and Conquest

Beginning around 1400, the Portuguese monarchy propelled Europe into overseas expansion. Portugal soon took a leading role in the African slave trade, while the newly unified kingdom of Spain undertook Europe's first conquests in the Americas. These two ventures, though not initially linked, eventually became cornerstones in the creation of the "Atlantic World," which connected Europe, Africa, and the Americas.

Portuguese Expansion

As a young soldier fighting in the Crusades, Prince Henry of Portugal (1394–1460) learned about the trans-Saharan trade in gold and slaves. Seeking a maritime route to the source of this trade in West Africa, Henry founded a center for oceanic navigation. Henry's mariners, challenged to find a way through the treacherous waters off the northwest African coast, designed a better-handling vessel, the caravel, which was rigged with a lateen (triangular) sail that enabled the ship to tack into the wind. This innovation allowed them to sail far into the Atlantic, where they discovered and colonized the Madeira and Azore islands. From there, they sailed in 1435 to sub-Saharan Sierra Leone, where they exchanged salt, wine, and fish for African ivory and gold.

Henry's efforts were soon joined to those of Italian merchants, who were being forced out of eastern Mediterranean trade routes by the rising power of the Ottoman Empire. Cut off from Asia, Genoese traders sought an Atlantic route to the lucrative

Banza in the Kingdom of Kongo, c. 1668   The city of Banza, or Mbanza Kongo, was the capital of the Kingdom of Kongo when Portuguese traders first arrived in 1483. Kongo's king, Nzinga a Nkuwu, chose to be baptized to cement an alliance with Portugal and took the name João I. Kongo became officially Christian, and Banza came to be known as São Salvador. Duarte Lopez visited and described the city in 1578; this engraving shows the city as it appeared a century later.   Banza in the Kingdom of Kongo, San Salvador, from Olfert Dapper, c. 1668. Picture Research Consultants & Archives.

markets of the Indian Ocean. They began to work with Portuguese and Castilian mariners and monarchs to finance trading voyages, and the African coast and its offshore islands opened to their efforts. European voyagers discovered the Canaries, the Cape Verde Islands, and São Tomé; all of them became laboratories for the expansion of Mediterranean agriculture.

On these Atlantic islands, planters transformed local ecosystems to experiment with a variety of familiar cash crops: wheat, wine grapes, and woad, a blue dye plant; livestock and honeybees; and, where the climate permitted, sugar. By 1500, Madeira was producing 2,500 metric tons a year, and Madeira sugar was available — in small, expensive quantities — in London, Paris, Rome, and Constantinople. Most of the islands were unpopulated. The Canaries were the exception; it took Castilian adventurers decades to conquer the Guanches who lived there. Once defeated, they were enslaved to labor in the Canaries or on Madeira, where they carved irrigation canals into the island's steep rock cliffs.

Europeans made no such inroads on the continent of Africa itself. The coastal kingdoms were well defended, and yellow fever, malaria, and dysentery quickly struck down Europeans who spent any time in the interior of West Africa. Instead they maintained small, fortified trading posts on offshore islands or along the coast, usually as guests of the local king.

Portuguese sailors continued to look for an Atlantic route to Asia. In 1488, Bartolomeu Dias rounded the Cape of Good Hope, the southern tip of Africa. Vasco da Gama reached East Africa in 1497 and India in the following year; his ships were mistaken for those of Chinese traders, the last pale-skinned men to arrive by sea. Although

MAP 1.4 The Eurasian Trade System and European Maritime Ventures, c. 1500
For centuries, the Mediterranean Sea was the meeting point for the commerce of Europe, North Africa, and Asia — via the Silk Road from China and the Spice Route from India. Beginning in the 1490s, Portuguese, Spanish, and Dutch rulers and merchants subsidized Christian maritime explorers who discovered new trade routes around Africa and new sources of wealth in the Americas. These initiatives undermined the commercial primacy of the Arab Muslim– dominated Mediterranean.

da Gama's inferior goods — tin basins, coarse cloth, honey, and coral beads — were snubbed by the Arab and Indian merchants along India's Malabar Coast, he managed to acquire a highly profitable cargo of cinnamon and pepper. Da Gama returned to India in 1502 with twenty-one fighting vessels, which outmaneuvered and outgunned the Arab fleets. Soon the Portuguese government set up fortified trading posts for its merchants at key points around the Indian Ocean, in Indonesia, and along the coast of China (Map 1.4). In a transition that sparked the momentous growth of European wealth and power, the Portuguese and then the Dutch replaced the Arabs as the leaders in Asian commerce.

IDENTIFY CAUSES
How did Europe's desire for an ocean route to Asia shape its contacts with Africa?

The African Slave Trade

Portuguese traders also ousted Arab merchants as the leading suppliers of African slaves. Coerced labor — through slavery, serfdom, or indentured servitude — was the norm in most premodern societies, and in Africa slavery was widespread. Some Africans were held in bondage as security for debts; others were sold into servitude by their kin in exchange for food in times of famine; many others were war captives. Slaves were a key commodity, sold as agricultural laborers, concubines, or military recruits. Sometimes their descendants were freed, but others endured hereditary bondage. Sonni Ali (r. 1464–1492), the ruler of the powerful Songhai Empire, personally owned twelve "tribes" of hereditary agricultural slaves, many of them seized in raids against neighboring peoples.

Slaves were also central to the trans-Saharan trade. When the renowned Tunisian adventurer Ibn Battuta crossed the Sahara from the Kingdom of Mali around 1350, he traveled with a caravan of six hundred female slaves, destined for domestic service or concubinage in North Africa, Egypt, and the Ottoman Empire. Between A.D. 700 and 1900, it is estimated that as many as nine million Africans were sold in the trans-Saharan slave trade.

Europeans initially were much more interested in trading for gold and other commodities than in trading for human beings, but gradually they discovered the enormous value of human trafficking. To exploit and redirect the existing African slave trade, Portuguese merchants established fortified trading posts like those in the Indian Ocean beginning at Elmina in 1482, where they bought gold and slaves from African princes and warlords. First they enslaved a few thousand Africans each year to work on sugar plantations on São Tomé, Cape Verde, the Azores, and Madeira; they also sold slaves in Lisbon, which soon had an African population of 9,000. After 1550, the Atlantic slave trade, a forced diaspora of African peoples, expanded enormously as Europeans set up sugar plantations across the Atlantic, in Brazil and the West Indies.

> **TRACE CHANGE OVER TIME**
> How was the African slave trade adapted to European needs?

Sixteenth-Century Incursions

As Portuguese traders sailed south and east, the Spanish monarchs Ferdinand II of Aragon and Isabella I of Castile financed an explorer who looked to the west. As Renaissance rulers, Ferdinand (r. 1474–1516) and Isabella (r. 1474–1504) saw national

The Map Behind Columbus's Voyage In 1489, Henricus Martellus, a German cartographer living in Florence, produced this huge (4 feet by 6 feet) view of the known world, probably working from a map devised by Christopher Columbus's brother, Bartholomew. The map uses the spatial projection of the ancient Greek philosopher Claudius Ptolemy (A.D. 90–168) and incorporates information from Marco Polo's explorations in Asia and Bartolomeu Dias's recent voyage around the tip of Africa. Most important, it greatly exaggerates the width of Eurasia, thereby suggesting that Asia lies only 5,000 miles west of Europe (rather than the actual distance of 15,000 miles). Using Martellus's map, Columbus persuaded the Spanish monarchs to support his westward voyage. bpk Bildagentur Berlin/Staatsbibliothek zu Berlin, Stiftung Preussischer Kulturbesitz/Ruth Schacht/Art Resource, NY.

unity and foreign commerce as the keys to power and prosperity. Married in an arranged match to combine their Christian kingdoms, the young rulers completed the centuries-long *reconquista*, the campaign by Spanish Catholics to drive Muslim Arabs from the European mainland, by capturing Granada, the last Islamic territory in Western Europe, in 1492. Using Catholicism to build a sense of "Spanishness," they launched the brutal Inquisition against suspected Christian heretics and expelled or forcibly converted thousands of Jews and Muslims.

Columbus and the Caribbean   Simultaneously, Ferdinand and Isabella sought trade and empire by subsidizing the voyages of Christopher Columbus, an ambitious and daring mariner from Genoa. Columbus believed that the Atlantic Ocean, long feared by Arab merchants as a 10,000-mile-wide "green sea of darkness," was a much narrower channel of water separating Europe from Asia. After six years of lobbying, Columbus persuaded Genoese investors and Ferdinand and Isabella to accept his dubious theories and finance a western voyage to Asia.

Columbus set sail in three small ships in August 1492. Six weeks later, after a perilous voyage of 3,000 miles, he disembarked on an island in the present-day Bahamas. Believing that he had reached Asia — "the Indies," in fifteenth-century parlance — Columbus called the native inhabitants Indians and the islands the West Indies. He was surprised by the crude living conditions but expected the Native peoples "easily [to] be made Christians." He claimed the islands for Spain and then explored the neighboring Caribbean islands, demanding tribute from the local Taino, Arawak, and Carib peoples. Columbus left forty men on the island of Hispaniola (present-day Haiti and the Dominican Republic) and returned triumphantly to Spain (Map 1.5).

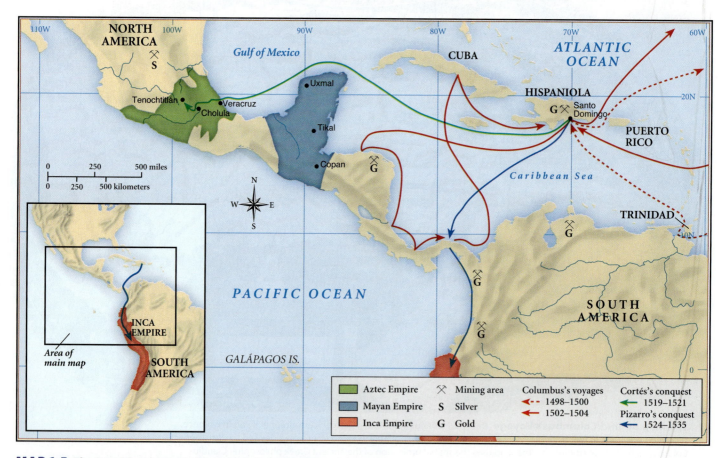

MAP 1.5 The Spanish Conquest of America's Great Empires
The Spanish first invaded the islands of the Caribbean, largely wiping out the Native peoples. Rumors of a gold-rich civilization led to Cortés's invasion of the Aztec Empire in 1519. By 1535, other Spanish conquistadors had conquered the Mayan temple cities and the Inca Empire in Peru, completing one of the great conquests in world history.

The Spanish monarchs supported three more voyages. Columbus colonized the West Indies with more than 1,000 Spanish settlers — all men — and hundreds of domestic animals. But he failed to find either golden treasures or great kingdoms, and his death in 1506 went virtually unnoticed.

A German geographer soon named the newly found continents "America" in honor of a different explorer. Amerigo Vespucci, a Florentine explorer who had visited the coast of present-day South America around 1500, denied that the region was part of Asia. He called it a *nuevo mundo*, a "new world." The Spanish crown called the two continents *Las Indias* ("the Indies") and wanted to make them a new Spanish world.

To see a longer excerpt of Columbus's views of the West Indies, along with other primary sources from this period, see **Sources for America's History**.

The Spanish Invasion After brutally subduing the Arawaks and Tainos on Hispaniola, the Spanish probed the mainland for gold and slaves. In 1513, Juan Ponce de León explored the coast of Florida and gave that peninsula its name. In the same year, Vasco Núñez de Balboa crossed the Isthmus of Darien (Panama) and became the first European to see the Pacific Ocean. Rumors of rich Indian kingdoms encouraged other Spaniards, including hardened veterans of the *reconquista*, to invade the mainland. The Spanish monarchs offered successful conquistadors noble titles, vast estates, and Indian laborers (Analyzing Voices).

With these inducements before him, in 1519 Hernán Cortés (1485–1547) led an army of 600 men to the Yucatán Peninsula. Gathering allies among Native peoples who chafed under Aztec rule, he marched on Tenochtitlán and challenged its ruler, Moctezuma. Awed by the Spanish invaders, Moctezuma received Cortés with great ceremony. But Cortés soon took the emperor captive, and after a long siege he and his men captured the city. The conquerors cut off the city's supply of food and water, causing great suffering for the residents of Tenochtitlán. By 1521, Cortés and his men had toppled the Aztec Empire.

The Spanish had a silent ally: disease. Having been separated from Eurasia for thousands of years, the inhabitants of the Americas had no immunities to common European diseases. After the Spaniards arrived, a massive smallpox epidemic ravaged Tenochtitlán, "striking everywhere in the city," according to an Aztec source, and killing Moctezuma's brother and thousands more. "They could not move, they could not stir. . . . Covered, mantled with pustules, very many people died of them." Subsequent outbreaks of smallpox, influenza, and measles killed hundreds of thousands of Indians and sapped the survivors' morale. Exploiting this advantage, Cortés quickly extended Spanish rule over the Aztec Empire. His lieutenants then moved against the Mayan city-states of the Yucatán Peninsula, eventually conquering them as well.

In 1524, Francisco Pizarro set out to accomplish the same feat in Peru. By the time he and his small force of 168 men and 67 horses finally reached their destination in 1532, half of the Inca population had already died from European diseases. Weakened militarily and divided between rival claimants to the throne, the Inca nobility was easy prey. Pizarro killed Atahualpa, the last Inca emperor, and seized his enormous wealth.

The Codex Mendoza Millions of people spoke Nahuatl, the language of the Aztec Empire. It was also a written language: a pictographic system allowed scribes to record histories, tribute lists, and other official texts. Spanish colonizers systematically destroyed Aztec records but later encouraged Native scribes to re-create them. The Codex Mendoza, which dates to the 1540s, gives a history of the Aztec Empire. This page depicts the conquests of Ahuitzotl, the figure in a white cloak and turquoise crown. The toppling temples surrounding him symbolize the city-states he conquered. © Bodleian Libraries/early 1540s/shelfmark Ms. Arch. Selden A. 1 fol. 013r/The Art Archive at Art Resource.

Primary sources are documents, images, or artifacts that were created during the time you are studying. To analyze a primary source, you need to ask some basic questions about the source:

A Spanish Priest Criticizes His Fellow Colonists

- Who is the author, and what circumstances led to the document's creation?
- Who was the author's intended audience?
- What was the author's goal in creating the document?
- What ideas, arguments, and images does the author use to make his or her point? How effective are they?
- What outside information can you bring to bear on this document? How does the primary source enhance your understanding of the textbook, and how does the textbook enhance your understanding of the source?
- What does this source tell you about the society in which it was produced?

These are general questions that you should have in mind whenever you read a primary source. Try to answer them for yourself as you read the following document. Then, once you have read it, answer the Questions for Analysis that follow.

BARTOLOMÉ DE LAS CASAS

A Short Account of the Destruction of the Indies

Bartolomé de las Casas first emigrated from Spain to the island of Hispaniola as a colonist and slave owner. After determining that Spain's treatment of Native Americans was cruel and unjust, Las Casas became a Dominican friar, or preacher, and argued that the Spanish king should intervene to protect Native populations. His writings persuaded King Charles V to impose the "New Laws of the Indies for the Good Treatment and Preservation of the Indians" (1542), which outlawed Indian slavery. Ironically, because they depicted Spanish cruelty to Native Americans so vividly, Las Casas's writings were quickly translated into other languages, including English, and Spain's enemies used these texts to support the so-called Black Legend — the view that Spanish colonization was uniquely exploitative and cruel.

SOURCE: *A Short Account of the Destruction of the Indies* by Bartolomé De Las Casas, edited and translated by Nigel Griffin, introduction by Anthony Pagden (Penguin Classics, 2008). The Translation and Notes copyright © Nigel Griffin, 1992. Introduction copyright © Anthony Pagden, 1992. Reproduced by permission of Penguin Books Ltd.

66 Most high and most mighty Lord:
As Divine Providence has ordained that the world shall, for the benefit and proper government of the human race, be divided into kingdoms and peoples and that these shall be ruled by kings, who are . . . the noblest and most virtuous of beings, there is no doubt . . . that these kings entertain nothing save that which is morally unimpeachable. It follows that if the commonwealth suffers from some . . . evil, the reason can only be that the ruler is unaware of it; once the matter is brought to his notice, he will work with the utmost diligence to set matters right. . . .

God made all the peoples of this area [the Americas], many and varied as they are, as open and as innocent as can be imagined. The simplest people in the world — unassuming, long-suffering, unassertive, and submissive — they are without malice or guile, and are utterly faithful and obedient both to their own native lords and to the Spaniards in whose service they now find themselves. . . . They are also among the poorest people on the face of the earth; they own next to nothing and

Although Inca resistance continued for a generation, the conquest was complete by 1535, and Spain was now the master of the wealthiest and most populous regions of the Western Hemisphere.

The Spanish invasion changed life forever in the Americas. Disease and warfare wiped out virtually all of the Indians of Hispaniola — at least 300,000 people. In Peru, the population of 9 million in 1530 plummeted to fewer than 500,000 a century later. Mesoamerica suffered the greatest losses: in one of the great demographic disasters in world history, its population of 20 million Native Americans in 1500 had dwindled to just 3 million in 1650.

Cabral and Brazil At the same time, Portuguese efforts to sail around the southern tip of Africa led to a surprising find. As Vasco da Gama and his contemporaries experimented with winds and currents, their voyages carried them ever farther away from the African coast and into the Atlantic. On one such voyage in 1500, the Portuguese have no urge to acquire material possessions. As a result they are neither ambitious nor greedy, and are totally uninterested in worldly power. . . . They are innocent and pure in mind and have a lively intelligence, all of which makes them particularly receptive to learning and understanding the truths of our Catholic faith and to being instructed in virtue. . . .

It was upon these gentle lambs, imbued by the Creator with all the qualities we have mentioned, that from the very first day they clapped eyes on them the Spanish fell like ravening wolves upon the fold, or like tigers and savage lions who have not eaten meat for days. The pattern established at the outset has remained unchanged to this day, and the Spaniards still do nothing save tear the natives to shreds, murder them and inflict upon them untold misery, suffering and distress, tormenting, harrying and persecuting them mercilessly. . . .

When the Spanish first journeyed there, the indigenous population of the island of Hispaniola stood at some three million; today only two hundred survive. The island of Cuba, which extends for a distance almost as great as that separating Valladolid from Rome, is now to all intents and purposes uninhabited; and two other large, beautiful and fertile islands, Puerto Rico and Jamaica, have been similarly devastated. Not a living soul remains today on any of the islands of the Bahamas. . . . On the mainland, we know for sure that our fellow-countrymen have, through their cruelty and wickedness, depopulated and laid waste an area which once boasted more than ten kingdoms, each of them larger in area than the whole of the Iberian Peninsula. . . . At a conservative estimate, the despotic and diabolical behaviour of the Christians has, over the last forty years, led to the unjust and totally unwarranted deaths of more than twelve million souls, women and children among them, and there are grounds for believing my own estimate of more than fifteen million to be nearer the mark.

There are two main ways in which those who have travelled to this part of the world pretending to be Christians have uprooted these pitiful peoples and wiped them from the face of the earth. First, they have waged war on them: unjust, cruel, bloody and tyrannical war. Second, they have murdered anyone and everyone who has shown the slightest sign of resistance, or even of wishing to escape the torment to which they have subjected him. This latter policy has been instrumental in suppressing the native leaders, and, indeed, given that the Spaniards normally spare only women and children, it has led to the annihilation of all adult males, whom they habitually subject to the harshest and most iniquitous and brutal slavery that man has ever devised for his fellow-men, treating them, in fact, worse than animals. . . .

The reason the Christians have murdered on such a vast scale and killed anyone and everyone in their way is purely and simply greed. They have set out to line their pockets with gold and to amass private fortunes as quickly as possible so that they can then assume a status quite at odds with that into which they were born. Their insatiable greed and overweening ambition know no bounds. . . .

One fact in all this is widely known and beyond dispute, for even the tyrannical murderers themselves acknowledge the truth of it: the indigenous peoples never did the Europeans any harm whatever; on the contrary, they believed them to have descended from the heavens, at least until they or their fellow-citizens had tasted, at the hands of these oppressors, a diet of robbery, murder, violence, and all other manner of trials and tribulations. **99**

QUESTIONS FOR ANALYSIS

1. Who is Las Casas's intended audience? What does the opening passage tell you about his view of royal authority?

2. How does Las Casas want the king to view Native Americans? Why does he think it is especially important to treat Native Americans humanely?

3. How does Las Casas want the king to view Spanish colonists? What imagery does he use to make his point?

4. How does the use of population figures strengthen the case Las Casas is presenting?

5. Using the information on pages 31–36, how would you place Las Casas's argument in context? What does Las Casas's writing tell you about Spanish colonial society?

---

commander Pedro Alvares Cabral and his fleet were surprised to see land loom in the west. Cabral named his discovery Ihla da Vera Cruz—the Island of the True Cross—and continued on his way toward India. Others soon followed and changed the region's name to Brazil after the indigenous tree that yielded a valuable red dye; for several decades, Portuguese sailors traded with the Tupi Indians for brazilwood. Then in the 1530s, to secure Portugal's claim, King Dom João III sent settlers, who began the long, painstaking process of carving out sugar plantations in the coastal lowlands.

For several decades, Native Americans supplied most of the labor for these operations, but African slaves gradually replaced them. Brazil would soon become the world's leading producer of sugar; it would also devour African lives. By introducing the **plantation system** to the Americas—a form of estate agriculture using slave labor that was pioneered by Italian merchants and crusading knights in the twelfth century and transplanted to the islands off the coast of Africa in the fifteenth century—the Portuguese

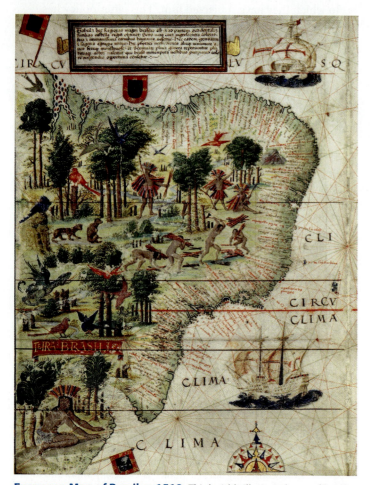

European Map of Brazil, c. 1519 This lavishly illustrated map of Brazil is drawn from the Miller Atlas, made by order of King Manuel I of Portugal around 1519. It features images of Indians harvesting brazilwood; macaws and other colorful birds; a monkey; and—improbably—a fire-breathing dragon. Note, too, the dense annotations and place names along the coast—a reminder that Portuguese familiarity with Brazil was confined almost entirely to the seaboard. Scala/White Images/Art Resource, NY.

set in motion one of the most significant developments of the early modern era.

By the end of the sixteenth century, the European colonization of the Americas had barely begun. Yet several of its most important elements were already taking shape. Spanish efforts demonstrated that densely populated empires were especially vulnerable to conquest and were also especially valuable sources of wealth. The Portuguese had discovered the viability of sugar plantations in the tropical regions of the Americas and pioneered the transatlantic slave trade as a way of manning them. And contacts with Native peoples revealed their devastating vulnerabilities to Eurasian diseases—one part of the larger phenomenon of the Columbian Exchange (discussed in Chapter 2).

> **IN YOUR OWN WORDS** What motivated Portuguese and Spanish expansion into the Atlantic, and what were its unintended consequences?

SUMMARY

Native American, European, and African societies developed independently over thousands of years before they experienced direct contacts with one another. In the Americas, residents of Mesoamerica and the Andes were fully sedentary (with individual ownership of land and intensive agriculture), but elsewhere societies were semisedentary (with central fields and villages that were occupied seasonally) or nonsedentary (hunter-gatherers). West and Central Africa also had a mix of sedentary, semisedentary, and nonsedentary settlements. Western Europe, by contrast, was predominantly sedentary. All three continents had a complex patchwork of political organizations, from empires, to kingdoms and chiefdoms, to principalities, duchies, and ministates; everywhere, rulership was imbued with notions of spiritual power. Ruling classes relied on warfare, trade, and tribute (or taxes) to dominate those around them and accumulate precious goods that helped to set them apart from ordinary laborers, but they also bore responsibility for the well-being of their subjects and offered them various forms of protection.

As sailors pushed into the Atlantic, they set in motion a chain of events whose consequences they could scarcely imagine. From a coastal trade with Africa that was secondary to their efforts to reach the Indian Ocean, from the miscalculations of Columbus and the happy accident of Cabral, developed a pattern of transatlantic exploration, conquest, and exploitation that no one could have foretold or planned. In the tropical zones of the Caribbean and coastal Brazil, invading Europeans enslaved Native Americans and quickly drove them into extinction or exile. The demands of plantation agriculture soon led Europeans to import slaves from Africa, initiating a transatlantic trade that would destroy African lives on both sides of the ocean. And two of the greatest empires in the world—the Aztec and Incan empires—collapsed in response to unseen biological forces that acted in concert with small invading armies.

TERMS TO KNOW

Identify and explain the significance of each term below.

Key Concepts and Events

hunters and gatherers (p. 8)

semisedentary societies (p. 8)

Mississippian culture (p. 11)

eastern woodlands (p. 11)

Algonquian cultures/languages (p. 11)

Iroquoian cultures/languages (p. 11)

Iroquois Confederacy (p. 13)

Great Lakes (p. 15)

Great Plains (p. 15)

Rocky Mountains (p. 15)

Great Basin (p. 15)

peasants (p. 19)

republic (p. 20)

Christianity (p. 21)

Islam (p. 22)

Crusades (p. 22)

Protestant Reformation (p. 23)

Counter-Reformation (p. 23)

plantation system (p. 35)

Key People

Hiawatha (p. 13)

Martin Luther (p. 23)

Christopher Columbus (p. 32)

Hernán Cortés (p. 33)

Moctezuma (p. 33)

Pedro Alvares Cabral (p. 35)

REVIEW QUESTIONS

Answer these questions to demonstrate your understanding of the chapter's main ideas.

1. What factors might best explain the variations among Native American societies and cultures?

2. How had recent developments changed Western Europe by 1491?

3. How was sub-Saharan Africa affected by the arrival of European traders?

4. What motivated Portuguese and Spanish expansion into the Atlantic, and what were its unintended consequences?

5. Review the events listed under "Work, Exchange, and Technology" and "Migration and Settlement" on the thematic timeline on pages 4–5. How did contacts among Europeans, Native Americans, and Africans alter the economies of the three continents?

MAKING CONNECTIONS

Recognize the larger developments and continuities within and across chapters by answering these questions.

1. The century following the first contacts among Europe, sub-Saharan Africa, and the Americas brought some of the most momentous changes in world history: a dramatic reconfiguration of human populations across the globe, new patterns of trade and warfare, and immense challenges to peoples' worldviews. Thinking about our contemporary world, what monumental changes are currently affecting our lives? How would you compare them with the events described in this chapter?

2. Return to the image of *The Beaune Altarpiece* on page 22. How does the emphasis on universal truth and everlasting punishment and reward make Christianity different from animism? How might faith in such a religious system shape the values and priorities of believers?

KEY TURNING POINTS

Refer to the chapter chronology on page 8 for help in answering the questions below.

The domestication of maize (6000 B.C.), the founding of Tenochtitlán (1325), and the conquest of the Aztec Empire (1519–1521): How did the domestication of maize make the city of Tenochtitlán possible? What characteristics of the Aztec Empire and its capital city made it vulnerable to conquest?

2

CHAPTER

American Experiments

1521–1700

IDENTIFY THE BIG IDEA

In what ways did European migrants transfer familiar patterns and institutions to their colonies in the Americas, and in what ways did they create new American worlds? How did Native Americans adapt to the growing presence of Europeans among them?

Beginning in the 1660s, legislators in Virginia and Maryland hammered out the legal definition of **chattel slavery**: the ownership of human beings as property. The institution of slavery—which would profoundly affect African Americans and shape much of American history—had been obsolete in England for centuries, and articulating its logic required lawmakers to reverse some of the most basic presumptions of English law. For example, in 1662 a Virginia statute declared, "all children borne in this country shalbe held bond or free only according to the condition of the mother." This idea—that a child's legal status derived from the mother, rather than the father—ran contrary to the patriarchal foundations of English law. The men who sat in Virginia's House of Burgesses would not propose such a thing lightly. Why would they decide that the principle of patriarchal descent, which was so fundamental to their own worlds, was inappropriate for their slaves?

The question needed to be addressed, according to the statute's preamble, since "doubts have arisen whether children got by an Englishman upon a negro woman should be slave or free." One such case involved Elizabeth Key, a woman whose father was a free Englishman and mother was an African slave. She petitioned for her freedom in 1656, based on her father's status. Her lawyer was an Englishman named William Greensted. He not only took Key's case, but he also fathered two of her children and, eventually, married her. Key won her case and her freedom from bondage. Elizabeth Key escaped her mother's fate—a life in slavery—because her father and her husband were both free Englishmen. The 1662 statute aimed to close Key's avenue to freedom.

The process by which the institution of chattel slavery was molded to the needs of colonial planters is just one example of the way Europeans adapted the principles they brought with them to the unfamiliar demands of their new surroundings. In the showdown between people like Elizabeth Key and William Greensted, on the one hand, and the members of Virginia's House of Burgesses on the other, we see how people in disorienting circumstances—some in positions of power, others in various states of subjection to their social and political superiors—scrambled to make sense of their world and bend its rules to their advantage. Through countless contests of power and authority like this one, the outlines of a new world gradually began to emerge from the collision of cultures.

By 1700, three distinct types of colonies had developed in the Americas. The tribute colonies created in Mexico and Peru relied initially on the wealth and labor of indigenous peoples. Plantation colonies produced sugar and other tropical and subtropical crops with bound labor. Finally, **neo-Europes** sought to replicate, or at least approximate, economies and social structures that colonists knew at home.

Power and Race in the Chesapeake In this 1670 painting by Gerard Soest, proprietor Lord Baltimore holds a map of Maryland, the colony he owned and which would soon belong to his grandson Cecil Calvert, shown in the painting as already grasping his magnificent inheritance. The presence of a young African servant foretells the importance of slave labor in the post-1700 economy of the Chesapeake colonies. Private Collection/Peter Newark American Pictures/Bridgeman Images.

As you read, ask yourself why this chapter begins and ends with these dates and then identify the links among related events.

1521	▶ Aztec Empire falls to the Spanish
1550–1630	▶ English crown supports mercantilism
1556–1598	▶ Reign of Philip II, king of Spain
1558–1603	▶ Reign of Elizabeth I, queen of England
1560–1620	▶ Growth of English Puritan movement
1577–1580	▶ Francis Drake's *Golden Hind* circles the globe, captures Spanish treasure fleet
1588	▶ Storms and English ships destroy Spanish Armada
1603–1625	▶ Reign of James I, king of England
1607	▶ English traders settle Jamestown (Virginia)
1608	▶ Samuel de Champlain founds Quebec
1609	▶ Henry Hudson explores North America for the Dutch
1614	▶ Dutch set up fur-trading post at Fort Orange (Albany)
1619	▶ First Africans arrive in Chesapeake region ▶ House of Burgesses convenes in Virginia
1620	▶ Pilgrims found Plymouth Colony
1620–1660	▶ Chesapeake colonies enjoy tobacco boom

1621	▶ Dutch West India Company chartered
1622	▶ Opechancanough's uprising
1624	▶ Virginia becomes royal colony
1625–1649	▶ Reign of Charles I, king of England
1630	▶ Puritans found Massachusetts Bay Colony
1634	▶ Colonists arrive in Maryland
1636	▶ Beginning of Puritan-Pequot War ▶ Roger Williams founds Providence
1637	▶ Anne Hutchinson banished from Massachusetts Bay
1640s	▶ Iroquois initiate wars over fur trade
1642–1659	▶ Puritan Revolution in England
1660	▶ Restoration of the English monarchy ▶ Tobacco prices fall and remain low
1664	▶ English conquer New Netherland
1675–1676	▶ Bacon's Rebellion in Virginia ▶ Metacom's War in New England
1692	▶ Salem witchcraft trials

Spain's Tribute Colonies

European interest in the Americas took shape under the influence of Spain's conquest of the Aztec and Inca empires. There, Spanish colonizers capitalized on preexisting systems of tribute and labor discipline to tap the enormous wealth of Mesoamerica and the Andes. Once native rulers were overthrown, the Spanish monarchs transferred their institutions — municipal councils, the legal code, the Catholic Church — to America; the empire was centrally controlled to protect the crown's immensely valuable holdings. The Spanish conquest also set in motion a global ecological transformation through a vast intercontinental movement of plants, animals, and diseases that historians call the Columbian Exchange. And the conquest triggered hostile responses from Spain's European rivals, especially the Protestant Dutch and English.

A New American World

After Cortés toppled Moctezuma and Pizarro defeated Atahualpa (see Chapter 1), leading conquistadors received *encomiendas* from the crown, which allowed them to claim tribute in labor and goods from Indian communities. Later these grants were repartitioned, but the pattern was set early: prominent men controlled vast resources and monopolized Indian labor. The value of these grants was dramatically enhanced by the discovery of gold and, especially, silver deposits in both Mexico and the Andes. In the decades after the conquest, mines were developed in Zacatecas, in Guanajuato, and — most famously — at Potosí, high in the Andes. There, Spanish officials co-opted the *mita* system, which had made laborers available to the Inca Empire, to force Indian workers into the mines. At its peak, Potosí alone produced 200 tons of silver per year, accounting for half the world's supply.

The two great indigenous empires of the Americas thus became the core of an astonishingly wealthy European empire. Vast amounts of silver poured across the

Pacific Ocean to China, where it was minted into money; in exchange, Spain received valuable Chinese silks, spices, and ceramics. In Europe, the gold that had formerly honored Aztec and Inca gods now flowed into the countinghouses of Spain and gilded the Catholic churches of Europe. The Spanish crown benefitted enormously from all this wealth—at least initially. In the long run, it triggered ruinous inflation. As a French traveler noted in 1603, "Everything is dear [expensive] in Spain, except silver."

A new society took shape on the conquered lands. Between 1500 and 1650, at least 350,000 Spaniards migrated to Mesoamerica and the Andes. About two-thirds were males drawn from a cross section of Spanish society, many of them skilled tradesmen. Also arriving were 250,000 to 300,000 Africans. Racial mixture was widespread, and such groups as mestizos (Spaniard-Indian) and mulattos (Spaniard-African) grew rapidly. Zambo (Indian-African) populations developed gradually as well. Over time, a system of increasingly complex racial categories developed—the **casta system**—buttressed by a legal code that differentiated among the principal groups.

Indians were always in the majority in Mexico and Peru, but profound changes came as their numbers declined and peoples of Spanish and mixed-race descent grew in number. Spaniards initially congregated in cities, but gradually they moved into the countryside, creating large estates (known as haciendas) and regional networks of market exchange. Most Indians remained in their Native communities, under the authority of Native rulers and speaking Native languages. However, Spanish priests suppressed religious ceremonies and texts and converted Natives to Christianity *en masse*. Catholicism was transformed in the process: Catholic parishes took their form from Indian communities; indigenous ideas and expectations reshaped Church practices; and new forms of Native American Christianity emerged in both regions.

The Columbian Exchange

The Spanish invasion permanently altered the natural as well as the human environment. Smallpox, influenza, measles, yellow fever, and other silent killers carried from Europe and Africa ravaged Indian communities, whose inhabitants had never encountered these diseases before and thus had no immunities to them. In the densely populated core areas, populations declined by 90 percent or more in the first century of contact with Europeans. On islands and in the tropical lowlands, the toll was even heavier; Native populations were often wiped out altogether. Syphilis was the only significant illness that traveled in the opposite direction: Columbus's sailors carried a virulent strain of the sexually transmitted disease back to Europe with them.

The movement of diseases and peoples across the Atlantic was part of a larger pattern of biological transformation that historians call the **Columbian Exchange** (Map 2.1). Foods of the Western Hemisphere—especially maize, potatoes, manioc, sweet potatoes, and tomatoes—significantly increased agricultural yields and population growth in other continents. Maize and potatoes, for example, reached China around 1700; in the following century, the Chinese population tripled from 100 million to 300 million. At the same time, many animals, plants, and germs were carried to the Americas. European livestock transformed American landscapes. While Native Americans domesticated very few animals—dogs and llamas were the principal exceptions—Europeans brought an enormous Old World bestiary to the Americas, including cattle, swine, horses, oxen, chickens, and honeybees. Eurasian grain crops—wheat, barley, rye, and rice—made the transatlantic voyage along with inadvertent imports like dandelions and other weeds.

> **PLACE EVENTS IN CONTEXT**
> How did the ecological context of colonization shape interactions between Europeans and Native Americans?

The Protestant Challenge to Spain

Beyond the core regions of its empire, Spain claimed vast American dominions but struggled to hold them. Controlling the Caribbean basin, which was essential for Spain's transatlantic shipping routes, was especially difficult, since the net of tiny islands

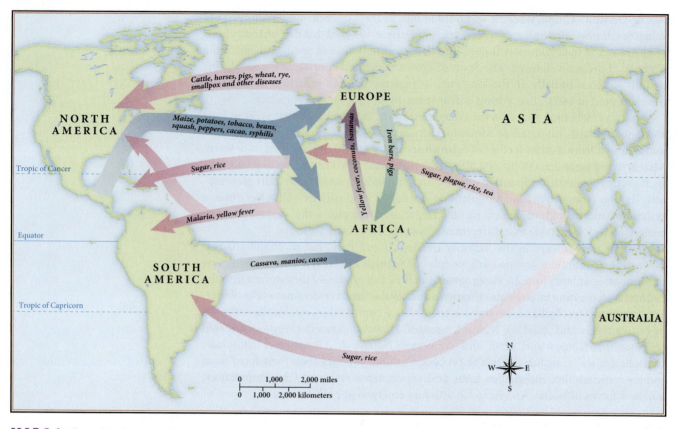

MAP 2.1 The Columbian Exchange

As European traders and adventurers traversed the world between 1430 and 1600, they began what historians call the Columbian Exchange, a vast intercontinental movement of plants, animals, and diseases that changed the course of historical development. The nutritious, high-yielding American crops of corn and potatoes enriched the diets of Europeans, Africans, and Asians. However, the Eurasian and African diseases of smallpox, diphtheria, malaria, and yellow fever nearly wiped out the native inhabitants of the Western Hemisphere and virtually ensured that they would lose control of their lands.

spanning the eastern Caribbean — the Lesser Antilles — provided many safe harbors for pirates and privateers. Fortified outposts in Havana (Cuba) and St. Augustine (Florida) provided some protection, but they were never sufficient to keep enemies at bay.

And Spain had powerful enemies, their animosity sharpened by the Protestant Reformation and the resulting split in European Christendom (see Chapter 1). In the wake of Martin Luther's attack on the Catholic Church, the Protestant critique of Catholicism broadened and deepened. Gold and silver from Mexico and Peru made Spain the wealthiest nation in Europe, and King Philip II (r. 1556–1598) — an ardent Catholic — its most powerful ruler. Philip was determined to root out challenges to the Catholic Church wherever they appeared. One such place was in the Spanish Netherlands, a collection of Dutch- and Flemish-speaking provinces that had grown wealthy from textile manufacturing and trade with Portuguese outposts in Africa and Asia. To protect their Calvinist faith and political liberties, they revolted against Spanish rule in 1566. After fifteen years of war, the seven northern provinces declared their independence, becoming the Dutch Republic (or Holland) in 1581.

The English king Henry VIII (r. 1509–1547) initially opposed Protestantism. However, when the pope refused to annul his marriage to the Spanish princess Catherine of Aragon in 1534, Henry broke with Rome and placed himself at the head of the new Church of England, which promptly granted an annulment. Although Henry's new church maintained most Catholic doctrines and practices, Protestant teachings continued to spread. Faced with popular pressure for reform, Henry's daughter and successor, Queen Elizabeth I (r. 1558–1603), approved a Protestant confession of faith. But she also retained the Catholic ritual of Holy Communion and left the Church in the hands of Anglican bishops and archbishops. Elizabeth's compromises angered radical Protestants, but the independent Anglican Church was anathema to the Spanish king, Philip II.

Elizabeth supported a generation of English seafarers who took increasingly aggressive actions against Spanish control of American wealth. The most famous of these Elizabethan "sea dogs" was Francis Drake, a rough-hewn, devoutly Protestant farmer's son from Devon who took to the sea and became a scourge to Philip's American interests. In 1577, he ventured into the Pacific to disrupt Spanish shipping to Manila. Drake's fleet lost three ships and a hundred men, but the survivors captured two Spanish treasure ships and completed the first English circumnavigation of the globe. When Drake's flagship, the *Golden Hind,* returned to England in 1580, it brought enough silver, gold, silk, and spices to bring his investors a 4,700 percent return on their investment.

At the same time, Elizabeth imposed English rule over Gaelic-speaking Catholic Ireland. Calling the Irish "wild savages" who were "more barbarous and more brutish in their customs . . . than in any other part of the world," English soldiers brutally massacred thousands, prefiguring the treatment of Indians in North America.

To meet Elizabeth's challenges, Philip sent a Spanish Armada — 130 ships and 30,000 men — against England in 1588. Philip intended to restore the Roman Church in England and then wipe out Calvinism in Holland. But he failed utterly: a fierce storm and English ships destroyed the Spanish fleet. Philip continued to spend his American gold and silver on religious wars, an ill-advised policy that diverted workers and resources from Spain's fledgling industries. The gold was like a "shewer of Raine," complained one critic, that left "no benefite behind." Oppressed by high taxes on agriculture and fearful of military service, more than 200,000 residents of Castile, once the most prosperous region of Spain, migrated to America. By the time of Philip's death in 1598, Spain was in serious economic decline.

By contrast, England's population soared from 3 million in 1500 to 5 million in 1630. English merchants had long supplied European weavers with high-quality wool; around 1500, they created their own textile industry. Merchants bought wool from the owners of great estates and sent it to landless peasants in small cottages to spin and weave into cloth. The government aided textile entrepreneurs by setting low wage rates and helped merchants by giving them monopolies in foreign markets.

This system of state-assisted manufacturing and trade became known as **mercantilism**. By encouraging textile production, Elizabeth reduced imports and increased exports. The resulting favorable balance of trade caused gold and silver to flow into England and stimulated further economic expansion. Increased trade with Turkey and India also boosted import duties, which swelled the royal treasury and the monarch's

Queen Elizabeth Receiving Dutch Ambassadors This sixteenth-century Dutch painting by an anonymous artist depicts a pair of Dutch ambassadors being received by England's Queen Elizabeth I. The seventeen provinces that constituted the Dutch Republic were in rebellion against Spanish rule in the later decades of the sixteenth century and hoped for Elizabeth's support. In 1585 Elizabeth signed the Treaty of Nonsuch, pledging her support for the Dutch cause. An undeclared war with Spain ensued, punctuated by the defeat of the Spanish Armada in 1588. Neue Galerie, Kessel, Germany © Museumslandschaft Hessen Kassel/Bridgeman Images.

TRACE CHANGE OVER TIME
Why did Spain's economy deteriorate and England's economy improve in the sixteenth century?

power. By 1600, Elizabeth's mercantile policies had laid the foundations for overseas colonization. Now the English had the merchant fleet and wealth needed to challenge Spain's control of the Western Hemisphere.

> **IN YOUR OWN WORDS**   How did Spanish colonization affect people in the Americas and in Europe?

Plantation Colonies

As Spain hammered out its American empire and struggled against its Protestant rivals, Portugal, England, France, and the Netherlands created successful plantation settlements in Brazil, Jamestown, Maryland, and the Caribbean islands (Map 2.2). Worldwide demand for sugar and tobacco fueled the growth of these new colonies, and the resulting influx of colonists diminished Spain's dominance in the New World. At the same time, they imposed dramatic new pressures on Native populations, who scrambled to survive and carve out pathways to the future.

Brazil's Sugar Plantations

Portuguese colonists transformed the tropical lowlands of coastal Brazil into a sugar plantation zone like the ones they had recently created on Madeira, the Azores, the Cape Verdes, and São Tomé. The work proceeded slowly, but by 1590 more than a

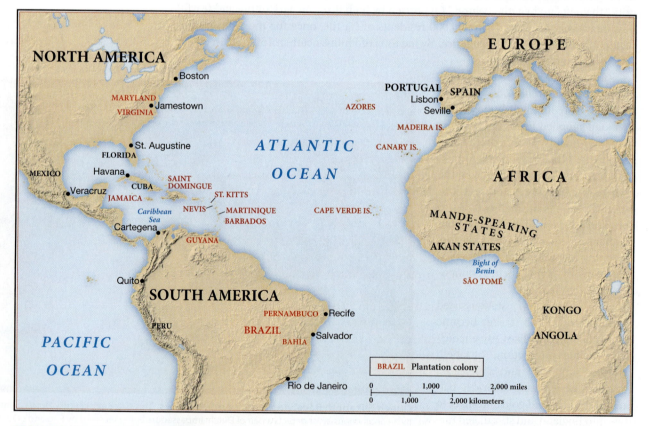

MAP 2.2 The Plantation Colonies
The plantation zone in the Americas extended from the tropical coast of Brazil northwestward through the West Indies and into the tropical and subtropical lowlands of southeastern North America. Sugar was the most important plantation crop in the Americas, but where the soil or climate could not support it planters experimented with a wide variety of other possibilities, including tobacco, indigo, cotton, cacao, and rice.

thousand sugar mills had been established in Pernambuco and Bahia. Each large plantation had its own milling operation: because sugarcane is extremely heavy and rots quickly, it must be processed on site. Thus sugar plantations combined backbreaking agricultural labor with milling, extracting, and refining processes that made them look like Industrial Revolution–era factories.

Initially, Portuguese planters hoped that Brazil's indigenous peoples would supply the labor required to operate their sugar plantations. But, beginning with a smallpox epidemic in 1559, unfamiliar diseases ravaged the coastal Indian population. As a result, planters turned to African slaves in ever-growing numbers; by 1620, the switch was complete. While Spanish colonies in Mexico and Peru took shape with astonishing speed following conquest, Brazil's development required both trial and error and prolonged hard work.

England's Tobacco Colonies

England was slow to pursue colonization in the Americas. There were fumbling attempts in the 1580s in Newfoundland and Maine, privately organized and poorly funded. Sir Walter Raleigh's three expeditions to North Carolina ended in disaster when 117 settlers on Roanoke Island, left unsupplied for several years, vanished. The fate of Roanoke—the "lost colony"—remains a compelling puzzle for modern historians.

The Jamestown Settlement Merchants then took charge of English expansion. In 1606, King James I (r. 1603–1625) granted to the Virginia Company of London all the lands stretching from present-day North Carolina to southern New York. To honor the memory of Elizabeth I, the never-married "Virgin Queen," the company's directors named the region Virginia (Map 2.3). This was a **joint-stock corporation** that pooled the resources of many investors, spreading the financial risk widely. Influenced by the Spanish example, in 1607 the Virginia Company dispatched an all-male group with no ability to support itself: there were no women, farmers, or ministers among the first arrivals. Instead the first colonists hoped to demand tribute from the region's Indian population while it searched out valuable commodities like pearls and gold. All they wanted, one of them said, was to "dig gold, refine gold, load gold."

But there was no gold, and the men fared poorly in their new environment. Arriving in Virginia after an exhausting four-month voyage, they settled on a swampy peninsula, which they named Jamestown to honor the king. There the adventurers lacked access to fresh water, refused to plant crops, and quickly died off; only 38 of the 120 men were alive nine months later. Death rates remained high: by 1611, the Virginia Company had dispatched 1,200 colonists to Jamestown, but fewer than half remained alive. "Our men were destroyed with cruell diseases, as Swellings, Fluxes, Burning Fevers, and by warres," reported one of the settlement's leaders, "but for the most part they died of meere famine."

Their plan to dominate the local Indian population ran up against the presence of Powhatan, the powerful paramount chief who oversaw some thirty subordinate chiefdoms between the James and Potomac rivers. He was willing to treat the English traders as potential allies who could provide valuable goods, but—just as the Englishmen expected tribute from the Indians—Powhatan expected tribute from the English. He provided the hungry English adventurers with corn; in return, he demanded "hatchets . . . bells, beads, and copper" as well as "two great guns" and expected

Carolina Indians Fishing, 1585 Though maize was a mainstay of the Indian diet, Native peoples along the Atlantic coast also harvested protein-rich fish, crabs, and oysters. In this watercolor by the English adventurer John White, Indians gather fish (in their "cannow," or dugout canoe) in the shallow waters of the Albemarle Sound, off present-day North Carolina. On the left, note the weir used both to catch fish and to store them live for later consumption. © The Trustees of the British Museum/Art Resource, NY.

John White's Map of Virginia This map, drawn by Roanoke colonist John White, may hold a clue to the fate of the so-called lost colony. The island of Roanoke is right of center, just off the mainland and within the barrier islands. Directly west, on the point where the Roanoke and Chowan rivers join, is a (barely visible) paper patch. When lit from behind, a red fort is clearly visible beneath the patch, suggesting that the Roanoke colonists may already have identified a settlement site there: when he left the colony, John White wrote that the remaining colonists "were prepared to remove from Roanoak 50 miles into the maine[land]." Archaeologists and historians plan to use this discovery to guide further explorations in the area. The Art Archive at Art Resource, NY.

Jamestown to become a dependent community within his chiefdom. Subsequently, Powhatan arranged a marriage between his daughter Pocahontas and John Rolfe, an English colonist (Thinking Like a Historian). But these tactics failed. The inability to decide who would pay tribute to whom led to more than a decade of uneasy relations, followed by a long era of ruinous warfare.

The war was precipitated by the discovery of a cash crop that — like sugar in Brazil — offered colonists a way to turn a profit but required steady expansion onto Indian lands. Tobacco was a plant native to the Americas, long used by Indians as a medicine and a stimulant. John Rolfe found a West Indian strain that could flourish in Virginia soil and produced a small crop — "pleasant, sweet, and strong" — that fetched a high price in England and spurred the migration of thousands of new settlers. The English soon came to crave the nicotine that tobacco contained. James I initially condemned the plant as a "vile Weed" whose "black stinking fumes" were "baleful to the nose, harmful to the brain, and dangerous to the lungs." But the king's attitude changed as taxes on imported tobacco bolstered the royal treasury. Powhatan, however, now accused the English of coming "not to trade but to invade my people and possess my country."

To encourage immigration, the Virginia Company allowed individual settlers to own land, granting 100 acres to every freeman and more to those who imported servants. The company also created a system of representative government: the **House of Burgesses**, first convened in 1619, could make laws and levy taxes, although the governor and the company council in England could veto its acts. By 1622, landownership, self-government, and a judicial system based on "the lawes of the realme of England" had attracted some 4,500 new recruits. To encourage the transition to a settler colony, the Virginia Company recruited dozens of "Maides young and uncorrupt to make wifes to the Inhabitants."

The Indian War of 1622 The influx of migrants sparked war with the neighboring Indians. The struggle began with an assault led by Opechancanough, Powhatan's younger brother and successor. In 1607, Opechancanough had attacked some of the first English invaders; subsequently, he "stood aloof" from the English settlers and "would not be drawn to any Treaty." In particular, he resisted English proposals to place Indian children in schools to be "brought upp in Christianytie." Upon becoming the paramount chief in 1621, Opechancanough told the leader of the neighboring Potomack Indians: "Before the end of two moons, there should not be an Englishman in all their Countries."

Opechancanough almost succeeded. In 1622, he coordinated a surprise attack by twelve Indian chiefdoms that killed 347 English settlers, nearly one-third of the population. The English fought back by seizing the fields and food of those they now called "naked, tanned, deformed Savages" and declared "a perpetual war without peace or truce" that lasted for a decade. They sold captured warriors into slavery, "destroy[ing] them who sought to destroy us" and taking control of "their cultivated places."

Shocked by the Indian uprising, James I revoked the Virginia Company's charter and, in 1624, made Virginia a **royal colony**. Now the king and his ministers appointed the governor and a small advisory council, retaining the locally elected House of

Burgesses but stipulating that the king's Privy Council (a committee of political advisors) must ratify all legislation. The king also decreed the legal establishment of the Church of England in the colony, which meant that residents had to pay taxes to support its clergy. These institutions—an appointed governor, an elected assembly, a formal legal system, and an established Anglican Church—became the model for royal colonies throughout English America.

Lord Baltimore Settles Catholics in Maryland

A second tobacco-growing colony developed in neighboring Maryland. King Charles I (r. 1625–1649), James's successor, was secretly sympathetic toward Catholicism, and in 1632 he granted lands bordering the vast Chesapeake Bay to Catholic aristocrat Cecilius Calvert, Lord Baltimore. Thus Maryland became a refuge for Catholics, who were subject to persecution in England. In 1634, twenty gentlemen, mostly Catholics, and two hundred artisans and laborers, mostly Protestants, established St. Mary's City at the mouth of the Potomac River. To minimize religious confrontations, the proprietor instructed the governor to allow "no scandall nor offence to be given to any of the Protestants" and to "cause All Acts of Romane Catholicque Religion to be done as privately as may be."

Maryland grew quickly because Baltimore imported many artisans and offered ample lands to wealthy migrants. But political conflict threatened the colony's stability. Disputing Baltimore's powers, settlers elected a representative assembly and insisted on the right to initiate legislation, which Baltimore grudgingly granted. Anti-Catholic agitation by Protestants also threatened his religious goals. To protect his coreligionists, Lord Baltimore persuaded the assembly to enact the Toleration Act (1649), which granted all Christians the right to follow their beliefs and hold church services. In Maryland, as in Virginia, tobacco quickly became the main crop, and that similarity, rather than any religious difference, ultimately made the two colonies very much alike in their economic and social systems.

The Caribbean Islands

Virginia's experiment with a cash crop that created a land-intensive plantation society ran parallel to developments in the Caribbean, where English, French, and Dutch sailors began looking for a permanent toehold. In 1624, a small English party under the command of Sir Thomas Warner established a settlement on St. Christopher (St. Kitts). A year later, Warner allowed a French group to settle the other end of the island so they could better defend their position from the Spanish. Within a few years, the English and French colonists on St. Kitts had driven the native Caribs from the island, weathered a Spanish attack, and created a common set of bylaws for mutual occupation of the island.

After St. Kitts, a dozen or so colonies were founded in the Lesser Antilles, including the French islands of Martinique, Guadeloupe, and St. Bart's; the English outposts of Nevis, Antigua, Montserrat, Anguilla, Tortola, and Barbados; and the Dutch colony of St. Eustatius. In 1655, an English fleet captured the Spanish island of Jamaica—one of the large islands of the Greater Antilles—and opened it to settlement as well. A few of these islands were unpopulated before Europeans settled there; elsewhere, native populations were displaced, and often wiped out, within a decade or so. Only on the largest islands did native populations hold out longer.

Colonists experimented with a wide variety of cash crops, including tobacco, indigo, cotton, cacao, and ginger. Beginning in the 1640s—and drawing on the example of

MAP 2.3 Eastern North America, 1650

By 1650, four European nations had permanent settlements along the eastern coast of North America, but only England had substantial numbers of settlers, some 25,000 in New England and another 15,000 in the Chesapeake region. French, Dutch, Swedish, and English colonists were also trading European manufactures to Native Americans in exchange for animal furs and skins, with far-reaching implications for Indian societies.

EXPLAIN CONSEQUENCES
How did the proximity of the Powhatan Chiefdom affect developments in early Virginia?

Who Was Pocahontas?

Matoaka — nicknamed Pocahontas — was born around 1596 in the region the English would soon name Virginia. A daughter of Chief Powhatan, her interactions with colonists were important at the time and have been mythologized ever since. Pocahontas left no writings, so what we know of her comes from others. From these accounts, we know that she acted as a mediator with the Jamestown settlers; she was the first Native American to marry an Englishman; and she traveled to England with her husband and son. Pocahontas fell ill and died in Gravesend, England, in June 1617.

1. **John Smith,** *Generall Historie of Virginia*, **1624.** *Smith's description of being a captive of Powhatan in 1607.*

   Having feasted [Smith] after their best barbarous manner they could, a long consultation was held, but the conclusion was, two great stones were brought before Powhatan: then as many as could layd hands on him, dragged him to them, and thereon laid his head, and being ready with their clubs, to beate out his braines, Pocahontas the Kings dearest daughter, when no entreaty could prevaile, got his head in her armes, and laid her owne upon his to save him from death: whereat the Emperour was contented he should live to make him hatchets, and her bells, beads, and copper.

2. **Robert Vaughn's engraving of Pocahontas saving Smith's life, from John Smith's** *Generall Historie of Virginia*, **1624.**

3. **John Smith,** *Generall Historie of Virginia*, **1624.** *Pocahontas visited Jamestown regularly in the years following Smith's capture. Smith returned to England in 1609; four years later Captain Samuel Argall kidnapped Pocahontas and held her captive in Jamestown.*

   [S]he too James towne [was brought.] A messenger forthwith was sent to her father, that his daughter Pocahontas he loved so dearely, he must ransome with our men, swords, peeces, tooles, &c. he treacherously had stolen. . . . [H]e . . . sent us word, that when we would deliver his daughter, he would make us satisfaction for all injuries done to us, and give us five hundred bushels of Corne, and for ever be friends with us. . . . [W]e could not believe the rest of our armes were either lost or stolen from him, and therefore till he sent them, we would keep his daughter. . . . [W]e heard no more from him a long time after. . . . .

   [Long before this, Master John Rolfe, an honest Gentleman of good behavior had been in love with Pocahontas, and she with him. . . . T]his marriage came soone to the knowledge of Powhatan, a thing acceptable to him, as appeared by his sudden consent, for within ten daies he sent Opachisco, an old Uncle of hers, and two of his sons, to see the manner of the marriage, and to do in that behalf what they were requested . . . which was accordingly done about the first of April: And ever since we have had friendly trade and commerce.

4. **John Rolfe, Letter to Sir Thomas Dale, 1614.** *Pocahontas and John Rolfe married in April 1614. In June, Rolfe defended his motives in this letter to Virginia's deputy-governor.*

   I freely subject my selfe to your grave and mature judgment, deliberation, approbation and determination. . . . [I am not led by] the unbridled desire of carnal affection: but for the good of this plantation, for the honour of our countrie, for the glory of God, for my owne salvation, and for the converting to the true knowledge of God and Jesus Christ, an unbeleeving creature, namely Pocahontas. To whom my hartie and best thoughts are, and have [for] a long time bin so intangled, and inthralled in so intricate a labyrinth, that I was even awearied to unwinde my selfe thereout. . . .

[I have often thought]: surely these are wicked instigations, hatched by him who seeketh and delighteth in man's destruction[.]

I say the holy spirit of God has often demanded of me, why I was created . . . but to labour in the Lord's vineyard. . . . Likewise adding hereunto her great appearance of love to me, her desire to be taught and instructed in the knowledge of God, her capableness of understanding, her aptness and willingness to receive any good impression, and also the spirituall, besides her owne incitements stirring me up hereunto. . . .

Now if the vulgar sort, who square all men's actions by the base rule of their owne filthiness, shall tax or taunt me in this my godly labour: let them know, it is not any hungry appetite, to gorge my selfe with incontinency; sure (if I would, and were so sensually inclined) I might satisfy such desire, though not without a seared conscience.

5. Portrait of Pocahontas by Simon Van De Pass, 1616. *In 1616, the Virginia Company of London sent Pocahontas, John Rolfe, and their son Thomas to England, where she met King James and sat for this portrait, the only surviving image of Pocahontas.*

Matoaks als Rebecka daughter to the mighty Prince
Powhatan Emperour of Attanoughskomouck als virginia
converted and baptized in the Christian faith, and
wife to the worll Mr Joh: Rolff.

S: Pass: sculp: Compton Holland excud:

6. John Smith, *Generall Historie of Virginia,* **1624.** *In 1624, John Smith recalled a meeting he had with Pocahontas during her 1616 tour of England.*

[H]earing shee was at Branford with divers of my friends, I went to see her: After a modest salutation, without any word, she turned about, obscured her face, as not seeming well contented; and in that humour her husband, with divers others, we all left her two or three houres. . . . But not long after, she began to talke, and remembred mee well what courtesies she had done: saying, ["]You did promise Powhatan what was yours should bee his, and he the like to you; you called him father being in his land a stranger, and by the same reason so must I doe you:["] which though I would have excused, I durst not allow of that title, because she was a Kings daughter; with a well set countenance she said, ["]Were you not afraid to come into my fathers Countrie, and caused feare in him and all his people (but mee) and feare you here I should call you father; I tell you then I will, and you shall call mee childe, and so I will bee for ever and ever your Countrieman. They did tell us [always] you were dead, and I knew no other till I came to [Plymouth]; yet Powhatan did command Uttamatomakkin to seeke you, and know the truth, because your Countriemen will lie much.["]

SOURCES: (1, 3, 6) John Smith, *Generall Historie of Virginia* (Glasgow: James MacLehose and Sons, 1907), 101, 218, 220, 238–239; (4) J. Franklin Jameson, *Narratives of Early Virginia* (New York: Charles Scribner's Sons, 1907), 237–244.

ANALYZING THE EVIDENCE

1. Most historians now believe that the event described and shown in sources 1 and 2 was a Powhatan ritual to make Smith an ally and that his life was not actually in danger. What elements of these sources suggest the validity of this interpretation? Why would Pocahontas — a child of eleven or twelve at the time — have had a role in such a ritual?

2. How does Vaughn (source 2) depict power relations and social hierarchy among the Powhatans? Where does Pocahontas fit within this hierarchy? What messages about Pocahontas do you think Van De Pass (source 5) intended to convey? How do these images contribute to the Pocahontas myth?

3. How does Rolfe explain his interest in Pocahontas (source 4)? What is his view of her? How do you interpret the letter?

4. Assess the reliability of sources 1, 3, and 6 and consider Smith's motive in including them in his *Historie*. Source 6 purports to record an actual conversation between Pocahontas and Smith. What is the tone of this encounter, and what might explain Pocahontas's remarks?

PUTTING IT ALL TOGETHER

Imagine the various encounters Pocahontas experienced with the Jamestown Englishmen from her point of view. Reflect on who Pocahontas was as described in these documents — savior and friend, captive, baptized wife, Virginia Company prize, and betrayed ally — and in a brief essay, use Pocahontas's experience to explore the uncertain nature of English-Powhatan relations in the first decade of contact.

A Sugar Mill in the French West Indies, 1655 Making sugar required both hard labor and considerable expertise. Field slaves labored strenuously in the hot tropical sun to cut the sugarcane and carry or cart it to an oxen- or wind-powered mill, where it was pressed to yield the juice. Then skilled slave artisans took over. They carefully heated the juice and, at the proper moment, added ingredients that granulated the sugar and separated it from the molasses, which was later distilled into rum.   Sarin Images/Granger, NYC.

Brazil — planters on many of the islands shifted to sugar cultivation. Where conditions were right, as they were in Barbados, Jamaica, Nevis, and Martinique, these colonies were soon producing substantial crops of sugar and, as a consequence, claimed some of the world's most valuable real estate.

Plantation Life

In North America and the Caribbean, plantations were initially small **freeholds**, farms of 30 to 50 acres owned and farmed by families or male partners. But the logic of plantation agriculture soon encouraged consolidation: large planters engrossed as much land as they could and experimented with new forms of labor discipline that maximized their control over production. In Virginia, the **headright system** guaranteed 50 acres of land to anyone who paid the passage of a new immigrant to the colony; thus, by buying additional indentured servants and slaves, the colony's largest planters also amassed ever-greater claims to land.

European demand for tobacco set off a forty-year economic boom in the Chesapeake. "All our riches for the present do consist in tobacco," a planter remarked in 1630. Exports rose from 3 million pounds in 1640 to 10 million pounds in 1660. After 1650, wealthy migrants from gentry or noble families established large estates along the coastal rivers, then acquired English indentured servants and enslaved Africans to work their lands. At about the same time, the switch to sugar production in Barbados caused the price of land there to quadruple, driving small landowners out.

For rich and poor alike, life in the plantation colonies of North America and the Caribbean was harsh. The scarcity of towns deprived settlers of community (Map 2.4). Families were equally scarce because there were few women, and marriages often ended with the early death of a spouse. Pregnant women were especially vulnerable to malaria, spread by mosquitoes that flourished in tropical and subtropical climates (Interpretations). Many mothers died after bearing a first or second child, so orphaned children (along with unmarried young men) formed a large segment of the society. Sixty percent of the children born in Middlesex County, Virginia, before 1680 lost one or both parents before they were thirteen. Death was pervasive. Although 15,000 English migrants arrived in Virginia between 1622 and 1640, the population rose only from 2,000 to 8,000. It was even harsher in the islands, where yellow fever epidemics killed indiscriminately. On Barbados, burials outnumbered baptisms in the second half of the seventeenth century by 4 to 1.

Indentured Servitude Still, the prospect of owning land continued to lure settlers. By 1700, more than 100,000 English migrants had come to Virginia and Maryland and over 200,000 had migrated to the islands of the West Indies, principally to Barbados; the vast majority to both destinations traveled as indentured servants. Shipping registers from the English port of Bristol reveal the backgrounds of 5,000 servants embarking for the Chesapeake. Three-quarters were young men. They came to Bristol searching for work; once there, merchants persuaded them to sign contracts to labor in America. **Indentured servitude** contracts bound the men — and the quarter who

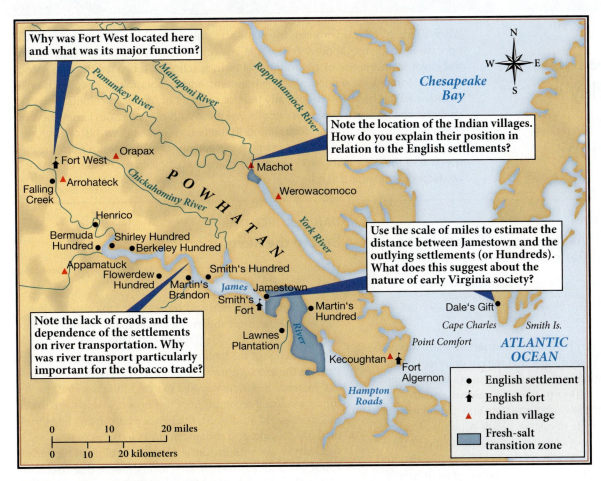

Why was Fort West located here and what was its major function?

Note the location of the Indian villages. How do you explain their position in relation to the English settlements?

Use the scale of miles to estimate the distance between Jamestown and the outlying settlements (or Hundreds). What does this suggest about the nature of early Virginia society?

Note the lack of roads and the dependence of the settlements on river transportation. Why was river transport particularly important for the tobacco trade?

MAP 2.4   River Plantations in Virginia, c. 1640
The first migrants settled in widely dispersed plantations along the James River, a settlement pattern promoted by the tobacco economy. From their riverfront plantations wealthy planter-merchants could easily load heavy hogsheads of tobacco onto oceangoing ships and offload supplies that they then sold to smallholding planters. Consequently, few substantial towns or trading centers developed in the Chesapeake region.

were women — to work for a master for four or five years, after which they would be free to marry and work for themselves.

For merchants, servants were valuable cargo: their contracts fetched high prices from Chesapeake and West Indian planters. For the plantation owners, indentured servants were a bargain if they survived the voyage and their first year in a harsh new disease environment, a process called "seasoning." During the Chesapeake's tobacco boom, a male servant could produce five times his purchase price in a single year. To maximize their gains, many masters ruthlessly exploited servants, forcing them to work long hours, beating them without cause, and withholding permission to marry. If servants ran away or became pregnant, masters went to court to increase the term of their service. Female servants were especially vulnerable to abuse. A Virginia law of 1692 stated that "dissolute masters have gotten their maids with child; and yet claim the benefit of their service." Planters got rid of uncooperative servants by selling their contracts. In Virginia, an Englishman remarked in disgust that "servants were sold up and down like horses."

Few indentured servants escaped poverty. In the Chesapeake, half the men died before completing the term of their contract, and another quarter remained landless. Only one-quarter achieved their quest for property and respectability. Female servants generally fared better. Because men had grown "very sensible of the Misfortune of

What Role Did Climate Play in American Colonization?

When a January blizzard grounds the plane scheduled to whisk us to our tropical vacation, we immediately appreciate the role environmental factors play in shaping our daily lives. With the rise of environmental history, scholars, too, have come to recognize the compelling influence of environment and geography in shaping human experience. This has been particularly true for scholars of American colonization who study Europeans and indigenous peoples wrestling with climate issues largely beyond their control or even their understanding. In the two excerpts below, historians Karen Kupperman and Daniel K. Richter examine the early history of America from the perspective of these peoples' experience with climate change. In each case, climate is a key factor in explaining that history.

KAREN KUPPERMAN

The Puzzle of the American Climate in the Early Colonial Period

SOURCE: Karen Kupperman, "The Puzzle of the American Climate in the Early Colonial Period," *American Historical Review* 87 (1982): 1288–1289. *The American Historical Review* © 1982 Oxford University Press. Used by permission of Oxford University Press and the author.

Throughout the early period of colonization, there was continuing tension between hope that the environment might meet English expectations and requirements and accommodation by English settlers to the environment actually encountered. The steady accumulation and assimilation of facts about the climate of eastern North America threatened the classical concept of climates — the belief that climate is constant in any latitude around the world. Yet colonists and promoters struggled to adapt the old concept to fit new evidence. . . . Newfoundland came to be rejected for colonization, although its importance as a fishing ground continued. New England was finally perceived as a rough country where settlement was possible. . . . In the early seventeenth-century southern mainland colonies, settlers continued to base their expectations on latitude and to hope they could eventually produce commodities comparable to those England imported from southern Europe.

DANIEL K. RICHTER

Before the Revolution

SOURCE: Daniel K. Richter, *Before the Revolution: America's Ancient Pasts* (Cambridge, MA: Belknap Press of Harvard University Press, 2010), 30–31.

Summer and winter, rain and snow, ceased to come predictably in the Southwest somewhat earlier than elsewhere in the northern hemisphere. . . . [D]ense populations had been living at the edge of the land's agricultural carrying capacity. . . . Perhaps the extraordinary religious fervor, political capital, and material resources devoted to agricultural ceremonies . . . shows a cultural recognition of just how unstable the balance was. In the arid Southwest, the balance had always been particularly delicate, and collapse appears to have come suddenly — not with the onset of global cooling in the early 1300s, but with a fifty-year-long local drought that struck the Chaco Canyon area after 1130. . . . All of the major Ancestral Puebloan and Hohokam urban centers were gradually abandoned in favor of new pueblos. . . . The former, stratified system of smaller supporting villages apparently disappeared in favor of a more egalitarian settlement pattern.

QUESTIONS FOR ANALYSIS

1. Name two key differences in the argument each historian makes about the role of climate in shaping the early history of America. What explains these differences?

2. What were the key differences in how European colonizers understood climate (excerpt 1) and how Native peoples in the Southwest understood climate (excerpt 2)?

3. To what extent does Chapter 2's examination of America's early history reflect each historian's emphasis on climate as a factor in explaining that history?

Wanting Wives," many propertied planters married female servants. Thus a few — very fortunate — men and women escaped early death or a life of landless poverty.

African Laborers The rigors of indentured servitude paled before the brutality that accompanied the large-scale shift to African slave labor. In Barbados and the other English islands, sugar production devoured laborers, and the supply of indentured servants quickly became inadequate to planters' needs. By 1690, blacks outnumbered whites on Barbados nearly 3 to 1, and white slave owners were developing a code of force and terror to keep sugar flowing and maintain control of the black majority that surrounded them. The first comprehensive slave legislation for the island, adopted in 1661, was called an "Act for the better ordering and governing of Negroes."

In the Chesapeake, the shift to slave labor was more gradual. In 1619, John Rolfe noted that "a Dutch man of warre . . . sold us twenty Negars" — slaves originally shipped by the Portuguese from the port of Luanda in Angola. For a generation, the number of Africans remained small. About 400 Africans lived in the Chesapeake colonies in 1649, just 2 percent of the population. By 1670, that figure had reached 5 percent. Most Africans served their English masters for life. However, since English common law did not acknowledge chattel slavery, it was possible for some Africans to escape bondage. Some were freed as a result of Christian baptism; some purchased their freedom from their owners; some — like Elizabeth Key, whose story was related at the beginning of the chapter — won their freedom in the courts. Once free, some ambitious Africans became landowners and purchased slaves or the labor contracts of English servants for themselves.

Social mobility for Africans ended in the 1660s with the collapse of the tobacco boom and the increasing political power of the gentry. Tobacco had once sold for 30 pence a pound; now it fetched less than one-tenth of that. The "low price of Tobacco requires it should bee made as cheap as possible," declared Virginia planter-politician Nicholas Spencer, and "blacks can make it cheaper than whites." As they imported more African workers, the English-born political elite grew more race-conscious. Increasingly, Spencer and other leading legislators distinguished English from African residents by color (white-black) rather than by religion (Christian-pagan). By 1671, the Virginia House of Burgesses had forbidden Africans to own guns or join the militia. It also barred them — "tho baptized and enjoying their own Freedom" — from owning English servants. Being black was increasingly a mark of inferior legal status, and slavery was fast becoming a permanent and hereditary condition. As an English clergyman observed, "These two words, Negro and Slave had by custom grown Homogeneous and convertible."

> **COMPARE AND CONTRAST**
> How were the experiences of indentured servants and slaves in the Chesapeake and the Caribbean similar? In what ways were they different?

> **IN YOUR OWN WORDS** How did the labor demands of plantation colonies transform the process of colonization?

Neo-European Colonies

While Mesoamerica and the Andes emerged at the heart of a tribute-based empire in Latin America, and tropical and subtropical environments were transformed into plantation societies, a series of colonies that more closely replicated European patterns of economic and social organization developed in the temperate zone along North America's Atlantic coast (America in Global Context). Dutch, French, and English sailors probed the continent's northern coastline, initially searching for a Northwest Passage through the continent to Asia. Gradually, they developed an interest in the region on its own terms. They traded for furs with coastal Native American populations, fished for cod on the Grand Banks off the coast of Newfoundland, and established freehold family farms and larger manors where they reproduced European patterns of agricultural life. Many migrants also came with aspirations to create godly communities, places of refuge where they could put religious ideals into practice. New France, New Netherland, and New England were the three pillars of neo-European colonization in the early seventeenth century.

New France

In the 1530s, Jacques Cartier ventured up the St. Lawrence River and claimed it for France. Cartier's claim to the St. Lawrence languished for three-quarters of a century,

Plantation Colonies Versus Neo-Europes

The prospects for Europeans who traveled to tropical plantations like Barbados differed dramatically from those traveling to neo-European colonies like Massachusetts Bay. In the former, planters employed small armies of servants and slaves; in the latter, the first generation of colonists worked hard, often in cold climates and rocky soils, to eke out a living.

HENRY WHISTLER'S JOURNAL, 1655

SOURCE: *The Narrative of General Venables* (New York: Longmans, Green, and Co., 1900), 145–146.

This Island [Barbados] is one of the Richest Spots of ground in the world and fully inhabited. . . . The gentry here doth Hue [appear] far better than ours do in England : they have most of them 100 or 2 or 3 of slaves[,] apes who they command as they please. . . . This Island is inhabited with all sorts : with English, French, Dutch, Scots, Irish, Spaniards they being Jews : with Indians and miserable Negroes borne to perpetual slavery they and their seed : these Negroes they do allow as many wives as they will have, some will have 3 or 4, according as they find their body able : our English here doth think a negro child the first day it is born to be worth £5, they cost them nothing the bringing up, they go all ways naked : some planters will have 30 more or les about 4 or 5 years old : they sell them from one to the other as we do sheep. This Island is the Dunghill whereon England doth cast forth its rubbish. . . . A rogue in England will hardly make a cheater here : a Bawd brought over puts on a demure comportment, a whore if handsome makes a wife for some rich planter.

WILLIAM WOOD, *NEW ENGLAND'S PROSPECT*, 1634

SOURCE: William Wood, *New England's Prospect* (Boston: The University of Massachusetts Press, 1993), 28–29, 68.

But it may be objected that it is too cold a country for our English men, who have been accustomed to a warmer climate. To which it may be answered . . . , there is wood good store and better cheap to build warm houses and make good fires, which makes the winter less tedious. . . . [T]rue it is that some venturing too nakedly in extremity of cold, being more foolhardy than wise, have for a time lost the use of their feet, others the use of their fingers; but time and surgery afterwards recovered them. Some have had their overgrown beards so frozen together that they could not get their strong-water bottles into their mouths. . . . [W]hereas many do disparage the land, saying a man cannot live without labor, in that they more disparage and discredit themselves in giving the world occasion to take notice of their dronish disposition that would live off the sweat of another man's brows. . . . For all in New England must be workers of some kind. . . . And howsoever they are accounted poor, they are well contented and look not so much at abundance as at competency.

QUESTIONS FOR ANALYSIS

1. Henry Whistler was a soldier who briefly visited Barbados on a military expedition to the West Indies, while William Wood lived for four years in Massachusetts Bay. How might that difference influence the tone of these two descriptions?

2. What core values does each author ascribe to the colony he writes about? What kinds of people were most likely to end up in each of these two colonies?

---

but in 1608 Samuel de Champlain returned and founded the fur-trading post of Quebec. Trade with the Cree-speaking Montagnais; Algonquian-speaking Micmacs, Ottawas, and Ojibwas; and Iroquois-speaking Hurons gave the French access to furs — mink, otter, and beaver — that were in great demand in Europe. To secure plush beaver pelts from the Hurons, who controlled trade north of the Great Lakes, Champlain provided them with manufactured goods. Selling pelts, an Indian told a French priest, "makes kettles, hatchets, swords, knives, bread." It also made guns, which Champlain sold to the Hurons.

The Hurons also became the first focus of French Catholic missionary activity. Hundreds of priests, most of them Jesuits, fanned out to live in Indian communities. They mastered Indian languages and came to understand, and sometimes respect, Indian values. Many Native peoples initially welcomed the French "Black Robes" as spiritually powerful beings, but when prayers to the Christian god did not protect them from disease, the Indians grew skeptical. A Peoria chief charged that a priest's "fables are good only in his own country; we have our own [beliefs], which do not make us die as his do." When a drought struck, Indians blamed the missionaries. "If you cannot make rain, they speak of nothing less than making away with you," lamented one Jesuit.

While New France became an expansive center of fur trading and missionary work, it languished as a farming settlement. In 1662, King Louis XIV (r. 1643–1714) turned New France into a royal colony and subsidized the migration of indentured servants. French servants labored under contract for three years, received a salary, and could eventually lease a farm — far more generous terms than those for indentured servants in the English colonies.

Nonetheless, few people moved to New France, a cold and forbidding country "at the end of the world," as one migrant put it. And some state policies discouraged migration. Louis XIV drafted tens of thousands of men into military service and barred Huguenots (French Calvinist Protestants) from migrating to New France, fearing they might win converts and take control of the colony. Moreover, the French legal system gave peasants strong rights to their village lands, whereas migrants to New France faced an oppressive, aristocracy- and church-dominated feudal system. In the village of Saint Ours in Quebec, for example, peasants paid 45 percent of their wheat crop to nobles and the Catholic Church. By 1698, only 15,200 Europeans lived in New France, compared to 100,000 in England's North American colonies.

The Fur Trade Luxuriant pelts like ermine and silver fox were always desirable, but the humble beaver dominated the early trade between Europeans and Indians in the Northeast. It had thick, coarse hair, but beneath that outer layer was soft "underfur." Those fine hairs were covered in microscopic barbs that allowed them to mat into a dense mass. European hatmakers pressed this fur into felt so strong and pliable that even broad-brimmed hats would hold their shape. As such hats became fashionable in Europe and the colonies, beavers were hunted to near-extinction in North America. Library and Archives Canada/NLC-3269.

Despite this small population, France eventually claimed a vast inland arc, from the St. Lawrence Valley through the Great Lakes and down the course of the Ohio and Mississippi rivers. Explorers and fur traders drove this expansion. In 1673, Jacques Marquette reached the Mississippi River in present-day Wisconsin; then, in 1681, Robert de La Salle traveled down the majestic river to the Gulf of Mexico. To honor Louis XIV, La Salle named the region Louisiana. By 1718, French merchants had founded the port of New Orleans at the mouth of the Mississippi. Eventually a network of about two dozen forts grew up in the Great Lakes and Mississippi. Soldiers and missionaries used them as bases of operations, while Indians, traders, and their métis (mixed-race) offspring created trading communities alongside them.

New Netherland

By 1600, Amsterdam had become the financial and commercial hub of northern Europe, and Dutch financiers dominated the European banking, insurance, and textile industries. Dutch merchants owned more ships and employed more sailors than did the combined fleets of England, France, and Spain. Indeed, the Dutch managed much of the world's commerce. During their struggle for independence from Spain and Portugal (ruled by Spanish monarchs, 1580–1640), the Dutch seized Portuguese forts in Africa and Indonesia and sugar plantations in Brazil. These conquests gave the Dutch control of the Atlantic trade in slaves and sugar and the Indian Ocean commerce in East Indian spices and Chinese silks and ceramics (Map 2.5).

In 1609, Dutch merchants sent the English mariner Henry Hudson to locate a navigable route to the riches of the East Indies. What he found as he probed the rivers of northeast America was a fur bonanza. Following Hudson's exploration of the river that

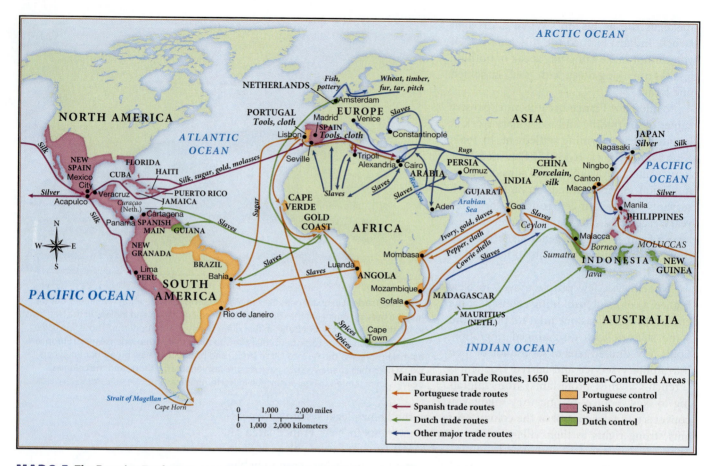

MAP 2.5 **The Eurasian Trade System and European Spheres of Influence, 1650**
Between 1550 and 1650, Spanish, Portuguese, and Dutch merchants took control of the maritime trade routes between Europe and India, Indonesia, and China. They also created two new trading connections. The South Atlantic System carried slaves, sugar, and manufactured goods between Europe, Africa, and the valuable plantation settlements in Brazil and the Caribbean islands. And a transpacific trade carried Spanish American silver to China in exchange for silks, ceramics, and other manufactures. (To trace long-term changes in trade and empires, see Map 1.4 on p. 30 and Map 5.1 on p. 143.)

now bears his name, the merchants built Fort Orange (Albany) in 1614 to trade for furs with the Munsee and Iroquois Indians. Then, in 1621, the Dutch government chartered the West India Company, which founded the colony of New Netherland, set up New Amsterdam (on Manhattan Island) as its capital, and brought in farmers and artisans to make the enterprise self-sustaining. The new colony did not thrive. The population of the Dutch Republic was too small to support much emigration — just 1.5 million people, compared to 5 million in Britain and 20 million in France — and its migrants sought riches in Southeast Asia rather than fur-trading profits in America. To protect its colony from rival European nations, the West India Company granted huge estates along the Hudson River to wealthy Dutchmen who promised to populate them. But by 1664, New Netherland had only 5,000 residents, and fewer than half of them were Dutch.

Like New France, New Netherland flourished as a fur-trading enterprise. Trade with the powerful Iroquois, though rocky at first, gradually improved. But Dutch settlers had less respect for their Algonquian-speaking neighbors. They seized prime farming land and disrupted Native American trade. In response, in 1643 the Algonquians launched attacks that nearly destroyed the colony. "Almost every place is abandoned," a settler lamented, "whilst the Indians daily threaten to overwhelm us." To defeat the Algonquians, the Dutch waged vicious warfare — maiming, burning, and killing hundreds of men, women, and children — and formed an alliance with the *t' Fort nieûw Amſterdam op de Manhatans*

New Amsterdam This early image of New Amsterdam shows a fictionalized scene. Although New Netherland was small and poorly defended, with nothing more than wooden palisades to protect the town, the engraver of this print hoped to reassure the viewer that all was well in the American colony. It is dominated by a large stone fort that appears to conform to the highest standards of European military engineering. Several Dutch merchant vessels ride at anchor, while Indians approach the shore in canoes hoping to trade their furs for European manufactures. Culture Club/Getty Images.

Mohawks, who were no less brutal. The grim progression of Euro-Indian relations — an uneasy welcome, followed by rising tensions and war — afflicted even the Dutch, who had few designs on Indian lands or on their "unregenerate" souls and were only looking to do business.

After the crippling Indian war, the West India Company ignored New Netherland and expanded its profitable trade in African slaves and Brazilian sugar. In New Amsterdam, Governor Peter Stuyvesant ruled in an authoritarian fashion, rejecting demands for a representative system of government and alienating the colony's diverse Dutch, English, and Swedish residents. Consequently, the residents of New Netherland offered little resistance when England invaded the colony in 1664. New Netherland became New York and fell under English control.

> **IDENTIFY CAUSES**
> Why did New France and New Netherland struggle to attract colonists?

The Rise of the Iroquois

Like other Native groups decimated by European diseases and warfare, the Five Nations of the Iroquois suffered as a result of colonization, but they were able to capitalize on their strategic location in central New York to dominate the region between the French and Dutch colonies. Obtaining guns and goods from Dutch merchants at Fort Orange, Iroquois warriors inflicted terror on their neighbors. Partly in response to a virulent smallpox epidemic in 1633, which cut their number by one-third, the Iroquois waged a series of devastating wars against the Hurons (1649), Neutrals (1651), Eries (1657), and Susquehannocks (1660) — all Iroquoian-speaking peoples. They razed villages, killing many residents and taking many more captive. The conquered Hurons ceased to exist as a distinct people; survivors trekked westward with displaced Algonquian peoples and formed a new nation, the Wyandots. Iroquois warriors pressed still farther — eastward into New England, south to the Carolinas, north to Quebec, and west via the Great Lakes to the Mississippi — dominating Indian groups along the way. Collectively known as the Beaver Wars, these Iroquois campaigns dramatically altered the map of northeastern North America.

Many Iroquois raids came at the expense of French-allied Algonquian Indians, and in the 1660s New France committed to all-out war against the Iroquois. In 1667, the Mohawks were the last of the Five Nations to admit defeat. As part of the peace settlement, the Five Nations accepted Jesuit missionaries into their communities. A minority of Iroquois—perhaps 20 percent of the population—converted to Catholicism and moved to the St. Lawrence Valley, where they settled in mission communities near Montreal (where their descendants still live today).

The Iroquois who remained in New York did not collapse, however. Forging a new alliance with the Englishmen who had taken over New Netherland, they would continue to be a dominant force in the politics of the Northeast for generations to come.

New England

In 1620, 102 English Protestants landed at a place they called Plymouth, near Cape Cod. A decade later, a much larger group began to arrive just north of Plymouth, in the newly chartered Massachusetts Bay Colony. By 1640, the region had attracted more than 20,000 migrants. Unlike the early arrivals in Virginia and Barbados, these were not parties of young male adventurers seeking their fortunes or bound to labor for someone else.

The Hurons' Feast of the Dead Hurons buried their dead in temporary raised tombs so they could easily care for their spirits. When they moved their villages in search of fertile soil and better hunting, the Hurons held a Feast of the Dead and reburied the bones of their own deceased (and often bones from other villages) in a common pit lined with beaver robes. This solemn ceremony united living and dead clan members, strengthening the bonds of the Huron Confederacy. It also was believed to release the spirits of the dead, allowing them to travel to the land where the first Huron, Aataentsic, fell from the sky, "made earth and man," and lived with her son and assistant, Iouskeha. Library of Congress.

They came in family groups to create communities like the ones they left behind, except that they intended to establish them according to Protestant principles, as John Calvin had done in Geneva. Their numbers were small compared to the Caribbean and the Chesapeake, but their balanced sex ratio and organized approach to community formation allowed them to multiply quickly. By distributing land broadly, they built a society of independent farm families. And by establishing a "holy commonwealth," they gave a moral dimension to American history that survives today.

The Pilgrims The **Pilgrims** were religious separatists—committed Protestants who had left the Church of England. When King James I threatened to drive them "out of the land, or else do worse," some chose to live among Dutch Calvinists in Holland. Subsequently, 35 of these exiles resolved to maintain their English identity by moving to America. Led by William Bradford and joined by 67 migrants from England, the Pilgrims sailed to America aboard the *Mayflower*. Because they lacked a royal charter, they combined themselves "together into a civill body politick," as their leader explained. This Mayflower Compact used the Pilgrims' self-governing religious congregation as the model for their political structure.

Only half of the first migrant group survived until spring, but thereafter Plymouth thrived; the cold climate inhibited the spread of mosquito-borne disease, and the Pilgrims' religious discipline encouraged a strong work ethic. Moreover, a smallpox epidemic in 1618 had devastated the local Wampanoags, minimizing the danger they posed. By 1640, there were 3,000 settlers in Plymouth. To ensure political stability, they established representative self-government, broad political rights, property ownership, and religious freedom of conscience.

Meanwhile, England plunged deeper into religious turmoil. When King Charles I repudiated certain Protestant doctrines, English Puritans, now powerful in Parliament, accused the king of "popery"—of holding Catholic beliefs. In 1629, Charles dissolved Parliament. When his archbishop, William Laud, began to purge Protestant ministers, thousands of **Puritans**—Protestants who (unlike the Pilgrims) did not separate from the Church of England but hoped to purify it of its ceremony and hierarchy—fled to America.

John Winthrop and Massachusetts Bay   The Puritan exodus began in 1630 with the departure of 900 migrants led by John Winthrop, a well-educated country squire who became the first governor of the Massachusetts Bay Colony. Calling England morally corrupt and "overburdened with people," Winthrop sought land for his children and a place in Christian history for his people. "We must consider that we shall be as a City upon a Hill," Winthrop told the migrants. "The eyes of all people are upon us." Like the Pilgrims, the Puritans envisioned a reformed Christian society with "authority in magistrates, liberty in people, purity in the church," as minister John Cotton put it. By their example, they hoped to inspire religious reform throughout Christendom.

Winthrop and his associates governed the Massachusetts Bay Colony from the town of Boston. Like the Virginia Company, the Massachusetts Bay Company was a joint-stock corporation. But the colonists transformed the company into a representative political system with a governor, council, and assembly. To ensure rule by the godly, the Puritans limited the right to vote and hold office to men who were church members. Rejecting the Plymouth Colony's policy of religious tolerance, the Massachusetts Bay Colony established Puritanism as the state-supported religion, barred other faiths from conducting services, and used the Bible as a legal guide. "Where there is no Law," they said, magistrates should rule "as near the law of God as they can." Over the next decade, about 10,000 Puritans migrated to the colony, along with 10,000 others fleeing hard times in England.

Seeing bishops as "traitours unto God," the New England Puritans placed power in the congregation of members—hence the name *Congregationalist* for their churches. Inspired by John Calvin, many Puritans embraced predestination, the idea that God saved only a few chosen people. Church members often lived in great anxiety, worried that God had not placed them among the "elect." Some hoped for a conversion experience, the intense sensation of receiving God's grace and being "born again." Other Puritans relied on "preparation," the confidence in salvation that came from spiritual guidance by their ministers. Still others believed that they were God's chosen people, the new Israelites, and would be saved if they obeyed his laws.

Roger Williams and Rhode Island   To maintain God's favor, the Massachusetts Bay magistrates purged their society of religious dissidents. One target was Roger Williams, the Puritan minister in Salem, a coastal town north of Boston. Williams opposed the decision to establish an official religion and praised the Pilgrims' separation of church and state. He advocated **toleration**, arguing that political magistrates had authority over only the "bodies, goods, and outward estates of men," not their spiritual lives. Williams also questioned the Puritans' seizure of Indian lands. The magistrates banished him from the colony in 1636.

Williams and his followers settled 50 miles south of Boston, founding the town of Providence on land purchased from the Narragansett Indians. Other religious dissidents settled nearby at Portsmouth and Newport. In 1644, these settlers obtained a corporate charter from Parliament for a new colony—Rhode Island—with full authority to rule themselves. In Rhode Island, as in Plymouth, there was no legally established church, and individuals could worship God as they pleased.

To see a longer excerpt of Winthrop's "City upon a Hill" sermon, along with other primary sources from this period, see *Sources for America's History*.

COMPARE AND CONTRAST
What made New England different from New France and New Netherland?

Anne Hutchinson The Massachusetts Bay magistrates saw a second threat to their authority in Anne Hutchinson. The wife of a merchant and mother of seven, Hutchinson held weekly prayer meetings for women and accused various Boston clergymen of placing undue emphasis on good behavior. Like Martin Luther, Hutchinson denied that salvation could be earned through good deeds. There was no "**covenant of works**" that would save the well-behaved, only a "**covenant of grace**" through which God saved those he predestined for salvation. Hutchinson likewise declared that God "revealed" divine truth directly to individual believers, a controversial doctrine that the Puritan magistrates denounced as heretical.

The magistrates also resented Hutchinson because of her sex. Like other Christians, Puritans believed that both men and women could be saved. But gender equality stopped there. Women were inferior to men in earthly affairs, said leading Puritan divines, who told married women: "Thy desires shall bee subject to thy husband, and he shall rule over thee." Puritan women could not be ministers or lay preachers, nor could they vote in church affairs. In 1637, the magistrates accused Hutchinson of teaching that inward grace freed an individual from the rules of the Church and found her guilty of holding heretical views. Banished, she followed Roger Williams into exile in Rhode Island.

Other Puritan groups moved out from Massachusetts Bay in the 1630s and settled on or near the Connecticut River. For several decades, the colonies of Connecticut, New Haven, and Saybrook were independent of one another; in 1660, they secured a charter from King Charles II (r. 1660–1685) for the self-governing colony of Connecticut. Like Massachusetts Bay, Connecticut had a legally established church and an elected governor and assembly; however, it granted voting rights to most property-owning men, not just to church members as in the original Puritan colony.

Puritan-Pequot War Many rival Indian groups lived in New England before Europeans arrived; by the 1630s, these groups were bordered by the Dutch colony of New Netherland to their west and the various English settlements to the east — Plymouth, Massachusetts Bay, Rhode Island, Connecticut, New Haven, and Saybrook. The region's Indian leaders created various alliances for the purposes of trade and defense: Wampanoags with Plymouth; Mohegans with Massachusetts and Connecticut; Pequots with New Netherland; and Narragansetts with Rhode Island.

Because of their alliance with the Dutch, the Pequots became a thorn in the side of English traders. A series of violent encounters began in July 1636 and escalated until May 1637, when a combined force of Massachusetts and Connecticut militiamen, accompanied by Narragansett and Mohegan warriors, attacked a Pequot village and massacred some five hundred men, women, and children. In the months that followed, the New Englanders drove the surviving Pequots into oblivion and divided their lands.

Believing they were God's chosen people, Puritans considered their presence to be divinely ordained. Initially, they pondered the morality of acquiring Native American lands. "By what right or warrant can we enter into the land of the Savages?" they asked themselves. Responding to such concerns, John Winthrop detected God's hand in a recent smallpox epidemic: "If God were not pleased with our inheriting these parts," he asked, "why doth he still make roome for us by diminishing them as we increase?" Experiences like the Pequot War confirmed New Englanders' confidence in their enterprise. "God laughed at the Enemies of his People," one soldier boasted after the 1637 massacre, "filling the Place with Dead Bodies."

Like Catholic missionaries, Puritans believed that their church should embrace all peoples. However, their strong emphasis on predestination — the idea that God saved only a few chosen people — made it hard for them to accept that Indians could be counted among the elect. "Probably the devil" delivered these "miserable savages" to America, Cotton Mather suggested, "in hopes that the gospel of the Lord Jesus Christ would never come here." A few Puritan ministers committed themselves to the effort to convert Indians. On Martha's Vineyard, Jonathan Mayhew helped to create an Indian-led community of Wampanoag Christians. John Eliot translated the Bible into Algonquian and created fourteen Indian praying towns. By 1670, more than 1,000 Indians lived in these settlements, but relatively few Native Americans were ever permitted to become full members of Puritan congregations.

The Puritan Revolution in England   Meanwhile, a religious civil war engulfed England. Archbishop Laud had imposed the Church of England prayer book on Presbyterian Scotland in 1637; five years later, a rebel Scottish army invaded England. Thousands of English Puritans (and hundreds of American Puritans) joined the Scots, demanding religious reform and parliamentary power. After years of civil war, parliamentary forces led by Oliver Cromwell emerged victorious. In 1649, Parliament beheaded King Charles I, proclaimed a republican Commonwealth, and banished bishops and elaborate rituals from the Church of England.

The Puritan triumph in England was short-lived. Popular support for the Commonwealth ebbed after Cromwell took dictatorial control in 1653. Following his death in 1658, moderate Protestants and a resurgent aristocracy restored the monarchy and the hierarchy of bishops. With Charles II (r. 1660–1685) on the throne, England's experiment in radical Protestant government came to an end.

For the Puritans in America, the restoration of the monarchy began a new phase of their "errand into the wilderness." They had come to New England expecting to return to Europe in triumph. When the failure of the English Revolution dashed that sacred mission, ministers exhorted congregations to create a godly republican society in America. The Puritan colonies now stood as outposts of Calvinism and the Atlantic republican tradition.

The Execution of Charles I, 1649   Charles I led the royalist army in the English Civil War until he was captured by Oliver Cromwell's rebelling New Model Army. Tried by members of the so-called Rump Parliament for treason, Charles was found guilty after three days of deliberation. On a platform erected in the street outside Whitehall, the royal palace in London, the king was beheaded on January 30, 1649. In this image, Charles — dressed in black, with head bowed — approaches the executioner and the chopping block as members of Parliament and throngs of Londoners look on. Private Collection/© Look and Learn/Peter Jackson Collection/Bridgeman Images.

Susanna Martin, Accused Witch

Before reading the document below, review again the questions you should ask of every primary source (p. 34). The answers to these questions are not always straight-forward. Consider the nature of the document and the motives of its creators as you read.

COTTON MATHER

Tryal of Susanna Martin in Salem, June 29, 1692

Susanna Martin was tried for witchcraft in Salem, Massachusetts, in the summer of 1692, during the height of the crisis there. Cotton Mather, a prominent Boston minister, published summaries of the testimony against her in the following year in *The Wonders of the Invisible World*, a book that sought to defend the colony's effort to root out the witches who he believed were doing the devil's work. "The New-Englanders are a people of God settled in those, which were once the Devil's Territories," he wrote. "The devil is now making one Attempt more upon us." Mather compiled the following testimony, but he is quoting witnesses who also must be treated, in a sense, as authors: witnesses with their own ideas and purposes, which may have been similar to Mather's but were not identical. In the bizarre stories they tell, we get a glimpse of how early New Englanders believed that the devil used people like Susanna Martin to act in the world.

SOURCE: "Tryal of Susanna Martin in Salem, June 29, 1692," in Cotton Mather, *The Wonders of the Invisible World* (London: J. R. Smith, 1862), 138–148.

❝ Susanna Martin, pleading *Not Guilty* to the Indictment of *Witchcraft*, brought in against her, there were produced the Evidences of many Persons very sensibly and grievously Bewitched; who all complained of the Prisoner at the Bar, as the Person whom they believed the cause of their Miseries. . . .

IV. *John Atkinson* testifi'd, That he exchanged a Cow with a Son of *Susanna Martin's*, whereat she muttered, and was unwilling he should have it. Going to receive this Cow, tho he Hamstring'd her, and Halter'd her, she, of a Tame Creature, grew so mad, that they could scarce get her along. She broke all the Ropes that were fastned unto her, and though she were ty'd fast unto a Tree, yet she made her escape, and gave them such further trouble, as they could ascribe to no cause but Witchcraft.

V. *Bernard Peache* testifi'd, That being in Bed, on the Lord's-day Night, he heard a scrabbling at the Window, whereat he then saw *Susanna Martin* come in, and jump down upon the Floor. She took hold of this Deponent's Feet, and drawing his Body up into an Heap, she lay upon him near Two Hours; in all which time he could neither speak nor stir. At length, when he could begin to move, he laid hold on her Hand, and pulling it up to his Mouth, he bit three of her Fingers, as he judged, unto the Bone. Whereupon she went from the Chamber, down the Stairs, out at the Door. This Deponent thereupon called unto the People of the House, to advise them of what passed; and he himself did follow her. The People saw her not; but there being a Bucket at the Left-hand of the Door, there was a drop of Blood found upon it; and several more drops of Blood upon the Snow newly fallen abroad: There was likewise the print of her 2 Feet just without the Threshold; but no more sign of any Footing further off. . . .

VI. *Robert Downer* testified, That this Prisoner being some Years ago prosecuted at Court for a Witch, he then said

---

Puritanism and Witchcraft Like Native Americans, Puritans believed that the physical world was full of supernatural forces. Devout Christians saw signs of God's (or Satan's) power in blazing stars, birth defects, and other unusual events. Noting after a storm that the houses of many ministers "had been smitten with Lightning," Cotton Mather, a prominent Puritan theologian, wondered "what the meaning of God should be in it."

Puritans were hostile toward people who they believed tried to manipulate these forces, and many were willing to condemn neighbors as Satan's "wizards" or "witches." People in the town of Andover "were much addicted to sorcery," claimed one observer, and "there were forty men in it that could raise the Devil as well as any astrologer." Between 1647 and 1662, civil authorities in New England hanged fourteen people for witchcraft, most of them older women accused of being "double-tongued" or of having "an unruly spirit" (Analyzing Voices).

The most dramatic episode of witch-hunting occurred in Salem in 1692. Several girls who had experienced strange seizures accused neighbors of bewitching them. When judges at the accused witches' trials allowed the use of "spectral" evidence — visions of evil beings and marks seen only by the girls — the accusations spun out of control. Eventually, Massachusetts Bay authorities tried 175 people for witchcraft and executed 19 of them. The causes of this mass hysteria were complex and are still debated.

unto her, *He believed she was a Witch*. Whereat she being dissatisfied, said, *That some She-Devil would shortly fetch him away!* Which words were heard by others, as well as himself. The Night following, as he lay in his Bed, there came in at the Window, the likeness of a *Cat*, which flew upon him, took fast hold of his Throat, lay on him a considerable while, and almost killed him. At length he remembered what *Susanna Martin* had threatned the Day before; and with much striving he cried out, *Avoid, thou She-Devil! In the Name of God the Father, the Son, and the Holy Ghost, Avoid!* Whereupon it left him, leap'd on the Floor, and flew out at the Window. . . .

VIII. *William Brown* testifi'd, That Heaven having blessed him with a most Pious and Prudent Wife, this Wife of his, one day met with *Susanna Martin*; but when she approach'd just unto her, *Martin* vanished out of sight, and left her extreamly affrighted. After which time, the said *Martin* often appear'd unto her, giving her no little trouble; and when she did come, was visited with Birds, that sorely peck'd and prick'd her; and sometimes, a Bunch, like a Pullet's Egg, would rise in her Throat, ready to choak her, till she cry'd out, *Witch, you shan't choak me!* While this good Woman was in this extremity, the Church appointed a Day of Prayer, on her behalf; whereupon her Trouble ceas'd; she saw not *Martin* as formerly; and the Church, instead of their Fast, gave Thanks for her Deliverance. But a considerable while after, she being Summoned to give in some Evidence at the Court, against this *Martin*, quickly thereupon, this Martin came behind her, while she was milking her Cow, and said unto her, *For thy defaming her at Court, I'll make thee the miserablest Creature in the World.* Soon after which, she fell into a strange kind of distemper, and became horribly frantick, and uncapable of any reasonable Action; the Physicians declaring, that her Distemper was preternatural, and that some Devil had certainly bewitched her; and in that condition she now remained.

IX. *Sarah Atkinson* testify'd, That *Susanna Martin* came from *Amesbury* to their House at *Newbury*, in an extraordinary Season, when it was not fit for any to Travel. She came (as she said, unto *Atkinson*), all that long way on Foot. She brag'd and shew'd how dry she was; nor could it be perceived that so much as the Soles of her Shoes were wet. *Atkinson* was amazed at it; and professed, that she should her self have been wet up to the knees, if she had then came so far; but *Martin* reply'd, *She scorn'd to be Drabbled!* It was noted, that this Testimony upon her Trial, cast her in a very singular Confusion. . . .

Note, this Woman was one of the most imprudent, scurrilous, wicked Creatures in the World; and she did now throughout her whole Tryal, discover [reveal] her self to be such an one. Yet when she was asked, what she had to say for her self? Her chief Plea was, *That she had lead a most virtuous and holy Life.* "

QUESTIONS FOR ANALYSIS

1. Who is Mather's intended audience? What was he trying to achieve in presenting this information to them?

2. How might the motives of the witnesses in Susanna Martin's trial have differed from Mather's? What were they trying to achieve?

3. What kinds of actions alienated Martin from her neighbors? What occurrences do her neighbors blame her for, and why?

4. Some witnesses describe events that are hard to imagine or understand. What should we make of their stories? Do we arrive at a clearer understanding of events if we try to explain them away, or is it best to accept the validity of their experiences?

5. Consider the discussion of New England culture on pages 58–65. How would you put this testimony in context? What aspects of New England society and culture predisposed people to view some of their neighbors as witches?

Some historians point to group rivalries: many accusers were the daughters or servants of poor farmers, whereas many of the alleged witches were wealthier church members or their friends. Because 18 of those put to death were women, other historians see the episode as part of a broader Puritan effort to subordinate women. Still others focus on political instability in Massachusetts Bay in the early 1690s and on fears raised by recent Indian attacks in nearby Maine, which had killed the parents of some of the young accusers. It is likely that all of these causes played some role in the executions.

Whatever the cause, the Salem episode marked a major turning point. Shaken by the number of deaths, government officials now discouraged legal prosecutions for witchcraft. Moreover, many influential people embraced the outlook of the European Enlightenment, a major intellectual movement that began around 1675 and promoted a rational, scientific view of the world. Increasingly, educated men and women explained strange happenings and sudden deaths by reference to "natural causes," not witchcraft. Unlike Cotton Mather (1663–1728), who believed that lightning was a supernatural sign, Benjamin Franklin (1706–1790) and other well-read men of his generation would investigate it as a natural phenomenon.

A Yeoman Society, 1630–1700 In building their communities, New England Puritans consciously rejected the feudal practices of English society. Many Puritans

Andover, 1650–1692
Nucleated to dispersed in fifty years

New houses
- ● By 1650
- ● By 1692
- ▲ Meeting House

0   2   4 miles

Meeting House

(after Vaughn)

The key to the right indicates that a central purpose of this map is to show the geographic distribution of nucleated and dispersed villages. Why are there so many nucleated towns in the Connecticut River Valley and so many dispersed settlements in eastern Massachusetts?

0   10   20 miles
0   10   20 kilometers

Village types
- ● Nucleated
- ◉ Initially nucleated, dispersed by 1700
- ○ Dispersed
- ◆ Indian settlements
- ▨ Continuous English settlements by 1700
- — Roads
- — Field boundaries

The map of Andover shows how an originally nucleated settlement changed over time into a dispersed town. New farms tended to be located farther and farther from the meeting house and town center, represented by a triangle on the town plan.

ATLANTIC OCEAN

ABENAKI

Hampton

Haverhill
Ipswich
Andover
Manchester
Salem
Newton
Sudbury
PENNACOOK
MASSACHUSETT
MAHICAN
Greenfield   Northfield
Deerfield   Sunderland
Hatfield
MASSACHUSETTS
Hadley
NIPMUCK
Worcester
Dedham
Medfield
Westfield
Oxford
Plymouth
Woodstock
NARRAGANSETT
RHODE ISLAND
Windsor   Hartford
PEQUOT
CONNECTICUT
WAMPANOAG
Farmington
Barnstable
MOHEGAN
Waterbury
Wallingford
SAKONNET
Newtown
Guilford
Derby

BERKSHIRE MOUNTAINS
Connecticut River
Housatonic River
Long Island

N
W   E
S

Wethersfield in 1640 is an example of a nucleated village, with house lots clustered around the meeting house and fields arranged in geometric patterns in the surrounding countryside.

The field boundaries in Wethersfield indicate that the land is flat in the Connecticut River Valley. In contrast, the pattern of roads and paths in Andover suggests a hilly topography. These uplands gave the Merrimack River a strong current and many rapids, which were later harnessed for industrial development. (See Map 8.3.)

(after Wood)

Wethersfield, 1640

0   0.5   1 mile

Meeting House

(after Andrews)

MAP 2.6 Settlement Patterns in New England Towns, 1630–1700
Throughout New England, colonists pressed onto desirable Indian lands. Initially, most Puritan towns were compact, or nucleated: families lived close to one another in village centers and traveled daily to work in the surrounding fields. This 1640 map of Wethersfield, Connecticut, a town situated on the broad plains of the Connecticut River Valley, shows this pattern clearly. The first settlers in Andover, Massachusetts, also chose to live in the village center. However, the rugged topography of eastern Massachusetts encouraged the townspeople to disperse. By 1692 (as the varied location of new houses shows), many Andover residents were living on farms distant from the village center.

came from middling families in East Anglia, a region of pasture lands and few manors, and had no desire to live as tenants of wealthy aristocrats or submit to oppressive taxation by a distant government. They had "escaped out of the pollutions of the world," the settlers of Watertown in Massachusetts Bay declared, and vowed to live "close togither" in self-governing communities. Accordingly, the General Courts of Massachusetts Bay and Connecticut bestowed land on groups of settlers, who then distributed it among the male heads of families.

Widespread ownership of land did not mean equality of wealth or status. "God had Ordained different degrees and orders of men," proclaimed Boston merchant John Saffin, "some to be Masters and Commanders, others to be Subjects, and to be commanded." Town proprietors normally awarded the largest plots to men of high social status who often became selectmen and justices of the peace. However, all families received some land, and most adult men had a vote in the **town meeting**, the main institution of local government (Map 2.6).

In this society of independent households and self-governing communities, ordinary farmers had much more political power than Chesapeake yeomen and European peasants did. Although Nathaniel Fish was one of the poorest men in the town of Barnstable — he owned just a two-room cottage, 8 acres of land, an ox, and a cow — he was a voting member of the town meeting. Each year, Fish and other Barnstable farmers levied taxes; enacted ordinances governing fencing, roadbuilding, and the use of common fields; and chose the selectmen who managed town affairs. The farmers also selected the town's representatives to the General Court, which gradually displaced the governor as the center of political authority. For Fish and thousands of other ordinary settlers, New England had proved to be a new world of opportunity.

> **IN YOUR OWN WORDS** What conditions were necessary to establish successful neo-European colonies?

Mrs. Elizabeth Freake and Baby Mary This portrait, completed around 1674 by an unknown artist, depicts the wife and youngest daughter of a wealthy Bostonian. Their clothes and surroundings illustrate the growing prosperity of well-to-do households. Mother and child both wear fine linen edged with fine lace. Elizabeth Freake's sleeve is decorated with colorful red and black ribbons and she wears a beaded bracelet on her wrist. They are seated on a chair colorfully upholstered in a style intended to imitate a Turkish carpet. Worcester Art Museum, Massachusetts, USA/ Bridgeman Images.

Instability, War, and Rebellion

Everywhere in Europe's American colonies, conflicts arose over the control of resources, the legitimacy of colonial leaders' claims to power, and attempts to define social and cultural norms. Periodically, these conflicts flared spectacularly into episodes of violence. Each episode has its own story — its own unique logic and narrative — but taken together, they also illustrate the way that, in their formative stages, colonial societies pressured people to accept new patterns of authority and new claims to power. When these claims were contested, the results could quickly turn deadly.

Native American Resistance

In the English Northeast and the Spanish Southwest, European claims to power and territory prompted Native American wars of resistance. In New England, Wampanoags and other Indian groups had maintained alliances with neighboring colonies for years. But these relations were unstable, and the potential for violence was never far from the surface. In the Spanish colony of New Mexico, soldiers and missionaries conquered Pueblo communities and ruled by force; there, too, violence was woven into colonial relations, and Native American resistance flared spectacularly.

Metacom's War, 1675–1676 By the 1670s, Europeans in New England outnumbered Indians by 3 to 1. The English population had multiplied to 55,000, while Native peoples had diminished from an estimated 120,000 in 1570 to barely 16,000. To the Wampanoag leader Metacom (also known as King Philip), the prospects for coexistence looked dim. When his people copied English ways by raising hogs and selling pork in Boston, Puritan officials accused them of selling at "an under rate" and restricted their trade. When Indians killed wandering hogs that devastated their corn-fields, authorities prosecuted them for violating English property rights.

Metacom concluded that the English colonists had to be expelled. In 1675, the Wampanoag leader forged a military alliance with the Narragansetts and Nipmucks and attacked white settlements throughout New England. Almost every day, settler William Harris fearfully reported, he heard new reports of the Indians' "burneing houses, takeing cattell, killing men & women & Children: & carrying others captive." Bitter fighting continued into 1676, ending only when the Indian warriors ran short of gunpowder and the Massachusetts Bay government hired Mohegan and Mohawk war-riors, who killed Metacom.

Metacom's War of 1675–1676 (which English settlers called King Philip's War) was a deadly affair. Indians destroyed one-fifth of the English towns in Massachusetts and Rhode Island and killed 1,000 settlers, nearly 5 percent of the adult population; for a time the Puritan experiment hung in the balance. But the Natives' losses — from famine and disease, death in battle, and sale into slavery — were much larger: about 4,500 Indians died, one-quarter of an already diminished population. Many of the surviving Wampanoag, Narragansett, and Nipmuck peoples moved west, intermarrying with Algonquian tribes allied to the French. Over the next century, these displaced Indian peoples would take their revenge, joining with French Catholics to attack their Puritan enemies. Metacom's War did not eliminate the presence of Native Americans in south-ern New England, but it effectively destroyed their existence as independent peoples.

The Pueblo Revolt From the time of their first arrival in Pueblo country in 1540, Spanish soldiers and Franciscan missionaries had attempted to dominate its Indian communities. They demanded tribute, labor, and forced conversions to Catholicism, and they ferociously suppressed resistance. A small minority ruling over a population of some 17,000 people, the Spanish were mistrusted and often hated. A drought begin-ning in 1660 compounded the Pueblos' misery; one priest wrote, "a great many Indians perished of hunger, lying dead along the roads, in the ravines, and in their huts." In this period of suffering, many Pueblos turned away from Christianity and back to their own holy men and traditional ceremonies. Seeking to suppress these practices, in 1675 Spanish officials hanged three Pueblo priests and whipped dozens of others as punish-ment for sorcery.

One of the convicted sorcerers was a religious leader from San Juan Pueblo named Popé. Five years later, he organized a complex military offensive against the Spanish that came to be known as the **Pueblo Revolt** (also called Popé's Rebellion). Drawing on warriors from two dozen pueblos spread across several hundred miles and speaking six languages, Popé orchestrated an uprising that liberated the pueblos and culminated in the capture of Santa Fe; 400 Spaniards were killed; the remaining 2,100 fled south. New Mexico was in Pueblo hands. Under the leadership of Diego de Vargas, the Spanish returned and recaptured Santa Fe in 1693; three years later, they had reclaimed most of the pueblos of New Mexico. But Spanish policy was redirected by the revolt. Officials reduced their labor demands on Pueblo communities, and across the Southwest — from Baja California to Tejas y Coahuila — Spain relied on Indian missions to create a defensive perimeter against their Ute, Apache, and Navajo neighbors.

In the century that followed, Jesuit and Franciscan missionaries built a dense net-work of missions extending north from Mexico along the coast of Baja and Alta (or lower and upper) California. From San José del Cabo in the south to San Francisco in the north, these institutions sought to pacify Native peoples and transform their ways of life. Massive waves of smallpox, typhus, and other diseases drove surviving Indians to the missions; their desperation often accomplished what the faithful labors of mis-sionaries could not. Throughout coastal California, remnant Indian populations grav-itated toward mission communities and the sustenance and protection they could offer.

CONSIDER POINTS OF VIEW
Compare the pressures that Native American groups faced from colonists in New England and New Mexico. What was similar, and in what ways did their circumstances differ?

Bacon's Rebellion

At about the same time that New England fought its war with Metacom and the Pueblos took up arms with Popé, Virginia was wracked by a rebellion that nearly toppled its government. It, too, grew out of a conflict with neighboring Indians, but this one inspired a popular uprising against the colony's royal governor. Like Metacom's War, it highlighted the way that a land-intensive settler colony created friction with Native American populations; in addition, it dramatized the way that ordinary colonists could challenge the authority of a new planter elite to rule over them.

By the 1670s, economic and political power in Virginia was in the hands of a small circle of men who amassed land, slaves, and political offices. Through headrights and royal grants, they controlled nearly half of all the settled land in Virginia. What they could not plant themselves, they leased to tenants. Freed indentured servants found it ever harder to get land of their own; many were forced to lease lands, or even sign new indentures, to make ends meet. To make matters worse, the price of tobacco fell until planters received only a penny a pound for their crops in the 1670s.

At the top of Virginia's narrow social pyramid was William Berkeley, governor between 1642 and 1652 and again after 1660. To consolidate power, Berkeley bestowed large land grants on members of his council. The councilors exempted these lands from taxation and appointed friends as justices of the peace and county judges. To win support in the House of Burgesses, Berkeley bought off legislators with land grants and lucrative appointments as sheriffs and tax collectors. But social unrest erupted when the Burgesses took the vote away from landless freemen, who by now constituted half the adult white men. Although property-holding yeomen retained their voting rights, they were angered by falling tobacco prices, political corruption, and "grievous taxations" that threatened the "utter ruin of us the poor commonalty." Berkeley and his allies were living on borrowed time.

Frontier War   An Indian conflict ignited the flame of social rebellion. In 1607, when the English intruded, 30,000 Native Americans resided in Virginia; by 1675, the Native population had dwindled to only 3,500. By then, Europeans numbered some 38,000 and Africans another 2,500. Most Indians lived on treaty-guaranteed territory along the frontier, where poor freeholders and landless former servants now wanted to settle, demanding that the Natives be expelled or exterminated. Their demands were ignored by wealthy planters, who wanted a ready supply of tenants and laborers, and by Governor Berkeley and the planter-merchants, who traded with the Occaneechee Indians for beaver pelts and deerskins.

Fighting broke out late in 1675, when a vigilante band of Virginia militiamen murdered thirty Indians. Defying Berkeley's orders, a larger force then surrounded a fortified Susquehannock village and killed five leaders who came out to negotiate. The Susquehannocks retaliated by attacking outlying plantations and killing three hundred whites. In response, Berkeley proposed a defensive strategy: a series of frontier forts to deter Indian intrusions. The settlers dismissed this scheme as a militarily useless plot by planter-merchants to impose high taxes and take "all our tobacco into their own hands."

Challenging the Government   Enter Nathaniel Bacon, a young, well-connected migrant from England who emerged as the leader of the rebels. Bacon held a position on the governor's council, but he was shut out of Berkeley's inner circle and differed with Berkeley on Indian policy. When the governor refused to grant him a military commission, Bacon mobilized his neighbors and attacked any Indians he could find. Condemning the frontiersmen as "rebels and mutineers," Berkeley expelled Bacon from the council and had him arrested. But Bacon's army forced the governor to release their leader and hold legislative elections. The newly elected House of Burgesses enacted far-reaching reforms that curbed the powers of the governor and council and restored voting rights to landless freemen.

These much-needed reforms came too late. Poor farmers and servants resented years of exploitation by wealthy planters, arrogant justices of the peace, and "wicked & pernicious Counsellors." As one yeoman rebel complained, "A poor man who has only his labour to maintain himself and his family pays as much [in taxes] as a man who has 20,000 acres." Backed by 400 armed men, Bacon issued a "Manifesto and Declaration of the People" that demanded the removal of Indians and an end to the rule of wealthy "parasites." "All the power and sway is got into the hands of the rich," Bacon proclaimed as his army burned Jamestown to the ground and plundered the plantations of Berkeley's allies. When Bacon died suddenly of dysentery in October 1676, the governor took revenge, dispersing the rebel army, seizing the estates of well-to-do rebels, and hanging 23 men.

In the wake of Bacon's Rebellion, Virginia's leaders worked harder to appease their humble neighbors. But the rebellion also coincided with the time when Virginia planters were switching from indentured servants, who became free after four years, to slaves, who labored for life. In the eighteenth century, wealthy planters would make common cause with poorer whites, while slaves became the colony's most exploited workers. That fateful change eased tensions within the free population but committed subsequent generations of Americans to a labor system based on racial exploitation. Bacon's Rebellion, like Metacom's War, reminds us that these colonies were unfinished worlds, still searching for viable foundations.

> **PLACE EVENTS IN CONTEXT**
> In what ways was Bacon's Rebellion symptomatic of social tensions in the colony of Virginia?

> **IN YOUR OWN WORDS** What did these three rebellions — Metacom's War, the Pueblo Revolt, and Bacon's Rebellion — have in common?

SUMMARY

During the sixteenth and seventeenth centuries, three types of colonies took shape in the Americas. In Mesoamerica and the Andes, Spanish colonists made indigenous empires their own, capitalizing on preexisting labor systems and using tribute and the discovery of precious metals to generate enormous wealth, which Philip II used to defend the interests of the Catholic Church in Europe. In tropical and subtropical regions, colonizers transferred the plantation complex — a centuries-old form of production and labor discipline — to places suited to growing exotic crops like sugar, tobacco, and indigo. The rigors of plantation agriculture demanded a large supply of labor, which was first filled in English colonies by indentured servants and later supplemented and eclipsed by African slaves. The third type of colony, neo-European settlement, developed in North America's temperate zone, where European migrants adapted familiar systems of social and economic organization in new settings.

Everywhere in the Americas, colonization was, first and foremost, a process of experimentation. As resources from the Americas flowed to Europe, monarchies were strengthened and the competition among them — sharpened by the schism between Protestants and Catholics — gained new force and energy. Establishing colonies demanded political, social, and cultural innovations that threw Europeans, Native Americans, and Africans together in bewildering circumstances, triggered massive ecological change through the Columbian Exchange, and demanded radical adjustments. In the Chesapeake and New England — the two earliest regions of English settlement on mainland North America — the adjustment to new circumstances sparked conflict with neighboring Indians and waves of instability within the colonies. These external and internal crises were products of the struggle to adapt to the rigors of colonization.

CHAPTER 2 REVIEW

TERMS TO KNOW

Identify and explain the significance of each term below.

Key Concepts and Events

chattel slavery (p. 38)

neo-Europes (p. 38)

encomienda (p. 40)

casta system (p. 41)

Columbian Exchange (p. 41)

mercantilism (p. 43)

joint-stock corporation (p. 45)

House of Burgesses (p. 46)

royal colony (p. 46)

freeholds (p. 50)

headright system (p. 50)

indentured servitude (p. 50)

Pilgrims (p. 58)

Puritans (p. 59)

toleration (p. 59)

covenant of works (p. 60)

covenant of grace (p. 60)

town meeting (p. 65)

Metacom's War (p. 66)

Pueblo Revolt (p. 66)

Key People

Philip II (p. 42)

Opechancanough (p. 46)

Lord Baltimore (p. 47)

John Winthrop (p. 59)

Roger Williams (p. 59)

Anne Hutchinson (p. 60)

Metacom (p. 65)

REVIEW QUESTIONS

Answer these questions to demonstrate your understanding of the chapter's main ideas.

1. How did Spanish colonization affect people in the Americas and in Europe?

2. How did the labor demands of plantation colonies transform the process of colonization?

3. What conditions were necessary to establish successful neo-European colonies?

4. What did these three rebellions — Metacom's War, the Pueblo Revolt, and Bacon's Rebellion — have in common?

5. Review the events listed under "Politics and Power" and "Culture and Society" on the thematic timeline on pages 4–5. How did political developments in seventeenth-century England impact the development of its American colonies?

MAKING CONNECTIONS

Recognize the larger developments and continuities within and across chapters by answering these questions.

1. In Chapter 1, we saw that there were many parallels between Native American, European, and African societies on the eve of contact. Yet Europeans ended up dominating both Native American and African populations in colonial American settings. Based on what you learned in Chapter 2, what factors help to explain that dominance?

2. Look closely at the depiction of the Hurons' Feast of the Dead on page 58. Where do you see the bodies of the dead? What do you think the people gathered around the fires are doing? Do you consider this image macabre? Reverent? How would you defend your interpretation?

KEY TURNING POINTS

Refer to the chapter chronology on page 40 for help in answering the questions below.

The Chesapeake tobacco boom (1620–1660), Opechancanough's uprising (1622), and the takeover of Virginia by the crown (1624): How were these events related to each other? What was their cumulative result?

2

PART

CHAPTER 3
The British Atlantic World, 1607–1750

CHAPTER 4
Growth, Diversity, and Conflict, 1720–1763

British North America and the Atlantic World

1607–1763

Between 1607 and 1763, English North America took root and flourished. From its unpromising beginnings in Jamestown, where colonists struggled simply to survive, England's colonies grew quickly in number and then, after 1680, became dramatically more populous and diverse. To begin Part 2, we reach back to 1607, the date when Jamestown was founded and permanent English colonization began. We end Part 2 a century and a half later, in 1763, with Britain's victory in the Great War for Empire. The choice to include the Great War in Part 2—thus ending in 1763 rather than 1754—allows us to understand how imperial rivalry and warfare underlay the colonial North American experience in the eighteenth century. By 1763, Britain became the dominant power in eastern North America, and its colonies contained nearly two million subjects.

The rise of British North America occurred amid great changes. Instead of a barrier to contact, the Atlantic Ocean became a watery highway carrying people, merchandise, and ideas. Trade caused more intensive interactions with Europe that knit together the increasingly diverse societies of British North America. After 1689, Europe plunged into a century of warfare that spilled over into North America. British, French, and Spanish colonies all turned to Indian allies for help, fundamentally changing the character of cross-cultural relations. The Great War for Empire transformed the map of North America, making Great Britain ascendant in eastern North America, while also creating new challenges for everyone living there.

We give particular attention in Part 2 to the following three main concepts: ▶

The Diversification of British North America

The American colonies of the various European nations gradually diverged from each other in character. The core of Spanish America developed into complex multiracial societies, while Portuguese Brazil was dominated by plantations and mining. The Dutch kept only a few tropical plantation colonies; the French also had valuable plantation colonies but struggled to populate their vast North American holdings. Britain's mainland colonies, by contrast, gradually stabilized and then grew and diversified rapidly. Britain came to dominate the Atlantic slave trade and brought more than two million slaves across the Atlantic. Most went to Jamaica and Barbados, but half a million found their way to the mainland. Slavery was a growing and thriving institution in British North America.

Many non-English Europeans also came to British North America, including more than 200,000 Germans and Scots-Irish. Most immigrated to Pennsylvania, which soon had the most ethnically diverse population of Europeans on the continent. These groups struggled to maintain their identities in a rapidly changing landscape.

© National Maritime Museum, London/The Image Works.

Rise of the British Atlantic World

These population movements were part of the larger growth and development of the British Atlantic world. Britain's transatlantic shipping networks laid the foundation for rising economic productivity and dramatic cultural transformations. The cultural impact of this change grew out of two further developments: the print revolution, which brought many ideas into circulation; and the consumer revolution, which flooded the Atlantic world with a variety of newly available merchandise.

Four new cultural developments emerged in the British Atlantic world. A transatlantic community interested in science and rationalism shared Enlightenment ideas; Pietists promoted the revival and expansion of Christianity; well-to-do colonists gained access to genteel values and the finery needed to put them into action; and colonial consumers went further into debt than they ever had before.

The New York Public Library/Art Resource, NY.

Contact and Conflict

In Europe, the period after 1689 has sometimes been called the Second Hundred Years' War, when Britain, France, and their European allies went to war against each other repeatedly. As these conflicts came to the North American theater, they decisively influenced Indian relations. The Columbian Exchange had devastated Native American populations. The rise of imperial warfare encouraged the process of tribalization, whereby Indians regrouped into political structures—called tribes by Europeans—to deal with their colonial neighbors and strike alliances in times of war. Europeans, in turn, used Indian allies as proxy warriors in their conflicts over North American territory.

This pattern culminated in the Great War for Empire, which began in North America and reshaped its map. The Treaty of Paris of 1763 gave Britain control of the entire continent east of the Mississippi. Events would soon show what a mixed blessing that outcome was, for Native Americans, colonists, and British administrators alike.

Courtesy of the John Carter Brown Library at Brown University.

British North America and the Atlantic World 1607–1763

Fogg Art Museum, Harvard Art Museums, USA/Bridgeman Images.

Thematic Understanding

This timeline organizes some of the important developments of this period into themes. How did the demographic changes outlined under the theme "Migration and Settlement" impact the developments that are listed under "Work, Exchange, and Technology"? ▶

	AMERICAN AND NATIONAL IDENTITY	POLITICS AND POWER	WORK, EXCHANGE, AND TECHNOLOGY	
1607	• English colonies founded without an overarching imperial system • English civil war allows colonial "big men" to govern themselves	• New England, Chesapeake, and West Indies elites establish their authority • King Charles I beheaded by Parliament (1649)	• Indentured servitude provides labor for the Chesapeake tobacco economy • Yeoman society takes root in New England	
1660	• Restoration makes England a monarchy again; royalist revival • The Glorious Revolution makes England a constitutional monarchy • Massachusetts loses its charter (1684) and gains a new one (1691)	• Dominion of New England (1686–1689) • Glorious Revolution (1688–1689) • War of the League of Augsburg (1689–1697) • Founding of the Restoration Colonies: the Carolinas (1663), New York (1664), New Jersey (1664), Pennsylvania (1681)	• South Atlantic System links plantation and neo-European colonies • Mercantilist legislation in England: Navigation Acts (1651, 1660, 1663) • New York inherits Hudson River Valley manors from the Dutch; Carolina proprietors fail to institute a manorial system • Migrants to Pennsylvania seek freehold lands • Rapid expansion of African slave imports undergirds sugar, tobacco, and rice plantation systems	
1690	• Colonists gain autonomy in the post–Glorious Revolution era • Tribalization develops among Native American peoples	• Parliament creates Board of Trade (1696) • War of the Spanish Succession (1702–1713)	• New England shipbuilding industry and merchant community dominate the coastal trade • Agricultural labor and artisanal skills in high demand in the Middle colonies	
1720	• African American community forms in the Chesapeake • Planter aristocracy emerges in the Chesapeake and South Carolina • Culture of gentility spreads among well-to-do	• Robert Walpole is prime minister (1720–1742) • Stono Rebellion (1739) • War of Jenkins's Ear (1739–1741) • War of the Austrian Succession (1740–1748)	• The price of wheat rises (doubles in Philadelphia, 1720–1770) • British trade dominates the Atlantic • Opportunity and inequality in the Middle colonies • Ohio Company of Virginia receives 200,000 acres (1749)	
1750	• Victory in the Great War for Empire sparks pro-British pride in the colonies • Desire for political autonomy and economic independence grows	• French and Indian War/Seven Years' War (1754–1763) • The Albany Congress (1754) • The Treaty of Paris (1763) • Pontiac's Rebellion (1763)	• Freehold society in crisis in New England • Half of Middle colonies' white men landless • Conflicts over western lands and political power (1750–1775) • British industry being mechanized; colonial debt crisis	

CULTURE AND SOCIETY	MIGRATION AND SETTLEMENT	GEOGRAPHY AND THE ENVIRONMENT	AMERICA IN THE WORLD	
• Puritan magistrates and tobacco planters govern the colonies	• Young male laborers dominate migration to the Chesapeake • Migration to New England brings intact households	• Tobacco takes root in the Chesapeake	• England intermittently ignores its American colonies	**1607**
• Collapse of the Puritan Commonwealth leads to toleration in England • Isaac Newton publishes *Principia Mathematica* (1687)	• The Middle Passage shapes Africans' experiences of arrival • Indian slave trade emerges in South Carolina • First Mennonites arrive in Pennsylvania (1683)	• Native American populations of the eastern woodlands decline catastrophically • African Americans are imported to tropical and semitropical colonies in large numbers	• England's proprietary colonies claim much of the Atlantic coast of North America	**1660**
• John Locke publishes *Two Treatises on Government* (1690) • Rise of toleration among colonial Protestants • Print revolution begins	• Quakers emigrate to Pennsylvania and New Jersey • Second wave of Germans arrives in Pennsylvania, Shenandoah Valley	• Rice cultivation begins in the Carolina and Georgia low country • New England fish feed southern Europe and Caribbean slaves	• European wars begin to spill onto American shores • Pennsylvania begins to draw large numbers of Scots-Irish and German migrants	**1690**
• George Whitefield's visit to America sparks the Great Awakening (1739) • Benjamin Franklin founds American Philosophical Society (1743)	• Scots-Irish begin migrating to Pennsylvania (c. 1720) • Parliament charters Georgia (1732) • Penns make Walking Purchase from the Delawares (1737)	• The pace of transatlantic shipping accelerates • A road network begins to knit together colonial towns	• The South Atlantic System connects America, Africa, and Europe • Mercantilism shapes England's policies toward its American colonies	**1720**
• New colleges, newspapers, magazines • At least twelve religious denominations in Philadelphia • Neolin promotes nativist revival among Ohio Indians (1763)	• 40,000 Germans and Swiss emigrate to Pennsylvania (1749–1756) • Anglo-Americans push onto backcountry lands	• The vast geographical scale of North America challenges European armies in the French and Indian War	• Britain wins the Great War for Empire and claims eastern North America	**1750**

3

CHAPTER

The British Atlantic World
1607–1750

For two weeks in June 1744, the town of Lancaster, Pennsylvania, hosted more than 250 Iroquois men, women, and children for a diplomatic conference with representatives from Pennsylvania, Maryland, and Virginia. Crowds of curious observers thronged Lancaster's streets and courthouse. The conference grew out of a diplomatic system between the colonies and the Iroquois designed to air grievances and resolve conflict: the Covenant Chain. Participants welcomed each other, exchanged speeches, and negotiated agreements in public ceremonies whose minutes became part of the official record of the colonies.

At Lancaster, the colonies had much to ask of their Iroquois allies. For one thing, they wanted them to confirm a land agreement. The Iroquois often began such conferences by resisting land deals; as the Cayuga orator Gachradodon said, "You know very well, when the White people came first here they were poor; but now they have got our Lands, and are by them become rich, and we are now poor; what little we have had for the Land goes soon away, but the Land lasts forever." In the end, however, they had little choice but to accept merchandise in exchange for land, since colonial officials were unwilling to take no for an answer. The colonists also announced that Britain was once again going to war with France, and they requested military support from their Iroquois allies. Canassatego—a tall, commanding Onondaga orator, about sixty years old, renowned for his eloquence—replied, "We shall never forget that you and we have but one Heart, one Head, one Eye, one Ear, and one Hand. We shall have all your Country under our Eye, and take all the Care we can to prevent any Enemy from coming into it."

The Lancaster conference—and dozens of others like it—demonstrates that the British colonies, like those of France and Spain, relied ever more heavily on alliances with Native Americans as they sought to extend their power in North America. Indian nations remade themselves in these same years, creating political structures—called "tribes" by Europeans—that allowed them to regroup in the face of population decline and function more effectively alongside neighboring colonies. The colonies, meanwhile, were drawn together into an integrated economic sphere—the South Atlantic System—that brought prosperity to British North America, while they achieved a measure of political autonomy that became essential to their understanding of what it meant to be British subjects.

> **IDENTIFY THE BIG IDEA**
>
> How did the South Atlantic System create an interconnected Atlantic world, and how did this system impact development in the British colonies?

English Tobacco Label, c. 1700 This label, which was used to advertise Virginia tobacco to London consumers, illustrates the growth of plantation economies in North America. Three well-to-do planters, bewigged and dressed in fashionable, colorful coats, take their ease with pipes of tobacco and glasses of liquor while slaves labor for them in the fields. The product's name — London's Virginia — highlights the relationship between production on colonial plantations and consumption in the English metropolis. The Granger Collection, New York.

CHAPTER CHRONOLOGY

As you read, ask yourself why this chapter begins and ends with these dates and then identify the links among related events.

1642–1651	▶ English civil war		1689–1713	▶ England, France, and Spain at war
1649	▶ Charles I beheaded		1696	▶ Parliament creates Board of Trade
1651	▶ First Navigation Act		1714–1750	▶ British policy of salutary neglect ▶ American assemblies gain power
1660–1685	▶ Reign of Charles II, king of England		1720–1742	▶ Robert Walpole leads Parliament
1663	▶ Charles II grants Carolina proprietorship		1720–1750	▶ African American communities form
1664	▶ English capture New Netherland, rename it New York			▶ Rice exports from South Carolina soar ▶ Planter aristocracy emerges ▶ Seaport cities expand
1669	▶ Virginia law declares that the murder of a slave cannot be treated as a felony		1732	▶ Parliament charters Georgia, challenging Spain ▶ Hat Act limits colonial enterprise
1681	▶ William Penn founds Pennsylvania		1733	▶ Molasses Act threatens distillers
1685–1688	▶ Reign of James II, king of England		1739	▶ Stono Rebellion in South Carolina
1686–1689	▶ Dominion of New England		1739–1748	▶ War with Spain in the Caribbean and France in Canada and Europe
1688–1689	▶ Glorious Revolution in England		1750	▶ Iron Act restricts colonial iron production
1689	▶ William and Mary ascend throne in England ▶ Revolts in Massachusetts, Maryland, and New York		1751	▶ Currency Act prohibits land banks and paper money

---

Colonies to Empire, 1607–1713

To see a longer excerpt of the Canassatego document mentioned in the chapter introduction, along with other primary sources from this period, see *Sources for America's History*.

Before 1660, England governed its New England and Chesapeake colonies haphazardly. Taking advantage of that laxness and the English civil war, local "big men" (Puritan magistrates and tobacco planters) ran their societies as they wished. Following the restoration of the monarchy in 1660, royal bureaucrats tried to impose order on the unruly settlements and, enlisting the aid of Indian allies, warred with rival European powers.

Self-Governing Colonies and New Elites, 1607–1660

In the years after its first American colonies were founded, England experienced a wrenching series of political crises. Disagreements between King Charles I and Parliament grew steadily worse until they culminated in the English civil war, which lasted from 1642 to 1651. A parliamentary army led by Oliver Cromwell fought against royalist forces for control of the country. Charles I was captured by Cromwell's army, tried for treason, and beheaded in 1649. Charles II, his son and successor, carried on the war for two more years but was defeated in 1651 and fled to France. England was no longer a monarchy. It was ruled by Parliament as a commonwealth, then fell under the personal rule of Oliver Cromwell, who was known as the Lord Protector. Cromwell's death in 1658 triggered a political crisis that led Parliament to invite Charles II to restore the monarchy and take up the throne.

During the long period of instability and crisis in England, its American colonies largely managed their own affairs. Neither crown nor Parliament devised a consistent system of imperial administration; in these years, England had colonies but no empire. Moreover, these were difficult years for all the colonies, when important decisions about the nature of the economy, the government, and the social system had to be worked out through trial and error (see Chapter 2). In this era of intense experimentation and struggle, emerging colonial elites often had to arrive at their own solutions to pressing problems. Leading men in Virginia, Maryland, the New England colonies, and the islands of the West Indies claimed authority and hammered out political systems that allowed the colonies to be largely self-governing. Even in colonies with crown-appointed governors, such as Sir William Berkeley in Virginia, it soon became apparent that those appointees had to make alliances with local leaders in order to be effective.

The restoration of the crown in 1660 marked a decisive end to this period of near-independence in the colonies. Charles II (r. 1660–1685) and his brother and successor, James II (r. 1685–1688), were deeply interested in England's overseas possessions and dramatically reshaped colonial enterprise. From England's early, prolonged, halting efforts to sponsor overseas activity, an empire finally began to take shape.

The Restoration Colonies and Imperial Expansion

Charles II expanded English power in Asia and America. In 1662, he married the Portuguese princess Catherine of Braganza, whose dowry included the islands of Bombay (present-day Mumbai, India). Then, in 1663, Charles initiated new outposts in America by authorizing eight loyal noblemen to settle Carolina, an area that had long been claimed by Spain and was populated by thousands of Indians. The following year, he awarded the just-conquered Dutch colony of New Netherland to his brother James, the Duke of York, who renamed the colony New York and then re-granted a portion of it, called New Jersey, to another group of proprietors. Finally, in 1681, Charles granted a vast tract to William Penn — Pennsylvania, or "Penn's Woods." In a great land grab, England had ousted the Dutch from North America, intruded into Spain's northern empire, and claimed all the land in between.

The Carolinas In 1660, English settlement was concentrated in New England and the Chesapeake. Five corporate colonies coexisted in New England: Massachusetts Bay, Plymouth, Connecticut, New Haven, and Rhode Island. (Connecticut absorbed New Haven in 1662, while Massachusetts Bay became a royal colony and absorbed Plymouth in 1692.) In the Chesapeake, Virginia was controlled by the crown while Maryland was in the hands of a Lord Proprietor. Like Lord Baltimore's Maryland, the new settlements in Carolina, New York, New Jersey, and Pennsylvania — the Restoration Colonies, as historians call them — were **proprietorships**. The Carolina and Jersey grantees, the Duke of York, and William Penn owned all the land in their new colonies and could rule them as they wished, provided that their laws conformed broadly to those of England (Table 3.1). Indeed, in New York, James II refused to allow an elective assembly and ruled by decree. The Carolina proprietors envisioned a traditional European society; they hoped to implement a manorial system, with a mass of serfs governed by a handful of powerful nobles.

The manorial system proved a fantasy. The first North Carolina settlers were a mixture of poor families and runaway servants from Virginia and English Quakers, an equality-minded Protestant sect (also known as the Society of Friends). Quakers "think there is no difference between a Gentleman and a labourer," complained an Anglican clergyman. Refusing to work on large manors, the settlers raised corn, hogs, and tobacco on modest family farms. Inspired by Bacon's Rebellion, they rebelled in 1677 against taxes on tobacco and again in 1708 against taxes to support the Anglican Church. Through their stubborn independence, residents forced the proprietors to abandon their dreams of a manorial society.

In South Carolina, the colonists also went their own way. The leading white settlers there were migrants from overcrowded Barbados. Hoping to re-create that island's hierarchical slave society, they used enslaved workers — both Africans and Native Americans — to raise cattle and food crops for export to the West Indies. Carolina merchants opened a lucrative trade in deerskins and Indian slaves with neighboring peoples. Then, around 1700, South Carolina planters hit upon rice cultivation. The swampy estuaries of the coastal low country could be modified with sluices, floodgates, and check dams to create ideal rice-growing conditions, and slaves could do the backbreaking work. By 1708, white South Carolinians relied upon a few thousand slaves to work

EXPLAIN CONSEQUENCES
How did the turmoil of the English civil war affect England's colonial enterprises?

TABLE 3.1

English Colonies Established in North America, 1660–1750					
Colony	Date	Original Colony Type	Religion	Status in 1775	Chief Export/ Economic Activity
Carolina	1663	Proprietary	Church of England	Royal	
North	1691				Farming, naval stores
South	1691				Rice, indigo
New Jersey	1664	Proprietary	Church of England	Royal	Wheat
New York	1664	Proprietary	Church of England	Royal	Wheat
Pennsylvania	1681	Proprietary	Quaker	Proprietary	Wheat
Georgia	1732	Trustees	Church of England	Royal	Rice
New Hampshire (separated from Massachusetts)	1741	Royal	Congregationalist	Royal	Mixed farming, lumber, naval stores
Nova Scotia	1749	Royal	Church of England	Royal	Fishing, mixed farming, naval stores

their coastal plantations; thereafter, the African population exploded. Blacks outnumbered whites by 1710 and constituted two-thirds of the population by 1740.

William Penn and Pennsylvania   In contrast to the Carolinas, which languished for decades with proprietors and colonists at odds, William Penn's colony was marked by unity of purpose: all who came hoped to create a prosperous neo-European settlement similar to the societies they knew at home. Penn, though born to wealth — he owned substantial estates in Ireland and England and lived lavishly — joined the **Quakers**, who condemned extravagance. Penn designed his colony as a refuge for his fellow Quakers, who were persecuted in England because they refused to serve in the military or pay taxes to support the Church of England. Penn himself had spent more than two years in jail in England for preaching his beliefs.

Like the Puritans, the Quakers sought to restore Christianity to its early simple spirituality. But they rejected the Puritans' pessimistic Calvinist doctrines, which restricted salvation to a small elect. The Quakers followed the teachings of two English visionaries, George Fox and Margaret Fell, who argued that God had imbued all men — and women — with an "inner light" of grace or understanding. Reflecting the sect's emphasis on gender equality, 350 Quaker women would serve as ministers in the colonies.

Mindful of the catastrophic history of Indian relations in the Chesapeake and New England, Penn exhorted colonists to "sit downe Lovingly" alongside the Native American inhabitants of the Delaware and Susquehanna valleys. He wrote a letter to the leaders of the Iroquois Confederacy alerting them to his intention to settle a colony, and in 1682 he arranged a public treaty with the Delaware Indians to purchase the lands that Philadelphia and the surrounding settlements would soon occupy.

Penn's Frame of Government (1681) applied the Quakers' radical beliefs to politics. It ensured religious freedom by prohibiting a legally established church, and it promoted political equality by allowing all property-owning men to vote and hold office. Cheered by these provisions, thousands of English Quakers flocked to Pennsylvania. To attract European Protestants, Penn published pamphlets in Germany promising cheap land and religious toleration. In 1683, migrants from Saxony founded Germantown (just outside Philadelphia), and thousands of other Germans soon followed. Ethnic diversity, pacifism, and freedom of conscience made Pennsylvania the most open and democratic of the Restoration Colonies.

From Mercantilism to Imperial Dominion

As Charles II distributed American land, his ministers devised policies to keep colonial trade in English hands. Since the 1560s, the English crown had pursued mercantilist policies, using government subsidies and charters to stimulate English manufacturing and foreign trade. Now it extended these mercantilist strategies to the American settlements through the **Navigation Acts**.

The Navigation Acts Dutch and French shippers were often buying sugar and other colonial products from English colonies and carrying them directly into foreign markets. To counter this practice, the Navigation Act of 1651 required that goods be carried on ships owned by English or colonial merchants. New parliamentary acts in 1660 and 1663 strengthened the ban on foreign traders: colonists could export sugar and tobacco only to England and import European goods only through England; moreover, three-quarters of the crew on English vessels had to be English. To pay the customs officials who enforced these laws, the Revenue Act of 1673 imposed a "plantation duty" on American exports of sugar and tobacco.

Edward Hicks, *Penn's Treaty*, c. 1830–1835 Edward Hicks was a Pennsylvania-born painter and preacher whose art expressed a religiously infused understanding of early Pennsylvania history. In more than a hundred paintings, Hicks depicted the colony as a "peaceable kingdom," in which lions lay down with lambs and colonists met peacefully with Native Americans. This painting, which features Hicks's characteristic folk art style, depicts William Penn's first meeting with the Lenni-Lenape peoples in 1683. A Quaker pacifist, Penn refused to seize Indian lands by force and instead negotiated their purchase. This spirit of peaceful cooperation eroded in the later colonial era, but Hicks chose to portray Penn's meeting with the Indians as the foundation of religious and civil liberty in America. Private Collection/Bridgeman Images.

The English government backed these policies with military force. In three wars between 1652 and 1674, the English navy drove the Dutch from New Netherland and contested Holland's control of the Atlantic slave trade by attacking Dutch forts and ships along the West African coast. Meanwhile, English merchants expanded their fleets, which increased in capacity from 150,000 tons in 1640 to 340,000 tons in 1690. This growth occurred on both sides of the Atlantic; by 1702, only London and Bristol had more ships registered in port than did the town of Boston.

Though colonial ports benefitted from the growth of English shipping, many colonists violated the Navigation Acts. Planters continued to trade with Dutch shippers, and New England merchants imported sugar and molasses from the French West Indies. The Massachusetts Bay assembly boldly declared: "The laws of England are bounded within the seas [surrounding it] and do not reach America." Outraged by this insolence, customs official Edward Randolph called for troops to "reduce Massachusetts to obedience." Instead, the Lords of Trade — the administrative body charged with colonial affairs — chose a less violent, but no less confrontational, strategy. In 1679, it denied the claim of Massachusetts Bay to New Hampshire and eventually established a separate royal colony there. Then, in 1684, the Lords of Trade persuaded an English court to annul the Massachusetts Bay charter by charging the Puritan government with violating the Navigation Acts and virtually outlawing the Church of England.

The Dominion of New England The Puritans' troubles had only begun, thanks to the accession of King James II (r. 1685–1688), an aggressive and inflexible ruler. During the reign of Oliver Cromwell, James had grown up in exile in France, and he admired its authoritarian king, Louis XIV. James wanted stricter control over the

MAP 3.1 The Dominion of New England, 1686–1689 In the Dominion, James II created a vast royal colony that stretched nearly 500 miles along the Atlantic coast. During the Glorious Revolution in England, politicians and ministers in Boston and New York City led revolts that ousted Dominion officials and repudiated their authority. King William and Queen Mary replaced the Dominion with governments that balanced the power held by imperial authorities and local political institutions.

PLACE EVENTS IN CONTEXT
How did the ambitions of Charles II and James II remake English North America?

colonies and targeted New England for his reforms. In 1686, the Lords of Trade revoked the charters of Connecticut and Rhode Island and merged them with Massachusetts Bay and Plymouth to form a new royal province, the **Dominion of New England**. James II appointed Sir Edmund Andros, a hard-edged former military officer, as governor of the Dominion. Two years later, James II added New York and New Jersey to the Dominion, creating a vast colony that stretched from Maine to Pennsylvania (Map 3.1).

The Dominion extended to America the authoritarian model of colonial rule that the English government had imposed on Catholic Ireland. James II ordered Governor Andros to abolish the existing legislative assemblies. In Massachusetts, Andros banned town meetings, angering villagers who prized local self-rule. Andros also advocated public worship in the Church of England, offending Puritan Congregationalists. Even worse, from the colonists' perspective, the governor invalidated all land titles granted under the original Massachusetts Bay charter. Andros offered to provide new deeds, but only if the colonists would pay an annual fee. James's plan for the Dominion of New England made it clear that he intended to rule his overseas possessions as an absolute monarch, rejecting the institutions and rights that colonists had come to expect.

The Glorious Revolution in England and America

Fortunately for the colonists, James II angered English political leaders as much as Andros alienated colonists. The king revoked the charters of English towns, rejected the advice of Parliament, and aroused popular opposition by openly practicing Roman Catholicism. Then, in 1688, James's Spanish Catholic wife gave birth to a son. Faced with a Catholic heir to the English throne, Protestant bishops and parliamentary leaders in the Whig Party invited William of Orange, a staunchly Protestant Dutch prince who was married to James's Protestant daughter, Mary Stuart, to come to England at the head of an invading army. With their support, William led a quick and nearly bloodless coup, and King James II was overthrown in an event dubbed the **Glorious Revolution** by its supporters. Whig politicians forced King William and Queen Mary to accept the Declaration of Rights, creating a constitutional monarchy that enhanced the powers of the House of Commons at the expense of the crown. The Whigs wanted political power, especially the power to levy taxes, to reside in the hands of the gentry, merchants, and other substantial property owners.

To justify their coup, the members of Parliament relied on political philosopher John Locke. In his *Two Treatises on Government* (1690), Locke rejected the divine-right monarchy celebrated by James II, arguing that the legitimacy of government rests on the consent of the governed and that individuals have inalienable natural rights to life, liberty, and property. Locke's celebration of individual rights and representative government had a lasting influence in America, where many political leaders wanted to expand the powers of the colonial assemblies.

Rebellions in America The Glorious Revolution sparked rebellions by Protestant colonists in Massachusetts, Maryland, and New York. When news of the coup reached Boston in April 1689, Puritan leaders and 2,000 militiamen seized Governor Andros and shipped him back to England. Heeding American complaints of authoritarian rule, the new monarchs broke up the Dominion of New England. However, they refused to restore the old Puritan-dominated government of Massachusetts Bay, instead creating in 1692 a new royal colony (which absorbed Plymouth and Maine). The new charter empowered the king to appoint the governor and customs officials, gave the vote to all male property owners (not just Puritan church members), and eliminated Puritan restrictions on the Church of England.

In Maryland, the uprising had economic as well as religious causes. Since 1660, falling tobacco prices had hurt poorer farmers, who were overwhelmingly Protestant, while taxes and fees paid to mostly Catholic proprietary officials continued to rise. When Parliament ousted James II, a Protestant association mustered 700 men and forcibly removed the Catholic governor. The Lords of Trade supported this Protestant initiative: they suspended Lord Baltimore's proprietorship, imposed royal government, and made the Church of England the legal religion in the colony. This arrangement lasted until 1715, when Benedict Calvert, the fourth Lord Baltimore, converted to the Anglican faith and the king restored the proprietorship to the Calvert family.

In New York, a Dutchman named Jacob Leisler led the rebellion against the Dominion of New England. Initially he enjoyed broad support, but he soon alienated many English-speaking New Yorkers and well-to-do Dutch residents. Leisler's heavy-handed tactics made him vulnerable; when William and Mary appointed Henry Sloughter as governor in 1691, Leisler was indicted for treason, hanged, and decapitated.

The Glorious Revolution of 1688–1689 began a new era in the politics of both England and its American colonies. In England, William and Mary ruled as **constitutional monarchs**; overseas, they promoted an empire based on commerce. They accepted the overthrow of James's disastrous Dominion of New England and allowed Massachusetts (under its new charter) and New York to resume self-government. In 1696, Parliament created a new body, the Board of Trade, to oversee colonial affairs. While the Board of Trade continued to pursue the mercantilist policies that made the colonies economically beneficial, it permitted local elites to maintain a strong hand in colonial affairs. As England plunged into a new era of European warfare, its leaders had little choice but to allow its colonies substantial autonomy.

King William III and Mary II   Rejecting James II's attempts to impose absolutism, a group of England's most powerful politicians invited William of Orange — a prince of the Dutch Republic — to invade England, depose James II, and occupy the throne jointly with his wife Mary. William's army quickly overthrew James in the so-called Glorious Revolution of 1688, an event that reverberated across the Atlantic in rebellions in Massachusetts, Maryland, and New York. This portrait, from the Guild Book of the Barber Surgeons of York, was probably painted to celebrate the coronation of William and Mary in 1689. © British Library/HIP/Art Resource, NY.

EXPLAIN CONSEQUENCES
How did the Glorious Revolution affect relations between England and its colonies?

IN YOUR OWN WORDS   Identify three new developments between 1660 and 1690 that helped shape England's American Empire.

Imperial Wars and Native Peoples

The price that England paid for bringing William of Orange to the throne was a new commitment to warfare on the continent. England wanted William because of his unambiguous Protestant commitments; William wanted England because of the resources it could bring to bear in European wars. Beginning with the War of the League of Augsburg in 1689, England embarked on an era sometimes called the **Second Hundred Years' War**, which lasted until the defeat of Napoleon at Waterloo in 1815. In that time, England (Britain after 1707) fought in seven major wars; the longest era of peace lasted only twenty-six years.

Imperial wars transformed North America. Prior to 1689, American affairs were distant from those of Europe, but the recurrent wars of the eighteenth century spilled over repeatedly into the colonies. Governments were forced to arm themselves and create new alliances with neighboring Native Americans, who tried to turn the fighting to their own advantage. Although war brought money to the American colonies in the form of war contracts, it also placed new demands on colonial governments to support the increasingly militant British Empire. To win wars in Western Europe, the Caribbean, and far-flung oceans, British leaders created a powerful central state that spent three-quarters of its revenue on military and naval expenses.

The "Four Indian Kings" in London, 1710 After a failed invasion of Canada in 1709, a colonial delegation went to London to ask the queen to try again. They brought four Indians with them — three Mohawks and a Mahican — and presented them in London as the "Four Indian Kings" of the Iroquois. The four kings met Queen Anne, dined with nobility, attended the theater, and toured the sites. They sat for several portraits, which were engraved for prints like this one. The queen agreed to make another try for Canada, but the 1711 invasion failed again. Bernard Lens the younger (1682–1740), Bernard Lens the elder (1659–1725), 1710, mezzotint on paper, Albany Institute of History & Art, bequest of Henry M. Sage, 1972.65.7.

Tribalization

For Native Americans, the rise of war intersected with a process scholars have called **tribalization**: the adaptation of stateless peoples to the demands imposed on them by neighboring states. In North America, tribalization occurred in catastrophic circumstances. Eurasian diseases rapidly killed off broad swaths of Native communities, disproportionately victimizing the old and the very young. In oral cultures, old people were irreplaceable repositories of knowledge, while the young were literally the future. With populations in free fall, many polities disappeared altogether. By the eighteenth century, the groups that survived had all been transformed. Some new tribes, like the Catawbas, had not existed before and were pieced together from remnants of formerly large groups. Other nations, like the Iroquois, declined in numbers but sustained themselves by adopting many war captives. In the Carolina borderlands, a large number of Muskogean-speaking communities came together as a nation known to the British as the "Creek" Indians, so named because some of them lived on Ochese Creek. Similarly, the Cherokees, the Delawares, and other groups that were culturally linked but politically fragmented became coherent "tribes" to deal more effectively with their European neighbors.

The rise of imperial warfare exposed Native American communities to danger, but it also gave them newfound leverage. The Iroquois were radically endangered by imperial conflict. A promised English alliance failed them, and in 1693 a combined force of French soldiers, militiamen, and their Indian allies burned all three Mohawk villages to the ground. Thereafter, the Iroquois devised a strategy for playing French and English interests off against each other. In 1701, they made alliances with both empires, declaring their intention to remain neutral in future conflicts between them. This did not mean that the Iroquois stayed on the sideline. Iroquois warriors often participated in raids during wartime, and Iroquois spokesmen met regularly with representatives of New York and New France to affirm their alliances and receive diplomatic gifts that included guns, powder, lead, clothing, and rum (from the British) or brandy (from the French). Their neutrality, paradoxically, made them more sought after as allies. For example, their alliance with New York, known as the **Covenant Chain**, soon became a model for relations between the British Empire and other Native American peoples.

Imperial warfare also reshaped Indian relations in the Southeast. During the War of the Spanish Succession (1702–1713), which pitted Britain against France and Spain, English settlers in the Carolinas armed the Creeks, whose 15,000 members farmed the fertile lands along the present-day border of Georgia and Alabama. A joint English-Creek expedition attacked Spanish Florida, burning the town of St. Augustine but failing to capture the fort. To protect Havana in nearby Cuba, the Spanish reinforced St. Augustine and unsuccessfully attacked Charleston, South Carolina.

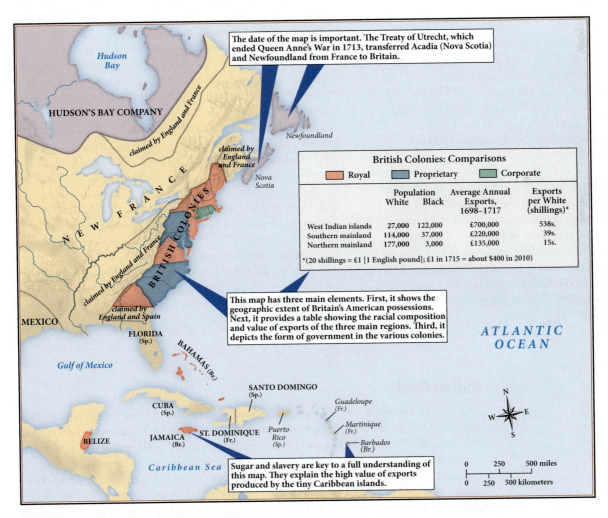

The date of the map is important. The Treaty of Utrecht, which ended Queen Anne's War in 1713, transferred Acadia (Nova Scotia) and Newfoundland from France to Britain.

British Colonies: Comparisons

	Royal		Proprietary		Corporate

	Population White	Black	Average Annual Exports, 1698–1717	Exports per White (shillings)*
West Indian islands	27,000	122,000	£700,000	538s.
Southern mainland	114,000	37,000	£220,000	39s.
Northern mainland	177,000	3,000	£135,000	15s.

*(20 shillings = £1 [1 English pound]; £1 in 1715 = about $400 in 2010)

This map has three main elements. First, it shows the geographic extent of Britain's American possessions. Next, it provides a table showing the racial composition and value of exports of the three main regions. Third, it depicts the form of government in the various colonies.

Sugar and slavery are key to a full understanding of this map. They explain the high value of exports produced by the tiny Caribbean islands.

MAP 3.2 Britain's American Empire, 1713
Many of Britain's possessions in the West Indies were tiny islands, mere dots on the Caribbean Sea. However, in 1713, these small pieces of land were by far the most valuable parts of the empire. Their sugar crops brought wealth to English merchants, commerce to the northern colonies, and a brutal life and early death to the hundreds of thousands of African slaves working on the plantations.

Native Americans and European Empires

Analyzing primary sources in which Europeans recorded Native American speech or actions can be especially challenging. In many cases, historians believe that recorded accounts of Native American speeches from the colonial era are essentially accurate. But often scholars consider it necessary to read *against the grain* of such sources — the document should be read closely and skeptically. Were the Native Americans speaking for themselves, or were others speaking for them? Who recorded their speech, and did they have any reason to alter the words they heard? What silences or contradictions can you see? These are good questions to apply to any primary source, but it's especially important when reading accounts of early Native Americans, who did not have written languages of their own to counterbalance the texts that were produced and archived by colonial powers. Try reading the two documents below "against the grain," and then answer the Questions for Analysis.

In 1710, four "Indian kings" traveled to London to strengthen the imperial alliance between Great Britain and the Iroquois. A London periodical printed the following account of their visit, including the speech they made to Queen Anne.

SOURCE: [Abel Boyer], *The History of the Reign of Queen Anne. Digested into Annals. Year the Ninth* (London, 1711), 189–192.

❝ On the 19th of *April*, . . . Four *Kings*, or *Chiefs* of the Six Nations in the *West-Indies*, which lye between *New-England*, and *New-France*, or *Canada*: Who lately came over with the *West-India* Fleet, and were Cloath'd and Entertain'd at the Queen's Expence, had a Publick Audience of Her Majesty at the Palace of St. *James*'s. . . . They made a Speech by their Interpreter, which Major *Pidgeon*, who was one of the Officers that came with them, read in *English* to Her Majesty, being as follows:
Great Queen!

We have undertaken a long and tedious Voyage, which none of our Predecessors could ever be prevail'd upon to undertake. The Motive that induc'd us was that we might see our *Great Queen*, and relate to Her those Things we thought absolutely necessary, for the Good of Her, and us, Her Allies, on the other side of the Great Water.

We doubt not but our *Great Queen* has been acquainted with our long and tedious War, in Conjunction with Her Children, (meaning Subjects) against Her Enemies the French; and that we have been as a strong Wall for their Security, even to the Loss of our best Men. The Truth of which . . . Colonel *Schuyler*, and . . . Colonel *Nicholson*, can testify, they having all our Proposals in Writing.

We were mightily rejoiced when we heard . . . that our Great Queen had resolved to send an Army to reduce *Canada*; . . . and in Token of our Friendship, we hung up the *Kettle*, and took up the *Hatchet*; and with one Consent, joined . . . Colonel *Schuyler*, and . . . Colonel *Nicholson*, in making Preparations . . . by building Forts, Store-Houses, Canows [canoes], and Battows [flat-bottomed boats]; whilst . . . Colonel *Vetch*, at the same time raised an Army at *Boston*, of which we were informed by our Ambassadors, who we sent thither for that Purpose. We waited long in Expectation of the Fleet from *England*, to join . . . Colonel *Vetch*, to go against *Quebec* by Sea, whilst [Nicholson, Schuyler], and we, went to *Port-Royal* by Land; but at last we were told, that our *Great Queen*, by some important Affair, was prevented in Her Design for that Season. This made us extream sorrowful, lest the *French*, who hitherto had dreaded us, should now think us unable to make War against them. The Reduction of *Canada* is of such Weight, that after the effecting thereof, we should have *Free Hunting*,

Indian Goals

The Creeks had their own agenda: to become the dominant tribe in the region, they needed to vanquish their longtime enemies, the pro-French Choctaws to the west and the Spanish-allied Apalachees to the south. Beginning in 1704, a force of Creek and Yamasee warriors destroyed the remaining Franciscan missions in northern Florida, attacked the Spanish settlement at Pensacola, and captured a thousand Apalachees, whom they sold to South Carolinian slave traders for sale in the West Indies. Simultaneously, a Carolina-supported Creek expedition attacked the Iroquois-speaking Tuscarora people of North Carolina, killing hundreds, executing 160 male captives, and sending 400 women and children into slavery. The surviving Tuscaroras joined the Iroquois in New York (who now became the Six Nations of the Iroquois). The Carolinians, having used the Creeks to kill Spaniards, now died at the hands of their former allies: when English traders demanded payment for trade debts in 1715, and a great Trade with our *Great Queen*'s Children; and as a Token of the Sincerity of the Six Nations, we do here, in the Name of all, present Our *Great Queen* with the *Belts* of *Wampum*.

Since we have been in Alliance with our *Great Queen*'s Children, we have had some Knowledge of the *Saviour* of the World; and have often been importuned by the *French*, both by the insinuations of their Priests, and by Presents, to come over to their Interest, but have always esteem'd them *Men of Falshood*: But if our *Great Queen* will be pleas'd to send over some Persons to instruct us, they shall find a most hearty Welcome. . . .

On *Friday*, the 21st of *April*, the Four *Indian* Princes went to see Dr. *Flamstead*'s House, and Mathematical Instruments in *Greenwich* Park; after which they were nobly treated by some of the Lords Commissioners of the Admiralty, in One of Her Majesty's Yachts. They staid about a Fortnight longer in *London*, where they were entertain'd by several Persons of Distinction, particularly by the Duke of *Ormond*, who regaled them likewise with a Review of the Four Troops of Life-Guards; And having seen all the Curiosities in and about this Metropolis, they went down to Portsmouth, through *Hampton-Court*, and *Windsor*, and embark'd on Board the *Dragon*, . . . and on the 15th of *July* arrived at *Boston* in *New England*. 🙾

In 1725, French officials in Louisiana organized a similar trip to Paris for five Native leaders representing the Missouris, Osages, Otos, and the Illinois confederacy. Jesuit missionaries had been active among the Illinois Indians for decades and had made many converts. Among them was Chikagou, a Michigamea headman (the Michigameas were one member nation of the Illinois confederacy) who was a staunch ally of the French. After a group of Natchez warriors attacked a French outpost in 1729, Chikagou and Mamantouensa, a headman of the Kaskaskias (another Illinois nation), appeared before the governor of Louisiana to offer their support in a counterattack. This account was recorded by a Jesuit missionary in attendance and included in a letter to his superior in Paris.

Source: Father le Petit to Father d'Avaugour, July 12, 1730, in *Jesuit Relations and Allied Documents*, ed. Reuben G. Thwaites, 73 vols. (Cleveland, 1896–1901), 68:201–203.

🙼 [The Illinois spokesman assured the governor,] 'We always place ourselves . . . before the enemies of the French; it is necessary to pass over our bodies to go to them, and to strike us to the heart before a single blow can reach them.' Their conduct is in accordance with this declaration, and has not in the least contradicted their words. . . . Chikagou, whom you saw in Paris, was at the head of the *Mitchigamias*, and *Mamantouensa* at the head of the *Kaskaskias*.

Chikagou spoke first. He spread out in the hall a carpet of deerskin, bordered with porcupine quills, on which he placed two calumets, with different savage ornaments, accompanying them with a present according to the usual custom. 'There,' said he, in showing these two calumets, 'are two messages which we bring you, the one of Religion, and the other of peace or war, as you shall determine. We have listened with respect to the Governors, because they bring us the word of the King our Father, and much more to the black Robes [Jesuit missionaries], because they bring us the word of God himself, who is the King of Kings. We have come from a great distance to weep with you for the death of the French, and to offer our Warriors to strike those hostile Nations whom you may wish to designate. You have but to speak. When I went over to France, the King promised me his protection for the Prayer, and recommended me never to abandon it. I will always remember it. Grant then your protection to us and to our black Robes.' He then gave utterance to the edifying sentiments with which he was impressed with regard to the Faith, as the Interpreter Baillarjon enabled us to half understand them in his miserable French. 🙾

QUESTIONS FOR ANALYSIS

1. What language was the speech of the "four kings" delivered in? How large a role do you think the four men played in shaping its content?

2. What requests did the "four kings" make of Queen Anne?

3. What language was Chikagou's speech delivered in? What points did he seek to make?

4. Which of these texts do you consider most reliable? Which gives you the clearest sense of a Native voice? What themes or concerns do they have in common?

---

the Creeks and Yamasees revolted, killing 400 colonists before being overwhelmed by the Carolinians and their new Indian allies, the Cherokees.

Native Americans also joined in the warfare between French Catholics in Canada and English Protestants in New England. With French aid, Catholic Mohawk and Abenaki warriors attacked their Puritan neighbors. They destroyed English settlements in Maine and, in 1704, attacked the western Massachusetts town of Deerfield, where they killed 48 residents and carried 112 into captivity. In response, New England militia attacked French settlements and, in 1710, joined with British naval forces to seize Port Royal in French Acadia (Nova Scotia). However, a major British–New England expedition against the French stronghold at Quebec, inspired in part by the visit of four Indian "kings" to London, failed miserably (Analyzing Voices).

Stalemated militarily in America, Britain won major territorial and commercial concessions through its victories in Europe. In the Treaty of Utrecht (1713), Britain obtained Newfoundland, Acadia, and the Hudson Bay region of northern Canada from

CONSIDER POINTS OF VIEW
What did Native Americans have to gain by participating in imperial wars?

France, as well as access through Albany to the western Indian trade. From Spain, Britain acquired the strategic fortress of Gibraltar at the entrance to the Mediterranean and a thirty-year contract to supply slaves to Spanish America. These gains advanced Britain's quest for commercial supremacy and brought peace to eastern North America for a generation (Map 3.2).

IN YOUR OWN WORDS What was tribalization, and how did it help Native Americans cope with their European neighbors?

The Imperial Slave Economy

Britain's focus on America reflected the growth of a new agricultural and commercial order — the **South Atlantic System** — that produced sugar, tobacco, rice, and other tropical and subtropical products for an international market. Its plantation societies were ruled by European planter-merchants and worked by hundreds of thousands of enslaved Africans (Figure 3.1).

The South Atlantic System

The South Atlantic System had its center in Brazil and the West Indies, and sugar was its primary product. Before 1500, there were few sweet foods in Europe — mostly honey and fruits — so when European planters developed vast sugarcane plantations in America, they found a ready market for their crop. (The craving for the potent new sweet food was so intense that, by 1900, sugar accounted for an astonishing 20 percent of the calories consumed by the world's people.)

European merchants, investors, and planters garnered the profits of the South Atlantic System. Following mercantilist principles, they provided the plantations with tools and equipment to grow and process the sugarcane and ships to carry it to Europe. But it was the Atlantic slave trade that made the system run. Between 1520 and 1650, Portuguese traders carried about 820,000 Africans across the Atlantic — about 4,000 slaves a year before 1600 and 10,000 annually thereafter. Over the next half century, the Dutch dominated the Atlantic slave trade; then, between 1700 and 1800, the British transported about 2.5 million of the total of 6.1 million Africans carried to the Americas.

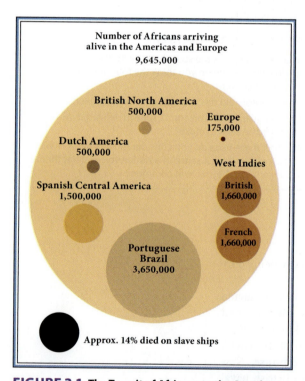

Number of Africans arriving alive in the Americas and Europe
9,645,000

British North America 500,000

Europe 175,000

Dutch America 500,000

West Indies

Spanish Central America 1,500,000

British 1,660,000

French 1,660,000

Portuguese Brazil 3,650,000

Approx. 14% died on slave ships

FIGURE 3.1 **The Transit of Africans to the Americas**
Though approximately 11 million enslaved Africans boarded ships to the Americas, about 1.5 million (14 percent) of them died en route. Two-thirds of the survivors ended up in Brazil (3.65 million) and the West Indies (3.32 million), where they worked primarily on sugar plantations. Half a million arrived directly from Africa in the present-day United States, while many thousands more were traded to the mainland from the West Indies.

England and the West Indies England was a latecomer to the plantation economy, but from the beginning the prospect of a lucrative cash crop drew large numbers of migrants. On St. Kitts, Nevis, Montserrat, and Barbados, most early settlers were small-scale English farmers (and their indentured servants) who exported tobacco and livestock hides; on this basis, they created small but thriving colonies. In 1650, there were more English residents in the West Indies (some 44,000) than in the Chesapeake (20,000) and New England (23,000) colonies combined.

After 1650, sugar transformed Barbados and the other islands into slave-based plantation societies, a change facilitated by English capital combined with the knowledge and experience of Dutch merchants. By 1680, an elite group of 175 planters, described by one anti-slavery writer of the time as "inhumane and barbarous," dominated Barbados's economy; they owned more than half of the island, thousands of indentured servants, and half of its more than 50,000 slaves. In 1692, exploited Irish servants and island-born African slaves staged a major uprising, which was brutally suppressed. The "leading principle" in a slave society, declared one West Indian planter, was to instill "fear" among workers and a commitment to "absolute coercive" force among masters. As social inequality and racial conflict increased, hundreds of English farmers fled to South Carolina and the large island of Jamaica. But the days of Caribbean smallholders were numbered. English sugar merchants soon invested heavily in Jamaica; by 1750, it had seven hundred large sugar plantations, worked by more than 105,000 slaves, and had become the wealthiest British colony.

Sugar was a rich man's crop because it could be produced most efficiently on large plantations. Scores of slaves planted and cut the sugarcane, which was then processed by expensive equipment — crushing mills, boiling houses, distilling apparatus — into raw sugar, molasses, and rum. The affluent planter-merchants who controlled the sugar industry drew annual profits of more than 10 percent on their investment. As Scottish economist Adam Smith noted in his famous treatise *The Wealth of Nations* (1776), sugar was the most profitable crop grown in America or Europe.

The Impact on Britain   The South Atlantic System generated enormous wealth and helped Europeans achieve world economic leadership. Most British West Indian plantations belonged to absentee owners who lived in England, where they spent their profits and formed a powerful sugar lobby. The Navigation Acts kept the British sugar trade in the hands of British merchants, who exported sugar to foreign markets, and by 1750 reshipments of American sugar and tobacco to Europe accounted for half of British exports. Enormous profits also flowed into Britain from the slave trade. The value of the guns, iron, rum, and cloth that were used to buy slaves was only about one-tenth (in the 1680s) to one-third (by the 1780s) of the value of the crops those slaves produced in America, allowing English traders to sell slaves in the West Indies for three to five times what they paid for them in Africa.

These massive profits drove the slave trade. At its height in the 1790s, Britain annually exported three hundred thousand guns to Africa, and a British ship carrying 300 to 350 slaves left an African port every other day. This commerce stimulated the entire British economy. English, Scottish, and American shipyards built hundreds of vessels, and thousands of people worked in trade-related industries: building port facilities and warehouses, refining sugar and tobacco, distilling rum from molasses, and manufacturing textiles and iron products for the growing markets in Africa and America. More than one thousand British merchant ships were plying the Atlantic by 1750, providing a supply of experienced sailors and laying the foundation for the supremacy of the Royal Navy.

> **EXPLAIN CONSEQUENCES**
> How did the South Atlantic System affect the British economy?

Africa, Africans, and the Slave Trade

As the South Atlantic System enhanced European prosperity, it imposed enormous costs on West and Central Africa. Between 1550 and 1870, the Atlantic slave trade uprooted 11 million Africans, draining lands south of the Sahara of people and wealth and changing African society (Map 3.3). By directing commerce away from the savannas and the Islamic world on the other side of the Sahara, the Atlantic slave trade changed the economic and religious dynamics of the African interior. It also fostered militaristic, centralized states in the coastal areas.

Africans and the Slave Trade   Warfare and slaving had been part of African life for centuries, but the South Atlantic System made slaving a favorite tactic of ambitious kings and plundering warlords. "Whenever the King of Barsally wants Goods or Brandy," an observer noted, "the King goes and ransacks some of his enemies' towns, seizing the people and selling them." Supplying slaves became a way of life in the West African state of Dahomey, where the royal house monopolized the sale of slaves and used European guns to create a military despotism. Dahomey's army, which included a contingent of 5,000 women, raided the interior for captives; between 1680 and 1730, Dahomey

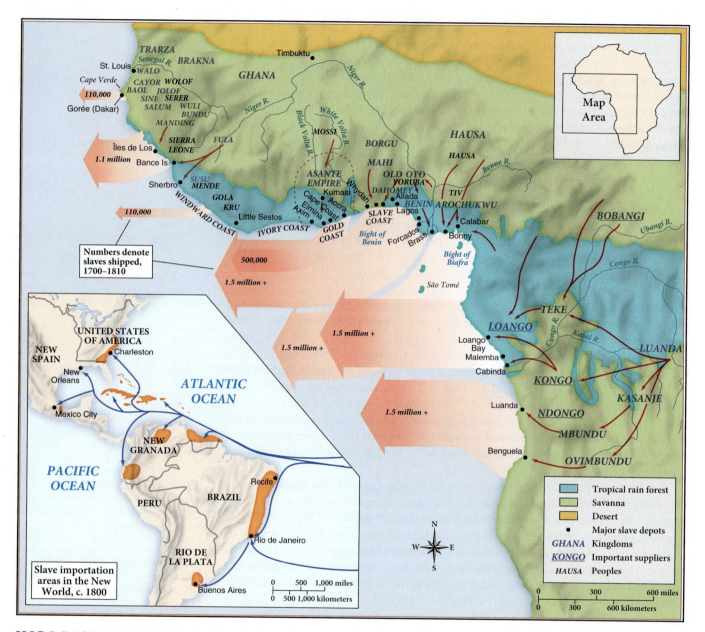

MAP 3.3 Africa and the Atlantic Slave Trade, 1700–1810

The tropical rain forest of West Africa was home to scores of peoples and dozens of kingdoms. With the rise of the slave trade, some of these kingdoms became aggressive slavers. Dahomey's army, for example, seized tens of thousands of captives in wars with neighboring peoples and sold them to European traders. About 14 percent of the captives died during the grueling Middle Passage, the transatlantic voyage between Africa and the Americas. Most of the survivors labored on sugar plantations in Brazil and the British and French West Indies.

annually exported 20,000 slaves from the ports of Allada and Whydah. The Asante kings likewise used slaving to conquer states along the Gold Coast as well as Muslim kingdoms in the savanna. By the 1720s, they had created a prosperous empire of 3 to 5 million people. Yet participation in the transatlantic slave trade remained a choice for Africans, not a necessity. The powerful kingdom of Benin, famous for its cast bronzes and carved ivory, prohibited for decades the export of all slaves, male and female.

The trade in humans produced untold misery. Hundreds of thousands of young Africans died, and millions more endured a brutal life in the Americas. In Africa itself, class divisions hardened as people of noble birth enslaved and sold those of lesser status. Gender relations shifted as well. Two-thirds of the slaves sent across the Atlantic were men, partly because European planters paid more for men and "stout men boys" and partly because Africans were more likely to sell enslaved women locally. The resulting sexual imbalance prompted more African men to take several wives. Finally, the expansion of the Atlantic slave trade increased the extent of slavery in Africa. Sultan Mawlay Ismail of Morocco (r. 1672–1727) owned 150,000 black slaves, obtained by trade in Timbuktu and in wars he waged in Senegal. In Africa, as in the Americas, slavery eroded the dignity of human life.

The Middle Passage and Beyond   Africans sold into the South Atlantic System suffered the bleakest fate. Torn from their villages, they were marched in chains to coastal ports, their first passage in slavery. Then they endured the perilous **Middle Passage** to the New World in hideously overcrowded ships. The captives had little to eat or drink, and some died from dehydration. The feces, urine, and vomit below decks prompted outbreaks of dysentery, which took more lives. "I was so overcome by the heat, stench, and foul air that I nearly fainted," reported a European doctor. Some slaves jumped overboard to drown rather than endure more suffering. Others staged violent shipboard revolts. Slave uprisings occurred on two thousand voyages, roughly one of every ten Atlantic passages. Nearly 100,000 slaves died in these insurrections, and nearly 1.5 million others — about 14 percent of those who were transported — died of disease or illness on the month-long journey (America in Global Context).

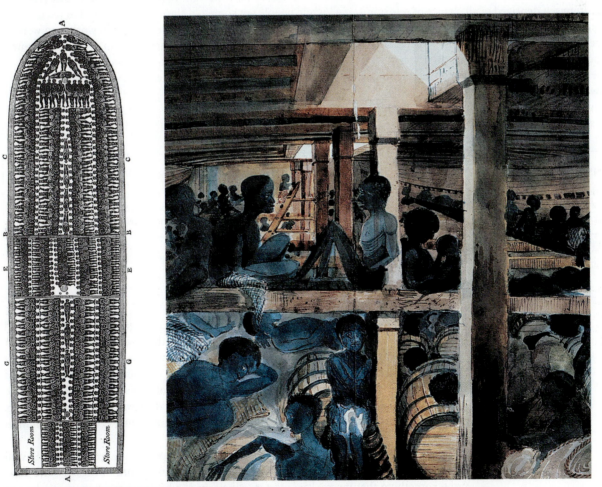

Two Views of the Middle Passage   An 1846 watercolor (on the right) shows the cargo hold of a slave ship en route to Brazil, which imported large numbers of African slaves until the 1860s. Painted by a ship's officer, the work minimizes the brutality of the Middle Passage — none of the slaves are in chains — and captures the Africans' humanity and dignity. The illustration on the left, which was printed by England's Abolitionist Society, shows the plan of a Liverpool slave ship designed to hold 482 Africans, packed in with no more respect than that given to hogsheads of sugar and tobacco. Records indicate that the ship actually carried as many as 609 Africans at once.   Left: Private Collection © Michael Graham-Stewart/Bridgeman Images. Right: © National Maritime Museum, London/The Image Works.

Olaudah Equiano: The Brutal "Middle Passage"

Olaudah Equiano claimed to have been born in Igboland (present-day southern Nigeria). But Vincent Carretta of the University of Maryland has discovered strong evidence that Equiano was born in South Carolina. He suggests that Equiano drew on conversations with African-born slaves to create a fictitious account of his kidnapping at the age of eleven and a traumatic passage across the Atlantic. After being purchased by an English sea captain, Equiano bought his freedom in 1766. In London, he became an antislavery activist, and in 1789 he published the memoir from which the following selections are drawn.

My father, besides many slaves, had a numerous family. . . . I was trained up from my earliest years in the art of war, . . . and my mother adorned me with emblems after the manner of our greatest warriors. One day, when all our people were gone out to their works as usual and only I and my dear sister were left to mind the house, two men and a woman got over our walls, and in a moment seized us both. . . .

I was . . . sold and carried through a number of places till . . . at the end of six or seven months after I had been kidnapped I arrived at the sea coast.

. . . I now saw myself deprived of all chance of returning to my native country. . . . I was soon put down under the decks, and there I received such a salutation in my nostrils as I had never experienced in my life; so that with the loathsomeness of the stench and crying together, I became so sick and low that I was not able to eat, nor had I the least desire to taste anything. I now wished for the last friend, death, to relieve me; but soon, to my grief, two of the white men offered me eatables, and on my refusing to eat, one of them held me fast by the hands and . . . tied my feet while the other flogged me severely. I had never experienced anything of this kind before, and . . . could I have got over the nettings, I would have jumped over the side. . . . One day, when we had a smooth sea and moderate wind, two of my wearied countrymen who were chained together . . . , preferring death to such a life of misery, somehow made it through the nettings and jumped into the sea. . . .

At last we came in sight of the island of Barbados; the white people got some old slaves from the land to pacify us. They told us we were not to be eaten but to work, and were soon to go on land where we should see many of our country people. This report eased us much; and sure enough soon after we were landed there came to us Africans of all languages.

Source: *The Interesting Narrative of the Life of Olaudah Equiano, or Gustavus Vassa, the African, Written by Himself* (London, 1789), 15, 22–23, 28–29.

QUESTIONS FOR ANALYSIS

1. What elements of Equiano's account might explain the average slave mortality rate of about 14 percent during the Atlantic crossing?

2. Assuming that Carretta is correct, and Equiano was not born in Africa, why do you think he composed this fictitious narrative of his childhood instead of describing his own childhood in slavery?

For those who survived the Atlantic crossing, things only got worse as they passed into endless slavery. Life on the sugar plantations of northwestern Brazil and the West Indies was one of relentless exploitation. Slaves worked ten hours a day under the hot tropical sun; slept in flimsy huts; and lived on a starchy diet of corn, yams, and dried fish. They were subjected to brutal discipline: "The fear of punishment is the principle [we use] . . . to keep them in awe and order," one planter declared. When punishments came, they were brutal. Flogging was commonplace; some planters rubbed salt, lemon juice, or urine into the resulting wounds.

Planters often took advantage of their power by raping enslaved women. Sexual exploitation was a largely unacknowledged but ubiquitous feature of master-slave relations, something that many slave masters considered to be an unquestioned privilege of their position. "It was almost a constant practice with our clerks, and other whites," Olaudah Equiano wrote, "to commit violent depredations on the chastity of the female slaves." Thomas Thistlewood was a Jamaica planter who kept an unusually detailed journal in which he noted every act of sexual exploitation he committed. In thirty-seven years as a Jamaica planter, Thistlewood recorded 3,852 sex acts with 138 enslaved women.

With sugar prices high and the cost of slaves low, many planters worked their slaves to death and then bought more. Between 1708 and 1735, British planters on Barbados imported about 85,000 Africans; however, in that same time the island's black population increased by only 4,000 (from 42,000 to 46,000). The constant influx of new slaves kept the population thoroughly "African" in its languages, religions, and culture. "Here," wrote a Jamaican observer, "each different nation of Africa meet and dance after the manner of their own country . . . [and] retain most of their native customs."

Slavery in the Chesapeake and South Carolina

West Indian–style slavery came to Virginia and Maryland following Bacon's Rebellion. Taking advantage of the expansion of the British slave trade (following the end of the Royal African Company's monopoly in 1698), elite planter-politicians led a "tobacco revolution" and bought more Africans, putting these slaves to work on ever-larger plantations. Scholars continue to debate the relationship between economic considerations and cultural values in their efforts to explain the rise of African slavery (Interpretations). By 1720, Africans made up 20 percent of the Chesapeake population; by 1740, nearly 40 percent. Slavery had become a core institution, no longer just one of several forms of unfree labor. Moreover, slavery was now defined in racial terms. Virginia legislators prohibited sexual intercourse between English and Africans and defined virtually all resident Africans as slaves: "All servants imported or brought into this country by sea or land who were not Christians in their native country shall be accounted and be slaves."

On the mainland as in the islands, slavery was a system of brutal exploitation. Violence was common, and the threat of violence always hung over master-slave relationships. In 1669, Virginia's House of Burgesses decreed that a master who killed a slave in the process of "correcting" him could not be charged with a felony, since it would be irrational to destroy his own property. From that point forward, even the most extreme punishments were permitted by law. Slaves could not carry weapons or gather in large numbers. Slaveholders were especially concerned to discourage slaves from running away. Punishments for runaways commonly included not only brutal whipping but also branding or scarring to make recalcitrant slaves easier to identify. Virginia laws spelled out the procedures for capturing and returning runaway slaves in detail. If a runaway slave was killed in the process of recapturing him, the county would reimburse the slave's owner for his full value. In some cases, slave owners could put runaway slaves up for trial; if they were found guilty and executed, the owner would be compensated for his loss (Thinking Like a Historian).

Despite the inherent brutality of the institution, slaves in Virginia and Maryland worked under better conditions than those in the West Indies. Many lived relatively long lives. Unlike sugar and rice, which were "killer crops" that demanded strenuous labor in a tropical climate, tobacco cultivation required steadier and less demanding labor in a more temperate environment. Workers planted young tobacco seedlings in spring, hoed and weeded the crop in summer, and in fall picked and hung the leaves to cure over the winter. Nor did diseases spread as easily in the Chesapeake, because plantation quarters were less crowded and more dispersed than those in the West Indies. Finally, because tobacco profits were lower than those from sugar, planters treated their slaves less harshly than West Indian planters did.

Many tobacco planters increased their workforce by buying female slaves and encouraging them to have children. In 1720, women made up more than one-third of the Africans in Maryland, and the black population had begun to increase naturally. "Be kind and indulgent to the breeding wenches," one slave owner told his overseer, "[and do not] force them when with child upon any service or hardship that will be injurious to them." By midcentury, more than three-quarters of the enslaved workers in the Chesapeake were American-born.

Why Did Americans Adopt Slavery?

Though most enslaved people who were imported to the Americas during the seventeenth century were shipped to the Caribbean and South America, a small portion ended up in Britain's North American colonies. The number of slaves in Britain's mainland colonies was still small in 1700, but it soared in the eighteenth century. On the eve of the American Revolution, there were nearly a quarter million Africans enslaved in the mainland colonies. The majority of these were concentrated on southern plantations, where they replaced white indentured servants as the primary laborers.

One question has puzzled historians more than most: why did American colonists turn to the enslavement of Africans to solve their labor problems? The answer is not straightforward, and historians have spent decades debating this question. While scholars have not agreed on a single answer, their debate has pointed to two major factors: white racism toward blacks and the economics of the plantation labor system. In the excerpts below, David Eltis and Robin Blackburn weigh in by offering competing answers to America's most difficult question.

DAVID ELTIS
The Rise of African Slavery in the Americas

SOURCE: David Eltis, *The Rise of African Slavery in the Americas* (New York: Cambridge University Press, 2000), 58, 66, 70, 84.

That Europeans used only non-Europeans as slaves . . . for primarily economic reasons has wide support [among scholars]. . . . [E]lites would surely use the cheapest option possible within the limits of mercantilist policies. . . . Yet such motives operated under the aegis of fundamental non-economic values. . . . One central issue here is perception of race, ethnicity, or, less controversially, who is to be considered an outsider and is therefore enslavable and who is an insider and thus unenslavable. . . . [F]rom the strictly economic standpoint there were strong arguments in support of using European rather than African slave labor. The crux of the matter was shipping costs. . . . [But] the barrier to European slaves in the Americas lay not only beyond shipping and enslavement costs but also beyond any strictly economic sphere. . . .

For elite and non-elite [Europeans] alike enslavement remained a fate for which only non-Europeans were qualified.

ROBIN BLACKBURN
The Making of New World Slavery

SOURCE: Robin Blackburn, *The Making of New World Slavery: From the Baroque to the Modern, 1492–1800* (London: Verso, 2010), 353.

The decision for slavery was implicit in the competitive commercial structure of planters and merchants. . . . Once planters and merchants competed to bring plantation produce to the market by the swiftest means possible, with a free hand to import slaves and exploit them, the transition to the slave-worked plantations was inevitable. The Atlantic slave trade option was supported by governments, deferring to the wishes of the main actors in the matter. For the planter who was seriously interested in maximizing output, and in the fortune this promised to make him, the decision to buy African slaves became a natural one.

QUESTIONS FOR ANALYSIS

1. Identify one way Eltis and Blackburn differ in their explanation of the origins of slavery in the Americas.
2. According to these historians, what role did economic considerations play in establishing the Atlantic slave system?

3. Based on your reading of this chapter's discussion of slavery, which argument about slavery's origins and justification is more persuasive and why?

Slaves in South Carolina labored under much more oppressive conditions. The colony grew slowly until 1700, when planters began to plant and export rice to southern Europe, where it was in great demand. Between 1720 and 1750, rice production increased fivefold. To expand production, planters imported thousands of Africans, some of them from rice-growing societies. By 1710, Africans formed a majority of the total population, eventually rising to 80 percent in rice-growing areas.

Most rice plantations lay in inland swamps, and the work was dangerous and exhausting. Slaves planted, weeded, and harvested the rice in ankle-deep mud. Pools of stagnant water bred mosquitoes, which transmitted diseases that claimed hundreds of African lives. Other slaves, forced to move tons of dirt to build irrigation works, died from exhaustion. "The labour required [for growing rice] is only fit for slaves," a Scottish traveler remarked, "and I think the hardest work I have seen them engaged in." In South Carolina, as in the West Indies and Brazil, there were many slave deaths and few births, and the arrival of new slaves continually "re-Africanized" the black population.

An African American Community Emerges

Slaves came from many peoples in West Africa and the Central African regions of Kongo and Angola. White planters welcomed ethnic diversity to deter slave revolts. "The safety of the Plantations," declared a widely read English pamphlet, "depends upon having Negroes from all parts of Guiny, who do not understand each other's languages and Customs and cannot agree to Rebel." By accident or design, most plantations drew laborers of many languages, including Kwa, Mande, and Kikongo. Among Africans imported after 1730 into the upper James River region of Virginia, 41 percent came from ethnic groups in present-day Nigeria, and another 25 percent from West-Central Africa. The rest hailed from the Windward and Gold coasts, Senegambia, and Sierra Leone. In South Carolina, plantation owners preferred laborers from the Gold Coast and Gambia, who had a reputation as hardworking farmers. But as African sources of slaves shifted southward after 1730, more than 30 percent of the colony's workers later came from Kongo and Angola.

Initially, the slaves did not think of themselves as Africans or blacks but as members of a specific family, clan, or people — Wolof, Hausa, Ibo, Yoruba, Teke, Ngola — and they sought out those who shared their language and customs. In the upper James River region, Ibo men and women arrived in equal numbers, married each other, and maintained their Ibo culture. In most places, though, this was impossible. Slaves from varying backgrounds were thrown together and only gradually discovered common ground.

Building Community   Through painful trial and error, slaves eventually discovered what limited freedoms their owners would allow them. Those who were not too rebellious or too recalcitrant were able to carve out precarious family lives — though they were always in danger of being disrupted by sale or life-threatening punishment — and build the rudiments of a slave community.

One key to the development of families and communities was a more or less balanced sex ratio that encouraged marriage and family formation. In South Carolina, the high death rate among slaves undermined ties of family and kinship; but in the Chesapeake, after 1725 some slaves, especially on larger plantations, were able to create strong nuclear families and extended kin relations. On one of Charles Carroll's estates in Maryland, 98 of the 128 slaves were members of two extended families. These African American kin groups passed on family names, traditions, and knowledge to the next generation, and thus a distinct culture gradually developed. As one observer suggested, blacks had created a separate world, "a Nation within a Nation."

As slaves forged a new identity, they carried on certain African practices but let others go. Many Africans arrived in America with ritual scars that white planters called "country markings"; these signs of ethnic identity fell into disuse on culturally diverse plantations. (Ironically, on some plantations these African markings were replaced by brands or scars that identified them with their owners.) But other tangible markers of African heritage persisted, including hairstyles, motifs used in wood carvings and pottery, the large wooden mortars and pestles used to hull rice, and the design of houses, in which rooms were arranged from front to back in a distinctive "I" pattern, not side by side as was common in English dwellings. Musical instruments — especially drums, gourd rattles, and a stringed instrument called a "molo," forerunner

Servitude and Slavery

Britain's American colonies relied heavily on bound labor. Two forms predominated: indentured servitude and African slavery. The idea of being bound to a master is alien to most of us today; the following texts allow us to glimpse some aspects of the experience. In what ways were these two institutions similar, and how did they differ?

1. **Slave advertisement from Charlestown, Virginia, July 24, 1769.**

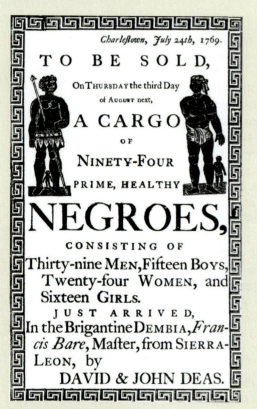

SOURCE: American Antiquarian Society, Worcester, Massachusetts, USA/Bridgeman Images.

2. **Indentured servant advertisement from the _Pennsylvania Gazette_, 1770.** _This advertisement offers to sell the remainder of a servant girl's indenture._

   TO BE SOLD, A HEALTHY servant GIRL'S Time, about 17 Years old, who has between 3 and 4 years to serve. She is sold for no other Reason, only there being more Servants than are needful in the family where she is.

   N. B. She has had the Small pox, can wash, and do all Sorts of Housework. Enquire of the Printers.

3. **Poem by James Revel, c. 1680.** _James Revel was an Englishman convicted of theft and transported to Virginia, where he served fourteen years as an indentured servant. Upon returning he published_ A Poor Unhappy Transported Felon's Sorrowful Account of His Fourteen Years' Transportation at Virginia, in America _(1680)._

   At last to my new master's house I came,

   At the town of Wicocc[o]moco call'd by name,

   Where my Europian clothes were took from me,

   Which never after I again could see.

   A canvas shirt and trowsers then they gave,

   With a hop-sack frock in which I was to slave:

   No shoes nor stockings had I for to wear,

   Nor hat, nor cap, both head and feet were bare.

   Thus dress'd into the Field I nex[t] must go,

   Amongst tobacco plants all day to hoe,

   At day break in the morn our work began,

   And so held to the setting of the Sun.

   My fellow slaves were just five Transports more,

   With eighteen Negroes, which is twenty four . . .

   We and the Negroes both alike did fare,

   Of work and food we had an equal share.

4. **Mechanisms used to control slaves, from Thomas Branagan, _The Penitential Tyrant; or, slave trader reformed_, 1807.** _The shackles and spurs (lower left) were intended to prevent escape; the faceguard with spiked collar (top and lower right) kept its wearer from either eating or lying down._

SOURCE: Library of Congress.

5. Court deposition of Joseph Mulders, July 31, 1649. *In a court case in Lower Norfolk County, Virginia indentured servant Joseph Mulders testified that his mistress, Deborah Fernehaugh, brutally beat her maidservant, Charity Dallen.*

[Mulders testified] That Deborah Fernehaugh, the Mistress of this deponent, did beate her mayd Sarvant in the quartering house before the dresser more Liken a dogge then a Christian, and that at a Certaine time, I felt her head, which was beaten as soft as a sponge, in one place, and that as there shee was a weeding, shee complained and sayd, her backe bone as shee thought was broken with beating, and that I did see the mayds arme naked which was full of blacke and blew bruises and pinches, and her necke Likewise and that after wards, I tould my Mistress of it and said, that two or three blowes, could not make her in such a Case, and after this my speeches shee Chidge [i.e., chided] the said mayd, for shewing her body to the men, and very often afterwards she [the maid] would have shoen mee, how shee had been beaten, but I refused to have seene it, saying it concernes me not, I will doe my worke and if my Mistress abuse you; you may complaine, and about 8 dayes since, being about the time shee last went to Complaine, I knew of her goeing, but would not tell my mistress of it, although shee asked mee, and sayd I could not chuse but know of it.

6. Runaway slave advertisement, Chestertown, Maryland, March 12, 1755. *Absconding from their masters was a common method of resistance for both slaves and servants, and masters frequently posted runaway advertisements in local newspapers.*

Chestertown, Maryland, March 12, 1755. TEN PISTOLES Reward. RAN away last night, from James Ringgold, of Eastern Neck, in Kent county, in the province of Maryland, the two following servant men; one named James Francis, an indented servant for five years, a middle siz'd young fellow, about 26 years of age, of a smooth fair complexion, his hair cut off, is an Englishman, and speaks a little in the west country dialect; was brought up to farming and husbandry: Had on, a country kersey jacket and breeches, blue fearnought jacket, and an old dark colour'd coat. The other a lusty young Mulatto fellow, named Toby, a slave about the same age, he is a well set, clean limb'd, stout fellow neither a very bright or very dark Mulatto, has large nostrils, is a likely fellow, and when he talks drawls his words out in a very slow manner, is no other way remarkable; he had on the same sort of clothes with the other servant, and one of them has a check or striped green and red everlasting jacket on or with them; and perhaps the Mulatto may set up for a cooper or carpenter, having work at both those business, and also understands plantation affairs. Whoever takes up and secures the above persons, and gives notice, so as their master gets them again, shall have Four Pistoles reward for the white servant, and Six Pistoles for the Mulatto. . . . That this slave should runaway, and attempt getting his liberty, is very alarming, as he has always been too kindly used, if any thing by his master, and one in whom his master has put great confidence, and depended on him to overlook the rest of his slaves, and he had no kind of provocation to go off. It seems to be the interest at least of every gentleman that has slaves, to be active in the beginning of these attempts . . . THOMAS RINGGOLD.

SOURCES: (2) *Pennsylvania Gazette*, May 3, 1770; (3) John Melville Jennings, ed., *The Virginia Magazine of History and Biography* 56 (April 1948), 187–194; (5) *Second to None: A Documentary History of American Women*, Vol. 1 (University of Nebraska Press, 1993), 67–68; (6) *Pennsylvania Gazette*, March 12, 1755.

ANALYZING THE EVIDENCE

1. What information do the traders in sources 1 and 2 want to convey to prospective buyers, and why? What similarities and differences do you see in the way sellers might choose to market servants and slaves?

2. What aspects of servitude did James Revel object to (source 3)? How did he compare the experiences of servants and slaves?

3. Source 4 appeared in an abolitionist work published in New York in 1807. How does that fact influence your interpretation of the images?

4. How does Mulders grapple with his position as a fellow servant as he testifies against his mistress (source 5)? Based on Mulders's testimony, the court removed Dallen from Fernehaugh's household. How might things have worked differently if either Mulders or Dallen had been a slave?

5. In source 6, what characteristics of each man does the ad emphasize? How does Ringgold view himself as a master, and what does his special plea to other slaveholders tell us about slaveholding culture?

PUTTING IT ALL TOGETHER

Using the sources above, along with what you learned in class and in Chapter 3, write a short essay that compares servitude and slavery. In what ways did African slavery in the British colonies grow out of servitude and bear close similarities to it, and in what ways were slaves set apart and treated fundamentally differently than their servant counterparts?

Hulling Rice in West Africa and Georgia Cultural practices often extend over time and space. The eighteenth-century engraving on the left shows West African women using huge wooden mortars and pestles to strip the tough outer hull from rice kernels. In the photo on the right, taken a century and a half later, African American women in Georgia use similar tools to prepare rice for their families. Left: Library of Congress. Right: Courtesy Georgia Archives, Vanishing Georgia Archives Collection, sap093.

of the banjo — helped Africans preserve cultural traditions and, eventually, shape American musical styles.

African values also persisted. Some slaves passed down Muslim beliefs, and many more told their children of the spiritual powers of conjurers, called *obeah* or *ifa*, who knew the ways of the African gods. Enslaved Yorubas consulted Orunmila, the god of fate, and other Africans (a Jamaican planter noted) relied on *obeah* "to revenge injuries and insults, discover and punish thieves and adulterers; [and] to predict the future."

Resistance and Accommodation Slaves' freedom of action was always dramatically circumscribed. It became illegal to teach slaves to read and write, and most slaves owned no property of their own. Because the institution of slavery rested on fear, planters had to learn a ferocious form of cruelty. Slaves might be whipped, restrained, or maimed for any infraction, large or small. A female cook in a Virginia household "was cruelly loaded with various kinds of iron machines; she had one particularly on her head, which locked her mouth so fast that she could scarcely speak; and could not eat nor drink." Thomas Jefferson, who witnessed such punishments on his father's Virginia plantation, noted that each generation of whites was "nursed, educated, and daily exercised in tyranny," and he concluded that the relationship "between master and slave is a perpetual exercise of the most unremitting despotism on the one part, and degrading submission on the other." A fellow Virginian, planter George Mason, agreed: "Every Master is born a petty tyrant."

The extent of white violence often depended on the size and density of the slave population. As Virginia planter William Byrd II complained of his slaves in 1736, "Numbers make them insolent." In the northern colonies, where slaves were few, white violence was sporadic. But plantation owners and overseers in the sugar- and rice-growing areas, where Africans outnumbered Europeans 8 or more to 1, routinely

COMPARE AND CONTRAST
How did the experiences of slaves in the Chesapeake differ from their experiences in South Carolina?

whipped assertive slaves. They also prohibited their workers from leaving the plantation without special passes and called on their poor white neighbors to patrol the countryside at night.

Despite the constant threat of violence, some slaves ran away, a very small number of them successfully. In some parts of the Americas — for example, in Jamaica — runaway slaves were able to form large, independent Maroon communities. But on the mainland, planters had the resources necessary to reclaim runaways, and such communities were unusual and precarious. More often, slaves who spoke English and possessed artisanal skills fled to colonial towns, where they tried to pass as free; occasionally they succeeded. Slaves who did not run away were engaged in a constant tug-of-war with their owners over the terms of their enslavement. Some blacks bartered extra work for better food and clothes; others seized a small privilege and dared the master to revoke it. In this way, Sundays gradually became a day of rest — asserted as a right, rather than granted as a privilege. When bargaining failed, slaves protested silently by working slowly or stealing.

Slave owners' greatest fear was that their regime of terror would fail and slaves would rise up to murder them in their beds. Occasionally that fear was realized. In the 1760s, in Amherst County, Virginia, a slave killed four whites; in Elizabeth City County, eight slaves strangled their master in bed. But the circumstances of slavery made any larger-scale uprising all but impossible. To rebel against their masters, slaves would have to be able to communicate secretly but effectively across long distances; choose leaders they could trust; formulate and disseminate strategy; accumulate large numbers of weapons; and ensure that no one betrayed their plans. This was all but impossible: in plantation slavery, the preponderance of force was on the side of the slave owners, and blacks who chose to rise up did so at their peril.

> **TRACE CHANGE OVER TIME**
> How much autonomy could slaves attain, and what did slave owners do to control them?

The Stono Rebellion   The largest slave uprising in the mainland colonies, South Carolina's **Stono Rebellion** of 1739, illustrates the impossibility of success. The Catholic governor of Spanish Florida instigated the revolt by promising freedom to fugitive slaves. By February 1739, at least 69 slaves had escaped to St. Augustine, and rumors circulated "that a Conspiracy was formed by Negroes in Carolina to rise and make their way out of the province." When war between England and Spain broke out in September, 75 Africans rose in revolt and killed a number of whites near the Stono River. According to one account, some of the rebels were Portuguese-speaking Catholics from the Kingdom of Kongo who hoped to escape to Florida. Displaying their skills as soldiers — decades of brutal slave raiding in Kongo had militarized the society there — the rebels marched toward Florida "with Colours displayed and two Drums beating."

Though their numbers and organization were impressive, the Stono rebels were soon met by a well-armed, mounted force of South Carolina militia. In the ensuing battle, 44 slaves were killed and the rebellion was suppressed, preventing any general uprising. In response, frightened South Carolinians cut slave imports and tightened plantation discipline.

The Rise of the Southern Gentry

As the southern colonies became full-fledged slave societies, life changed for whites as well as for blacks. Consider the career of William Byrd II (1674–1744). Byrd's father, a successful planter-merchant in Virginia, hoped to marry his children into the English gentry. To smooth his son's entry into landed society, Byrd sent him to England for his education. But his status-conscious classmates shunned young Byrd, calling him a "colonial," a first bitter taste of the gradations of rank in English society.

Other English rejections followed. Lacking aristocratic connections, Byrd was denied a post with the Board of Trade, passed over three times for the royal governorship of Virginia, and rejected as a suitor by a rich Englishwoman. In 1726, at age fifty-two, Byrd finally gave up and moved back to Virginia, where he sometimes felt he was "being buried alive." Accepting his lesser destiny as a member of the colony's elite, Byrd built an elegant brick mansion on the family's estate at Westover, sat in "the best pew in the church," and won an appointment to the governor's council.

William Byrd II's experience mirrored that of many planter-merchants, trapped in Virginia and South Carolina by their inferior colonial status. They used their wealth to rule over white yeomen families and tenant farmers and relied on violence to exploit enslaved blacks. Planters used Africans to grow food, as well as tobacco; to build houses, wagons, and tobacco casks; and to make shoes and clothes. By making their plantations self-sufficient, the Chesapeake elite survived the depressed tobacco market between 1670 and 1720.

White Identity and Equality To prevent uprisings like Bacon's Rebellion, the Chesapeake gentry found ways to assist middling and poor whites. They gradually lowered taxes; in Virginia, for example, the annual head tax (on each adult man) fell from 45 pounds of tobacco in 1675 to just 5 pounds in 1750. They also encouraged smallholders to improve their economic lot by using slave labor, and many did so. By 1770, 60 percent of English families in the Chesapeake owned at least one slave. On the political front, planters now allowed poor yeomen and some tenants to vote. The strategy of the leading families — the Carters, Lees, Randolphs, and Robinsons — was to bribe these voters with rum, money, and the promise of minor offices in county governments. In return, they expected the yeomen and tenants to elect them to office and defer to their rule. This horse-trading solidified the authority of the planter elite, which used its control of the House of Burgesses to limit the power of the royal governor. Hundreds of yeomen farmers benefitted as well, tasting political power and garnering substantial fees and salaries as deputy sheriffs, road surveyors, estate appraisers, and grand jurymen.

Even as wealthy Chesapeake gentlemen formed political ties with smallholders, they took measures to set themselves apart culturally. As late as the 1720s, leading planters were boisterous, aggressive men who lived much like the common folk — hunting, drinking, gambling on horse races, and demonstrating their manly prowess by forcing themselves on female servants and slaves. As time passed, however, planters like William Byrd II began to model themselves on the English aristocracy, remaining sexual predators but learning from advice books how to act like gentlemen in other regards: "I must not sit in others' places; Nor sneeze, nor cough in people's faces. Nor with my fingers pick my nose, Nor wipe my hands upon my clothes." Cultivating **gentility** — a lifestyle that stressed refinement and self-control — they replaced their modest wooden houses with mansions of brick and mortar. Planters educated their sons in London as lawyers and gentlemen. But unlike Byrd's father, they expected them to return to America, marry local heiresses, and assume their fathers' roles: managing plantations, socializing with fellow gentry, and running the political system.

Wealthy Chesapeake and South Carolina women likewise emulated the English elite. They read English newspapers and fashionable magazines, wore the finest English clothes, and dined in the English fashion, including an elaborate afternoon tea. To enhance their daughters' gentility (and improve their marriage prospects), parents hired English tutors. Once married, planter women deferred to their husbands, reared pious children, and maintained complex social networks, in time creating a new ideal: the southern gentlewoman. Using the profits generated by enslaved Africans in the South Atlantic System of commerce, wealthy planters formed an increasingly well-educated, refined, and stable ruling class.

IDENTIFY CAUSES
How did the planter elite maintain alliances with their smallholder neighbors?

IN YOUR OWN WORDS How did their ties to Great Britain and Africa change the lives of American planters?

The Northern Maritime Economy

The South Atlantic System had a broad geographical reach. As early as the 1640s, New England farmers supplied the sugar islands with bread, lumber, fish, and meat. As a West Indian explained, planters "had rather buy foode at very deare rates than produce it by labour, soe infinite is the profitt of sugar works." By 1700, the economies of the West Indies and New England were closely interwoven. Soon farmers and merchants in New York, New Jersey, and Pennsylvania were also shipping wheat, corn, and bread to the Caribbean. By the 1750s, about two-thirds of New England's exports and half of those from the Middle Atlantic colonies went to the British and French sugar islands.

The sugar economy linked Britain's entire Atlantic empire. In return for the sugar they sent to England, West Indian planters received credit, in the form of bills of exchange, from London merchants. The planters used these bills to buy slaves from Africa and to pay North American farmers and merchants for their provisions and shipping services. The mainland colonists then exchanged the bills for British manufactures, primarily textiles and iron goods.

The Urban Economy

The West Indian trade created the first American merchant fortunes and the first urban industries. Merchants in Boston, Newport, Providence, Philadelphia, and New York invested their profits in new ships; some set up manufacturing enterprises, including twenty-six refineries that processed raw sugar into finished loaves. Mainland distilleries turned West Indian molasses into rum, producing more than 2.5 million gallons in Massachusetts alone by the 1770s. Merchants in Salem, Marblehead, and smaller New England ports built a major fishing industry by selling salted mackerel and cod to the sugar islands and to southern Europe. Baltimore merchants transformed their town into a major port by developing a bustling export business in wheat, while traders in Charleston shipped deerskins, indigo, and rice to European markets (Map 3.4).

As transatlantic commerce expanded — from five hundred voyages a year in the 1680s to fifteen hundred annually in the 1730s — American port cities grew in size and complexity. By 1750, the populations of Newport and Charleston were nearly 10,000; Boston had 15,000 residents; and New York had almost 18,000. The largest port was Philadelphia, whose population by 1776 had reached 30,000, the size of a large European provincial city. Smaller coastal towns emerged as centers of the lumber and shipbuilding industries. Seventy sawmills lined the Piscataqua River in New Hampshire, providing low-cost wood for homes, warehouses, and especially shipbuilding. Hundreds of shipwrights turned out oceangoing vessels, while other artisans made ropes, sails, and metal fittings for the new fleet. By the 1770s, colonial-built ships made up one-third of the British merchant fleet.

The South Atlantic System extended far into the interior. A fleet of small vessels sailed back and forth on the Hudson and Delaware rivers, delivering cargoes of European manufactures and picking up barrels of flour and wheat to carry to New York and Philadelphia for export to the West Indies and Europe. By the 1750s, hundreds of professional teamsters in Maryland were transporting 370,000 bushels of wheat and corn and 16,000 barrels of flour to urban markets each year — more than 10,000 wagon trips. To service this traffic, entrepreneurs and artisans set up taverns, horse stables, and barrel-making shops in towns along the wagon roads. Lancaster (the town that hosted the Iroquois conference described in the chapter opening), in a prosperous wheat-growing area of Pennsylvania, boasted more than 200 German and English artisans and a dozen merchants.

EXPLAIN CONSEQUENCES
How did the rise of the South Atlantic System impact economic development in the northern colonies?

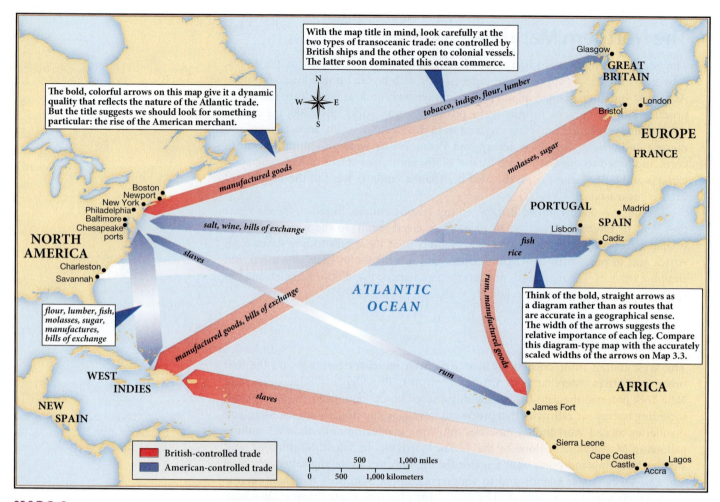

With the map title in mind, look carefully at the two types of transoceanic trade: one controlled by British ships and the other open to colonial vessels. The latter soon dominated this ocean commerce.

The bold, colorful arrows on this map give it a dynamic quality that reflects the nature of the Atlantic trade. But the title suggests we should look for something particular: the rise of the American merchant.

Think of the bold, straight arrows as a diagram rather than as routes that are accurate in a geographical sense. The width of the arrows suggests the relative importance of each leg. Compare this diagram-type map with the accurately scaled widths of the arrows on Map 3.3.

tobacco, indigo, flour, lumber

manufactured goods

salt, wine, bills of exchange

slaves

molasses, sugar

fish
rice

manufactured goods, bills of exchange

rum, manufactured goods

rum

flour, lumber, fish, molasses, sugar, manufactures, bills of exchange

slaves

ATLANTIC OCEAN

NORTH AMERICA

Boston
Newport
New York
Philadelphia
Baltimore
Chesapeake ports
Charleston
Savannah

WEST INDIES

NEW SPAIN

GREAT BRITAIN

Glasgow
Bristol
London

EUROPE
FRANCE
PORTUGAL
Lisbon
SPAIN
Madrid
Cadiz

AFRICA
James Fort
Sierra Leone
Cape Coast Castle
Accra
Lagos

■ British-controlled trade
■ American-controlled trade

0   500   1,000 miles
0   500   1,000 kilometers

MAP 3.4   The Growing Power of American Merchants, 1750
Throughout the colonial era, British merchant houses dominated the transatlantic trade in manufactures, sugar, tobacco, and slaves. However, by 1750, American-born merchants in Boston, New York, and Philadelphia had seized control of the commerce between the mainland and the West Indies. In addition, Newport traders played a small role in the slave trade from Africa, and Boston and Charleston merchants grew rich carrying fish and rice to southern Europe.

Urban Society

Wealthy merchants dominated the social life of seaport cities. In 1750, about forty merchants controlled more than 50 percent of Philadelphia's trade. Like the Chesapeake gentry, urban merchants imitated the British upper classes, importing architectural design books from England and building Georgian-style mansions to display their wealth. Their wives strove to create a genteel culture by buying fine furniture and entertaining guests at elegant dinners.

Artisan and shopkeeper families, the middle ranks of seaport society, made up nearly half the population. Innkeepers, butchers, seamstresses, shoemakers, weavers, bakers, carpenters, masons, and dozens of other skilled workers toiled to gain an income sufficient to maintain their families in modest comfort. Wives and husbands often worked as a team and taught the "mysteries of the craft" to their children. Some artisans aspired to wealth and status, an entrepreneurial ethic that prompted them to hire apprentices and expand production. However, most artisans were not well-to-do. During his working life, a tailor was lucky to accumulate £30 worth of property, far less than the £2,000 owned at death by an ordinary merchant or the £300 listed in the probate inventory of a successful blacksmith.

Laboring men and women formed the lowest ranks of urban society. Merchants needed hundreds of dockworkers to unload manufactured goods and molasses from inbound ships and reload them with barrels of wheat, fish, and rice. For these demanding jobs, merchants used enslaved blacks and indentured servants, who together made up 30 percent of the workforce in Philadelphia and New York City until the 1750s; otherwise, they hired unskilled wageworkers. Poor white and black women eked out a living by washing clothes, spinning wool, or working as servants or prostitutes. To make ends meet, laboring families sent their children out to work.

Periods of stagnant commerce threatened the financial security of merchants and artisans alike. For laborers, seamen, and seamstresses — whose household budgets left no margin for sickness or unemployment — depressed trade meant hunger, dependence on public charity, and (for the most desperate) petty thievery or prostitution. The sugar- and slave-based South Atlantic System, and cycles of imperial warfare, brought economic uncertainty as well as opportunity to the people of the northern colonies.

The Greenwood-Lee Family, 1747   Born in Massachusetts and apprenticed as an engraver, John Greenwood (1727–1792) painted dozens of commissioned works there before moving to Surinam in 1752. He painted this scene of his own family at the age of twenty. Group portraits with so many people were rare in the colonies, and it is a technically impressive composition. Greenwood himself is at the right rear, wigless (he wears a velvet cap to keep his head warm) and holding a palette and brushes. The table displays a basket of needlework and a volume of *The Spectator*, the popular London periodical published by Joseph Addison and Richard Steele.   Museum of Fine Arts, Boston, Massachusetts, USA/Bequest of Henry Lee Shattuck in memory of the late Morris Gray/Bridgeman Images.

> **IN YOUR OWN WORDS**   What economic activities drove the northern maritime economy?

The New Politics of Empire, 1713–1750

The South Atlantic System also changed the politics of empire. British ministers, pleased with the wealth produced by the trade in slaves, sugar, rice, and tobacco, ruled the colonies with a gentle hand. The colonists took advantage of that leniency to strengthen their political institutions and eventually to challenge the rules of the mercantilist system.

The Rise of Colonial Assemblies

After the Glorious Revolution, representative assemblies in America copied the English Whigs and limited the powers of crown officials. In Massachusetts during the 1720s, the assembly repeatedly ignored the king's instructions to provide the royal governor with a permanent salary, and legislatures in North Carolina, New Jersey, and Pennsylvania did the same. Using such tactics, the legislatures gradually took control of taxation and appointments, angering imperial bureaucrats and absentee proprietors. "The people in power in America," complained William Penn during a struggle with the Pennsylvania assembly, "think nothing taller than themselves but the Trees."

Leading the increasingly powerful assemblies were members of the colonial elite. Although most property-owning white men had the right to vote, only men of wealth and status stood for election. In New Jersey in 1750, 90 percent of assemblymen came from influential political families. In Virginia, seven members of the wealthy Lee family sat in the House of Burgesses and, along with other powerful families, dominated its major committees. In New England, affluent descendants of the original Puritans formed a core of political leaders. "Go into every village in New England," John Adams wrote in 1765, "and you will find that the office of justice of the peace, and even the place of representative, have generally descended from generation to generation, in three or four families at most."

However, neither elitist assemblies nor wealthy property owners could impose unpopular edicts on the people. Purposeful crowd actions were a fact of colonial life. An uprising of ordinary citizens overthrew the Dominion of New England in 1689. In New York, mobs closed houses of prostitution; in Salem, Massachusetts, they ran people with infectious diseases out of town; and in New Jersey in the 1730s and 1740s, mobs of farmers battled with proprietors who were forcing tenants off disputed lands. When officials in Boston restricted the sale of farm produce to a single public market, a crowd destroyed the building, and its members defied the authorities to arrest them. "If you touch One you shall touch All," an anonymous letter warned the sheriff, "and we will show you a Hundred Men where you can show one." These expressions of popular discontent, combined with the growing authority of the assemblies, created a political system that was broadly responsive to popular pressure and increasingly resistant to British control.

IDENTIFY CAUSES
What explains the increasing political autonomy of the colonies in the eighteenth century?

Salutary Neglect

British colonial policy during the reigns of George I (r. 1714–1727) and George II (r. 1727–1760) allowed for this rise of American self-government as royal bureaucrats, pleased by growing trade and import duties, relaxed their supervision of internal colonial affairs. In 1775, British political philosopher Edmund Burke would praise this strategy as **salutary neglect**.

Salutary neglect was a by-product of the political system developed by Sir Robert Walpole, the Whig leader in the House of Commons from 1720 to 1742. Walpole relied on **patronage** — the practice of giving offices and salaries to political allies — to create a strong Court Party. Under his leadership, Britain's government achieved a new measure of financial and political stability. But critics — the so-called Country Party — charged that Walpole's policies of high taxes and a bloated royal bureaucracy threatened British liberties.

These arguments were echoed in North America, where colonial legislators complained that royal governors abused their patronage powers. To preserve American liberty, the colonists strengthened the powers of the representative assemblies, unintentionally laying the foundation for the American independence movement.

Protecting the Mercantile System

In 1732, Walpole provided a parliamentary subsidy for the new colony of Georgia. While Georgia's reform-minded trustees envisioned the colony as a refuge for Britain's poor, Walpole had little interest in social reform; he subsidized Georgia to protect the valuable rice-growing colony of South Carolina. But the new colony had the opposite effect. Britain's expansion into Georgia outraged Spanish officials, who were already angry about the rising tide of smuggled British manufactures in New Spain. To counter Britain's commercial imperialism, Spanish naval forces stepped up their seizure of illegal traders, in the process cutting off the ear of an English sea captain, Robert Jenkins.

Yielding to parliamentary pressure, Walpole declared war on Spain in 1739. The so-called War of Jenkins's Ear (1739–1741) was a fiasco for Britain. In 1740, British regulars failed to capture St. Augustine because South Carolina whites, still shaken by the Stono Rebellion, refused to commit militia units to the expedition. A year later, an assault on the prosperous seaport of Cartagena (in present-day Colombia) also

The Siege and Capture of Louisbourg, 1745 In 1760, as British and colonial troops moved toward victory in the French and Indian War (1754–1763), the London artist J. Stevens sought to bolster imperial pride by celebrating an earlier Anglo-American triumph. In 1745, a British naval squadron led a flotilla of colonial ships and thousands of New England militiamen in an attack on the French fort at Louisbourg, on Cape Breton Island, near the mouth of the St. Lawrence River. After a siege of forty days, the Anglo-American force captured the fort, long considered impregnable. The victory was bittersweet because the Treaty of Aix-la-Chapelle (1748) returned the island to France. Anne S. K. Brown Military Collection, Brown University Library.

failed; 20,000 British sailors and soldiers and 2,500 colonial troops died in the attack, mostly from tropical diseases.

The War of Jenkins's Ear quickly became part of a general European conflict, the War of the Austrian Succession (1740–1748). Massive French armies battled British-subsidized German forces in Europe, and French naval forces roamed the West Indies, vainly trying to conquer a British sugar island. In 1745, three thousand New England militiamen and a British naval squadron captured Louisbourg, the French fort guarding the entrance to the St. Lawrence River. To the dismay of New England Puritans, who feared invasion from Catholic Quebec, the Treaty of Aix-la-Chapelle (1748) returned Louisbourg to France. The treaty made it clear to colonial leaders that England would act in its own interests, not theirs.

Mercantilism and the American Colonies

Though Parliament prohibited Americans from manufacturing textiles (Woolen Act, 1699), hats (Hat Act, 1732), and iron products such as plows, axes, and skillets (Iron Act, 1750), and also curbed the colonies' ability to print their own paper money (Currency Act, 1751), it could not prevent the colonies from maturing economically. American merchants soon controlled over 75 percent of the transatlantic trade in manufactures and 95 percent of the commerce between the mainland and the British West Indies (see Map 3.4).

Moreover, by the 1720s, the British sugar islands could not absorb all the flour, fish, and meat produced by mainland settlers. So, ignoring Britain's intense rivalry with France, colonial merchants sold their produce to the French sugar islands. When American rum distillers began to buy cheap molasses from the French islands, the West Indian sugar lobby in London persuaded Parliament to pass the Molasses Act of 1733. The act placed a high tariff on French molasses, so high that it would no

A View of Savannah, 1734 This idealized view of Savannah, Georgia, portrays the infant settlement as a scene of perfect order carved out of vacant wilderness. Dedicated to the colony's trustees, this engraving imagines the town as they would have hoped to see it. Steps ascend the steep riverbank, while public buildings and house lots are beginning to appear. At the far left a guardhouse and row of cannons defend the site from the water, while construction has commenced on a wall of pickets surrounding the perimeter, reminders that the town is always in danger of being attacked. Library of Congress.

longer be profitable for American merchants to import it. Colonists protested that the Molasses Act would cripple the distilling industry; cut farm exports; and, by slashing colonial income, reduce the mainland's purchases of British goods. When Parliament ignored these arguments, American merchants smuggled in French molasses by bribing customs officials.

These conflicts angered a new generation of English political leaders. In 1749, Charles Townshend of the Board of Trade charged that the American assemblies had assumed many of the "ancient and established prerogatives wisely preserved in the Crown," and he vowed to replace salutary neglect with more rigorous imperial control.

The wheel of empire had come full circle. In the 1650s, England had set out to create a centrally managed Atlantic empire and, over the course of a century, achieved the military and economic aspects of that goal. Mercantilist legislation, maritime warfare, commercial expansion, and the forced labor of a million African slaves brought prosperity to Britain. However, internal unrest (the Glorious Revolution) and a policy of salutary neglect had weakened Britain's political authority over its American colonies. Recognizing the threat self-government posed to the empire, British officials in the late 1740s vowed to reassert their power in America — an initiative with disastrous results.

> **IN YOUR OWN WORDS** How could Great Britain maintain its mercantilist policies and permit the "salutary neglect" of its colonies at the same time?

SUMMARY

In this chapter, we examined processes of change in politics and society. The political story began in the 1660s as Britain imposed controls on its American possessions. Parliament passed the Acts of Trade and Navigation to keep colonial products and trade in English hands. Then King James II abolished representative institutions in the northern colonies and created the authoritarian Dominion of New England. Following the Glorious Revolution, the Navigation Acts remained in place and tied the American economy to that of Britain. But the uprisings of 1688–1689 overturned James II's policy of strict imperial control, restored colonial self-government, and ushered in an era of salutary political neglect. It also initiated a long era of imperial warfare, in which Native American peoples allied themselves to the colonies and often served as proxy warriors against French- and Spanish-allied peoples, pursuing their own goals in the process.

The social story centers on the development of the South Atlantic System of production and trade, which involved an enormous expansion in African slave raiding; the Atlantic slave trade; and the cultivation of sugar, rice, and tobacco in America. This complex system created an exploited African American labor force in the southern mainland and West Indian colonies, while it allowed European American farmers, merchants, and artisans on the North American mainland to prosper. How would the two stories play out? In 1750, slavery and the South Atlantic System seemed firmly entrenched, but the days of salutary neglect appeared numbered.

CHAPTER 3 REVIEW

TERMS TO KNOW
Identify and explain the significance of each term below.

Key Concepts and Events

proprietorship (p. 77)

Quakers (p. 78)

Navigation Acts (p. 79)

Dominion of New England (p. 80)

Glorious Revolution (p. 80)

constitutional monarchy (p. 81)

Second Hundred Years' War (p. 82)

tribalization (p. 82)

Covenant Chain (p. 83)

South Atlantic System (p. 86)

Middle Passage (p. 89)

Stono Rebellion (p. 97)

gentility (p. 98)

salutary neglect (p. 102)

patronage (p. 102)

Key People

William Penn (p. 77)

Edmund Andros (p. 80)

William of Orange (p. 80)

John Locke (p. 80)

Jacob Leisler (p. 81)

William Byrd II (p. 96)

Robert Walpole (p. 102)

REVIEW QUESTIONS
Answer these questions to demonstrate your understanding of the chapter's main ideas.

1. Identify three new developments between 1660 and 1690 that helped shape England's American Empire.

2. What was tribalization, and how did it help Native Americans cope with their European neighbors?

3. How did their ties to Great Britain and Africa change the lives of American planters?

4. What economic activities drove the northern maritime economy?

5. How could Great Britain maintain its mercantilist policies and permit the "salutary neglect" of its colonies at the same time?

6. Trace the developments outlined in the section entitled "Politics and Power" from 1660 to 1750 on the thematic timeline on page 72. What pattern of political evolution do you see in colonial interactions with Britain?

MAKING CONNECTIONS
Recognize the larger developments and continuities within and across chapters by answering these questions.

1. In Chapter 2, we traced the emergence of three distinct colonial types in the Americas during the sixteenth and seventeenth centuries: tribute, plantation, and neo-European colonies. In Chapter 3, we have seen how Britain's plantation and neo-European colonies became more closely interconnected after 1700. What developments caused them to become more closely tied to each other? How did they benefit from these ties? Can you see any disadvantages to the colonies in a more fully integrated Atlantic system?

2. Consider the illustrations of women hulling rice in West Africa and Georgia on page 96. Historians have long debated the role Africans played in developing rice cultivation in the South Carolina and Georgia low country. These debates have focused primarily on methods of cultivation: Did Africans who had prior experience with rice teach English planters how to grow it? How can these two images contribute to the debate and expand our perspective on the question of African influences in American rice production?

KEY TURNING POINTS
Refer to the chapter chronology on page 76 for help in answering the questions below.

The Glorious Revolution (1688–1689), salutary neglect and the rise of the assemblies (1714–1750), and the Hat, Molasses, Iron, and Currency Acts (1732–1751): How do these developments reflect Britain's new attitude toward its colonies? In what matters did Parliament seek to control the colonies, and in what did it grant them autonomy?

4

CHAPTER

Growth, Diversity, and Conflict
1720–1763

In 1736, Alexander MacAllister left the Highlands of Scotland for the backcountry of North Carolina, where his wife and three sisters soon joined him. MacAllister prospered as a landowner and mill proprietor and had only praise for his new home. Carolina was "the best poor man's country," he wrote to his brother Hector, urging him to "advise all poor people . . . to take courage and come." In North Carolina, there were no landlords to keep "the face of the poor . . . to the grinding stone," and so many Highlanders were arriving that "it will soon be a new Scotland." Here, on the far margins of the British Empire, people could "breathe the air of liberty, and not want the necessarys of life." Some 300,000 European migrants—primarily Highland Scots, Scots-Irish, and Germans—heeded MacAllister's advice and helped swell the population of Britain's North American settlements from 400,000 in 1720 to almost 2 million by 1765.

MacAllister's "air of liberty" did not last forever, as the rapid increase in white settlers and the arrival of nearly 300,000 enslaved Africans transformed life throughout mainland British North America. Long-settled towns in New England became overcrowded, and antagonistic ethnic and religious communities jostled uneasily with one another in the Middle Atlantic colonies; in 1748, there were more than a hundred German Lutheran and Reformed congregations in Quaker-led Pennsylvania. By then, the MacAllisters and thousands of other Celtic and German migrants had altered the social landscape and introduced religious conflict into the southern backcountry.

Everywhere, two European cultural movements, the Enlightenment and Pietism, changed the tone of intellectual and spiritual life. Advocates of "rational thought" viewed human beings as agents of moral self-determination and urged Americans to fashion a better social order. Religious Pietists outnumbered them and had more influence. Convinced of the weakness of human nature, evangelical ministers told their followers to seek regeneration through divine grace. Amidst this intellectual and religious ferment, migrants and the landless children of long-settled families moved inland and sparked wars with the Native peoples and with France and Spain. A generation of dynamic growth produced a decade of deadly warfare that would set the stage for a new era in American history.

IDENTIFY THE BIG IDEA

In what ways were Britain's American colonies affected by events across the Atlantic, and how were their societies taking on a life of their own?

John Collet, *George Whitefield Preaching* No painting could capture English minister George Whitefield's charismatic appeal, although this image conveys his open demeanor and religious intensity. When Whitefield spoke to a crowd near Philadelphia, an observer noted that his words were "sharper than a two-edged sword. . . . Some of the people were pale as death; others were wringing their hands . . . and most lifting their eyes to heaven and crying to God for mercy." An astute businessman as well as a charismatic preacher, Whitefield tirelessly promoted the sale of his sermons and books. *George Whitefield Preaching*/Collet, John (c. 1725–1780)/Private Collection/Bridgeman Images.

CHAPTER CHRONOLOGY

As you read, ask yourself why this chapter begins and ends with these dates and then identify the links among related events.

1695	▶ Licensing Act lapses in England, triggering the print revolution
1710s–1730s	▶ Enlightenment ideas spread from Europe to America ▶ Germans and Scots-Irish settle in Middle colonies ▶ Theodore Jacob Frelinghuysen preaches Pietism to German migrants
1720s–1730s	▶ William and Gilbert Tennent lead Presbyterian revivals among Scots-Irish ▶ Jonathan Edwards preaches in New England
1729	▶ Benjamin Franklin buys the *Pennsylvania Gazette*
1739	▶ George Whitefield sparks Great Awakening
1740s–1760s	▶ Conflict between Old Lights and New Lights ▶ Shortage of farmland in New England threatens freehold ideal ▶ Growing ethnic and religious pluralism in Middle Atlantic colonies ▶ Religious denominations establish colleges
1743	▶ Benjamin Franklin founds American Philosophical Society ▶ Samuel Morris starts Presbyterian revivals in Virginia

1748	▶ Ohio Company receives grant of 200,000 acres from the crown
1749	▶ Connecticut farmers form Susquehanna Company
1750s	▶ Industrial Revolution begins in England ▶ British shipping dominates North Atlantic ▶ Consumer purchases increase American imports and debt
1754	▶ French and Indian War begins ▶ Iroquois and colonists meet at Albany Congress ▶ Franklin's Plan of Union
1756	▶ Britain begins Great War for Empire
1759–1760	▶ Britain completes conquest of Canada
1760s	▶ Land conflict along New York and New England border ▶ Baptist revivals win converts in Virginia
1763	▶ Pontiac's Rebellion leads to Proclamation of 1763 ▶ Treaty of Paris ends Great War for Empire ▶ Scots-Irish Paxton Boys massacre Indians in Pennsylvania
1771	▶ Royal governor puts down Regulator revolt in North Carolina

New England's Freehold Society

In the 1630s, the Puritans had fled England, where a small elite of nobles and gentry owned 75 percent of the arable land, while **tenants** (renters) and propertyless workers farmed it. In New England, the Puritans created a yeoman society of relatively equal landowning farm families. But by 1750, the migrants' numerous descendants had parceled out the best farmland, threatening the future of the freehold ideal.

Farm Families: Women in the Household Economy

The Puritans' vision of social equality did not extend to women, and their ideology placed the husband firmly at the head of the household. In *The Well-Ordered Family* (1712), the Reverend Benjamin Wadsworth of Boston advised women, "Since he is thy Husband, God has made him the head and set him above thee." It was a wife's duty "to love and reverence" her husband.

Women learned this subordinate role throughout their lives. Small girls watched their mothers defer to their fathers, and as young women, they were told to be "silent in company." They saw the courts prosecute more women than men for the crime of fornication (sex outside of marriage), and they found that their marriage portions would be inferior to those of their brothers. Thus Ebenezer Chittendon of Guilford, Connecticut, left his land to his sons, decreeing that "Each Daughter [shall] have half so much as Each Son, one half in money and the other half in Cattle."

Throughout the colonies, women assumed the role of dutiful helpmeets (helpmates) to their husbands. In addition to tending gardens, farmwives spun thread and yarn from flax and wool and then wove it into cloth for shirts and gowns. They knitted sweaters and stockings, made candles and soap, churned milk into butter, fermented malt for beer, preserved meats, and mastered dozens of other household tasks. "Notable women" — those who excelled at domestic arts — won praise and high status (Thinking Like a Historian).

Bearing and rearing children were equally important tasks. Most women in New England married in their early twenties and by their early forties had given birth to six or seven children, delivered with the help of a female neighbor or a midwife. One Massachusetts mother confessed that she had little time for religious activities because "the care of my Babes takes up so large a portion of my time and attention." Yet most Puritan congregations were filled with women: "In a Church of between *Three* and *Four* Hundred *Communicants*," the eminent minister Cotton Mather noted, "there are but few more than *One* Hundred *Men*; all the Rest are Women."

Women's lives remained tightly bound by a web of legal and cultural restrictions. Ministers praised women for their piety but excluded them from an equal role in the church. When Hannah Heaton, a Connecticut farmwife, grew dissatisfied with her Congregational minister, thinking him unconverted and a "blind guide," she sought out equality-minded Quaker and evangelist Baptist churches that welcomed questioning women such as herself and treated "saved" women equally with men. However, by the 1760s, many evangelical congregations had reinstituted men's dominance over women. "The government of Church and State must be . . . family government" controlled by its "king," declared the Danbury (Connecticut) Baptist Association.

> **CONSIDER POINTS OF VIEW**
> What ideas, institutions, and responsibilities shaped New England farm women's lives?

Farm Property: Inheritance

By contrast, European men who migrated to the colonies escaped many traditional constraints, including the curse of landlessness. "The hope of having land of their own & becoming independent of Landlords is what chiefly induces people into America," an official noted in the 1730s. Owning property gave formerly dependent peasants a new social identity.

Unlike the adventurers seeking riches in other parts of the Americas, most New England migrants wanted farms that would provide a living for themselves and ample land for their children. In this way, they hoped to secure a **competency** for their families: the ability to keep their households solvent and independent and to pass that ability on to the next generation. Parents who could not give their offspring land placed these children as indentured servants in more prosperous households. When the indentures ended at age eighteen or twenty-one, propertyless sons faced a decades-long climb up the agricultural ladder, from laborer to tenant and finally to freeholder.

Sons and daughters in well-to-do farm families were luckier: they received a marriage portion when they were in their early twenties. That portion — land, livestock, or farm equipment — repaid them for their past labor and allowed parents to choose their marriage partners. Parents' security during old age depended on a wise choice of son- or daughter-in-law. Although the young people could refuse

Prudence Punderson (1758–1784), *The First, Second and Last Scenes of Mortality* This powerful image reveals both the artistic skills of colonial women in the traditional medium of needlework and the Puritans' continuing cultural concern with the inevitability of death. Prudence Punderson, the Connecticut woman who embroidered this scene, rejected a marriage proposal and followed her Loyalist father into exile on Long Island in 1778. Sometime later, she married a cousin, Timothy Rossiter, and bore a daughter, Sophia, who may well be the baby in the cradle being rocked by "Jenny," a slave owned by Prudence's father. Long worried by "my ill state of health" and perhaps now anticipating her own death, Prudence has inscribed her initials on the coffin — and, in creating this embroidery, transformed her personal experience into a broader meditation on the progression from birth, to motherhood, to death. Embroidery, 1776–1783, Gift of Newton C. Brainard, accession no. 1962.28.4, the Connecticut Historical Society.

Women's Labor

As these documents show, women bore the responsibility for a wide variety of work, from keeping up households to supporting themselves independently.

1. **Thomas Tusser, *Five Hundred Pointes of Good Husbandrie*, 1557.** *Advice manuals like Tusser's circulated for generations and offered guidance on household management. In this couplet, Tusser stresses the virtues of a wife's economy and hard work.*

Wife, make thine own candle,

Spare penny to handle.

Provide for thy tallow ere frost cometh in,

And make thine own candle ere winter begin.

2. **Eliza Lucas, letters, 1740–1742.** *George Lucas owned three South Carolina plantations, but, as lieutenant governor of Antigua, he was frequently absent. When his daughter was sixteen, he gave her responsibility for managing them. She introduced indigo cultivation in South Carolina, and it soon became the colony's second-leading cash crop. These letters were written when she was between the ages of eighteen and twenty.*

May 2, 1740

"I have the business of 3 plantations to transact, which requires much writing and more business and fatigue of other sorts than you can imagine. But least you should imagine it too burthensom to a girl at my early time of life, give me leave to answer you: I assure you I think myself happy that I can be useful to so good a father, and by rising very early I find I can go through much business."

July 1740

"Wrote my Father a very long letter on his plantation affairs and on . . . the pains I had taken to bring the Indigo, Ginger, Cotton and Lucerne and Casada to perfection, and had greater hopes from the Indigo . . . than any of the rest of the things I tried."

February 6, 1741

" . . . I have a Sister to instruct and a parcel of little Negroes whom I have undertaken to teach to read."

April 23, 1741

"Wrote to my Father informing him of the loss of a Negro man — also the boat being overset in Santilina [Saint Helena] Sound and 20 barrels of Rice lost."

[1742]

"Wont you laugh at me if I tell you I am so busey in providing for Posterity I hardly allow my self time to Eat or sleep. . . . I am making a large plantation of Oaks which I look upon as my own property, whether my father gives me the land or not; and therefore I design many years hence when oaks are more valueable than they are now — which you know they will be when we come to build fleets."

[c. June 1742]

"I am engaged with the rudiments of the law to which I am yet but a stranger. . . . If You will not laugh too immoderately at me I'll Trust you with a secrett. I have made two wills already."

3. **Mary Vial Holyoke, diary excerpts, 1761.** *Mary Vial Holyoke, wife of a prominent physician in Salem, Massachusetts, kept a diary that offers a glimpse of the range of household tasks women faced.*

[1761]

Jan. 16: Began upon the firkin of butter of 40 lb. . . .

22: Bo't hog, weighed 182 pounds, at 2/5. Salted hog with half Lisbon & half saltertudas [Tortugas] salt. . . .

Mar. 4: Ironing. . . .

7: Scower'd pewter. . . .

17: Made the Dr. six Cravats marked H. . . .

Apr. 17: Made soap. . . .

23: Dressed a Calves Head turtle fashion. . . .

May 20: Began to whitewash. . . .

28: Ironed. . . .

30: Scower'd pewter. . . .

July 7: Scowered rooms. . . .

4. **Colonial house interiors in Germantown, Pennsylvania, and Augusta, Maine.** *These images show the dining room of Benjamin Chew, a wealthy Philadelphia lawyer (below), and the kitchen of the Howards, an extended family of soldiers and merchants on the Maine frontier (opposite).*

Source: © Ron Blunt.

5. **Business advertisement in the *Pennsylvania Gazette*, 1758.** *Not all women's work was done in the home. Hannah Breintnall, a Philadelphia widow, ran a tavern before opening a shop specializing in eyeglasses.*

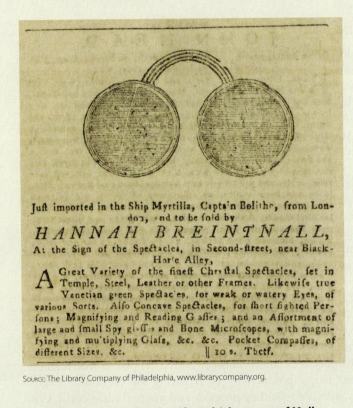

6. ***Hilliad Magna: Being the Life and Adventures of Moll Placket-Hole*, 1765.** *Moll Placket-Hole was a satirical, seven-page pamphlet that purported to describe the life of a Philadelphia prostitute.* Moll *was an eighteenth-century term for a loose woman or prostitute, while* placket-hole *referred to a slit that might be found in a woman's skirt.*

MOLL PLACKET-HOLE was born in a *Bawdy House* in a *Lane* in the City of *Brotherly Love*. . . . [A]t the Age of twelve (Shocking to consider!) . . . [her] Mother *sold* her Virginity — *sold* it for the Trifling Consideration of *Ten Pounds*. Her Purchaser was soon cloyed and abandoned her. Virtue lost and good Reputation (if ever she had it) gone, she commenced open Prostitute and dealt out her Favours to the highest Bidder. . . . [S]he understood the Trade and set up a *Bawdy-House*. . . . It was necessary, however, that a Man should live with her, that they might appear to the Publick, as *honest* Housekeepers. . . . The Trade became at last so publick, that it gave Offence to her sober Neighbours. . . . [T]he Town tired out with her Insolence, and her Escape from Justice in a regular Manner, set a Mob (many of whom had been her Beneficiaries) upon her. They pulled down her House, and destroyed her Furniture &c. She stormed and raged and swore if her Customers would not build her a better House, she would expose them. . . . They opened a Subscription, and a hundred Pounds were subscribed in one Day.

SOURCES: (1) Alice Morse Earle, *Home Life in the Colonial Days* (New York: The Macmillan Company, 1898), 35; (2) From *The Letterbook of Eliza Lucas Pinckney, 1739–1762*, edited by Elise Pinckney, University of North Carolina Press, 1972. Based on original documents from the South Carolina Historical Society. Courtesy of the South Carolina Historical Society; (3) George Francis Dow, ed., *The Holyoke Diaries, 1709–1856* (Salem, MA: The Essex Institute, 1911), 49–51; (6) *Hilliad Magna: Being the Life and Adventures of Moll Placket-Hole* ([Philadelphia]: Printed [by Anthony Armbruster], 1765).

ANALYZING THE EVIDENCE

1. Compare the advice manual (source 1) with Eliza Lucas's letters and Mary Vial Holyoke's diary. What themes do they share in common, and how do these women's experiences deviate from the expectations of the advice book authors?

2. Eliza Lucas supervised slave labor, and Mary Vial Holyoke very likely employed servants. How do these facts affect the way you interpret sources 2 and 3?

3. Compare the two house interiors (source 4). What work would women have done in these spaces? The Chews were a slaveholding family, and the Howards probably employed servants. With that in mind, consider the relationship between supervisory and manual labor.

4. Hannah Breintnall was a well-to-do widow, while Moll Placket-Hole was a fictional stereotype. What does Breintnall's experience tell us about the prospects of a woman living without a male protector? How does Moll Placket-Hole shed light on popular attitudes toward such women?

PUTTING IT ALL TOGETHER

With all these sources in mind, write a short essay that considers the role of hierarchy and social power in women's work. How did economic and social status affect the work that was expected of women? How did the women whose lives are documented here navigate the challenges and opportunities they faced? And how does the satire of Moll Placket-Hole illuminate popular attitudes toward women's work and its place in colonial society?

an unacceptable match, they did not have the luxury of falling in love with and marrying whomever they pleased.

Marriage under eighteenth-century English common law was not a contract between equals. Under the legal principle of **coverture**, which placed married women under the protection and authority of their husbands, a bride relinquished to her husband the legal ownership of all her property. After his death, she received a dower right, the right to use (though not sell) one-third of the family's property. On the widow's death or remarriage, her portion was divided among the children. Thus the widow's property rights were subordinate to those of the family line, which stretched across the generations.

A father's duty was to provide inheritances for his children so that one day they could "be for themselves." Men who failed to do so lost status in the community. Some fathers willed the family farm to a single son and provided other children with money, an apprenticeship, or uncleared frontier tracts. Other yeomen moved their families to the frontier, where life was hard but land was cheap and abundant. "The Squire's House stands on the Bank of the Susquehannah," traveler Philip Fithian reported from the Pennsylvania backcountry in the early 1760s. "He tells me that he will be able to settle all his sons and his fair Daughter Betsy on the Fat of the Earth."

Freehold Society in Crisis

Because of rapid natural increase, New England's population doubled each generation, from 100,000 in 1700, to nearly 200,000 in 1725, to almost 400,000 in 1750. After being divided and then subdivided, farms became so small — 50 acres or less — that parents could provide only one child with an adequate inheritance. In the 1740s, the Reverend Samuel Chandler of Andover, Massachusetts, was "much distressed for land for his children," seven of them young boys. A decade later, in nearby Concord, about 60 percent of the farmers owned less land than their fathers had.

Because parents had less to give their sons and daughters, they had less control over their children's lives. The traditional system of arranged marriages broke down, as young people engaged in premarital sex and then used the urgency of pregnancy to win permission to marry. Throughout New England, premarital conceptions rose dramatically, from about 10 percent of firstborn children in the 1710s to more than 30 percent in the 1740s. Given another chance, young people "would do the same again," an Anglican minister observed, "because otherwise they could not obtain their parents' consent to marry."

Even as New England families changed, they maintained the freeholder ideal. Some parents chose to have smaller families and used birth control to do so: abstention, coitus interruptus, or primitive condoms. Other families petitioned the provincial government for frontier land grants and hacked new farms out of the forests of central Massachusetts, western Connecticut, and eventually New Hampshire and Vermont. Still others improved their farms' productivity by replacing the traditional English crops of wheat and barley with high-yielding potatoes and maize (Indian corn). Corn was an especially wise choice: good for human consumption, as well as for feeding cattle and pigs, which provided milk and meat. Gradually, New England changed from a grain to a livestock economy, becoming a major exporter of salted meat to the plantations of the West Indies.

As the population swelled, New England farmers developed the full potential of what one historian has called the "**household mode of production**," in which families swapped labor and goods. Women and children worked in groups to spin yarn, sew quilts, and shuck corn. Men loaned neighbors tools, draft animals, and grazing land. Farmers plowed fields owned by artisans and shopkeepers, who repaid them with shoes, furniture, or store credit. Partly because currency was in short supply, no cash changed hands. Instead, farmers, artisans, and shopkeepers recorded debits and credits

IDENTIFY CAUSES
What factors threatened the freeholder ideal in midcentury New England, and what strategies did farming families use to preserve this ideal?

and "balanced" the books every few years. This system helped New Englanders to maximize agricultural output and preserve the freehold ideal.

> **IN YOUR OWN WORDS**   What goals and values shaped New England society in the eighteenth century?

Diversity in the Middle Colonies

The Middle colonies — New York, New Jersey, and Pennsylvania — became home to peoples of differing origins, languages, and religions. Scots-Irish Presbyterians, English and Welsh Quakers, German Lutherans and Moravians, Dutch Reformed Protestants, and others all sought to preserve their cultural and religious identities as they pursued economic opportunity. At the same time, rapid population growth throughout the region strained public institutions, pressured Indian lands, and created a dynamic but unstable society.

Economic Growth, Opportunity, and Conflict

Previously home to New Netherland and New Sweden, the Mid-Atlantic region was already ethnically diverse before England gained control of it. The founding of Pennsylvania and New Jersey amplified this pattern. Fertile land seemed abundant, and grain exports to Europe and the West Indies financed the colonies' rapid settlement (America in Global Context). Between 1720 and 1770, a growing demand for wheat, corn, and flour doubled their prices and brought people and prosperity to the region. Yet that very growth led to conflict, both within the Middle colonies and in their relations with Native American neighbors.

Tenancy in New York   In New York's fertile Hudson River Valley, wealthy Dutch and English families presided over the huge manors created by the Dutch West India Company and English governors. Like Chesapeake planters, the New York landlords aspired to live in the manner of the European gentry but found that few migrants wanted to labor as peasants. To attract tenants, the manorial lords granted long leases, with the right to sell improvements such as houses and barns to the next tenant. They nevertheless struggled to populate their estates.

Most tenant families hoped that with hard work and ample sales they could eventually buy their own farmsteads. But preindustrial technology limited output. A worker with a hand sickle could reap only half an acre of wheat, rye, or oats a day. The cradle scythe, a tool introduced during the 1750s, doubled or tripled the amount of grain one worker could cut. Even so, a family with two adult workers could reap only about 12 acres of grain, or roughly 150 to 180 bushels of wheat. After saving enough grain for food and seed, the surplus might be worth £15 — enough to buy salt and sugar, tools, and cloth, but little else. The road to landownership was not an easy one.

Conflict in the Quaker Colonies   In Quaker-dominated Pennsylvania and New Jersey, wealth was initially distributed more evenly than in New York, but the proprietors of each colony, like the manor lords of New York, had enormous land claims. The first migrants lived simply in small, one- or two-room houses with a sleeping loft, a few benches or stools, and some wooden platters and cups. Economic growth brought greater prosperity, along with conflicts between ordinary settlers and the proprietors who tried to control their access to land, resources, and political power.

William Penn's early appeals to British Quakers and continental Protestants led to a boom in immigrants. When these first arrivals reported that Pennsylvania and New

Transatlantic Migration, 1500–1760

The following graph compares the number of European and African migrants who arrived in the American colonies of Spain, Portugal, Britain, France, and the Netherlands. It also charts change over time: while immigrants in the sixteenth and early seventeenth centuries went predominantly to the colonies of Spain and Portugal, Britain's colonies became the principal destination for both Europeans and Africans between 1640 and 1760.

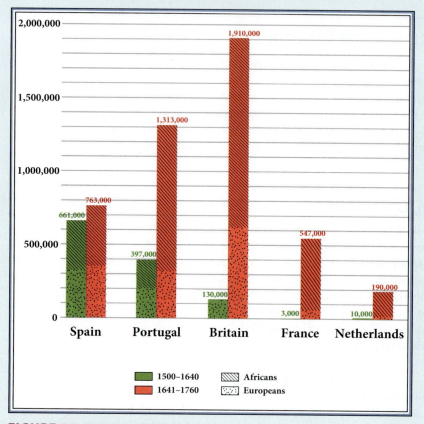

FIGURE 4.1 **Transatlantic Migration**

Source of data: Stanley L. Engerman and Kenneth L. Sokoloff, "Factor Endowments, Institutions, and Differential Paths of Growth Among New World Economies: A View from Economic Historians of the United States," in *How Latin America Fell Behind: Economic Histories of Brazil and Mexico, 1800–1914*, ed. Stephen Haber (Palo Alto, CA: Stanford University Press, 1997), 264.

QUESTIONS FOR ANALYSIS

1. What relationship do you see between the number of European emigrants and the importation of African slaves? Which nation's colonies had the highest percentage of Africans relative to Europeans? Which had the lowest? Which time periods had the highest and lowest percentages of Africans?

2. Compare France and the Netherlands to Spain, Portugal, and Britain. Why do you suppose that the ratio of Africans to Europeans is so much higher in French and Dutch colonies than in the other nations? Which type of colony — tribute, plantation, or neo-European — was likely to have been most important to the French and Dutch?

Jersey were "the best poor man's country in the world," thousands more followed. Soon the proprietors of both colonies were overwhelmed by the demand for land. By the 1720s, many new migrants were forced to become **squatters**, settling illegally on land they hoped eventually to be able to acquire on legal terms.

Frustration over the lack of land led the Penn family to perpetrate one of the most infamous land frauds of the eighteenth century, the so-called Walking Purchase of 1737, in which they fraudulently exploited an Indian deed to claim more than a million acres of prime farmland north of Philadelphia. This purchase, while opening new lands to settlement, poisoned Indian relations in the colony. Delaware and Shawnee migration to western Pennsylvania and the Ohio Valley, which was already under way, accelerated rapidly in response.

Immigrants flooded into Philadelphia, which grew from 2,000 people in 1700 to 25,000 by 1760. Many families came in search of land; for them, Philadelphia was only a temporary way station. Other migrants came as laborers, including a large number of indentured servants. Some were young, unskilled men, but the colony's explosive growth also created a strong demand for all kinds of skilled laborers, especially in the construction trades.

Pennsylvania and New Jersey grew prosperous but contentious. New Jersey was plagued by contested land titles, and ordinary settlers rioted against the proprietors in the 1740s and the 1760s. By the 1760s, eastern Pennsylvania landowners with large farms were using slaves and poor Scots-Irish migrants to grow wheat. Other ambitious men were buying up land and dividing it into small tenancies, which they lent out on profitable leases. Still others sold farming equipment and manufactured goods or ran mills. These large-scale farmers, rural landlords, speculators, storekeepers, and gristmill operators formed a distinct class of agricultural capitalists. They built large stone houses for their families, furnishing them with four-poster beds and expensive mahogany tables, on which they laid elegant linen and imported Dutch dinnerware.

By contrast, one-half of the Middle colonies' white men owned no land and little personal property. Some were the sons of smallholding farmers and would eventually inherit some land. But many were Scots-Irish or German "inmates"—single men or families, explained a tax assessor, "such as live in small cottages and have no taxable property, except a cow." In the predominantly German township of Lancaster, Pennsylvania, a merchant noted an "abundance of Poor people" who "maintain their Families with great difficulty by day Labour." Although these workers hoped eventually to become landowners, rising land prices prevented many from realizing their dreams.

> **EXPLAIN CONSEQUENCES**
> How did rapid immigration and economic growth trigger conflict in the Middle colonies?

Cultural Diversity

The Middle Atlantic colonies were not a melting pot. Most European migrants held tightly to their traditions, creating a patchwork of ethnically and religiously diverse communities (Figure 4.2). In 1748, a Swedish traveler counted no fewer than twelve religious denominations in Philadelphia, including Anglicans, Baptists, Quakers, Swedish and German Lutherans, Mennonites, Scots-Irish Presbyterians, and Roman Catholics.

Migrants preserved their cultural identity by marrying within their ethnic groups. A major exception was the Huguenots, Calvinists who had been expelled from Catholic France in the 1680s and resettled in Holland, England, and the British colonies. Huguenots in American port cities such as Boston, New York, and Charleston quickly lost their French identities by intermarrying with other Protestants. More typical were the Welsh Quakers in Chester County, Pennsylvania: 70 percent of the children of the original Welsh migrants married other Welsh Quakers, as did 60 percent of the third generation.

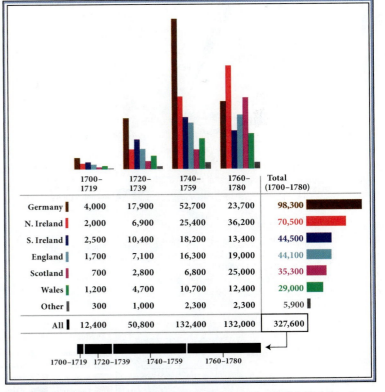

	1700–1719	1720–1739	1740–1759	1760–1780	Total (1700–1780)
Germany	4,000	17,900	52,700	23,700	98,300
N. Ireland	2,000	6,900	25,400	36,200	70,500
S. Ireland	2,500	10,400	18,200	13,400	44,500
England	1,700	7,100	16,300	19,000	44,100
Scotland	700	2,800	6,800	25,000	35,300
Wales	1,200	4,700	10,700	12,400	29,000
Other	300	1,000	2,300	2,300	5,900
All	12,400	50,800	132,400	132,000	327,600

1700–1719 1720–1739 1740–1759 1760–1780

FIGURE 4.2 Estimated European Migration to the British Mainland Colonies, 1700–1780
After 1720, European migration to British North America increased dramatically, peaking between 1740 and 1780, when more than 264,000 settlers arrived in the mainland colonies. Emigration from Germany peaked in the 1740s, but the number of migrants from Ireland, Scotland, England, and Wales continued to increase during the 1760s and early 1770s. Most migrants, including those from Ireland, were Protestants.

In Pennsylvania and western New Jersey, Quakers shaped the culture because of their numbers, wealth, and social cohesion. Most Quakers came from English counties with few landlords and brought with them traditions of local village governance, popular participation in politics, and social equality. But after 1720, the growth of German and Scots-Irish populations challenged their dominance.

The German Influx   The Quaker vision of a "peaceable kingdom" attracted 100,000 German migrants who had fled their homelands because of military conscription, religious persecution, and high taxes. First to arrive, in 1683, were the Mennonites, religious dissenters drawn by the promise of freedom of worship. In the 1720s, a larger wave of German migrants arrived from the overcrowded villages of southwestern Germany and Switzerland. "Wages were far better" in Pennsylvania, Heinrich Schnee-beli reported to his friends in Zurich, and "one also enjoyed there a free unhindered exercise of religion." A third wave of Germans and Swiss — nearly 40,000 strong — landed in Philadelphia between 1749 and 1756. To help pay the costs of the expensive trip from the Rhine Valley, German immigrants pioneered the **redemptioner** system, a flexible form of indentured servitude that allowed families to negotiate their own terms upon arrival. Families often indentured one or more children while their parents set up a household of their own.

Germans soon dominated many districts in eastern Pennsylvania, and thousands more moved down the fertile Shenandoah Valley into the western backcountry of Maryland, Virginia, and the Carolinas (Map 4.1). Many migrants preserved their cultural identity by settling in German-speaking Lutheran and Reformed communities that endured well beyond 1800. A minister in North Carolina admonished young people "not to contract any marriages with the English or Irish," arguing that "we owe it to our native country to do our part that German blood and the German language be preserved in America."

These settlers were willing colonial subjects of Britain's German-born and German-speaking Protestant monarchs, George I (r. 1714–1727) and George II (r. 1727–1760). They generally avoided politics except to protect their cultural practices; for example, they insisted that married women have the legal right to hold property and write wills, as they did in Germany.

Scots-Irish Settlers   Migrants from Ireland, who numbered about 115,000, were the most numerous of the incoming Europeans. Some were Irish and Catholic, but most were Scots and Presbyterian, the descendants of the Calvinist Protestants sent to Ireland during the seventeenth century to solidify English rule there. Once in Ireland, the Scots faced hostility from both Irish Catholics and English officials and landlords. The Irish Test Act of 1704 restricted voting and office holding to members of the Church of England, English mercantilist

MAP 4.1   Ethnic and Racial Diversity in the British Colonies, 1775
In 1700, most colonists in British North America were of English origin; by 1775, settlers of English descent constituted only about 50 percent of the total population. African Americans now accounted for one-third of the residents of the South, while tens of thousands of German and Scots-Irish migrants added ethnic and religious diversity in the Middle colonies, the southern backcountry, and northern New England (see Figure 4.2).

regulations placed heavy import duties on linens made by Scots-Irish weavers, and farmers paid heavy taxes. This persecution made America seem desirable. "Read this letter, Rev. Baptist Boyd," a migrant to New York wrote back to his minister, "and tell all the poor folk of ye place that God has opened a door for their deliverance . . . all that a man works for is his own; there are no revenue hounds to take it from us here."

Lured by such reports, thousands of Scots-Irish families sailed for the colonies. By 1720, most migrated to Philadelphia, attracted by the religious tolerance there (Interpretations). Seeking cheap land, they moved to central Pennsylvania and to the fertile Shenandoah Valley to the south. Governor William Gooch of Virginia welcomed the Scots-Irish presence to secure "the Country against the Indians." An Anglican planter, however, thought them as dangerous as "the Goths and Vandals of old" had been to the Roman Empire. Like the Germans, the Scots-Irish retained their culture, living in ethnic communities and holding firm to the Presbyterian Church.

IDENTIFY CAUSES
What attracted German and Scots-Irish migrants to Pennsylvania in such large numbers?

Religion and Politics

In Western Europe, the leaders of church and state condemned religious diversity. "To tolerate all [religions] without controul is the way to have none at all," declared an Anglican clergyman. Orthodox church officials carried such sentiments to Pennsylvania. "The preachers do not have the power to punish anyone, or to force anyone to go to church," complained Gottlieb Mittelberger, an influential German minister. As a result, "Sunday is very badly kept. Many people plough, reap, thresh, hew or split wood and the like." He concluded: "Liberty in Pennsylvania does more harm than good to many people, both in soul and body."

Mittelberger was mistaken. Although ministers in Pennsylvania could not invoke government authority to uphold religious values, the result was not social anarchy. Instead, religious sects enforced moral behavior through communal self-discipline. Quaker families attended a weekly meeting for worship and a monthly meeting for business; every three months, a committee reminded parents to provide proper religious instruction. The committee also supervised adult behavior; a Chester County meeting, for example, disciplined a member "to reclaim him from drinking to excess and keeping vain company." Significantly, Quaker meetings allowed couples to marry only if they had land and livestock sufficient to support a family. As a result, the children of well-to-do Friends usually married within the sect, while poor Quakers remained unmarried, wed later in life, or married without permission — in which case they were often ousted from the meeting. These marriage rules helped the Quakers build a self-contained and prosperous community.

In the 1740s, the flood of new migrants reduced Quakers to a minority — a mere 30 percent of Pennsylvanians. Moreover, Scots-Irish settlers in central Pennsylvania demanded an aggressive Indian policy, challenging the pacifism of the assembly. To retain power, Quaker politicians sought an alliance with those German religious groups that also embraced pacifism and voluntary (not compulsory) militia service. In response, German leaders demanded more seats in the assembly and laws that respected their inheritance customs.

By the 1750s, politics throughout the Middle colonies roiled with conflict. In New York, a Dutchman declared that he "Valued English Law no more than a Turd," while in Pennsylvania, Benjamin Franklin disparaged the "boorish" character and "swarthy complexion" of German migrants. Yet there was broad agreement on the importance of economic opportunity and liberty of conscience. The unstable balance between shared values and mutual mistrust prefigured tensions that would pervade an increasingly diverse American society in the centuries to come.

CONSIDER POINTS OF VIEW
What issues divided the various ethnic and religious groups of the Middle colonies? What core values did they agree upon?

IN YOUR OWN WORDS How were the goals of immigrants to the Middle colonies similar to those of New England colonists, and how did they differ?

Did Diversity Lead to Toleration?

What must it have been like to be a newcomer in colonial America? In some places, new immigrants found themselves to be religious, racial, or ethnic minorities. The Middle colonies were especially diverse. As Sally Schwartz, author of the first excerpt below, notes, a third of Pennsylvania's population was English. Another third was German and, with the exception of a small group of Africans and Native Americans, the rest hailed from other parts of northern Europe. They claimed membership in more than sixteen different faith communities. With such divergent identities, traditions, and cultures, how did they live together? Schwartz and Peter Silver, author of the second passage, agree that Pennsylvania and the Middle colonies were unusually diverse, but disagree about how tolerant their societies were.

SALLY SCHWARTZ

A Mixed Multitude

SOURCE: Sally Schwartz, "A Mixed Multitude": The Struggle for Toleration in Colonial Pennsylvania (New York: New York University Press, 1987), 1–2.

The extremely heterogeneous population confronted Pennsylvania with a unique set of problems that could have impeded the creation of a stable society. Nevertheless, despite the inevitable tensions, exacerbated by waves of new immigration, wars, and religious conflict, colonial Pennsylvanians managed to develop new ideals of pluralism and tolerance on which they built their province. . . . William Penn . . . set forth a new, ideological basis for pluralism and tolerance that transformed the tentative pattern of relative harmony and toleration into one of official policy . . . [H]e drafted a series of constitutions that guaranteed religious freedom and promoted his colony not only in the British Isles but on the Continent as well.

PETER SILVER

Our Savage Neighbors

SOURCE: Peter Silver, Our Savage Neighbors: How Indian War Transformed Early America (New York: W. W. Norton & Company, 2008), xviii–xix.

Pennsylvania . . . New Jersey, Delaware, northern Maryland, and parts of New York — colonies that together made the eighteenth-century mid-Atlantic perhaps the most racially, ethnically, and religiously mixed place in the world . . . were the unintended byproducts of a force that is now alien: early modern settler colonialism, in which huge numbers of Europeans and Africans were drawn across the ocean, in freedom and bondage, and replanted in new landscapes. . . . With few exceptions, living together made the different sorts of people there feel frightened of one another's intentions. Forced proximity brought many groups to a fresh appreciation for their own distinctive ways, ways they thought of as 'traditional' and fought to recover amid the disturbing novelties that came with diversity. Most strove both to make the other peoples around them act more like themselves and to keep, if they could, from coming to resemble those neighbors, making for a jittery, culturally competitive society.

QUESTIONS FOR ANALYSIS

1. How do these historians differ in their assessment of colonial America's tolerance of differences in race, ethnicity, and religion?
2. Identify two factors that Schwartz and Silver contend either promoted or undermined colonial tolerance in the face of cultural diversity.
3. Which of these interpretations is best supported by the narrative in Chapter 4?

Commerce, Culture, and Identity

After 1720, transatlantic shipping grew more frequent and Britain and its colonies more closely connected, while a burgeoning print culture flooded the colonies with information and ideas. Two great European cultural movements — the **Enlightenment**, which emphasized the power of human reason to understand and shape the world; and **Pietism**, an evangelical Christian movement that stressed the individual's personal relationship with God — reached America as a result. At the same time, an abundance of imported goods began to reshape material culture, bringing new comforts into the lives of the middling sort while allowing prosperous merchants and landowners to set themselves apart from their neighbors in new ways.

Transportation and the Print Revolution

In the eighteenth century, improved transportation networks opened Britain's colonies in new ways, and British shipping came to dominate the North Atlantic. In 1700, Britain had 40,000 sailors; by 1750, the number had grown to 60,000, while many more hailed from the colonies. An enormous number of vessels plied Atlantic waters: in the late 1730s, more than 550 ships arrived in Boston annually. About a tenth came directly from Britain or Ireland; the rest came mostly from other British colonies, either on the mainland or in the West Indies.

A road network slowly took shape as well, though roadbuilding was expensive and difficult. In 1704, Sarah Kemble Knight traveled from Boston to New York on horseback. The road was "smooth and even" in some places, treacherous in others; it took eight days of hard riding to cover 200 miles. Forty years later, a physician from Annapolis, Maryland, traveled along much better roads to Portsmouth, New Hampshire, and back—more than 1,600 miles in all. He spent four months on the road, stopping frequently to meet the locals and satisfy his curiosity. By the mid-eighteenth century, the "Great Wagon Road" carried migrating families down the Shenandoah Valley as far as the Carolina backcountry.

All of these water and land routes carried people, produce, and finished merchandise. They also carried information, as letters, newspapers, pamphlets, and crates of books began to circulate widely. The trip across the Atlantic took seven to eight weeks on average, so the news arriving in colonial ports was not fresh by our standard, but compared to earlier years, the colonies were awash in information.

Until 1695, the British government had the power to censor all printed materials. In that year, Parliament let the Licensing Act lapse, and the floodgates opened. Dozens of new printshops opened in London and Britain's provincial cities. They printed newspapers and pamphlets; poetry, ballads, and sermons; and handbills, tradesman's cards, and advertisements. Larger booksellers also printed scientific treatises, histories, travelers' accounts, and novels. The result was a print revolution. In Britain and throughout Europe, print was essential to the transmission of new ideas, and both the Enlightenment and Pietism took shape in part through its growing influence.

All this material crossed the Atlantic and filled the shops of colonial booksellers. The colonies also began printing their own newspapers. In 1704, the *Boston Newsletter* was founded; by 1720, Boston had five printing presses and three newspapers; and by 1776, the thirteen colonies that united in declaring independence had thirty-seven newspapers among them. This world of print was essential to their ability to share grievances and join in common cause.

The Enlightenment in America

To explain the workings of the natural world, some colonists relied on folk wisdom. Swedish migrants in Pennsylvania attributed magical powers to the great white mullein, a common wildflower, and treated fevers by tying the plant's leaves around their feet and arms. Traditionally, Christians believed that the earth stood at the center of the universe, and God (and Satan) intervened directly and continuously in human affairs. The scientific revolution of the sixteenth and seventeenth centuries challenged these ideas, and educated people—most of them Christians—began to modify their views accordingly.

The European Enlightenment In 1543, the Polish astronomer Copernicus published his observation that the earth traveled around the sun, not vice versa. Copernicus's discovery suggested that humans occupied a more modest place in the universe than Christian theology assumed. In the next century, Isaac Newton, in his *Principia Mathematica* (1687), used the sciences of mathematics and physics to explain the movement of the planets around the sun (and invented calculus in the process). Though Newton was himself profoundly religious, in the long run his work undermined the traditional Christian understanding of the cosmos.

In the century between the *Principia Mathematica* and the French Revolution of 1789, the philosophers of the European Enlightenment used empirical research and scientific reasoning to study all aspects of life, including social institutions and human behavior. Enlightenment thinkers advanced four fundamental principles: the lawlike order of the natural world, the power of human reason, the "natural rights" of individuals (including the right to self-government), and the progressive improvement of society.

English philosopher John Locke was a major contributor to the Enlightenment. In his *Essay Concerning Human Understanding* (1690), Locke stressed the impact of environment and experience on human behavior and beliefs, arguing that the character of individuals and societies was not fixed but could be changed through education, rational thought, and purposeful action. Locke's *Two Treatises of Government* (1690) advanced the revolutionary theory that political authority was not given by God to monarchs, as James II had insisted (see Chapter 3). Instead, it derived from social compacts that people made to preserve their **natural rights** to life, liberty, and property. In Locke's view, the people should have the power to change government policies — or even their form of government.

> **PLACE EVENTS IN CONTEXT**
> What conditions and ideas lay behind the emergence of the Enlightenment in America?

Some clergymen responded to these developments by devising a rational form of Christianity. Rejecting supernatural interventions and a vengeful Calvinist God, Congregational minister Andrew Eliot maintained that "there is nothing in Christianity that is contrary to reason." The Reverend John Wise of Ipswich, Massachusetts, used Locke's philosophy to defend giving power to ordinary church members. Just as the social compact formed the basis of political society, Wise argued, so the religious covenant among the lay members of a congregation made them — not the bishops of the Church of England or even ministers like himself — the proper interpreters of religious truth. The Enlightenment influenced Puritan minister Cotton Mather as well. When a measles epidemic ravaged Boston in the 1710s, Mather thought that only God could end it; but when smallpox struck a decade later, he used his newly acquired knowledge of inoculation — gained in part from a slave, who told him of the practice's success in Africa — to advocate this scientific preventive for the disease.

Franklin's Contributions   Benjamin Franklin was the exemplar of the American Enlightenment. Born in Boston in 1706 to devout Calvinists, he grew to manhood during the print revolution. Apprenticed to his brother, a Boston printer, Franklin educated himself through voracious reading. At seventeen, he fled to Philadelphia, where he became a prominent printer, and in 1729 he founded the *Pennsylvania Gazette*, which became one of the colonies' most influential newspapers. Franklin also formed a "club of mutual improvement" that met weekly to discuss "Morals, Politics, or Natural Philosophy." These discussions, as well as Enlightenment literature, shaped his thinking. As Franklin explained in his *Autobiography* (1771), "From the different books I read, I began to doubt of Revelation [God-revealed truth]."

Like a small number of urban artisans, wealthy Virginia planters, and affluent seaport merchants, Franklin became a deist.

Benjamin Franklin's Rise   This portrait of Benjamin Franklin, attributed to Robert Feke and executed around 1746, portrays Franklin as a successful businessman. His ruffled collar and cuffs, his fashionably curly wig, and his sober but expensive suit reveal his social ambitions. In later portraits, after he gained fame as an Enlightenment sage, he dispensed with the wig and chose more unaffected poses; but in 1746, he was still establishing his credentials as a young Philadelphia gentleman on the rise. Fogg Art Museum, Harvard Art Museums, USA/Bridgeman Images.

Deism was a way of thinking, not an established religion. "My own mind is my own church," said deist Thomas Paine. "I am of a sect by myself," added Thomas Jefferson. Influenced by Enlightenment science, deists such as Jefferson believed that a Supreme Being (or Grand Architect) created the world and then allowed it to operate by natural laws but did not intervene in people's lives. Rejecting the divinity of Christ and the authority of the Bible, deists relied on "natural reason," their innate moral sense, to define right and wrong. Thus Franklin, a onetime slave owner, came to question the morality of slavery, repudiating it once he recognized the parallels between racial bondage and the colonies' political bondage to Britain.

Franklin popularized the practical outlook of the Enlightenment in *Poor Richard's Almanack* (1732–1757), an annual publication that was read by thousands. He also founded the American Philosophical Society (1743–present) to promote "useful knowledge." Adopting this goal in his own life, Franklin invented bifocal lenses for eyeglasses, the Franklin stove, and the lightning rod. His book on electricity, published in England in 1751, won praise as the greatest contribution to science since Newton's discoveries. Inspired by Franklin, ambitious printers in America's seaport cities published newspapers and gentlemen's magazines, the first significant nonreligious periodicals to appear in the colonies. The European Enlightenment, then, added a secular dimension to colonial cultural life, foreshadowing the great contributions to republican political theory by American intellectuals of the Revolutionary era: John Adams, James Madison, and Thomas Jefferson.

Enlightenment Philanthropy: Pennsylvania Hospital, Philadelphia Using public funds and private donations, Philadelphia reformers built this imposing structure in 1753. The new hospital embodied two principles of the Enlightenment: that purposeful actions could improve society, and that the products of these actions should express reason and order, exhibited here in the building's symmetrical facade. Etchings like this one from the 1760s (*A Perspective View of the Pennsylvania Hospital*, by John Streeper and Henry Dawkins) circulated widely and bolstered Philadelphia's reputation as the center of the American Enlightenment. The New York Public Library/Art Resource, NY.

American Pietism and the Great Awakening

As some colonists turned to deism, thousands of others embraced Pietism, a Christian movement originating in Germany around 1700 and emphasizing pious behavior (hence the name). In its emotional worship services and individual striving for a mystical union with God, Pietism appealed to believers' hearts rather than their minds (Analyzing Voices). In the 1720s, German migrants carried Pietism to America, sparking a religious **revival** (or renewal of religious enthusiasm) in Pennsylvania and New Jersey, where Dutch minister Theodore Jacob Frelinghuysen preached passionate sermons to German settlers and encouraged church members to spread the message of spiritual urgency. A decade later, William Tennent and his son Gilbert copied Frelinghuysen's approach and led revivals among Scots-Irish Presbyterians throughout the Middle Atlantic region.

New England Revivalism Simultaneously, an American-born Pietist movement appeared in New England. Revivals of Christian zeal were built into the logic of Puritanism. In the 1730s, Jonathan Edwards, a minister in Northampton, Massachusetts, encouraged a revival there that spread to towns throughout the Connecticut River Valley. Edwards

Analyzing primary sources often involves comparing and contrasting documents that represent multiple points of view. In such cases, we ask the same analytical questions of each document, but we also think about the sources in relation to each other. How does one person's perspective on an important issue shed light on other points of view? In the documents that follow, four individuals offer statements that describe formative experiences and link them to core beliefs. As you read, consider the ways in which each person's experience shapes his or her views.

Evangelical Religion and Enlightenment Rationalism

Two great historical movements, Enlightenment thought and Pietistic religion, swept across British North America in the eighteenth century and offered radically different — indeed, almost completely contradictory — worldviews. Pietism sparked religious revivals based on passion and emotion, while Enlightenment rationalism encouraged personal restraint and intellectual logic. Both movements shaped American cultural development: Pietism transformed American religious life, and Enlightenment thinking influenced the principles of the American government.

SARAH LIPPET
Death as a Passage to Life

Sarah Lippet was a longtime member of the Baptist church of Middletown in eastern New Jersey. She died in October 1767 at the age of sixty-one; fellow parishioners reported her sentiments as she lay, for four days, on her deathbed.

SOURCE: "The Triumphant Christian," in *Historical and Genealogical Miscellany*, ed. John E. Stillwell (New York, 1964), 3: 465–466.

66 All my lifetime I have been in fears and doubts, but now am delivered. He hath delivered them who through fear of death were all their lifetime subject to bondage. For the love I have for Christ I am willing to part with all my friends to be with Him, for I love Him above all; yet it is nothing in me, for I know if I had my desert I should be in Hell. I believe in Christ, and I know that I put my whole trust in Him, and he that believeth in Him shall not be ashamed nor be confounded. . . .

Why do you mourn when I rejoice? You should not; it is no more for me to die and leave my friends for the great love I have for Christ than for me to go to sleep. I have no fears of death in my mind. Christ has the keys of death and hell, and blessed are the dead that die in the Lord. I can't bear to see a tear shed. You should not mourn. 99

NATHAN COLE
The Struggle for Salvation

Connecticut farmer Nathan Cole found God after listening to a sermon by George Whitefield, the great English evangelist. But Cole's spiritual quest was not easy. He struggled for two years before coming to believe that he was saved.

SOURCE: "The Spiritual Travels of Nathan Cole, 1741" in *The Great Awakening: Documents on the Revival of Religion, 1740–1745*, ed. Richard L. Bushman (New York: Atheneum, 1970), 68–70.

66 [After hearing Whitefield] I began to think I was not Elected, and that God made some for heaven and me for hell. And I thought God was not Just in so doing. . . . My heart then rose against God exceedingly, for his making me for hell; Now this distress lasted Almost two years — Poor Me — Miserable me. . . . I was loaded with the guilt of Sin. . . .

Hell fire was most always in my mind; and I have hundreds of times put my fingers into my pipe when I have been smoking to feel how fire felt: And to see how my Body could bear to lye in Hell fire for ever and ever. . . . And while these thoughts were in my mind God appeared unto me and made me Skringe: before whose face the heavens and the earth fled away; and I was Shrinked into nothing; I knew not whether I was in the body or out, I seemed to hang in open Air before God, and he seemed to Speak to me in an angry and Sovereign way[:] What? Won't you trust your Soul with God?; My heart answered O yes, yes, yes. . . .

When God disappeared or in some measure withdrew, every thing was in its place again and I was on my Bed. . . . I was set free, my distress was gone, and I was filled with a pineing desire to see Christs own words in the bible; . . . I got the bible up under my Chin and hugged it; it was sweet and lovely; the word was nigh [near] me in my hand, then I began to pray and to praise God. 99

BENJAMIN FRANKLIN
The Importance of a Virtuous Life

Franklin stood at the center of the American Enlightenment. In his *Autobiography*, he outlined his religious views and his human-centered moral principles.

SOURCE: Louis P. Masur, ed., *The Autobiography of Benjamin Franklin, with Related Documents*, 2nd ed. (Boston: Bedford/St. Martin's, 2003), 73–74, 93–94, 108.

66 My Parents had early given me religious Impressions, and brought me through my Childhood piously in the Dissenting Way. But I was scarce 15 when, after doubting by turns of several Points as I found them disputed in the different Books I read, I began to doubt of Revelation itself. Some Books against Deism fell into my Hands. . . . It happened that they wrought an Effect on me quite contrary to what was intended by them: For the Arguments of the Deists [that were quoted in those books] appeared to me much Stronger than the Refutations. In short I soon became a thorough Deist. . . .

I grew convinc'd that Truth, Sincerity & Integrity in Dealings between Man & Man, were of the utmost Importance to the Felicity of Life, and I form'd written Resolutions, (which still remain in my Journal Book) to practice them ever while I lived. . . .

About the Year 1734. There arrived among us from Ireland, a young Presbyterian Preacher named Hemphill, who delivered with a good Voice, & apparently extempore, most excellent Discourses, which drew together considerable Numbers of different Persuasions, who join'd in admiring them. Among the rest I became one of his constant Hearers, his Sermons pleasing me as they had little of the dogmatical kind, but inculcated strongly the Practice of Virtue, or what in the religious Stile are called Good Works. Those however, of our Congregation, who considered themselves as orthodox Presbyterians, disapprov'd his Doctrine, and were join'd by most of the old Clergy, who arraign'd him of Heterodoxy before the Synod, in order to have him silenc'd. I became his zealous Partisan. . . .

I never was without some religious Principles; I never doubted, for instance, the Existance of the Deity, that he made the World, & govern'd it by his Providence; that the most acceptable Service of God was the doing Good to Man; that our Souls are immortal; and that all Crime will be punished & Virtue rewarded either here or hereafter; these I esteem'd the Essentials of every Religion. 99

JOHN WISE

The Primacy of Human Reason and Natural Laws

Reverend John Wise (1652–1725) served for many years as a pastor in Ipswich, Massachusetts. A graduate of Harvard College, Wise used the Enlightenment doctrines of John Locke and Samuel von Pufendorf to justify the democratic structure of New England Congregational churches.

SOURCE: John Wise, *A Vindication of the Government of New England Churches* (Boston: J. Allen, for N. Boone, 1717), 32–40.

66 I Shall disclose several Principles of Natural Knowledge; plainly discovering the Law of Nature; or the true sentiments of Natural Reason, with Respect to Mans Being and Government. . . . I shall consider Man in a state of Natural Being, as a Free-Born Subject under the Crown of Heaven, and owing Homage to none but God himself. It is certain Civil Government in General, is a very Admirable Result of Providence, and an Incomparable Benefit to Mankind, yet must needs be acknowledged to be the Effect of Humane Free-Compacts and not of Divine Institution; it is the Produce of Mans Reason, of Humane and Rational Combinations, and not from any direct Orders of Infinite Wisdom. . . .

The Prime Immunity in Mans State, is that he is most properly the Subject of the Law of Nature. He is the Favourite Animal on Earth; in that this Part of Gods Image, viz. Reason is Congenate with his Nature, wherein by a Law Immutable, Instampt upon his Frame, God has provided a Rule for Men in all their Actions; obliging each one to the performance of that which is Right, not only as to Justice, but likewise as to all other Moral Vertues, which is nothing but the Dictate of Right Reason founded in the Soul of Man. . . .

The Second Great Immunity of Man is an Original Liberty Instampt upon his Rational Nature. He that intrudes upon this Liberty, Violates the Law of Nature. . . .

The Third Capital Immunity belonging to Mans Nature, is an equality amongst Men; Which is not to be denied by the Law of Nature, till Man has Resigned himself with all his Rights for the sake of a Civil State; and then his Personal Liberty and Equality is to be cherished, and preserved to the highest degree. 99

QUESTIONS FOR ANALYSIS

1. All of these writers declare a belief in God. How do their beliefs and outlooks differ?
2. These writers were variously influenced by the Great Awakening, the Enlightenment, and rational Christianity. How are these movements reflected in the passages above?
3. What roles do fear and anxiety play in the experiences of Sarah Lippet and Nathan Cole? What difference does it make that neither Franklin nor Wise expresses fear, either of God or of his own sinfulness?
4. Benjamin Franklin and John Wise stress the importance of reason and virtue as guides to human conduct. How would Nathan Cole and Sarah Lippet react to that emphasis?

guided and observed the process and then published an account entitled *A Faithful Narrative of the Surprising Work of God*, printed first in London (1737), then in Boston (1738), and then in German and Dutch translations. Its publication history highlights the transatlantic network of correspondents that gave Pietism much of its vitality.

COMPARE AND CONTRAST
What did the Enlightenment and Pietism have in common, and how did they differ?

Whitefield's Great Awakening English minister George Whitefield transformed the local revivals of Edwards and the Tennents into a Great Awakening. After Whitefield had his personal awakening upon reading the German Pietists, he became a follower of John Wesley, the founder of English Methodism. In 1739, Whitefield carried Wesley's fervent message to America, where he attracted huge crowds from Georgia to Massachusetts.

Whitefield had a compelling presence. "He looked almost angelical; a young, slim, slender youth . . . cloathed with authority from the Great God," wrote a Connecticut farmer. Like most evangelical preachers, Whitefield did not read his sermons but spoke from memory. More like an actor than a theologian, he gestured eloquently, raised his voice for dramatic effect, and at times assumed a female persona — as a woman in labor struggling to deliver the word of God. When the young preacher told his spellbound listeners that they had sinned and must seek salvation, some suddenly felt a "new light" within them. As "the power of god come down," Hannah Heaton recalled, "my knees smote together . . . [and] it seemed to me I was a sinking down into hell . . . but then I resigned my distress and was perfectly easy quiet and calm . . . [and] it seemed as if I had a new soul & body both." Strengthened and self-confident, these converts, the so-called New Lights, were eager to spread Whitefield's message.

The rise of print intersected with this enthusiasm. "Religion is become the Subject of most Conversations," the *Pennsylvania Gazette* reported. "No books are in Request but those of Piety and Devotion." Whitefield and his circle did their best to answer the demand for devotional reading. As he traveled, Whitefield regularly sent excerpts of his journal to be printed in newspapers. Franklin printed Whitefield's sermons and journals by subscription and found them to be among his best-selling titles. Printed accounts of Whitefield's travels, conversion narratives, sermons, and other devotional literature helped to confirm Pietists in their faith and strengthen the communication networks that sustained them.

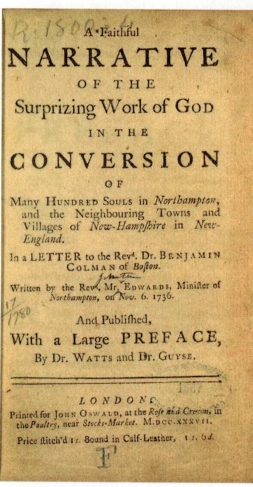

The Print Revolution and the Great Awakening
A local revival in Northampton, Massachusetts, gained transatlantic importance through the power of print. Jonathan Edwards's *A Faithful Narrative of the Surprising Works of God* began as a letter to a fellow clergyman describing events in his congregation. Two English evangelicals, Isaac Watts and John Guyse, learned of the letter and encouraged Edwards to expand it into a book. Edwards sent them an enlarged version; Watts and Guyse gave it a title and shepherded it into print in London in 1737, complete with extensive editorial commentary. A year later the first American edition was published in Boston. It became an important evangelical text in England, Scotland, and North America, and Dutch and German translations also made the book available to Pietists on the continent. Rare Book and Special Collections Division, Library of Congress.

Religious Upheaval in the North

Like all cultural explosions, the Great Awakening was controversial. Conservative ministers — passionless **Old Lights**, according to the evangelists — condemned the "cryings out, faintings and convulsions" in revivalist meetings and the New Lights' claims of "working Miracles or speaking with Tongues." Boston minister Charles Chauncy attacked the Pietist **New Lights** for allowing women to speak in public: it was "a plain breach of that commandment of the lord, where it is said, Let your women keep silence in the churches." In Connecticut, Old Lights persuaded the legislature to prohibit evangelists from speaking to a congregation without the minister's permission. But the New Lights refused to be silenced. Dozens of farmers, women, and artisans roamed the countryside, condemning the Old Lights as "unconverted" and willingly accepting imprisonment: "I shall bring glory to God in my bonds," a dissident preacher wrote from jail.

The Great Awakening undermined legally established churches and their tax-supported ministers. In New England, New Lights left the Congregational Church and founded 125 "separatist" churches that supported their ministers through voluntary contributions (Figure 4.3). Other religious dissidents joined Baptist congregations, which also condemned government support of churches: "God never allowed any civil state upon earth to impose religious taxes," declared Baptist preacher Isaac Backus. In New York and New Jersey, the Dutch Reformed Church split in two as New Lights refused to accept doctrines imposed by conservative church authorities in Holland.

The Great Awakening also appealed to Christians whose established churches could not serve their needs. By 1740, Pennsylvania's German Reformed and Lutheran congregations suffered from a severe lack of university-trained pastors. In the colony's Dutch Reformed, Dutch and Swedish Lutheran, and even its Anglican congregations, half the pulpits were empty. In this circumstance, itinerant preachers who stressed the power of "heart religion" and downplayed the importance of formal ministerial training found a ready audience.

The Great Awakening challenged the authority of all ministers whose status rested on respect for their education and knowledge of the Bible. In an influential pamphlet, *The Dangers of an Unconverted Ministry* (1740), Gilbert Tennent asserted that ministers' authority should come not from theological knowledge but from the conversion experience. Reaffirming Martin Luther's belief in the priesthood of all Christians, Tennent suggested that anyone who had felt God's redeeming grace could speak with ministerial authority. Sarah Harrah Osborn, a New Light "exhorter" in Rhode Island, refused "to shut up my mouth . . . and creep into obscurity" when silenced by her minister.

As religious enthusiasm spread, churches founded new colleges to educate their young men and to train ministers. New Light Presbyterians established the College of New Jersey (Princeton) in 1746, and New York Anglicans founded King's College (Columbia) in 1754. Baptists set up the College of Rhode Island (Brown) in 1764; two years later, the Dutch Reformed Church subsidized Queen's College (Rutgers) in New Jersey. However, the main intellectual legacy of the Great Awakening was not education for the privileged few but a new sense of authority among the many. A European visitor to Philadelphia remarked in surprise, "The poorest day-laborer . . . holds it his right to advance his opinion, in religious as well as political matters, with as much freedom as the gentleman."

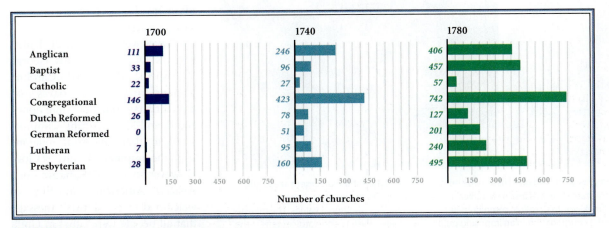

FIGURE 4.3 Church Growth by Denomination, 1700–1780
In 1700, and again in 1740, the Congregational and Anglican churches had the most members. By 1780, however, largely because of their enthusiastic evangelical message, Presbyterian and Baptist congregations outnumbered those of the Anglicans. The growth of immigrant denominations, such as the German Reformed and Lutheran, was equally impressive.

Social and Religious Conflict in the South

In the southern colonies, where the Church of England was legally established, religious enthusiasm triggered social conflict. Anglican ministers generally ignored the spiritual needs of African Americans and landless whites, who numbered 40 percent and 20 percent of the population, respectively. Middling white freeholders (35 percent of the residents) formed the core of most Church of England congregations. But prominent planters (just 5 percent) held the real power, using their control of parish finances to discipline ministers. One clergyman complained that dismissal awaited any minister who "had the courage to preach against any Vices taken into favor by the leading Men of his Parish."

The Presbyterian Revival Soon, a democratization of religion challenged the dominance of both the Anglican Church and the planter elite. In 1743, bricklayer Samuel Morris, inspired by reading George Whitefield's sermons, led a group of Virginia Anglicans out of their congregation. Seeking a deeper religious experience, Morris invited New Light Presbyterian Samuel Davies to lead their prayer meetings. Davies's sermons, filled with erotic devotional imagery and urging Christians to feel "ardent Passion," sparked Presbyterian revivals across the Tidewater region, threatening the social authority of the Virginia gentry. Traditionally, planters and their well-dressed families arrived at Anglican services in fancy carriages drawn by well-bred horses and flaunted their power by sitting in the front pews. Such ritual displays of the gentry's superiority were meaningless if freeholders attended other churches. Moreover, religious pluralism threatened the tax-supported status of the Anglican Church.

To halt the spread of New Light ideas, Virginia governor William Gooch denounced them as "false teachings," and Anglican justices of the peace closed Presbyterian churches. This harassment kept most white yeomen and poor tenant families in the Church of England.

The Baptist Insurgency During the 1760s, the vigorous preaching and democratic message of New Light Baptist ministers converted thousands of white farm families. The Baptists were radical Protestants whose central ritual was adult (rather than infant) baptism. Once men and women had experienced the infusion of grace — had been "born again" — they were baptized in an emotional public ceremony, often involving complete immersion in water.

Slaves were welcome at Baptist revivals. During the 1740s, George Whitefield had urged Carolina planters to bring their slaves into the Christian fold, but white opposition and the Africans' commitment to their ancestral religions kept the number of converts low. However, in the 1760s, native-born African Americans in Virginia welcomed the Baptists' message that all people were equal in God's eyes. Sensing a threat to the system of racial slavery, the House of Burgesses imposed heavy fines on Baptists who preached to slaves without their owners' permission.

A Contrast in Styles and Values These two church interiors highlight the divergent styles and values of traditional state churches and new, radical Protestant ones. On the left is St. James' Anglican Church in Goose Creek, South Carolina, completed in 1719. It embodies traditional values. The minister is elevated above the congregation in an imposing pulpit. The ornate pilasters and cornices reflect the importance of classical architecture in gentry culture, while the shield featuring a lion and unicorn — a symbol of the British monarchy — emphasizes the tie between church and state. On the right, the Mount Shiloh Baptist Church in Faber, Virginia, exhibits the plain style and egalitarian values of the Baptist movement. The minister is not elevated above the congregation, the pews are plain and open, and the room lacks any special ornamentation. This building dates to the nineteenth century, but its predecessors would have been similar in style. Left: Library of Congress. Right: Virginia Baptist Historical Society.

Baptists threatened gentry authority because they repudiated social distinctions and urged followers to call one another "brother" and "sister." They also condemned the planters' decadent lifestyle. As planter Landon Carter complained, the Baptists were "destroying pleasure in the Country; for they encourage ardent Prayer . . . & an intire Banishment of *Gaming, Dancing,* & Sabbath-Day Diversions." The gentry responded with violence. In Caroline County, an Anglican posse attacked Brother John Waller at a prayer meeting. Waller "was violently jerked off the stage; they caught him by the back part of his neck, beat his head against the ground, and a gentleman gave him twenty lashes with his horsewhip."

Despite these attacks, Baptist congregations multiplied. By 1775, about 15 percent of Virginia's whites and hundreds of enslaved blacks had joined Baptist churches. To signify their state of grace, some Baptist men "cut off their hair, like Cromwell's round-headed chaplains." Others forged a new evangelical masculinity, "crying, weeping, lifting up the eyes, groaning" when touched by the Holy Spirit.

The Baptist revival in the Chesapeake challenged customary authority in families and society but did not overturn it. Rejecting the pleas of evangelical women, Baptist men kept church authority in the hands of "free born male members," and Anglican slaveholders retained control of the political system. Still, the Baptist insurgency infused the lives of poor tenant families with spiritual meaning and empowered yeomen to defend their economic interests. Moreover, as Baptist ministers spread Christianity among slaves, the cultural gulf between blacks and whites shrank, undermining one justification for slavery and giving some blacks a new religious identity. Within a generation, African Americans would develop distinctive versions of Protestant Christianity.

> **IN YOUR OWN WORDS** How did the accelerating pace of travel and communication affect colonial society and culture?

The Midcentury Challenge: War, Trade, and Social Conflict, 1750–1763

Between 1750 and 1763, three significant events transformed colonial life. First, Britain went to war against the French in America, sparking a worldwide conflict: the Great War for Empire. Second, a surge in trade boosted colonial consumption but caused Americans to become deeply indebted to British creditors. Third, westward migration sparked warfare with Indian peoples, violent disputes between settlers and land speculators, and backcountry rebellions against eastern-controlled governments.

The French and Indian War

In 1754, overlapping French and British claims in North America came to a head (Map 4.2). The French maintained their vast claims through a network of forts and trading posts that sustained alliances with neighboring Indians. The soft underbelly of this sprawling empire was the Ohio Valley, where French claims were tenuous. Native peoples were driven out of the valley by Iroquois attacks in the seventeenth century, but after 1720 displaced Indian populations—especially Delawares and Shawnees from Pennsylvania—resettled there in large numbers. In the 1740s, British traders from Pennsylvania began traveling down the Ohio River. They traded with Delawares and Shawnees in the upper valley and began to draw French-allied Indians into their orbit and away from French posts. Then, in 1748, the Ohio Company of Virginia, a partnership of prominent colonial planters and London merchants, received a 200,000-acre grant from the crown to establish a new settlement on the upper Ohio, threatening French claims to the region.

MAP 4.2 European Spheres of Influence in North America, 1754

In the mid-eighteenth century, France, Spain, and the British-owned Hudson's Bay Company laid claim to the vast areas of North America still inhabited primarily by Indian peoples. British settlers had already occupied much of the land east of the Appalachian Mountains. To safeguard their lands west of the mountains, Native Americans played off one European power against another. As a British official remarked: "To preserve the Ballance between us and the French is the great ruling Principle of Modern Indian Politics." When Britain expelled France from North America in 1763, Indians had to face encroaching Anglo-American settlers on their own.

Conflict in the Ohio Valley   By midcentury, Britain relied on the Iroquois Confederacy as its partner in Indian relations throughout the Northeast. By extending the Covenant Chain, the Iroquois had become a kind of Indian Empire in their own right, claiming to speak for other groups throughout the region based on their seventeenth-century conquests. The Delawares, Shawnees, and other groups who repopulated the Ohio Valley did so in part to escape the Iroquois yoke. To maintain influence on the Ohio, the Iroquois sent two "half-kings," Tanaghrisson (an adopted Seneca) and Scarouady (an Oneida), to the Native settlement of Logstown, a trading town on the upper Ohio, where Britain recognized them as leaders.

French authorities, alarmed by British inroads, built a string of forts from Lake Erie to the headwaters of the Ohio, culminating with Fort Duquesne on the site of present-day Pittsburgh. To reassert British claims, Governor Dinwiddie dispatched an expedition led by Colonel George Washington, a twenty-two-year-old Virginian whose half-brothers were Ohio Company stockholders. Washington discovered that most of the Ohio Indians had decided to side with the French; only the Iroquois half-kings and a few of their followers supported his efforts. After Washington's party fired on a French detachment, Tanaghrisson rushed in and killed a French officer to ensure war — a prospect that would force British arms to support Iroquois interests in the valley.

Washington's party was soon defeated by a larger French force. The result was an international incident that prompted Virginian and British expansionists to demand war. But war in North America was a worrisome prospect: the colonies were notoriously incapable of cooperating in their own defense, and the Covenant Chain was badly in need of repair.

The Albany Congress   The Iroquois Confederacy was unhappy with its British alliance and believed that the British were neglecting the Iroquois while settlers from New York pressed onto their lands. Moreover, the Ohio Indians, France, and Britain were all acting in the Ohio Valley without consulting them. To mend relations with the Iroquois, the British Board of Trade called a meeting at Albany in June 1754. There, a prominent Mohawk leader named Hendrick Peters Theyanoguin challenged Britain to defend its interests more vigorously, while Benjamin Franklin proposed a "Plan of Union" among the colonies to counter French expansion.

The Albany Plan of Union proposed that "one general government . . . be formed in America, including all the said colonies." It would have created a continental assembly to manage trade, Indian policy, and the colonies' defense. Though it was attractive to a few reform-minded colonists and administrators, the plan would have compromised the independence of colonial assemblies and the authority of Parliament. It never received serious consideration, but that did not stop the push toward war.

The War Hawks Win   In Parliament, the fight for the Ohio prompted a debate over war with France. Henry Pelham, the British prime minister, urged calm: "There is such a load of debt, and such heavy taxes already laid upon the people, that nothing but an absolute necessity can justifie our engaging in a new War." But two expansionist-minded war hawks — rising British statesman William Pitt and Lord Halifax, the new head of the Board of Trade — persuaded Pelham to launch an American war. In June 1755, British and New England troops captured Fort Beauséjour in the disputed territory of Nova Scotia (which the French called Acadia). Soldiers from Puritan Massachusetts then forced nearly 10,000 French settlers from their lands, arguing they were "rebels" without property rights, and deported them to France,

> To see a longer excerpt of the Albany Plan of Union, along with other primary sources from this period, see *Sources for America's History.*

Hendrick Peters Theyanoguin, Chief of the Mohawks   Great Britain's alliance with the Iroquois Confederacy — the Covenant Chain — was central to its Indian policy in the mid-eighteenth century, and the Mohawk warrior and sachem Hendrick Peters Theyanoguin emerged as its most powerful spokesman. His speech at the Albany Congress of 1754, in which he urged Great Britain toward war, was reported in newspapers in Britain and the colonies and made him a transatlantic celebrity. This print was advertised for sale in London bookstalls just as his death at the Battle of Lake George (1755) was being reported in newspapers there. Hendrick wears a rich silk waistcoat, an overcoat trimmed with gold lace, a ruffled shirt, and a tricorn hat — gifts from his British allies — while he holds a wampum belt in one hand and a tomahawk in the other.   Courtesy of the John Carter Brown Library at Brown University.

the West Indies, and Louisiana (where "Acadians" became "Cajuns"). English and Scottish Protestants took over the farms the French Catholics left behind.

This Anglo-American triumph was quickly offset by a stunning defeat. In July 1755, General Edward Braddock advanced on Fort Duquesne with a force of 1,500 British regulars and Virginia militiamen. Braddock and his fellow officers were persuaded that British arms could easily triumph in the American backcountry, but instead they were routed by a French and Indian force. Braddock was killed, and more than half his troops were dead or wounded. "We have been beaten, most shamefully beaten, by a handfull of Men," George Washington complained bitterly as he led the survivors back to Virginia.

The Great War for Empire

By 1756, the American conflict had spread to Europe, where it was known as the Seven Years' War, and pitted Britain and Prussia against France, Spain, and Austria. When Britain mounted major offensives in India, West Africa, and the West Indies as well as in North America, the conflict became the Great War for Empire.

William Pitt emerged as the architect of the British war effort. Pitt was a committed expansionist with a touch of arrogance. "I know that I can save this country and that I alone can," he boasted. A master strategist, he planned to cripple France by seizing its colonies. In North America, he enjoyed a decisive demographic advantage, since George II's 2 million subjects outnumbered the French 14 to 1. To mobilize the colonists, Pitt paid half the cost of their troops and supplied them with arms and equipment, at a cost of £1 million a year. He also committed a fleet of British ships and 30,000 British soldiers to the conflict in America.

Beginning in 1758, the powerful Anglo-American forces moved from one triumph to the next, in part because they brought Indian allies back into the fold. They forced the French to abandon Fort Duquesne (renamed Fort Pitt) and then captured Fort Louisbourg, the stronghold at the mouth of the St. Lawrence that had been captured in 1745, only to be returned at the close of the previous war. In 1759, an armada led by British general James Wolfe sailed down the St. Lawrence and took Quebec, the heart of France's American Empire. The Royal Navy prevented French reinforcements from crossing the Atlantic, allowing British forces to complete the conquest of Canada in 1760 by capturing Montreal (Map 4.3).

Elsewhere, the British likewise had great success. From Spain, the British won Cuba and the Philippine Islands. Fulfilling Pitt's dream, the East India Company ousted French traders from India, and British forces seized French Senegal in West Africa. They also captured the rich sugar islands of Martinique and Guadeloupe in the French West Indies, but at the insistence of the West Indian sugar lobby (which wanted to protect its monopoly), the ministry returned the islands to France in the Treaty of Paris of 1763. Despite that controversial decision, the treaty confirmed Britain's triumph. It granted Britain sovereignty over half of North America, including French Canada, all French territory east of the Mississippi River, Spanish Florida, and the recent conquests in Africa and India. Britain had forged a commercial and colonial empire that was nearly worldwide.

Though Britain had won cautious support from some Native American groups in the late stages of the war, its territorial acquisitions alarmed many Native peoples from New York to the Mississippi, who preferred the presence of a few French traders to an influx of thousands of Anglo-American settlers. To encourage the French to return, the Ottawa chief Pontiac declared, "I am French, and I want to die French." Neolin, a Delaware prophet, went further, calling for the expulsion of all white-skinned invaders: "If you suffer the English among you, you are dead men. Sickness, smallpox, and their poison [rum] will destroy you entirely." In 1763, inspired by Neolin's nativist vision, Pontiac led a major uprising at Detroit. Following his example, Indians throughout the Great Lakes and Ohio Valley seized nearly every British military garrison west of Fort Niagara, besieged Fort Pitt, and killed or captured more than 2,000 settlers.

British military expeditions defeated the Delawares near Fort Pitt and broke the siege of Detroit, but it took the army nearly two years to reclaim all the posts it had lost.

MAP 4.3 The Anglo-American Conquest of New France
After full-scale war with France began in 1756, it took almost three years for the British ministry to equip colonial forces and dispatch a sizable army to far-off America. In 1758, British and colonial troops attacked the heartland of New France, capturing Quebec in 1759 and Montreal in 1760. This conquest both united and divided the allies. Colonists celebrated the great victory: "The Illuminations and Fireworks exceeded any that had been exhibited before," reported the *South Carolina Gazette*. However, British officers had little respect for colonial soldiers. Said one, "[They are] the dirtiest, most contemptible, cowardly dogs you can conceive."

In the peace settlement, Pontiac and his allies accepted the British as their new political "fathers." The British ministry, having learned how expensive it was to control the trans-Appalachian west, issued the Royal Proclamation of 1763, which confirmed Indian control of the region and declared it off-limits to colonial settlement. It was an edict that many colonists would ignore.

British Industrial Growth and the Consumer Revolution

Britain owed its military and diplomatic success to its unprecedented economic resources. Since 1700, when it had wrested control of many oceanic trade routes from the Dutch, Britain had become the dominant commercial power in the Atlantic and Indian oceans. By 1750, it was also becoming the first country to use new manufacturing technology and work discipline to expand output. This combination of commerce and industry would soon make Britain the most powerful nation in the world.

Mechanical power was key to Britain's Industrial Revolution. British artisans designed and built water mills and steam engines that efficiently powered a wide array of machines: lathes for shaping wood, jennies and looms for spinning and weaving textiles, and hammers for forging iron. Compared with traditional manufacturing methods, the new power-driven machinery produced woolen and linen textiles, iron tools, furniture, and chinaware in greater quantities — and at lower cost. Moreover, the entrepreneurs running the new workshops drove their employees hard, forcing them to keep pace with the machines and work long hours. To market the abundant factory-produced goods, English and Scottish merchants extended credit to colonial shopkeepers for a full year instead of the traditional six months. Americans soon were purchasing 30 percent of all British exports.

> **EXPLAIN CONSEQUENCES**
> How did the Seven Years' War reshape Britain's empire in North America and affect Native peoples?

> **EXPLAIN CONSEQUENCES**
> How did the prosperity of the British Empire improve and endanger the lives and interests of colonists?

Nicholas Boylston, c. 1769
Merchants in the coastal and transatlantic trades gained enormous wealth in the mid-eighteenth century and displayed it in new ways. Among the most flamboyant was Nicholas Boylston. Of Boylston's home John Adams wrote, "A Seat it is for a noble Man, a Prince." In this portrait, painted by John Singleton Copley in 1769, Boylston flaunts his exotic possessions. In place of the wig he would have worn outside his home, Boylston wears a red velvet turban to keep his shaved head warm. His morning gown of heavy silk damask covers a rich waistcoat, casually unbuttoned in the middle to reveal his elegant ruffled shirt. Boylston rests his left elbow on two thick account books, an unmistakable reminder of the source of his wealth. Museum of Fine Arts, Boston, Massachusetts, USA/Bridgeman Images.

To pay for British manufactures, mainland colonists increased their exports of tobacco, rice, indigo, and wheat. Using credit advanced by Scottish merchants, planters in Virginia bought land, slaves, and equipment to grow tobacco, which they exported to expanding markets in France and central Europe. In South Carolina, rice planters used British government subsidies to develop indigo and rice plantations. New York, Pennsylvania, Maryland, and Virginia became the breadbasket of the Atlantic World, supplying Europe's exploding population with wheat.

Americans used their profits and the generous credit extended from overseas to buy English manufactures. When he was practicing law in Boston, John Adams visited the home of Nicholas Boylston, one of the city's wealthiest merchants, "to view the Furniture, which alone cost a thousand Pounds sterling," he wrote. "[T]he Marble Tables, the rich Beds with Crimson Damask Curtains and Counterpins, the Beautiful Chimny Clock, the Spacious Garden, are the most magnificent of any Thing I have ever seen." Through their possessions, well-to-do colonists set themselves apart from their humbler — or, as they might have said, more vulgar — neighbors.

Although Britain's **consumer revolution** raised living standards, it landed many consumers — and the colonies as a whole — in debt (Figure 4.4). Even during the war-time boom of the 1750s, exports paid for only 80 percent of British imports. Britain financed the remaining 20 percent — the Americans' trade deficit — through the extension of credit and Pitt's military expenditures. When the military subsidies ended in 1763, the colonies fell into an economic recession. Merchants looked anxiously at their overstocked warehouses and feared bankruptcy. "I think we have a gloomy prospect before us," a Philadelphia trader noted in 1765. The increase in transatlantic trade had made Americans more dependent on overseas credit and markets.

The Struggle for Land in the East

In good times and bad, the population continued to grow, intensifying the demand for arable land. Consider the experience of Kent, Connecticut. Like earlier generations, Kent's residents had moved inland to establish new farms, but Kent stood at the colony's western boundary. To provide for the next generation, many Kent families joined the Susquehanna Company (1749), which speculated in lands in the Wyoming Valley in present-day northeastern Pennsylvania. As settlers took up farmsteads there, the company urged the Connecticut legislature to claim the region on the basis of Connecticut's

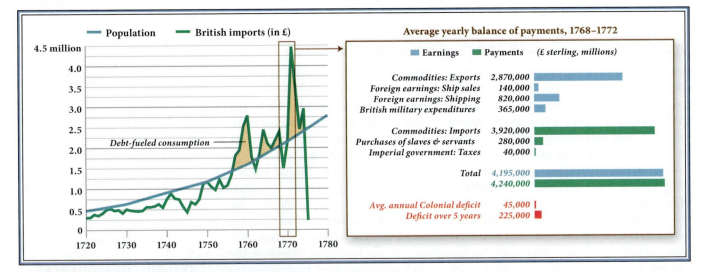

FIGURE 4.4 Mainland Population and British Imports
Around 1750, British imports were growing at a faster rate than the American population, indicating that the colonists were consuming more per capita. But Americans went into debt to pay for these goods, running an annual trade deficit with their British suppliers that by 1772 had created a cumulative debt of £2 million.

"sea-to-sea" royal charter of 1662. However, Charles II had also granted the Wyoming Valley to William Penn, and the Penn family had sold farms there to Pennsylvania residents. By the late 1750s, settlers from Connecticut and Pennsylvania were at war, burning down their rivals' houses and barns. Delawares with their own claim to the valley were caught in the crossfire. In April 1763, the Delaware headman Teedyuscung was burned to death in his cabin; in retaliation, Teedyuscung's son Captain Bull led a war party that destroyed a community of Connecticut settlers.

Simultaneously, three distinct but related land disputes broke out in the Hudson River Valley (Map 4.4). Dutch tenant farmers, Wappinger Indians, and migrants from Massachusetts asserted ownership rights to lands long claimed by manorial families such as the Van Rensselaers and the Livingstons. When the manor lords turned to the legal system to uphold their claims, Dutch and English farmers in Westchester, Dutchess, and Albany counties rioted to close the courts. In response, New York's royal governor ordered British troops to assist local sheriffs and manorial bailiffs: they suppressed the tenant uprisings, intimidated the Wappingers, and evicted the Massachusetts squatters.

Other land disputes erupted in New Jersey and the southern colonies, where landlords and English aristocrats had successfully revived legal claims based on long-dormant seventeenth-century charters. One court decision allowed Lord Granville, the heir of an original Carolina proprietor, to collect an annual tax on land in North Carolina; another decision awarded ownership of the entire northern neck of Virginia (along the Potomac River) to Lord Fairfax.

The revival of these proprietary claims by manorial lords and English nobles testified to the rising value of land along the Atlantic coastal plain. It also underscored the increasing similarities between rural societies in Europe and America. To avoid the status of European peasants, native-born yeomen and tenant families joined the stream of European migrants searching for cheap land near the Appalachian Mountains.

Western Rebels and Regulators

As would-be landowners moved west, they sparked conflicts over Indian policy, political representation, and debts. During the war with France, Delaware and Shawnee warriors had exacted revenge for Thomas Penn's land swindle of 1737 by destroying frontier farms in Pennsylvania and killing hundreds of residents. Scots-Irish settlers demanded the expulsion of all Indians, but Quaker leaders refused. So in 1763, a group of Scots-Irish frontiersmen called the Paxton Boys massacred twenty Conestoga Indians, an assimilated community that had lived alongside their colonist neighbors peacefully for many years. When Governor John Penn tried to bring the murderers to justice, 250 armed Scots-Irishmen advanced on Philadelphia. Benjamin Franklin intercepted the angry mob at Lancaster and arranged a truce, averting a battle with the militia. Prosecution of the Paxton Boys failed for lack of witnesses, and the episode gave their defenders the opportunity to excoriate Pennsylvania's government for protecting Indians while it neglected the interests of backcountry colonists.

The South Carolina Regulators Violence also broke out in the backcountry of South Carolina, where land-hungry Scottish and Anglo-American settlers clashed repeatedly with Cherokees during the war with France. After the fighting ended in 1763, a group of landowning vigilantes known as the **Regulators** demanded that the eastern-controlled government provide western districts with more courts, fairer taxation, and greater representation in the assembly. "We

MAP 4.4 Westward Expansion and Land Conflicts, 1750–1775

Between 1750 and 1775, the mainland colonial population more than doubled—from 1.2 million to 2.5 million—triggering westward migrations and legal battles over land, which had become increasingly valuable. Violence broke out in eastern areas, where tenant farmers and smallholders contested landlords' property claims based on ancient titles; and in the backcountry, where migrating settlers fought with Indians, rival claimants, and the officials of eastern-dominated governments.

are *Free-Men* — British Subjects — Not Born *Slaves*," declared a Regulator manifesto. Fearing slave revolts, the lowland rice planters who ran the South Carolina assembly compromised. In 1767, the assembly created western courts and reduced the fees for legal documents; but it refused to reapportion the legislature or lower western taxes. Like the Paxton Boys in Pennsylvania, the South Carolina Regulators won attention to backcountry needs but failed to wrest power from the eastern elite.

Civil Strife in North Carolina In 1766, a more radical Regulator movement arose in North Carolina. When the economic recession of the early 1760s brought a sharp fall in tobacco prices, many farmers could not pay their debts. When creditors sued these farmers for payment, judges directed sheriffs to seize the debtors' property. Many backcountry farmers lost their property or ended up in jail for resisting court orders.

To save their farms, North Carolina's debtors defied the government's authority. Disciplined mobs intimidated judges, closed courts, and freed their comrades from jail. The Regulators proposed a series of reforms, including lower legal fees and tax payments in the "produce of the country" rather than in cash. They also demanded greater representation in the assembly and a just revenue system that would tax each person "in proportion to the profits arising from his estate." All to no avail. In May 1771, Royal Governor William Tryon mobilized British troops and the eastern militia, which defeated a large Regulator force at the Alamance River. When the fighting ended, thirty men lay dead, and Tryon summarily executed seven insurgent leaders. Not since Bacon's Rebellion in Virginia in 1675 and the colonial uprisings during the Glorious Revolution of 1688 (see Chapters 2 and 3) had a colonial dispute caused so much political agitation.

In 1771, as in 1675 and 1688, colonial conflicts became linked with imperial politics. In Connecticut, the Reverend Ezra Stiles defended the North Carolina Regulators. "What shall an injured & oppressed people do," he asked, "[when faced with] Oppression and tyranny?" Stiles's remarks reflected growing resistance to recently imposed British policies of taxation and control. The American colonies still depended primarily on Britain for their trade and military defense. However, by the 1760s, the mainland settlements had evolved into complex societies with the potential to exist independently. British policies would play a crucial role in determining the direction the maturing colonies would take.

> **IN YOUR OWN WORDS** How did midcentury developments reflect Britain's deepening connections to North America?

SUMMARY

In this chapter, we observed dramatic changes in British North America between 1720 and 1763. An astonishing surge in population — from 400,000 to almost 2 million — was the combined result of natural increase, European migration, and the African slave trade. The print revolution and the rise of the British Atlantic world brought important new influences: the European Enlightenment and European Pietism transformed the world of ideas, while a flood of British consumer goods and the genteel aspirations of wealthy colonists reshaped the colonies' material culture.

Colonists confronted three major regional challenges. In New England, crowded towns and ever-smaller farms threatened the yeoman ideal of independent farming, prompting families to limit births, move to the frontier, or participate in an "exchange" economy. In the Middle Atlantic colonies, Dutch, English, German, and Scots-Irish residents maintained their religious and cultural identities while they competed for access to land and political power. Across the backcountry, new interest in western lands triggered conflicts with Indian peoples, civil unrest among whites, and, ultimately, the Great War for Empire. In the aftermath of the fighting, Britain stood triumphant in Europe and America.

TERMS TO KNOW

Identify and explain the significance of each term below.

Key Concepts and Events

tenancy (p. 108)

competency (p. 109)

coverture (p. 112)

household mode of production (p. 112)

squatters (p. 114)

redemptioner (p. 116)

Enlightenment (p. 118)

Pietism (p. 118)

natural rights (p. 120)

deism (p. 121)

revival (p. 121)

Old Lights (p. 124)

New Lights (p. 124)

consumer revolution (p. 132)

Regulators (p. 133)

Key People

Isaac Newton (p. 120)

John Locke (p. 120)

Benjamin Franklin (p. 120)

Jonathan Edwards (p. 121)

George Whitefield (p. 124)

Tanaghrisson (p. 129)

William Pitt (p. 129)

Pontiac (p. 130)

REVIEW QUESTIONS

Answer these questions to demonstrate your understanding of the chapter's main ideas.

1. What goals and values shaped New England society in the eighteenth century?

2. How were the goals of immigrants to the Middle colonies similar to those of New England colonists, and how did they differ?

3. How did the accelerating pace of travel and communication affect colonial society and culture?

4. How did midcentury developments reflect Britain's deepening connections to North America?

5. Review the events listed under "American and National Identity" and "Work, Exchange, and Technology" for the period 1720–1750 on the thematic timeline on page 72. How did economic developments in the colonies influence the formation of new cultural identities in this era?

MAKING CONNECTIONS

Recognize the larger developments and continuities within and across chapters by answering these questions.

1. In Chapter 3 we saw the rise of the South Atlantic System, an engine of economic growth that tied Britain's colonies more closely together and generated prosperity throughout the British Atlantic world. What consequences of that integration and prosperity are evident in the topics discussed in this chapter? How was the Great War for Empire grounded in earlier economic developments? And how did the postwar debt crisis grow out of the South Atlantic System?

2. Return to the John Collet painting of George Whitefield that opened the chapter (p. 107). How does Collet portray Whitefield's audience? Consider the postures and facial expressions of individual members of the crowd and imagine what might have been running through their minds as they listened. What do the various elements of this painting (the crowd, tankard of ale, sleeping dog, setting) suggest about the Great Awakening's appeal? About Collet's attitude toward evangelical preaching?

KEY TURNING POINTS

Refer to the chapter chronology on page 108 for help in answering the questions below.

The Ohio Company grant (1748), the formation of the Susquehanna Company (1749), land conflict along the New York and New England border (1760s), and the defeat of the North Carolina Regulators (1771): How do these events reveal tensions over the question of who would control the development of frontier lands in Britain's mainland North American colonies? What were the effects of these conflicts on Native American populations?

Revolution and Republican Culture

1754–1800

Although Part 3 is dominated by the causes and consequences of the War of Independence, it opens in 1754 to capture the changes wrought by the Great War for Empire, which were revolutionary in themselves — Britain had triumphed in the war, only to see its American empire unravel and descend into rebellion. Against all odds, thirteen colonies first united to win their independence, and then formed a federal republic that could claim a place among the nations of the world. "The American war is over," Philadelphia Patriot Benjamin Rush declared in 1787, "but this is far from being the case with the American Revolution. On the contrary, nothing but the first act of the great drama is closed. It remains yet to establish and perfect our new forms of government."

The republican revolution extended far beyond politics. It challenged many of the values and institutions that had prevailed for centuries in Europe and the Atlantic world. After 1776, Americans reconsidered basic assumptions that structured their societies, cultures, families, and communities. These social and cultural effects of the Revolution were only beginning to take shape by 1800, but we end Part 3 there, when the essential characteristics of the United States were becoming clear. (Chapter 7 carries the political story forward to 1820 in order to trace key themes to their conclusion, but Part 4 takes 1800 as its start date.) This periodization — 1754 to 1800 — captures a critical phase in American history: the transition from imperial rivalry and wars among European powers and Native societies to the founding of a new nation-state and its political institutions. Three principal developments are discussed in Part 3: ▶

From British North America to the United States of America

To administer the vast new American territory it gained in 1763, Britain had to reform its empire. Until that time, its colonies had been left largely free to manage their own affairs. Now, Parliament hoped to pay the costs of empire by taxing the colonies, while at the same time extending control over its new lands in the continental interior. Colonial radicals resisted these reforms. Calling themselves Patriots, they insisted on preserving local control over taxes. As Britain pressured local communities, colonists created intercolonial institutions and developed a broad critique of British rule that combined older, republican political principles with radical ideas of natural rights and the equality of all men. Their protests grew more strident, eventually resulting in open warfare with Great Britain and a declaration of independence.

The Granger Collection, New York.

Experiments in Government

At the same time they fought a war against Great Britain, Patriot leaders in the newly independent states had to create new governments. They drafted constitutions for their states while maintaining a loose confederacy to bind them together. In 1787, reformers put forward a new plan of government: a constitution that would bind the states into a single nation.

The new American republic emerged fitfully. Experiments in government took shape across an entire generation, and it took still longer to decide how much power the federal republic should wield over the states. Political culture was unformed and slow to develop. Political parties, for example, were an unexpected development. At first they were widely regarded as illegitimate, but by 1800 they had become essential to managing political conflict, heightening some forms of competition while blunting others. In the last half of the eighteenth century, American political culture was transformed as newly created governments gained the allegiance of their citizens.

The Granger Collection, New York.

Conquest, Competition, and Consolidation

One uncontested value of the Revolutionary era was a commitment to economic opportunity. To achieve this, people migrated in large numbers, creating new pressures on the United States to meet the needs of its citizens. The federal government acted against westerners who tried to rebel or secede, fought Indian wars to claim new territory, and turned back challenges from Britain and France to maintain its control over western lands. By 1820, the United States had dramatically expanded its boundaries and extended control far beyond the original seaboard states.

Even as the borders of the United States expanded, its diversity inhibited the effort to define an American culture and identity. Native Americans still lived in their own clans and nations; black Americans were developing a distinct African American culture; and white Americans were enmeshed in vigorous regional ethnic communities. But by 1800, to be an American meant, for many members of the dominant white population, to be a republican, a Protestant, and an enterprising individual.

Smithsonian American Art Museum, Washington, DC/ Art Resource, NY.

Revolution and Republican Culture 1754–1800

The Granger Collection, New York.

Thematic Understanding

This timeline arranges some of the important events of this period into themes. Consider the items listed under the theme "Culture and Society." How did the American Revolution challenge existing social arrangements? Consider the role of religion in American life, the status of women, and the institution of slavery. What tensions developed as a result of those challenges? ▶

	AMERICAN AND NATIONAL IDENTITY	POLITICS AND POWER	WORK, EXCHANGE, AND TECHNOLOGY	
1763	• Concept of popular sovereignty gains force • Colonists claim rights of Englishmen	• Stamp Act Congress (1765) • First Continental Congress (1774) • Second Continental Congress (1775)	• Merchants defy Sugar and Stamp Acts • Patriots mount three boycotts of British goods, in 1765, 1767, and 1774 • Boycotts spur Patriot women to make textiles	
1776	• Thomas Paine's *Common Sense* (1776) causes colonists to rethink political loyalties • New state constitutions rely on property qualifications to define citizenship rights	• The Declaration of Independence (1776) • States adopt republican constitutions (1776 on) • Articles of Confederation ratified (1781) • Treaty of Paris (1783)	• Manufacturing expands during the war • Cutoff of trade and severe inflation threaten economy • War debt grows	
1787	• Indians form Western Confederacy (1790) • Second Great Awakening (1790–1860) • Emerging political divide between South and North	• U.S. Constitution drafted (1787) • Conflict over Alexander Hamilton's economic policies • First national parties: Federalists and Republicans	• Bank of the United States founded (1791) • Land speculation increases in the West • Whiskey producers rebel against taxes (1794) • War in Europe raises wheat prices in Chesapeake and Middle colonies • Invention of cotton gin creates boom in cotton production	
1800	• Marshall's Supreme Court affirms national over state powers	• Jefferson reduces activism of national government; end of First Party System • Chief Justice Marshall asserts federal judicial powers • "Era of Good Feeling" in politics	• Congress cuts off Atlantic slave trade (1808) • Eastern farmers change crop mix and upgrade equipment	

CULTURE AND SOCIETY	MIGRATION AND SETTLEMENT	GEOGRAPHY AND THE ENVIRONMENT	AMERICA IN THE WORLD	
• Patriots call for American unity • The idea of natural rights challenges the institution of chattel slavery	• Migration into the Ohio Valley after Pontiac's Rebellion • Quebec Act (1774) allows Catholicism	• The trans-Appalachian west attracts the interest of settlers and investors • Ohio Indians resist Anglo-American expansion	• France and Spain cede all their territories east of the Mississippi River to Britain in the Treaty of Paris (1763) • Patriots invade Canada (1775)	**1763**
• Judith Sargent Murray publishes "On the Equality of the Sexes" (1779) • Emancipation of slaves begins in the North • Virginia enacts religious freedom (1786)	• Declining immigration from Europe (1775–1820) enhances American identity • African American slaves seek freedom through military service	• The vast geographical scale of the American Revolution poses challenges for its combatants	• Thomas Paine's *Common Sense* (1776) assaults monarchy • U.S. alliances with France (1778) and Spain (1779) virtually ensure a Patriot victory	**1776**
• Politicians and ministers deny vote to women; praise republican motherhood • Bill of Rights ratified (1791) • Sedition Act limits freedom of the press (1798)	• State cessions, land ordinances, and Indian wars create national domain in the West • The Alien Act makes it harder for immigrants to become citizens and allows for deporting aliens (1798)	• The Northwest Ordinance and sham Indian treaties open western land to settlement	• War between Britain and France puts American neutrality at risk • The French Revolution divides Americans	**1787**
• Handsome Lake preaches a middle path between Indian and Christian traditions	• Conflicts with Native Americans increase as settlers move west	• The Louisiana Purchase (1803) nearly doubles the size of the United States • The West is explored by Lewis and Clark (1804–1806)	• Napoleonic Wars lead to British impressment of American sailors • Jefferson enacts Embargo Act of 1807 • Battle of Tippecanoe eliminates threat from Western Confederacy • War of 1812 fought; Jackson's victory raises nation's pride • Monroe Doctrine (1823) asserts American leadership in Western Hemisphere	**1800**

5

CHAPTER

The Problem of Empire
1754–1776

In June 1775, the city of New York faced a perplexing dilemma. Word arrived that George Washington, who had just been named commander in chief of the newly formed Continental army, was coming to town. But on the same day, William Tryon, the colony's crown-appointed governor, was scheduled to return from Britain. Local leaders orchestrated a delicate dance. Though the Provincial Congress was operating illegally in the eyes of the crown, it did not wish to offend Governor Tryon. It instructed the city's newly raised volunteer battalion to divide in two. One company awaited Washington's arrival, while another prepared to greet the governor. The "residue of the Battalion" was to be "ready to receive either the General or Governour *Tryon*, which ever shall first arrive." Washington arrived first. He was met by nine companies of the volunteer battalion and a throng of well-wishers, who escorted him to his rooms in a local tavern. Many of this same crowd then crossed town to join the large group assembled to greet the governor, whose ship was just landing. The crowd met him with "universal shouts of applause" and accompanied him home.

This awkward moment in the history of one American city reflects a larger crisis of loyalty that plagued colonists throughout British North America in the years between 1763 and 1776. The outcome of the Great War for Empire left Great Britain the undisputed master of eastern North America. But that success pointed the way to catastrophe. Convinced of the need to reform the empire and tighten its administration, British policymakers imposed a series of new administrative measures on the colonies. Accustomed as they were to governing their own affairs, colonists could not accept these changes. Yet the bonds of loyalty were strong, and the unraveling of British authority was tortuous and complex. Only gradually — as militancy slowly mounted on both sides — were the ties of empire broken and independence declared.

IDENTIFY THE BIG IDEA

Was colonial independence inevitable, and was war the only way to achieve it?

The Great New York Fire of 1776 In the wake of the Declaration of Independence, General William Howe's first objective was to capture New York, with its strategic location and excellent harbor. Patriot forces under George Washington's command attempted to defend the city but were forced into retreat and abandoned it to the British in September 1776. Early in the morning of September 21, a fire broke out near the southern tip of Manhattan and burned northwestward, driven by a strong wind. As many as a quarter of the town's buildings were destroyed; residents, already distressed by the fighting, fled into the streets with whatever possessions they could carry. Each side accused the other of arson, but that charge was never proven. From The New York Public Library, http://digitalcollections.nypl.org/items/510d47e3-b9b0-a3d9-e040-e00a18064a99.

CHAPTER CHRONOLOGY

As you read, ask yourself why this chapter begins and ends with these dates and then identify the links among related events.

1763	▶ Proclamation Line limits white settlement		**1772**	▶ Committees of correspondence form	
1764	▶ Sugar Act and Currency Act		**1773**	▶ Tea Act leads to Boston Tea Party	
	▶ Colonists oppose vice-admiralty courts		**1774**	▶ Coercive Acts punish Massachusetts	
1765	▶ Stamp Act imposes direct tax			▶ Dunmore's War against the Shawnees	
	▶ Quartering Act requires barracks for British troops			▶ Continental Congress meets	
	▶ Stamp Act Congress meets			▶ Third American boycott	
	▶ Americans boycott British goods		**1775**	▶ General Gage marches to Lexington and Concord	
1766	▶ First compromise: Stamp Act repealed			▶ Second Continental Congress creates Continental army	
	▶ Declaratory Act passed			▶ Lord Dunmore recruits Loyalist slaves	
1767	▶ Townshend duties			▶ Patriots invade Canada and skirmish with Loyalists in South	
1768	▶ Second American boycott			▶ Western settlers occupy Kentucky	
1770	▶ Second compromise: partial repeal of Townshend Act		**1776**	▶ Thomas Paine's *Common Sense*	
	▶ Boston Massacre			▶ Declaration of Independence	

An Empire Transformed

The war that began as the French and Indian War in 1754 and culminated in the Great War for Empire of 1756–1763 (Chapter 4) transformed the British Empire in North America. The British ministry could no longer let the colonies manage their own affairs while it minimally oversaw Atlantic trade. Its interests and responsibilities now extended far into the continental interior — a much more costly and complicated proposition than it had ever faced before. And neither its American colonies nor their Native American neighbors were inclined to cooperate in the transformation.

British administrators worried about their American colonists, who, according to former Georgia governor Henry Ellis, felt themselves "entitled to a greater measure of Liberty than is enjoyed by the people of England." Ireland had been closely ruled for decades, and recently the East India Company set up dominion over millions of non-British peoples (Map 5.1 and America in Global Context). Britain's American possessions were likewise filled with aliens and "undesirables": "French, Dutch, Germans innumerable, Indians, Africans, and a multitude of felons from this country," as one member of Parliament put it. Consequently, declared Lord Halifax, "The people of England" considered Americans "as foreigners."

Contesting that status, wealthy Philadelphia lawyer John Dickinson argued that his fellow colonists were "not [East Indian] Sea Poys, nor Marattas, but *British subjects* who are born to liberty, who know its worth, and who prize it high." Thus was the stage set for a struggle between the conceptions of identity — and empire — held by British ministers, on the one hand, and many American colonists on the other.

EXPLAIN CONSEQUENCES
What was the impact of the Great War for Empire on British policymakers and the colonies?

The Costs of Empire

The Great War for Empire imposed enormous costs on Great Britain. The national debt soared from £75 million to £133 million and was, an observer noted, "becoming the alarming object of every British subject." By war's end, interest on the debt alone consumed 60 percent of the nation's budget, and the ministry had to raise taxes. During the eighteenth century, taxes were shifting from land — owned by the gentry and aristocracy — to consumables, and successive ministries became ever more ingenious in devising new ways to raise money. Excise (or sales) taxes were levied on all kinds of ordinary goods — salt and beer, bricks and candles, paper (in the form of a stamp tax) — that were consumed by middling and poor Britons. In the 1760s, the per capita tax burden was 20 percent of income.

MAP 5.1 Eurasian Trade and European Colonies, c. 1770

By 1770, the Western European nations that had long dominated maritime trade had created vast colonial empires and spheres of influence. Spain controlled the western halves of North and South America, Portugal owned Brazil, and Holland ruled Indonesia. Britain, a newer imperial power, boasted settler societies in North America, rich sugar islands in the West Indies, slave ports in West Africa, and a growing presence on the Indian subcontinent. France had lost its possessions on mainland North America but retained lucrative sugar islands in the Caribbean.

To collect the taxes, the government doubled the size of the tax bureaucracy (Figure 5.1). Customs agents patrolled the coasts of southern Britain, seizing tons of contraband French wines, Dutch tea, and Flemish textiles. Convicted smugglers faced heavy penalties, including death or forced "transportation" to America as indentured servants. (Despite colonial protests, nearly fifty thousand English criminals had already been shipped to America to be sold as indentured servants.)

The price of empire abroad was thus larger government and higher taxes at home. Members of two British opposition parties, the Radical Whigs and the Country Party, complained that the huge war debt placed the nation at the mercy of the "monied interests," the banks and financiers who reaped millions of pounds' interest from government bonds. To reverse the growth of government and the threat to personal liberty and property rights, British reformers demanded that Parliament represent a broader spectrum of the property-owning classes. The Radical Whig John Wilkes condemned rotten boroughs — sparsely populated, aristocratic-controlled electoral districts — and demanded greater representation for rapidly growing commercial and manufacturing cities. The war thus transformed British politics.

The war also revealed how little power Britain wielded in its American colonies. In theory, royal governors had extensive political powers; in reality, they shared power with the colonial assemblies, which outraged British officials. Moreover, colonial merchants had evaded trade duties for decades by bribing customs officials. To end that

Britain's Atlantic and Asian Empires

The following table enumerates the economic benefits derived by Great Britain from its various colonies, which sent a wide variety of goods to Britain and also served as markets for British exports.

TABLE 5.1

English/British Imports and Exports (annual averages in pounds sterling)

	England*		Britain*	
	1700–1701	**1750–1751**	**1772–1773**	**1789–1790**
Imports from Asia, Africa, and America				
North America	372,000	877,000	1,997,000	1,351,000
The Fisheries**	0	7,000	27,000	188,000
West Indies	785,000	1,484,000	3,222,000	4,045,000
Africa	24,000	43,000	80,000	87,000
East Indies	775,000	1,101,000	2,203,000	3,256,000
Total	1,956,000	3,512,000	7,529,000	8,927,000
Exports to America, Asia, and Africa				
North America	362,000	1,355,000	3,254,000	3,763,000
West Indies	336,000	589,000	1,402,000	1,892,000
Africa	145,000	188,000	777,000	799,000
East India	125,000	653,000	893,000	2,173,000
Total	968,000	2,785,000	6,326,000	8,627,000

*The "England" column shows data for England and Wales; "Britain" includes Scotland as well.
**Includes Massachusetts Bay, Maine, and Newfoundland; by the 1760s more than £500,000 worth of fish was being sent annually to the West Indies and southern Europe.

SOURCE: Adapted from *The Oxford History of the British Empire*, vol. 2, ed. P. J. Marshall (Oxford: Oxford University Press, 1998), 101.

QUESTIONS FOR ANALYSIS

1. Compare Britain's colonies in their roles as producers of British imports to their roles as consumers of British exports. Why are the mainland colonies of North America a distant third as producers of imports, but ranked first as consumers of exports?

2. How did the American Revolution (1776–1783) impact the economic relationship between Great Britain and its mainland colonies? Is it reasonable to conclude that political independence did not bring economic independence?

practice, Parliament passed the Revenue Act of 1762. The ministry also instructed the Royal Navy to seize American vessels carrying food crops from the mainland colonies to the French West Indies. It was absurd, declared a British politician, that French armies attempting "to Destroy one English province . . . are actually supported by Bread raised in another."

Britain's military victory brought another fundamental shift in policy: a new peacetime deployment of 15 royal battalions—some 7,500 troops—in North America. In part the move was strategic. The troops would maintain Britain's hold on its vast new North American territory: they would prevent colonists from defying the Proclamation of 1763 (see Chapter 4), while managing relations with Native Americans and 60,000 French residents of Canada, Britain's newly conquered colony (Map 5.2).

In part, too, the move had financial implications. The cost of supporting these troops was estimated at £225,000 per year, and Parliament expected that the colonies would bear the cost of the troops stationed in America. The king's ministers agreed that Parliament could no longer let them off the hook for the costs of empire. The greatest gains from the war had come in North America, where the specter of French encirclement had finally been lifted, and the greatest new postwar expenses were being incurred in North America as well.

George Grenville and the Reform Impulse

The challenge of raising revenue from the colonies fell first to George Grenville. Widely regarded as "one of the ablest men in Great Britain," Grenville understood the need for far-reaching imperial reform. He first passed the Currency Act of 1764, which banned the American colonies from using paper money as legal tender. Colonial shopkeepers, planters, and farmers had used local currency, which was worth less than British pounds sterling, to pay their debts to British merchants. The Currency Act ensured that merchants would no longer be paid in money printed in the colonies, boosting their profits and British wealth.

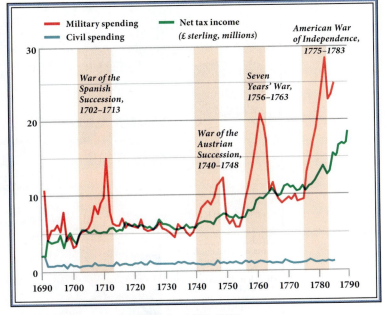

FIGURE 5.1 **The Cost of Empire, 1690–1790**
It cost money to build and maintain an empire. As Britain built a great navy, subsidized the armies of European allies, and fought four wars against France and Spain between 1702 and 1783, military expenditures soared. Tax revenues did not keep pace, so the government created a large national debt by issuing bonds for millions of pounds. This policy created a class of wealthy financiers, led to political protests, and eventually prompted attempts to tax the American colonists.

The Sugar Act Grenville also won parliamentary approval of the **Sugar Act of 1764** to replace the widely ignored Molasses Act of 1733 (see Chapter 3). The earlier act had set a tax rate of 6 pence per gallon on French molasses, in effect outlawing the trade, since such a high tax made it unprofitable. Rather than pay it, colonial merchants bribed customs officials at the going rate of 1.5 pence per gallon. Grenville intended to allow the trade and settled on a duty of 3 pence per gallon, which merchants could pay and still turn a profit.

This carefully crafted policy garnered little support in America. New England merchants, among them John Hancock of Boston, had made their fortunes smuggling French molasses. In 1754, Boston merchants paid customs duties on a mere 400 hogsheads of molasses, yet they imported 40,000 hogsheads for use by 63 Massachusetts rum distilleries. Publicly, the merchants claimed that the Sugar Act would ruin the distilling industry; privately, they vowed to evade the duty by smuggling or by bribing officials.

The End of Salutary Neglect More important, colonists raised constitutional objections to the Sugar Act. In Massachusetts, the leader of the assembly argued that the new legislation was "contrary to a fundamental Principall of our Constitution: That all Taxes ought to originate with the people." In Rhode Island, Governor Stephen Hopkins warned: "They who are taxed at pleasure by others cannot possibly have any property, and they who have no property, can have no freedom." The Sugar Act raised other constitutional issues as well. Merchants prosecuted under the act would be tried in **vice-admiralty courts**, tribunals governing the high seas and run by British-appointed judges. Previously, merchants accused of Navigation Acts violations were tried by local common-law courts, where friendly juries often acquitted them. The Sugar Act instead extended the jurisdiction of the vice-admiralty courts to all customs offenses.

The Sugar Act revived old American fears. The influential Virginia planter Richard Bland emphasized that the American colonists "were not sent out to be the Slaves but

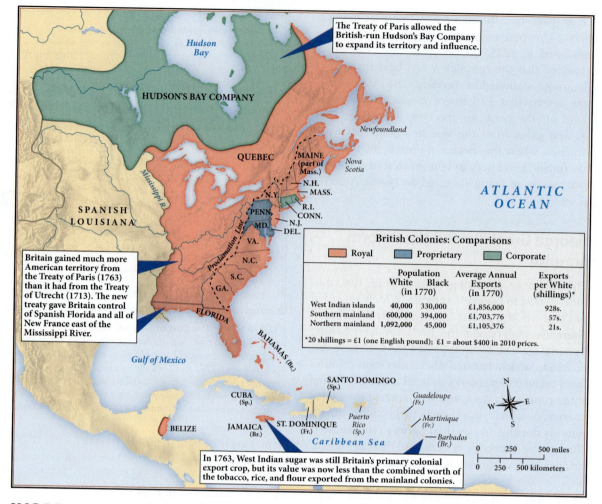

The Treaty of Paris allowed the British-run Hudson's Bay Company to expand its territory and influence.

Britain gained much more American territory from the Treaty of Paris (1763) than it had from the Treaty of Utrecht (1713). The new treaty gave Britain control of Spanish Florida and all of New France east of the Mississippi River.

British Colonies: Comparisons

| | Royal | Proprietary | Corporate |

	Population White	Population Black	Average Annual Exports (in 1770)	Exports per White (shillings)*
	(in 1770)			
West Indian islands	40,000	330,000	£1,856,000	928s.
Southern mainland	600,000	394,000	£1,703,776	57s.
Northern mainland	1,092,000	45,000	£1,105,376	21s.

*20 shillings = £1 (one English pound); £1 = about $400 in 2010 prices.

In 1763, West Indian sugar was still Britain's primary colonial export crop, but its value was now less than the combined worth of the tobacco, rice, and flour exported from the mainland colonies.

MAP 5.2 Britain's American Empire in 1763

The Treaty of Paris gave Britain control of the eastern half of North America and returned a few captured sugar islands in the West Indies to France. To protect the empire's new mainland territories, British ministers dispatched troops to Florida and Quebec. They also sent troops to uphold the terms of the Proclamation of 1763, which prohibited Anglo-American settlement west of the Appalachian Mountains.

To see a longer excerpt of the Richard Bland document, along with other primary sources from this period, see *Sources for America's History.*

to be the Equals of those that remained behind." John Adams, the young Massachusetts lawyer defending John Hancock on a charge of smuggling, argued that the vice-admiralty courts diminished this equality by "degrad[ing] every American . . . below the rank of an Englishman."

In fact, accused smugglers in Britain were also tried in vice-admiralty courts, so there was no discrimination against Americans. The real issue was the growing power of the British state. After decades of salutary neglect, Americans saw that the new imperial regime would deprive them "of some of their most essential Rights as British subjects," as a committee of the Massachusetts assembly put it. In response, Royal Governor Francis Bernard replied: "The rule that a British subject shall not be bound by laws or liable to taxes, but what he has consented to by his representatives must be confined to the inhabitants of Great Britain only." To Bernard, Grenville, and other imperial reformers, Americans were second-class subjects of the king, with rights limited by the Navigation Acts, parliamentary laws, and British interests.

An Open Challenge: The Stamp Act

Another new tax, the **Stamp Act of 1765**, sparked the first great imperial crisis. Grenville hoped the Stamp Act would raise £60,000 per year. The act would require a tax stamp on all printed items, from college diplomas, court documents, land titles, and contracts to newspapers, almanacs, and playing cards. It was ingeniously designed. Like its counterpart in England, it bore more heavily on the rich, since it charged only a penny a sheet for newspapers and other common items but up to £10 for a lawyer's license. It also required no new bureaucracy; stamped paper would be delivered to colonial ports and sold to printers in lieu of unstamped stock.

Benjamin Franklin, agent of the Pennsylvania assembly, proposed a different solution: American representation in Parliament. "If you chuse to tax us," he wrote, "give us Members in your Legislature, and let us be one People." With the exception of William Pitt, British politicians rejected Franklin's idea as too radical. They

Protesting the Stamp Act in Portsmouth, New Hampshire   Throughout the colonies, disciplined mobs protesting the Stamp Act forced stamp distributors to resign their offices. In this engraving, protesters in the small city of Portsmouth, New Hampshire, stone an effigy of the distributor as other members of the mob carry off a coffin representing the death of American "Liberty."   Illustration from "Interesting Events in the History of the U.S." by J. W. Barber, 1829/Picture Research Consultants & Archives.

argued that the colonists already had **virtual representation** in Parliament because some of its members were transatlantic merchants and West Indian sugar planters. Colonial leaders were equally skeptical of Franklin's plan. Americans were "situate at a great Distance from their Mother Country," the Connecticut assembly declared, and therefore "cannot participate in the general Legislature of the Nation."

The House of Commons ignored American opposition and passed the act by an overwhelming majority of 205 to 49. At the request of General Thomas Gage, the British military commander in America, Parliament also passed the **Quartering Act of 1765**, which required colonial governments to provide barracks and food for British troops. Finally, Parliament approved Grenville's proposal that violations of the Stamp Act be tried in vice-admiralty courts.

Using the doctrine of parliamentary supremacy, Grenville had begun to fashion a centralized imperial system in America much like that already in place in Ireland: British officials would govern the colonies with little regard for the local assemblies. Consequently, the prime minister's plan provoked a constitutional confrontation on the specific issues of taxation, jury trials, and military quartering as well as on the general question of representative self-government.

> **CONSIDER POINTS OF VIEW**
> Why did most British and colonial leaders reject the idea that the colonies should be represented in Parliament?

> **IN YOUR OWN WORDS**   What changes in Britain's imperial policy were triggered by its victory in the Great War for Empire?

The Dynamics of Rebellion, 1765–1770

In the name of reform, Grenville had thrown down the gauntlet to the Americans. The colonists had often resisted unpopular laws and aggressive governors, but they had faced an all-out attack on their institutions only once before — in 1686, when James II had unilaterally imposed the Dominion of New England. Now the danger was even greater because both the king and Parliament backed reform. But the Patriots, as the defenders of American rights came to be called, met the challenge posed by Grenville and his successor, Charles Townshend. They organized protests — formal and informal, violent as well as peaceful — and fashioned a compelling ideology of resistance.

Formal Protests and the Politics of the Crowd

Virginia's House of Burgesses was the first formal body to complain. In May 1765, hot-headed young Patrick Henry denounced Grenville's legislation and attacked George III (r. 1760–1820) for supporting it. He compared the king to Charles I, whose tyranny had led to his overthrow and execution in the 1640s. These remarks, which bordered on treason, frightened the Burgesses; nonetheless, they condemned the Stamp Act's "manifest Tendency to Destroy American freedom." In Massachusetts, James Otis, another republican-minded firebrand, persuaded the House of Representatives to call a meeting of all the mainland colonies "to implore Relief" from the act.

The Stamp Act Congress   Nine assemblies sent delegates to the **Stamp Act Congress**, which met in New York City in October 1765. The congress protested the loss of American "rights and liberties," especially the right to trial by jury. It also challenged the constitutionality of both the Stamp and Sugar Acts by declaring that only the colonists' elected representatives could tax them. Still, moderate-minded delegates wanted compromise, not confrontation. They assured Parliament that Americans "glory in being subjects of the best of Kings" and humbly petitioned for repeal of the Stamp Act. Other influential Americans favored active (but peaceful) resistance, organizing a boycott of British goods.

Crowd Actions   Popular opposition also took a violent form, however. When the Stamp Act went into effect on November 1, 1765, disciplined mobs demanded the resignation of stamp-tax collectors. In Boston, a group calling itself the **Sons of Liberty** burned an effigy of collector Andrew Oliver and then destroyed Oliver's new brick warehouse. Two weeks later, Bostonians attacked the house of Lieutenant Governor Thomas Hutchinson, Oliver's brother-in-law and a prominent defender of imperial authority, breaking his furniture, looting his wine cellar, and setting fire to his library.

Wealthy merchants and Patriot lawyers, such as John Hancock and John Adams, encouraged the mobs, which were usually led by middling artisans and minor merchants. In New York City, nearly three thousand shopkeepers, artisans, laborers, and seamen marched through the streets breaking windows and crying "Liberty!" Resistance to the Stamp Act spread far beyond the port cities. In nearly every colony, angry crowds—the "rabble," their detractors called them—intimidated royal officials. Near Wethersfield, Connecticut, five hundred farmers seized tax collector Jared Ingersoll and forced him to resign his office in "the Cause of the People."

The Motives of the Crowd   Such crowd actions were common in both Britain and America, and protesters had many motives. Roused by the Great Awakening, evangelical Protestants resented arrogant British military officers and corrupt royal bureaucrats. In New England, where rioters invoked the antimonarchy sentiments of their great-grandparents, an anonymous letter sent to a Boston newspaper promising to save "all the Freeborn Sons of America" was signed "Oliver Cromwell," the English republican revolutionary of the 1650s. In New York City, Sons of Liberty leaders Isaac Sears and Alexander McDougall were minor merchants and Radical Whigs who feared that imperial reform would undermine political liberty. The mobs also included apprentices, day laborers, and unemployed sailors: young men with their own notions of liberty who—especially if they had been drinking—were quick to resort to violence.

Nearly everywhere popular resistance nullified the Stamp Act. Fearing an assault on Fort George, New York lieutenant governor Cadwallader Colden called on General Gage to use his small military force to protect the stamps. Gage refused. "Fire from the Fort might disperse the Mob, but it would not quell them," he told Colden, and the result would be "an Insurrection, the Commencement of Civil War." The tax was collected in Barbados and Jamaica, but frightened collectors resigned their offices in all thirteen colonies that would eventually join in the Declaration of Independence. This

COMPARE AND CONTRAST
Why did the Stamp Act arouse so much more resistance than the Sugar Act?

popular insurrection gave a democratic cast to the emerging Patriot movement. "Nothing is wanting but your own Resolution," declared a New York rioter, "for great is the Authority and Power of the People."

The Ideological Roots of Resistance

Some Americans couched their resistance in constitutional terms. Many were lawyers or well-educated merchants and planters. Composing pamphlets of remarkable political sophistication, they gave the resistance movement its rationale, its political agenda, and its leaders.

Patriot writers drew on three intellectual traditions. The first was **English common law**, the centuries-old body of legal rules and procedures that protected the lives and property of the monarch's subjects. In the famous *Writs of Assistance* case of 1761, Boston lawyer James Otis invoked English legal precedents to challenge open-ended search warrants. In demanding a jury trial for John Hancock in the late 1760s, John Adams appealed to the Magna Carta (1215), the ancient document that, said Adams, "has for many Centuries been esteemed by Englishmen, as one of the . . . firmest Bulwarks of their Liberties." Other lawyers protested that new strictures violated specific "liberties and privileges" granted in colonial charters or embodied in Britain's "ancient constitution."

Enlightenment rationalism provided Patriots with a second important intellectual resource. Virginia planter Thomas Jefferson and other Patriots drew on the writings of John Locke, who had argued that all individuals possessed certain **natural rights**—life, liberty, and property—that governments must protect (see Chapter 4). And they turned to the works of French philosopher Montesquieu, who had maintained that a "separation of powers" among government departments prevented arbitrary rule.

The republican and Whig strands of the English political tradition provided a third ideological source for American Patriots. Puritan New England had long venerated the Commonwealth era (1649–1660), when England had been a republic (see Chapter 2). After the Glorious Revolution of 1688–1689, many colonists praised the English Whigs for creating a constitutional monarchy that prevented the king from imposing taxes and other measures. Joseph Warren, a physician and a Radical Whig Patriot, suggested that the Stamp Act was part of a ministerial plot "to force the colonies into rebellion" and justify the use of "military power to reduce them to servitude." John Dickinson's *Letters from a Farmer in Pennsylvania* (1768) urged colonists to "remember your ancestors and your posterity" and oppose parliamentary taxes. The letters circulated widely and served as an early call to resistance. If Parliament could tax the colonies without their consent, he wrote, "our boasted liberty is but A sound and nothing else."

Such arguments, widely publicized in newspapers and pamphlets, gave intellectual substance to the Patriot movement and turned a series of impromptu riots, tax protests, and boycotts of British manufactures into a formidable political force.

Another Kind of Freedom

"We are taxed without our own consent," Dickinson wrote in one of his *Letters*. "We are therefore—SLAVES." As Patriot writers argued that taxation without representation made colonists the slaves of Parliament, many, including Benjamin Franklin in

Phillis Wheatley Born in West Africa and enslaved as a child, Phillis Wheatley was purchased by Boston merchant and tailor John Wheatley when she was eight. Tutored by Wheatley's children, Phillis learned to read English, Greek, and Latin by the age of twelve. This engraving, which pictures her at a writing desk, was the frontispiece for her *Poems on Various Subjects, Religious and Moral* (1773), which was praised by George Washington and gained attention in both Britain and the colonies. Freed upon the death of her master, Wheatley married John Peters, a free black man. He was later imprisoned for debt, forcing Wheatley to take employment as a maid. She died in 1784 at age thirty-one; none of her three children survived infancy. Library of Congress.

Philadelphia and James Otis in Massachusetts, also began to condemn the institution of chattel slavery itself as a violation of slaves' natural rights. African Americans made the connection as well. In Massachusetts, slaves submitted at least four petitions to the legislature asking that slavery be abolished. As one petition noted, slaves "have in common with other men, a natural right to be free, and without molestation, to enjoy such property, as they may acquire by their industry."

In the southern colonies, where slaves constituted half or more of the population and the economy depended on their servitude, the quest for freedom alarmed slaveholders. In November 1773, a group of Virginia slaves hoped to win their freedom by supporting British troops that, they heard, would soon arrive in the colony. Their plan was uncovered, and, as James Madison wrote, "proper precautions" were taken "to prevent the Infection" from spreading. He fully understood how important it was to defend the colonists' liberties without allowing the idea of natural rights to undermine the institution of slavery. "It is prudent," he wrote, "such things should be concealed as well as suppressed." Throughout the Revolution, the quest for African American rights and liberties would play out alongside that of the colonies, but unlike national independence, the liberation of African Americans would not be fulfilled for many generations.

COMPARE AND CONTRAST
Why were southerners more threatened by challenges to the institution of slavery than northerners?

Parliament and Patriots Square Off Again

When news of the Stamp Act riots and the boycott reached Britain, Parliament was already in turmoil. Disputes over domestic policy had led George III to dismiss Grenville as prime minister. However, Grenville's allies demanded that imperial reform continue, if necessary at gunpoint. "The British legislature," declared Chief Justice Sir James Mansfield, "has authority to bind every part and every subject, whether such subjects have a right to vote or not."

Yet a majority in Parliament was persuaded that the Stamp Act was cutting deeply into British exports and thus doing more harm than good. "The Avenues of Trade are all shut up," a Bristol merchant told Parliament: "We have no Remittances and are at our Witts End for want of Money to fulfill our Engagements with our Tradesmen." Grenville's successor, the Earl of Rockingham, forged a compromise. He repealed the Stamp Act and reduced the duty on molasses imposed by the Sugar Act to a penny a gallon. Then he pacified imperial reformers and hardliners with the **Declaratory Act of 1766**, which explicitly reaffirmed Parliament's "full power and authority to make laws and statutes . . . to bind the colonies and people of America . . . in all cases whatsoever." By swiftly ending the Stamp Act crisis, Rockingham hoped it would be forgotten just as quickly.

Charles Townshend Steps In Often the course of history is changed by a small event—an illness, a personal grudge, a chance remark. That was the case in 1767, when George III named William Pitt to head a new government. Pitt, chronically ill and often absent from parliamentary debates, left chancellor of the exchequer Charles Townshend in command. Pitt was sympathetic toward America; Townshend was not. He had strongly supported the Stamp Act, and in 1767 he promised to find a new source of revenue in America.

Celebrating Repeal This British cartoon mocking supporters of the Stamp Act — "The Repeal, or the Funeral Procession of Miss Americ-Stamp"—was probably commissioned by merchants trading with America. Preceded by two flag bearers, George Grenville, the author of the legislation, carries a miniature coffin (representing the act) to a tomb, as a dog urinates on the leader of the procession. Two bales on the wharf, labeled "Stamps from America" and "Black cloth return'd from America," testify to the failure of the act. The Granger Collection, New York.

The new tax legislation, the **Townshend Act of 1767**, had both fiscal and political goals. It imposed duties on colonial imports of paper, paint, glass, and tea that were expected to raise about £40,000 a year. Though Townshend did allocate some of this revenue for American military expenses, he earmarked most of it to pay the salaries of royal governors, judges, and other imperial officials, who had always previously been paid by colonial assemblies. Now, he hoped, royal appointees could better enforce parliamentary laws and carry out the king's instructions. Townshend next devised the Revenue Act of 1767, which created a board of customs commissioners in Boston and vice-admiralty courts in Halifax, Boston, Philadelphia, and Charleston. By using parliamentary taxes to finance imperial administration, Townshend intended to undermine American political institutions.

The Townshend duties revived the constitutional debate over taxation. During the Stamp Act crisis, some Americans, including Benjamin Franklin, distinguished between external and internal taxes. They suggested that external duties on trade (such as those long mandated by the Navigation Acts) were acceptable to Americans, but that direct, or internal, taxes were not. Townshend thought this distinction was "perfect nonsense," but he indulged the Americans and laid duties only on trade.

A Second Boycott and the Daughters of Liberty

Even so, most colonial leaders rejected the legitimacy of Townshend's measures. In February 1768, the Massachusetts assembly condemned the Townshend Act, and Boston and New York merchants began a new boycott of British goods. Throughout Puritan New England, ministers and public officials discouraged the purchase of "foreign superfluities" and promoted the domestic manufacture of cloth and other necessities.

American women, ordinarily excluded from public affairs, became crucial to the **nonimportation movement**. They reduced their households' consumption of imported goods and produced large quantities of homespun cloth. Pious farmwives spun yarn at their ministers' homes. In Berwick, Maine, "true Daughters of Liberty" celebrated American products by "drinking rye coffee and dining on bear venison." Other women's groups supported the boycott with charitable work, spinning flax and wool for the needy. Just as Patriot men followed tradition by joining crowd actions, so women's protests reflected their customary concern for the well-being of the community.

Newspapers celebrated these exploits of the Daughters of Liberty. One Massachusetts town proudly claimed an annual output of 30,000 yards of cloth; East Hartford, Connecticut, reported 17,000 yards. This surge in domestic production did not offset the loss of British imports, which had averaged about 10 million yards of cloth annually, but it brought thousands of women into the public arena.

The boycott mobilized many American men as well. In the seaport cities, the Sons of Liberty published the names of merchants who imported British goods and harassed their employees and customers.

Edenton Ladies' Tea Party In October 1774, a group of fifty-one women from Edenton, North Carolina, led by Penelope Barker, created a local association to support a boycott of British goods. Patriots in the colonies praised the Edenton Tea Party, which was one of the first formal female political associations in North America, but it was ridiculed in Britain, where this cartoon appeared in March 1775. The women are given a mannish appearance, and the themes of promiscuity and neglect to their female duties are suggested by the presence of a slave and an amorous man, the neglected child, and the urinating dog. Library of Congress.

MAP 5.3 British Troop Deployments, 1763 and 1775

As the imperial crisis deepened, British military priorities changed. In 1763, most British battalions were stationed in Canada to deter Indian uprisings and French Canadian revolts. After the Stamp Act riots of 1765, the British placed large garrisons in New York and Philadelphia. By 1775, eleven battalions of British regulars occupied Boston, the center of the Patriot movement.

By March 1769, the nonimportation movement had spread to Philadelphia; two months later, the members of the Virginia House of Burgesses vowed not to buy duties articles, luxury goods, or imported slaves. Reflecting colonial self-confidence, Benjamin Franklin called for a return to the pre-1763 mercantilist system: "Repeal the laws, renounce the right, recall the troops, refund the money, and return to the old method of requisition."

Despite the enthusiasm of Patriots, nonimportation — accompanied by pressure on merchants and consumers who resisted it — opened fissures in colonial society. Not only royal officials, but also merchants, farmers, and ordinary folk, were subject to new forms of surveillance and coercion — a pattern that would only become more pronounced as the imperial crisis unfolded.

EXPLAIN CONSEQUENCES
How did the nonimportation movement bring women into the political sphere?

Troops to Boston   American resistance only increased British determination. When the Massachusetts assembly's letter opposing the Townshend duties reached London, Lord Hillsborough, the secretary of state for American affairs, branded it "unjustifiable opposition to the constitutional authority of Parliament." To strengthen the "Hand of Government" in Massachusetts, Hillsborough dispatched General Thomas Gage and 2,000 British troops to Boston (Map 5.3). Once in Massachusetts, Gage accused its leaders of "Treasonable and desperate Resolves" and advised the ministry to "Quash this Spirit at a Blow." In 1765, American resistance to the Stamp Act had sparked a parliamentary debate; in 1768, it provoked a plan for military coercion.

The Problem of the West

At the same time that successive ministries addressed the problem of raising a colonial revenue, they quarreled over how to manage the vast new inland territory — about half a billion acres—acquired in the Treaty of Paris in 1763 (see Chapter 4). The Proclamation Line had drawn a boundary between the colonies and Indian country. The line was originally intended as a temporary barrier. It prohibited settlement "for the present, and until our further Pleasure be known." The Proclamation also created three new mainland colonies—Quebec, East Florida, and West Florida—and thus opened new opportunities at the northern and southern extremities of British North America.

But many colonists looked west rather than north or south. Four groups in the colonies were especially interested in westward expansion. First, gentlemen who had invested in numerous land speculation companies were petitioning the crown for large land grants in the Ohio country. Second, officers who served in the Seven Years' War were paid in land warrants—up to 5,000 acres for field officers—and some, led by George Washington, were exploring possible sites beyond the Appalachians. Third, Indian traders who had received large grants from the Ohio Indians hoped to sell land titles. And fourth, thousands of squatters were following the roads cut to the Ohio by the Braddock and Forbes campaigns during the Seven Years' War to take up lands in the hope that they could later receive a title to them. "The roads are . . . alive with Men, Women, Children, and Cattle from Jersey, Pennsylvania, and Maryland," wrote one astonished observer (Thinking Like a Historian).

All of this activity antagonized the Ohio Indians. In 1770, Shawnees invited hundreds of Indian leaders to gather at the town of Chillicothe on the Scioto River. There they formed the Scioto Confederacy, which pledged to oppose any further expansion into the Ohio country. Some British officers and administrators tried to protect Indian interests, while others encouraged their exploitation, leading to interpretive disagreements among historians (Interpretations).

Meanwhile, in London, the idea that the Proclamation Line was only temporary gave way to the view that it should be permanent. Hillsborough, who became colonial secretary in 1768, adamantly opposed westward expansion, believing it would antagonize the Indians without benefitting the empire. Moreover, he owned vast Irish estates, and he was alarmed by the number of tenants who were leaving Ireland for America. To preserve Britain's laboring class, as well as control costs, Hillsborough wanted to make the Proclamation Line permanent.

For colonists who were already moving west to settle in large numbers, this shift in policy caused confusion and frustration. Eventually, like the Patriots along the seaboard, they would take matters into their own hands.

Parliament Wavers

In Britain, the colonies' nonimportation agreement was taking its toll. In 1768, the colonies had cut imports of British manufactures in half; by 1769, the mainland colonies had a trade surplus with Britain of £816,000. Hard-hit by these developments, British merchants and manufacturers petitioned Parliament to repeal the Townshend duties. Early in 1770, Lord North became prime minister. A witty man and a skillful politician, North designed a new compromise. Arguing that it was foolish to tax British exports to America (thereby raising their price and decreasing consumption), he persuaded Parliament to repeal most of the Townshend duties. However, North retained the tax on tea as a symbol of Parliament's supremacy (Figure 5.2).

> **IDENTIFY CAUSES**
> What groups were most interested in western lands, and why did Hillsborough oppose them?

FIGURE 5.2 Trade as a Political Weapon, 1763–1776
Political upheaval did not affect the mainland colonies' exports to Britain, which rose slightly over the period, but imports fluctuated greatly. The American boycott of 1765–1766 prompted a dip in imports, but the second boycott of 1768–1770 led to a sharp drop in imports of British textiles, metal goods, and ceramics. Imports of manufactures soared after the repeal of the Townshend duties, only to plummet when the First Continental Congress proclaimed a third boycott in 1774.

Beyond the Proclamation Line

Though the Royal Proclamation of 1763 called the territory between the Appalachian Mountains and the Mississippi River "Indian country," the reality was more complex than this phrase indicates. The following documents illustrate some of the patterns that shaped life beyond the Proclamation Line between 1763 and 1776.

1. **Colonel John Bradstreet's Thoughts on Indian Affairs, 1764.** *Colonel John Bradstreet led a force of British redcoats to Fort Niagara in response to Pontiac's Rebellion. He drafted these remarks shortly afterward.*

   Of all the Savages upon the continent, the most knowing, the most intriguing, the less useful, and the greatest Villains, are those most conversant with the Europeans, and deserve most the attention of Govern[men]t by way of correction, and these are the Six Nations, Shawanese and Delawares; they are well acquainted with the defenceless state of the Inhabitants, who live on the Frontiers, and think they will ever have it in their power to distress and plunder them, and never cease raising the jealousy of the Upper Nations against us, by propagating amongst them such stories, as make them believe the English have nothing so much at heart as the extirpation of all Savages. The apparent design of the Six Nations, is to keep us at war with all Savages, but themselves, that they may be employed as mediators between us and them.

2. **William Johnson to the British Lords of Trade, 1763.** *William Johnson, a New Yorker with extensive experience in Indian relations, was the crown's superintendent for Indian affairs in the northern colonies.*

   [T]he Colonies, had all along neglected to cultivate a proper understanding with the Indians, and from a mistaken notion, have greatly dispised them, without considering, that it is in their power at pleasure to lay waste and destroy the Frontiers. . . . Without any exageration, I look upon the Northern Indians to be the most formidable of any uncivilized body of people in the World. Hunting and War are their sole occupations, and the one qualifies them for the other, they have few wants, and those are easily supplied, their properties of little value, consequently, expeditions against them however successful, cannot distress them, and they have courage sufficient for their manner of fighting, the nature and situation of their Countrys, require not more.

3. **"Indians Giving a Talk to Colonel Bouquet," 1766.** *Based on a painting by Benjamin West, this engraving from a book about Bouquet's campaign to the Ohio following Pontiac's Rebellion depicts a meeting with Delaware, Seneca, and Shawnee representatives in October 1764.*

SOURCE: The Granger Collection, New York.

4. **David Jones's journal, 1773.** *David Jones was a Baptist minister who traveled down the Ohio River in 1772 and 1773. His journal offers a compelling glimpse of life in the valley's trading communities.*

   FRIDAY [January] 22, in company with Mr. Irwine, set out for Chillicaathee. . . . Here Mr. Irwine kept an assortment of goods, and for that purpose rented an house from an Indian whose name is *Waappee Monneeto*, often called the White Devil. . . . Went to see Mr. Moses Henry a gunsmith and trader from Lancaster. This gentleman has lived for some years in this town, and is lawfully married to a white woman, who was captivated so young that she speaks the language as well as any Indian. . . .

Mr. Henry lives in a comfortable manner, having plenty of good beef, pork, milk, &c. . . . Chillicaathee is the chief town of the Shawanee Indians — it is situated north of a large plain adjacent to a branch of Paint Creek. This plain is their corn-field, which supplies great part of their town. Their houses are made of logs. . . .

WEDNESDAY [February] 10. . . . This is a small town consisting of Delawares and Shawanees. The chief is a Shawanee woman, who is esteemed very rich — she entertains travelers — there were four of us in company, and for our use, her negro quarter was evacuated this night, which had a fire in the middle without any chimney. This woman has a large stock, and supplied us with milk. Here we also got corn for our horses at a very expensive price. . . .

FRIDAY [February] 12 . . . We passed [the Delaware chief] Captain White Eye's Town. . . . He told me that he intended to be religious, and have his children educated. He saw that their way of living would not answer much longer — game grew scarce — they could not much longer pretend to live by hunting, but must farm, &c. — But said, he could not attend to matters of religion now, for he intended to make a great *hunt* down Ohio, and take the skins himself to Philadelphia.

5. Killbuck to the governors of Pennsylvania, Maryland, and Virginia, December 1771. *John Killbuck Jr., or Gelelemend, a Delaware headman, aired grievances on behalf of Ohio Delaware, Munsie, and Mahican Indians.*

Great numbers more of your people have come over the Great Mountains and settled throughout this country, and we are sorry to tell you, that several quarrels have happened between your people and ours, in which people have been killed on both sides, and that we now see the nations round us and your people ready to embroil in a quarrel, which gives our nations great concerns, as we, on our parts, want to live in friendship with you. As you have always told us, you have laws to govern your people by, — but we do not see that you have; therefore, brethren, unless you can fall upon some method of governing your people who live between the Great Mountains and the Ohio River and who are now very numerous, it will be out of the Indians' power to govern their young men, for we assure you the black clouds begin to gather fast in this country. . . . We find your people are very fond of our rich land. We see them quarrelling every day about land and burning one another's houses, so that we do not know how soon they may come over the river Ohio and drive us from our villages, nor do we see you, brothers, take any care to stop them.

6. Aeneas MacKay to Pennsylvania governor John Penn, April 4, 1774. *MacKay, a magistrate of Pennsylvania's Westmoreland County, reported on Virginia's effort to create a competing jurisdiction in the vicinity of Pittsburgh. Dr. John Connolly, appointed by Governor Dunmore as commander of the militia in Pittsburgh, was at the center of the controversy.*

Since the return of the Celebrated Doctor Connelly from Virginia last to this place, which he did on the 28th of March, our village is become the scene of anarchy and Confusion. . . .

The Doctor now is in actual possession of the Fort, with a Body Guard of Militia about him, Invested, as we are told, with both Civil & military power, to put the Virginia Law in Force in these parts, and a considerable Number of the Inhabitants of these back Parts of this Country, Ready to join him on any emergency, every artifice are used to seduce the people, some by being promoted to Civil or military employments, and others with the promises of grants of Lands, on easy Terms, & the giddy headed mobs are so Infatuated as to suffer themselves to be carried away by these Insinuating Delusions. . . .

The Indians are greatly alarmed at seeing parties of armed men patrolling through our streets Daily, not knowing but there is hostility intended against them and their country.

SOURCES: (1, 2) E. B. O'Callaghan and Berthold Fernow, eds., *Documents Relative to the Colonial History of the State of New York*, 15 vols. (Albany, 1856–1887), 7: 690–694, 574; (4) David Jones, *A Journal of Two Visits Made to Some Nations of Indians on the West Side of the River Ohio, in the Years 1772 and 1773* (Burlington, 1774 [rep. NY, 1971]); (5) K. G. Davies, ed., *Documents of the American Revolution, 1770–1783*, 19 vols. (Shannon and Dublin, 1972–1981), 3: 254–255; (6) Samuel Hazard, ed., *Pennsylvania Archives*, series 1, 12 vols. (Philadelphia: Joseph Severns & Co., 1856), 4: 484–486.

ANALYZING THE EVIDENCE

1. John Bradstreet, a career British army officer, based his observations (source 1) on his wartime experiences in the West. William Johnson (source 2) had lived in close proximity to Iroquois Indians for many years. Compare their views: what do they agree upon, and where do they differ?

2. Charles Grignion's engraving (source 3) appeared in print a short time after Pontiac's Rebellion. How does it portray the Ohio Indians? Compare Grignion's image with the descriptions in sources 1 and 2 and John Killbuck's speech (source 5). What parallels or differences do you see?

3. What do you find most surprising about source 4? What evidence of European influence do you see in the Indian towns Jones describes?

4. Sources 5 and 6 describe the state of affairs on the upper Ohio shortly before the outbreak of Dunmore's War. What concerns does Killbuck express? Why was Virginia's willingness to organize a militia so important to the residents of the region?

PUTTING IT ALL TOGETHER

Using these documents and what you have learned in Chapter 5, write a short essay that surveys British and Anglo-American attitudes toward the Ohio Indians and explores the contradictions between these attitudes and the reality of life in the Ohio country.

Did British Administrators Try to Protect or Exploit Native Americans?

Despite official British policy to prohibit colonial settlement west of the Proclamation Line of 1763, Anglo-American colonists nonetheless continued to push into the Ohio Valley (see Map 5.5, p. 164). Not surprisingly, the Indian peoples living in the Ohio Valley continued to be alarmed at the influx. In an effort to manage the empire and the potential for conflict, British officials had to balance relations with the Indian nations while also preventing conflict between Indians and Anglo-American colonists. In the excerpts below, historians Eric Hinderaker (one of the authors of this textbook) and Gregory Evans Dowd highlight one aspect of this conflict: British imperial policy toward the Indian nations.

ERIC HINDERAKER

SOURCE: Eric Hinderaker, *Elusive Empires: Constructing Colonialism in the Ohio Valley, 1673–1800* (Cambridge: Cambridge University Press, 1997), 175.

Officers of empire and Indian leaders had consistently sought, through long years of association, to create patterns of leadership and diplomacy that would mute conflict and encourage accommodation. . . . The collapse of British authority in the Ohio Valley dealt the final blow to the already badly weakened principles of accommodation and mediation.

GREGORY EVANS DOWD

SOURCE: Gregory Evans Dowd, *War Under Heaven: Pontiac, the Indian Nations, & the British Empire* (Baltimore: The Johns Hopkins University Press, 2002), 175.

Official policy, highly confused though it was, tended to place Indians far beyond the rule of law, and it intended, even in the long run, to keep them there by pushing them away from any civil jurisdiction in the colonies. . . . During the war . . . officers urged, ordered, and approved the indiscriminate slaughter of Indians.

QUESTIONS FOR ANALYSIS

1. Identify the major difference between these two historians' arguments concerning British policy toward Native Americans.

2. How does each historian assess the effectiveness of British imperial officials in managing relations with Native Americans?

3. How does the textbook's discussion of Anglo-American settlers in the Ohio Valley support or challenge each of the historians' arguments regarding British policy?

The Boston Massacre Even as Parliament was debating North's repeal, events in Boston guaranteed that reconciliation between Patriots and Parliament would be hard to achieve. Between 1,200 and 2,000 troops had been stationed in Boston for a year and a half. Soldiers were also stationed in New York, Philadelphia, several towns in New Jersey, and various frontier outposts in these years, with a minimum of conflict or violence. But in Boston — a small port town on a tiny peninsula — the troops numbered 10 percent of the local population, and their presence wore on the locals. On the night of March 5, 1770, a group of nine British redcoats fired into a crowd and killed five townspeople. A subsequent trial exonerated the soldiers, but Boston's Radical Whigs, convinced of a ministerial conspiracy against liberty, labeled the incident a "massacre" and used it to rally sentiment against imperial power.

Sovereignty Debated When news of North's compromise arrived in the colonies in the wake of the Boston Massacre, the reaction was mixed. Most of Britain's colonists remained loyal to the empire, but five years of conflict had taken their toll. In 1765, American leaders had accepted Parliament's authority; the Stamp Act Resolves had opposed only certain "unconstitutional" legislation. By 1770, the most outspoken Patriots — Benjamin Franklin in Pennsylvania, Patrick Henry in Virginia, and Samuel Adams in Massachusetts — repudiated parliamentary supremacy and claimed equality for the American assemblies within the empire. Franklin suggested that the colonies were now "distinct and separate states" with "the same Head, or Sovereign, the King."

Patriot Propaganda Silversmith Paul Revere issued this engraving of the confrontation between British redcoats and snowball-throwing Bostonians in the days after it occurred. To whip up opposition to the military occupation of their town, Revere and other Patriots labeled the incident "The Boston Massacre." The shooting confirmed their Radical Whig belief that "standing armies" were instruments of tyranny. Library of Congress.

Franklin's suggestion outraged Thomas Hutchinson, the American-born royal governor of Massachusetts. Hutchinson emphatically rejected the idea of "two independent legislatures in one and the same state." He told the Massachusetts assembly, "I know of no line that can be drawn between the supreme authority of Parliament and the total independence of the colonies."

There the matter rested. The British had twice imposed revenue acts on the colonies, and American Patriots had twice forced a retreat. If Parliament insisted on a policy of constitutional absolutism by imposing taxes a third time, some Americans were prepared to pursue violent resistance. Nor did they flinch when reminded that George III condemned their agitation. As the Massachusetts House replied to Hutchinson, "There is more reason to dread the consequences of absolute uncontrolled supreme power, whether of a nation or a monarch, than those of total independence." Fearful of civil war, Lord North's ministry hesitated to force the issue.

> **TRACE CHANGE OVER TIME**
> What was Benjamin Franklin's position on colonial representation in 1765, and why had his view changed by 1770?

> **IN YOUR OWN WORDS** What was the relationship between formal protests against Parliament and popular resistance in the years between 1765 and 1770?

The Road to Independence, 1771–1776

Repeal of the Townshend duties in 1770 restored harmony to the British Empire, but strong feelings and mutual distrust lay just below the surface. In 1773, those emotions erupted, destroying any hope of compromise. Within two years, the Americans and the British clashed in armed conflict. Despite widespread resistance among loyal colonists, Patriot legislators created provisional governments and military forces, the two essentials for independence.

A Compromise Repudiated

Once aroused, political passions are not easily quieted. In Boston, Samuel Adams and other radical Patriots continued to warn Americans of imperial domination and, late in 1772, persuaded the town meeting to set up a committee of correspondence "to state the Rights of the Colonists of this Province." Soon, eighty Massachusetts towns had similar committees. When British officials threatened to seize the Americans responsible for the burning of the customs vessel *Gaspée* and prosecute them in Britain, the Virginia House of Burgesses and several other assemblies set up their own **committees of correspondence**. These standing committees allowed Patriots to communicate with leaders in other colonies when new threats to liberty occurred. By 1774, among the colonies that would later declare independence, only Pennsylvania was without one.

The East India Company and the Tea Act
These committees sprang into action when Parliament passed the **Tea Act of May 1773**. The act provided financial relief for the East India Company, a royally chartered private corporation that served as the instrument of British imperialism. The company was deeply in debt; it also had a huge surplus of tea as a result of high import duties, which led Britons and colonists alike to drink smuggled Dutch tea instead. The Tea Act gave the company a government loan and, to boost its revenue, canceled the import duties on tea the company exported to Ireland and the American colonies. Now even with the Townshend duty of 3 pence a pound on tea, high-quality East India Company tea would cost less than the Dutch tea smuggled into the colonies by American merchants.

Radical Patriots accused the British ministry of bribing Americans with the cheaper East India Company tea so they would give up their principled opposition to the tea tax. As an anonymous woman wrote to the *Massachusetts Spy*, "The use of [British] tea is considered not as a private but as a public evil . . . a handle to introduce a variety of . . . oppressions amongst us." Merchants joined the protest because the East India Company planned to distribute its tea directly to shopkeepers, excluding American wholesalers from the trade's profits. "The fear of an Introduction of a Monopoly in this Country," British general Frederick Haldimand reported from New York, "has induced the mercantile part of the Inhabitants to be very industrious in opposing this Step and added Strength to a Spirit of Independence already too prevalent."

The Tea Party and the Coercive Acts
The Sons of Liberty prevented East India Company ships from delivering their cargoes in New York, Philadelphia, and Charleston. In Massachusetts, Royal Governor Hutchinson was determined to land the tea and collect the tax. To foil the governor's plan, artisans and laborers disguised as Indians boarded three ships — the *Dartmouth*, the *Eleanor*, and the *Beaver* — on December 16, 1773, broke open 342 chests of tea (valued at about £10,000, or about $900,000 today), and threw them into the harbor. "This destruction of the Tea . . . must have so important Consequences," John Adams wrote in his diary, "that I cannot but consider it as an Epoch in History."

The king was outraged. "Concessions have made matters worse," George III declared. "The time has come for compulsion." Early in 1774, Parliament passed four **Coercive Acts** to force Massachusetts to pay for the tea and to submit to imperial

CONSIDER POINTS OF VIEW
Why did colonists react so strongly against the Tea Act, which imposed a small tax and actually lowered the price of tea?

authority. The Boston Port Bill closed Boston Harbor to shipping; the Massachusetts Government Act annulled the colony's charter and prohibited most town meetings; a new Quartering Act mandated new barracks for British troops; and the Justice Act allowed trials for capital crimes to be transferred to other colonies or to Britain.

Patriot leaders throughout the colonies branded the measures "Intolerable" and rallied support for Massachusetts. In Georgia, a Patriot warned the "Freemen of the Province" that "every privilege you at present claim as a birthright, may be wrested from you by the same authority that blockades the town of Boston." "The cause of Boston," George Washington declared in Virginia, "now is and ever will be considered as the cause of America." The committees of correspondence had created a firm sense of Patriot unity.

In 1774, Parliament also passed the Quebec Act, which allowed the practice of Roman Catholicism in Quebec. This concession to Quebec's predominantly Catholic population reignited religious passions in New England, where Protestants associated Catholicism with arbitrary royal government. Because the act extended Quebec's boundaries into the Ohio River Valley, it also angered influential land speculators in Virginia and Pennsylvania and ordinary settlers by the thousands (Map 5.4). Although the ministry did not intend the Quebec Act as a coercive measure, many colonists saw it as further proof of Parliament's intention to control American affairs.

The Continental Congress Responds

In response to the Coercive Acts, Patriot leaders convened a new continent-wide body, the **Continental Congress**. Twelve mainland colonies sent representatives. Four recently acquired colonies — Florida, Quebec, Nova Scotia, and Newfoundland — refused to send delegates, as did Georgia, where the royal governor controlled the legislature. The assemblies of Barbados, Jamaica, and the other sugar islands, although wary of British domination, were even more fearful of revolts by their predominantly African populations and therefore declined to attend.

The delegates who met in Philadelphia in September 1774 had different agendas. Southern representatives, fearing a British plot "to overturn the constitution and introduce a system of arbitrary government," advocated a new economic boycott. Independence-minded representatives from New England demanded political union and defensive military preparations. Many delegates from the Middle Atlantic colonies favored compromise.

Led by Joseph Galloway of Pennsylvania, these men of "loyal principles" proposed a new political system similar to Benjamin Franklin's proposal at the Albany Congress of 1754: each colony would retain its assembly to legislate on local matters, and a new continent-wide body would handle general American affairs. The king would appoint a president-general to preside over a legislative council selected by the colonial assemblies. Galloway's plan failed by a single vote; a bare majority thought it was too conciliatory (Analyzing Voices).

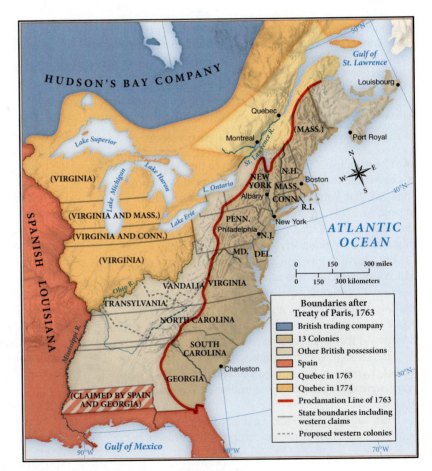

MAP 5.4 British Western Policy, 1763–1774
The Proclamation of 1763 prohibited white settlement west of the Appalachian Mountains. Nonetheless, Anglo-American settlers and land speculators proposed the new colonies of Vandalia and Transylvania to the west of Virginia and North Carolina. The Quebec Act of 1774 designated most western lands as Indian reserves and vastly enlarged the boundaries of Quebec, dashing speculators' hopes and eliminating the old sea-to-sea land claims of many seaboard colonies. The act especially angered New England Protestants, who condemned it for allowing French residents to practice Catholicism, and colonial political leaders, who protested its failure to provide Quebec with a representative assembly.

The Debate over Representation and Sovereignty

These two documents offer formal statements of political principles. To analyze them effectively, think carefully about the ways in which the abstract ideas they express might shape the lives of ordinary people. Why did Parliament believe the taxing power was essential to its authority? Why would colonists disagree? And why would people like Joseph Galloway want to find a way to reconcile their differences? Consider what motivated the authors of these documents as you read them; then turn to the Questions for Analysis that follow.

Speaking before the House of Commons, Benjamin Franklin declared that before 1763 Americans had paid little attention to the question of Parliament's "right to lay taxes and duties" in the colonies. The reason was simple, Franklin said: "A right to lay internal taxes was never supposed to be in Parliament, as we are not represented there." Franklin recognized that representation was central to the imperial debate. As the following selections show, the failure to solve the problem of representation, and the closely related issue of parliamentary sovereignty, led to the American rebellion.

JARED INGERSOLL
Report on the Debates in Parliament (1765)

Connecticut lawyer Jared Ingersoll (1722–1781) served as his colony's agent, or lobbyist, in Britain. In this 1765 letter to the governor of Connecticut, Ingersoll summarizes the debate then under way in Parliament over the Stamp Act. When the act passed, he returned home to become the stamp distributor in Connecticut. A mob forced him to resign that post. Ingersoll later served as a vice-admiralty judge in Philadelphia and, during the Revolution, remained loyal to Britain.

SOURCE: New Haven Colony Historical Society, *Papers* (1918), 9: 306–315.

❝ The principal Attention has been to the Stamp bill that has been preparing to Lay before Parliament for taxing America. The Point of the Authority of Parliament to impose such Tax I found on my Arrival here was so fully and Universally yielded [accepted], that there was not the least hopes of making any impressions that way. . . .

I beg leave to give you a Summary of the Arguments which are made use of in favour of such Authority. The House of Commons, say they, is a branch of the supreme legislature of the Nation, and which in its Nature is supposed to represent, or rather to stand in the place of, the Commons, that is, of the great body of the people. . . .

That this house of Commons, therefore, is now . . . a part of the Supreme unlimited power of the Nation, as in every State there must be some unlimited Power and Authority. . . .

They say a Power to tax is a necessary part of every Supreme Legislative Authority, and that if they have not that

Power over America, they have none, and then America is at once a Kingdom of itself.

On the other hand those who oppose the bill say, it is true the Parliament have a supreme unlimited Authority over every Part and Branch of the Kings dominions and as well over Ireland as any other place.

Yet [they say] we believe a British parliament will never think it prudent to tax Ireland [or America]. Tis true they say, that the Commons of England and of the British Empire are all represented in and by the house of Commons, but this representation is confessedly on all hands by Construction and Virtual [because most British subjects] . . . have no hand in choosing the representatives. . . .

[They say further] that the Effects of this implied Representation here and in America must be infinitely different in the Article of Taxation. . . . By any Mistake an act of Parliament is made that prove injurious and hard the Member of Parliament here [in Britain] sees with his own Eyes and is moreover very accessible to the people. . . . [Also,] the taxes are laid equally by one Rule and fall as well on the Member himself as on the people. But as to America, from the great distance in point of Situation [they are not represented in the same way]. . . .

[Finally, the opponents of the Act say] we already by the Regulations upon their trade draw from the Americans all that they can spare. . . . This Step [of taxation] should not take place until or unless the Americans are allowed to send Members to Parliament.

Thus I have given you, I think, the Substance of the Arguments on both sides of that great and important

---

Instead, the delegates demanded the repeal of the Coercive Acts and stipulated that British control be limited to matters of trade. They also approved a program of economic retaliation: Americans would stop importing British goods in December 1774. If Parliament did not repeal the Coercive Acts by September 1775, the Congress vowed to cut off virtually all colonial exports to Britain, Ireland, and the British West Indies. Ten years of constitutional conflict had culminated in a threat of all-out commercial warfare.

Question of the right and also of the Expediency of taxing America by Authority of Parliament. . . . [But] upon a Division of the house upon the Question, there was about 250 to about 50 in favour of the Bill. 99

JOSEPH GALLOWAY
Plan of Union (1775)

Speaker of the Pennsylvania assembly Joseph Galloway was a delegate to the First Continental Congress, where he proposed a plan that addressed the issue of representation. The colonies would remain British but operate under a continental government with the power to veto parliamentary laws that affected America. Radical Patriots in the Congress, who favored independence, prevented a vote on Galloway's plan and suppressed mention of it in the records. Galloway remained loyal to the crown, fought on the British side in the War for Independence, and moved to England in 1778.

SOURCE: Joseph Galloway, *Historical and Political Reflections on the Rise and Progress of the American Rebellion* (London, 1780), 70.

66 If we sincerely mean to accommodate the difference between the two countries, . . . we must take into consideration a number of facts which led the Parliament to pass the acts complained of. . . . [You will recall] the dangerous situation of the Colonies from the intrigues of France, and the incursions of the Canadians and their Indian allies, at the commencement of the last war. . . . Great-Britain sent over her fleets and armies for their protection. . . .

In this state of the Colonies, it was not unreasonable to expect that Parliament would have levied a tax on them proportionate to their wealth, . . . Parliament was naturally led to exercise the power which had been, by its predecessors, so often exercised over the Colonies, and to pass the Stamp Act. Against this act, the Colonies petitioned Parliament, and denied its authority . . . [declaring] that the Colonies could not be represented in that body. This justly alarmed the British Senate. It was thought and called by the ablest men [in] Britain, a clear and explicit declaration of the American Independence, and compelled the Parliament to pass the Declaratory Act, in order to save its ancient and incontrovertible right of supremacy over all the parts of the empire. . . .

Having thus briefly stated the arguments in favour of parliamentary authority, . . . I am free to confess that the exercise of that authority is not perfectly constitutional in respect to the Colonies. We know that the whole landed interest of Britain is represented in that body, while neither the land nor the people of America hold the least participation in the legislative authority of the State. . . . Representation, or a participation in the supreme councils of the State, is the great principle upon which the freedom of the British Government is established and secured.

I wish to see . . . the right to participate in the supreme councils of the State extended, in some form . . . to America . . . [and therefore] have prepared the draught of a plan for uniting America more intimately, in constitutional policy, with Great-Britain. . . . I am certain when dispassionately considered, it will be found to be the most perfect union in power and liberty with the Parent State, next to a representation in Parliament, and I trust it will be approved of by both countries.

The Plan
That the several [colonial] assemblies shall [form an American union and] choose members for the grand council. . . .

That the Grand Council . . . shall hold and exercise all the like rights, liberties and privileges, as are held and exercised by and in the House of Commons of Great-Britain. . . .

That the President-General shall hold his office during the pleasure of the King, and his assent shall be requisite to all acts of the Grand Council, and it shall be his office and duty to cause them to be carried into execution. . . .

That the President-General, by and with the advice and consent of the Grand-Council, hold and exercise all the legislative rights, powers, and authorities, necessary for regulating and administering all the general police and affairs of the colonies. . . .

That the said President-General and the Grand Council, be an inferior and distinct branch of the British legislature, united and incorporated with it, . . . and that the assent of both [Parliament and the Grand Council] shall be requisite to the validity of all such general acts or statutes [that affect the colonies]. 99

QUESTIONS FOR ANALYSIS

1. According to Ingersoll, what were the main arguments of those in Parliament who opposed the Stamp Act? Did those opposing the Stamp Act agree with the act's supporters that Parliament had the right to tax the colonies?

2. How did Galloway's plan solve the problem of colonial representation in Parliament? How would the British ministers who advocated parliamentary supremacy have reacted to the plan?

3. The framers of the U.S. Constitution addressed the problem of dividing authority between state governments and the national government by allowing the states to retain legal authority over most matters and delegating limited powers to the national government. Could such a solution have been implemented in the British Empire? Why or why not?

A few British leaders still hoped for compromise. In January 1775, William Pitt, now sitting in the House of Lords as the Earl of Chatham, asked Parliament to renounce its power to tax the colonies and to recognize the Continental Congress as a lawful body. In return, he suggested, the Congress should acknowledge parliamentary supremacy and provide a permanent source of revenue to help defray the national debt.

Lord North Frederick North, the second earl of Guilford, served as George III's prime minister from 1770 until the end of the American Revolution. He began his term of service by seeking reconciliation with the colonies. In that spirit, he championed the repeal of most of the Townshend duties. After the destruction of the East India Company tea in Boston, however, Lord North pursued a hard line, sponsoring the Coercive Acts and insisting that Boston should pay for the tea it destroyed. In taking this approach, North had the full support of the king, who was appalled by the destruction of the tea and believed that the colonies had to be pressed to acknowledge British authority. The Granger Collection, New York.

> **COMPARE AND CONTRAST**
> Why did Parliament prefer North's solution to the Boston Tea Party to William Pitt's?

The British ministry rejected Pitt's plan. Twice it had backed down in the face of colonial resistance; a third retreat was impossible. Branding the Continental Congress an illegal assembly, the ministry rejected Lord Dartmouth's proposal to send commissioners to negotiate a settlement. Instead, Lord North set stringent terms: Americans must pay for their own defense and administration and acknowledge Parliament's authority to tax them. To put teeth in these demands, North imposed a naval blockade on American trade with foreign nations and ordered General Gage to suppress dissent in Massachusetts. "Now the case seemed desperate," the prime minister told Thomas Hutchinson, whom the Patriots had forced into exile in London. "Parliament would not — could not — concede." North predicted that the crisis "must come to violence."

The Rising of the Countryside

The fate of the urban-led Patriot movement would depend on the colonies' large rural population. Most farmers had little interest in imperial affairs. Their lives were deeply rooted in the soil, and their prime allegiance was to family and community. But imperial policies had increasingly intruded into the lives of farm families by sending their sons to war and raising their taxes. In 1754, farmers on Long Island, New York, had paid an average tax of 10 shillings; by 1756, thanks to the Great War for Empire, their taxes had jumped to 30 shillings.

The Continental Association The boycotts of 1765 and 1768 raised the political consciousness of rural Americans. When the First Continental Congress established the **Continental Association** in 1774 to enforce a third boycott of British goods, it quickly set up a rural network of committees to do its work. In Concord, Massachusetts, 80 percent of the male heads of families and a number of single women signed a "Solemn League and Covenant" supporting nonimportation. In other farm towns, men blacked their faces, disguised themselves in blankets "like Indians," and threatened violence against shopkeepers who traded "in rum, molasses, & Sugar, &c." in violation of the boycott.

Patriots likewise warned that British measures threatened the yeoman tradition of landownership. In Petersham, Massachusetts, the town meeting worried that new British taxes would drain "this People of the Fruits of their Toil." Arable land was now scarce and expensive in older communities, and in new settlements merchants were seizing farmsteads for delinquent debts. By the 1770s, many northern yeomen felt personally threatened by British policies, which, a Patriot pamphlet warned, were "paving the way for reducing the country to lordships" (Table 5.2).

Southern Planters Fear Dependency Despite their higher standard of living, southern slave owners had similar fears. Many Chesapeake planters were deeply in debt to British merchants. Accustomed to being absolute masters on their slave-labor plantations and seeing themselves as guardians of English liberties, planters resented their financial dependence on British creditors and dreaded the prospect of political subservience to British officials.

That danger now seemed real. If Parliament used the Coercive Acts to subdue Massachusetts, then it might turn next to Virginia, dissolving its representative assembly and assisting British merchants to seize debt-burdened properties. Consequently, the Virginia gentry supported demands by indebted yeomen farmers to close the law courts so that they could bargain with merchants over debts without the threat of legal action. "The spark of liberty is not yet extinct among our people," declared one planter, "and if properly fanned by the Gentlemen of influence will, I make no doubt, burst out again into a flame."

Loyalists and Neutrals

Yet in many places, the Patriot movement was a hard sell. In Virginia, Patriot leaders were nearly all wealthy planters, and many of their poorer neighbors regarded the

TABLE 5.2		
Patriot Resistance, 1762–1776		
Date	**British Action**	**Patriot Response**
1762	Revenue Act	Merchants complain privately
1763	Proclamation Line	Land speculators voice discontent
1764	Sugar Act	Merchants and Massachusetts legislature protest
1765	Stamp Act	Sons of Liberty riot; Stamp Act Congress; first boycott of British goods
1765	Quartering Act	New York assembly refuses to fund until 1767
1767–1768	Townshend Act; military occupation of Boston	Second boycott of British goods; harassment of pro-British merchants
1772	Royal commission to investigate *Gaspée* affair	Committees of correspondence form
1773	Tea Act	Widespread resistance; Boston Tea Party
1774	Coercive Acts; Quebec Act	First Continental Congress; third boycott of British goods
1775	British raids near Boston; king's Proclamation for Suppressing Rebellion and Sedition	Armed resistance; Second Continental Congress; invasion of Canada; cutoff of colonial exports
1776	Military attacks led by royal governors in South	Paine's *Common Sense*; Declaration of Independence

movement with suspicion. In regions where great landowners became Patriots — the Hudson River Valley of New York, for example — many tenant farmers supported the king because they hated their landlords. Similar social conflicts prompted some Regulators in the North Carolina backcountry and many farmers in eastern Maryland to oppose the Patriots there.

There were many reasons to resist the Patriot movement. Skeptics believed that Patriot leaders were subverting British rule only to advance their own selfish interests. Peter Oliver wrote of Samuel Adams, for example, "He was so thorough a Machiavilian, that he divested himself of every worthy Principle, & would stick at no Crime to accomplish his Ends." Some "Gentlemen of influence" worried that resistance to Britain would undermine all political institutions and "introduce Anarchy and disorder and render life and property here precarious." Their fears increased when the Sons of Liberty used intimidation and violence to uphold the boycotts. One well-to-do New Yorker complained, "No man can be in a more abject state of bondage than he whose Reputation, Property and Life are exposed to the discretionary violence . . . of the community." As the crisis deepened, such men became Loyalists — so called because they remained loyal to the British crown.

Many other colonists simply hoped to stay out of the fray. Some did so on principle: in New Jersey and Pennsylvania, thousands of pacifist Quakers and Germans resisted conscription and violence out of religious conviction. Others were ambivalent or confused about the political crisis unfolding around them. The delegate elected to New York's Provincial Congress from Queen's County, on Long Island, chose not to attend since "the people [he represented] seemed to be much inclined to remain peaceable and quiet." More than three-fourths of Queen's County voters, in fact, opposed sending any delegate at all. Many loyal or neutral colonists hoped, above all, to preserve their families' property and independence, whatever the outcome of the imperial crisis.

Historians estimate that some 15 to 20 percent of the white population — perhaps as many as 400,000 colonists — were loyal to the crown. Some managed to avoid persecution, but many were pressured by their neighbors to join the boycotts and subjected to violence and humiliation if they refused. As Patriots took over the reins of local government throughout the colonies, Loyalists were driven out of their homes or forced into silence. At this crucial juncture, Patriots commanded the allegiance, or at least the acquiescence, of the majority of white Americans.

> **IN YOUR OWN WORDS** What actions did the Continental Association take to support the efforts of the Continental Congress?

Violence East and West

By 1774, British authority was wavering. At the headwaters of the Ohio, the abandonment of Fort Pitt left a power vacuum that was filled by opportunistic men, led by a royally appointed governor acting in defiance of his commission. In Massachusetts, the attempt to isolate and punish Boston and the surrounding countryside backfired as Patriots resisted military coercion. Violence resulted in both places, and with it the collapse of imperial control.

Lord Dunmore's War

In the years since the end of Pontiac's Rebellion, at least 10,000 people had traveled along Braddock's and Forbes's Roads to the headwaters of the Ohio River, where Fort Pitt had replaced Fort Duquesne during the Great War for Empire, and staked claims to land around Pittsburgh (Map 5.5). They relied for protection on Fort Pitt, which remained one of Britain's most important frontier outposts. But the revenue crisis forced General Gage to cut expenses, and in October 1772, the army pulled down the fort's log walls and left the site to the local population. Settler relations with the neighboring Ohio Indians were tenuous and ill-defined, and the fort's abandonment left them exposed and vulnerable.

In the ensuing power vacuum, Pennsylvania and Virginia both claimed the region. Pennsylvania had the better claim on paper. It had organized county governments, established courts, and collected taxes there. But—in keeping with its pacifist Quaker roots—it did not organize a militia. In this omission, Virginia's royal governor, the Earl of Dunmore, recognized an opportunity. Appointed to his post in 1771, Dunmore was an irascible and unscrupulous man who clashed repeatedly with the House of Burgesses. But when it suited him, he was just as willing to defy the crown. In 1773, he traveled to Pittsburgh, where, he later wrote, "the people flocked about me and beseeched me . . . to appoint magistrates and officers of militia." He organized a local militia; soon, men armed by Virginia were drilling near the ruins of Fort Pitt.

In the summer of 1774, Dunmore took the next step. In defiance of both his royal instructions and the House of Burgesses, he called out Virginia's militia and led a force of 2,400 men against the Ohio Shawnees, who had a long-standing claim to Kentucky as a hunting

MAP 5.5 The Ohio Country, 1774–1775
The erosion of British imperial authority caused chaos in the Ohio country. Pennsylvania and Virginia each claimed Pittsburgh and the surrounding countryside, while the Indian communities on the upper Ohio increasingly feared colonist aggression. Their fears were realized in the summer of 1774, when Lord Dunmore led a force of Virginia militia into the valley. After defeating a Shawnee force in the Battle of Point Pleasant, many Virginians began surveying and staking claims to land in the Kentucky bluegrass. In the summer of 1775, perhaps a dozen new towns were settled there, in violation of the Royal Proclamation of 1763 and the Quebec Act of 1774.

ground. They fought a single battle, at Point Pleasant; the Shawnees were defeated, and Dunmore and his militia forces claimed Kentucky as their own. A participant justified his actions shortly afterward: "When without a king," he wrote, "[one] doeth according to the freedom of his own will." Years of neglect left many colonists in the backcountry feeling abandoned by the crown. **Dunmore's War** was their declaration of independence.

PLACE EVENTS IN CONTEXT
What led to Dunmore's War, and why did western settlers support it?

Armed Resistance in Massachusetts

Meanwhile, as the Continental Congress gathered in Philadelphia in September 1774, Massachusetts was also defying British authority. In August, a Middlesex County Congress had urged Patriots to close the existing royal courts and to transfer their political allegiance to the popularly elected House of Representatives. Subsequently, armed crowds harassed Loyalists and ensured Patriot rule in most of New England.

In response, General Thomas Gage, now the military governor of Massachusetts, ordered British troops in Boston in September 1774 to seize Patriot armories in nearby Charlestown and Cambridge. An army of 20,000 militiamen quickly mobilized to safeguard other Massachusetts military depots. The Concord town meeting raised a defensive force, the famous **Minutemen**, to "Stand at a minutes warning in Case of alarm." Increasingly, Gage's authority was limited to Boston, where it rested on the bayonets of his 3,500 troops. Meanwhile, the Patriot-controlled Massachusetts assembly met in nearby Salem in open defiance of Parliament, collecting taxes, bolstering the militia, and assuming the responsibilities of government.

In London, the colonial secretary, Lord Dartmouth, proclaimed Massachusetts to be in "open rebellion" and ordered Gage to march against the "rude rabble." On the night of April 18, 1775, Gage dispatched 700 soldiers to capture colonial leaders and supplies at Concord. However, Paul Revere and a series of other riders warned Patriots in many towns, and at dawn, militiamen confronted the British regulars first at Lexington and then at Concord. Those first skirmishes took a handful of lives, but as the British retreated to Boston, militia from neighboring towns repeatedly ambushed them. By the end of the day, 73 British soldiers were dead, 174 wounded, and 26 missing. British fire had killed 49 Massachusetts militiamen and wounded 39. Twelve years of economic and constitutional conflict had ended in violence.

The Second Continental Congress Organizes for War

A month later, in May 1775, Patriot leaders gathered in Philadelphia for the **Second Continental Congress**. As the Congress opened, 3,000 British troops attacked American fortifications on Breed's Hill and Bunker Hill overlooking Boston. After three assaults and 1,000 casualties, they finally dislodged the Patriot militia. Inspired by his countrymen's valor, John Adams exhorted the Congress to rise to the "defense of American liberty" by creating a continental army. He nominated George Washington to lead it. After bitter debate, the Congress approved the proposals, but, Adams lamented, only "by bare majorities."

Congress Versus King George   Despite the bloodshed in Massachusetts, a majority in the Congress still hoped for reconciliation. Led by John Dickinson of Pennsylvania, these moderates won approval of a petition expressing loyalty to George III and asking for repeal of oppressive parliamentary legislation. But Samuel Adams, Patrick Henry, and other zealous Patriots drummed up support for a Declaration of the Causes and Necessities of Taking Up Arms. Americans dreaded the "calamities of civil war," the declaration asserted, but were "resolved to die Freemen rather than to live [as] slaves." George III failed to exploit the divisions among the Patriots; instead, in August 1775, he issued a Proclamation for Suppressing Rebellion and Sedition.

EXPLAIN CONSEQUENCES
How did the violence around Boston in the spring of 1775 affect proceedings in the Second Continental Congress?

Before the king's proclamation reached America, the radicals in the Congress had won support for an invasion of Canada to prevent a British attack from the north. Patriot forces easily defeated the British at Montreal; but in December 1775, they failed to capture Quebec City and withdrew. Meanwhile, American merchants waged the financial warfare promised at the First Continental Congress by cutting off exports to Britain and its West Indian sugar islands. Parliament retaliated with the Prohibitory Act, which outlawed all trade with the rebellious colonies.

Fighting in the South   Skirmishes between Patriot and Loyalist forces now broke out in the southern colonies. In Virginia, Patriots ousted Governor Dunmore and forced him to take refuge on a British warship in Chesapeake Bay. Branding the rebels "traitors," the governor organized two military forces: one white, the Queen's Own Loyal Virginians; and one black, the Ethiopian Regiment, which enlisted 1,000 slaves who had fled their Patriot owners. In November 1775, Dunmore issued a controversial proclamation promising freedom to black slaves and white indentured servants who joined the Loyalist cause. White planters denounced this "Diabolical scheme," claiming it "point[ed] a dagger to their Throats." A new rising of the black and white underclasses, as in Bacon's Rebellion in the 1670s, seemed a possibility. In Fincastle County in southwestern Virginia, Loyalist planter John Hiell urged workers to support the king, promising "a Servant man" that soon "he and all the negroes would get their freedom." Frightened by Dunmore's aggressive tactics, Patriot yeomen and tenants called for a final break with Britain.

In North Carolina, too, military clashes prompted demands for independence. Early in 1776, Josiah Martin, the colony's royal governor, raised a Loyalist force of 1,500 Scottish Highlanders in the backcountry. In response, Patriots mobilized the lowcountry militia and, in February, defeated Martin's army at the Battle of Moore's Creek Bridge, capturing more than 800 Highlanders. Following this victory, radical Patriots in the North Carolina assembly told its representatives to the Continental Congress to join with "other Colonies in declaring Independence, and forming foreign alliances." In May, the Virginia gentry followed suit: led by James Madison, Edmund Pendleton, and Patrick Henry, the Patriots met in convention and resolved unanimously to support independence.

Occupying Kentucky   Beginning in the spring of 1775, in the wake of Dunmore's War, independent parties of adventurers began to occupy the newly won lands of Kentucky. Daniel Boone led one group to the banks of the Kentucky River, where they established the town of Boonesborough; nearby was Lexington, named in honor of the Massachusetts town that had resisted British troops a few months earlier. The Shawnees and other Ohio Indians opposed the settlers, and colonists built their tiny towns in the form of stations to protect themselves — groups of cabins connected by palisades to form small forts.

These western settlers had complex political loyalties. Many had marched under Dunmore and hoped to receive recognition for their claims from the crown. But as the rebellion unfolded, most recognized that the Patriots' emphasis on liberty and equality

Daniel Boone Escorting Settlers Through the Cumberland Gap   In 1775 Daniel Boone led a group of prospective settlers into Kentucky on behalf of Richard Henderson, a North Carolina judge and self-appointed proprietor of a land speculation venture called the Transylvania Colony. Henderson's venture soon collapsed, but Boonesborough was one of perhaps a dozen towns founded in Kentucky in violation of crown policy that summer. Boone became a folk hero, and in the mid-nineteenth century George Caleb Bingham painted this memorable scene. Using biblical imagery (the woman on horseback recalls Mary riding into Bethlehem on a donkey) and dramatic lighting, Bingham portrays Boone as an agent of progress bringing civilization to a howling and dangerous wilderness. Washington University, St. Louis, USA/Bridgeman Images.

squared with their view of the world. They soon petitioned Virginia's rebel government, asking it to create a new county that would include the Kentucky settlements. They had "Fought and bled" for the land in Dunmore's War and now wanted to fight against the crown and its Indian allies in the Ohio country. Virginia agreed: in 1776, it organized six new frontier counties and sent arms and ammunition to Kentucky. In July, the Continental Congress followed suit, dispatching troops and arms to the Ohio River as well.

Thomas Paine's *Common Sense*

As military conflicts escalated, Americans were divided in their opinions of King George III. Many blamed him for supporting oppressive legislation and ordering armed retaliation, but other influential colonists held out the hope that he might mediate their conflict with Parliament. John Dickinson, whose *Letters* did so much to arouse Patriot resistance in 1768, nevertheless believed that war with Great Britain would be folly. In July 1775, he persuaded Congress to send George III the Olive Branch Petition, which pleaded with the king to negotiate. John Adams, a staunch supporter of independence, was infuriated by Dickinson's waffling. But Dickinson had many supporters, both inside and outside of Congress. For example, many of Philadelphia's Quaker and Anglican merchants were neutrals or Loyalists. In response to their passivity, Patriot artisans in the city organized a Mechanics' Association to protect America's "just Rights and Privileges."

With popular sentiment in flux, a single brief pamphlet helped tip the balance. In January 1776, Thomas Paine published *Common Sense*, a rousing call for independence and a republican form of government. Paine had served as a minor customs official in England until he was fired for joining a protest against low wages. In 1774, Paine migrated to Philadelphia, where he met Benjamin Rush and other Patriots who shared his republican sentiments.

In *Common Sense*, Paine assaulted the traditional monarchical order in stirring language. "Monarchy and hereditary succession have laid the world in blood and ashes," Paine proclaimed, leveling a personal attack at George III, "the hard hearted sullen Pharaoh of England." Mixing insults with biblical quotations, Paine blasted the British system of "mixed government" that balanced power among the three estates of king, lords, and commoners. Paine granted that the system "was noble for the dark and slavish times" of the past, but now it yielded only "monarchical tyranny in the person of the king" and "aristocratical tyranny in the persons of the peers."

Paine argued for American independence by turning the traditional metaphor of patriarchal authority on its head: "Is it the interest of a man to be a boy all his life?" he asked. Within six months, *Common Sense* had gone through twenty-five editions and reached hundreds of thousands of people. "There is great talk of independence," a worried New York Loyalist noted, "the unthinking multitude are mad for it. . . . A pamphlet called Common Sense has carried off . . . thousands." Paine urged Americans to create independent republican states: "A government of our own is our natural right, 'tis time to part."

Independence Declared

Inspired by Paine's arguments and beset by armed Loyalists, Patriot conventions urged a break from Britain. In June 1776, Richard Henry Lee presented Virginia's resolution to the Continental Congress: "That these United Colonies are, and of right ought to be, free and independent states." Faced with certain defeat, staunch Loyalists and anti-independence moderates withdrew from the Congress, leaving committed Patriots to take the fateful step. On July 4, 1776, the Congress approved the **Declaration of Independence** (see Documents, p. D-1).

The Declaration's main author, Thomas Jefferson of Virginia, had mobilized resistance to the Coercive Acts with the pamphlet *A Summary View of the Rights of British America* (1774). Now, in the Declaration, he justified independence and republicanism to Americans and the world by vilifying George III: "He has plundered our seas, ravaged our coasts, burned our towns, and destroyed the lives of our people." Such a prince

La Destruction de la Statue Royale, Paris On July 9, 1776 — just days after the Continental Congress approved the Declaration of Independence — a New York crowd removed symbols of the monarchy from buildings throughout the city and smashed or burned them. The crowd then proceeded to Bowling Green on the southern end of Manhattan and pulled down a statue of King George III on horseback. Constructed of gilded lead, the two-ton statue was beheaded. The horse and its headless rider were melted down to make bullets. Patriots intended to place the king's head on a spike, but British soldiers recovered it and shipped it to England. In this engraving, printed in Paris, the work is being done by slaves, suggesting how Europeans imagined life in the American colonies. Library of Congress.

was a "tyrant," Jefferson concluded, and "is unfit to be the ruler of a free people."

Employing the ideas of the European Enlightenment, Jefferson proclaimed a series of "self-evident" truths: "that all men are created equal"; that they possess the "unalienable rights" of "Life, Liberty, and the pursuit of Happiness"; that government derives its "just powers from the consent of the governed" and can rightly be overthrown if it "becomes destructive of these ends." By linking these doctrines of individual liberty, **popular sovereignty** (the principle that ultimate power lies in the hands of the electorate), and republican government with American independence, Jefferson established them as the defining political values of the new nation.

For Jefferson, as for Paine, the pen proved mightier than the sword. The Declaration won wide support in France and Germany; at home, it sparked celebrations in rural hamlets and seaport cities, as crowds burned effigies and toppled statues of the king. On July 8, 1776, in Easton, Pennsylvania, a "great number of spectators" heard a reading of the Declaration, "gave their hearty assent with three loud huzzahs, and cried out, 'May God long preserve and unite the Free and Independent States of America.'"

IN YOUR OWN WORDS How did the colonies' long controversy with Parliament influence the ideals that shaped the independence movement?

SUMMARY

Chapter 5 has focused on a short span of time — little more than a decade — and outlined the plot of a political drama. Act I of that drama resulted from the Great War for Empire, which prompted British political leaders to implement a program of imperial reform and taxation. Act II is full of dramatic action, as colonial mobs riot, colonists chafe against restrictions on western lands, Patriot pamphleteers articulate ideologies of resistance, and British ministers search for compromise between claims of parliamentary sovereignty and assertions of colonial autonomy. Act III takes the form of tragedy: the once-proud British Empire dissolves into civil war, an imminent nightmare of death and destruction.

Why did this happen? More than two centuries later, the answers still are not clear. Certainly, the lack of astute leadership in Britain was a major factor. But British leaders faced circumstances that limited their actions: a huge national debt and deep commitments to both a powerful fiscal-military state and the absolute supremacy of Parliament. Moreover, in America, decades of salutary neglect strengthened Patriots' demands for political autonomy and economic opportunity. Artisans, farmers, and aspiring western settlers all feared an oppressive new era in imperial relations. The trajectories of their conflicting intentions and ideas placed Britain and its American possessions on course for a disastrous and fatal collision.

CHAPTER 5 REVIEW

TERMS TO KNOW
Identify and explain the significance of each term below.

Key Concepts and Events

Sugar Act of 1764 (p. 145)

vice-admiralty courts (p. 145)

Stamp Act of 1765 (p. 146)

virtual representation (p. 147)

Quartering Act of 1765 (p. 147)

Stamp Act Congress (p. 148)

Sons of Liberty (p. 148)

English common law (p. 149)

natural rights (p. 149)

Declaratory Act of 1766 (p. 150)

Townshend Act of 1767 (p. 151)

nonimportation movement (p. 151)

committees of correspondence (p. 158)

Tea Act of May 1773 (p. 158)

Coercive Acts (p. 158)

Continental Congress (p. 159)

Continental Association (p. 162)

Dunmore's War (p. 165)

Minutemen (p. 165)

Second Continental Congress (p. 165)

Declaration of Independence (p. 167)

popular sovereignty (p. 168)

Key People

George Grenville (p. 145)

John Dickinson (p. 149)

Charles Townshend (p. 150)

Lord North (p. 153)

Samuel Adams (p. 158)

Lord Dunmore (p. 164)

Thomas Paine (p. 167)

Thomas Jefferson (p. 167)

REVIEW QUESTIONS
Answer these questions to demonstrate your understanding of the chapter's main ideas.

1. What changes in Britain's imperial policy were triggered by its victory in the Great War for Empire?

2. What was the relationship between formal protests against Parliament and popular resistance in the years between 1765 and 1770?

3. What actions did the Continental Association take to support the efforts of the Continental Congress?

4. How did the colonies' long controversy with Parliament influence the ideals that shaped the independence movement?

5. Consider the events listed under "Politics and Power" and "Work, Exchange, and Technology" for the period 1763–1776 on the thematic timeline on page 138. How important were the linkages between economic developments and political ones in these years?

MAKING CONNECTIONS
Recognize the larger developments and continuities within and across chapters by answering these questions.

1. Chapter 4 presented a turbulent era, marked by social and cultural conflict and imperial warfare, during which the regions of British North America were disparate and without unity. Yet by 1776 — only thirteen years after the Treaty of Paris ending the Great War for Empire — thirteen of Britain's mainland colonies were prepared to unite in a Declaration of Independence. What happened in that intervening time to strengthen and deepen colonists' sense of common cause? As they drew together to resist imperial authority, what political and cultural resources did they have in common?

2. Return to the Paul Revere engraving of the Boston Massacre on page 157. This image was an instrument of political propaganda. What features of the image are most important to its political purpose? Consider his depiction of both the soldiers and the townspeople. Look, too, at the buildings surrounding the crowd, especially the Custom House on the right. List the ways in which Revere invokes the idea of tyranny in this image.

KEY TURNING POINTS
Refer to the chapter chronology on page 142 for help in answering the questions below.

The Boston Tea Party (1773), the Coercive Acts (1774), and the First Continental Congress (1774): What did Parliament hope to achieve with the Coercive Acts? How did the decision to convene a continent-wide congress demonstrate the failure of Parliament's efforts?

6

CHAPTER

Making War and Republican Governments

1776–1789

IDENTIFY THE BIG IDEA

How revolutionary was the American Revolution? What political, social, and economic changes did it produce, and what stayed the same?

When Patriots in Frederick County, Maryland, demanded his allegiance to their cause in 1776, Robert Gassaway would have none of it. "It was better for the poor people to lay down their arms and pay the duties and taxes laid upon them by King and Parliament than to be brought into slavery and commanded and ordered about [by you]," he told them. The story was much the same in Farmington, Connecticut, where Patriot officials imprisoned Nathaniel Jones and seventeen other men for "remaining neutral." In Pennsylvania, Quakers accused of Loyalism were rounded up, jailed, and charged with treason, and some were hanged for aiding the British cause. Everywhere, the outbreak of fighting in 1776 forced families to choose the Loyalist or the Patriot side.

The Patriots' control of most local governments gave them an edge in this battle. Patriot leaders organized militia units and recruited volunteers for the Continental army, a ragtag force that surprisingly held its own on the battlefield. "I admire the American troops tremendously!" exclaimed a French officer. "It is incredible that soldiers composed of every age, even children of fifteen, of whites and blacks, almost naked, unpaid, and rather poorly fed, can march so well and withstand fire so steadfastly."

Military service created political commitment, and vice versa. Many Patriot leaders encouraged Americans not only to support the war but also to take an active role in government. As more people did so, their political identities changed. Previously, Americans had lived within a social world dominated by the links of family, kinship, and locality. Now, the abstract bonds of citizenship connected them directly to more distant institutions of government. "From subjects to citizens the difference is immense," remarked South Carolina Patriot David Ramsay. By repudiating monarchical rule and raising a democratic army, the Patriots launched the age of republican revolutions.

Soon republicanism would throw France into turmoil and inspire revolutionaries in Spain's American colonies. The independence of the Anglo-American colonies, remarked the Venezuelan political leader Francisco de Miranda, who had been in New York and Philadelphia at the end of the American Revolution, "was bound to be . . . the infallible preliminary to our own [independence movement]." The Patriot uprising of 1776 set in motion a process that gradually replaced an Atlantic colonial system that spanned the Americas with an American system of new nations.

General Washington, 1781 By war's end, George Washington was a hero on both sides of the Atlantic. This engraving, printed in Paris in 1781, shows him with various British bills and declarations in tatters at his feet while he holds copies of the Declaration of Independence and the Treaty of Alliance with France. In the background of this vaguely Orientalized scene, a black slave — presumably William Lee, Washington's valet and constant companion during the Revolution — saddles his horse. Anne S. K. Brown Military Collection, Brown University Library.

As you read, ask yourself why this chapter begins and ends with these dates and then identify the links among related events.

1776
- ▶ Second Continental Congress declares independence
- ▶ Howe forces Washington to retreat from New York and New Jersey
- ▶ Pennsylvania approves democratic state constitution
- ▶ John Adams publishes *Thoughts on Government*

1777
- ▶ Articles of Confederation create central government
- ▶ Howe occupies Philadelphia (September)
- ▶ Gates defeats Burgoyne at Saratoga (October)

1778
- ▶ Franco-American alliance (February)
- ▶ Lord North seeks political settlement
- ▶ Congress rejects negotiations
- ▶ British adopt southern strategy
- ▶ British capture Savannah (December)

1778–1781
- ▶ Severe inflation of Continental currency

1779
- ▶ British and American forces battle in Georgia

1780
- ▶ Clinton seizes Charleston (May)
- ▶ French troops land in Rhode Island

1781
- ▶ Cornwallis invades Virginia (April), surrenders at Yorktown (October)
- ▶ States finally ratify Articles of Confederation

1783
- ▶ Treaty of Paris (September 3) officially ends war

1784–1785
- ▶ Congress enacts political and land ordinances for new states

1786
- ▶ Nationalists hold convention in Annapolis, Maryland
- ▶ Shays's Rebellion roils Massachusetts

1787
- ▶ Congress passes Northwest Ordinance
- ▶ Constitutional Convention in Philadelphia

1787–1788
- ▶ Jay, Madison, and Hamilton write *The Federalist*
- ▶ Eleven states ratify U.S. Constitution

The Trials of War, 1776–1778

The Declaration of Independence appeared just as the British launched a full-scale military assault. For two years, British troops manhandled the Continental army. A few inspiring American victories kept the rebellion alive, but during the winters of 1776 and 1777, the Patriot cause hung in the balance.

War in the North

Once the British resorted to military force, few Europeans gave the rebels a chance. The population of Great Britain was 11 million; the colonies, 2.5 million, 20 percent of whom were enslaved Africans. Moreover, the British government had access to the immense wealth generated by the South Atlantic System and the emerging Industrial Revolution. Britain also had the most powerful navy in the world, a standing army of 48,000 Britons plus thousands of German (Hessian) soldiers, and the support of thousands of American Loyalists and powerful Indian coalitions. In the Carolinas, the Cherokees resisted colonists' demands for their lands by allying with the British, as did four of the six Iroquois nations of New York (Map 6.1). In the Ohio country, Shawnees and their allies, armed by the British, attacked the new Kentucky settlements.

By contrast, the Americans were economically and militarily weak. They lacked a strong central government and a reliable source of tax revenue. Their new Continental army, commanded by General George Washington, consisted of 18,000 poorly trained and inexperienced recruits.

To demonstrate Britain's military superiority, Prime Minister Lord North ordered General William Howe to capture New York City. His strategy was to seize control of the Hudson River and thereby isolate the radical Patriots in New England from the colonies to the south. As the Second Continental Congress declared independence in Philadelphia in July 1776, Howe landed 32,000 troops — British regulars and German mercenaries — outside New York City. In August 1776, Howe defeated the Americans in the **Battle of Long Island** and forced their retreat to Manhattan Island. There, Howe outflanked Washington's troops and nearly trapped them. Outgunned and outmaneuvered, the Continental army again retreated, eventually crossing the Hudson River to New Jersey. By December, the British army had pushed the rebels across New Jersey and over the Delaware River into Pennsylvania.

Joseph Brant Mohawk chief Thayendanegea, known to whites as Joseph Brant, was a devout member of the Church of England and helped to translate the Bible into the Mohawk language. Brant persuaded four of the six Iroquois nations to support Britain in the war. He received a captain's commission in the British army and led Iroquois warriors and Tory rangers in devastating attacks on American settlements in the Wyoming Valley of Pennsylvania and Cherry Valley in New York. After the war, he was instrumental in resettling Mohawks and other British-allied Indians on the Grand River in Ontario, Canada. Brant was depicted many times by painters and sculptors. In this 1786 portrait, painted during one of his trips to England, Gilbert Stuart depicts his hybrid identity and captures a haunting sense of melancholy. Corbis Historical/Getty Images.

From the Patriots' perspective, winter came just in time. Following eighteenth-century custom, the British halted their military campaign for the cold months, allowing the Americans to catch them off guard. On Christmas night 1776, Washington crossed the Delaware River and staged a successful surprise attack on Trenton, New Jersey, where he forced the surrender of 1,000 German soldiers. In early January 1777, the Continental army won a small victory at nearby Princeton (Map 6.2). But these minor triumphs could not mask British military superiority. "These are the times," wrote Thomas Paine, "that try men's souls."

Armies and Strategies

Thanks in part to General Howe, the rebellion survived. Howe had opposed the Coercive Acts of 1774 and still hoped for a political compromise. So he did not try to destroy the American army but instead tried to show its weakness and persuade the Continental Congress to give up the struggle. Howe's restrained tactics cost Britain the opportunity to nip the rebellion in the bud. For his part, Washington acted cautiously to avoid a major defeat: "On our Side the War should be defensive," he told Congress. His strategy was to draw the British away from the seacoast, extend their lines of supply, and sap their morale.

Congress had promised Washington a regular force of 75,000 men, but the Continental army never reached even a third of that number. Yeomen, refusing to be "Haras'd with callouts" that took them away from their families and farms, would serve only in local militias. When the Virginia gentry imposed a military draft and three years of service on propertyless men — the "Lazy fellows who lurk about and are pests to Society" — they resisted so fiercely that the legislature had to pay them substantial bounties and agree to shorter terms of service. The Continental soldiers recruited in Maryland by General William Smallwood were poor American youths and older foreign-born men, often British ex-convicts and former indentured servants. Most enlisted for the $20 cash bonus (about $2,000 today) and the promise of 100 acres of land.

Molding such recruits into an effective fighting force was nearly impossible. Inexperienced soldiers panicked in the face of British attacks; thousands deserted, unwilling to submit to the discipline of military life. The soldiers who stayed resented the contempt their officers had for the "camp followers," the women who made do with the meager supplies provided to feed and care for the troops. General Philip Schuyler of New York complained that his troops were "destitute of provisions, without camp equipage, with little ammunition, and not a single piece of cannon."

The Continental army was not only poorly supplied but was also held in suspicion by Radical Whig Patriots, who believed that a standing army was a threat to liberty. Even in wartime, they preferred militias to a professional fighting force. Given these handicaps, Washington and his army were fortunate to have escaped an overwhelming defeat.

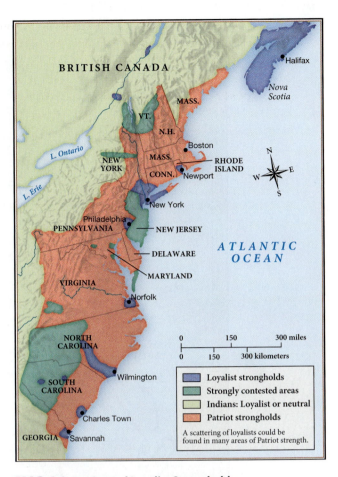

MAP 6.1 Patriot and Loyalist Strongholds

Patriots were in the majority in most of the thirteen mainland colonies and used their control of local governments to funnel men, money, and supplies to the rebel cause. Although Loyalists could be found in every colony, their strongholds were limited to Nova Scotia, eastern New York, New Jersey, and certain areas in the South. However, most Native American peoples favored the British cause and bolstered the power of Loyalist militias in central New York (see Map 6.3) and in the Carolina backcountry.

CONSIDER POINTS OF VIEW

Why was control of New York City Britain's first military objective in the emerging war?

IDENTIFY CAUSES

What factors made it difficult for the Continental Congress to create an effective army?

Victory at Saratoga

After Howe failed to achieve an overwhelming victory, Lord North and his colonial secretary, Lord George Germain, launched another major military campaign in 1777.

MAP 6.2 The War in the North, 1776–1777
In 1776, the British army drove Washington's forces across New Jersey into Pennsylvania. The Americans counterattacked successfully at Trenton and Princeton and then set up winter headquarters in Morristown. In 1777, British forces stayed on the offensive. General Howe attacked the Patriot capital, Philadelphia, from the south and captured it in early October. Meanwhile, General Burgoyne and Colonel St. Leger launched simultaneous invasions from Canada. With the help of thousands of New England militiamen, American troops commanded by General Horatio Gates defeated Burgoyne in August at Bennington, Vermont, and in October at Saratoga, New York, the military turning point in the war.

Isolating New England remained the primary goal. To achieve it, Germain planned a three-pronged attack converging on Albany, New York. General John Burgoyne would lead a large contingent of regulars south from Quebec, Colonel Barry St. Leger and a force of Iroquois would attack from the west, and General Howe would lead troops north from New York City.

Howe instead decided to attack Philadelphia, the home of the Continental Congress, hoping to end the rebellion with a single decisive blow. Howe's troops easily outflanked the American positions along Brandywine Creek in Delaware and, in late September, marched triumphantly into Philadelphia. However, the capture of the rebels' capital did not end the uprising; the Continental Congress, determined to continue the struggle, fled to the countryside.

In the north, Burgoyne's troops had at first advanced quickly, overwhelming the American defenses at Fort Ticonderoga in early July and driving south toward the Hudson River. Then they stalled. Burgoyne—nicknamed "Gentleman Johnny"—was used to high living and had fought in Europe in a leisurely fashion; underestimating the extent of popular support for the rebels, he stopped early each day to pitch comfortable tents and eat elaborate dinners with his officers. The American troops led by General Horatio Gates also slowed Burgoyne's progress by felling huge trees in his path and raiding British supply lines to Canada.

At summer's end, Burgoyne's army of 6,000 British and German troops and 600 Loyalists and Indians was stuck near Saratoga, New York. Desperate for food and horses, in August the British raided nearby Bennington, Vermont, but were beaten back by 2,000 American militiamen. Patriot forces in the Mohawk Valley also threw St. Leger and the Iroquois into retreat. Making matters worse, the British commander in New York City recalled 4,000 troops he had sent toward Albany and ordered them to Philadelphia to bolster Howe's force. While Burgoyne waited in vain for help, thousands of Patriot militiamen from Massachusetts, New Hampshire, and New York joined Gates. The Patriots "swarmed around the army like birds of prey," reported an English sergeant, and in October 1777, they forced Burgoyne to surrender.

The victory at the **Battle of Saratoga** was the turning point of the war. The Patriots captured more than 5,000 British troops and ensured the diplomatic success of American representatives in Paris, who won a military alliance with France.

The Perils of War

The Patriots' triumph at Saratoga was tempered by wartime difficulties. A British naval blockade cut off supplies of European manufactures and disrupted the New England fishing industry; meanwhile, the British occupation of Boston, New York, and Philadelphia reduced trade. As Patriots, along with unemployed artisans and laborers, moved to the countryside, New York City's population declined from 21,000 to 10,000. The British blockade cut tobacco exports in the Chesapeake, so planters grew grain to sell to the contending armies. All across the land, farmers and artisans adapted to a war economy.

With goods now scarce, governments requisitioned military supplies directly from the people. In 1776, Connecticut officials asked the citizens of Hartford to provide 1,000 coats and 1,600 shirts, and soldiers echoed their pleas. After losing all his shirts "except the one on my back" in the Battle of Long Island, Captain Edward Rogers told his wife that "the making of Cloath . . . must go on." Patriot women responded; in Elizabeth, New Jersey, they promised "upwards of 100,000 yards of linnen and woolen cloth." Other women assumed the burdens of farmwork while their men were away at war and acquired a taste for decision making. "We have sow'd our oats as you desired," Sarah Cobb Paine wrote to her absent husband. "Had I been master I should have planted it to

Victory at Saratoga The surrender of General John Burgoyne to American forces at Saratoga, New York, in October 1777 was the most important Patriot victory in the early years of the war. General Horatio Gates, wearing the blue and buff officers' uniform of the Continental army, stands at the center of this painting by John Trumbull, which hangs in the U.S. Capitol. Burgoyne, in the scarlet uniform of the British army, forlornly offers Gates his sword as Gates invites him into his tent. The Patriots' victory at Saratoga, which unfolded over several weeks in a complex set of military maneuvers, proved to their allies and enemies alike that they could defeat a British army in the field. Architect of the Capitol.

American Militiamen Beset by continuing shortages of cloth, the Patriot army dressed in a variety of uniforms and fabrics. This German engraving, taken from a drawing by a Hessian officer, shows two American militiamen (one of them barefoot) wearing hunting shirts and trousers made of ticking, the strong linen fabric often used to cover mattresses and pillows. Anne S. K. Brown Military Collection, Brown University Library.

Corn." Their self-esteem boosted by wartime activities, some women expected greater legal rights in the new republican society.

Still, goods remained scarce and pricey. Hard-pressed consumers assailed shop-keepers as "enemies, extortioners, and monopolizers" and called for government regulation. But when the New England states imposed price ceilings in 1777, many farmers and artisans refused to sell their goods. Ultimately, a government official admitted, consumers had to pay the higher market prices "or submit to starving."

The fighting endangered tens of thousands of civilians. A British officer, Lord Rawdon, favored giving "free liberty to the soldiers to ravage [the country] at will, that these infatuated creatures may feel what a calamity war is." As British and American armies marched back and forth across New Jersey, they forced Patriot and Loyalist families to flee their homes to escape arrest — or worse. Soldiers and partisans looted farms, and disorderly troops harassed and raped women and girls. "An army, even a friendly one, are a dreadful scourge to any people," wrote one Connecticut soldier. "You cannot imagine what devastation and distress mark their steps."

The war divided many farm communities. Patriots formed committees of safety to collect taxes and seized the property of those who refused to pay. "Every Body submitted to our Sovereign Lord the Mob," lamented a Loyalist preacher. In parts of Maryland, the number of "nonassociators" — those who refused to join either side — was so large that they successfully defied Patriot mobs. "Stand off you dammed rebel sons of bitches," shouted Robert Davis of Anne Arundel County, "I will shoot you if you come any nearer."

Financial Crisis

Such defiance exposed the weakness of Patriot governments. Most states were afraid to raise taxes, so officials issued bonds to secure gold or silver from wealthy individuals. When those funds ran out, individual states financed the war by issuing so much paper money — some $260 million all told — that it lost worth, and most people refused to accept it at face value. In North Carolina, even tax collectors eventually rejected the state's currency.

The finances of the Continental Congress collapsed, too, despite the efforts of Philadelphia merchant Robert Morris, the government's chief treasury official. Because the Congress lacked the authority to impose taxes, Morris relied on funds requisitioned from the states, but the states paid late or not at all. So Morris secured loans from France and Holland and sold Continental loan certificates to some thirteen thousand firms and individuals. All the while, the Congress was issuing paper money — some $200 million between 1776 and 1779 — which, like state currencies, quickly fell in value. In 1778, a family needed $7 in Continental bills to buy goods worth $1 in gold or silver. As the exchange rate deteriorated — to 42 to 1 in 1779, 100 to 1 in 1780, and 146 to 1 in 1781 — it sparked social upheaval. In Boston, a mob of women accosted merchant Thomas Boyleston, "seazd him by his Neck," and forced him to sell his wares at traditional prices. In rural Ulster County, New York, women told the committee of safety to lower food prices or "their husbands and sons shall fight no more." As morale crumbled, Patriot leaders feared the rebellion would collapse.

Paper Currency Testifying to their independent status, the new state governments printed their own currencies. Rejecting the English system of pounds and shillings, Virginia used the Spanish gold dollar as its basic unit of currency, although the equivalent in English pounds is also shown. Initially, $1,200 was equal to £360 — a ratio of 3.3 to 1. By 1781, Virginia had printed so much paper money to pay its soldiers and wartime expenses that the value of its currency had depreciated. It now took $40 in Virginia currency to buy the same amount of goods as £1 sterling. Courtesy of the American Numismatic Society.

Valley Forge

Fears reached their peak during the winter of 1777. While Howe's army lived comfortably in Philadelphia, Washington's army retreated 20 miles to **Valley Forge**, where

12,000 soldiers and hundreds of camp followers suffered horribly. "The army . . . now begins to grow sickly," a surgeon confided to his diary. "Poor food — hard lodging — cold weather — fatigue — nasty clothes — nasty cookery. . . . Why are we sent here to starve and freeze?" Nearby farmers refused to help. Some were pacifists, Quakers and German sectarians unwilling to support either side. Others looked out for their own families, selling grain for gold from British quartermasters but refusing depreciated Continental currency. "Such a dearth of public spirit, and want of public virtue," lamented Washington. By spring, more than 200 officers had resigned, 1,000 hungry soldiers had deserted, and another 3,000 had died from malnutrition and disease. That winter at Valley Forge took as many American lives as had two years of fighting.

In this dark hour, Baron von Steuben raised the readiness of the American army. A former Prussian military officer, von Steuben was one of a handful of republican-minded foreign aristocrats who joined the American cause. Appointed as inspector general of the Continental army, he instituted a strict drill system and encouraged officers to become more professional. Thanks to von Steuben, the smaller army that emerged from Valley Forge in the spring of 1778 was a much tougher and better-disciplined force.

> **IN YOUR OWN WORDS** What challenges did Patriot forces confront in the first two years of the war, and what were their key achievements?

The Path to Victory, 1778–1783

Wars are often won by astute diplomacy, and so it was with the War of Independence. The Patriots' prospects improved dramatically in 1778, when the Continental Congress concluded a military alliance with France, the most powerful nation in Europe. The alliance gave the Americans desperately needed money, supplies, and, eventually, troops. And it confronted Britain with an international war that challenged its domination of the Atlantic and Indian oceans.

The French Alliance

France and America were unlikely partners. France was Catholic and a monarchy; the United States was Protestant and a federation of republics. From 1689 to 1763, the two peoples had been enemies: New Englanders had brutally uprooted the French population from Acadia (Nova Scotia) in 1755, and the French and their Indian allies had raided British settlements. But the Comte de Vergennes, the French foreign minister, was determined to avenge the loss of Canada during the Great War for Empire (see Chapter 4) and persuaded King Louis XVI to provide the rebellious colonies with a secret loan and much-needed gunpowder. When news of the rebel victory at Saratoga reached Paris in December 1777, Vergennes sought a formal alliance.

Benjamin Franklin and other American diplomats craftily exploited France's rivalry with Britain to win an explicit commitment to American independence. The Treaty of Alliance of February 1778 specified that once France entered the war, neither partner would sign a separate peace without the "liberty, sovereignty, and independence" of the United States. In return, the Continental Congress agreed to recognize any French conquests in the West Indies. "France and America," warned Britain's Lord Stormont, were "indissolubly leagued for our destruction."

The alliance gave new life to the Patriots' cause. "There has been a great change in this state since the news from France," a Patriot soldier reported from Pennsylvania. Farmers — "mercenary wretches," he called them — were "as eager for Continental Money now as they were a few weeks ago for British gold." Its confidence bolstered, the

EXPLAIN CONSEQUENCES
What were the most important results of the Patriot victory at Saratoga?

Continental Congress addressed the demands of the officer corps. Most officers were gentlemen who equipped themselves and raised volunteers; in return, they insisted on lifetime military pensions at half pay. John Adams condemned the officers for "scrambling for rank and pay like apes for nuts," but General Washington urged the Congress to grant the pensions: "The salvation of the cause depends upon it." The Congress reluctantly granted the officers half pay, but only for seven years.

Meanwhile, the war had become unpopular in Britain. At first, George III was determined to crush the rebellion. If America won independence, he warned Lord North, "the West Indies must follow them. Ireland would soon follow the same plan and be a separate state, then this island would be reduced to itself, and soon would be a poor island indeed." Stunned by the defeat at Saratoga, however, the king changed his mind. To thwart an American alliance with France, he authorized North to seek a negotiated settlement. In February 1778, North persuaded Parliament to repeal the Tea and Prohibitory Acts and, amazingly, to renounce its power to tax the colonies. But the Patriots, now allied with France and committed to independence, rejected North's overture.

War in the South

The French alliance did not bring a rapid end to the war. When France entered the conflict in June 1778, it hoped to seize all of Britain's sugar islands. Spain, which joined the war against Britain in 1779, aimed to regain Florida and the fortress of Gibraltar at the entrance to the Mediterranean Sea.

Britain's Southern Strategy For its part, the British government revised its military strategy to defend the West Indies and capture the rich tobacco- and rice-growing colonies: Virginia, the Carolinas, and Georgia. Once conquered, the ministry planned to use the Scottish Highlanders in the Carolinas and other Loyalists to hold them. It had already mobilized the Cherokees and Delawares against the land-hungry Americans and knew that the Patriots' fears of slave uprisings weakened them militarily (Map 6.3). As South Carolina Patriots admitted to the Continental Congress, they could raise only a few recruits "by reason of the great proportion of citizens necessary to remain at home to prevent insurrection among the Negroes."

MAP 6.3 **Native Americans and the War in the West, 1778–1779**
Many Indian peoples remained neutral, but others, fearing land-hungry Patriot farmers, used British-supplied guns to raid American settlements. To thwart attacks by militant Shawnees, Cherokees, and Delawares, a Patriot militia led by George Rogers Clark captured the British fort and supply depot at Vincennes on the Wabash River in February 1779. To the north, Patriot generals John Sullivan and James Clinton defeated pro-British Indian forces near Tioga (on the New York–Pennsylvania border) in August 1779 and then systematically destroyed villages and crops throughout the lands of the Iroquois.

The large number of slaves in the South made the Revolution a "triangular war," in which African Americans constituted a strategic problem for Patriots and a tempting, if dangerous, opportunity for the British. Britain actively recruited slaves to its cause. The effort began with Dunmore's controversial proclamation in November 1775 recruiting slaves to his Ethiopian Regiment (see Chapter 5). In 1779, the **Philipsburg Proclamation** declared that any slave who deserted a rebel master would receive protection, freedom, and land from Great Britain. Together, these proclamations led some 30,000 African Americans to take refuge behind British lines. George Washington initially barred blacks from the Continental army, but he relented in 1777. By war's end, African Americans could enlist in every state but South Carolina and Georgia, and some 5,000 — slave and free — fought for the Patriot cause (Thinking Like a Historian).

It fell to Sir Henry Clinton — acutely aware of the role slaves might play — to implement Britain's southern strategy. From the British army's main base in New York City, Clinton launched a seaborne attack on Savannah, Georgia. Troops commanded by Colonel Archibald Campbell captured the town in December 1778. Mobilizing hundreds of blacks to transport supplies, Campbell moved inland and captured Augusta early in 1779. By year's end, Clinton's forces and local Loyalists controlled coastal Georgia and had 10,000 troops poised for an assault on South Carolina.

In 1780, British forces marched from victory to victory (Map 6.4). In May, Clinton forced the surrender of Charleston, South Carolina, and its garrison of 5,000 troops. Then Lord Charles Cornwallis assumed control of the British forces and, at Camden, defeated an American force commanded by General Horatio Gates, the hero of Saratoga. Only 1,200 Patriot militiamen joined Gates at Camden, a fifth of the number at Saratoga. Cornwallis took control of South Carolina, and hundreds of African Americans fled to freedom behind British lines. The southern strategy was working.

Then the tide of battle turned. Thanks to another republican-minded European aristocrat, the Marquis de Lafayette, France finally dispatched troops to the American mainland. A longtime supporter of the American cause, Lafayette persuaded King Louis XVI to send General Comte de Rochambeau and 5,500 men to Newport, Rhode Island, in 1780. There, they threatened the British forces holding New York City.

Guerrilla Warfare in the Carolinas Meanwhile, Washington dispatched General Nathanael Greene to recapture the Carolinas, where he found "a country that has been ravaged and plundered by both friends and enemies." Greene put local militiamen, who had been "without discipline and addicted to plundering," under strong leaders and unleashed them on less mobile British forces. In October 1780, Patriot militia defeated a regiment of Loyalists at King's Mountain, South Carolina, taking about one thousand prisoners. American guerrillas commanded by the "Swamp Fox," General Francis Marion, also won a series of small but fierce battles. Then, in January 1781, General Daniel Morgan led an American

Francis Marion Crossing the Pedee River Francis Marion was a master of the ferocious guerrilla fighting that characterized the war in South Carolina. Though Patriot general Horatio Gates had little confidence in him, Marion led an irregular militia brigade in several successful attacks. After chasing Marion into a swamp, British general Banastre Tarleton declared, "As for this damned old fox, the Devil himself could not catch him." Soon Patriots began calling Marion the Swamp Fox. In 1851, William T. Ranney painted Marion (on horseback in a white shirt and blue coat) and his men crossing the Pedee River in flatboats. Ranney included an unidentified (and possibly fictionalized) black oarsman. William T. Ranney, *Marion Crossing the Pedee*, 1850, oil on canvas. Amon Carter Museum, Fort Worth, Texas, 1983.126.

The Black Soldier's Dilemma

For African American slaves, the Revolution offered no clear path to freedom. Some slaves agreed to fight for Britain because of its promise to liberate slaves who fought against their masters. While some were freed, many others died fighting, were forced into servitude in the army, or even sold into slavery in the West Indies. Patriots at first refused the service of black soldiers, then enlisted them in small numbers, but always upheld the property rights of masters.

1. **Dunmore's Proclamation, 1775.** *Virginia's Governor Dunmore issued this proclamation in response to the emerging rebellion and formed his recruits into the so-called Ethiopian Regiment.*

To defeat such unreasonable Purposes . . . that the Peace, and good Order of this Colony may be again restored . . . I have thought fit to issue this my Proclamation, hereby declaring, that until the aforesaid good Purposes can be obtained, I do in Virtue of the Power and Authority to me given, by His majesty, determine to execute Martial Law, and cause the same to be executed throughout this Colony: and to the end that Peace and good Order may the sooner be [effected], I do require every Person capable of bearing Arms, to [resort] to His majesty's standard, or be looked upon as Traitors to His [majesty] . . . I do hereby further declare all indentured Servants, Negroes, or others, (appertaining to Rebels,) free that are able and willing to bear Arms, they joining His majesty's Troops as soon as may be, for the more speedily reducing this Colony to a proper Sense of their Duty.

2. **Virginia's response to Dunmore's Proclamation, 1775.** *A month later, Virginia's General Assembly issued the following response.*

WHEREAS lord Dunmore, by his proclamation, dated on board the ship William, off Norfolk, the 7th day of November 1775, hath offered freedom to such able-bodied slaves as are willing to join him, and take up arms, against the good people of this colony, giving thereby encouragement to a general insurrection . . . it is enacted, that all negro or other slaves, conspiring to rebel or make insurrection, shall suffer death. . . . We think it proper to declare, that all slaves who have been, or shall be seduced, by his lordship's proclamation, or other arts, to desert their masters' service, and take up arms against

the inhabitants of this colony, shall be liable to such punishment as shall hereafter be directed by the General Convention. . . . [A]ll such, who have taken this unlawful and wicked step, may return in safety to their duty, and escape the punishment due their crimes. . . . And we do farther earnestly recommend it to all humane and benevolent persons in this colony to explain and make known this our offer of mercy to those unfortunate people.

3. **Runaway advertisement, 1775.** *Titus — or, as he was later known, Captain Tye of the Ethiopian Regiment — abandoned his Delaware master in response to Dunmore's Proclamation.*

THREE POUNDS Reward.

RUN away from the subscriber, living in Shrewsbury, in the county of Monmouth, New-Jersey, a NEGROE man, named TITUS, but may probably change his name; he is about 21 years of age, not very black, near 6 feet high; had on a grey homespun coat, brown breeches, blue and white stockings, and took with him a wallet, drawn up at one end with a string, in which was a quantity of clothes. Whoever takes up said Negroe, and secures him in any goal, or brings him to me, shall be entitled to the above reward of Three Pounds proc. and all reasonable charges, paid by

Nov. 8, 1775. § JOHN CORLIS.

SOURCE: American Antiquarian Society, Worcester, Massachusetts, USA/Bridgeman Images.

4. **Report of Bernardo de Gálvez, 1780.** *Fighting against the British in support of the Patriots, Louisiana governor Bernardo de Gálvez raised a mixed regiment, almost half of whom were slaves and free people of color from New Orleans. He praised their efforts in this report of his campaign.*

No less deserving of eulogy are the companies of Negroes and free Mulattoes who were continually occupied in the outposts, in false attacks, and discoveries,

force to a bloody victory at Cowpens, South Carolina. In March, Greene's soldiers fought Cornwallis's seasoned army to a draw at North Carolina's Guilford Court House. Weakened by this war of attrition, the British general decided to concede the Carolinas to Greene and seek a decisive victory in Virginia. There, many Patriot militiamen had refused to take up arms, claiming that "the Rich wanted the Poor to fight for them."

Exploiting these social divisions, Cornwallis moved easily through the Tidewater region of Virginia in the early summer of 1781. Reinforcements sent from New York exchanging shots with the enemy . . . conduct[ing] themselves with as much valor and generosity as the whites.

5. **Boston King gains his freedom, 1783.** *In 1780, Boston King, like many other southern slaves, escaped to the British army. Here he describes his experiences at war's end.*

About this time, peace was restored between America and Great Britain which diffused universal joy among all parties except us, who had escaped slavery and taken refuge in the English army; for a report prevailed at New-York that all the slaves, in number two thousand, were to be delivered up to their masters, altho' some of them had been three or four years among the English. This dreadful rumour filled us with inexpressible anguish and terror, especially when we saw our old masters coming from Virginia, North-Carolina and other parts and seizing upon slaves in the streets of New-York, or even dragging them out of their beds. Many of the slaves had very cruel masters, so that the thought of returning home with them embittered life to us. For some days we lost our appetite for food, and sleep departed from our eyes. The English had compassion upon us in the day of our distress, and issued out a Proclamation importing "That all slaves should be free who had taken refuge in the British lines and claimed the sanction and privileges of the Proclamations respecting the security and protection of Negroes." In consequence of this, each of us received a certificate from the commanding officer at New-York, which dispelled our fears and filled us with joy and gratitude.

6. **Jehu Grant is re-enslaved, 1778.** *Jehu Grant of Narragansett, Rhode Island, was owned by a Loyalist. In August 1777 he escaped and joined the Patriot side; ten months later, his master tracked him down and reclaimed him. In 1837 Grant applied for a pension from the U.S. government and supplied the following narrative of his experience. His application was denied.*

[I] enlisted as a soldier but was put to the service of a teamster in the summer and a waiter in the winter . . . I was then grown to manhood, in the full vigor and strength of life, and heard much about the cruel and arbitrary things done by the British. Their ships lay within a few miles of my master's house, which stood near the shore, and I was confident that my master traded with them, and I suffered much from fear that I

should be sent aboard a ship of war. This I disliked. But when I saw liberty poles and the people all engaged for the support of freedom, I could not but like and be pleased with such thing (God forgive me if I sinned in so feeling). And living on the borders of Rhode Island, where whole companies of colored people enlisted, it added to my fears and dread of being sold to the British. These considerations induced me to enlist into the American army, where I served faithful about ten months, when my master found and took me home. Had I been taught to read or understand the precepts of the Gospel, "Servants obey your master," I might have done otherwise, notwithstanding the songs of liberty that saluted my ear, thrilled through my heart.

SOURCES: (1) Lord Dunmore's Proclamation, Learn NC, North Carolina Digital History "Revolutionary North Carolina," www.learnnc.org; (2) J. N. Brenaman, *A History of Virginia Conventions* (Richmond: J. L. Hill Printing Company, 1902), p. 30; (4) Thomas Truxtun Moebs, *Black Soldiers-Black Sailors-Black Ink: Research Guide on African-Americans in U. S. Military History, 1526–1900* (Chesapeake Bay, Paris: Moebs Publishing Company, 1994), 1125; (5) Boston King, *Book of Negroes* (New York, 1783), in Simon Schama, *Rough Crossings: Britain, the Slaves and the American Revolution* (New York: HarperCollins, 2006), 107, 150; (6) Jehu Grant, To Hon. J. L. Edwards, Commissioner of Pension, 1836, in *The Revolution Remembered: Eyewitness Accounts of the War for Independence*, ed. John C. Dann (Chicago: University of Chicago Press, 1980), 27–28.

ANALYZING THE EVIDENCE

1. Why was Dunmore willing to offer freedom to slaves (source 1) when they were a recognized form of property under the British Empire? What assumptions about the loyalties of slaves underlie the response of the Virginia assembly (source 2)?

2. Why might Louisiana governor Bernardo de Gálvez (source 4) have made a point of praising the contributions of black soldiers to the Patriot cause?

3. Compare the runaway ad for Titus (source 3) and the narratives of Boston King and Jehu Grant (sources 5 and 6). What goals did British officers hope to achieve in their relations with slaves? What Patriot values trumped slaves' individual liberties during and after the war?

PUTTING IT ALL TOGETHER

Considering these sources along with the chapter contents and what you've learned in class, write a short essay that explains how the presence of slaves created a "triangular war" in the South, assesses the choices that individual slaves had to make during the Revolution, and considers how the differences in the institution of slavery between northern and southern colonies shaped slaves' experiences in the war.

and commanded by General Benedict Arnold, the infamous Patriot traitor, bolstered his ranks. As Arnold and Cornwallis sparred with an American force led by Lafayette near the York Peninsula, Washington was informed that France had finally sent its powerful West Indian fleet to North America, and he devised an audacious plan. Feigning an assault on New York City, he secretly marched General Rochambeau's army from Rhode Island to Virginia. Simultaneously, the French fleet took control of Chesapeake Bay. By the time the British discovered Washington's scheme, Cornwallis was surrounded, his 9,500-man army outnumbered 2 to 1 on land and cut off from

MAP 6.4 The War in the South, 1778–1781
Britain's southern military strategy started well. British forces captured Savannah in December 1778, took control of Georgia during 1779, and vanquished Charleston in May 1780. Over the next eighteen months, brutal warfare between the British troops and Loyalist units and the Continental army and militia raged in the interior of the Carolinas and ended in a stalemate. Hoping to break the deadlock, British general Charles Cornwallis carried the battle into Virginia in 1781. A Franco-American army led by Washington and Lafayette, with the help of the French fleet under Admiral de Grasse, surrounded Cornwallis's forces on the Yorktown Peninsula and forced their surrender.

reinforcement or retreat by sea. In a hopeless position, at the conclusion of the **Battle of Yorktown** Cornwallis surrendered in October 1781.

The Franco-American victory broke the resolve of the British government. "Oh God! It is all over!" Lord North exclaimed. Isolated diplomatically in Europe, stymied militarily in America, and lacking public support at home, the British ministry gave up active prosecution of the war on the American mainland.

The Patriot Advantage

How could mighty Britain, victorious in the Great War for Empire, lose to a motley rebel army? The British ministry pointed to a series of blunders by the military

IDENTIFY CAUSES
What were the keys to the Patriot victory in the South?

leadership. Why had Howe not ruthlessly pursued Washington's army in 1776? Why had Howe and Burgoyne failed to coordinate their attacks in 1777? Why had Cornwallis marched deep into the Patriot-dominated state of Virginia in 1781?

Historians acknowledge British mistakes, but they also attribute the rebels' victory to French aid and the inspired leadership of George Washington. Astutely deferring to elected officials, Washington won the support of the Continental Congress and the state governments. Confident of his military abilities, he pursued a defensive strategy that minimized casualties and maintained the morale of his officers and soldiers through five difficult years of war. Moreover, the Patriots' control of local governments gave Washington a greater margin for error than the British generals had. Local militiamen provided the edge in the 1777 victory at Saratoga and forced Cornwallis from the Carolinas in 1781.

In the end, it was the American people who decided the outcome, especially the one-third of the white colonists who were zealous Patriots. Tens of thousands of these farmers and artisans accepted Continental bills in payment for supplies, and thousands of soldiers took them as pay, even as the currency literally depreciated in their pockets. Rampant inflation meant that every paper dollar held for a week lost value, imposing a hidden "**currency tax**" on those who accepted the paper currency. Each individual tax was small—a few pennies on each dollar. But as millions of dollars changed hands multiple times, the currency taxes paid by ordinary citizens financed the American military victory.

> **TRACE CHANGE OVER TIME**
> Despite being at a clear disadvantage at the start of the war, the American Patriots won. Why?

Diplomatic Triumph

After Yorktown, diplomats took two years to conclude a peace treaty. Talks began in Paris in April 1782, but the French and Spanish, still hoping to seize a West Indian island or Gibraltar, stalled for time. Their tactics infuriated American diplomats Benjamin Franklin, John Adams, and John Jay. So the Americans negotiated secretly with the British, prepared if necessary to ignore the Treaty of Alliance and sign a separate peace. British ministers were equally eager: Parliament wanted peace, and they feared the loss of a rich sugar island.

Consequently, the American diplomats secured extremely favorable terms. In the **Treaty of Paris of 1783**, signed in September, Great Britain formally recognized American independence and relinquished its claims to lands south of the Great Lakes and east of the Mississippi River. The British negotiators did not insist on a separate territory for their Indian allies. "In endeavouring to assist you," a Wea Indian complained to a British general, "it seems we have wrought our own ruin." The Cherokees were forced to relinquish claims to 5 million acres—three-quarters of their territory—in treaties with Georgia, the Carolinas, and Virginia, while New York and the Continental Congress pressed the Iroquois and Ohio Indians to cede much of their land as well. British officials, like those of other early modern empires, found it easy to abandon allies they had never really understood (America in Global Context).

The Paris treaty also granted Americans fishing rights off Newfoundland and Nova Scotia, prohibited the British from "carrying away any negroes or other property," and guaranteed freedom of navigation on the Mississippi to American citizens "forever." In return, the American government allowed British merchants to pursue legal claims for prewar debts and encouraged the state legislatures to return confiscated property to Loyalists and grant them citizenship.

In the Treaty of Versailles, signed simultaneously, Britain made peace with France and Spain. Neither American ally gained very much. Spain reclaimed Florida from Britain, but not the strategic fortress at Gibraltar. France received the Caribbean island of Tobago, small consolation for a war that had sharply raised taxes and quadrupled France's national debt. Just six years later, cries for tax relief and political liberty would spark the French Revolution. Only Americans profited handsomely; the treaties gave them independence and access to the trans-Appalachian west.

> **IN YOUR OWN WORDS**   What were the keys to Patriot victory in the American Revolution?

China's Growing Empire

As Britain was losing control of its multiethnic empire in North America, China's Qing [pronounced Ching] dynasty was consolidating its authority over borderlands peoples during the eighteenth century. And just as Europeans relied on ethnographic descriptions of Native Americans to understand the peoples and territories they hoped to control, Chinese authorities used ethnographic manuals that included prose, poetry, and illustrations to make sense of their new subjects. These excerpts from a set of "Miao albums" illustrate the cultural characteristics they observed in, or ascribed to, one such group of these non-Chinese (or non-Han) peoples.

BULONG (BASKET-REPAIRING) ZHONGJIA

The Bulong Zhongjia are located in Dinfan and Guangshun Districts. Their customs are similar to those of the Kayou. For them, the New Year begins in the twelfth month. They greet it by striking a bronze drum. When they dig in the ground and find a drum, they consider it to be the legacy of Zhuge Liang [an ancient Chinese hero claimed as a forebear]. The rich must pay a high price to buy the drum. At funerals, cattle are butchered and dressed, and relatives and friends are invited. Drinking from the "ox horn of happiness," the guests often get drunk and sometimes even wind up killing each other. The host does not usually eat meat but only fish and shrimp. After burial, the grave is covered by an umbrella. By nature the Bulong are alert and fierce. When coming and going they carry sharp knives. They will avenge even an angry look.

NONG (AGRICULTURAL) MIAO

The Nong Miao are located in the Zhenfeng District, which once belonged to Guangxi. . . . Men shave their heads and dress just like Han people. Women wear short tunics and long skirts, and cover their heads with colorful scarves. They still follow Miao customs. Their nature is fierce and cruel; they enjoy killing.

GEDOU MIAO

The Gedou Miao are found in Zhenyuan, Shibing, and Huangping. They are as good at hunting as the Turen. Women wear their hair up, inclined toward one side, with a comb inserted. Their short tunics are collarless, and their skirts do not reach beyond the knee. They embroider in five colors on the bust and the sleeves, and ornament themselves with seashells [shaped] like silkworm cocoons, stringing them together like real pearls. If a man is injured by one of their poisoned arrows he will die immediately. They are not, however, given to thievery.

SOURCE: Deal, David, and Laura Hostetler. Introduction by Laura Hostetler. Preface by Charles F. McKhann. *The Art of Ethnography: A Chinese "Miao Album"* © 2006. Reprinted with permission of the University of Washington Press.

QUESTIONS FOR ANALYSIS

1. What attributes seemed especially meaningful to the authors of these descriptions?
2. Why would the authors have singled out the particular qualities that are remarked upon here? How does this compare to the ways in which the British viewed the Native Americans?

Creating Republican Institutions, 1776–1787

When the Patriots declared independence, they confronted the issue of political authority. "Which of us shall be the rulers?" asked a Philadelphia newspaper. The question was multifaceted. Would power reside in the national government or the states? Who would control the new republican institutions: traditional elites or average citizens? Would women have greater political and legal rights? What would be the status of slaves in the new republic?

The State Constitutions: How Much Democracy?

In May 1776, the Second Continental Congress urged Americans to reject royal authority and establish republican governments. Most states quickly complied. "Constitutions employ every pen," an observer noted. Within six months, Virginia, Maryland, North Carolina, New Jersey, Delaware, and Pennsylvania had all ratified new constitutions, and Connecticut and Rhode Island had revised their colonial charters to delete references to the king.

Republicanism meant more than ousting the king. The Declaration of Independence stated the principle of popular sovereignty: governments derive "their just powers from the consent of the governed." In the heat of revolution, many Patriots gave this clause a further democratic twist. In North Carolina, the backcountry farmers of Mecklenburg County told their delegates to the state's constitutional convention to "oppose everything that leans to aristocracy or power in the hands of the rich." In Virginia, voters elected a new assembly in 1776 that, an eyewitness remarked, "was composed of men not quite so well dressed, nor so politely educated, nor so highly born" as colonial-era legislatures (Figure 6.1).

To see a longer excerpt of the Mecklenburg delegates' document, along with other primary sources from this period, see *Sources for America's History*.

Pennsylvania's Controversial Constitution

This democratic impulse flowered in Pennsylvania, thanks to a coalition of Scots-Irish farmers, Philadelphia artisans, and Enlightenment-influenced intellectuals. In 1776, these insurgents ousted every officeholder of the Penn family's proprietary government, abolished property ownership as a qualification for voting, and granted all taxpaying men the right to vote and hold office. The **Pennsylvania constitution of 1776** also created a unicameral (one-house) legislature with complete power; there was no governor to exercise a veto. Other provisions mandated a system of elementary education and protected citizens from imprisonment for debt.

Pennsylvania's democratic constitution alarmed many leading Patriots. From Boston, John Adams denounced the unicameral legislature as "so democratical that it must produce confusion and every evil work." Along with other conservative Patriots, Adams wanted to restrict office holding to "men of learning, leisure and easy circumstances" and warned of oppression under majority rule: "If you give [ordinary citizens] the command or preponderance in the . . . legislature, they will vote all property out of the hands of you aristocrats."

COMPARE AND CONTRAST
What aspects of the Pennsylvania constitution were most objectionable to Adams, and what did he advocate instead?

Tempering Democracy

To counter the appeal of the Pennsylvania constitution, Adams published *Thoughts on Government* (1776). In that treatise, he adapted the British Whig theory of **mixed government** (a sharing of power among the monarch, the House of Lords, and the Commons) to a republican society. To disperse authority and preserve liberty, he insisted on separate institutions: legislatures would make laws, the executive would administer them, and the judiciary would enforce them. Adams also demanded a bicameral (two-house) legislature with an upper house of substantial property owners to offset the popular majorities in the lower one. As further curbs on democracy, he proposed an elected governor with veto power and an appointed — not elected — judiciary.

Conservative Patriots endorsed Adams's governmental system. In New York's constitution of 1777, property qualifications for voting excluded 20 percent of white men from assembly elections and 60 percent from casting ballots for the governor and the upper house. In South Carolina, elite planters used property rules to disqualify about 90 percent of white men from office holding. The 1778 constitution required candidates for governor to have a debt-free estate of £10,000 (about $700,000 today), senators to be worth £2,000, and assemblymen to own property valued at £1,000. Even in

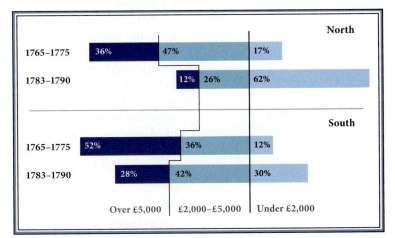

FIGURE 6.1 Middling Men Enter the Halls of Government, 1765–1790
Before the Revolution, wealthy men (with assets of £2,000 or more, as measured by tax lists and probate records) dominated most colonial assemblies. The power of money was especially apparent in the southern colonies, where representatives worth at least £5,000 formed a majority of the legislators. However, in the new American republic, the proportion of middling legislators (yeomen farmers and others worth less than £2,000) increased dramatically, especially in the northern states. Adapted from Jackson T. Main, "Government by the People: The American Revolution and the Democratization of the Legislatures," *William and Mary Quarterly*, series 3, 23 (1966). Used by permission of *William and Mary Quarterly*.

Judith Sargent Murray Judith Sargent Murray was perhaps the most accomplished female essayist of the Revolutionary era. Publishing under various pen names, she advocated for economic independence and better educational opportunities for women. Two years before Mary Wollstonecraft's *A Vindication of the Rights of Woman* (1792), she published "On the Equality of the Sexes" in the *Massachusetts Magazine.* Her letter books, which run to twenty volumes, were discovered only in 1984; the Judith Sargent Murray Society (http://www.jsmsociety.com/Home.html) is now transcribing and indexing them for publication. This striking portrait by John Singleton Copley hints at her intelligence and sardonic wit. John Singleton Copley, *Portrait of Mrs. John Stephens* (Judith Sargent, later Mrs. John Murray). Daniel J. Terra Art Acquisition Endowment Fund, 2000.6. Terra Foundation for American Art, Chicago/Art Resource, NY.

IDENTIFY CAUSES
What impact did republican ideals have on gender roles and expectations during the Revolutionary era?

traditionally democratic Massachusetts, the 1780 constitution, authored primarily by Adams, raised property qualifications for voting and office holding and skewed the lower house toward eastern, mercantile interests.

The political legacy of the Revolution was complex. Only in Pennsylvania and Vermont were radical Patriots able to create truly democratic institutions. Yet in all the new states, representative legislatures had acquired more power, and average citizens now had greater power at the polls and greater influence in the halls of government.

Women Seek a Public Voice

The extraordinary excitement of the Revolutionary era tested the dictum that only men could engage in politics. Men controlled all public institutions — legislatures, juries, government offices — but upper-class women engaged in political debate and, defying men's scorn, filled their letters, diaries, and conversations with opinions on public issues. "The men say we have no business [with politics]," Eliza Wilkinson of South Carolina complained in 1783. "They won't even allow us liberty of thought, and that is all I want."

As Wilkinson's remark suggests, most women did not insist on civic equality with men; many sought only an end to restrictive customs and laws. Abigail Adams demanded equal legal rights for married women, who under common law could not own property, enter into contracts, or initiate lawsuits. The war bonds she purchased had to be held in a trust run by a male relative. "Men would be tyrants" if they continued to hold such power over women, Adams declared to her husband, John, criticizing him and other Patriots for "emancipating all nations" from monarchical despotism while "retaining absolute power over Wives."

Most politicians ignored women's requests, and most men insisted on traditional sexual and political prerogatives. Long-married husbands remained patriarchs who dominated their households, and even young men who embraced the republican ideal of "companionate marriage" did not support legal equality for their wives and daughters. Except in New Jersey, which until 1807 allowed unmarried and widowed female property holders to vote, women remained disenfranchised. In the new American republic, only white men enjoyed full citizenship.

Nevertheless, the republican belief in an educated citizenry created opportunities for some women. In her 1779 essay "On the Equality of the Sexes," Judith Sargent Murray argued that men and women had equal capacities for memory and that women had superior imaginations. She conceded that most women were inferior to men in judgment and reasoning, but only from lack of training: "We can only reason from what we know," she argued, and most women had been denied "the opportunity of acquiring knowledge." That situation changed in the 1790s, when the attorney general of Massachusetts declared that girls had an equal right to schooling under the state constitution. By 1850, the literacy rates of women and men in the northeastern states were equal, and educated women again challenged their subordinate legal and political status.

The War's Losers: Loyalists, Native Americans, and Slaves

The success of republican institutions was assisted by the departure of as many as 100,000 Loyalists, many of whom suffered severe financial losses. Some Patriots demanded revolutionary justice: the seizure of all Loyalist property and its distribution to needy Americans. But most officials were unwilling to go so far. When state governments did seize Loyalist property, they often auctioned it to the highest bidders; only rarely did small-scale farmers benefit. In the cities, Patriot merchants replaced Loyalists at the top of the economic ladder, supplanting a traditional economic elite — who often invested profits from trade in real estate — with republican entrepreneurs who tended to promote new trading ventures and domestic manufacturing. This shift facilitated America's economic development in the years to come.

Though the Revolution did not result in widespread property redistribution, it did encourage yeomen, middling planters, and small-time entrepreneurs to believe that their new republican governments would protect their property and ensure widespread access to land. In western counties, former Regulators demanded that the new governments be more responsive to their needs; beyond the Appalachians, thousands of squatters who had occupied lands in Kentucky and Tennessee expected their claims to be recognized and lands to be made available on easy terms. If the United States were to secure the loyalty of westerners, it would have to meet their needs more effectively than the British Empire had.

This meant, among other things, extinguishing Native American claims to land as quickly as possible. At war's end, George Washington commented on the "rage for speculating" in Ohio Valley lands. "Men in these times, talk with as much facility of fifty, a hundred, and even 500,000 Acres as a Gentleman formerly would do of 1000 acres." "If we make a right use of our natural advantages," a Fourth of July orator observed, "we soon must be a truly great and happy people." Native American land claims stood as a conspicuous barrier to the "natural advantages" he imagined.

For southern slaveholders, the Revolution was fought to protect property rights, and any sentiment favoring slave emancipation met with violent objections. When Virginia Methodists called for general emancipation in 1785, slaveholders used Revolutionary principles to defend their right to human property. They "risked [their] Lives and Fortunes, and waded through Seas of Blood" to secure "the Possession of [their] Rights of Liberty and Property," only to hear of "a very subtle and daring Attempt" to "dispossess us of a very important Part of our Property." Emancipation would bring "Want, Poverty, Distress, and Ruin to the Free Citizen." The liberties coveted by ordinary white Americans bore hard on the interests of Native Americans and slaves.

> **EXPLAIN CONSEQUENCES**
> How did the Revolutionary commitment to liberty and the protection of property affect enslaved African Americans and western Indians?

The Articles of Confederation

As Patriots embraced independence in 1776, they envisioned a central government with limited powers. Carter Braxton of Virginia thought the Continental Congress should "regulate the affairs of trade, war, peace, alliances, &c." but "should by no means have authority to interfere with the internal police [governance] or domestic concerns of any Colony."

That idea informed the **Articles of Confederation**, which were approved by the Continental Congress in November 1777. The Articles provided for a loose union in which "each state retains its sovereignty, freedom, and independence." As an association of equals, each state had one vote regardless of its size, population, or wealth. Important laws needed the approval of nine of the thirteen states, and changes in the Articles required unanimous consent. Though the Confederation had significant powers on paper—it could declare war, make treaties with foreign nations, adjudicate disputes between the states, borrow and print money, and requisition funds from the states "for the common defense or general welfare"—it had major weaknesses as well. It had neither a chief executive nor a judiciary. Though it could make treaties, it could not enforce their provisions, since the states remained sovereign. Most important, it lacked the power to tax either the states or the people.

Although the Congress exercised authority from 1776—raising the Continental army, negotiating the treaty with France, and financing the war—the Articles won formal ratification only in 1781. The delay stemmed from conflicts over western lands. The royal charters of Virginia, Massachusetts, Connecticut, and other states set boundaries stretching to the Pacific Ocean. States without western lands—Maryland and Pennsylvania—refused to accept the Articles until the land-rich states relinquished these claims to the Confederation. Threatened by Cornwallis's army in 1781, Virginia gave up its claims, and Maryland, the last holdout, finally ratified the Articles (Map 6.5).

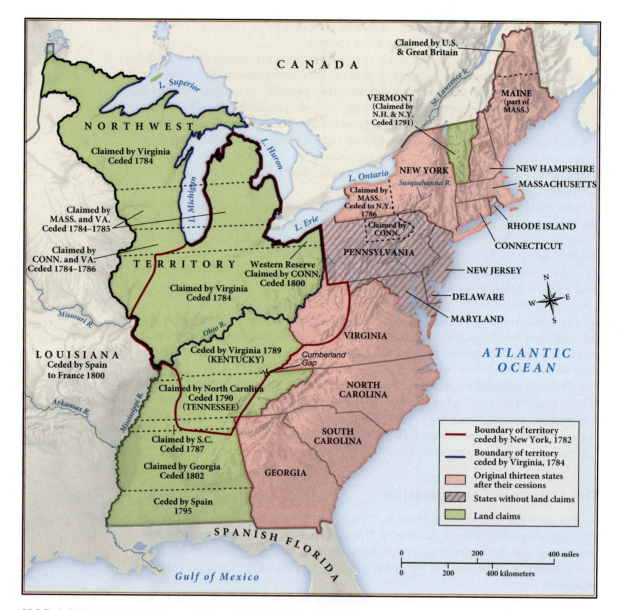

MAP 6.5 The Confederation and Western Land Claims, 1781–1802
The Congress formed by the Articles of Confederation had to resolve conflicting state claims to western lands. For example, the territories claimed by New York and Virginia on the basis of their royal charters overlapped extensively. Beginning in 1781, the Confederation Congress and, after 1789, the U.S. Congress persuaded all of the states to cede their western claims, creating a "national domain" open to all citizens. In the Northwest Ordinance (1787), the Congress divided the domain north of the Ohio River into territories and set up democratic procedures by which they could eventually join the Union as states. South of the Ohio River, the Congress allowed the existing southern states to play a substantial role in settling the ceded lands.

Continuing Fiscal Crisis By 1780, the central government was nearly bankrupt, and General Washington called urgently for a national tax system; without one, he warned, "our cause is lost." Led by Robert Morris, who became superintendent of finance in 1781, nationalist-minded Patriots tried to expand the Confederation's authority. They persuaded Congress to charter the Bank of North America, a private institution in Philadelphia, arguing that its notes would stabilize the inflated Continental currency. Morris also created a central bureaucracy to manage the Confederation's finances and urged Congress to enact a 5 percent import tax. Rhode Island and New York rejected the tax proposal. His state had opposed British import duties, New York's representative declared, and it would not accept them from Congress. To raise revenue, Congress looked to the sale of western lands. In 1783, it asserted that the recently signed Treaty of Paris had extinguished the Indians' rights to those lands and made them the property of the United States.

The Northwest Ordinance   By 1784, more than 30,000 settlers had already moved to Kentucky and Tennessee, despite the uncertainties of frontier warfare, and after the war their numbers grew rapidly. In that year, the residents of what is now eastern Tennessee organized a new state, called it Franklin, and sought admission to the Confederation. To preserve its authority over the West, Congress refused to recognize Franklin. Subsequently, Congress created the Southwest and Mississippi Territories (the future states of Tennessee, Alabama, and Mississippi) from lands ceded by North Carolina and Georgia. Because these cessions carried the stipulation that "no regulation . . . shall tend to emancipate slaves," these states and all those south of the Ohio River allowed human bondage.

However, the Confederation Congress banned slavery north of the Ohio River. Between 1784 and 1787, it issued three important ordinances organizing the "Old Northwest." The Ordinance of 1784, written by Thomas Jefferson, established the principle that territories could become states as their populations grew. The Land Ordinance of 1785 mandated a rectangular-grid system of surveying and specified a minimum price of $1 an acre. It also required that half of the townships be sold in single blocks of 23,040 acres each, which only large-scale speculators could afford, and the rest in parcels of 640 acres each, which restricted their sale to well-to-do farmers (Map 6.6).

Finally, the **Northwest Ordinance of 1787** created the territories that would eventually become the states of Ohio, Indiana, Illinois, Michigan, and Wisconsin. The ordinance prohibited slavery and earmarked funds from land sales for the support of schools. It also specified that Congress would appoint a governor and judges to administer each new territory until the population reached 5,000 free adult men, at which point the citizens could elect a territorial legislature. When the population reached 60,000, the legislature could devise a republican constitution and apply to join the Confederation.

The land ordinances of the 1780s were a great and enduring achievement of the Confederation Congress. They provided for orderly settlement and the admission of new states on the basis of equality; there would be no politically dependent "colonies" in the West. But they also extended the geographical division between slave and free areas that would haunt the nation in the coming decades. And they implicitly invalidated Native American claims to an enormous swath of territory — a corollary that would soon lead the newly independent nation, once again, into war.

> **COMPARE AND CONTRAST**
> In what ways did the Confederation function effectively, and what were its greatest failings?

Shays's Rebellion

Though many national leaders were optimistic about the long-term prospects of the United States, postwar economic conditions were grim. The Revolution had crippled American shipping and cut exports of tobacco, rice, and wheat. The British Navigation Acts, which had nurtured colonial commerce, now barred Americans from legal trade with the British West Indies. Moreover, low-priced British manufactures (and some from India as well) were flooding American markets, driving urban artisans and wartime textile firms out of business.

The fiscal condition of the state governments was dire, primarily because of war debts. Well-to-do merchants and landowners (including Abigail Adams) had invested in state bonds during the war; others had speculated in debt certificates, buying them on the cheap from hard-pressed farmers and soldiers. Now creditors and speculators demanded that the state governments redeem the bonds and certificates quickly and at full value, a policy that would require tax increases and a decrease in the amount of paper currency. Most legislatures — now including substantial numbers of middling farmers and artisans — refused. Instead they authorized new issues of paper currency

MAP 6.6 Land Division in the Northwest Territory

Throughout the Northwest Territory, government surveyors imposed a rectangular grid on the landscape, regardless of the local topography, so that farmers bought neatly defined tracts of land. The right-angled property lines in Muskingum County, Ohio (lower left), contrasted sharply with those in Baltimore County, Maryland (lower right), where — as in most of the eastern and southern states — boundaries followed the contours of the land.

and allowed debtors to pay private creditors in installments. Although wealthy men deplored these measures as "intoxicating Draughts of Liberty" that destroyed "the just rights of creditors," such political intervention prevented social upheaval.

In Massachusetts, however, the new constitution placed power in the hands of a mercantile elite that owned the bulk of the state's war bonds. Ignoring the interests of ordinary citizens, the legislature increased taxes fivefold to pay off wartime debts — and it stipulated that they be paid in hard currency. Even for substantial farmers, this was a crushing burden. When cash-strapped farmers could not pay both their taxes and their debts, creditors threatened lawsuits. Debtor Ephraim Wetmore heard a rumor that merchant Stephan Salisbury "would have my Body Dead or Alive in case I did not pay." To protect their livelihoods, farmers called extralegal conventions to protest high taxes and property seizures. Then mobs of angry farmers, including men of high status, closed the courts by force. "[I] had no Intensions to Destroy the Publick Government," declared Captain Adam Wheeler, a former town selectman; his goal was simply to prevent "Valuable and Industrious members of Society [being] dragged from their families to prison" because of their debts. These crowd actions grew into a full-scale revolt led by Captain Daniel Shays, a Continental army veteran.

As a revolt against taxes imposed by an unresponsive government, **Shays's Rebellion** resembled American resistance to the British Stamp Act. Consciously linking themselves to the Patriot movement, Shays's men placed pine twigs in their hats just as Continental troops had done. "The people have turned against their teachers the doctrines which were inculcated to effect the late revolution," complained Fisher Ames, a conservative Massachusetts lawmaker. Some of the radical Patriots of 1776 likewise condemned the Shaysites: "[Men who] would lessen the Weight of Government lawfully exercised must be Enemies to our happy Revolution and Common Liberty," charged Samuel Adams. To put down the rebellion, the Massachusetts legislature passed the Riot Act, and wealthy bondholders equipped a formidable fighting force, which Governor James Bowdoin used to disperse Shays's ragtag army during the winter of 1786–1787.

Although Shays's Rebellion failed, it showed that many middling Patriot families felt that American oppressors had replaced British tyrants. Massachusetts voters turned Governor Bowdoin out of office, and debt-ridden farmers in New York, northern Pennsylvania, Connecticut, and New Hampshire closed courthouses and forced their governments to provide economic relief. British officials in Canada predicted the imminent demise of the United States; and American leaders urged purposeful action to save their republican experiment. Events in Massachusetts, declared nationalist Henry Knox, formed "the strongest arguments possible" for the creation of "a strong general government."

> **PLACE EVENTS IN CONTEXT**
> How did the Shaysites draw on the Revolution for inspiration?

> **IN YOUR OWN WORDS** What were the most important challenges facing governments in the 1780s?

The Constitution of 1787

These issues ultimately led to the drafting of a national constitution. From its creation, the U.S. Constitution was a controversial document, both acclaimed for solving the nation's woes and condemned for perverting its republican principles. Critics charged that republican institutions worked only in small political units — the states. Advocates replied that the Constitution extended republicanism by adding another level of government elected by the people. In the new two-level political federation created by the Constitution, the national government would exercise limited, delegated powers, and the existing state governments would retain authority over all other matters.

The Rise of a Nationalist Faction

Money questions — debts, taxes, and tariffs — dominated the postwar political agenda. Americans who had served the Confederation as military officers, officials, and diplomats viewed these issues from a national perspective and advocated a stronger central government. George Washington, Robert Morris, Benjamin Franklin, John Jay, and John Adams wanted Congress to control foreign and interstate trade and tariff policy. However, lawmakers in Massachusetts, New York, and Pennsylvania — states with strong commercial traditions — insisted on controlling their own tariffs, both to protect their artisans from low-cost imports and to assist their merchants. Most southern states opposed tariffs because planters wanted to import British textiles and ironware at the lowest possible prices.

Nonetheless, some southern leaders became nationalists because their state legislatures had cut taxes and refused to redeem state war bonds. Such policies, lamented wealthy bondholder Charles Lee of Virginia, led taxpayers to believe they would "never be compelled to pay" the public debt. Creditors also condemned state laws that "stayed" (delayed) the payment of mortgages and other private debts. "While men are madly accumulating enormous debts, their legislators are making provisions for their nonpayment," complained a South Carolina merchant. To undercut the democratic majorities in the state legislatures, creditors joined the movement for a stronger central government.

Delegates from five states met in Annapolis, Maryland, in September 1786 to consider solutions to the confederation's economic problems. They recommended that another convention, with representatives from all the states, meet in Philadelphia in 1787. Spurred on by Shays's Rebellion, nationalists in Congress secured a resolution calling for such a convention to revise the Articles of Confederation. Only an "efficient plan from the Convention," a fellow nationalist wrote to James Madison, "can prevent anarchy first & civil convulsions afterwards."

The Philadelphia Convention

In May 1787, fifty-five delegates arrived in Philadelphia. They came from every state except Rhode Island, where the legislature opposed increasing central authority. Most were strong nationalists; forty-two had served in the Confederation Congress. They were also educated and propertied: merchants, slaveholding planters, and "monied men." There were no artisans, backcountry settlers, or tenants, and only a single yeoman farmer.

Some influential Patriots missed the convention. John Adams and Thomas Jefferson were serving as American ministers to Britain and France, respectively. The Massachusetts General Court rejected Samuel Adams as a delegate because he opposed a stronger national government, and his fellow firebrand from Virginia, Patrick Henry, refused to attend because he "smelt a rat." Just as politically engaged citizens disagreed in 1787 whether a new form of government was needed, historians have argued ever since about whether the Constitution was necessary (Interpretations).

The absence of experienced leaders and contrary-minded delegates allowed capable younger nationalists to set the agenda. Declaring that the convention would "decide for ever the fate of Republican Government," James Madison insisted on increased national authority. Alexander Hamilton of New York likewise demanded a strong central government to protect the republic from "the imprudence of democracy."

James Madison, Statesman Throughout his long public life, Madison kept the details of his private life to himself. His biography, he believed, should be a record of his public accomplishments, not his private affairs. Future generations celebrated him not as a great man (like Hamilton or Jefferson) or as a great president (like Washington), but as an original and incisive political thinker. The chief architect of the U.S. Constitution and the Bill of Rights, Madison was the preeminent republican political theorist of his generation. Mead Art Museum, Amherst College, MA, USA/Bequest of Herbert L. Pratt (Class of 1895)/Bridgeman Images.

Was the Constitution Necessary?

Political debate during the 1780s focused on the efficacy of the Articles of Confederation, ratified in 1781. For those leery of a strong central government, the Confederation placed authority properly with the states and safeguarded the rights of the people against tyranny. To others, the national Congress lacked the authority and power to restrain popular excesses, maintain order, and establish sound financial policies. Commercial growth convinced some Americans that the young country was thriving, but others saw the chase for money as a sign of moral weakness. These divergent views came to a head in May 1787 when representatives from the states met in Philadelphia to revise the Articles of Confederation. Instead they drafted an entirely new form of government. Two historians — Merrill Jensen and Gordon S. Wood — offer interpretations of the 1780s from differing points of view, highlighting factors pushing some to support and others to reject the Articles of Confederation.

MERRILL JENSEN

SOURCE: Merrill Jensen, *The New Nation: A History of the United States During the Confederation, 1781–1789* (New York: Alfred A. Knopf, 1950), 423–424.

[T]he often violent expression of such discontents in politics should not blind us to the fact that the period was one of extraordinary economic growth. Merchants owned more ships at the end of the 1780s than they had at the beginning of the Revolution . . . [and] the export of agricultural produce was double. . . . American cities grew rapidly. . . . There can be no question but that freedom from the British Empire resulted in a surge of activity in all phases of American life . . . [T]here is no evidence of stagnation and decay in the 1780s. Instead the story is one of a newly free people who seized upon every means to improve and enrich themselves in a nation which they believed had a golden destiny.

GORDON S. WOOD

SOURCE: Gordon S. Wood, *The Creation of the American Republic, 1776–1787* (New York: W. W. Norton & Company, 1969), 415–417.

Viewing the state as analogous to the human body, Americans saw their country stricken by a serious sickness. The 1780s seemed to mark the point in the life of the young nation where a decisive change had to occur, leading either to recovery or death. . . . The signs of disease spread everywhere. Merchants and farmers were seeking their own selfish ends; hucksters were engrossing products to raise prices. Even government officials . . . were using their public positions to fill their own pockets. The fluctuation in the value of money . . . was putting a premium on selfishness. . . . Instead of bringing about the moral reformation they had anticipated from victory, the Revolution had only aggravated America's corruption and sin.

QUESTIONS FOR ANALYSIS

1. Identify and explain two differences between these historians' interpretations of America during the 1780s.
2. Using the two historians' descriptions of the 1780s, identify the factors that might have led some Americans to support — and others to reject — the Articles of Confederation.
3. Explain how this chapter's sections on "The Articles of Confederation" and "The Constitution of 1787" support one or the other historian's interpretation of the 1780s.

The Virginia and New Jersey Plans The delegates elected George Washington as their presiding officer and voted to meet behind closed doors. Then — momentously — they decided not to revise the Articles of Confederation but rather to consider the so-called **Virginia Plan**, a scheme for a powerful national government devised by James Madison. Just thirty-six years old, Madison was determined to fashion national political institutions run by men of high character. A graduate of Princeton, he had read classical and modern political theory and served in both the Confederation Congress and the Virginia assembly. Once an optimistic Patriot, Madison had grown discouraged because of the "narrow ambition" and outlook of state legislators.

Madison's Virginia Plan differed from the Articles of Confederation in three crucial respects. First, the plan rejected state sovereignty in favor of the "supremacy of national authority," including the power to overturn state laws. Second, it called for the national government to be established by the people (not the states) and for national laws to operate directly on citizens of the various states. Third, the plan proposed a three-tier election system in which ordinary voters would elect only the lower house of the national legislature. This lower house would then select the upper house, and both houses would appoint the executive and judiciary.

From a political perspective, Madison's plan had two fatal flaws. First, most state politicians and citizens resolutely opposed allowing the national government to veto state laws. Second, the plan based representation in the lower house on population; this provision, a Delaware delegate warned, would allow the populous states to "crush the small ones whenever they stand in the way of their ambitious or interested views."

So delegates from Delaware and other small states rallied behind a plan devised by William Paterson of New Jersey. The **New Jersey Plan** gave the Confederation the power to raise revenue, control commerce, and make binding requisitions on the states. But it preserved the states' control of their own laws and guaranteed their equality: as in the Confederation Congress, each state would have one vote in a unicameral legislature. Delegates from the more populous states vigorously opposed this provision. After a month-long debate on the two plans, a bare majority of the states agreed to use Madison's Virginia Plan as the basis of discussion.

This decision raised the odds that the convention would create a more powerful national government. Outraged by this prospect, two New York delegates, Robert Yates and John Lansing, accused their colleagues of exceeding their mandate to revise the Articles and left the convention. The remaining delegates met six days a week during the summer of 1787, debating both high principles and practical details. Experienced politicians, they looked for a plan that would be acceptable to most citizens and existing political interests. Pierce Butler of South Carolina invoked a classical Greek precedent: "We must follow the example of Solon, who gave the Athenians not the best government he could devise but the best they would receive."

The Great Compromise   As the convention grappled with the central problem of the representation of large and small states, the Connecticut delegates suggested a possible solution. They proposed that the national legislature's upper chamber (the Senate) have two members from each state, while seats in the lower chamber (the House of Representatives) be apportioned by population (determined every ten years by a national census). After bitter debate, delegates from the populous states reluctantly accepted this "Great Compromise."

Other state-related issues were quickly settled by restricting (or leaving ambiguous) the extent of central authority. Some delegates opposed a national system of courts, predicting that "the states will revolt at such encroachments" on their judicial authority. This danger led the convention to vest the judicial power "in one supreme Court" and allow the new national legislature to decide whether to establish lower courts within the states. The convention also refused to set a property requirement for voting in national elections. "Eight or nine states have extended the right of suffrage beyond the freeholders," George Mason of Virginia pointed out. "What will people there say if they should be disfranchised?" Finally, the convention specified that state legislatures would elect members of the upper house, or Senate, and the states would select the electors who would choose the president. By allowing states to have important roles in the new constitutional system, the delegates hoped that their citizens would accept limits on state sovereignty.

Negotiations over Slavery   The shadow of slavery hovered over many debates, and Gouverneur Morris of New York brought it into view. To safeguard property rights, Morris wanted life terms for senators, a property qualification for voting in national elections, and a strong president with veto power. Nonetheless, he rejected the legitimacy of two traditional types of property: the feudal dues claimed by aristocratic landowners and the ownership of slaves. An advocate of free markets and personal liberty, Morris condemned slavery as "a nefarious institution."

Many slave-owning delegates from the Chesapeake region, including Madison and George Mason, recognized that slavery contradicted republican principles and hoped for its eventual demise. They supported an end to American participation in the Atlantic slave trade, a proposal the South Carolina and Georgia delegates angrily rejected. Unless the importation of African slaves continued, these rice planters and merchants declared, their states "shall not be parties to the Union." At their insistence, the convention denied Congress the power to regulate immigration—and so the slave trade—until 1808 (Analyzing Voices).

The delegates devised other slavery-related compromises. To mollify southern planters, they wrote a "fugitive clause" that allowed masters to reclaim enslaved blacks (or white indentured servants) who fled to other states. But in acknowledgment of the antislavery sentiments of Morris and other northerners, the delegates excluded the words *slavery* and *slave* from the Constitution; it spoke only of citizens and "all other Persons." Because slaves lacked the vote, antislavery delegates wanted their census numbers excluded when apportioning seats in Congress. Southerners—ironically, given that they considered slaves property—demanded that slaves be counted in the census the same as full citizens, to increase the South's representation. Ultimately, the delegates agreed that each slave would count as three-fifths of a free person for purposes of representation and taxation, a compromise that helped southern planters dominate the national government until 1860.

National Authority   Having addressed the concerns of small states and slave states, the convention created a powerful national government. The Constitution declared that congressional legislation was the "supreme" law of the land. It gave the new government the power to tax, raise an army and a navy, and regulate foreign and interstate commerce, with the authority to make all laws "necessary and proper" to implement those and other provisions. To assist creditors and establish the new government's fiscal integrity, the Constitution required the United States to honor the existing national debt and prohibited the states from issuing paper money or enacting "any Law impairing the Obligation of Contracts."

The proposed constitution was not a "perfect production," Benjamin Franklin admitted, as he urged the delegates to sign it in September 1787. But the great statesman confessed his astonishment at finding "this system approaching so near to perfection." His colleagues apparently agreed; all but three signed the document.

> **COMPARE AND CONTRAST**
> How did the Constitution, in its final form, differ from the plan that James Madison originally proposed?

The People Debate Ratification

The procedure for ratifying the new constitution was as controversial as its contents. Knowing that Rhode Island (and perhaps other states) would reject it, the delegates did not submit the Constitution to the state legislatures for their unanimous consent, as required by the Articles of Confederation. Instead, they arbitrarily—and cleverly—declared that it would take effect when ratified by conventions in nine of the thirteen states. Moreover, they insisted that the conventions could only approve or disapprove the plan; they could not suggest alterations. As George Mason put it, the conventions would "take this or take nothing."

As the constitutional debate began in early 1788, the nationalists seized the initiative with two bold moves. First, they called themselves **Federalists**, suggesting that they supported a federal union—a loose, decentralized system—and obscuring their commitment to a strong national government. Second, they launched a coordinated campaign in pamphlets and newspapers to explain and justify the Philadelphia constitution.

The Antifederalists   The opponents of the Constitution, called by default the **Antifederalists**, had diverse backgrounds and motives. Some, like Governor George Clinton of New York, feared that state governments would lose power. Rural

The First National Debate over Slavery

In this part of the text, we trace the impact of republican ideology on American politics and society. What happened when republicanism collided head-on with the well-established practice of slavery? After the Revolution, the Massachusetts courts abolished slavery, but in 1787, slavery was legal in the rest of the Union and was the bedrock of social order and agricultural production in the southern states. A look at the debates on the issue of the African slave trade at the Philadelphia convention and in a state ratifying convention shows that slavery was an extremely divisive issue at the birth of the nation—a dark cloud threatening the bright future of the young republic.

THE CONSTITUTIONAL CONVENTION

Slavery was not a major topic of discussion at the Philadelphia convention, but it surfaced a number of times, notably in the important debate over representation (which produced the three-fifths clause). A discussion of the Atlantic slave trade began when Luther Martin, a delegate from Maryland, proposed a clause allowing Congress to impose a tax on or prohibit the importation of slaves.

Source: Max Farrand, ed., *The Records of the Federal Convention of 1787* (New Haven: Yale University Press, 1911), 2: 364–365, 369–372.

Mr. Martin proposed to vary article 7, sect. 4 so as to allow a prohibition or tax on the importation of slaves. . . . [He believed] it was inconsistent with the principles of the Revolution, and dishonorable to the American character, to have such a feature [promoting the slave trade] in the Constitution.

Mr. [John] Rutledge [of South Carolina declared that] religion and humanity had nothing to do with this question. Interest alone is the governing principle with nations. The true question at present is whether the Southern states shall or shall not be parties to the Union. . . . Mr. [Oliver] Ellsworth [of Connecticut] was for leaving the clause as it stands. Let every state import what it pleases. The morality or wisdom of slavery are considerations belonging to the states themselves. . . . The old Confederation had not meddled with this point, and he did not see any greater necessity for bringing it within the policy of the new one.

Mr. [Charles C.] Pinckney [said] South Carolina can never receive the plan [for a new constitution] if it prohibits the slave trade. In every proposed extension of the powers of Congress, that state has expressly and watchfully excepted that of meddling with the importation of Negroes. . . .

Mr. [Roger] Sherman [of Connecticut] was for leaving the clause as it stands. He disapproved of the slave trade; yet, as the states were now possessed of the right to import slaves, . . . and as it was expedient to have as few objections as possible to the proposed scheme of government, he thought it best to leave the matter as we find it.

Col. [George] Mason [of Virginia stated that] this infernal trade originated in the avarice of British merchants. The British government constantly checked the attempts of Virginia to put a stop to it. The present question concerns not the importing states alone, but the whole Union. . . . Maryland and Virginia, he said, had already prohibited the importation of slaves expressly. North Carolina had done the same in substance. All this would be in vain if South Carolina and Georgia be at liberty to import. The Western people are already calling out for slaves for their new lands, and will fill that country with slaves, if they can be got through South Carolina and Georgia. Slavery discourages arts and manufactures. The poor despise labor when performed by slaves. They prevent the immigration of whites, who really enrich and strengthen a country. . . .

Every master of slaves is born a petty tyrant. They bring the judgment of Heaven on a country. As nations cannot be rewarded or punished in the next world, they must be in this. By an inevitable chain of causes and effects, Providence punishes national sins by national calamities. . . . He held it essential, in every point of view, that the general government should have power to prevent the increase of slavery.

democrats protested that the proposed document, unlike most state constitutions, lacked a declaration of individual rights; they also feared that the central government would be run by wealthy men. "Lawyers and men of learning and monied men expect to be managers of this Constitution," worried a Massachusetts farmer. "[T]hey will swallow up all of us little folks . . . just as the whale swallowed up Jonah." Giving political substance to these fears, Melancton Smith of New York argued that the large electoral districts prescribed by the Constitution would restrict office holding to wealthy men, whereas the smaller districts used in state elections usually produced legislatures "composed principally of respectable yeomanry." John Quincy Adams agreed: if only

Mr. Ellsworth, as he had never owned a slave, could not judge of the effects of slavery on character. He said, however, that if it was to be considered in a moral light, we ought to go further, and free those already in the country. . . . Let us not intermeddle. As population increases, poor laborers will be so plenty as to render slaves useless. Slavery, in time, will not be a speck in our country. . . .

Gen. [Charles C.] Pinckney [argued that] South Carolina and Georgia cannot do without slaves. As to Virginia, she will gain by stopping the importations. Her slaves will rise in value, and she has more than she wants. It would be unequal to require South Carolina and Georgia to confederate on such unequal terms. . . . He contended that the importation of slaves would be for the interest of the whole Union. The more slaves, the more produce to employ the carrying trade; the more consumption also; and the more of this, the more revenue for the common treasury. . . . [He] should consider a rejection of the [present] clause as an exclusion of South Carolina from the Union. 99

THE MASSACHUSETTS RATIFYING CONVENTION

In Philadelphia, the delegates agreed on a compromise: they gave Congress the power to tax or prohibit slave imports, as Luther Martin had proposed, but withheld that power for twenty years. In the Massachusetts convention, the delegates split on this issue and on many others. They ratified the Constitution by a narrow margin, 187 to 168.

SOURCE: Jonathan Elliot, ed., *The Debates . . . on the Adoption of the Federal Constitution* (Philadelphia: J. B. Lippincott, 1836), 1: 103–105, 107, 112, 117.

66 Mr. Neal (from Kittery) [an Antifederalist] went over the ground of objection to . . . the idea that slave trade was allowed to be continued for 20 years. His profession, he said, obliged him to bear witness against any thing that should favor the making merchandize of the bodies of men, and unless his objection was removed, he could not put his hand to the constitution. Other gentlemen said, in addition to this idea, that there was not even a proposition that the negroes ever shall be free: and Gen. Thompson exclaimed — 'Mr. President, shall it be said, that after we have established our own independence and freedom, we make slaves of others? Oh! Washington . . . he has immortalized himself! but he holds those in slavery who have a good right to be free as he is. . . .'

On the other side, gentlemen said, that the step taken in this article, towards the abolition of slavery, was one of the beauties of the constitution. They observed, that in the confederation there was no provision whatever for its ever being abolished; but this constitution provides, that Congress may after twenty years, totally annihilate the slave trade. . . .

Mr. Heath (Federalist): . . . I apprehend that it is not in our power to do any thing for or against those who are in slavery in the southern states. No gentleman within these walls detests every idea of slavery more than I do: it is generally detested by the people of this commonwealth, and I ardently hope that the time will soon come, when our brethren in the southern states will view it as we do, and put a stop to it; but to this we have no right to compel them.

Two questions naturally arise: if we ratify the Constitution, shall we do any thing by our act to hold the blacks in slavery or shall we become the partakers of other men's sins? I think neither of them: each state is sovereign and independent to a certain degree, and they have a right, and will regulate their own internal affairs, as to themselves appears proper. . . . We are not in this case partakers of other men's sins. . . .

The federal convention went as far as they could; the migration or immigration &c. is confined to the states, now existing only, new states cannot claim it. Congress, by their ordnance for erecting new states, some time since, declared that there shall be no slavery in them. But whether those in slavery in the southern states, will be emancipated after the year 1808, I do not pretend to determine: I rather doubt it. 99

QUESTIONS FOR ANALYSIS

1. At the Constitutional Convention in Philadelphia, what were the main arguments for and against federal restrictions on the Atlantic slave trade? How do you explain the position taken by the Connecticut delegates in Philadelphia and Mr. Heath in the Massachusetts debate?

2. What argument does George Mason, a Virginia slave owner, make in favor of prohibiting the Atlantic slave trade?

3. What evidence of regional tensions appears in the documents? Several men from different states — Mason from Virginia, Ellsworth from Connecticut, and Heath from Massachusetts — offered predictions about the future of slavery. How accurate were they?

"*eight* men" would represent Massachusetts, "they will infallibly be chosen from the aristocratic part of the community."

Smith summed up the views of Americans who held traditional republican values. To keep government "close to the people," they wanted the states to remain small sovereign republics tied together only for trade and defense — not the "United States" but the "States United." Citing the French political philosopher Montesquieu, Antifederalists argued that republican institutions were best suited to small polities. "No extensive empire can be governed on republican principles," declared James Winthrop of Massachusetts. Patrick Henry worried that the Constitution would re-create British rule: high taxes, an oppressive bureaucracy, a standing army, and a "great and mighty President . . . supported in extravagant munificence." As another Antifederalist put it, "I had rather be a free citizen of the small republic of Massachusetts than an oppressed subject of the great American Empire." Many Americans found themselves somewhere in the middle, supporting a stronger central government in principle but worried about countless details that made the Constitution appear flawed.

Federalists Respond In New York, where ratification was hotly contested, James Madison, John Jay, and Alexander Hamilton defended the proposed constitution in a series of eighty-five essays written in 1787 and 1788, collectively titled *The Federalist*. This work influenced political leaders throughout the country and subsequently won acclaim as an important treatise of practical republicanism. Its authors denied that a centralized government would lead to domestic tyranny. Drawing on Montesquieu's theories and John Adams's *Thoughts on Government*, Madison, Jay, and Hamilton pointed out that authority would be divided among the president, a bicameral legislature, and a judiciary. Each branch of government would "check and balance" the others and so preserve liberty.

In "**Federalist No. 10**," Madison challenged the view that republican governments only worked in small polities, arguing that a large state would better protect republican liberty. It was "sown in the nature of man," Madison wrote, for individuals to seek power and form factions. Indeed, "a landed interest, a manufacturing interest, a mercantile interest, a moneyed interest, with many lesser interests, grow up of necessity in civilized nations." A free society should welcome all factions but keep any one of them from becoming dominant — something best achieved in a large republic. "Extend the sphere and you take in a greater variety of parties and interests," Madison concluded, inhibiting the formation of a majority eager "to invade the rights of other citizens."

The Constitution Ratified The delegates debating these issues in the state ratification conventions included untutored farmers and middling artisans as well as educated gentlemen. Generally, backcountry delegates were especially skeptical, while those from coastal areas were more likely to support the new constitution. In Pennsylvania, a coalition of Philadelphia merchants and artisans and commercial farmers ensured its ratification. Other early Federalist successes came in four less populous states — Delaware, New Jersey, Georgia, and Connecticut — where delegates hoped that a strong national government would offset the power of large neighboring states (Map 6.7).

The Constitution's first real test came in January 1788 in Massachusetts, a hotbed of Antifederalist sentiment. Influential Patriots, including Samuel Adams and Governor John Hancock, opposed the new constitution, as did many followers of Daniel Shays. But Boston artisans, who wanted tariff protection from British imports, supported ratification. To win over other delegates, Federalist leaders suggested nine amendments that the Massachusetts delegation would submit to the new Congress for consideration once the Constitution was ratified. By a close vote of 187 to 168, the Federalists carried the day.

Spring brought Federalist victories in Maryland, South Carolina, and New Hampshire, reaching the nine-state quota required for ratification. But it took the powerful arguments advanced in *The Federalist* and more talk of amendments to secure the Constitution's adoption in the essential states of Virginia and New York. The votes were again close: 89 to 79 in Virginia and 30 to 27 in New York.

Testifying to their respect for popular sovereignty and majority rule, most Americans accepted the verdict of the ratifying conventions. "A decided majority" of the New Hampshire assembly had opposed the "new system," reported Joshua Atherton, but now they said, "It is adopted, let us try it." In Virginia, Patrick Henry vowed to "submit as a quiet citizen" and fight for amendments "in a constitutional way." And during the first session of Congress, James Madison set to work drafting a set of amendments to

MAP 6.7 Ratifying the Constitution of 1787

In 1907, geographer Owen Libby mapped the votes of members of the state conventions that ratified the Constitution. His map showed that most delegates from seaboard or commercial farming districts (which sent many delegates to the conventions) supported the Constitution, while those from sparsely represented, subsistence-oriented backcountry areas opposed it. Subsequent research has confirmed Libby's socioeconomic interpretation of the voting patterns in North and South Carolina and in Massachusetts. However, other states' delegates were influenced by different factors. For example, in Georgia, delegates from all regions voted for ratification.

satisfy some of the most pressing concerns that had arisen in the ratification process (see Chapter 7).

Unlike in France, where the Revolution of 1789 divided the society into irreconcilable factions for generations, the American Constitutional Revolution of 1787 created a national republic that enjoyed broad popular support. Federalists celebrated their triumph by organizing great processions in the seaport cities. By marching in an orderly fashion—in conscious contrast to the riotous Revolutionary mobs—Federalist-minded citizens affirmed their allegiance to a self-governing but elite-ruled republican nation.

IN YOUR OWN WORDS   What were the most important compromises struck in the Philadelphia convention of 1787?

SUMMARY

In this chapter, we examined the unfolding of two related sets of events. The first was the war between Britain and its rebellious colonies that began in 1776 and ended in 1783. The two great battles of Saratoga (1777) and Yorktown (1781) determined the outcome of that conflict. Surprisingly, given the military might of the British Empire, both were American victories. These triumphs testify to the determination of George Washington, the resilience of the Continental army, and support for the Patriot cause from hundreds of local militias and tens of thousands of taxpaying citizens.

This popular support reflected the Patriots' second success: building effective institutions of republican government. These elected institutions of local and state governance evolved out of colonial-era town meetings and representative assemblies. They were defined in the state constitutions written between 1776 and 1781, and their principles informed the first national constitution, the Articles of Confederation. Despite the challenges posed by conflicts over suffrage, women's rights, and fiscal policy, these self-governing political institutions carried the new republic successfully through the war-torn era and laid the foundation for the Constitution of 1787, the national charter that endures today.

CHAPTER 6 REVIEW

TERMS TO KNOW   *Identify and explain the significance of each term below.*

Key Concepts and Events

Battle of Long Island (1776) (p. 172)

Battle of Saratoga (1777) (p. 175)

Valley Forge (p. 176)

Philipsburg Proclamation (p. 179)

Battle of Yorktown (1781) (p. 182)

currency tax (p. 183)

Treaty of Paris of 1783 (p. 183)

Pennsylvania constitution of 1776 (p. 185)

mixed government (p. 185)

Articles of Confederation (p. 187)

Northwest Ordinance of 1787 (p. 189)

Shays's Rebellion (p. 191)

Virginia Plan (p. 193)

New Jersey Plan (p. 194)

Federalists (p. 195)

Antifederalists (p. 195)

Federalist No. 10 (p. 198)

Key People

General George Washington (p. 172)

General William Howe (p. 172)

General Horatio Gates (p. 175)

Robert Morris (p. 176)

Baron von Steuben (p. 177)

Judith Sargent Murray (p. 186)

James Madison (p. 192)

REVIEW QUESTIONS   *Answer these questions to demonstrate your understanding of the chapter's main ideas.*

1. What challenges did Patriot forces confront in the first two years of the war, and what were their key achievements?

2. What were the keys to Patriot victory in the American Revolution?

3. What were the most important challenges facing governments in the 1780s?

4. What were the most important compromises struck in the Philadelphia convention of 1787?

5. Consider the events listed under "Politics and Power" and "Work, Exchange, and Technology" for the period 1776–1787 on the thematic timeline on page 138. How did war debt and inflation influence the development of political institutions during these years?

MAKING CONNECTIONS

Recognize the larger developments and continuities within and across chapters by answering these questions.

1. In Chapter 5, we saw the way that protests against imperial policy grew until colonists chose to declare their independence rather than submit to Parliament's authority. By 1787, the problems created by the Revolutionary War forced leaders of the newly independent states to consider plans for their own powerful central government. What problems led nationalists to believe such a step was necessary? How did Antifederalists draw on Revolutionary ideas to make their case against the Constitution? What claims did nationalists make in response to dampen Antifederalist fears?

2. Look again at Map 6.5 on page 188 showing western land claims in the 1780s. If these claims had not been ceded to the Continental Congress, what would have been the likely result? Why was it so important to the survival of the Confederation that individual states give up their claims to these western lands?

KEY TURNING POINTS

Refer to the chapter chronology on page 172 for help in answering the questions below.

Gates defeats Burgoyne at Saratoga (1777), the Franco-American alliance (1778), and Cornwallis surrenders at Yorktown (1781): How were these three events linked? How important was the French alliance to the Patriot victory?

7
C H A P T E R

Hammering Out a Federal Republic
1787–1820

IDENTIFY THE BIG IDEA

What was required to make the United States a viable independent republic, and how did debates over the Constitution shape relations between the national government and the states?

Like an earthquake, the American Revolution shook the European monarchical order, and its aftershocks reverberated for decades. By "creating a new republic based on the rights of the individual, the North Americans introduced a new force into the world," the eminent German historian Leopold von Ranke warned the king of Bavaria in 1854, a force that might cost the monarch his throne. Before 1776, "a king who ruled by the grace of God had been the center around which everything turned. Now the idea emerged that power should come from below [from the people]."

Other republican-inspired upheavals—England's Puritan Revolution of the 1640s and the French Revolution of 1789—ended in political chaos and military rule. Similar fates befell many Latin American republics that won independence from Spain in the early nineteenth century. But the American states escaped both anarchy and dictatorship. Having been raised in a Radical Whig political culture that viewed standing armies and powerful generals as instruments of tyranny, General George Washington left public life in 1783 to manage his plantation, astonishing European observers but bolstering the authority of elected Patriot leaders. "'Tis a Conduct so novel," American painter John Trumbull reported from London, that it is "inconceivable to People [here]."

The great task of fashioning representative republican governments absorbed the energy and intellect of an entire generation and was rife with conflict. Seeking to perpetuate the elite-led polity of the colonial era, Federalists celebrated "natural aristocrats" such as Washington and condemned the radical republicanism of the French Revolution. In response, Jefferson and his Republican followers claimed the Fourth of July as their holiday and "we the people" as their political language. "There was a grand democrat procession in Town on the 4th of July," came a report from Baltimore: "All the farmers, tanners, black-smiths, shoemakers, etc. were there . . . and afterwards they went to a grand feast."

Many people of high status worried that the new state governments were too attentive to the demands of such ordinary workers and their families. When considering a bill, Connecticut conservative Ezra Stiles grumbled, every elected official "instantly thinks how it will affect his constituents" rather than how it would enhance the general welfare. What Stiles criticized as irresponsible, however, most Americans welcomed. The concerns of ordinary citizens were now paramount, and traditional elites trembled.

An Emblem of America, 1800 In the first years of independence, citizens of the United States searched for a symbolic representation of their new nation. This engraving shows many of the choices: Should the symbol of "America" have an ideological meaning, as in the Goddess of Liberty? Or should it enshrine national heroes, as in the stone Memorial to Washington? Or should America's symbol be found among its unique features, such as Niagara Falls (pictured in the background) or the presence of Africans and Indians (as represented by the black youth to the right and the spear-brandishing figure in front of the falls)? Or, finally, should its symbol be the national flag? Courtesy of the John Carter Brown Library at Brown University.

CHAPTER CHRONOLOGY

As you read, ask yourself why this chapter begins and ends with these dates and then identify the links among related events.

1784–1789	▶ Contested Indian treaties: Fort Stanwix (1784), Fort McIntosh (1785), Fort Finney (1786), and Fort Harmar (1789)
1789–1799	▶ French Revolution
1789	▶ Judiciary Act establishes federal courts
1790	▶ Hamilton's public credit system approved
1790–1791	▶ Western Confederacy defeats U.S. armies
1791–1803	▶ Haitian Revolution
1791	▶ Bill of Rights ratified ▶ Bank of the United States chartered
1792	▶ Kentucky joins Union
1793	▶ War between Britain and France
1794	▶ Madison and Jefferson found Republican Party ▶ Whiskey Rebellion ▶ Battle of Fallen Timbers
1795	▶ Jay's Treaty with Great Britain ▶ Pinckney's Treaty with Spain ▶ Treaty of Greenville accepts Indian land rights

1796	▶ Tennessee joins Union
1798	▶ XYZ Affair ▶ Alien, Sedition, and Naturalization Acts ▶ Virginia and Kentucky Resolutions
1800	▶ Jefferson elected president
1801–1812	▶ Gallatin reduces national debt
1803	▶ Louisiana Purchase ▶ *Marbury v. Madison* asserts judicial review
1804–1806	▶ Lewis and Clark explore West
1807	▶ Embargo Act cripples American shipping
1808	▶ Madison elected president
1809	▶ Tecumseh and Tenskwatawa revive Western Confederacy
1812–1815	▶ War of 1812
1817–1825	▶ Era of Good Feeling
1819	▶ Adams-Onís Treaty ▶ *McCulloch v. Maryland; Dartmouth College v. Woodward*

The Political Crisis of the 1790s

The final decade of the eighteenth century brought fresh challenges for American politics. The Federalists split into two factions over financial policy and the French Revolution, and their leaders, Alexander Hamilton and Thomas Jefferson, offered contrasting visions of the future. Would the United States remain an agricultural nation governed by local officials, as Jefferson hoped? Or would Hamilton's vision of a strong national government and an economy based on manufacturing become reality?

The Federalists Implement the Constitution

The Constitution expanded the dimensions of political life by allowing voters to choose national leaders as well as local and state officials. The Federalists swept the election of 1788, winning forty-four seats in the House of Representatives; only eight Antifederalists won election. As expected, members of the electoral college chose George Washington as president. John Adams received the second-highest number of electoral votes and became vice president.

Devising the New Government Once the military savior of his country, Washington now became its political father. At age fifty-seven, the first president possessed great personal dignity and a cautious personality. To maintain continuity, he adopted many of the administrative practices of the Confederation and asked Congress to reestablish the existing executive departments: Foreign Affairs (State), Finance (Treasury), and War. To head the Department of State, Washington chose Thomas Jefferson, a fellow Virginian and an experienced diplomat. For secretary of the treasury, he turned to Alexander Hamilton, a lawyer and his former military aide. The president designated Jefferson, Hamilton, and Secretary of War Henry Knox as his cabinet, or advisory body.

The Constitution mandated a supreme court, but the Philadelphia convention gave Congress the task of creating a national court system. The Federalists wanted strong national institutions, and the **Judiciary Act of 1789** reflected their vision. The act established a federal district court in each state and three circuit courts to hear appeals from the districts, with the Supreme Court having the final say. The Judiciary Act also specified that cases arising in state courts that involved federal laws could be appealed to the Supreme Court. This provision ensured that federal judges would determine the meaning of the Constitution.

The Bill of Rights   The Federalists kept their promise to consider amendments to the Constitution. James Madison, now a member of the House of Representatives, submitted nineteen amendments to the First Congress; by 1791, ten had been approved by Congress and ratified by the states. These ten amendments, known as the **Bill of Rights**, safeguard fundamental personal rights, including freedom of speech and religion, and mandate legal procedures, such as trial by jury. By protecting individual citizens, the amendments eased Antifederalists' fears of an oppressive national government and secured the legitimacy of the Constitution. They also addressed the issue of federalism: the proper balance between the authority of the national and state governments. But that question was constantly contested until the Civil War and remains important today.

Hamilton's Financial Program

George Washington's most important decision was choosing Alexander Hamilton as secretary of the treasury. An ambitious self-made man of great intelligence, Hamilton married into the Schuyler family, influential Hudson River Valley landowners, and was a prominent lawyer in New York City. At the Philadelphia convention, he condemned the "democratic spirit" and called for an authoritarian government and a president with near-monarchical powers.

As treasury secretary, Hamilton devised bold policies to enhance national authority and to assist financiers and merchants. He outlined his plans in three pathbreaking reports to Congress: on public credit (January 1790), on a national bank (December 1790), and on manufactures (December 1791). These reports outlined a coherent program of national mercantilism—government-assisted economic development. Hamilton's system was controversial at the time, and historians continue to debate whether the powers they gave the national government were necessary or excessive (Interpretations).

Public Credit: Redemption and Assumption   The financial and social implications of Hamilton's "**Report on the Public Credit**" made it instantly controversial. Hamilton asked Congress to redeem at face value the $55 million in Confederation securities held by foreign and domestic investors (Figure 7.1). His reasons were simple: as an underdeveloped nation, the United States needed good credit to secure loans from Dutch and British financiers. However, Hamilton's redemption plan would give enormous profits to speculators, who had bought up depreciated securities. For example, the Massachusetts firm of Burrell & Burrell had paid $600 for Confederation notes with a face value of $2,500; it stood to reap a profit of $1,900. Such windfall gains offended a majority of Americans, who condemned the speculative practices of capitalist financiers. Equally controversial was Hamilton's proposal to pay the Burrells and other note holders with new interest-bearing securities, thereby creating a permanent national debt and tying the interests of wealthy creditors to the survival of the new nation.

Patrick Henry condemned this plan "to erect, and concentrate, and perpetuate a large monied interest" and warned that it would prove "fatal to the existence of American liberty." James Madison demanded that Congress recompense those who originally owned Confederation securities: the thousands of shopkeepers, farmers, and soldiers who had bought or accepted them during the dark days of the war. However, it

Did Hamilton's Economic System Endanger the Legacy of the Revolution?

Alexander Hamilton became the nation's first secretary of the treasury in 1789 and immediately set to work organizing the new government's finances. Detailed in three major reports to Congress on public credit, a national bank, and manufacturing, Hamilton's financial plan corrected for the limitations the national government experienced under the Articles of Confederation. He wanted to establish a stable currency to encourage investment, to impose tariffs on goods imported into the country to stimulate domestic manufacturing, and to repay Revolutionary war debts with revenue from an excise tax on whiskey and other luxuries. His ambitious proposals depended on the power and authority of a strong central government and pointed toward a commercial and manufacturing future for America. While many people embraced Hamilton's vision for America's future, others grew suspicious. Historians Forrest McDonald and Lance Banning offer contrasting assessments of Hamilton's economic system and its political consequences.

FORREST McDONALD

Source: Forrest McDonald, *Alexander Hamilton: A Biography* (New York: W. W. Norton & Company, 1979), 117.

Hamilton's assigned duty, upon becoming minister of the nation's finances, would be to devise a way of managing the Revolutionary War debts so as to place public credit upon firm foundations. . . . Hamilton set for himself "the task of making the citizens in every regard more well-behaved, healthier, wiser, richer, and more secure." Specifically, he proposed to use his administration of the public finances as an instrument for forging the American people into a prosperous, happy, and respected nation.

LANCE BANNING

Source: Lance Banning, *The Jeffersonian Persuasion: Evolution of a Party Ideology* (Ithaca: Cornell University Press, 1978), 128.

His [Alexander Hamilton's] plans . . . were not only a catalyst for sectional confrontation. They seemed an excellent confirmation of persistent Antifederalist suspicions of an engulfing federal power. . . . Coming in conjunction with the high style of the new government, the antipopulistic pronouncements of some of its supporters, and measures such as an excise tax and a professional army, the Hamiltonian program might as well have been designed to awaken specific expectations about the course and nature of governmental decay that were never very far beneath the surface of revolutionary minds.

QUESTIONS FOR ANALYSIS

1. How does each historian characterize the political effects of Hamilton's economic plans?
2. From the two historians' excerpts, what can you infer about the political ideologies of Hamilton's supporters and opponents?
3. Identify two factors from this chapter that either support or refute the idea that Hamilton's economic policies threatened the legacy of the American Revolution.

---

would have been difficult to trace the original owners; moreover, nearly half the members of the House of Representatives owned Confederation securities and would profit personally from Hamilton's plan. Melding practicality with self-interest, the House rejected Madison's suggestion.

Hamilton then proposed that the national government further enhance public credit by assuming the war debts of the states. This assumption plan, costing $22 million, also favored well-to-do creditors such as Abigail Adams, who had bought depreciated Massachusetts government bonds with a face value of $2,400 for only a few hundred dollars and would reap a windfall profit. Still, Adams was a long-term investor, not a speculator like Assistant Secretary of the Treasury William Duer. Knowing Hamilton's intentions in advance, Duer and his associates secretly bought up $4.6 million of the war bonds of southern states at bargain rates. Congressional critics condemned Duer's speculation. They also pointed out that some states had already paid off their war debts; in response, Hamilton promised to reimburse those states. To win the votes of congressmen from Virginia and Maryland, the treasury chief arranged another deal: he agreed that the permanent national capital would be built along the Potomac River, where

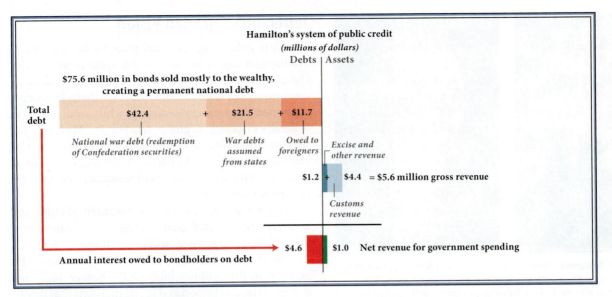

FIGURE 7.1 **Hamilton's Fiscal Structure, 1792**
As treasury secretary, Alexander Hamilton established a national debt by issuing government bonds and using the proceeds to redeem Confederation securities and assume the war debts of the states. To pay the annual interest due on the bonds, he used the revenue from excise taxes and customs duties. Hamilton deliberately did not attempt to redeem the bonds because he wanted to tie the interests of the wealthy Americans who owned them to the new national government.

suspicious southerners could easily watch its operations. Such astute bargaining gave Hamilton the votes he needed to enact his redemption and assumption plans.

Creating a National Bank   In December 1790, Hamilton asked Congress to charter the **Bank of the United States**, which would be jointly owned by private stockholders and the national government. Hamilton argued that the bank would provide stability to the specie-starved American economy by making loans to merchants, handling government funds, and issuing bills of credit — much as the Bank of England had done in Great Britain. These potential benefits persuaded Congress to grant Hamilton's bank a twenty-year charter and to send the legislation to the president for his approval.

At this critical juncture, Secretary of State Thomas Jefferson joined with James Madison to oppose Hamilton's financial initiatives. Jefferson charged that Hamilton's national bank was unconstitutional. "The incorporation of a Bank," Jefferson told President Washington, was not a power expressly "delegated to the United States by the Constitution." Jefferson's argument rested on a *strict* interpretation of the Constitution. Hamilton preferred a *loose* interpretation; he told Washington that Article 1, Section 8, empowered Congress to make "all Laws which shall be necessary and proper" to carry out the provisions of the Constitution. Agreeing with Hamilton, the president signed the legislation.

Raising Revenue Through Tariffs   Hamilton now sought revenue to pay the annual interest on the national debt. At his insistence, Congress imposed excise taxes, including a duty on whiskey distilled in the United States. These taxes would yield $1 million a year. To raise another $4 million to $5 million, the treasury secretary proposed higher tariffs on foreign imports. Although Hamilton's "**Report on Manufactures**" (1791) urged the expansion of American manufacturing, he did not support high protective tariffs that would exclude foreign products. Rather, he advocated moderate revenue tariffs that would pay the interest on the debt and other government expenses.

Hamilton's scheme worked brilliantly. As American trade increased, customs revenue rose steadily and paid down the national debt. Controversies notwithstanding, the treasury secretary had devised a strikingly modern and successful fiscal system; as entrepreneur Samuel Blodget Jr. declared in 1801, "the country prospered beyond all former example."

CONSIDER POINTS OF VIEW
Why did Hamilton believe a national debt would strengthen the United States and help to ensure its survival?

Two Visions of America Thomas Jefferson (left) and Alexander Hamilton confront each other in these portraits, as they did in the political battles of the 1790s. Jefferson was pro-French, Hamilton pro-British. Jefferson favored farmers and artisans; Hamilton supported merchants and financiers. Jefferson believed in democracy and rule by legislative majorities; Hamilton argued for strong executives and judges. Still, in the contested presidential election of 1800, Hamilton (who detested candidate Aaron Burr) threw his support to Jefferson and secured the presidency for his longtime political foe. Left: White House Collection/White House Historical Association. Right: Yale University Art Gallery.

COMPARE AND CONTRAST
How did Jefferson's idea of an agrarian republic differ from the economic vision put forward by Alexander Hamilton?

To see a longer excerpt of Jefferson's *Notes on the State of Virginia*, along with other primary sources from this period, see **Sources for America's History**.

Jefferson's Agrarian Vision

Hamilton paid a high political price for his success. As Washington began his second four-year term in 1793, Hamilton's financial measures had split the Federalists into bitterly opposed factions. Most northern Federalists supported the treasury secretary, while most southern Federalists joined a group headed by Madison and Jefferson. By 1794, the two factions had acquired names. Hamiltonians remained Federalists; the allies of Madison and Jefferson called themselves Democratic Republicans or simply Republicans.

Thomas Jefferson spoke for southern planters and western farmers. Well-read in architecture, natural history, agricultural science, and political theory, Jefferson embraced the optimism of the Enlightenment. He believed in the "improvability of the human race" and deplored the corruption and social divisions that threatened its progress. Having seen the poverty of laborers in British factories, Jefferson doubted that wageworkers had the economic and political independence needed to sustain a republican polity.

Jefferson therefore set his democratic vision of America in a society of independent yeomen farm families. "Those who labor in the earth are the chosen people of God," he wrote. The grain and meat from their homesteads would feed European nations, which "would manufacture and send us in exchange our clothes and other comforts." Jefferson's notion of an international division of labor resembled that proposed by Scottish economist Adam Smith in *The Wealth of Nations* (1776).

Turmoil in Europe brought Jefferson's vision closer to reality. The French Revolution began in 1789; four years later, the First French Republic (1792–1804) went to war against a British-led coalition of monarchies. As fighting disrupted European farming, wheat prices leaped from 5 to 8 shillings a bushel and remained high for twenty years, bringing substantial profits to Chesapeake and Middle Atlantic farmers. "Our farmers have never experienced such prosperity," remarked one observer. Simultaneously, a boom in the export of raw cotton, fueled by the invention of the cotton gin and the mechanization of cloth production in Britain, boosted the economies of Georgia and South Carolina. As Jefferson had hoped, European markets brought prosperity to American agriculture.

The French Revolution Divides Americans

American merchants profited even more handsomely from the European war. In 1793, President Washington issued a **Proclamation of Neutrality**, allowing U.S. citizens to trade with all belligerents. As neutral carriers, American merchant ships claimed a right to pass through Britain's naval blockade of French ports, and American firms quickly took over the lucrative sugar trade between France and its West Indian islands. Commercial earnings rose spectacularly, averaging $20 million annually in the 1790s — twice the value of cotton and tobacco exports. As the American merchant fleet increased from 355,000 tons in 1790 to 1.1 million tons in 1808, northern shipbuilders and merchants provided work for thousands of shipwrights, sailmakers, dockhands, and seamen. Carpenters, masons, and cabinetmakers in Boston, New York, and Philadelphia easily found work building warehouses and fashionable "Federal-style" town houses for newly affluent merchants.

Ideological Politics As Americans profited from Europe's struggles, they argued passionately over its ideologies. Most Americans had welcomed the **French Revolution**

(1789–1799) because it abolished feudalism and established a constitutional monarchy. The creation of the First French Republic was more controversial. Many applauded the end of the monarchy and embraced the democratic ideology of the radical **Jacobins**. Like the Jacobins, they formed political clubs and began to address one another as "citizen." However, Americans with strong religious beliefs condemned the new French government for closing Christian churches and promoting a rational religion based on "natural morality." Fearing social revolution at home, wealthy Americans condemned revolutionary leader Robespierre and his followers for executing King Louis XVI and three thousand aristocrats.

Their fears were well founded, because Hamilton's economic policies quickly sparked a domestic insurgency. In 1794, western Pennsylvania farmers mounted the so-called **Whiskey Rebellion** to protest Hamilton's excise tax on spirits (Thinking Like a Historian). This tax had cut demand for the corn whiskey the farmers distilled and bartered for eastern manufactures. Like the Sons of Liberty in 1765 and the Shaysites in 1786, the Whiskey Rebels assailed the tax collectors who sent the farmers' hard-earned money to a distant government. Protesters waved banners proclaiming the French revolutionary slogan "Liberty, Equality, Fraternity!" To deter popular rebellion and uphold national authority, President Washington raised a militia force of 12,000 troops and dispersed the Whiskey Rebels.

Jay's Treaty   Britain's maritime strategy intensified political divisions in America. Beginning in late 1793, the British navy seized 250 American ships carrying French sugar and other goods. Hoping to protect merchant property through diplomacy,

The Whiskey Rebellion, 1794   This painting of Washington reviewing the militia forces that would march against the Whiskey Rebels in western Pennsylvania expresses a Federalist vision of hierarchy (in the form of officers on horseback) and order (represented by the ranks of troops). The reality was messier: Militias were called up from four states, but when volunteers were too few the states resorted to a draft, which prompted protests and riots. In the end, the militia force of more than 12,000 men was larger than the Continental army itself had been through much of the Revolution. Upon its approach, the rebellion evaporated. Twenty-four men were indicted for treason; two were sentenced to hang, but Washington pardoned them to encourage peaceful reconciliation. The Granger Collection, New York.

The Social Life of Alcohol

Alcohol was ubiquitous in post-Revolutionary America. Expensive wines and distilled spirits traveled through the channels of Atlantic trade; molasses was imported from the West Indies and distilled into rum in American port towns; and cider, beer, and whiskey were produced on a small scale everywhere in the countryside. Taverns were centers of social and political activity. Alcohol both mirrored and reinforced the economic and geographical divisions in American life.

1. James Newport's ad in the *Pennsylvania Gazette*, 1790.

JAMES NEWPORT, At his *Wine, Spirit and Cordial Stores*, in Second street, at the upper corner of Carter's alley, has, by Wholesale and Retail, MADEIRA, Sherry, Lisbon, Teneriffe, Malaga, Fayal, and Port Wines, Jamaica spirits, Antigua rum, Philadelphia ditto, Holland gin, Philadelphia ditto, very excellent, in cases, Coniac [sic] brandy, American ditto, good flavor, choice shrub. CORDIALS, &c. Anniseed water, clove water, all-fours, Cinnamon water, prime wine and rum colouring, wine bitters. Spirits of wine. Retail Stores and Tavern-keepers will in particular, find their interest in buying here, the articles being all the best in their kind, and selling at the most reduced prices. Philadelphia, April 30, 1790.

2. Benjamin Chew on providing alcohol to his slaves, 1794.

The instructions of a prominent Philadelphia lawyer and land-owner to his overseer about giving rum to his slaves during the harvest.

I have written . . . to let you have [illegible] Rum & other necessaries for the Harvest. But as these articles are so [illegible] dear I must recommend it to you to be as sparing of them as possible. . . . I must rely on you good man [to conduct] the Business. . . . I would have you let the People have a little Rum — let them be cautious in using too much Spirits during Harvest — it will be well to mix some molasses with water to drink — it is very wholesome & much recommended. . . . I need not caution you that a great deal depends upon your own proper attention to yourself and that you are careful of good Conduct during Harvest.

3. Anonymous, *The Toast*, c. 1810–1815.

SOURCE: John P. Nugent Collection, Newburgh, Indiana.

4. **John Lewis Krimmel, *Village Tavern*, 1814.** *This painting of a postman arriving at a Pennsylvania tavern with letters and newspapers reminds us that taverns were not merely places to drink.*

Source: John Lewis Krimmel (American, 1786–1821), *Village Tavern*, 1813–1814, oil on canvas, 16 7/8 x 22 1/2 inches, Toledo Museum of Art (Toledo, Ohio). Purchased with funds from the Florence Scott Libbey Bequest in Memory of her Father, Maurice A. Scott. 1954.13. Photo Credit: Richard Goodbody, New York.

virtuous principles of republican liberty, and shall receive punishment according to the nature of the offense.

And whereas, a certain John Reed, now resident in Washington, and being at his place near Pittsburgh, called Reedsburgh, and having a set of stills employed at said Reedsburgh, entered on the excise docket, contrary to the will and good pleasure of his fellow citizens, and came not forth to assist in the suppression of the execution of said law, by aiding and assisting in the late expedition, have, by delinquency, manifested his approbation to the execution of the aforesaid law, is hereby charged forthwith to cause the contents of this paper, without adding or diminishing, to be published in the Pittsburgh Gazette, the ensuing week, under the no less penalty than the consumption of his distillery.

Given under my hand, this 19th day of July, one thousand seven hundred and ninety-four.

Sources: (1) James Newport, *Pennsylvania Gazette*, May 5, 1790; (2) Chew Family Papers, Box 773, ff. 25, 10, Historical Society of Pennsylvania; (5) *Pennsylvania Gazette*, October 1, 1794; (6) *Pennsylvania Archives*, 2nd ser., 4:61–62 (Harrisburg: E. K. Meyers, State Printer, 1890).

5. **Public notice from the *Pennsylvania Gazette*, 1794.** *Here, a tavern serves as the gathering place for citizens interested in nominating candidates for election to office.*

THE INHABITANTS of the County of Chester, are hereby requested to meet at the Centre house, kept by Abraham Marshall, in West Bradford, on FRIDAY the 10th Day of October next, at 10 o'clock, A. M. in order to form a TICKET for the ensuing Election.

6. **Tom the Tinker demands compliance, July 23, 1794.** *During the Whiskey Rebellion, "Tom the Tinker" pinned this notice to a tree near John Reed's distillery. Reed had it published in a Pittsburgh newspaper.*

In taking a survey of the troops under my direction in the late expedition against that insolent exciseman, John Neville, I find there were a great number of delinquents, even among those who carry on distilling. It will, therefore, be observed that I, Tom the Tinker, will not suffer any certain class or set of men to be excluded [from] the service of this my district, when notified to attend on any expedition carried on in order to obstruct the execution of the excise law, and obtain a repeal thereof.

And I do declare on my solemn word, that if such delinquents do not come forth on the next alarm, with equipments, and give their assistance in opposing the execution and obtaining a repeal of the excise law, he or they will be deemed as enemies and stand opposed to

ANALYZING THE EVIDENCE

1. Who is the intended audience for an advertisement like James Newport's (source 1)? How many Atlantic ports of call are represented in the products he advertises?

2. The two paintings (sources 3 and 4), set in the interiors of a private home and a tavern, depict mostly men. What have they gathered for in each case? *Village Tavern* is set during the War of 1812. How does that fact influence your interpretation of the scene? What do you think the woman and child are doing in the tavern?

3. *Village Tavern* (source 4) and the ad calling for a political gathering (source 5) both suggest the way that politics and drinking often mixed. How might the fact that taverns were gathering places for political discussion and decision making have influenced outcomes?

4. What concerns does Benjamin Chew express in his correspondence with his overseer (source 2)? Given those worries, why do you think he provides rum to his slaves at all?

5. Tom the Tinker expressed the collective will of whiskey distillers in western Pennsylvania during the Whiskey Rebellion (source 6). Why would it have been important to enforce unanimous action during the uprising?

PUTTING IT ALL TOGETHER

Using the sources here and what you know about the trade and consumption of alcohol, social stratification in the early republic, and differences between urban and rural communities, write a short essay that considers the ways in which taverns and alcohol helped unite people in some ways while differentiating or dividing them in others.

Toussaint L'Ouverture, Haitian Revolutionary and Statesman The American Revolution of 1776 constituted a victory for republicanism; the Haitian revolt of the 1790s represented a triumph of liberty over slavery and a demand for racial equality. After leading the black army that ousted French planters and British invaders from Haiti, Toussaint formed a constitutional government in 1801. A year later, when French troops invaded the island, he negotiated a treaty that halted Haitian resistance in exchange for a pledge that the French would not reinstate slavery. Subsequently, the French seized Toussaint and imprisoned him in France, where he died in 1803. This image, engraved in France in 1802, places Toussaint on horseback to emphasize his military prowess. Photo12/UIG/Getty Images.

IDENTIFY CAUSES
How did events abroad during the 1790s sharpen political divisions in the United States?

Washington dispatched John Jay to Britain. But Jay returned with a controversial treaty that ignored the American claim that "free ships make free goods" and accepted Britain's right to stop neutral ships. The treaty also required the U.S. government to make "full and complete compensation" to British merchants for pre–Revolutionary War debts owed by American citizens. In return, the agreement allowed Americans to submit claims for illegal seizures and required the British to remove their troops and Indian agents from the Northwest Territory. Despite Republican charges that **Jay's Treaty** was too conciliatory, the Senate ratified it in 1795, but only by the two-thirds majority required by the Constitution. As long as the Federalists were in power, the United States would have a pro-British foreign policy.

The Haitian Revolution The French Revolution inspired a revolution closer to home that would also impact the United States. The wealthy French plantation colony of Saint-Domingue in the West Indies was deeply divided: a small class of elite planters stood atop the population of 40,000 free whites and dominated the island's half million slaves. In between, some 28,000 *gens de couleur* — free men of color — were excluded from most professions, forbidden from taking the names of their white relatives, and prevented from dressing like whites. The French Revolution intensified conflict between planters and free blacks, giving way to a massive slave uprising in 1791 that aimed to abolish slavery. The uprising touched off years of civil war, along with Spanish and British invasions. In 1798, black Haitians led by Toussaint L'Ouverture — himself a former slave-owning planter — seized control of the country. After five more years of fighting, in 1803 Saint-Domingue became the independent nation of Haiti: the first black republic in the Atlantic world.

The **Haitian Revolution** profoundly impacted the United States. In 1793, thousands of refugees — planters, slaves, and free blacks alike — fled the island and traveled to Charleston, Norfolk, Baltimore, Philadelphia, and New York, while newspapers detailed the horrors of the unfolding war. Many slaveholders panicked, fearful that the "contagion" of black liberation would undermine their own slave regimes. U.S. policy toward the rebellion presented a knotty problem. The first instinct of the Washington administration was to supply aid to the island's white population. Adams — strongly antislavery and no friend of France — changed course, aiding the rebels and strengthening commercial ties. Jefferson, though sympathetic to moral arguments against slavery, was himself a southern slaveholder; he was, moreover, an ardent supporter of France. When he became president, he cut off aid to the rebels, imposed a trade embargo, and refused to recognize an independent Haiti. For many Americans, an independent nation of liberated citizen-slaves was a horrifying paradox, a perversion of the republican ideal (America in Global Context).

The Rise of Political Parties

The appearance of Federalists and Republicans marked a new stage in American politics — what historians call the First Party System. Colonial legislatures had factions based on family, ethnicity, or region, but they did not have organized political parties. Nor did the new state and national constitutions make any provision for political societies. Indeed, most Americans believed that parties were dangerous because they looked out for themselves rather than serving the public interest.

But a shared understanding of the public interest collapsed in the face of sharp conflicts over Hamilton's fiscal policies. Most merchants and creditors supported the Federalist Party, as did wheat-exporting slaveholders in the Tidewater districts of the Chesapeake. The emerging Republican coalition included southern tobacco and rice planters, debt-conscious western farmers, Germans and Scots-Irish in the southern backcountry, and subsistence farmers in the Northeast.

Party identity crystallized in 1796. To prepare for the presidential election, Federalist and Republican leaders called caucuses in Congress and conventions in the states. They

The Haitian Revolution and the Problem of Race

The slave uprising on the French island of Saint-Domingue triggered international war, created a refugee crisis, and ended with the creation of a new republic. The American Revolution did all these things as well, yet the United States did not support either the rebellion or the republic of Haiti.

SAVANNAH CITY COUNCIL'S RESOLUTION IN RESPONSE TO THE HAITIAN UPRISING, 1795

Whereas, from the mischiefs which the people of St. Domingo, and other French islands, have experienced, from the insurrection of their Negroes and People of Colour, the precautions taken by the people of South Carolina . . . to prevent the importation or landing of any such Negroes or Mulattoes amongst them, and the information the Citizens now assembled have received, that a vessel is now lying at Cockspur, recently from Kingston, with near one hundred Negroes on board, whose landing may be dangerous to the inhabitants of this state, with the daily expectation of many more; therefore, to prevent the evils that may arise from suffering people of this description, under any pretense whatever, from being introduced amongst us, the Citizens pledge themselves unanimously to support the City Council in any salutary measures they may adopt[.]

SOURCE: Schomburg Center for Research in Black Culture, Manuscripts, Archives and Rare Books Division, Image ID 1243998, digitalgallery.nypl.org.

EXCERPTS FROM THE CONSTITUTION OF 1801 ESTABLISHED BY THE CENTRAL ASSEMBLY OF SAINT-DOMINGUE

Article 1. – Saint-Domingue in its entire expanse, and Samana, La Tortue, La Gonave, Les Cayemites, L'Ile-a-Vache, La Saone and other adjacent islands form the territory of a single colony, which is part of the French Empire, but ruled under particular laws. . . .

Article 3. – There cannot exist slaves on this territory, servitude is therein forever abolished. All men are born, live and die free and French.

Article 4. – All men, regardless of color, are eligible to all employment.

Article 5. – There shall exist no distinction other than those based on virtue and talent, and other superiority afforded by law in the exercise of a public function.

The law is the same for all whether in punishment or in protection.

SOURCE: *Haitian Constitution of 1801* (English), The Louverture Project, thelouvertureproject.org.

QUESTIONS FOR ANALYSIS

1. How does the first document express the fears of American slaveholders? Why do you suppose the Savannah City Council perceived Haitian refugees to be a danger?

2. How does the excerpt from the 1801 Constitution echo themes of the American Revolution? What differences do you see? Comparing the second document to the first, how would you say that the two revolutions impacted views of race in Georgia and in Haiti?

---

also mobilized popular support by organizing public festivals and processions: the Federalists held banquets in February to celebrate Washington's birthday, and the Republicans marched through the streets on July 4 to honor the Declaration of Independence.

In the election, voters gave Federalists a majority in Congress and made John Adams president. Jefferson, narrowly defeated, became vice president. Adams continued Hamilton's pro-British foreign policy and strongly criticized French seizures of American merchant ships. When the French foreign minister Talleyrand solicited a loan and a bribe from American diplomats to stop the seizures, Adams charged that Talleyrand's agents, whom he dubbed X, Y, and Z, had insulted America's honor. In response to the **XYZ Affair**, Congress cut off trade with France in 1798 and authorized American privateering (licensing private ships to seize French vessels). This undeclared maritime war curtailed American trade with the French West Indies and resulted in the capture of nearly two hundred French and American merchant vessels.

The Naturalization, Alien, and Sedition Acts of 1798 As Federalists became more hostile to the French Republic, they also took a harder line against their Republican critics. When Republican-minded immigrants from Ireland vehemently attacked Adams's policies, a Federalist pamphleteer responded in kind: "Were I president, I would hang them for otherwise they would murder me." To silence the critics, the Federalists enacted three coercive laws limiting individual rights and threatening the fledgling party system. The **Naturalization Act** lengthened the residency requirement for American citizenship from five to fourteen years, the **Alien Act** authorized the deportation of foreigners, and the **Sedition Act** prohibited the publication of insults or malicious attacks on the president or members of Congress. "He that is not for us is against us," thundered the Federalist *Gazette of the United States*. Using the Sedition Act, Federalist prosecutors arrested more than twenty Republican newspaper editors and politicians, accused them of sedition, and convicted and jailed a number of them.

This repression sparked a constitutional crisis. Republicans charged that the Sedition Act violated the First Amendment's prohibition against "abridging the freedom of speech, or of the press." However, they did not appeal to the Supreme Court because the Court's power to review congressional legislation was uncertain and because most of the justices were Federalists. Instead, Madison and Jefferson looked to the state legislatures. At their urging, the Kentucky and Virginia legislatures issued resolutions in 1798 declaring the Alien and Sedition Acts to be "unauthoritative, void, and of no force." The **Virginia and Kentucky Resolutions** set forth a states' rights interpretation of the Constitution, asserting that the states had a "right to judge" the legitimacy of national laws.

The conflict over the Sedition Act set the stage for the presidential election of 1800. Jefferson, once opposed on principle to political parties, now asserted that they could "watch and relate to the people" the activities of an oppressive government. Meanwhile, John Adams reevaluated his foreign policy. Rejecting Hamilton's advice to declare war against France (and benefit from the resulting upsurge in patriotism), Adams put country ahead of party and used diplomacy to end the maritime conflict.

The "Revolution of 1800" The campaign of 1800 was a bitter, no-holds-barred contest. The Federalists launched personal attacks on Jefferson, branding him an irresponsible pro-French radical and, because he opposed state support of religion in Virginia, "the arch-apostle of irreligion and free thought." Both parties changed state election laws to favor their candidates, and rumors circulated of a Federalist plot to stage a military coup.

The election did not end these worries. Thanks to a surprising Republican victory in New York, low Federalist turnout in Virginia and Pennsylvania, and the three-fifths rule (which boosted electoral votes in the southern states), Jefferson won a narrow 73-to-65 victory over Adams in the electoral college. However, the Republican electors also gave 73 votes to Aaron Burr of New York, who was Jefferson's vice-presidential running mate (Map 7.1). The Constitution specified that in the case of a tie vote, the House of Representatives would choose between the

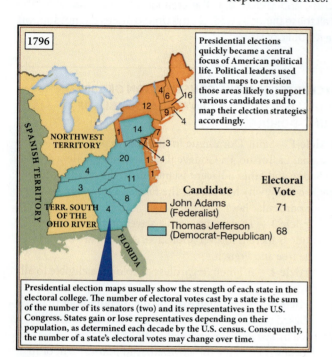

Presidential election maps usually show the strength of each state in the electoral college. The number of electoral votes cast by a state is the sum of the number of its senators (two) and its representatives in the U.S. Congress. States gain or lose representatives depending on their population, as determined each decade by the U.S. census. Consequently, the number of a state's electoral votes may change over time.

Candidate	Electoral Vote
John Adams (Federalist)	71
Thomas Jefferson (Democrat-Republican)	68

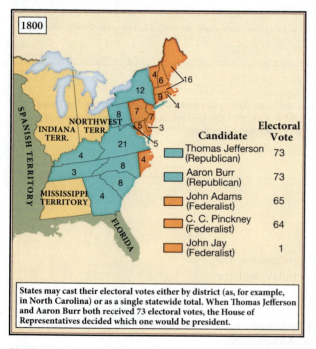

States may cast their electoral votes either by district (as, for example, in North Carolina) or as a single statewide total. When Thomas Jefferson and Aaron Burr both received 73 electoral votes, the House of Representatives decided which one would be president.

Candidate	Electoral Vote
Thomas Jefferson (Republican)	73
Aaron Burr (Republican)	73
John Adams (Federalist)	65
C. C. Pinckney (Federalist)	64
John Jay (Federalist)	1

MAP 7.1 The Presidential Elections of 1796 and 1800
Both elections pitted Federalist John Adams of Massachusetts against Republican Thomas Jefferson of Virginia, and both saw voters split along regional lines. Adams carried every New England state and, reflecting Federalist strength in maritime and commercial areas, the eastern districts of the Middle Atlantic states; Jefferson won most of the agricultural-based states of the South and West (Kentucky and Tennessee). New York was the pivotal swing state. It gave its 12 electoral votes to Adams in 1796 and, thanks to the presence of Aaron Burr on the Republican ticket, bestowed them on Jefferson in 1800.

candidates. For thirty-five rounds of balloting, Federalists in the House blocked Jefferson's election, prompting rumors that Virginia would raise a military force to put him into office.

Ironically, arch-Federalist Alexander Hamilton ushered in a more democratic era by supporting Jefferson. Calling Burr an "embryo Caesar" and the "most unfit man in the United States for the office of president," Hamilton persuaded key Federalists to allow Jefferson's election. The Federalists' concern for political stability also played a role. As Senator James Bayard of Delaware explained, "It was admitted on all hands that we must risk the Constitution and a Civil War or take Mr. Jefferson."

Jefferson called the election the "Revolution of 1800," and so it was. The bloodless transfer of power showed that popularly elected governments could be changed in an orderly way, even in times of bitter partisan conflict. In his inaugural address in 1801, Jefferson praised this achievement, declaring, "We are all Republicans, we are all Federalists."

> **CONSIDER POINTS OF VIEW**
> Why did Jefferson consider his election in 1800 to be revolutionary?

> **IN YOUR OWN WORDS** What were the most important differences between Federalists and Republicans in the 1790s?

A Republican Empire Is Born

In the Treaty of Paris of 1783, Great Britain gave up its claims to the trans-Appalachian region and, said one British diplomat, left the Indian nations "to the care of their [American] neighbours." *Care* was hardly the right word: many white Americans wanted to destroy Native communities. "Cut up every Indian Cornfield and burn every Indian town," proclaimed Congressman William Henry Drayton of South Carolina, so that their "nation be extirpated and the lands become the property of the public." Other leaders, including Henry Knox, Washington's first secretary of war, favored assimilating Native peoples into Euro-American society. Knox proposed the division of tribal lands among individual Indian families, who would become citizens of the various states. Indians resisted both forms of domination and fought to retain control of their lands and cultures. In the ensuing struggle, the United States emerged as an expansive power, determined to control the future of the continent.

Sham Treaties and Indian Lands

As in the past, the major struggle between Natives and Europeans centered on land rights. Invoking the Paris treaty and regarding Britain's Indian allies as conquered peoples, the U.S. government asserted both sovereignty over and ownership of the trans-Appalachian west. Indian nations rejected both claims, pointing out they had not been conquered and had not signed the Paris treaty. "Our lands are our life and our breath," declared Creek chief Hallowing King; "if we part with them, we part with our blood." Brushing aside such objections and threatening military action, U.S. commissioners forced the pro-British Iroquois peoples — Mohawks, Onondagas, Cayugas, and Senecas — to cede huge tracts in New York and Pennsylvania in the Treaty of Fort Stanwix (1784). New York land speculators used liquor and bribes to take a million more acres, confining the once powerful Iroquois to reservations — essentially colonies of subordinate peoples.

American negotiators used similar tactics to grab Ohio Valley lands. At the Treaties of Fort McIntosh (1785) and Fort Finney (1786), they pushed the Chippewas, Delawares, Ottawas, Wyandots, and Shawnees to cede most of the future state of Ohio. The tribes quickly repudiated the agreements, justifiably claiming they were made under duress. Recognizing the failure of these agreements, American negotiators

PLACE EVENTS IN CONTEXT
Why did the United States go to war against western Indians so quickly after the Revolution?

arranged for a comprehensive agreement at Fort Harmar (1789), but it, too, failed. To defend their lands, these tribes joined with the Miami and Potawatomi Indians to form the Western Confederacy. Led by Miami chief Little Turtle, confederacy warriors crushed American expeditionary forces sent by President Washington in 1790 and 1791.

The Treaty of Greenville Fearing an alliance between the Western Confederacy and the British in Canada, Washington doubled the size of the U.S. Army and ordered General "Mad Anthony" Wayne to lead a new expedition. In August 1794, Wayne defeated the confederacy in the Battle of Fallen Timbers (near present-day Toledo, Ohio). However, continuing Indian resistance forced a compromise. In the **Treaty of Greenville** (1795), American negotiators acknowledged Indian ownership of the land, and, in return for various payments, the Western Confederacy ceded most of Ohio (Map 7.2). The Indian peoples also agreed to accept American sovereignty, placing themselves "under the protection of the United States, and no other Power whatever." These American advances caused Britain to agree, in Jay's Treaty (1795), to reduce its trade and military aid to Indians in the trans-Appalachian region.

The Greenville treaty sparked a wave of white migration. Kentucky already had a population of 73,000 in 1790, and in 1792 it was admitted to the Union as the fifteenth state (Vermont entered a year earlier). Tennessee, Kentucky's neighbor to the south, was admitted in 1796. By 1800, more than 375,000 people had moved into the Ohio and Tennessee valleys; in 1805, the new state of Ohio alone had more than 100,000 residents. Thousands more farm families moved into the future states of Indiana and Illinois, sparking new conflicts with Native peoples over land and hunting rights. Between 1790 and 1810, farm families settled as much land as they had during the entire colonial period. The United States "is a country in flux," a visiting French aristocrat observed in 1799, and "that which is true today as regards its population, its establishments, its prices, its commerce will not be true six months from now."

Assimilation Rejected To dampen further conflicts, the U.S. government encouraged Native Americans to assimilate into white society. The goal, as one Kentucky Protestant minister put it, was to make the Indian "a farmer, a citizen of the United States, and a Christian." Most Indians rejected wholesale assimilation; even those who joined Christian churches retained many ancestral values and religious beliefs. To think of themselves as individuals or members of a nuclear family, as white Americans were demanding, meant repudiating the clan, the very essence of Indian life. To preserve "the old Indian way," many Native communities expelled white missionaries and forced Christianized Indians to participate in tribal rites. As a Munsee prophet declared, "There are two ways to God, one for the whites and one for the Indians."

MAP 7.2 Indian Cessions and State Formation, 1776–1840
By virtue of the Treaty of Paris (1783) with Britain, the United States claimed sovereignty over the entire trans-Appalachian west. The Western Confederacy contested this claim, but the U.S. government upheld it with military force. By 1840, armed diplomacy had forced most Native American peoples to move west of the Mississippi River. White settlers occupied their lands, formed territorial governments, and eventually entered the Union as members of separate — and equal — states. By 1860, the trans-Appalachian region constituted an important economic and political force in American national life.

A few Indian leaders sought a middle path in which new beliefs overlapped with old practices. Among the Senecas, the prophet Handsome Lake encouraged traditional animistic rituals that gave thanks to the sun, the earth, water, plants, and animals. But he included Christian elements in his teachings—the concepts of heaven and hell and an emphasis on personal morality—to deter his followers from alcohol, gambling, and witchcraft. Handsome Lake's teachings divided the Senecas into hostile factions. Led by Chief Red Jacket, traditionalists condemned European culture as evil and demanded a complete return to ancestral ways.

Most Indians also rejected the efforts of American missionaries to turn warriors into farmers and women into domestic helpmates. Among eastern woodland peoples, women grew corn, beans, and squash—the mainstays of the Indians' diet—and land cultivation rights passed through the female line. Consequently, women exercised considerable political influence, which they were eager to retain. Nor were Indian men interested in becoming farmers. When war raiding and hunting were no longer possible, many turned to grazing cattle and sheep.

Migration and the Changing Farm Economy

Native American resistance slowed the advance of white settlers but did not stop it. Nothing "short of a Chinese Wall, or a line of Troops," Washington declared, "will restrain . . . the Incroachment of Settlers, upon the Indian Territory." During the 1790s, two great streams of migrants moved out of the southern states.

Southern Migrants   One stream, composed primarily of white tenant farmers and struggling yeomen families, flocked through the Cumberland Gap into Kentucky and Tennessee. "Boundless settlements open a door for our citizens to run off and leave us," a worried Maryland landlord lamented, "depreciating all our landed property and disabling us from paying taxes." In fact, many migrants were fleeing from this planter-controlled society. They wanted more freedom and hoped to prosper by growing cotton and hemp, which were in great demand.

Many settlers in Kentucky and Tennessee lacked ready cash to buy land. Like the North Carolina Regulators in the 1770s, poorer migrants claimed a customary right to occupy "back waste vacant Lands" sufficient "to provide a subsistence to themselves and their Posterity." Virginia legislators, who administered the Kentucky Territory, had a more elitist vision. Although they allowed poor settlers to buy up to 1,400 acres of land at reduced prices, they sold or granted huge tracts of 100,000 acres to twenty-one groups of speculators and leading men. In 1792, this landed elite owned one-fourth of the state, while half the white men owned no land and lived as quasi-legal squatters or tenant farmers.

Widespread landlessness—and opposition to slavery—prompted a new migration across the Ohio River into the future states of Ohio, Indiana, and Illinois. In a free community, thought Peter Cartwright, a Methodist lay preacher from southwestern Kentucky who moved to Illinois, "I would be entirely clear of the evil of slavery . . . [and] could raise my children to work where work was not thought a degradation." Yet land distribution in Ohio was almost exactly as unequal as in Kentucky: in 1810, a quarter of its real estate was owned by 1 percent of the population, while more than half of its white men were landless.

Meanwhile, a second stream of southern planters and slaves from the Carolinas moved along the coastal plain toward the Gulf of Mexico. Some set up new estates in the interior of Georgia and South Carolina, while others moved into the future states of Alabama, Mississippi, and Louisiana. "The Alabama Feaver rages here with great violence," a North Carolina planter remarked, "and has carried off vast numbers of our Citizens."

Cotton was the key to this migratory surge. Around 1750, the demand for raw wool and cotton increased dramatically as water-powered spinning jennies, weaving mules, and other technological innovations of the Industrial Revolution boosted textile production in England. South Carolina and Georgia planters began growing cotton, and American inventors, including Connecticut-born Eli Whitney, built machines (called gins) that efficiently extracted seeds from its strands. To grow more cotton, white planters imported about 115,000 Africans between 1776 and 1808, when Congress cut off the Atlantic slave trade. The cotton boom financed the rapid settlement of Mississippi and Alabama—in a single year, a government land office in Huntsville, Alabama, sold $7 million of uncleared land—and the two states entered the Union in 1817 and 1819, respectively.

Exodus from New England   As southerners moved across the Appalachians and along the Gulf Coast, a third stream of migrants flowed out of the overcrowded communities of New England. Previous generations of Massachusetts and Connecticut farm families had moved north and east, settling New Hampshire, Vermont, and Maine. Now New England farmers moved west. Seeking land for their children, thousands of parents migrated to New York. "The town of Herkimer," noted one traveler, "is entirely populated by families come from Connecticut." By 1820, almost 800,000 New Englanders lived in a string of settlements stretching from Albany to Buffalo, and many others had traveled on to Ohio and Indiana. Soon, much of the Northwest Territory consisted of New England communities that had moved inland.

In New York, as in Kentucky and Ohio, well-connected speculators snapped up much of the best land, leasing farms to tenants for a fee. Imbued with the "homestead" ethic, many New England families preferred to buy farms. They signed contracts with the Holland Land Company, a Dutch-owned syndicate of speculators, that allowed settlers to pay for their farms as they worked them, or moved west again in an elusive search for land on easy terms.

Innovation on Eastern Farms   The new farm economy in New York, Ohio, and Kentucky forced major changes in eastern agriculture. Unable to compete with lower-priced western grains, farmers in New England switched to potatoes, which were high yielding and nutritious. To make up for the labor of sons and daughters who had moved inland, Middle Atlantic farmers bought more efficient farm equipment. They replaced metal-tipped wooden plows with cast-iron models that dug deeper and required a single yoke of oxen instead of two. Such changes in crop mix and technology kept production high.

Easterners also adopted the progressive farming methods touted by British agricultural reformers. "Improvers" in Pennsylvania doubled their average yield per acre by rotating their crops. Yeomen farmers raised sheep and sold the wool to textile manufacturers. Many farmers adopted a year-round planting cycle, sowing corn in the spring for animal fodder and then planting winter wheat in September for market sale. Women and girls milked the family cows and made butter and cheese to sell in the growing towns and cities.

Whether hacking fields out of western forests or carting manure to replenish eastern soils, farmers now worked harder and longer, but their increased productivity brought them a better standard of living. European demand for American produce was high in these years, and westward migration—the settlement and exploitation of Indian lands—boosted the farming economy throughout the country.

> **IDENTIFY CAUSES**
> Why were westward migration and agricultural improvement so widespread in the late eighteenth and early nineteenth centuries?

The Jefferson Presidency

From 1801 to 1825, three Republicans from Virginia—Thomas Jefferson, James Madison, and James Monroe—each served two terms as president. Supported by farmers in the South and West and strong Republican majorities in Congress, this "Virginia Dynasty" completed what Jefferson had called the Revolution of 1800. It reversed many Federalist policies and actively supported westward expansion.

When Jefferson took office in 1801, he inherited an old international conflict. Beginning in the 1780s, the Barbary States of North Africa had raided merchant ships in the Mediterranean, and like many European nations, the United States had paid an annual bribe—massive in relation to the size of the federal budget—to protect its vessels. Initially Jefferson refused to pay this "tribute" and ordered the U.S. Navy to attack the pirates' home ports. After four years of intermittent fighting, in which the United States bombarded Tripoli and captured the city of Derna, the Jefferson administration cut its costs. It signed a peace treaty that included a ransom for returned prisoners, and Algerian ships were soon taking American sailors hostage again. Finally, in 1815, President Madison sent a fleet of ten warships to the Barbary Coast under the command of Commodore Stephen Decatur, which forced leaders in Algiers, Tunis, and Tripoli to sign a treaty respecting American sovereignty.

At home, Jefferson inherited a national judiciary filled with Federalist appointees, including the formidable John Marshall of Virginia, the new chief justice of the Supreme Court. To add more Federalist judges, the outgoing Federalist Congress had passed the Judiciary Act of 1801. The act created sixteen new judgeships and various other positions, which President Adams filled at the last moment with "midnight appointees." The Federalists "have retired into the judiciary as a stronghold," Jefferson complained, "and from that battery all the works of Republicanism are to be beaten down and destroyed."

Jefferson's fears were soon realized. When Republican legislatures in Kentucky and Virginia repudiated the Alien and Sedition Acts as unconstitutional, Marshall declared that only the Supreme Court held the power of constitutional review. The Court claimed this authority for itself when James Madison, the new secretary of state, refused to deliver the commission of William Marbury, one of Adams's midnight appointees. In **Marbury v. Madison (1803)**, Marshall asserted that Marbury had the right to the appointment but that the Court did not have the constitutional power to enforce it. In defining the Court's powers, Marshall voided a section of the Judiciary Act of 1789, in effect asserting the Court's authority to review congressional legislation and interpret the Constitution. "It is emphatically the province and duty of the judicial department to say what the law is," the chief justice declared, directly challenging the Republican view that the state legislatures had that power.

Ignoring this setback, Jefferson and the Republicans reversed other Federalist policies. When the Alien and Sedition Acts expired in 1801, Congress branded them unconstitutional and refused to extend them. It also amended the Naturalization Act, restoring the original waiting period of five years for resident aliens to become citizens. Charging the Federalists with grossly expanding the national government's size and power, Jefferson had the Republican Congress shrink it. He abolished all internal taxes, including the excise tax that had sparked the Whiskey Rebellion of 1794. To quiet Republican fears of a military coup, Jefferson reduced the size of the permanent army. He also secured repeal of the Judiciary Act of 1801, ousting forty of Adams's midnight appointees. Still, Jefferson retained competent Federalist officeholders, removing only 69 of 433 properly appointed Federalists during his eight years as president.

Jefferson likewise governed tactfully in fiscal affairs. He tolerated the economically important Bank of the United States, which he had once condemned as unconstitutional. But he chose as his secretary of the treasury Albert Gallatin, a fiscal conservative who believed that the national debt was "an evil of the first magnitude." By limiting expenditures and using customs revenue to redeem government bonds, Gallatin reduced the

America in the Middle East, 1804 To protect American merchants from capture and captivity in the Barbary States, President Thomas Jefferson sent in the U.S. Navy. This 1846 lithograph, created by the famous firm of Currier & Ives, depicts one of the three attacks on the North African port of Tripoli by Commodore Edward Preble in August 1804. As the USS *Constitution* and other large warships lob shells into the city, small American gunboats defend the fleet from Tripolitan gunboats. "Our loss in Killed & Wounded has been considerable," Preble reported, and "the Enemy must have suffered very much . . . among their Shipping and on shore." The Granger Collection, New York.

debt from $83 million in 1801 to $45 million in 1812. With Jefferson and Gallatin at the helm, the nation's fiscal affairs were no longer run in the interests of northeastern creditors and merchants.

Jefferson and the West

Jefferson had long championed settlement of the West. He celebrated the yeoman farmer in *Notes on the State of Virginia* (1785); wrote one of the Confederation's western land ordinances; and supported Pinckney's Treaty (1795), the agreement between the United States and Spain that reopened the Mississippi River to American trade and allowed settlers to export crops via the Spanish-held port of New Orleans.

As president, Jefferson pursued policies that made it easier for farm families to acquire land. In 1796, a Federalist-dominated Congress had set the price of land in the national domain at $2 per acre; by the 1830s, Jefferson-inspired Republican Congresses had enacted more than three hundred laws that cut the cost to $1.25, eased credit terms, and allowed illegal squatters to buy their farms. Eventually, in the Homestead Act of 1862, Congress gave farmsteads to settlers for free.

The Louisiana Purchase   International events challenged Jefferson's vision of westward expansion. In 1799, Napoleon Bonaparte seized power in France and sought to reestablish France's American Empire. In 1801, he coerced Spain into signing a secret treaty that returned Louisiana to France and restricted American access to New Orleans, violating Pinckney's Treaty. Napoleon also launched an invasion to restore French rule in Saint-Domingue. It was once the richest sugar colony in the Americas, but its civil war had ruined the economy and cost France a fortune. Napoleon wanted to crush the rebellion and restore its planter class.

Napoleon's actions in Haiti and Louisiana prompted Jefferson to question his pro-French foreign policy. "The day that France takes possession of New Orleans, we must marry ourselves to the British fleet and nation," the president warned, dispatching James Monroe to Britain to negotiate an alliance. To keep the Mississippi River open to western farmers, Jefferson told Robert Livingston, the American minister in Paris, to negotiate the purchase of New Orleans.

Jefferson's diplomacy yielded a magnificent prize: the entire territory of Louisiana. By 1802, the French invasion of Saint-Domingue was faltering in the face of disease and determined black resistance, a new war threatened in Europe, and Napoleon feared an American invasion of Louisiana. Acting with characteristic decisiveness, the French ruler offered to sell the entire territory of Louisiana for $15 million (about $500 million today). "We have lived long," Livingston remarked to Monroe as they concluded the **Louisiana Purchase** in 1803, "but this is the noblest work of our lives."

The Louisiana Purchase forced Jefferson to reconsider his strict interpretation of the Constitution. He had long believed that the national government possessed only the powers expressly delegated to it in the Constitution, but there was no provision for adding new territory. So Jefferson pragmatically accepted a loose interpretation of the Constitution and used its treaty-making powers to complete the deal with France. The new western lands, Jefferson wrote, would be "a means of tempting all our Indians on the East side of the Mississippi to remove to the West."

Secessionist Schemes   The acquisition of Louisiana brought new political problems. Some New England Federalists, fearing that western expansion would hurt their region and party, talked openly of leaving the Union and forming a confederacy of northeastern states. The secessionists won the support of Aaron Burr, the ambitious vice president. After Alexander Hamilton accused Burr of planning to destroy the Union, the two fought an illegal pistol duel that led to Hamilton's death.

EXPLAIN CONSEQUENCES
How was Jefferson's agrarian vision reflected in his policies affecting western lands?

This tragedy propelled Burr into another secessionist scheme, this time in the Southwest. When his term as vice president ended in 1805, Burr moved west to avoid prosecution. There, he conspired with General James Wilkinson, the military governor of the Louisiana Territory, either to seize territory in New Spain or to establish Louisiana as a separate nation. But Wilkinson, himself a Spanish spy and incipient traitor, betrayed Burr and arrested him. In a highly politicized trial presided over by Chief Justice John Marshall, the jury acquitted Burr of treason.

The Louisiana Purchase had increased party conflict and generated secessionist schemes in both New England and the Southwest. Such sectional differences would continue, challenging Madison's argument in "Federalist No. 10" that a large and diverse republic was more stable than a small one.

A Mandan Village This Mandan settlement in North Dakota, painted by George Catlin around 1837, resembled those in which the Lewis and Clark expedition spent the winter of 1804–1805. Note the palisade of logs that surrounds the village, as protection from the Sioux and other marauding Plains peoples, and the solidly built mud lodges that provided warm shelter from the bitter cold of winter. Smithsonian American Art Museum, Washington, DC/Art Resource, NY.

Lewis and Clark Meet the Mandans and Sioux A scientist as well as a statesman, Jefferson wanted information about Louisiana: its physical features, plant and animal life, and Native peoples. He was also worried about intruders: the British-run Hudson's Bay Company and Northwest Company were actively trading for furs on the upper Missouri River. So in 1804, Jefferson sent his personal secretary, Meriwether Lewis, to explore the region with William Clark, an army officer. From St. Louis, Lewis, Clark, and their party of American soldiers and frontiersmen traveled up the Missouri for 1,000 miles to the fortified, earth-lodge towns of the Mandan and Hidatsa peoples (near present-day Bismarck, North Dakota), where they spent the winter.

The Mandans lived primarily by horticulture, growing corn, beans, and squash. They had acquired horses by supplying food to nomadic Plains Indians and secured guns, iron goods, and textiles by selling buffalo hides and dried meat to European traders. However, the Mandans (and neighboring Arikaras) had been hit hard by the smallpox epidemics that swept across the Great Plains in 1779–1781 and 1801–1802. Now they were threatened by Sioux peoples: Tetons, Yanktonais, and Oglalas. Originally, the Sioux had lived in the prairie and lake region of northern Minnesota. As their numbers rose and fish and game grew scarce, the Sioux moved westward, acquired horses, and hunted buffalo, living as nomads in portable skin tepees. The Sioux became ferocious fighters who tried to reduce the Mandans and other farming tribes to subject peoples. According to Lewis and Clark, they were the "pirates of the Missouri." Soon the Sioux would dominate the buffalo trade throughout the upper Missouri region.

In the spring of 1805, Lewis and Clark began an epic 1,300-mile trek into unknown country. Their party now included Toussaint Charbonneau, a French Canadian fur trader, and his Shoshone wife, Sacagawea, who served as a guide and translator. After following the Missouri River to its source on the Idaho-Montana border, they crossed the Rocky Mountains, and — venturing far beyond the Louisiana Purchase — traveled

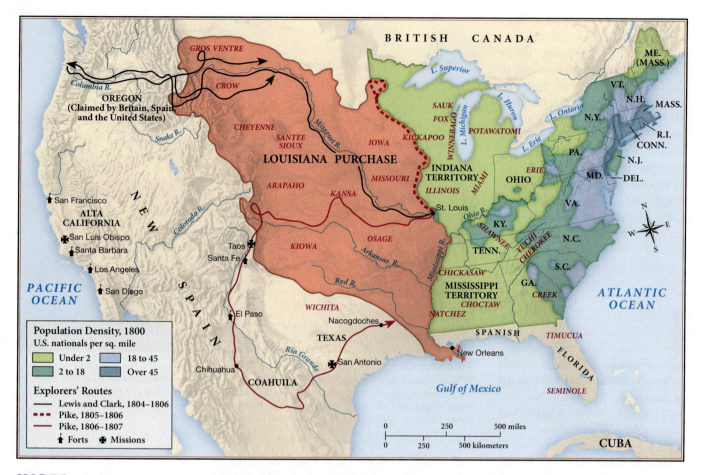

MAP 7.3 U.S. Population Density in 1803 and the Louisiana Purchase

When the United States purchased Louisiana from France in 1803, much of the land to its east — the vast territory between the Appalachian Mountains and the Mississippi River — remained in Indian hands. The equally vast lands beyond the Mississippi were virtually unknown to Anglo-Americans, even after the epic explorations of Meriwether Lewis and William Clark. Still, President Jefferson predicted quite accurately that the huge Mississippi River Valley "from its fertility . . . will ere long yield half of our whole produce, and contain half of our whole population."

down the Columbia River to the Pacific Ocean. Nearly everywhere, Indian peoples asked for guns so they could defend themselves from other armed tribes. In 1806, Lewis and Clark capped off their pathbreaking expedition by providing Jefferson with the first maps of the immense wilderness and a detailed account of its natural resources and inhabitants (Map 7.3). Their report prompted some Americans to envision a nation that would span the continent.

> **IN YOUR OWN WORDS** How were the principles of the Jeffersonian Republicans reflected in this era of dramatic growth and development?

The War of 1812 and the Transformation of Politics

The Napoleonic Wars that ravaged Europe after 1802 brought new attacks on American merchant ships. American leaders struggled desperately to protect the nation's commerce while avoiding war. When this effort finally failed, it sparked dramatic political changes that destroyed the Federalist Party and split the Republicans into National and Jeffersonian factions.

Conflict in the Atlantic and the West

As Napoleon conquered European countries, he cut off their commerce with Britain and seized American merchant ships that stopped in British ports. The British ministry responded with a naval blockade and seized American vessels carrying sugar and molasses from the French West Indies. The British navy also searched American merchant ships for British deserters and used these raids to replenish its crews, a practice known as impressment. Between 1802 and 1811, British naval officers impressed nearly 8,000 sailors, including many U.S. citizens. In 1807, American anger boiled over when a British warship attacked the U.S. Navy vessel *Chesapeake*, killing three, wounding eighteen, and seizing four alleged deserters. "Never since the battle of Lexington have I seen this country in such a state of exasperation as at present," Jefferson declared.

The Embargo of 1807   To protect American interests, Jefferson pursued a policy of peaceful coercion. The **Embargo Act of 1807** prohibited American ships from leaving their home ports until Britain and France stopped restricting U.S. trade. A drastic maneuver, the embargo overestimated the reliance of Britain and France on American shipping and underestimated the resistance of merchants, who feared the embargo would ruin them. In fact, the embargo cut the American gross national product by 5 percent and weakened the entire economy. Exports plunged from $108 million in 1806 to $22 million in 1808, hurting farmers as well as merchants. "All was noise and bustle" in New York City before the embargo, one visitor remarked; afterward, everything was closed up as if "a malignant fever was raging in the place."

Despite popular discontent over the embargo, voters elected Republican James Madison to the presidency in 1808. A powerful advocate for the Constitution, the architect of the Bill of Rights, and a prominent congressman and party leader, Madison had served the nation well. But John Beckley, a loyal Republican, worried that Madison would be "too timid and indecisive as a statesman," and events proved him right. Acknowledging the embargo's failure, Madison replaced it with new economic restrictions, which also failed to protect American commerce.

Western War Hawks   Republican congressmen from the West were certain that Britain was the primary offender. They pointed to its trade with Indians in the Ohio River Valley in violation of the Treaty of Paris and Jay's Treaty. Bolstered by British guns and supplies, the Shawnee war chief Tecumseh revived the Western Confederacy in 1809. His brother, the prophet Tenskwatawa, provided the confederacy with a powerful nativist ideology. He urged Indian peoples to shun Americans, "the children of the Evil Spirit . . . who have taken away your lands"; renounce alcohol; and return to traditional ways. The Shawnee leaders found their greatest support among Kickapoo, Potawatomi, Winnebago, Ottawa, and Chippewa warriors: Indians of the western Great Lakes who had so far been largely shielded from the direct effects of U.S. westward expansion. They flocked to Tenskwatawa's holy village, Prophetstown, in the Indiana Territory.

As Tecumseh mobilized the western Indian peoples for war, William Henry Harrison, the governor of the Indiana Territory, decided on a preemptive strike. In November 1811, when Tecumseh went south to seek support from the Chickasaws, Choctaws, and Creeks, Harrison took advantage of his absence and attacked Prophetstown. The governor's 1,000 troops and militiamen traded heavy casualties with the confederacy's warriors at the **Battle of Tippecanoe** and then destroyed the holy village.

With Britain assisting Indians in the western territories and seizing American ships in the Atlantic, Henry Clay of Kentucky, the new Speaker of the House of Representatives, and John C. Calhoun, a rising young congressman from South Carolina, pushed Madison toward war. Like other Republican "war hawks" from the West and South, they wanted to seize territory in British Canada and Spanish Florida. With national elections approaching, Madison issued an ultimatum to Britain. When Britain failed to respond quickly, the

Tenskwatawa, "The Prophet," 1830 Tenskwatawa added a spiritual dimension to Native American resistance by urging a holy war against the invading whites and calling for a return to sacred ancestral ways. His dress reflects his teachings: note the animal-skin shirt and the heavily ornamented ears. However, some of Tenskwatawa's religious rituals reflected the influence of French Jesuits; he urged his followers to finger a sacred string of beads (such as those in his left hand) that were similar to the Catholic rosary, thereby "shaking hands with the Prophet." Whatever its origins, Tenskwatawa's message transcended the cultural differences among Indian peoples and helped his brother Tecumseh create a formidable political and military alliance. Smithsonian American Art Museum, Washington, DC/Art Resource, NY.

president asked Congress for a declaration of war. In June 1812, a sharply divided Senate voted 19 to 13 for war, and the House of Representatives concurred, 79 to 49.

The causes of the War of 1812 have been much debated. Officially, the United States went to war because Britain had violated its commercial rights as a neutral nation. But the Federalists in Congress who represented the New England and Middle Atlantic merchants voted against the war; and in the election of 1812, those regions cast their 89 electoral votes for the Federalist presidential candidate, De Witt Clinton of New York. Madison amassed most of his 128 electoral votes in the South and West, where voters and congressmen strongly supported the war. Many historians therefore argue that the conflict was actually "a western war with eastern labels" (Analyzing Voices).

The War of 1812

The War of 1812 was a near disaster for the United States. An invasion of British Canada in 1812 quickly ended in a retreat to Detroit. Nonetheless, the United States stayed on the offensive in the West. In 1813, American raiders burned the Canadian capital of York (present-day Toronto), Commodore Oliver Hazard Perry defeated a small British flotilla on Lake Erie, and General William Henry Harrison overcame a British and Indian force at the Battle of the Thames, taking the life of Tecumseh, now a British general.

In the East, political divisions prevented a wider war. New England Federalists opposed the war and prohibited their states' militias from attacking Canada. Boston merchants and banks refused to lend money to the federal government, making the war difficult to finance. In Congress, Daniel Webster, a dynamic young politician from New Hampshire, led Federalists opposed to higher tariffs and national conscription of state militiamen.

Gradually, the tide of battle turned in Britain's favor. When the war began, American privateers had captured scores of British merchant vessels, but by 1813 British warships were disrupting American commerce and threatening seaports along the Atlantic coast. In 1814, a British fleet sailed up the Chesapeake Bay, and troops stormed ashore to attack Washington City. Retaliating for the destruction of York, the invaders burned the U.S. Capitol and government buildings. After two years of fighting, the United States was stalemated along the Canadian frontier and on the defensive in the Atlantic, and its new capital city lay in ruins. The only U.S. victories came in the Southwest. There, a rugged slave-owning planter named Andrew Jackson and a force of Tennessee militiamen defeated British- and Spanish-supported Creek Indians in the Battle of Horseshoe Bend (1814) and forced the Indians to cede 23 million acres of land (Map 7.4).

IDENTIFY CAUSES

What do you think is the most persuasive explanation for the United States's decision to declare war on Great Britain in 1812?

MAP 7.4 The War of 1812

Unlike the War of Independence, the War of 1812 had few large-scale military campaigns. In 1812 and 1813, most of the fighting took place along the Canadian border, as small American military forces attacked British targets with mixed success (nos. 1–4). The British took the offensive in 1814, launching a successful raid on Washington, but their attack on Baltimore failed, and they suffered heavy losses when they invaded the United States along Lake Champlain (nos. 5–7). Near the Gulf of Mexico, American forces moved from one success to another: General Andrew Jackson defeated the pro-British Creek Indians at the Battle of Horseshoe Bend, won a victory in Pensacola, and, in the single major battle of the war, routed an invading British army at New Orleans (nos. 8–10).

Factional Politics and the War of 1812

In the quarter-century following the ratification of the U.S. Constitution, American leaders had to deal with the wars of the French Revolution and Napoleon. These European conflicts posed two dangers to the United States. First, the naval blockades imposed by the British and the French hurt American commerce and prompted calls for a military response. Second, European ideological and political struggles intensified party conflicts in the United States. On three occasions, the American republic faced danger from the combination of an external military threat and internal political turmoil. In 1798, the Federalist administration of John Adams almost went to war with France to help American merchants and to undermine the Republican Party. In 1807, Thomas Jefferson's embargo on American commerce shocked Federalists and sharply increased political tensions. And, as the following selections show, the political divisions during the War of 1812 threatened the very existence of the American republic.

GEORGE WASHINGTON
Farewell Address, 1796

Washington's support for Alexander Hamilton's economic policies promoted political factionalism. Ignoring his own role in creating that political divide, Washington condemned factionalism and, as his presidency proceeded, tried to stand above party conflicts. In his farewell address, Washington warned Americans to stand united and avoid the "Spirit of Party."

SOURCE: James D. Richardson, ed., *A Compilation of the Messages and Papers of the Presidents, 1789–1896* (Washington, D.C.: U.S. Government Printing Office, 1896), 1: 213–215.

66 A solicitude for your welfare [prompts me] . . . to offer . . . the disinterested warnings of a parting friend, who can possibly have no personal motive to bias his counsels. . . .

The Unity of Government which constitutes you one people . . . is a main Pillar in the Edifice of your real independence . . . your tranquility at home; your peace abroad. . . . But it is easy to foresee, that, from different causes, and from different quarters, much pains will be taken, many artifices employed, to weaken in your minds the conviction of this truth. . . .

I have already intimated to you the danger of parties in the State, with particular reference to founding them on geographical discriminations. Let me now take a more comprehensive view, and warn you, in the most solemn manner, against the baneful effects of the Spirit of Party, generally.

This spirit, unfortunately, is inseparable from our nature, having its root in the strongest passions of the human mind. It exists under different shapes, in all governments, more or less stifled, controlled or repressed; but in those of the popular form, it is seen in its greatest rankness, and is truly their worst enemy.

The alternate dominion of one faction over another, sharpened by the spirit of revenge . . . , is itself a frightful despotism; but this leads at length to a more formal and permanent despotism. 99

JOSIAH QUINCY ET AL.
Federalists Protest "Mr. Madison's War"

The United States — and its two political parties — divided sharply over the War of 1812. As Congress debated the issue of going to war against Great Britain, Josiah Quincy and other antiwar Federalist congressmen published a manifesto that questioned the justifications for the war offered by President Madison and the military strategy proposed by Republican war hawks.

SOURCE: *Annals of Congress*, 12th Cong., 1st sess., vol. 2, cols. 2219–2221.

66 How will war upon the land [an invasion of British Canada] protect commerce upon the ocean? What balm has Canada for wounded honor? How are our mariners benefited by a war which exposes those who are free, without promising release to those who are impressed?

But it is said that war is demanded by honor. Is national honor a principle which thirsts after vengeance, and is appeased only by blood? . . . If honor demands a war with England, what opiate lulls that honor to sleep over the wrongs done us by France? On land, robberies, seizures, imprisonments, by French authority; at sea, pillage, sinkings, burnings, under French orders. These are notorious. Are they unfelt because they are French? . . .

Federalists Oppose the War American military setbacks increased opposition to the war in New England. In 1814, Massachusetts Federalists called for a convention "to lay the foundation for a radical reform in the National Compact." When New England Federalists met in Hartford, Connecticut, some delegates proposed secession, but most wanted to revise the Constitution. To end Virginia's domination of the presidency, the Hartford Convention proposed a constitutional amendment limiting the office to a single four-year term and rotating it among citizens from different states.

There is . . . a headlong rushing into difficulties, with little calculation about the means, and little concern about the consequences. With a navy comparatively [small], we are about to enter into the lists against the greatest marine [power] on the globe. With a commerce unprotected and spread over every ocean, we propose to make a profit by privateering, and for this endanger the wealth of which we are honest proprietors. An invasion is threatened of the [British colonies in Canada, but Britain] . . . without putting a new ship into commission, or taking another soldier into pay, can spread alarm or desolation along the extensive range of our seaboard. . . .

What are the United States to gain by this war? Will the gratification of some privateersmen compensate the nation for that sweep of our legitimate commerce by the extended marine of our enemy which this desperate act invites? Will Canada compensate the Middle states for [the loss of] New York; or the Western states for [the loss of] New Orleans?

Let us not be deceived. A war of invasion may invite a retort of invasion. When we visit the peaceable, and as to us innocent, colonies of Great Britain with the horrors of war, can we be assured that our own coast will not be visited with like horrors? **99**

HEZEKIAH NILES

A Republican Defends the War

In 1814, what the Federalists feared had come to pass: British ships blockaded American ports, and British troops invaded American territory. In January 1815, Republican editor Hezekiah Niles used the pages of his influential Baltimore newspaper, *Niles' Weekly Register*, to explain current Republican policies and blame the Federalists for American reverses.

66 It is universally known that the causes for which we declared war are no obstruction to peace. The practice of blockade and impressment having ceased by the general pacification of Europe, our government is content to leave the principle as it was. . . .

We have no further business in hostility, than such as is purely defensive; while that of Great Britain is to humble or subdue us. The war, on our part, has become a contest for life, liberty and property — on the part of our enemy, of revenge or ambition. . . .

What then are we to do? Are we to encourage him by divisions among ourselves — to hold out the hope of a separation of the states and a civil war — to refuse to bring forth

the resources of the country against him? . . . I did think that in a defensive war — a struggle for all that is valuable — that all parties would have united. But it is not so — every measure calculated to replenish the treasury or raise men is opposed [by Federalists] as though it were determined to strike the 'star spangled banner' and exalt the bloody cross. Look at the votes and proceedings of congress — and mark the late spirit [to secede from the Union] . . . that existed in Massachusetts, and see with what unity of action every thing has been done [by New England Federalists] to harass and embarrass the government. Our loans have failed; and our soldiers have wanted their pay, because those [New England merchants] who had the greater part of the monied capital covenanted with each other to refuse its aid to the country. They had a right, legally, to do this; and perhaps, also, by all the artifices of trade or power that money gave them, to oppress others not of their 'stamp' and depress the national credit — but history will shock posterity by detailing the length to which they went to bankrupt the republic. . . .

To conclude — why does the war continue? It is not the fault of the government — we demand no extravagant thing. I answer the question, and say — *it lasts because Great Britain depends on the exertions of her 'party' in this country to destroy our resources, and compel 'unconditional submission.'*

Thus the war began, and is continued, by our divisions. **99**

Source: *Niles' Weekly Register*, January 28, 1815.

QUESTIONS FOR ANALYSIS

1. According to Washington, what is the ultimate cause of political factionalism? Why does Washington believe that factionalism is most dangerous in "popular" — that is, republican — governments?

2. Compare and contrast the Quincy and Niles documents. What specific dangers did Josiah Quincy and the Federalists foresee with regard to Republican war policies? According to Hezekiah Niles, what were the war goals of the Republican administration?

3. Read the section on the War of 1812 on pages 224–228, and then discuss the accuracy of the Federalists' predictions.

4. How had Republican war goals changed since the start of the war? Niles charged the Federalists and their supporters with impeding the American war effort. What were his specific charges? Did they have any merit? How might the Federalists have defended their stance with respect to the war?

The convention also suggested amendments restricting commercial embargoes to sixty days and requiring a two-thirds majority in Congress to declare war, prohibit trade, or admit a new state to the Union.

As a minority party, the Federalists could prevail only if the war continued to go badly — a very real prospect. The war had cost $88 million, raising the national debt to $127 million. And now, as Albert Gallatin warned Henry Clay in May 1814, Britain's triumph over Napoleon in Europe meant that a "well organized and large army is [now

Washington, D.C., Burns, 1814 This chaotic image depicts the events of August 24, 1814, when British forces under the command of Major-General Robert Ross captured Washington, D.C. Ross and his men, with three cannons captured from American forces, command the heights above the city (right). The American flotilla (foreground) is defeated and the dockyard and arsenal are in flames. In the background, more of the city is burning, including a bridge over the Potomac River, the War Office, the Treasury, the Senate building, and the White House (center, far background). Ross's army then proceeded to Baltimore, where American forces at Fort McHenry held out against the British. A lawyer named Francis Scott Key, observing the fort's bombardment, dashed off a poem entitled "Defense of Fort McHenry." Later set to music, it came to be known as "The Star-Spangled Banner." Library of Congress.

ready] . . . to act immediately against us." When an attack from Canada came in the late summer of 1814, only an American naval victory on Lake Champlain stopped the British from marching down the Hudson River Valley. A few months later, thousands of seasoned British troops landed outside New Orleans, threatening American control of the Mississippi River. With the nation politically divided and under attack from north and south, Gallatin feared that "the war might prove vitally fatal to the United States."

Peace Overtures and a Final Victory Fortunately for the young American republic, by 1815 Britain wanted peace. The twenty-year war with France had sapped its wealth and energy, so it began negotiations with the United States in Ghent, Belgium. At first, the American commissioners — John Quincy Adams, Gallatin, and Clay — demanded territory in Canada and Florida, while British diplomats sought an Indian buffer state between the United States and Canada. Both sides quickly realized that these objectives were not worth the cost of prolonged warfare. The **Treaty of Ghent**, signed on Christmas Eve 1814, retained the prewar borders of the United States.

That result hardly justified three years of war, but before news of the treaty reached the United States, a final military victory lifted Americans' morale. On January 8, 1815, General Jackson's troops crushed the British forces attacking New Orleans. Fighting from carefully constructed breastworks, the Americans rained "grapeshot and cannister bombs" on the massed British formations. The British lost 700 men, and 2,000 more were wounded or taken prisoner; just 13 Americans died, and only 58 suffered wounds. A newspaper headline proclaimed: "Almost Incredible Victory!! Glorious News." The victory made Jackson a national hero, redeemed the nation's battered pride, and undercut the Hartford Convention's demands for constitutional revision.

The Federalist Legacy

The War of 1812 ushered in a new phase of the Republican political revolution. Before the conflict, Federalists had strongly supported Alexander Hamilton's program of national mercantilism — a funded debt, a central bank, and tariffs — while Jeffersonian Republicans had opposed it. After the war, the Republicans split into two camps. Led by Henry Clay, National Republicans pursued Federalist-like policies. In 1816, Clay pushed legislation through Congress creating the Second Bank of the United States and persuaded President Madison to sign it. In 1817, Clay won passage of the Bonus Bill, which created a national fund for roads and other internal improvements. Madison vetoed it. Reaffirming traditional Jeffersonian Republican principles, he argued that the national government lacked the constitutional authority to fund internal improvements.

Meanwhile, the Federalist Party crumbled. As one supporter explained, the National Republicans in the eastern states had "destroyed the Federalist party by the adoption of its principles" while the favorable farm policies of Jeffersonians maintained the Republican Party's dominance in the South and West. "No Federal character can run with success," Gouverneur Morris of New York lamented, and the election of 1818 proved him right: Republicans outnumbered Federalists 37 to 7 in the Senate and 156 to 27 in the House. Westward expansion and the success of Jefferson's Revolution of 1800 had shattered the First Party System.

Marshall's Federalist Law However, Federalist policies lived on thanks to John Marshall's long tenure on the Supreme Court. Appointed chief justice by President John Adams in January 1801, Marshall had a personality and intellect that allowed him to dominate the Court until 1822 and strongly influence its decisions until his death in 1835.

Three principles informed Marshall's jurisprudence: judicial authority, the supremacy of national laws, and traditional property rights (Table 7.1). Marshall claimed the right of judicial review for the Supreme Court in *Marbury v. Madison* (1803), and the

***John Marshall*, by Chester Harding, c. 1830** Even at the age of seventy-five, John Marshall (1755–1835) had a commanding personal presence. After he became chief justice of the U.S. Supreme Court in 1801, Marshall elevated the Court from a minor department of the national government to a major institution in American legal and political life. His decisions on judicial review, contract rights, the regulation of commerce, and national banking permanently shaped the character of American constitutional law. © Boston Athenaeum, USA/Bridgeman Images.

TABLE 7.1

Major Decisions of the Marshall Court

	Date	Case	Significance of Decision
Judicial Authority	1803	*Marbury v. Madison*	Asserts principle of judicial review
Property Rights	1810	*Fletcher v. Peck*	Protects property rights through broad reading of Constitution's contract clause
	1819	*Dartmouth College v. Woodward*	Safeguards property rights, especially of chartered corporations
Supremacy of National Law	1819	*McCulloch v. Maryland*	Interprets Constitution to give broad powers to national government
	1824	*Gibbons v. Ogden*	Gives national government jurisdiction over interstate commerce

Court frequently used that power to overturn state laws that, in its judgment, violated the Constitution.

Asserting National Supremacy The important case of *McCulloch v. Maryland* **(1819)** involved one such law. When Congress created the Second Bank of the United States in 1816, it allowed the bank to set up state branches that competed with state-chartered banks. In response, the Maryland legislature imposed a tax on notes issued by the Baltimore branch of the Second Bank. The Second Bank refused to pay, claiming that the tax infringed on national powers and was therefore unconstitutional. The state's lawyers then invoked Jefferson's argument: that Congress lacked the constitutional authority to charter a national bank. Even if a national bank was legitimate, the lawyers argued, Maryland could tax its activities within the state.

Marshall and the nationalist-minded Republicans on the Court firmly rejected both arguments. The Second Bank was constitutional, said the chief justice, because it was "necessary and proper," given the national government's control over currency and credit, and Maryland did not have the power to tax it.

The Marshall Court again asserted the dominance of national over state statutes in *Gibbons v. Ogden* (1824). The decision struck down a New York law granting a monopoly to Aaron Ogden for steamboat passenger service across the Hudson River to New Jersey. Asserting that the Constitution gave the federal government authority over interstate commerce, the chief justice sided with Thomas Gibbons, who held a federal license to run steamboats between the two states.

Upholding Vested Property Rights Finally, Marshall used the Constitution to uphold Federalist notions of property rights. During the 1790s, Jefferson Republicans had celebrated "the will of the people," prompting Federalists to worry that popular sovereignty would result in a "tyranny of the majority." If state legislatures enacted statutes infringing on the property rights of wealthy citizens, Federalist judges vowed to void them.

Marshall was no exception. Determined to protect individual property rights, he invoked the contract clause of the Constitution to do it. The contract clause (in Article I, Section 10) prohibits the states from passing any law "impairing the obligation of contracts." Economic conservatives at the Philadelphia convention had inserted the clause to prevent "stay" laws, which kept creditors from seizing the lands and goods of delinquent debtors. In *Fletcher v. Peck* (1810), Marshall greatly expanded its scope. The Georgia legislature had granted a huge tract of land to the Yazoo Land Company. When a new legislature cancelled the grant, alleging fraud and bribery, speculators who had purchased Yazoo lands appealed to the Supreme Court to uphold their titles. Marshall did so by ruling that the legislative grant was a contract that could not be revoked. His decision was controversial and far-reaching. It limited state power; bolstered vested property rights; and, by protecting out-of-state investors, promoted the development of a national capitalist economy.

The Court extended its defense of vested property rights in *Dartmouth College v. Woodward* (1819). Dartmouth College was a private institution created by a royal charter issued by King George III. In 1816, New Hampshire's Republican legislature enacted a statute converting the school into a public university. The Dartmouth trustees opposed the legislation and hired Daniel Webster to plead their case. A renowned constitutional lawyer and a leading Federalist, Webster cited the Court's decision in *Fletcher v. Peck* and argued that the royal charter was an unalterable contract. The Marshall Court agreed and upheld Dartmouth's claims.

CONSIDER POINTS OF VIEW
Why do historians think the decisions of the Marshall Court constitute a Federalist legacy?

The Diplomacy of John Quincy Adams Even as John Marshall incorporated important Federalist principles into the American legal system, voting citizens and political leaders embraced the outlook of the Republican Party. The political career of John Quincy Adams was a case in point. Although he was the son of Federalist

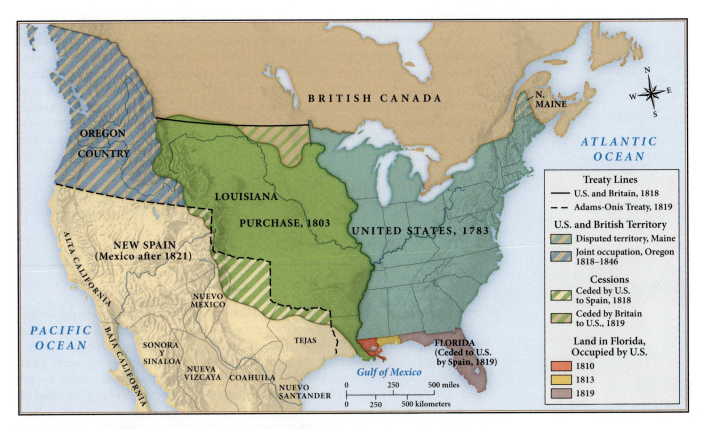

MAP 7.5   Defining the National Boundaries, 1800–1820

After the War of 1812, American diplomats negotiated treaties with Great Britain and Spain that defined the boundaries of the Louisiana Purchase, with British Canada to the north and New Spain (which in 1821 became the independent nation of Mexico) to the south and west. These treaties eliminated the threat of border wars with neighboring states for a generation, giving the United States a much-needed period of peace and security.

president John Adams, John Quincy Adams had joined the Republican Party before the War of 1812. He came to national attention for his role in negotiating the Treaty of Ghent, which ended the war.

Adams then served brilliantly as secretary of state for two terms under James Monroe (1817–1825). Ignoring Republican antagonism toward Great Britain, in 1817 Adams negotiated the Rush-Bagot Treaty, which limited American and British naval forces on the Great Lakes. In 1818, he concluded another agreement with Britain setting the forty-ninth parallel as the border between Canada and the lands of the Louisiana Purchase. Then, in the **Adams-Onís Treaty** of 1819, Adams persuaded Spain to cede the Florida territory to the United States (Map 7.5). In return, the American government accepted Spain's claim to Texas and agreed to a compromise on the western boundary for the state of Louisiana, which had entered the Union in 1812.

Finally, Adams persuaded President Monroe to declare American national policy with respect to the Western Hemisphere. At Adams's behest, Monroe warned Spain and other European powers to keep their hands off the newly independent republics in Latin America. The American continents were not "subject for further colonization," the president declared in 1823—a policy that thirty years later became known as the **Monroe Doctrine**. In return, Monroe pledged that the United States would not "interfere in the internal concerns" of European nations. Thanks to John Quincy Adams, the United States had successfully asserted its diplomatic leadership in the Western Hemisphere and won international acceptance of its northern and western boundaries.

The appearance of political consensus after two decades of bitter party conflict prompted observers to dub James Monroe's presidency (1817–1825) the "Era of Good Feeling." This harmony was real but transitory. The Republican Party was now split between the National faction, led by Clay and Adams, and the Jeffersonian faction, soon to be led by Martin Van Buren and Andrew Jackson. The two groups differed sharply over federal support for roads and canals and many other issues. As the aging Jefferson himself complained, "You see so many of these new [National] republicans maintaining in Congress the rankest doctrines of the old federalists." This division in the Republican Party would soon produce the Second Party System, in which national-minded Whigs and state-focused Democrats would confront each other. By the early 1820s, one cycle of American politics and economic debate had ended, and another was about to begin.

> **IN YOUR OWN WORDS**   What elements of Federalist political philosophy survived the end of the First Party System?

SUMMARY

In this chapter, we traced three interrelated themes: public policy, westward expansion, and party politics. We began by examining the contrasting public policies advocated by Alexander Hamilton and Thomas Jefferson. A Federalist, Hamilton supported a strong national government and created a fiscal infrastructure (the national debt, tariffs, and a national bank) to spur trade and manufacturing. By contrast, Jefferson wanted to preserve the authority of state governments, and he envisioned an America enriched by farming rather than industry.

Jefferson and the Republicans promoted a westward movement that transformed the agricultural economy and sparked new wars with Indian peoples. Expansion westward also shaped American diplomatic and military policy, leading to the Louisiana Purchase, the War of 1812, and the treaties negotiated by John Quincy Adams.

Finally, there was the unexpected rise of the First Party System. As Hamilton's policies split the political elite, the French Revolution divided Americans into hostile ideological groups. The result was two decades of bitter conflict and controversial measures: the Federalists' Sedition Act, the Republicans' Embargo Act, and Madison's decision to go to war with Britain. Although the Federalist Party faded away, it left as its enduring legacy Hamilton's financial innovations and John Marshall's constitutional jurisprudence.

CHAPTER 7 REVIEW

TERMS TO KNOW   *Identify and explain the significance of each term below.*

Key Concepts and Events

Judiciary Act of 1789 (p. 205)	**Proclamation of Neutrality** (p. 208)	**Naturalization, Alien, and Sedition Acts** (p. 214)	**Embargo Act of 1807** (p. 223)
Bill of Rights (p. 205)	**French Revolution** (p. 208)	**Virginia and Kentucky Resolutions** (p. 214)	**Battle of Tippecanoe** (p. 223)
Report on the Public Credit (p. 205)	**Jacobins** (p. 209)	**Treaty of Greenville** (p. 216)	**Treaty of Ghent** (p. 228)
Bank of the United States (p. 207)	**Whiskey Rebellion** (p. 209)	*Marbury v. Madison* **(1803)** (p. 219)	*McCulloch v. Maryland* **(1819)** (p. 230)
Report on Manufactures (p. 207)	**Jay's Treaty** (p. 212)	**Louisiana Purchase** (p. 220)	**Adams-Onís Treaty** (p. 231)
	Haitian Revolution (p. 212)		**Monroe Doctrine** (p. 231)
	XYZ Affair (p. 213)		

Key People

Alexander Hamilton (p. 204)

Thomas Jefferson (p. 204)

John Adams (p. 204)

Little Turtle (p. 216)

John Marshall (p. 219)

Tecumseh (p. 223)

Henry Clay (p. 223)

John Quincy Adams (p. 228)

REVIEW QUESTIONS

Answer these questions to demonstrate your understanding of the chapter's main ideas.

1. What were the most important differences between Federalists and Republicans in the 1790s?

2. How were the principles of the Jeffersonian Republicans reflected in this era of dramatic growth and development?

3. What elements of Federalist political philosophy survived the end of the First Party System?

4. Look at the events listed under "Politics and Power" and "Work, Exchange, and Technology" for the period 1787–1800 on the thematic timeline on page 138. What was the relationship in these years between disagreements over the national government and developments in the American economy?

MAKING CONNECTIONS

Recognize the larger developments and continuities within and across chapters by answering these questions.

1. In Chapter 6, thirteen former British colonies cooperated in war and established new republican institutions of self-government. After 1789, unforeseen divisions developed in American politics. Why did Hamiltonians and Jeffersonians disagree so sharply on key questions of national policy? Which of the factions in the First Party System — Federalists or Republicans — best embodied the principles of the Revolution? How did westward expansion and international relations force the United States to modify its Revolutionary republican ideals?

2. Return to the Currier & Ives print depicting the bombardment of Tripoli on page 219. What message does it convey about America's position in the world? How well does that message square with the actual outcome of the First Barbary War? What does this suggest about the artist's purpose?

KEY TURNING POINTS

Refer to the chapter chronologies on pages 172 and 204 for help in answering the questions below.

The Northwest Ordinance (1787; Chapter 6), Kentucky and Tennessee join the Union (1792, 1796), and Jefferson is elected president (1800): How were developments in the West tied into national politics in the 1790s? Why did the Federalists steadily lose ground to the Republicans?

PART

4

Overlapping Revolutions
1800–1848

We begin Part 4 in 1800 because important structural changes were reshaping American life at the beginning of the new century. They included new banking, credit, and transportation systems; the invention of the cotton gin and the transformation of American slavery; innovations in political structures and practices; and new religious and cultural expressions. We have chosen 1848 as a useful end point for this period because that was the year that the U.S.-Mexico War ended and the continental ambitions of the new American nation were fully realized.

Historians often call these decades the antebellum (prewar) era because, looking back, we know that in 1861 the Civil War pitted North against South. But many of the developments of this era worked to unite northern and southern interests. Policymakers and entrepreneurs built canals and banks, expanded the reach of plantation slavery, opened textile factories in the North to process slave-grown cotton from the South, hired wageworkers to tend the water-powered looms, and sold northern products back to southern planters. By the 1830s, a few radical abolitionists criticized this system for binding "Lords of the Loom and Lords of the Lash" in one vast cycle of exploitative enterprise.

Four transformations marked the United States in the early nineteenth century. One was economic: the expansion of commercial agriculture, the rise of manufacturing, and development of the cotton complex triggered unprecedented economic growth. Another was political, as new democratic political forms took shape. A third transformation was the emergence of evangelical Christianity, reform movements, and utopian experiments that remade American culture and society. Finally, the geographical boundaries of the United States expanded enormously in these years. Part 4 of *America's History* explains how these momentous changes happened and shows how closely intertwined they were. Building on these transformations, three principal developments are discussed in Part 4: ▶

234

A Commercial Slaveholding Republic

The economic revolution of the early 1800s rested on innovations in transportation and technology, from the cotton gin to the steam-powered loom. It also relied on steady acquisitions of frontier lands, where farmers specialized in agricultural products that could be shipped to an increasingly industrial Northeast.

The rise of the "cotton complex" vastly expanded slavery in the South. It also sharpened social and economic class divisions among business elites, planters, middle-class merchants and professionals, artisans, wageworkers, and the urban poor. At first, Americans hoped manufacturing would increase prosperity for all, but by the end of the period some desperate immigrants from Ireland, and others who labored in low-skill jobs, lived in shocking poverty. Like many other transformations, the commercial revolution had unintended consequences.

Bettmann/Getty Images.

Democratic Citizenship and Culture

Americans celebrated the expansion of political rights and the rise of mass political parties, starting with the Democrats under the charismatic leadership of Andrew Jackson. Jacksonian Democrats cut federal and state government aid to financiers, merchants, and corporations. Beginning in the 1830s, the Democrats faced challenges from the Whigs, who devised a competing program that stressed state-sponsored economic development, moral reform, and individual social mobility. The parties wrestled over such issues as Jackson's Indian Removal Act of 1830 and high protective tariffs on manufactured goods, the latter of which many farmers and planters opposed.

New democratic forms flourished in culture as well as politics. The expanding urban middle class created a distinct religious culture and an ideal of domesticity or "separate spheres" for women, as well as an array of reform movements, from temperance to moral reform. Wage-earning workers in the growing cities, including poor immigrants from Germany and Ireland, participated in a vibrant popular culture of their own. New England intellectuals launched the distinctly American movement of transcendentalism, while utopians founded cooperative experiments and religious communities such as those of the Shakers and Mormons.

© Collection of the New-York Historical Society, USA/ Bridgeman Images.

Claiming an Empire

Territorial expansion between 1800 and 1848 was vast and violent. Moving into Texas at the behest of Mexican authorities, who were struggling to populate Mexico's northern areas, southern cotton planters brought slavery and a spirit of independence that soon triggered the Texas revolution for separation from Mexico. Other Americans, especially on the midwestern frontier, pushed ardently for annexation of Oregon and by the 1840s began a drive to the Pacific. Most decisive was the election in 1844 of James K. Polk, an expansionist Democrat who promised to claim all of Oregon from the United States's chief rival— Britain—and to annex Texas even if it precipitated war with Mexico. Though the former conflict was arbitrated, the latter triggered a war that brought in not only Texas but also a vast new domain including California and the Southwest— acquisitions that would lead to sectional crisis.

West Point Museum, United States Military Academy, West Point, NY.

Overlapping Revolutions 1800–1848

© Collection of the New-York Historical Society, USA/Bridgeman Images.

Thematic Understanding

This timeline arranges some of the important events of this period into themes. How did economic, political, and cultural developments influence one another in this era? ▶

	AMERICAN AND NATIONAL IDENTITY	POLITICS AND POWER	WORK, EXCHANGE, AND TECHNOLOGY	
1800	• Neomercantilist policies support banking, transportation, and communication systems	• Jefferson reduces activism of national government • Chief Justice Marshall begins to assert federal judicial powers	• Cotton output and demand for African labor expands • Congress approves funds for a National Road (1806)	
1810	• Emma Willard founds Middlebury Female Seminary for young women (1814) • American Colonization Society founded (1817) • Notion of the self-made man spreads	• Expansion of white male political rights begins • Martin Van Buren creates first statewide political machine (1817–1821) • Missouri crisis (1819–1821) over slavery	• Construction on National Road begins (1811) • First American textile factory opens in Waltham, Massachusetts (1814)	
1820	• David Walker's *Appeal . . . to the Colored Citizens* (1829) attacks slavery • Public schools, female academies strengthen literacy and civic engagement • Domesticity and ideal of "separate spheres" emerge in middle class	• Rise of Andrew Jackson and Democratic Party • Anti-Masonic and Working Men's parties rise and decline	• Erie Canal completed (1825) • Henry Clay proposes "American System" of government-assisted development	
1830	• More distinct middle-class and working-class identities emerge with industrialization • Nat Turner's uprising in Virginia (1831) • American Anti-Slavery Society founded (1833) • First wave of married women's property laws (1839–1845) • Abolitionist Grimké sisters defend public roles for women	• Tariff battles and nullification crisis (1828, 1832) • Whig Party forms (1834) • Jackson destroys Second National Bank, expands executive power • Congress adopts "gag rule" to block antislavery petitions (1836)	• U.S. textiles compete with British goods • Canal systems expand trade in eastern United States • Cotton complex expands • Financial panic of 1837 begins six-year depression	
1840	• Margaret Fuller publishes *Woman in the Nineteenth Century* (1844) • Seneca Falls Convention seeks women's equal rights (1848)	• Heyday of Second Party System (Democrats vs. Whigs) • Liberty Party runs James G. Birney for president (1844) • U.S.-Mexico War (1846–1848)	• American machine tool industry expands	

CULTURE AND SOCIETY	MIGRATION AND SETTLEMENT	GEOGRAPHY AND THE ENVIRONMENT	AMERICA IN THE WORLD	
• Rural white Americans share a common culture	• Congress outlaws Atlantic slave trade (1808)	• Louisiana Purchase nearly doubles the land mass of the United States (1803) • Lewis and Clark explore the West (1804–1806)	• Embargo Act prohibits trade with Great Britain (1807)	**1800**
• African Methodist Episcopal Church founded (1816)	• Andrew Jackson forces Creeks to relinquish millions of acres during War of 1812	• Road and turnpike construction facilitate travel • The cotton frontier moves inland	• Africans from Congo region influence black culture for decades • U.S. and Great Britain agree to joint control of Oregon Country (1818)	**1810**
• Second Great Awakening; Charles Finney begins Protestant revival campaigns (1823)	• Internal slave trade forces thousands of African Americans west in cotton boom • Rise of cities and manufacturing towns prompts migration from rural areas • Violence drives over a thousand African Americans out of Cincinnati (1829)	• Canals and steamboats shrink space • Major Stephen H. Long labels the Great Plains the "Great American Desert"	• Mexico gains independence from Spain (1821)	**1820**
• Emerson champions transcendentalism • Benevolent Empire of reform movements • Immense popularity of blackface minstrel shows • Joseph Smith founds Mormon church (Latter-day Saints) (1830) • Horace Mann begins public school expansion in Massachusetts (1837)	• Indian Removal Act (1830) forces Native peoples west • Cherokee Trail of Tears (1838)	• U.S. immigration into Texas accelerates • Emergence of commercial cities in the Old Northwest • Indian Removal Act (1830) leads to mass relocation	• Emerson and others draw on European romanticism in developing transcendentalist ideas • Texas declares its independence from Mexico (1836)	**1830**
• Dorothea Dix promotes hospitals for the mentally ill (1841) • Henry Thoreau spends a year at Walden Pond (1845) • John Humphrey Noyes establishes cooperative experiment at Oneida (1848)	• Brigham Young leads Mormons to Salt Lake (1846) • Increased immigration from Ireland and Germany	• Immigration to the Oregon Country increases dramatically	• United States declares war on Mexico (1846) • Treaty with Britain divides Oregon Country (1846) • American troops capture Mexico City (1847)	**1840**

8
CHAPTER

Economic Transformations
1800–1848

In 1804, life turned grim for eleven-year-old Chauncey Jerome. His father died suddenly, and Jerome became an indentured servant on a Connecticut farm. Quickly learning that few farmers "would treat a poor boy like a human being," Jerome bought out his indenture by making dials for clocks and then found a job with clockmaker Eli Terry. A manufacturing wizard, Terry used water power to drive precision saws and woodworking lathes. Soon his shop, and dozens of outworkers, were turning out thousands of tall clocks with wooden works. Then, in 1816, Terry patented an enormously popular desk clock with brass parts, an innovation that turned Waterbury, Connecticut, into the clockmaking center of the United States.

In 1822, Chauncey Jerome set up his own clock factory. By organizing work more efficiently and using new machines that stamped out interchangeable metal parts, he drove down the price of a simple clock from $20 to $5 and then to less than $2. By the 1840s, Jerome was selling his clocks in England, the hub of the Industrial Revolution; a decade later, his workers were turning out 400,000 clocks a year. By 1860, the United States was not only the world's leading exporter of cotton and wheat but also the third-ranked manufacturing nation behind Britain and France.

"Business is the very soul of an American: the fountain of all human felicity," author Francis Grund observed shortly after arriving from Europe. Stimulated by America's entrepreneurial culture, thousands of artisan-inventors like Chauncey Jerome propelled the country into the Industrial Revolution, a new system of production based on water and steam power and machine technology. To bring their products to market, they relied on important innovations in travel and communication. By 1848, northern entrepreneurs — and their southern counterparts who invested in cotton planting — had created a new economic order.

Not all Americans embraced the new business-dominated society, and many failed to share in the new prosperity. The increase in manufacturing, commerce, and finance created class divisions that challenged the founders' vision of an agricultural republic with few distinctions of wealth. As the philosopher Ralph Waldo Emerson warned in 1839: "The invasion of Nature by Trade with its Money, its Credit, its Steam, [and] its Railroad threatens to . . . establish a new, universal Monarchy."

> **IDENTIFY THE BIG IDEA**
>
> How did the economic transformations of the first half of the nineteenth century reshape northern and southern society and culture?

The First Cotton Gin, drawn by William L. Sheppard The economic lives of northerners and southerners alike were transformed by technological innovation and new forms of labor discipline in the years between 1800 and 1848. In this image, two male slaves operate a cotton gin in a process that crushed the hard, stubborn cotton bolls and removed the seeds, while an enslaved woman brings a heavy new load for processing. In the background, a planter and a buyer closely inspect the finished product, which would soon be shipped to a textile mill in the North or in England. This was the cotton complex, a set of economic activities that drove forward economic change in both the northern and southern states. Bettmann/Getty Images.

As you read, ask yourself why this chapter begins and ends with these dates and then identify the links among related events.

1790 ▶ Samuel Slater reproduces Arkwright's inventions in Providence, Rhode Island	**1820–1840** ▶ Urban population surges in Northeast and Midwest; shoe entrepreneurs adopt division of labor
1792 ▶ Congress passes Post Office Act	**1820s** ▶ New England women take textile jobs ▶ Entrepreneurial planters in Cotton South turn to gang labor
1793 ▶ Eli Whitney devises cotton gin	
1800s ▶ Natural increase produces surplus of slaves in Old South ▶ Domestic slave trade expands, disrupting black family life	**1824** ▶ *Gibbons v. Ogden* promotes interstate trade
	1830s ▶ Emergence of western commercial cities ▶ Boom in cotton production ▶ Labor movement gains strength ▶ Middle-class culture emerges
1807 ▶ Embargo Act prohibits trade with Great Britain	
1808 ▶ African slave trade abolished by Congress	
1812 ▶ Louisiana becomes a state and its sugar output increases	**1837** ▶ South Carolina Senator John C. Calhoun argues that slavery is a "positive good"
1814 ▶ Boston Manufacturing Company opens factory in Waltham, Massachusetts	**1840s** ▶ Gradual emancipation completed in North ▶ Maturation of machine-tool industry
1816–1828 ▶ Congress levies protective tariffs	**1842** ▶ *Commonwealth v. Hunt* legitimizes trade unions
1817 ▶ Erie Canal begun (completed in 1825) ▶ Mississippi becomes a state; Alabama follows (1819)	

Foundations of a New Economic Order

The emerging economic order was based on core principles grounded in republican ideals. Private property, market exchange, and individual opportunity were widely shared values, and throughout the nation, activist state governments pursued **neomercantilist** policies to help achieve them. New systems of banking and credit, often supported by state charters, increased the money supply and made capital more widely available to American entrepreneurs. State legislatures also issued charters to turnpike and canal companies, whose new roads and waterways reduced the cost of transportation and stimulated economic activity. As a result, beginning around 1800 the average per capita income of Americans increased by more than 1 percent a year — more than 30 percent in a single generation.

Credit and Banking

America was "a Nation of Merchants," a British visitor reported from Philadelphia in 1798, "keen in the pursuit of wealth in all the various modes of acquiring it." Acquire it they did, making spectacular profits as the wars of the French Revolution and Napoleon (1793–1815) crippled European firms. Merchants John Jacob Astor and Robert Oliver became the nation's first millionaires. After working for an Irish-owned linen firm in Baltimore, Oliver struck out on his own, achieving affluence by trading West Indian sugar and coffee. Astor, who migrated from Germany to New York in 1784, began by selling dry-goods and became wealthy carrying furs from the Pacific Northwest to China and investing in New York City real estate (Thinking Like a Historian).

To finance their ventures, Oliver, Astor, and other merchants needed capital, from either their own savings or loans. Before the American Revolution, colonial merchants often relied on credit from British suppliers. In 1781, the Confederation Congress chartered the Bank of North America in Philadelphia, and traders in Boston and New York soon founded similar institutions to raise and loan money. "Our monied capital has so much increased from the Introduction of Banks, & the Circulation of the Funds,"

The China Trade   Following the Revolution, New England merchants traded actively with the major Asian manufacturing centers of China and India. In this painting by George Chinnery (1774–1852), the American flag flies prominently, alongside other national banners, in front of the warehouse district in Canton (modern Guangzhou). There, merchants exchanged bundles of American furs for cargoes of Chinese tea, silks, and porcelain plates, cups, and serving dishes. © Peabody Essex Museum, Salem, Massachusetts, USA/Bridgeman Images.

Philadelphia merchant William Bingham boasted in 1791, "that the Necessity of Soliciting Credits from England will no longer exist."

That same year, Federalists in Congress chartered the Bank of the United States (Chapter 7). By 1805, the bank had branches in eight seaport cities, profits that averaged a handsome 8 percent annually, and clients with easy access to capital. As trader Jesse Atwater noted, "the foundations of our [merchant] houses are laid in bank paper."

But Jeffersonians attacked the bank as an unconstitutional expansion of federal power "supported by public creditors, speculators, and other insidious men." When the bank's charter expired in 1811, the Jeffersonian Republican–dominated Congress refused to renew it. Merchants, artisans, and farmers quickly persuaded state legislatures to charter banks — in Pennsylvania, no fewer than 41. By 1816, when Congress (now run by National Republicans) chartered a new national bank (the Second Bank of the United States), there were 246 state-chartered banks with tens of thousands of stockholders and $68 million in banknotes in circulation. These state banks were often shady operations that issued notes without adequate specie reserves, made loans to insiders, and lent generously to farmers buying overpriced land.

Bad banking policies helped bring on the **Panic of 1819** (just as they caused the financial crisis of 2008), but broader forces were equally important. As the Napoleonic Wars ended in 1815, American imports of English woolen and cotton goods spiked. Then, in 1818, farmers and planters faced an abrupt 30 percent drop in world agricultural prices. As farmers' income declined, they could not pay debts owed to stores and banks, many of which went bankrupt. "A deep shadow has passed over our land," lamented one New Yorker, as land prices dropped by 50 percent. The panic gave

The Entrepreneur and the Community

Americans of the early republic believed that with hard work and virtue, even the lowliest of white men might rise to economic and political respectability, if not prominence. In the Revolutionary generation, Benjamin Franklin, born into a large and impoverished Boston family, had become a successful businessman and an international celebrity. Franklin's success reflected the optimism that laboring men felt when contemplating the new nation's seemingly boundless opportunity.

1. **Banner of the Society of Pewterers of the City of New York, carried in the Federal Procession, July 23, 1788, celebrating the ratification of the U.S. Constitution.** *The ribbon at top right reads "The Federal Plan Most Solid & Secure/Americans Their Freedom Will Endure/All Art Shall Flourish in Columbia's Land/And All her Sons Join as One Social Band."*

SOURCE: © Collection of the New-York Historical Society, USA/Bridgeman Images.

2. **John Jacob Astor quoted in Elbert Hubbard, *Little Journeys to the Homes of Great Business Men*, 1909.** *John Jacob Astor's (1763–1848) story is a parable of American entrepreneurial triumph. Arriving in America in 1783 from Germany, Astor worked in the fur industry treating pelts and, with capital borrowed from his brother, started up a musical instrument* shop and fur business in 1786. Over the next three decades, Astor's American Fur Company prospered by trading furs in China, making Astor America's first millionaire. Apparently influenced by Benjamin Franklin's aphorism "Early to bed and early to rise, makes a man healthy wealthy and wise," Astor wrote:

> The man who makes it the habit of his life to go to bed at nine o'clock, usually gets rich and is always reliable. Of course, going to bed does not make him rich — I merely mean that such a man will in all probability be up early in the morning and do a big day's work . . . good habits in America make any man rich.

3. **Anonymous, "A Working Man's Recollections of America," *Knight's Penny Magazine*, 1846.** *A cabinetmaker penned this account after returning to England following an unsuccessful stint seeking success in New York.*

> I was a cabinet-maker by trade, and one of the many who, between the years 1825–35, expatriated themselves in countless thousands, drawn by the promise of fair wages for faithful work, and driven by the scanty remuneration offered to unceasing toil at home. . . . On landing in New York I made up my mind to lose none of the advantages it uttered by want of diligence on my part. During the first two years I took but one holiday. . . . In summer we began work at six; at eight took half an hour for breakfast, and then worked till twelve, when one an hour for dinner; after which we kept on till six, seven, or eight. . . . A relative who arrived from England held out to me bright prospects of advantages to be realized by the employment of a little capital, combined with a removal to some inland town. I sold off nearly the whole

---

EXPLAIN CONSEQUENCES
Why were banks important to American economic development?

Americans their first taste of a business cycle, the periodic boom and bust inherent to an unregulated market economy.

Transportation and the Market Revolution

Economic expansion also depended on improvements in transportation, where governments once again played a crucial role. As with bank charters, legislative charters for turnpikes and canal companies reflected the ideology of mercantilism — government-assisted economic development. Just as Parliament had used the Navigation Acts to spur British prosperity, so American legislatures enacted laws "of great public utility" to increase the "common wealth." Following Jefferson's embargo of 1807, which cut off goods and credit from Europe, the New England states awarded charters to two hundred iron-mining, textile-manufacturing, and banking companies, while Pennsylvania granted more than eleven hundred. By 1820, state governments had created a of our moveables . . . [and committed all my savings to this enterprise. However,] our scheme . . . completely failed, and I had no resources but my industry and chest of tools to meet the impending difficulties.

4. **Diary entry by Philip Hone, March 29, 1848.** *Philip Hone (1780–1851), a conservative Whig, was a successful merchant and entrepreneur and mayor of New York City from 1826 to 1827. Hone's marvelous diary (1828–1851) records the changing character of New York City, as well as his contempt for Jacksonian Democracy and its Irish immigrant supporters.*

John Jacob Astor died this morning, at nine o'clock, in the eighty-fifth year of his age . . . and left reluctantly his unbounded wealth. His property is estimated at $20,000,000, some judicious persons say $30,000,000; but, at any rate, he was the richest man in the United States in productive and valuable property; and this immense, gigantic fortune was the fruit of his own labor, unerring sagacity, and far-seeing penetration. He came to this country at twenty years of age; penniless, friendless, without inheritance, without education . . . but with a determination to be rich, and ability to carry it into effect. His capital consisted of a few trifling musical instruments, which he got from his brother, George Astor, in London, a dealer in music. . . . The fur trade was the philosopher's stone of this modern Croesus; beaver-skins and musk-rats furnished the oil for the supply of Aladdin's lamp. His traffic was the shipment of furs to China, where they brought immense prices, for he monopolized the business; and the return cargoes of teas, silks, and rich productions of China brought further large profits. . . . My brother and I found in Mr. Astor a valuable customer. . . . All he touched turned to gold.

5. **Editorial in the *New York Herald*, April 5, 1848.** *John Jacob Astor's will included a bequest of $400,000 for the establishment of what became the New York Public Library. This editorial questioned whether this relatively meager bequest adequately repaid residents.*

If we had been an associate of John Jacob Astor the first idea that we should have put into his head would

have been that one-half of his immense property — ten million at least — belonged to the people of the city of New York. During the last fifty years of the life of John Jacob Astor, his property has been augmented and increased in the value by the aggregate intelligence, industry, enterprise and commerce of New York, fully to the amount of one-half its value. The farms and lots of ground which he bought forty, twenty and ten and five years ago, have all increased in value entirely by the industry of the citizens of New York . . . half of his immense estate, in its actual value, has accrued to him by the industry of the community.

SOURCES: (2) Elbert Hubbard, *Little Journeys to the Homes of Great Business Men* (New York: Wm. H. Wise & Co., 1916), 201; (3) *Knight's Penny Magazine*, Vol. 1 (London: Charles Knight & Co., 1846), 97, 107, 108; (4) Philip Hone, *The Diary of Philip Hone, 1828–1851*, Vol. 2 (New York: Dodd, Mead and Company, 1889), 347–348; (5) Gustavus Myers, *History of the Great American Fortunes*, Vol. 1 (Chicago: Charles H. Kerr & Company, 1910), 199–200.

ANALYZING THE EVIDENCE

1. What does the Pewterer's Banner (source 1) suggest about personal and by extension national success in the post-Revolutionary era?

2. According to John Jacob Astor (source 2) and the cabinet-maker (source 3), what traits are important in work?

3. Sources 2, 4, and 5 all deal with John Jacob Astor. What do these sources suggest about the road to wealth in America?

4. Compare and contrast Hone's view of Astor (source 4) with that of the *Herald*'s editorial (source 5).

PUTTING IT ALL TOGETHER

As these sources indicate, Americans had a divided view of the place of wealth in their society. For many, the opportunity to reap the benefits of hard work was essential to American liberty, and the wealth of John Jacob Astor was his just reward. Others, in keeping with older, republican values, believed that Astor's great wealth came at the expense of others, and that the fortunes of the individual and the community should rise together. Considering these sources and what you have learned in Chapter 8, write an essay that explores this tension in American economic ideals.

---

republican political economy: a **Commonwealth System** that funneled state aid to private businesses whose projects would improve the general welfare.

Transportation projects were among the greatest beneficiaries of the Commonwealth System. Between 1793 and 1812, for example, the Massachusetts legislature granted charters to more than one hundred private turnpike corporations. These charters gave the companies special legal status and often included monopoly rights to a transportation route. Pennsylvania issued fifty-five charters, including one to the Lancaster Turnpike Company, which built a 65-mile graded and graveled toll road to Philadelphia. The road quickly boosted the regional economy. A farm woman noted, "The turnpike is finished and we can now go to town at all times and in all weather." New turnpikes soon connected dozens of inland market centers to seaport cities. Westward migration beyond the seaboard states created a rapidly growing demand for new transportation routes.

The vital precondition for westward migration was the dispossession of Native American peoples. In the War of 1812, the United States defeated the confederation of

Great Lakes and Ohio Indians led by Tecumseh and Tenskwatawa and claimed their lands, along with 23 million acres ceded by the Creeks after the Battle of Horseshoe Bend. Subsequent treaties with the Creeks, Cherokees, Chickasaws, and Choctaws in the South and with the Miamis, Ottawas, Sauks, Fox, and other nations in the North brought millions more acres into the public domain. (See Map 7.2, p. 216.)

For farmers, artisans, and merchants to capitalize on these new lands, however, they needed access to transportation routes. Farmers in Kentucky, Tennessee, southern Ohio, Indiana, and Illinois settled near the Ohio River and its many tributaries, so they could easily get goods to market. Similarly, speculators hoping to capitalize on the expansion of commerce bought up property in the cities along the banks of major rivers: Cincinnati, Louisville, Chattanooga, and St. Louis. Farmers and merchants built barges to carry cotton, grain, and meat downstream to New Orleans, which by 1815 was exporting about $5 million in agricultural products yearly.

But natural waterways were not enough, by themselves, to connect east and west. To link westward migrants to the seaboard states, Congress approved funds for a National Road constructed of compacted gravel. The project began in 1811 at Cumberland in western Maryland, at the head of navigation of the Potomac River; reached Wheeling, Virginia (now West Virginia), on the Ohio River in 1818; and ended in Vandalia, Illinois, in 1839. As migrants traveled west on the National Road and other interregional highways, they passed livestock herds heading in the opposite direction, destined for eastern markets.

Shrinking Space: Canals Even on well-built gravel roads, overland travel was slow and expensive. As U.S. territory expanded and artisans, farmers, and manufacturers produced an ever expanding array of goods, legislators and businessmen created faster and cheaper ways to get those products to consumers. To carry people, crops, and manufactures to and from the great Mississippi River basin, public money and private businesses developed a water-borne transportation system of unprecedented size, complexity, and cost. State governments and private entrepreneurs dredged shallow rivers and constructed canals to bypass waterfalls and rapids. Around 1820, they began constructing a massive system of canals and roads linking states along the Atlantic coast with new states in the trans-Appalachian west.

This transportation system set in motion a mass migration of people to the Greater Mississippi River basin. This huge area, drained by six river systems (the Missouri, Arkansas, Red, Ohio, Tennessee, and Mississippi), contains the largest and most productive contiguous acreage of arable land in the world. By 1860, nearly one-third of the nation's citizens lived in eight of its states — the "Midwest," consisting of the five states carved out of the Northwest Territory (Ohio, Indiana, Illinois, Michigan, and Wisconsin) along with Missouri, Iowa, and Minnesota. There they created a rich agricultural economy and an industrializing society.

The key event was the New York legislature's 1817 financing of the **Erie Canal**, a 364-mile waterway connecting the Hudson River and Lake Erie. Previously, the longest canal in the United States was just 28 miles long — reflecting the huge capital cost of canals and the lack of American engineering expertise. New York's ambitious project had three things working in its favor: the vigorous support of New York City's merchants, who wanted access to western markets; the backing of New York's governor, De Witt Clinton, who proposed to finance the waterway from tax revenues, tolls, and bond sales to foreign investors; and the relatively gentle terrain west of Albany. Even so, the task was enormous. Workers — many of them Irish immigrants — dug out millions of cubic yards of soil, quarried thousands of tons of rock for the huge locks that raised and lowered the boats, and constructed vast reservoirs to ensure a steady supply of water.

The first great engineering project in American history, the Erie Canal altered the ecology of an entire region. As farming communities and market towns sprang up along the waterway, settlers cut down millions of trees to provide wood for houses and barns and to open the land for growing crops and grazing animals. Cows and sheep

View of the Erie Canal This pastoral view of the Erie Canal near Lockport, New York, painted by artist John William Hill, hints at this waterway's profound impact on American life. Without the canal, the town in the background would not exist and farmers such as the man in the foreground would not have a regional market for their cattle and grain. The success of the Erie Canal had led to the construction of a vast system of canals by 1860. This infrastructure was as important to the nation as the railroad network of the late nineteenth century and the interstate highway and airport transportation systems of the late twentieth century. Bettmann/Getty Images.

foraged in pastures that had recently been forests occupied by deer and bears, and spring rains caused massive erosion of the denuded landscape.

Whatever its environmental consequences, the Erie Canal was an instant economic success. The first 75-mile section opened in 1819 and quickly yielded enough revenue to repay its construction cost. When workers finished the canal in 1825, a 40-foot-wide ribbon of water stretched from Buffalo, on the eastern shore of Lake Erie, to Albany, where it joined the Hudson River for the 150-mile trip to New York City. The canal's water "must be the most fertilizing of all fluids," suggested novelist Nathaniel Hawthorne, "for it causes towns with their masses of brick and stone, their churches and theaters, their business and hubbub, their luxury and refinement, their gay dames and polished citizens, to spring up."

The Erie Canal brought prosperity to the farmers of central and western New York and the entire Great Lakes region. Northeastern manufacturers shipped clothing, boots, and agricultural equipment to farm families; in return, farmers sent grain, cattle, hogs, and raw materials (leather, wool, and hemp, for example) to eastern cities and foreign markets. Two horses pulling a wagon overland could tow 4 tons of freight; now, those same two horses working the towpaths of the Erie Canal could pull 100-ton freight barges at a steady 30 miles a day, cutting transportation costs and accelerating the flow of goods. In 1818, the mills in Rochester, New York, processed 26,000 barrels of flour for export. Ten years later their output soared to 200,000 barrels, and by 1840 it was at 500,000 barrels.

The spectacular benefits of the Erie Canal prompted a national canal boom. Civic and business leaders in Philadelphia and Baltimore proposed waterways to link their cities to the Midwest. Copying New York's fiscal innovations, they persuaded their state legislatures to invest directly in canal companies or to force state-chartered banks to do so, and to offer guarantees that encouraged British and Dutch investors. Soon, artificial

MAP 8.1 The Transportation Revolution: Roads and Canals, 1820–1850
By 1850, the United States had an efficient system of water-borne transportation with three distinct parts. Short canals and navigable rivers carried cotton, tobacco, and other products from the countryside of the southern seaboard states into the Atlantic commercial system. A second system, centered on the Erie, Chesapeake and Ohio, and Pennsylvania Mainline canals, linked northeastern seaports to the vast trans-Appalachian region. Finally, a set of regional canals in the Midwest connected most of the Great Lakes region to the Ohio and Mississippi rivers and the port of New Orleans.

waterways connected Philadelphia and Baltimore, via the Pennsylvania Canal and the Chesapeake and Ohio Canal, to the Great Lakes region. The Michigan and Illinois Canal (finished in 1848), which linked Chicago to the Mississippi River, completed an inland all-water route from New York City to New Orleans, the two most important port cities in North America (Map 8.1). Historians have labeled the economic boom resulting from these new banking and transportation systems the **Market Revolution**. Americans had greater access to capital, more financial liquidity, and more opportunities to buy and sell products over long distances, than they had ever had before.

Shrinking Space: Steamboats The steamboat, another product of the industrial age, added crucial flexibility to the Mississippi basin's river-based transportation system. In 1807, engineer-inventor Robert Fulton piloted the first American steamboat, the *Clermont*, up the Hudson River. To navigate shallow western rivers, engineers broadened steamboats' hulls to reduce their draft and enlarge their cargo capacity. These vessels halved the cost of upstream river transport and dramatically increased the flow of goods, people, and news. In 1830, a traveler or a letter from New York could reach Buffalo or Pittsburgh by water in less than a week and Detroit, Chicago, or St. Louis in two weeks. In 1800, the same journeys had taken twice as long.

Slave-owning planters from the Lower South settled in Missouri (admitted to the Union in 1821) and pushed on to Arkansas (admitted in 1836). Simultaneously, yeomen families from the Upper South joined migrants from New England and New York in farming the fertile lands near the Great Lakes. Once Indiana and Illinois were settled, American-born farmers poured into Michigan (1837), Iowa (1846), and Wisconsin (1848)—where they resided among tens of thousands of hardworking immigrants from Germany. To meet the demand for cheap farmsteads, Congress in 1820 reduced the price of federal land from $2.00 an acre to $1.25. For $100, a farmer could buy 80 acres, the minimum required under federal law. By the 1840s, this generous policy had enticed about 5 million people to states and territories west of the Appalachians (Map 8.2).

While state legislatures subsidized canals, the national government created a vast postal system, the first network for the exchange of information. Thanks to the Post Office Act of 1792, there were more than eight thousand post offices by 1830, and the postal service had more employees than all the rest of the government's civilian employees combined. They safely delivered thousands of letters and banknotes worth millions of dollars, along with newspapers that carried information from the Atlantic seaboard to the Mississippi basin. The U.S. Supreme Court, headed by John Marshall, likewise encouraged interstate trade by firmly establishing federal authority over interstate commerce (Chapter 7). In *Gibbons v. Ogden* (1824), the Court voided a New York law that created a monopoly on steamboat travel into New York City. That

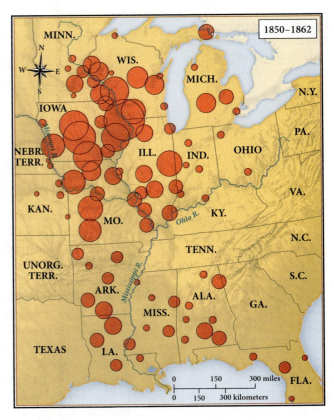

MAP 8.2 Western Land Sales, 1830–1839 and 1850–1862
The federal government set up local offices to sell land in the national domain to settlers. During the 1830s, the offices sold huge amounts of land in the corn and wheat belt of the Midwest (Ohio, Indiana, Illinois, and Michigan) and the cotton belt to the south (especially Alabama and Mississippi). As settlers moved westward in the 1850s, most sales were in the upper Mississippi River Valley (particularly Iowa and Wisconsin). Each circle indicates the relative amount of land sold at a local office.

decision prevented local or state monopolies — or tariffs — from impeding the flow of goods, people, and news across the nation.

Shrinking Space: The Telegraph An efficient postal service was a great boon to merchants and manufacturers doing business across long distances. But for decades, inventors who were familiar with the properties of electricity dreamed of a much faster form of communication: electrical telegraphy. Across Europe, scientists experimented with various methods of using electrical impulses to send messages, but they struggled to devise a practical way to represent the alphabet. In 1837, a Massachusetts painter-turned-inventor, Samuel F. B. Morse, devised a telegraph capable of sending signals through miles of wire. Of equal importance, Morse and his collaborator, machinist and inventor Alfred Vail, invented a code for transmitting letters and numbers along a single wire by means of a contact key. A telegraph line was strung between Washington, D.C., and Baltimore in 1844; a year later, the Magnetic Telegraph Company was founded to create the first network of telegraph lines. By 1848, telegraph wires connected New York and Chicago. Western Union was formed in 1856 to consolidate the operations of smaller companies, and in 1861 it completed a transcontinental telegraph line connecting New York with San Francisco.

All these innovations — roads and turnpikes, canals and steamboats, the postal service and the telegraph — helped to shrink the vast spaces of North America. They enabled farmers and merchants to sell goods in distant markets, helped entrepreneurs to coordinate business activity, aided immigrants as they relocated, and created a

IDENTIFY CAUSES
How did advances in technology and engineering advance the Market Revolution?

network of information that shaped politics and culture on a national scale. Together, they constituted the foundation of a new social order.

> **IN YOUR OWN WORDS** What was the relationship between government support and private enterprise in economic development?

The Cotton Complex: Northern Industry and Southern Agriculture

In 1800, the economy of the United States remained overwhelmingly agricultural and manufacturing was still in its infancy. Nevertheless, in the first half of the nineteenth century the **Industrial Revolution** came to the United States. At its center was the **cotton complex**: the relationship between northern industry and southern agriculture that drove a major economic transformation. In the Northeast, merchants and manufacturers invested in new textile mills that relied on the labor of young women drawn from nearby farms. These northeastern mills, and many more like them in Great Britain, created vast demand for cotton, which transformed the southern economy as well. As northern merchants and manufacturers reorganized work routines and increased output, goods that were once luxury items became part of everyday life. Southern planters poured capital into land and slaves, revolutionizing agricultural production and sentencing additional generations of African American slaves to the miseries of plantation life.

The American Industrial Revolution

The Industrial Revolution had its roots in Great Britain, where textile manufacturing had undergone major changes in the last half of the eighteenth century. Clothmaking was an ancient enterprise common to Asia, Africa, Europe, and the Americas, but until this time it was driven by small-scale production. For millennia, spinning and weaving—whether wool, cotton, linen, or silk—were crafts that were plied in the home, using technology that had been very slow to change. Strands of fiber were spun into thread and yarn by hand or using foot-driven spinning wheels, while yarn was woven into cloth on foot-powered looms.

A series of technical innovations in Britain in the eighteenth century made cloth-making increasingly efficient. The flying shuttle, invented in 1733, made it possible to weave cloth much more rapidly than yarn could be spun. Then, beginning in the 1760s, a series of devices for spinning fibers into yarn were invented: first a spinning jenny, then a water frame, and then a mule. Because the water frame and the mule were machines that relied on water or steam power, spinning moved out of households and into factories built alongside rivers that could drive the apparatus. Water-powered spinning mills could now produce abundant yarn, and cloth production soared. In India, it took 50,000 hours of labor to spin 100 pounds of raw cotton. In Britain in 1790, workers using a spinning mule could do the same work in 1,000 hours; by 1825, it took only 135 hours. This was a revolution in productivity.

To protect its textile industry from American competition, Great Britain prohibited the export of textile machinery and the emigration of the skilled craftsmen who could replicate the mills. But the promise of higher wages brought thousands of these skilled **mechanics** to the United States illegally.

Samuel Slater, the most important émigré mechanic, came to America in 1789 after working for Richard Arkwright, who had invented the most advanced British machinery for spinning cotton. A year later, Slater reproduced Arkwright's innovations in merchant Moses Brown's cotton mill in Providence, Rhode Island—the first in North

America. The fast-flowing rivers that cascaded down from the Appalachian foothills to the coastal plain provided a cheap source of energy. From Massachusetts to Delaware, these waterways were soon lined with industrial villages and textile mills as large as 150 feet long, 40 feet wide, and four stories high (Map 8.3). The Industrial Revolution had arrived on American shores.

American and British Advantages British textile manufacturers nevertheless easily undersold their American competitors, for two reasons. First, they enjoyed the benefit of efficient shipping networks, which brought raw cotton to Britain at bargain prices, and low interest rates, which enabled mill owners to borrow money cheaply to support and expand their operations. Second, Britain had cheap labor: it had a larger population — about 12.6 million in 1810 compared to 7.3 million Americans — and thousands of landless laborers prepared to accept low-paying factory jobs, while in the United States labor was scarce and well paid.

To offset these advantages, American entrepreneurs relied on help from the federal government: in 1816, 1824, and 1828, Congress passed tariff bills that placed high taxes on imported cotton and woolen cloth. However, in the 1830s, Congress reduced tariffs because southern planters, western farmers, and urban consumers demanded inexpensive imports.

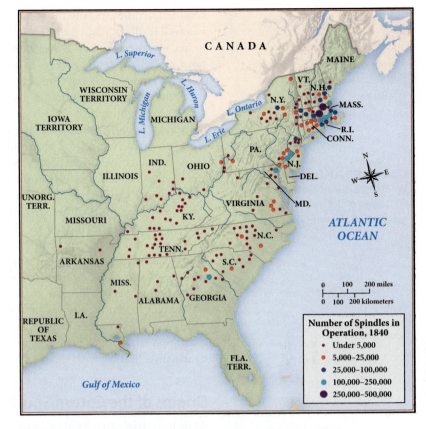

MAP 8.3 New England's Dominance in Cotton Spinning, 1840
Although the South grew the nation's cotton, it did not process it. Prior to the Civil War, entrepreneurs in Massachusetts and Rhode Island built most of the factories that spun and wove raw cotton into cloth. Their factories made use of the abundant water power available in New England and the region's surplus labor force. Initially, factory managers hired young farmwomen to work the machines; later, they relied on immigrants from Ireland and the French-speaking Canadian province of Quebec.

Better Machines, Cheaper Workers American producers used two other strategies to compete with their British rivals. First, they improved on British technology. In 1811, Francis Cabot Lowell, a wealthy Boston merchant, toured British textile mills, secretly making detailed drawings of their power machinery. Paul Moody, an experienced American mechanic, then copied the machines and improved their design. In 1814, Lowell joined with merchants Nathan Appleton and Patrick Tracy Jackson to form the Boston Manufacturing Company. Having raised the staggering sum of $400,000, they built a textile plant in Waltham, Massachusetts — the first American factory to perform all clothmaking operations under one roof. Thanks to Moody's improvements, Waltham's power looms operated at higher speeds than British looms and needed fewer workers.

The second strategy was to tap a cheaper source of labor. In the 1820s, the Boston Manufacturing Company recruited thousands of young women from farm families, providing them with rooms in boardinghouses and with evening lectures and other cultural activities. To reassure parents about their daughters' moral welfare, the mill owners enforced strict curfews, prohibited alcoholic beverages, and required regular church attendance. At Lowell (1822), Chicopee (1823), and other sites in Massachusetts and New Hampshire, the company built new factories that used this labor system, known as the **Waltham-Lowell System**.

By the early 1830s, more than 40,000 New England women were working in textile mills. As an observer noted, the wages were "more than could be obtained by the hitherto ordinary occupation of housework," the living conditions were better than those in

To see a longer excerpt of the Lucy Larcom document, along with other primary sources from this period, see **Sources for America's History**.

COMPARE AND CONTRAST
What were the advantages and strategies of British and American textile manufacturers?

crowded farmhouses, and the women had greater independence. Lucy Larcom became a Lowell textile operative at age eleven to avoid being "a trouble or burden or expense" to her widowed mother. Other women operatives used wages to pay off their father's farm mortgages, send brothers to school, or accumulate a marriage dowry for themselves (America in Global Context).

Some operatives just had a good time. Susan Brown, who worked as a Lowell weaver for eight months, spent half her earnings on food and lodging and the rest on plays, concerts, lectures, and a two-day excursion to Boston. Like most textile workers, Brown soon tired of the rigors of factory work and the never-ceasing clatter of the machinery, which ran twelve hours a day, six days a week. After she quit, she lived at home for a time and then moved to another mill. Whatever the hardships, waged work gave young women a sense of freedom. "Don't I feel independent!" a woman mill worker wrote to her sister. "The thought that I am living on no one is a happy one indeed to me." The owners of the Boston Manufacturing Company were even happier. By combining tariff protection with improved technology and cheap female labor, they could undersell their British rivals. Their textiles were also cheaper than those made in New York and Pennsylvania, where farmworkers were paid more than in New England and textile wages consequently were higher. Manufacturers in those states garnered profits by using advanced technology to produce higher-quality cloth. Even Thomas Jefferson, the great champion of yeoman farming, was impressed. "Our manufacturers are now very nearly on a footing with those of England," he boasted in 1825.

Origins of the Cotton South

As its industrial capacity grew in the eighteenth century, Great Britain began to import cotton in larger quantities. But the world supply was relatively small because cotton production was immensely labor-intensive. A revolution in cotton cloth production would require a revolution in cotton agriculture, based on new forms of cheap labor. The black belt of the American Southeast — an arc of fertile soil stretching from western South Carolina through central Georgia, Alabama, and Mississippi — provided a landscape that was ideal for cotton cultivation, and the slave plantation complex offered a system of labor discipline that could bring cotton to world markets on an entirely new scale.

The Decline of Slavery, 1776–1800 The possibility that cotton production would lead to a boom in African slavery would have come as a surprise to the generation that lived through the American Revolution, because in that era slavery was in a steep decline. Whites and blacks alike perceived a contradiction between the colonies' pursuit of liberty and the institution of slavery. "I wish most sincerely there was not a Slave in the province," Abigail Adams confessed to her husband, John. "It always appeared a most iniquitous Scheme to me — to fight ourselves for what we are daily robbing and plundering from those who have as good a right to freedom as we do."

The North Ends Slavery — Slowly Beginning in the 1750s, Quaker evangelist John Woolman urged Friends to free their slaves, and many did so. In 1780, antislavery activists in Pennsylvania passed the first **gradual emancipation** law in the United States. Though it freed no one, the law set an important precedent. In subsequent years, legislators in Connecticut (1784), Rhode Island (1784), New York (1799), and New Jersey (1804) adopted gradual emancipation statutes as well (Map 8.4). These laws recognized white property rights by requiring slaves to buy their freedom by years — even decades — of additional labor. For example, the New York Emancipation Act of 1799 allowed slavery to continue until 1828 and freed slave children only at the age of twenty-five. Consequently, as late as 1810, almost 30,000 blacks in the northern states — nearly one-fourth of the African Americans living there — were still enslaved.

AMERICA IN GLOBAL CONTEXT

The Fate of the American and Indian Textile Industries

In 1776, the United States declared its independence from the British Empire. At about the same time, Britain began to create in India what historians call the Second British Empire. By 1860, Britain had become the world's leading industrial economy and dominated the princely states and peoples of the Indian subcontinent. The following tables trace the impact of political decisions on the American and Indian textile industries. As the legislature of an independent republic, the U.S. Congress could impose tariffs (taxes on imported goods) on British textiles; as colonies, Indian governments could not do so.

TABLE 8.1

Cotton Textile Production and Consumption in India

Year	Population (millions)	Imports from Britain (mill. yds.)	Production for Domestic Consumption (mill. yds.)	Exports to Britain (pieces, avg./year)
1751	190	0	1,598	632,000 (1750–1754)
1801	207	0	1,741	1,355,304 (1800–1804)
1821	205	20	1,704	542,117 (1820–1824)
1841	212	141	1,642	192,965 (1830–1834)
1861	242	514	1,538	Data not available

TABLE 8.2

Textile Production in the United States

Year	Number of Cotton Mill Workers	Number of Spindles (avg./decade)[1]	Imports from Britain (mill. yds.)	Average U.S. Tariff (as % of item's value)
1810		215,000		
1815			70.81	25.0%
1820	12,000	936,000		
1827			52.86	53.8%
1830	55,000	1,038,000		
1835			74.96	40.4%
1840	72,000	1,243,000		
1850	92,000	1,709,000	104.23	27.1%
1859			225.15	19.6%
1860	122,000			

[1]Entries in Spindle column are the average per year across the decade; i.e., there were perhaps 100,000 spindles in 1810 and 350,000 in 1820, yielding an average of 215,000 between 1810 and 1819.

QUESTIONS FOR ANALYSIS

1. Compare changes in Indian production ("Production for Domestic Consumption" and "Exports to Britain") with changes in American production ("Number of Cotton Mill Workers" and "Number of Spindles") between 1800 and 1861. Which country is "industrializing," and which is "deindustrializing"?

2. How do American tariffs change over time? (Chapter 10 will explain the reasons for these changes.) What is the impact of American tariff rates on the import of British textiles?

3. What insights does this material provide into the political and economic aspects of American industrialization?

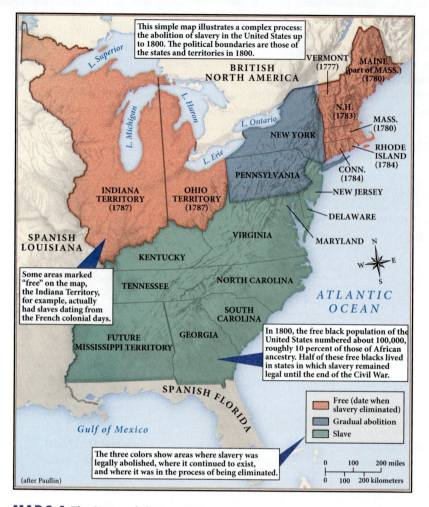

This simple map illustrates a complex process: the abolition of slavery in the United States up to 1800. The political boundaries are those of the states and territories in 1800.

Some areas marked "free" on the map, the Indiana Territory, for example, actually had slaves dating from the French colonial days.

In 1800, the free black population of the United States numbered about 100,000, roughly 10 percent of those of African ancestry. Half of these free blacks lived in states in which slavery remained legal until the end of the Civil War.

The three colors show areas where slavery was legally abolished, where it continued to exist, and where it was in the process of being eliminated.

(after Paullin)

Legend:
- Free (date when slavery eliminated)
- Gradual abolition
- Slave

MAP 8.4 The Status of Slavery, 1800

In 1775, racial slavery was legal in all of the British colonies in North America. By the time the confederated states achieved their independence in 1783, the New England region was mostly free of slavery. By 1800, all of the states north of Maryland had provided for the gradual abolition of slavery except New Jersey, whose legislature finally acted in 1804, but the process of gradual emancipation dragged on until the 1830s. Some slave owners in the Chesapeake region manumitted a number of their slaves, leaving only the whites of the Lower South firmly committed to racial bondage.

Freed blacks faced severe prejudice from whites who feared job competition and racial melding. When Massachusetts judges abolished slavery through case law in 1784, the legislature reenacted an old statute that prohibited whites from marrying blacks, mulattos, or Indians. For African Americans in the North, freedom meant second-class citizenship; nevertheless, the institution of slavery was being ushered slowly out of existence.

Manumission in the Chesapeake The coming of war encouraged many southern slaves to expect that the Revolution would bring their freedom. A black preacher in Georgia told his fellow slaves that King George III "was about to alter the World, and set the Negroes free." Similar rumors, prompted in part by Royal Governor Lord Dunmore's proclamation of 1775 and the Philipsburg Proclamation of 1779 (see Chapters 5 and 6), led thousands of African Americans to flee behind British lines. Two neighbors of Virginia Patriot Richard Henry Lee lost "every slave they had in the world," as did many other planters. In 1781, when the British army evacuated Charleston, more than 6,000 former slaves went with them; another 4,000 left from Savannah. All told, about 30,000 blacks fled their owners.

Yet thousands of African Americans supported the Patriot cause as well. In Maryland, some slaves took up arms for the rebels in return for the promise of freedom. Enslaved Virginians struck informal bargains with their Patriot owners, trading loyalty in wartime for the hope of liberty. Following the Virginia legislature's passage of a **manumission** act in 1782, allowing owners to free their slaves, 10,000 slaves won their freedom.

The southern states faced the most glaring contradiction between liberty and property rights because enslaved blacks represented a huge financial investment. But in the Chesapeake, slavery was in decline for three reasons. First, the tobacco economy was chronically depressed, and many tobacco planters were shifting to wheat and livestock production, a less labor-intensive form of farming that gave them an oversupply of slaves. Second, many leading planters were committed to the principle of human liberty and saw, in the institution of slavery, the same contradiction that their northern counterparts did. Third, evangelical Christianity encouraged some planters to regard their slaves as spiritual equals. In 1784, a conference of Virginia Methodists declared that slavery was "contrary to the Golden Law of God on which hang all the Law and the Prophets." Under these influences, many Chesapeake slave owners manumitted their slaves or allowed them to buy their freedom by working as artisans or laborers. In 1785 a Powhatan planter named Joseph Mayo manumitted all of his slaves, 150 to 170 in number; in the 1790s, Robert "Councillor" Carter manumitted more than 500 slaves and provided them with land. John Randolph of Roanoke manumitted hundreds of slaves in his will, and also left money to buy them land. Widespread manumission gradually brought freedom to one-third of the African Americans in Maryland.

Slavery Resurgent But slavery still had powerful advocates. In Virginia, slave owners pushed back against the wave of manumissions. Fearing the possibility of total emancipation, hundreds of slave owners petitioned the Virginia legislature to repeal the manumission act and thereby protect "the most valuable and indispensible Article of our Property, our Slaves." In 1792, legislators forbade further manumissions. Following the lead of Thomas Jefferson, who owned more than a hundred slaves, political leaders now argued that slavery was a "necessary evil" required to maintain white supremacy and the luxurious planter lifestyle. In North Carolina, legislators condemned private Quaker manumissions as "highly criminal and reprehensible."

Farther south, in the rice-growing states of South Carolina and Georgia, slavery was even more deeply entrenched. Yet rice plantations were confined to the seaboard; at the time of the Revolution, there was no cash crop that could support plantation agriculture farther inland. Cotton was about to change that. In 1786, responding to rising prices resulting from Great Britain's mechanized processing, Georgia planters on the Sea Islands harvested their first crop of long-staple cotton. Its silky fibers produced a high grade of cotton, but — like rice and indigo — Sea Island cotton would not grow in the uplands. Hardier varieties of short-staple cotton could thrive in rich inland soils, but their bolls, with tightly packed fibers, required machine processing. American inventors immediately put their minds to the problem. In 1793, Massachusetts native Eli Whitney devised a machine, called a cotton engine (or cotton "gin" for short), that could quickly separate the seeds of a short-staple cotton boll from their delicate fibers, an innovation that increased the speed of cotton processing fiftyfold. The cotton rush was on.

> **PLACE EVENTS IN CONTEXT**
> Why was slavery in retreat in the Revolutionary era, and what caused its resurgence?

The Cotton Boom and Slavery

In the early nineteenth century, slave plantations pushed into the interior of North America in two directions at once: westward, from the coastal states of South Carolina and Georgia; and northward from New Orleans up the Mississippi (Map 8.5). In the lower Mississippi Valley, sugar was a viable crop; thus, a combination of sugar and cotton drove the development of formerly French Louisiana (admitted as a state in 1812) and Mississippi (admitted in 1817). After crossing the Appalachians, westward-moving cotton planters settled in southern Tennessee (admitted 1796) and Alabama (1819), then pushed into Missouri (1821), Arkansas (1836), and Texas (1845). These migratory streams converged in the rich alluvial soils of the black belt, which stretched from western South Carolina all the way to east Texas. Between 1800 and 1848, the new cotton-growing lands of the American Southeast became some of the most valuable real estate in the world.

The cotton boom immediately tripled the value of good southern farmland. As Creeks, Choctaws, and Chickasaws ceded land, the federal government made it available to southern planters as quickly as possible. Capital investments from overseas helped to speed the process, as wealthy British investors like banker and cotton merchant Thomas Baring loaned money to bring the lands under cultivation. Cotton was wildly profitable; in 1807, a Mississippi cotton plantation returned 22.5 percent a year on its investment. As cotton cultivation expanded, it became the cornerstone of the nation's economy: between 1815 and 1860, it accounted for more than half of all U.S. exports. By 1840, the South produced and exported 1.5 million bales of raw cotton a year, over two-thirds of the world's supply. The cotton-producing capacity of the South dwarfed the industrial capacity of the Northeast. In the first half of the nineteenth century, more than 85 percent of the U.S. cotton crop was sold in Liverpool to be processed in Great Britain, while only a small fraction could be absorbed by American mills. "Cotton is King," boasted the *Southern Cultivator*.

To plant this vast new inland frontier, white planters first imported enslaved laborers from Africa. Between 1776 and 1808, when Congress outlawed the Atlantic slave trade, planters purchased about 115,000 Africans. "The Planter will . . . Sacrifice every

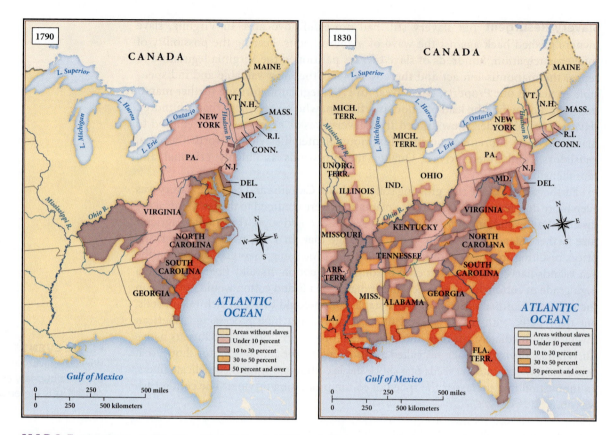

MAP 8.5 Distribution of the Slave Population in 1790 and 1830
The cotton boom shifted the African American population to the South and West. In 1790, most slaves lived and worked on Chesapeake tobacco and Carolina rice and indigo plantations. By 1830, those areas were still heavily populated by black families, but hundreds of thousands of slaves also labored on the cotton and sugar lands of the lower Mississippi Valley and on cotton plantations in Georgia, northern Florida, and Alabama. In the decades to come, the cotton frontier would push across Mississippi and Louisiana and into Texas.

thing to attain Negroes," declared one slave trader. But demand far exceeded the supply. Planters also imported new African workers illegally, through the Spanish colony of Florida until 1819 and then through the Mexican province of Texas. Yet these Africans — about 50,000 between 1810 and 1865 — did not satisfy the demand either.

The Upper South Exports Slaves Planters seeking labor also looked to the Chesapeake region, where the African American population was growing by natural increase at an average of 27 percent a decade, creating a surplus of enslaved workers on many plantations. The result was a growing domestic trade in slaves. Between 1818 and 1829, planters in just one Maryland tobacco-growing county — Frederick — sold at least 952 slaves to traders or cotton planters. Plantation owners in Virginia sold 75,000 slaves during the 1810s and again during the 1820s. That number jumped to nearly 120,000 during the 1830s and then averaged 85,000 during the 1840s and 1850s. By 1860, the "mania for buying negroes" from the Upper South had resulted in a massive transplantation of more than 1 million slaves (Figure 8.1). A majority of African Americans now lived and worked in the Deep South, the lands that stretched from Georgia to Texas.

This African American migration took two forms: transfer and sale. Looking for new opportunities, thousands of Chesapeake and Carolina planters sold their existing plantations and moved their slaves to the Southwest. Many other planters gave slaves to sons and daughters who moved west. Such transfers accounted for about 40 percent of the African American migrants. The rest — about 60 percent of the 1 million migrants — were sold south through traders.

One set of trading routes ran to the Atlantic coast and sent thousands of slaves to rapidly developing sugar plantations in Louisiana. As sugar output soared, slave traders scoured the countryside near the port cities of Baltimore, Alexandria, Richmond, and Charleston — searching, as one of them put it, for "likely young men such as I think would suit the New Orleans market." Because this **coastal trade** in laborers was highly visible, it elicited widespread condemnation by northern abolitionists. Sugar was a "killer" crop, and Louisiana (like the eighteenth-century West Indies) soon had a well-deserved reputation among African Americans "as a place of slaughter." Maryland farmer John Anthony Munnikhuysen refused to allow his daughter Priscilla to marry a Louisiana sugar planter, declaring: "Mit has never been used to see negroes flayed alive and it would kill her."

The **inland system** that fed slaves to the Cotton South was less visible than the coastal trade but more extensive. Professional slave traders went from one rural village to another buying "young and likely Negroes." The traders marched their purchases in coffles — columns of slaves bound to one another — to Alabama, Mississippi, and Missouri in the 1830s and to Arkansas and Texas in the 1850s.

Chesapeake and Carolina planters provided the human cargo. Some planters sold slaves when they ran into debt. "Trouble gathers thicker and thicker around me," Thomas B. Chaplin of South Carolina lamented in his diary. "I will be compelled to send about ten prime Negroes to Town on next Monday, to be sold." Many more planters doubled as slave traders, earning substantial profits by traveling south to sell some of their slaves and those of their neighbors. Colonel E. S. Irvine, a member of the South Carolina legislature and "a highly respected gentleman" in white circles, traveled frequently "to sell a drove of Negroes." Prices marched in step with those for cotton; during a boom year in the 1850s, a planter noted that a slave "will fetch $1000, cash, quick."

The domestic slave trade was crucial to the prosperity of the fast-developing Cotton South. Equally important, it sustained the wealth of slave owners in the East. By selling surplus black workers, planters in the Chesapeake and Carolinas added about 20 percent to their income. As a Maryland newspaper remarked in 1858, "[The trade serves as] an almost universal resource to raise money. A prime able-bodied slave is worth three times as much to the cotton or sugar planter as to the Maryland agriculturalist."

The Impact on Blacks For African American families, the domestic slave trade was a personal disaster that underlined their status — and

FIGURE 8.1 Forced Slave Migration to the Lower South, 1790–1860
The cotton boom set in motion a vast redistribution of the African American population. Between 1790 and 1860, white planters moved or sold more than a million enslaved people from the Upper to the Lower South, a process that broke up families and long-established black communities. Based on data in Robert William Fogel and Stanley L. Engerman, *Time on the Cross: The Economics of American Negro Slavery*, by Robert W. Fogel and Stanley L. Engerman. Copyright © 1974 Little Brown and in *Speculators and Slaves: Masters, Traders, and Slaves in the Old South*, by Michael Tadman, University of Wisconsin Press, 1996.

The Inland Slave Trade Mounted whites escort a convoy of slaves from Virginia to Tennessee in Lewis Miller's *Slave Trader, Sold to Tennessee* (1853). For white planters, the interstate trade in slaves was lucrative; it pumped money into the declining Chesapeake economy and provided young workers for the expanding plantations of the cotton belt. For blacks, it was a traumatic journey, a new Middle Passage that broke up their families and communities. "Arise! Arise! and weep no more, dry up your tears, we shall part no more," the slaves sing sorrowfully as they journey to new lives in Tennessee. The Colonial Williamsburg Foundation. Gift of Dr. Richard M. Kain in memory of George Hay Kain.

vulnerability — as chattel slaves. In law, they were the movable personal property of the whites who owned them. As Lewis Clark, a fugitive from slavery, noted: "Many a time i've had 'em say to me, 'You're my property.'" "The being of slavery, its soul and its body, lives and moves in the **chattel principle**, the property principle, the bill of sale principle," declared former slave James W. C. Pennington. As a South Carolina master put it, "[The slave's earnings] belong to me because I bought him."

Slave property underpinned the entire southern economic system. Whig politician Henry Clay noted that the "immense amount of capital which is invested in slave property . . . is owned by widows and orphans, by the aged and infirm, as well as the sound and vigorous. It is the subject of mortgages, deeds of trust, and family settlements."

As a slave owner, Clay also knew that property rights were key to slave discipline. "I govern them . . . without the whip," another master explained, "by stating . . . that I should sell them if they do not conduct themselves as I wish." The threat was effective. "The Negroes here dread nothing on earth so much as this," a Maryland observer noted. "They regard the south with perfect horror, and to be sent there is considered as the worst punishment." Thousands of slaves suffered that fate, which destroyed about one in every four slave marriages. "Why does the slave ever love?" asked black abolitionist Harriet Jacobs in her autobiography, *Incidents in the Life of a Slave Girl*, when her partner "may at any moment be wrenched away by the hand of violence?" After being sold, one Georgia slave lamented, "My Dear wife for you and my Children my pen cannot Express the griffe I feel to be parted from you all."

The interstate slave trade often focused on young adults. In northern Maryland, planters sold away boys and girls at an average age of seventeen years. "Dey sole my sister Kate," Anna Harris remembered decades later, "and I ain't seed or heard of her since." The trade also separated almost a third of all slave children under the age of fourteen from one or both of their parents. Sarah Grant remembered, "Mamma used to cry when she had to go back to work because she was always scared some of us kids would be sold while she was away."

Despite these sales, 75 percent of slave marriages remained unbroken, and the majority of children lived with one or both parents until puberty. Consequently, the sense of family among African Americans remained strong. Sold from Virginia to Texas in 1843, Hawkins Wilson carried with him a mental picture of his family. Twenty-five years later and now a freedman, Wilson set out to find his "dearest relatives" in Virginia. "My sister belonged to Peter Coleman in Caroline County and her name was Jane. . . . She had three children, Robert, Charles and Julia, when I left — Sister Martha belonged to Dr. Jefferson. . . . Sister Matilda belonged to Mrs. Botts."

During the decades between sale and freedom, Hawkins Wilson and thousands of other African Americans constructed new lives for themselves in the Mississippi Valley. Undoubtedly, many did so with a sense of foreboding, knowing from personal experience that their owners could disrupt their lives at any moment. Like Charles Ball, some "longed to die, and escape from the bonds of my tormentors." The darkness of slavery shadowed even moments of joy. Knowing that sales often ended slave marriages, a white minister blessed one couple "for so long as God keeps them together."

The Inherent Brutality of Slavery Like all systems of forced labor, American racial slavery relied ultimately on physical coercion. Slave owners and overseers routinely whipped slaves who worked slowly or defied their orders. On occasion, they applied the whip with such ferocity that the slave was permanently injured or killed. This photograph of a Mississippi slave named Gordon, taken after he fled to the Union army in Louisiana in 1863 and published in *Harper's Weekly*, stands as graphic testimony to the inherent brutality of the system. Smith Collection/Gado/Getty Images.

The Ideology and Reality of "Benevolence"
The planter aristocracy flourished around the periphery of the South's booming

Cotton Belt—in Virginia, South Carolina, and Louisiana—and took the lead in defending slavery. Within a generation after the Revolution, southern apologists rejected the view that slavery was, at best, a "necessary evil." In 1837, South Carolina Senator John C. Calhoun argued that the institution was a **"positive good"** because it subsidized an elegant lifestyle for a white elite and provided tutelage for genetically inferior Africans. "As a race, the African is inferior to the white man," declared Alexander Stephens, the future vice president of the Confederacy. "Subordination to the white man is his normal condition." Apologists depicted planters and their wives as aristocratic models of "disinterested benevolence," who provided food and housing for their workers and cared for them in old age. One wealthy Georgian declared, "Plantation government should be eminently patriarchal. . . . The paterfamilias, or head of the family, should, in one sense, be the father of the whole concern, negroes and all."

Those planters who embraced Christian stewardship tried to shape the religious lives of their chattel. They built churches on their plantations, welcomed evangelical preachers, and required their slaves to attend services. A few encouraged African Americans with spiritual "gifts" to serve as exhorters and deacons. Most of these planters acted from sincere Christian belief, but they also hoped to counter abolitionist criticism and to use religious teachings to control their workers.

Indeed, slavery's defenders increasingly used religious justifications for human bondage. Protestant ministers in the South pointed out that the Hebrews, God's chosen people, had owned slaves and that Jesus Christ had never condemned slavery. As James Henry Hammond told a British abolitionist in 1845: "What God ordains and Christ sanctifies should surely command the respect and toleration of man." In making their case, slavery's advocates rarely acknowledged its day-to-day brutality and exploitation. "I was at the plantation last Saturday and the crop was in fine order," a son wrote to his absentee father, "but the negroes are most brutally scarred & several have run off."

Despite the violence inherent in the chattel principle, many white planters considered themselves benevolent masters, committed to the welfare of "my family, black and white." Historians have labeled this idea **paternalism**. Some masters gave substance to the paternalist ideal by treating kindly "loyal and worthy" slaves—black overseers, the mammy who raised their children, and trusted house servants. By preserving the families of these slaves, many planters could believe that they "sold south" only "coarse" troublemakers who had "little sense of family." Other owners were more honest about the human cost of their pursuit of wealth. "Tomorrow the negroes are to get off [to Kentucky]," a slave-owning woman in Virginia wrote to a friend, "and I expect there will be great crying and moaning, with children Leaving there mothers, mothers there children, and women there husbands."

Whether or not they acknowledged the slaves' pain, few southern whites questioned the morality of the slave trade. Responding to abolitionists' criticism, the city council of Charleston, South Carolina, declared that "the removal of slaves from place to place, and their transfer from master to master, by gift, purchase, or otherwise" was completely consistent "with moral principle and with the highest order of civilization" (Analyzing Voices).

The Chattel Principle This public notice for a New Orleans raffle in which the prizes are a horse and buggy and a female slave named Sarah dramatically illustrates the "chattel principle" governing the institution of slavery, which made slaves the property of their owners. Joseph Jennings, the store owner conducting the raffle, has valued Sarah at nine hundred dollars. The Granger Collection, New York.

EXPLAIN CONSEQUENCES
How did the internal slave trade affect planter-slave relations and black families?

IN YOUR OWN WORDS How were industrial development in the North and the expansion of cotton agriculture in the South connected?

The Debate over Free and Slave Labor

As the abolitionist assault on slavery mounted, its rhetoric shaped the debate over the emergent system of wage labor in the northern states. By the 1850s, New York senator William Seward starkly contrasted the political systems of the South and the North in terms of their labor systems: "the one resting on the basis of servile or slave labor, the other on voluntary labor of freemen." Seward strongly favored the "free-labor system," crediting to it "the strength, wealth, greatness, intelligence, and freedom, which the whole American people now enjoy." As the following documents show, some Americans agreed with Seward, while others, such as *New York Tribune* editor Horace Greeley and South Carolina senator James Henry Hammond (who is quoted often in this chapter), contested his premises and conclusions.

SOUTH CAROLINA SENATOR JAMES HENRY HAMMOND
Speech to the Senate, March 4, 1858

In response to New York senator Seward, Senator Hammond urged admission of Kansas under the proslavery Lecompton Constitution and, by way of argument, celebrated the success of the South's cotton economy and its political and social institutions.

SOURCE: *The Congressional Globe* (Washington, DC, March 6, 1858), 962.

66 In all social systems there must be a class to do the menial duties, to perform the drudgery of life. . . . Such a class you must have, or you would not have that other class which leads progress, civilization, and refinement. It constitutes the very mud-sill of society and of political government. . . . Fortunately for the South, she found a race adapted to that purpose to her hand. A race inferior to her own, but eminently qualified in temper, in vigor, in docility, in capacity to stand the climate, to answer all her purposes. We use them for our purpose, and call them slaves. . . .

The Senator from New York said yesterday that the whole world had abolished slavery. Aye, the name, but not the thing; . . . for the man who lives by daily labor, and scarcely lives at that, and who has to put out his labor in the market, and take the best he can get for it; in short, your whole hireling class of manual laborers and 'operatives,' as you call them, are essentially slaves. The difference between us is, that our slaves are hired for life and well compensated; there is no starvation, no begging, no want of employment among our people, and not too much employment either. Yours are hired by the day, not cared for, and scantily compensated, which may be proved in the

most painful manner, at any hour in any street in any of your large towns. 99

NEW YORK PROTESTANT EPISCOPAL CHURCH MISSION SOCIETY
Sixth Annual Report, 1837

This excerpt demonstrates the society's belief that a class-bound social order could be avoided by encouraging "a spirit of independence and self-estimation" among the poor.

SOURCE: New York Protestant Episcopal Church Mission Society, Sixth Annual Report (New York, 1837), 15–16.

66 In the older countries of Europe, there is a CLASS OF POOR: families born to poverty, living in poverty, dying in poverty. With us there are none such. In our bounteous land individuals alone are poor; but they form no poor class, because with them poverty is but a transient evil . . . save [except] paupers and vagabonds . . . all else form one common class of citizens; some more, others less advanced in the career of honorable independence. 99

HORACE GREELEY
Public Letter Declining an Invitation to Attend an Antislavery Convention in Cincinnati, Ohio, June 3, 1845

This letter from the editor of the *New York Tribune* explains his broad definition of slavery.

SOURCE: Horace Greeley, *Hints Toward Reform in Lectures, Addresses, and Other Writings* (New York: Harper & Brothers, 1850), 352–355.

Technological Innovation and Labor

The technical advances that spurred the rise of cotton mills in the North were part of a larger pattern of economic innovation and change. Americans became inventive, seeking countless ways to improve and simplify production. Machines were at the center of many of these improvements, and American mechanics led the world in creating devices that worked faster and better than before. But workers did not always

66 Dear Sir:— I received, weeks since, your letter inviting me to be present at a general convention of opponents of Human Slavery. . . . What is Slavery? You will probably answer; 'The legal subjection of one human being to the will and power of another.' But this definition appears to me inaccurate. . . .

I understand by Slavery, that condition in which one human being exists mainly as a convenience for other human beings. . . . In short, . . . where the relation [is one] of authority, social ascendency and power over subsistence on the one hand, and of necessity, servility, and degradation on the other — there, in my view, is Slavery. . . . If I am less troubled concerning the Slavery prevalent in Charleston or New-Orleans, it is because I see so much Slavery in New-York. . . .

Wherever Opportunity to Labor is obtained with difficulty, and is so deficient that the Employing class may virtually prescribe their own terms and pay the Laborer only such share as they choose of the produce, there is a strong tendency to Slavery. 99

EDITORIAL IN THE *STAUNTON SPECTATOR*, 1859

Entitled "Freedom and Slavery," this editorial argues that "the black man's lot as a slave, is vastly preferable to that of his free brethren at the North."

SOURCE: *Staunton Spectator*, December 6, 1859, p. 2, c. 1.

66 The intelligent, christian slave-holder at the South is the best friend of the negro. He does not regard his bondsmen as mere chattel property, but as human beings to whom he owes duties. While the Northern Pharisee will not permit a negro to ride on the city railroads, Southern gentlemen and ladies are seen every day, side by side, in cars and coaches, with their faithful servants. Here the honest black man is not only protected by the laws and public sentiment, but he is respected by the community as truly as if his skin were white. Here there are ties of genuine friendship and affection between whites and blacks, leading to an interchange of all the comities of life. The slave nurses his master in sickness, and sheds tears of genuine sorrow at his grave. 99

JAMES HENRY HAMMOND

Private Letter to His Son Harry Hammond, 1856

This letter regards the future of Hammond's slave mistress, Sally Johnson, her son Henderson, and her daughter Louisa, who was the common mistress of father and son, and Louisa's children whom they sired.

SOURCE: James Hammond to Harry Hammond, February 19, 1856, in JHH Papers, SCL, quoted in Drew Gilpin Faust, *James Henry Hammond and the Old South: A Design for Mastery* (Baton Rouge: Louisiana State University Press, 1982), 87.

66 In the last will I made I left to you . . . Sally Johnson the mother of Louisa & all the children of both. Sally says Henderson is my child. It is possible, but I do not believe it Yet act on her's rather than my opinion. Louisa's first child may be mine. I think not. Her second I believe is mine. Take care of her & her children who are both of your blood if not of mine. . . . The services of the rest will compensate for indulgence to these. I cannot free these people & send them North. It would be cruelty to them. Nor would I like that any but my own blood should own as slaves my own blood or Louisa. I leave them to your charge, believing that you will best appreciate & most independently carry out my wishes in regard to them. Do not let Louisa or any of my children or possible children be the Slaves of Strangers. Slavery in the family will be their happiest earthly condition. 99

QUESTIONS FOR ANALYSIS

1. Which of these documents argue for slave owners as benevolent paternalists and the institution of slavery as a "positive good"? What other points of view are represented?

2. Given the discussion of "class" and "honorable independence" in the Mission Society statement, how would an Episcopalian reply to Hammond's critique of the northern labor system?

3. How can we understand Hammond's treatment of Sally Johnson and her daughter, as well as his refusal to free his and his son's children, in the context of his 1858 speech and the *Staunton Spectator*'s editorial?

4. Using the principles asserted in his letter, how would Horace Greeley analyze the southern labor system, as described by Hammond and the *Staunton Spectator*? Why does Greeley suggest that the northern system has only "a strong tendency to Slavery"?

5. Consider the sources above in the light of this Abraham Lincoln comment: "although volume upon volume is written to prove slavery a very good thing, we never hear of the man who wishes to take the good of it, by being a slave himself."

---

benefit. Skilled laborers formed unions to strengthen their bargaining position with employers. Lower-skilled workers in factory jobs, who often performed repetitive labor under close supervision, tried to organize as well, but they often faced legal obstacles. In the first half of the nineteenth century, many Americans struggled to understand their place in an increasingly complex social order. Urban growth was one sign of change, as wageworkers swelled the size of older cities and prompted the creation of many new ones.

The Spread of Innovation

By the 1820s, American-born artisans had replaced British immigrants at the cutting edge of technological innovation. In the Philadelphia region, the remarkable Sellars family produced the most important inventors. Samuel Sellars Jr. invented a machine for twisting worsted woolen yarn to give it an especially smooth surface. His son John improved the efficiency of the waterwheels powering the family's sawmills and built a machine to weave wire sieves. John's sons and grandsons ran machine shops that turned out riveted leather fire hoses, papermaking equipment, and eventually locomotives. In 1824, the Sellars and other mechanics founded the Franklin Institute in Philadelphia. Named after Benjamin Franklin, whom the mechanics admired for his work ethic and scientific accomplishments, the institute published a journal; provided high-school-level instruction in chemistry, mathematics, and mechanical design; and organized exhibits of new products. Craftsmen in Ohio and other states established similar institutes to disseminate technical knowledge and encourage innovation. Between 1820 and 1860, the number of patents issued by the U.S. Patent Office rose from two hundred to four thousand a year.

American craftsmen pioneered the development of **machine tools** — machines that made parts for other machines. Eli Whitney was a key innovator. At the age of fourteen, Whitney began fashioning nails and knife blades; later, he made women's hatpins. Aspiring to wealth and status, Whitney won admission to Yale College and subsequently worked as a tutor on a Georgia cotton plantation. He capitalized on his expertise in making hatpins to design his cotton gin. Although Whitney patented the machine, other manufacturers improved on his design and captured the market.

Still seeking his fortune, Whitney decided in 1798 to manufacture military weapons. He eventually designed and built machine tools that could rapidly produce interchangeable musket parts, bringing him the wealth and fame he had long craved. After Whitney's death in 1825, his partner John H. Hall built an array of metalworking machine tools, such as turret lathes, milling machines, and precision grinders.

Technological innovation now swept through American manufacturing. Mechanics in the textile industry invented lathes, planers, and boring machines that turned out standardized parts for new spinning jennies and weaving looms. Despite being mass-produced, these jennies and looms were precisely made and operated at higher speeds than British equipment. Richard Garsed nearly doubled the speed of the power looms in his father's Delaware factory and patented a cam-and-harness device that allowed damask and other elaborately designed fabrics to be machine-woven. Meanwhile, the mechanics employed by Samuel W. Collins built a machine for pressing and hammering hot metal into dies (cutting forms). Using this machine, a worker could make three hundred ax heads a day — compared to twelve using traditional methods. In Richmond, Virginia, Welsh- and American-born mechanics at the Tredegar Iron Works produced low-cost parts for complicated manufacturing equipment. As a group of British observers noted admiringly, many American products were made "with machinery applied to almost every process . . . all reduced to an almost perfect system of manufacture."

McCormick's Reaper The economic revolution was the result, in part, of increased output created by power-driven machinery used in factories. However, machines also dramatically increased farm productivity. The mechanical reaper invented by Cyrus McCormick, first patented in 1834, revolutionized the harvesting process. Using McCormick's reaper and a horse, a farmer and his son could cut as much grain in a day as seven men with scythes. They could now plant more acres and not worry about the wheat sprouting (and becoming worthless) before it could be harvested. Threshing machines similarly allowed farmers to use animal power to process the grain. Eventually, a single horse-drawn machine — the combine harvester, or combine — could execute both operations. Oxford Science Archive/Print Collector/Getty Images.

As mass production spread, the American Industrial Revolution came of age. Reasonably priced products such as Remington rifles, Singer sewing machines, and Yale locks became household names in the United States and abroad. After winning praise at the Crystal Palace Exhibition in London in 1851 — the first major international display of industrial goods — Remington, Singer, and other American firms became multinational businesses, building factories in Great Britain and selling goods throughout Europe. By 1877, the Singer Manufacturing Company controlled 75 percent of the world market for sewing machines.

> **TRACE CHANGE OVER TIME**
> What new types of products came out of American factories by the 1840s and 1850s?

Wageworkers and the Labor Movement

As the Industrial Revolution gathered momentum, it changed the nature of workers' lives. Following the American Revolution, many craft workers espoused **artisan republicanism**, an ideology of production based on liberty and equality. They saw themselves as small-scale producers, equal to one another and free to work for themselves. The poet Walt Whitman summed up their outlook: "Men must be masters, under themselves."

Free Workers Form Unions However, as the outwork and factory systems spread, more and more workers became wage earners who labored under the control of an employer. Unlike young women, who embraced factory work because it freed them from parental control and domestic service, men bridled at their status as supervised wageworkers. To assert their independence, male wageworkers rejected the traditional terms of *master* and *servant* and used the Dutch word *boss* to refer to their employer. Likewise, lowly apprentices refused to allow masters to control their private (nonwork) lives and joined their mates in building a robust plebeian culture. Still, as hired hands, they received meager wages and had little job security. The artisan-republican ideal of "self-ownership" confronted the harsh reality of waged work in an industrializing capitalist society. Labor had become a commodity, to be bought and sold.

Some wage earners worked in carpentry, stonecutting, masonry, and cabinetmaking — traditional crafts that required specialized skills. Their strong sense of identity, or trade consciousness, enabled these workers to form **unions** and bargain with their master-artisan employers. They resented low wages and long hours, which restricted their family life and educational opportunities. In Boston, six hundred carpenters went on strike in 1825. That protest failed, but in 1840, craft workers in St. Louis secured a ten-hour day, and President Van Buren issued an executive order setting a similar workday for federal workers.

Artisans in other occupations were less successful in preserving their pay and working conditions. As aggressive entrepreneurs and machine technology took command, shoemakers, hatters, printers, furniture makers, and weavers faced low-paid factory work. In response, some artisans in these trades moved to small towns, while in New York City, 800 highly skilled cabinetmakers made fashionable furniture. In status and income, these cabinetmakers outranked a group of 3,200 semitrained, wage-earning workers who made cheaper tables and chairs in factories. Thus the new industrial system split the traditional artisan class into self-employed craftsmen and wage-earning workers.

When wage earners banded together to form unions, they faced a legal hurdle: English and American common law branded such groups as illegal "combinations." As a Philadelphia judge put it, unions interfered with a "master's" authority over his "servant." Other lawsuits accused unions of "conspiring" to raise wages and thereby injure employers. "It is important to the best interests of society that the price

Woodworker, c. 1850 Skilled makers took great pride in their furniture, which was often intricately designed and beautifully executed. To underline the dignity of his occupation, this woodworker poses in formal dress and proudly displays the tools of his craft. A belief in the value of their labor was an important ingredient of the artisan-republican ideology held by many workers. Library of Congress.

of labor be left to regulate itself," the New York Supreme Court declared in 1835, while excluding employers from this rule. Clothing manufacturers in New York City collectively agreed to set wage rates and to dismiss members of the Society of Journeymen Tailors.

Labor Ideology Despite such obstacles, during the 1830s journeymen shoemakers founded mutual benefit societies in Lynn, Massachusetts, and other shoemaking centers. As the workers explained, "The capitalist has no other interest in us, than to get as much labor out of us as possible." To exert more pressure on their employers, in 1834 local unions from Boston to Philadelphia formed the National Trades Union, the first regional union of different trades.

Workers found considerable popular support for their cause. When a New York City court upheld a conspiracy verdict against their union, tailors warned that the "Freemen of the North are now on a level with the slaves of the South," and organized a mass meeting of 27,000 people to denounce the decision. In 1836, local juries hearing conspiracy cases acquitted shoemakers in Hudson, New York; carpet makers in Thompsonville, Connecticut; and plasterers in Philadelphia. Then, in *Commonwealth v. Hunt* (1842), Chief Justice Lemuel Shaw of the Massachusetts Supreme Judicial Court upheld the right of workers to form unions and call strikes to enforce closed-shop agreements that limited employment to union members. But many judges continued to resist unions by forbidding strikes.

Union leaders expanded artisan republicanism to include wageworkers. Arguing that wage earners were becoming "slaves to a monied aristocracy," they condemned the new factory system in which "capital and labor stand opposed." To create a just society in which workers could "live as comfortably as others," they advanced a **labor theory of value**. Under this theory, the price of goods should reflect the labor required to make them, and the income from their sale should go primarily to the producers, not to factory owners, middlemen, or storekeepers. "The poor who perform the work, ought to receive at least half of that sum which is charged" to the consumer, declared minister Ezra Stiles Ely. Union activists agreed, organizing nearly fifty strikes for higher wages in 1836. Appealing to the spirit of the American Revolution, which had destroyed the aristocracy of birth, they called for a new revolution to demolish the aristocracy of capital.

Women textile operatives were equally active. Competition in the woolen and cotton textile industries was fierce because mechanization caused output to grow faster than consumer demand. As textile prices fell, manufacturers' revenues declined. To maintain profits, employers reduced workers' wages and imposed tougher work rules. In 1828 and again in 1834, women mill workers in Dover, New Hampshire, went on strike and won some relief. In Lowell, two thousand women operatives backed a strike by withdrawing their savings from an employer-owned bank. "One of the leaders mounted a pump," the *Boston Transcript* reported, "and made a flaming . . . speech on the rights of women and the iniquities of the 'monied aristocracy.' " Increasingly, young New England women refused to enter the mills, and impoverished Irish (and later French Canadian) immigrants took their places (Interpretations).

> **CONSIDER POINTS OF VIEW**
> How did the capitalist-run industrial economy conflict with artisan republicanism, and how did workers respond?

The Growth of Cities and Towns

The expansion of industry and trade dramatically increased America's urban population. In 1820, there were 58 towns with more than 2,500 inhabitants; by 1840, there were 126 such towns, located mostly in the Northeast and Midwest. During those two decades, the total number of city dwellers grew more than fourfold, from 443,000 to 1,844,000 (Map 8.6).

The fastest growth occurred in the new industrial towns that sprouted along the "fall line," where rivers descended rapidly from the Appalachian Mountains to the coastal plain. In 1822, the Boston Manufacturing Company built a complex of mills in

Did the Market Revolution Expand Opportunities for Women?

The Market Revolution of the early nineteenth century produced important changes in patterns of work. Two opportunities that the revolution opened for women are highlighted by Paul E. Johnson and Mary H. Blewett. Johnson describes the emergence of the factory system in Lowell, Massachusetts, pioneered by the Boston Manufacturing Company, which employed young, unmarried women in the production of textiles. Mostly from rural New England towns, the "Lowell girls" worked in the factories and lived together in the company's boardinghouses until they married and left the wage economy. The New England farmwomen whom Blewett describes also participated in the market economy but indirectly and from home. Often wives and mothers, these women squeezed piecework between their domestic chores to supplement the family income. In this case, they stitched the leather uppers of a shoe and then shipped them to a "shoe boss" whose shop finished the shoe's manufacture by stitching the upper to its leather sole.

PAUL E. JOHNSON

SOURCE: Paul E. Johnson, *The Early American Republic, 1789–1829* (New York: Oxford University Press, 2007), 79.

The brick mills and prim boarding houses . . . occupied by sober, well-behaved farm girls . . . produced a self-respecting sisterhood of independent, wage-earning women. Twice in the 1830s the women of Lowell went out on strike, proclaiming that they were not wage slaves but "the daughters of freemen." . . . [M]any [former] Lowell women entered public life as reformers. Most of them married and became housewives but not on the same terms their mothers had known. . . . Thus the [male factory owners] kept their promise to produce cotton cloth profitably without creating a permanent working class. But they did not succeed in shuttling young women between rural and urban paternalism and back again. Wage labor, the ultimate degradation for agrarian-republican men, opened a road to independence for thousands of young women.

MARY H. BLEWETT

SOURCE: From Mary H. Blewett, "Work, Gender and the Artisan Tradition in New England Shoemaking, 1780–1860," *Journal of Social History* by George Mason University. Reproduced with permission of George Mason University in the format Book via Copyright Clearance Center.

Sharing the bonds of womanhood both in work and in their domestic sphere, shoebinders in 1834 tried to organize themselves in terms of a female community of workers. . . . [But] . . . the conditions under which many shoebinders labored — isolated from each other, employed by the shoe boss outside a group labor system and combining wage work with domestic responsibilities — discouraged collective activity. The tensions between their relationship to the artisan system and its equal rights ideology and their subordinate role as females in the family were exposed by their arguments for a just wage for women. Neither the social relations of the artisan family nor the realities of working as a woman for a shoe boss encouraged . . . [her] . . . to identify with her working sister in the Lowell mills or conceive of herself as a worker capable of supporting herself who could unite with her peers to protest mistreatment.

QUESTIONS FOR ANALYSIS

1. Identify two factors that explain the different conclusions drawn by Johnson and Blewett regarding women's opportunities in the market economy.

2. To what extent did the women these two historians describe see their work as a means to claim political, social, or economic rights?

3. Comparing these excerpts with Chapter 8's discussion of the development of the market economy, identify two ways women's work experiences differed from men's.

---

a sleepy Merrimack River village that quickly became the bustling textile factory town of Lowell, Massachusetts. The towns of Hartford, Connecticut; Trenton, New Jersey; and Wilmington, Delaware, also became urban centers as mill owners exploited the water power of their rivers and recruited workers from the countryside.

Western commercial cities such as Pittsburgh, Cincinnati, and New Orleans grew almost as fast. They began as transit centers, where workers transferred goods from farmers' rafts and wagons to flatboats or steamboats. As the midwestern population grew during the 1830s and 1840s, St. Louis, Detroit, and especially Buffalo and Chicago

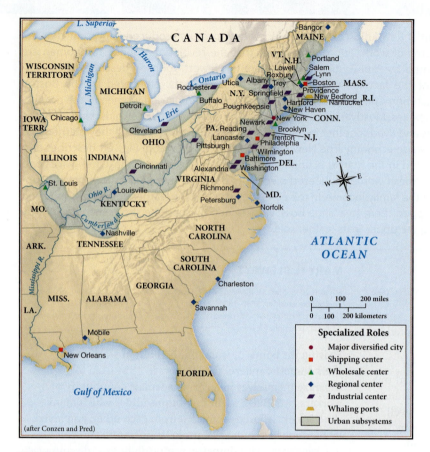

MAP 8.6 **The Nation's Major Cities, 1840**
By 1840, the United States boasted three major conglomerations of cities. The long-settled ports on the Atlantic — from Boston to Baltimore — served as centers for import merchants, banks, insurance companies, and manufacturers of ready-made clothing, and their financial reach extended far into the interior — nationwide in the case of New York City. A second group of cities stretched along the Great Lakes and included the commercial hubs of Buffalo, Detroit, and Chicago, as well as the manufacturing center of Cleveland. A third urban system extended along the Ohio River, comprising the industrial cities of Pittsburgh and Cincinnati and the wholesale centers of Louisville and St. Louis.

also emerged as dynamic centers of commerce. "There can be no two places in the world," journalist Margaret Fuller wrote from Chicago in 1843, "more completely thoroughfares than this place and Buffalo. . . . The life-blood [of commerce] rushes from east to west, and back again from west to east." Chicago's merchants and bankers developed the marketing, provisioning, and financial services essential to farmers and small-town shopkeepers in its vast hinterland. "There can be no better [market] any where in the Union," declared a farmer in Paw Paw, Illinois.

These midwestern hubs quickly became manufacturing centers. Capitalizing on the cities' links to rivers and canals, entrepreneurs built warehouses, flour mills, packing plants, and machine shops, creating work for hundreds of artisans and factory laborers. In 1846, Cyrus McCormick moved his reaper factory from western Virginia to Chicago to be closer to his midwestern customers.

The old Atlantic seaports — Boston, Philadelphia, Baltimore, Charleston, and especially New York City — remained important for their foreign commerce and, increasingly, as centers of finance and small-scale manufacturing. New York City and nearby Brooklyn grew at a phenomenal rate: between 1820 and 1860, their combined populations increased nearly tenfold to 1 million people, thanks to the arrival of hundreds of thousands of German and Irish immigrants. Drawing on these workers, New York became a center of the ready-made clothing industry, which relied on thousands of low-paid seamstresses. "The wholesale clothing establishments are . . . absorbing the business of the country," a "Country Tailor" complained to the *New York Tribune*, "casting many an honest and hardworking man out of employment [and helping] . . . the large cities to swallow up the small towns."

New York City had the best harbor in the United States and, thanks to the Erie Canal, was the best gateway to the Midwest and the best outlet for western grain. Recognizing the city's advantages, in 1818 four English Quaker merchants founded the Black Ball Line to carry cargo, people, and mail between New York and London, Liverpool, and Le Havre, establishing the first regularly scheduled transatlantic shipping service. By 1840, its port handled almost two-thirds of foreign imports into the United States, almost half of all foreign trade, and much of the immigrant traffic. New York likewise monopolized trade with the newly independent South American nations of Brazil, Peru, and Venezuela, and its merchants took over the trade in cotton by offering finance, insurance, and shipping to southern planters and merchants.

COMPARE AND CONTRAST
What different types of cities emerged between 1820 and 1848, and what caused their growth?

IN YOUR OWN WORDS How did technological innovation improve the lives of ordinary people, and what challenges did it present to them?

***View of Cincinnati*, by John Caspar Wild, c. 1835** Thanks to its location on the Ohio River (a tributary of the Mississippi), Cincinnati quickly became one of the major processing centers for grain and hogs in the trans-Appalachian west. By the 1820s, passenger steamboats and freight barges connected the city with Pittsburgh to the north and the ocean port of New Orleans far to the south. Museum of Fine Arts, Boston. Gift of Maxim Karolik for the M. and M. Karolik Collection of American Watercolors and Drawings, 1800–1875, 57.298. Photograph © 2016 Museum of Fine Arts, Boston. All rights reserved/Bridgeman Images.

New Social Classes and Cultures

The economic changes of the early nineteenth century improved the lives of many Americans, who now lived in larger houses, cooked on iron stoves, and wore better-made clothes, but they also created a more stratified society. In 1800, white Americans thought of their society in terms of rank: "notable" families had higher status than those from the "lower orders." Yet in rural areas, people of different ranks often shared a common culture. Gentlemen farmers talked easily with yeomen about crop yields, while their wives conversed about the art of quilting. In the South, humble tenants and aristocratic slave owners enjoyed the same amusements: gambling, cockfighting, and horse racing. Rich and poor attended the same Quaker meetinghouse or Presbyterian church. "Almost everyone eats, drinks, and dresses in the same way," a European visitor to Hartford, Connecticut, reported in 1798, "and one can see the most obvious inequality only in the dwellings."

The rise of the cotton complex heightened economic inequality. In the South, the cotton boom sharpened distinctions between poorer and wealthier whites and concentrated slaves on larger plantations. In the booming cities, the new economic order spawned distinct social classes: a small but wealthy business elite, a substantial middle class, and a mass of propertyless wage earners. By creating a class-divided society, industrialization posed a momentous challenge to America's republican ideals.

A Slave Family Picking Cotton Picking cotton—thousands of small bolls attached to 3-foot-high woody and often prickly stalks—was a tedious and time-consuming task, taking up to four months on many plantations. However, workers of both sexes and all ages could pick cotton, and masters could measure output by weighing the baskets of each picker or family, chastising those who failed to meet their quotas. What does this early photograph of a family of pickers, taken on a plantation near Savannah, Georgia, suggest about women's and children's lives, family relations, and living conditions? © Collection of the New-York Historical Society, USA/Bridgeman Images.

Planters, Yeomen, and Slaves

By the time of the American Revolution, tobacco and rice planting in the South had already created a three-tiered slave society. Large planters who owned dozens, or even hundreds, of slaves dominated the life of the Chesapeake and the Carolina lowcountry, while poorer whites with less land and fewer slaves deferred to their wealthy neighbors' leadership. African American slaves possessed little or nothing of their own and lived at the mercy of their owners. After 1800, South Carolina rice planters remained at the apex of the seaboard plantation aristocracy. In 1860, the fifteen proprietors of the vast plantations in All Saints Parish in South Carolina owned 4,383 slaves—nearly 300 apiece—who annually grew and processed 14 million pounds of rice. As inexpensive Asian rice entered the world market in the 1820s, the Carolina rice planters sold some slaves and worked the others harder to maintain their lifestyle.

In tobacco-growing regions, the planter aristocracy followed a different path. Slave ownership had always been more widely diffused: in the 1770s, about 60 percent of white families in the Chesapeake owned at least one slave. As wealthy tobacco planters moved their estates and slaves to the Cotton South, middling whites (who owned between five and twenty slaves) came to dominate the Chesapeake economy. The descendants of the old tobacco aristocracy remained influential, but increasingly as slave-owning grain farmers, lawyers, merchants, industrialists, and politicians. They hired out surplus slaves, sold them south, or allowed them to purchase their freedom.

In the Cotton South, ambitious planters worked their slaves ferociously as they sought to establish themselves. A Mississippi planter put it plainly: "Everything has to give way to large crops of cotton." It was a demanding crop. Frederick Law Olmsted, the future architect of New York's Central Park, noted during his travels that slaves in the Cotton South worked "much harder and more unremittingly" than those in the tobacco regions. To increase output, profit-seeking cotton planters began during the 1820s to use a rigorous **gang-labor system**. Previously, many planters had supervised workers only sporadically, or had assigned them tasks to complete at their own pace. Now masters with twenty or more slaves organized disciplined teams, or "gangs," supervised by black drivers and white overseers. They worked the gangs at a steady pace, clearing and plowing land or hoeing and picking cotton.

The gang-labor system enhanced profits by increasing productivity. Because slaves in gangs finished tasks in thirty-five minutes that took a white yeoman planter an hour to complete, gang labor became ever more prevalent. As the price of raw cotton surged after 1846, the wealth of the planter class skyrocketed. And no wonder: nearly 2 million enslaved African Americans now labored on the plantations of the Cotton South and annually produced 4 million bales of the valuable fiber.

On the eve of the Civil War, southern slave owners accounted for nearly two-thirds of all American men with wealth of $100,000 or more. Other white southerners—backcountry yeoman farmers and cotton-planting tenants in particular—occupied some of the lowest rungs of the nation's social order. The expansion of southern slavery, like the flowering of northern capitalism, increased inequalities of wealth and status.

IDENTIFY CAUSES
How did the rise of cotton agriculture affect the social structure of the South?

The Northern Business Elite

In the North, the Industrial Revolution altered the older agrarian social order. The urban economy made a few city residents — the merchants, manufacturers, bankers, and landlords who made up the business elite — very rich. In 1800, the richest 10 percent of the nation's families owned about 40 percent of the wealth; by 1860, they held nearly 70 percent. In New York, Chicago, Baltimore, and New Orleans, the superrich — the top 1 percent — owned more than 40 percent of the land, buildings, and other tangible property and an even higher share of intangible property, such as stocks and bonds.

Government tax policies facilitated the accumulation of wealth. There were no federal taxes on individual and corporate income. Rather, the U.S. Treasury raised most of its revenue from tariffs: regressive taxes on textiles and other imported goods purchased mostly by ordinary citizens. State and local governments also favored the wealthy. They taxed real estate (farms, city lots, and buildings) and tangible personal property (furniture, tools, and machinery), but almost never taxed stocks and bonds or the inheritances the rich passed on to their children.

Hartford Family   Completely at home in their elegant drawing room, this elite family in Hartford, Connecticut, enjoys the fruits of the father's business success. As the father lounges in his silk robe, his eldest son (and presumptive heir) adopts an air of studied nonchalance, and his daughter fingers a piano, signaling her musical accomplishments and the family's gentility. A diminutive African American servant (her size suggesting her status) serves fruit to the lavishly attired woman of the house. The sumptuously appointed drawing room reflects the owners' prosperity and their aesthetic and cultural interests.   White House Collection/White House Historical Association.

As cities expanded in size and wealth, affluent families set themselves apart. They dressed in well-tailored clothes, rode in fancy carriages, and bought expensively furnished houses tended by butlers, cooks, and other servants. The women no longer socialized with those of lesser wealth, and the men no longer labored side by side with their employees. Instead, they became managers and directors and relied on trusted subordinates to supervise their employees. Merchants, manufacturers, and bankers placed a premium on privacy and lived in separate neighborhoods, often in exclusive central areas or at the city's edge. The geographic isolation of privileged families and the massive flow of immigrants into separate districts divided cities spatially along lines of class, race, and ethnicity.

> **TRACE CHANGE OVER TIME**
> How and why did elite families change between 1800 and 1848?

The Middle Class

Standing between wealthy owners and propertyless wage earners was a growing **middle class** — the social product of increased commerce. The "middling class," a Boston printer explained, was made up of "the farmers, the mechanics, the manufacturers, the traders, who carry on professionally the ordinary operations of buying, selling, and exchanging merchandize." Professionals with other skills — building contractors, lawyers, surveyors, and so on — were suddenly in great demand and well compensated, as were middling business owners and white-collar clerks. In the Northeast, men with these qualifications numbered about 30 percent of the population in the 1840s. But they also could be found in small towns of the agrarian Midwest and South. In 1854, the cotton boomtown of Oglethorpe, Georgia (population 2,500), boasted eighty "business houses" and eight hotels.

The emergence of the middle class reflected a dramatic rise in prosperity. Between 1830 and 1857, the per capita income of Americans increased by about 2.5 percent a year, a remarkable rate that has never since been matched. This surge in income, along with an abundance of inexpensive mass-produced goods, fostered a distinct middle-class urban culture. Middle-class husbands earned enough to save about 15 percent of their income, which they used to buy well-built houses in a "respectable part of town." Middle-class wives became purveyors of genteel culture, buying books, pianos, lithographs, and comfortable furniture for their front parlors. Upper-middle-class families hired Irish or African American domestic servants, while less prosperous folk enjoyed the comforts provided by new industrial goods. For their homes they acquired furnaces (to warm the entire house and heat water for bathing), cooking stoves with ovens, and Singer's treadle-operated sewing machines. Some urban families now kept their perishable food in iceboxes, which ice-company wagons periodically refilled.

If material comfort was one distinguishing mark of the middle class, moral and mental discipline was another. Middle-class writers denounced raucous carnivals and festivals as a "chaos of sin and folly, of misery and fun" and, by the 1830s, had largely suppressed them. Ambitious parents were equally concerned with their children's moral and intellectual development, providing a high school education (in an era when most white children received only five years of schooling) and stressing the importance of discipline and hard work. American Protestants had long believed that diligent work in an earthly "calling" was a

[Fig. 130. Plain Timber Cottage-Villa.]

[Fig. 131. Principal Floor.]

Architecture for the Emergent Middle Class This dwelling was well suited for a "farmer of wealth" or a middle-class suburbanite, according to Andrew Downing, author of *The Architecture of Country Houses* (1850). The exterior of the house exhibited "a considerable degree of elegance," while the interior boasted a substantial drawing room and dining room, for the entertainment of guests, and a parlor for more intimate conversations among family and friends. Downing's books helped to define the culture of the growing middle class and diffuse it across the nation. Andrew J. Downing, *The Architecture of Country Houses*, 1850/Picture Research Consultants & Archives.

duty owed to God. Now the business elite and the middle class gave this idea a secular twist by celebrating work as the key to individual social mobility and national prosperity.

Young, middle-class men saved their money, adopted temperate habits, and aimed to rise in the world. There was an "almost universal ambition to get forward," observed Hezekiah Niles, editor of *Niles' Weekly Register*. Warner Myers, a Philadelphia house-painter, rose from poverty by saving his wages, borrowing from his family and friends, and becoming a builder, eventually constructing and selling sixty houses. Countless children's books, magazine stories, self-help manuals, and novels recounted the tales of similar individuals. The **self-made man** became a central theme of American popular culture. Just as the yeoman ethic had served as a unifying ideal in pre-1800 agrarian America, so the gospel of personal achievement linked the middle and business classes of the new industrializing society.

Urban Workers and the Poor

As thoughtful business leaders surveyed their society, they concluded that the yeoman farmer and artisan-republican ideal — a social order of independent producers — was no longer possible. "Entire independence ought not to be wished for," Ithamar A. Beard, the paymaster of the Hamilton Manufacturing Company (in Lowell, Massachusetts), told a mechanics' association in 1827. "In large manufacturing towns, many more must fill subordinate stations and must be under the immediate direction and control of a master or superintendent, than in the farming towns."

Beard had a point. In 1840, all of the nation's slaves, some 2.5 million people, and about half of its adult white workers, another 3 million (of a total population of 17 million), were laboring for others. The bottom 10 percent of white wage earners consisted of casual workers hired on a short-term basis for arduous jobs. Poor women washed clothes; their husbands and sons carried lumber and bricks for construction projects, loaded ships, and dug out dirt and stones to build canals. Even when they could find jobs, they could never save enough "to pay rent, buy fire wood and eatables" when the job market or the harbor froze up. During business depressions, casual laborers suffered and died; in good times, their jobs were temporary and dangerous.

Other laborers had greater security of employment, but few were prospering. In Massachusetts in 1825, an unskilled worker earned about two-thirds as much as a mechanic did; two decades later, it was less than half as much. A journeyman carpenter in Philadelphia reported that he was about "even with the World" after several years of work but that many of his coworkers were in debt. Only the most fortunate working-class families could afford to educate their children, buy apprenticeships for their sons, or accumulate small dowries for their daughters. Most families sent ten-year-old children out to work, and the death of a parent often threw the survivors into dire poverty. As a charity worker noted, "What can a bereaved widow do, with 5 or 6 little children, destitute of every means of support but what her own hands can furnish (which in a general way does not amount to more than 25 cents a day)?"

Impoverished workers congregated in dilapidated housing in bad neighborhoods. Single men and women lived in crowded boardinghouses, while families jammed themselves into tiny apartments in the basements and attics of small houses. As immigrants poured in after 1840, urban populations soared, and developers squeezed more and more dwellings and foul-smelling outhouses onto a single lot. By 1848, America's largest cities were deeply divided between the genteel dwellings of the middle and upper classes and the impoverished neighborhoods of the working poor.

> **CONSIDER POINTS OF VIEW**
> What were the moral values and material culture of the urban middle class?

> **PLACE EVENTS IN CONTEXT**
> How did the increasingly urban, capitalist economy of the northeastern states affect the lives of poor workers?

> **IN YOUR OWN WORDS**   How was the structure of American society different in 1848 than it had been in 1800?

SUMMARY

This chapter examined the causes of the economic transformation of the first half of the nineteenth century. The Market Revolution enabled long-distance travel, trade, and communication, while a revolution in productivity — the Industrial Revolution in the North and the expansion of cotton production in the South — dramatically increased economic output. Water, steam, and minerals such as coal and iron were essential to this transformation; so, too, were technological innovation and labor discipline. Together they helped the United States to master and exploit its vast new territory.

We also explored the consequences of that transformation. In the South, the institution of slavery expanded its geographical reach, with millions of new laborers exploited more intensively than ever before. In the North, where new urban centers developed and older cities grew, workers struggled to control the terms of their employment. The Northeast and the Midwest shared important cultural affinities, while the resurgence of slavery in the South set it apart, but in every region the social order was growing more divided by race and class. As the next chapter suggests, Americans looked to their political system, which was becoming increasingly democratic, to address these social divisions. In fact, the tensions among economic inequality, cultural diversity, and political democracy became a troubling — and enduring — part of American life.

CHAPTER 8 REVIEW

TERMS TO KNOW   *Identify and explain the significance of each term below.*

Key Concepts and Events

neomercantilism (p. 240)

Panic of 1819 (p. 241)

Commonwealth System (p. 243)

Erie Canal (p. 244)

Market Revolution (p. 246)

Industrial Revolution (p. 248)

cotton complex (p. 248)

mechanics (p. 248)

Waltham-Lowell System (p. 249)

gradual emancipation (p. 250)

manumission (p. 252)

coastal trade (p. 255)

inland system (p. 255)

chattel principle (p. 256)

"positive good" (p. 257)

paternalism (p. 257)

machine tools (p. 260)

artisan republicanism (p. 261)

unions (p. 261)

labor theory of value (p. 262)

gang-labor system (p. 266)

middle class (p. 268)

self-made man (p. 269)

Key People

John Jacob Astor (p. 240)

Samuel F. B. Morse (p. 247)

Samuel Slater (p. 248)

Francis Cabot Lowell (p. 249)

Sellars Family (p. 260)

Eli Whitney (p. 260)

Cyrus McCormick (p. 260)

REVIEW QUESTIONS

Answer these questions to demonstrate your understanding of the chapter's main ideas.

1. What was the relationship between government support and private enterprise in economic development?

2. How were industrial development in the North and the expansion of cotton agriculture in the South connected?

3. How did technological innovation improve the lives of ordinary people, and what challenges did it present to them?

4. How was the structure of American society different in 1848 than it had been in 1800?

5. Review the events listed under "Work, Exchange, and Technology" on the thematic timeline on page 236. What were the most important changes in the economy between 1800 and 1848, and how did they affect people's lives?

MAKING CONNECTIONS

Recognize the larger developments and continuities within and across chapters by answering these questions.

1. How did the economic revolution described in this chapter affect the lives of women in various social groups, and how did it make their experiences different from those of their mothers, whose political and social lives were explored in Chapter 6 on the American Revolution, and their grandmothers, whose work lives and cultural experiences were considered in Chapter 4?

2. Look again at three images, the slave family picking cotton (p. 266), the woodworker (p. 261), and the Hartford family (p. 267). Taken together, what insights do they provide into the different aspects and social consequences of the economic changes discussed in this chapter?

KEY TURNING POINTS

Refer to the chapter chronology on page 240 for help in answering the question below.

Many of the early chronology entries concern economic matters, while later entries refer to other subjects. Based on your reading of the chapter, when and why does this change in emphasis occur?

A Democratic Revolution
1800–1848

IDENTIFY THE BIG IDEA

What were the main features of the Democratic Revolution, and what role did Andrew Jackson play in its outcome?

Europeans who visited the United States in the 1830s mostly praised its republican society but not its political parties and politicians. "The gentlemen spit, talk of elections and the price of produce, and spit again," Frances Trollope reported in *Domestic Manners of the Americans* (1832). In her view, American politics was the sport of self-serving party politicians who reeked of "whiskey and onions." Other Europeans lamented the low intellectual level of American political debate. The "clap-trap of praise and pathos" from a Massachusetts politician "deeply disgusted" Harriet Martineau, while the shallow arguments advanced by the inept "farmers, shopkeepers, and country lawyers" who sat in the New York assembly astonished Basil Hall.

The negative verdict was nearly unanimous. "The most able men in the United States are very rarely placed at the head of affairs," French aristocrat Alexis de Tocqueville concluded in *Democracy in America* (1835). The reason, said Tocqueville, lay in the character of democracy itself. Most citizens ignored important policy issues, jealously refused to elect their intellectual superiors, and listened in awe to "the clamor of a mountebank [a charismatic fraud] who knows the secret of stimulating their tastes."

These Europeans were witnessing the American Democratic Revolution. Before 1815, men of ability had sat in the seats of government, and the prevailing ideology had been republicanism, or rule by "men of TALENTS and VIRTUE," as a newspaper put it. Many of those leaders feared popular rule, so they wrote constitutions with Bills of Rights, bicameral legislatures, and independent judiciaries, and they criticized overambitious men who campaigned for public office. But history took a different course. By the 1820s and 1830s, the watchwords were *democracy* and *party politics*, a system run by men who avidly sought office and rallied supporters through newspapers, broadsides, and great public processions. Politics became a sport—a competitive contest for the votes of ordinary men. "That the majority should govern was a fundamental maxim in all free governments," declared Martin Van Buren, the most talented of the new breed of professional politicians. By encouraging ordinary Americans to burn with "election fever" and support party principles, he and other politicians redefined the meaning of democratic government and made it work.

The Politics of Democracy As ordinary American men asserted a claim to a voice in government affairs, politicians catered to their preferences and prejudices. Aspiring candidates took their messages to voters, in rural hamlets as well as large towns. This detail from George Caleb Bingham's *Stump Speaking* (1855) shows a swanky, tail-coated politician on an improvised stage seeking the votes of an audience of well-dressed gentlemen and local farmers — identified by their broad-brimmed hats and casual attire. Private Collection/Bridgeman Images.

As you read, ask yourself why this chapter begins and ends with these dates and then identify the links among related events.

1810s ▶ States expand white male voting rights ▶ Martin Van Buren creates disciplined party in New York	**1833** ▶ Congress enacts compromise tariff
	1834 ▶ Whig Party formed by Clay, Calhoun, and Daniel Webster
1825 ▶ House of Representatives selects John Quincy Adams as president ▶ Adams endorses Henry Clay's American System	**1835** ▶ Roger Taney named Supreme Court chief justice
	1836 ▶ Van Buren elected president
1828 ▶ Working Men's Parties win support ▶ Tariff of Abominations raises duties ▶ Andrew Jackson elected president ▶ John C. Calhoun's *South Carolina Exposition and Protest*	**1837** ▶ *Charles River Bridge* case weakens chartered monopolies ▶ Panic of 1837 derails economy and labor movement
1830 ▶ Jackson vetoes National Road bill ▶ Congress enacts Jackson's Indian Removal Act	**1838** ▶ Many Cherokees die in Trail of Tears march to Indian Territory
1831 ▶ *Cherokee Nation v. Georgia* denies Indians' independence, but *Worcester v. Georgia* (1832) upholds their political autonomy	**1839– 1843** ▶ Defaults on bonds by state governments spark international financial crisis and depression
	1840 ▶ Whigs win "log cabin campaign"
1832 ▶ Massacre of 850 Sauk and Fox warriors at Bad Axe ▶ Jackson vetoes renewal of Second Bank ▶ South Carolina adopts Ordinance of Nullification	**1841** ▶ John Tyler succeeds William Henry Harrison as president

The Rise of Popular Politics

Expansion of the **franchise** (the right to vote) dramatically symbolized the Democratic Revolution. By the 1830s, most states allowed nearly all white men to vote. Nowhere else in the world did ordinary farmers and wage earners exercise such political influence; in England, the Reform Bill of 1832 extended the vote to only 600,000 out of 6 million men — a mere 10 percent. Equally important, political parties provided voters with the means to express their preferences. At the same time, state legislatures barred women and free African Americans from exercising the franchise. As political democracy took shape in the United States, participation was restricted to white men.

The Decline of the Notables and the Rise of Parties

The American Revolution weakened the elite-run society of the colonial era but did not overthrow it. Only two states — Pennsylvania and Vermont — gave the vote to all male taxpayers, and many families of low rank continued to defer to their social "betters." Consequently, wealthy **notables** — northern landlords, slave-owning planters, and seaport merchants — dominated the political system in the new republic. And rightly so, said John Jay, the first chief justice of the Supreme Court: "Those who own the country are the most fit persons to participate in the government of it." Jay and other notables managed local elections by building up an "interest": lending money to small farmers, giving business to storekeepers, and treating their tenants to rum. An outlay of $20 for refreshments, remarked one poll watcher, "may produce about 100 votes." This gentry-dominated system kept men who lacked wealth and powerful family connections from seeking office.

The Rise of Democracy To broaden voting rights, Maryland reformers in the 1810s invoked the equal rights rhetoric of republicanism. They charged that property qualifications for voting were a "tyranny" because they endowed "one class of men with privileges which are denied to another." In response, legislators in Maryland and other seaboard states grudgingly expanded the franchise. The new voters often rejected candidates who wore "top boots, breeches, and shoe buckles," their hair in "powder and queues." Instead, they elected men who dressed simply and endorsed popular rule.

Farmers and laborers in the Midwest and Southwest also challenged the old order. The constitutions of the new states of Indiana (1816), Illinois (1818), and Alabama (1819) prescribed a broad male franchise, and voters usually elected middling men to local and state offices. A well-to-do migrant in Illinois was surprised to learn that the man who plowed his fields "was a colonel of militia, and a member of the legislature." Once in public office, men from modest backgrounds restricted imprisonment for debt, kept taxes low, and allowed farmers to claim squatters' rights to unoccupied land.

By 1830, most state legislatures had given the vote to all white men or to all men who paid taxes or served in the militia. Only two — North Carolina and Rhode Island — still required the possession of freehold property (Map 9.1). Equally significant, between 1818 and 1821, Connecticut, Massachusetts, and New York wrote more democratic constitutions that reapportioned legislative districts on the basis of population and stipulated that judges and justices of the peace would be elected rather than appointed.

Democratic politics was contentious and, because it attracted ambitious men, often corrupt. Powerful entrepreneurs and speculators — both notables and self-made men — demanded government assistance and paid bribes to get it. Speculators won land grants by paying off the members of important committees, and bankers distributed shares of stock to key legislators. When the Seventh Ward Bank of New York City received a legislative charter in 1833, the bank's officials set aside one-third of the 3,700 shares of stock for themselves and their friends and almost two-thirds for state legislators and bureaucrats, leaving just 40 shares for public sale (America in Global Context).

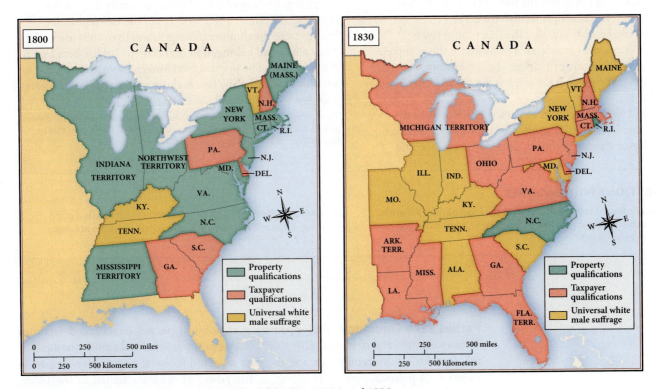

MAP 9.1   The Expansion of Voting Rights for White Men, 1800 and 1830
Between 1800 and 1830, the United States moved steadily toward political equality for white men. Many existing states revised their constitutions and replaced a property qualification for voting with less restrictive criteria, such as paying taxes or serving in the militia. Some new states in the West extended the suffrage to all adult white men. As parties sought votes from a broader electorate, the tone of politics became more open and competitive — swayed by the interests and values of ordinary people.

Alexis de Tocqueville: Letter to Louis de Kergorlay, June 29, 1831

In 1831, the French aristocrat Alexis de Tocqueville (1805–1859) came to the United States to report on its innovative penal system. Instead, he produced a brilliant analysis of the new republican society and politics, *Democracy in America* (1835, 1840). This letter to a French friend reveals his thinking and insights.

Do you know what, in this country's political realm, makes the most vivid impression on me? The effect of laws governing inheritance. . . . The English had exported their laws of primogeniture, according to which the eldest acquired three-quarters of the father's fortune. This resulted in a host of vast territorial domains passing from father to son and wealth remaining in families. My American informants tell me that there was no aristocracy but, instead, a class of great landowners leading a simple, rather intellectual life characterized by its air of good breeding, its manners, and a strong sense of family pride. . . . Since then, inheritance laws have been revised.

Primogeniture gave way to equal division, with almost magical results. Domains split up, passing into other hands. Family spirit disappeared. The aristocratic bias that marked the republic's early years was replaced by a democratic thrust of irresistible force. . . . I've seen several members of these old families. . . . They regret the loss of everything aristocratic: patronage, family pride, high tone. . . .

There can be no doubt that the inheritance law is responsible in some considerable measure for this complete triumph of democratic principles. The Americans . . . agree that "it has made us what we are, it is the foundation of our republic." . . .

When I apply these ideas to France, I cannot resist the thought that Louis XVIII's charter [of 1814 sought to restore the pre-Revolutionary regime by creating] . . . aristocratic institutions in political law, but [by mandating equality before the law and retaining the Revolutionary-era inheritance laws giving all children, irrespective of sex, an equal share of the parental estate] within the domain of civil law gave shelter to a democratic principle so vigorous that it was bound before long to destroy the foundations of the edifice it raised. . . . We are moving toward an unrestricted democracy . . . that . . . would not suit France at all. . . . [However,] there is no human power capable of changing the law of inheritance, and with this change our families will disappear, possessions will pass into other hands, wealth will be increasingly equalized, the upper class will melt into the middle, the latter will become immense and shape everything to its level. . . .

What I see in America leaves me doubting that government by the multitude, even under the most favorable circumstances — and they exist here — is a good thing. There is general agreement that in the early days of the republic, statesmen and members of the two legislative houses were much more distinguished than they are today. They almost all belonged to that class of landowners I mentioned above. The populace no longer chooses with such a sure hand. It generally favors those who flatter its passions and descend to its level.

SOURCE: From *Letters from America: Alexis de Tocqueville*, edited, translated, and with an introduction by Frederick Brown, Yale University Press, 2010. Copyright © 2010 by Frederick Brown. Reprinted by permission of Yale University Press.

QUESTIONS FOR ANALYSIS

1. According to Tocqueville, what is the legal basis of American social equality and political democracy? What is the comparable situation in France?

2. Why does Tocqueville doubt that democratic rule is a good thing, even in the United States, and "would not suit France at all"?

Parties Take Command The appearance of political parties encouraged vigorous debates over government policy. Revolutionary-era Americans had condemned political "factions" as antirepublican, and the new state and national constitutions made no mention of political parties. However, as the power of notables waned in the 1820s, disciplined political parties appeared in a number of states. Usually they were run by professional politicians, often middle-class lawyers and journalists. One observer called the new parties **political machines** because, like the new power-driven textile looms, they efficiently wove together the interests of diverse social and economic groups.

Martin Van Buren of New York was the chief architect of the emerging system of party government. The ambitious son of a Jeffersonian tavern keeper, Van Buren grew up in the landlord-dominated society of the Hudson River Valley. Trained as a lawyer, he sought an alternative to the system of deferring to local notables. He wanted to create a political order based on party identity, not family connections. Van Buren rejected the traditional republican belief that political factions were dangerous and claimed that the opposite was true. In his autobiography he wrote, "All men of sense know that political parties are inseparable from free government," because they restrain an elected official's inherent "disposition to abuse power."

Between 1817 and 1821 in New York, Van Buren turned his "Bucktail" supporters (who wore a deer's tail on their hats) into the first statewide political machine. He purchased a newspaper, the *Albany Argus*, and used it to promote his policies and get out the vote. Patronage was an even more important tool. When Van Buren's Bucktails won control of the New York legislature in 1821, they acquired the power to appoint some six thousand of their friends to positions in New York's legal bureaucracy of judges, justices of the peace, sheriffs, deed commissioners, and coroners. Critics called this ruthless distribution of offices a **spoils system**, but Van Buren argued it was fair, operating "sometimes in favour of one party, and sometimes of another." Party government was thoroughly republican, he added, because it reflected the preferences of a majority of the citizenry. To ensure the passage of the party's legislative program, Van Buren insisted on disciplined voting as determined by a **caucus**, a meeting of party leaders. On one crucial occasion, the "Little Magician" — a nickname reflecting Van Buren's short stature and political dexterity — honored seventeen New York legislators for sacrificing "individual preferences for the general good" of the party.

Racial Exclusion and Republican Motherhood

The rise of a more democratic political system did not lead to universal voting rights. Old cultural rules — and new laws — denied the vote to most women and free African American men. When women and free blacks asked for voting rights, legislators wrote explicit race and gender restrictions into the law. In 1802, Ohio disenfranchised African Americans, and the New York constitution of 1821 imposed a property-holding requirement on black voters. A striking case of sexual discrimination occurred in New Jersey, where the state constitution of 1776 had granted the voting franchise to all property holders. As Federalists and Republicans competed for power, they ignored customary gender rules and urged property-owning single women and widows to vote. Sensing a threat to men's monopoly on politics, the New Jersey legislature in 1807 invoked both biology and custom to limit voting to men only: "Women, generally, are neither by nature, nor habit, nor education, nor by their necessary condition in society fitted to perform this duty with credit to themselves or advantage to the public."

Republican Motherhood   The controversy over women's political rights mirrored a debate over authority within the household. Traditionally, most American women had spent their active adult years working as farmwives and bearing and nurturing children. However, after 1800, the birthrate in the northern states dropped significantly. In the farming village of Sturbridge in central Massachusetts, women now bore an average of six children; their grandmothers had usually given birth to eight or nine. In the growing seaport cities, native-born white women now bore an average of only four children.

To see a longer excerpt from Martin Van Buren's autobiography, along with other primary sources from this period, see *Sources for America's History*.

Martin Van Buren   Martin Van Buren's skills as a lawyer and a politician won him many admirers, as did his personal charm, sharp intellect, and imperturbable composure. "Little Van" — a mere 5 feet 6 inches in height — had almost as many detractors. Davy Crockett, Kentucky frontiersman, land speculator, and congressman, labeled him "an artful, cunning, intriguing, selfish lawyer," concerned only with "office and money." In truth, Van Buren was a complex man, a middle-class lawyer with republican values and aristocratic tastes who nonetheless created a democratic political party. National Portrait Gallery, Smithsonian Institution/Art Resource, NY.

IDENTIFY CAUSES
What was the relationship between the growth of democracy and the emergence of political parties?

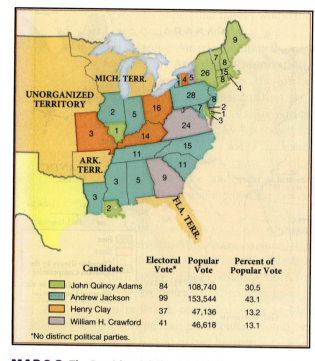

Candidate	Electoral Vote*	Popular Vote	Percent of Popular Vote
John Quincy Adams	84	108,740	30.5
Andrew Jackson	99	153,544	43.1
Henry Clay	37	47,136	13.2
William H. Crawford	41	46,618	13.1

*No distinct political parties.

MAP 9.3 The Presidential Election of 1824
Regional voting was the dominant pattern in 1824. John Quincy Adams captured every electoral vote in New England and most of those in New York; Henry Clay carried Ohio and Kentucky, the most populous trans-Appalachian states, as well as Missouri; and William Crawford took the southern states of Virginia and Georgia. Only Andrew Jackson claimed a national constituency, winning Pennsylvania and New Jersey in the East, Indiana and most of Illinois in the Midwest, and much of the South. Only 356,000 Americans voted, about 27 percent of the eligible electorate.

CONSIDER POINTS OF VIEW
Why did Jacksonians consider the political deal between Adams and Clay "corrupt"?

and use tariff revenues to finance **internal improvements**, that is, public works such as roads and canals. His nationalistic program won praise in the Northwest, which needed better transportation, but elicited sharp criticism in the South, which relied on rivers to market its cotton and had few manufacturing industries to protect. William Crawford of Georgia, an ideological heir of Thomas Jefferson, denounced Clay's American System as a scheme to "consolidate" political power in Washington. Concluding that he could not defeat Crawford, John C. Calhoun of South Carolina withdrew from the race and endorsed Andrew Jackson.

As the hero of the Battle of New Orleans, Jackson benefitted from the surge of patriotism after the War of 1812. Born in the Carolina backcountry, Jackson settled in Nashville, Tennessee, where he formed ties to influential families through marriage and a career as an attorney and a slave-owning cotton planter. His rise from common origins symbolized the new democratic age, and his reputation as a "plain solid republican" attracted voters in all regions. Still, Jackson's strong showing in the electoral college surprised most political leaders. The Tennessee senator received 99 electoral votes; Adams, 84 votes; Crawford, struck down by a stroke during the campaign, won 41; and Clay finished with 37 (Map 9.3).

Because no candidate received an absolute majority, the Twelfth Amendment to the Constitution (ratified in 1804) set the rules: the House of Representatives would choose the president from among the three highest vote-getters. This procedure hurt Jackson because many congressmen feared that the rough-hewn "military chieftain" might become a tyrant. Excluded from the race, Henry Clay used his influence as Speaker of the House to thwart Jackson's election. Clay assembled a coalition of representatives from New England and the Ohio River Valley that voted Adams into the presidency in 1825. Adams showed his gratitude by appointing Clay his secretary of state, the traditional stepping-stone to the presidency. Clay's appointment was politically fatal for both men: Jackson's supporters accused Clay and Adams of making a **corrupt bargain**, and they vowed to oppose Adams's policies and to prevent Clay's rise to the presidency.

The Last Notable President: John Quincy Adams

As president, Adams called for bold national action. "The moral purpose of the Creator," he told Congress, was to use the president to "improve the conditions of himself and his fellow men." Adams called for the establishment of a national university in Washington, scientific explorations in the Far West, and a uniform standard of weights and measures. Most important, he endorsed Henry Clay's American System and its three key elements: protective tariffs to stimulate manufacturing, federally subsidized roads and canals to facilitate commerce, and a national bank to control credit and provide a uniform currency.

The Demise of the American System Manufacturers, entrepreneurs, and farmers in the Northeast and Midwest welcomed Adams's proposals. However, his policies won little support in the South, where planters opposed protective tariffs because these taxes raised the price of manufactures. Southern smallholders also feared powerful banks that could force them into bankruptcy. From his deathbed, Thomas Jefferson condemned Adams for promoting the rule of a monied "aristocracy" over "the plundered ploughman and beggared yeomanry."

Other politicians objected to the American System on constitutional grounds. In 1817, President Madison had vetoed the Bonus Bill, which proposed using the national government's income from the Second Bank of the United States to fund improvement projects in the states. Such projects, Madison argued, were the sole responsibility of the states, a sentiment shared by the Republican followers of Thomas Jefferson. In 1824, Martin Van Buren likewise declared his allegiance to the constitutional "doctrines of the Jefferson School" and his opposition to "consolidated government," a powerful and potentially oppressive national administration. Now a member of the U.S. Senate, Van Buren helped to defeat most of Adams's proposed subsidies for roads and canals.

The Tariff Battle   The major battle of the Adams administration came over tariffs. The Tariff of 1816 had placed relatively high duties on imports of cheap English cotton cloth, allowing New England textile producers to control that segment of the market. In 1824, Adams and Clay secured a new tariff that protected New England and Pennsylvania manufacturers from more expensive woolen and cotton textiles and also English iron goods. Without these tariffs, British imports would have dominated the market and slowed American industrial development. (See Chapter 8, America in Global Context, p. 251.)

Recognizing the appeal of tariffs, Van Buren and his Jacksonian allies hopped on the bandwagon. By increasing duties on wool, hemp, and other imported raw materials, they hoped to win the support of farmers in New York, Ohio, and Kentucky for Jackson's presidential candidacy in 1828. The tariff had become a political weapon. "I fear this tariff thing," remarked Thomas Cooper, the president of the College of South Carolina and an advocate of free trade. "By some strange mechanical contrivance [it has become] . . . a machine for manufacturing Presidents, instead of broadcloths, and bed blankets." Disregarding southern protests, northern Jacksonians joined with supporters of Adams and Clay to enact the Tariff of 1828, which raised duties significantly on raw materials, textiles, and iron goods.

The new tariff cost southerners about $100 million a year. Planters had to buy either higher-cost American textiles and iron goods, thus enriching northeastern businesses and workers, or highly taxed British imports, thus paying the expenses of the national government. The new tariff was "little less than legalized pillage," an Alabama legislator declared, calling it a **Tariff of Abominations**. Ignoring the Jacksonians' support for the Tariff of 1828, most southerners heaped blame on President Adams.

Southern governments also criticized Adams's Indian policy. A deeply moral man, the president supported the treaty-guaranteed land rights of Native Americans against expansion-minded whites. In 1825, U.S. commissioners had secured a treaty from one faction of Creeks ceding its lands in Georgia to the United States for eventual sale to the state's citizens. When the Creek National Council claimed the treaty was fraudulent, Adams called for new negotiations. In response, Georgia governor George M. Troup attacked the president as a "public enemy . . . the unblushing ally of the savages." Mobilizing Georgia's congressional delegation, Troup persuaded Congress to extinguish the Creeks' land titles, forcing most Creeks to leave the state.

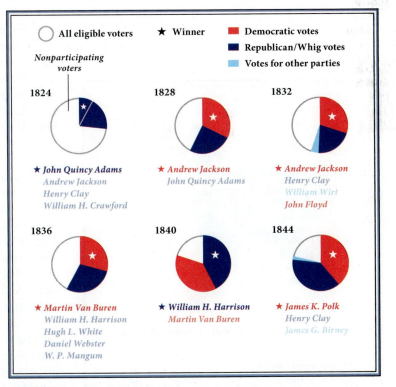

FIGURE 9.1 **The Rise of Voter Turnout, 1824–1844**
As the shrinking white sections of these pie graphs indicate, the proportion of eligible voters who cast ballots in presidential elections increased dramatically over time. In 1824, 27 percent voted; in 1840 and thereafter, about 80 percent went to the polls. Voter participation soared first in 1828, when Andrew Jackson and John Quincy Adams contested for the White House, and again in 1840, as competition heated up between Democrats and Whigs, who advocated different policies and philosophies of government. Democrats won most of these contests because their policies had greater appeal to ordinary citizens.

EXPLAIN CAUSES
What were the successes and failures of John Adams's presidency, and what accounted for those outcomes?

Elsewhere, Adams's primary weakness was his out-of-date political style. He was aloof, inflexible, and paternalistic. When Congress rejected his economic policies, Adams accused its members of following the whims of public opinion and told them not to be enfeebled "by the will of our constituents." Rather than "run" for reelection in 1828, Adams "stood" for it, telling friends, "If my country wants my services, she must ask for them."

"The Democracy" and the Election of 1828

Martin Van Buren and the politicians handling Andrew Jackson's campaign for the presidency had no reservations about running for office. To put Jackson in the White House, Van Buren revived the political coalition created by Thomas Jefferson, championing policies that appealed to both southern planters and northern farmers and artisans, the "plain Republicans of the North." John C. Calhoun, Jackson's running mate, brought his South Carolina allies into Van Buren's party, and Jackson's close friends in Tennessee rallied voters throughout the Old Southwest. The Little Magician hoped that a national party would reconcile the diverse "interests" that, as James Madison suggested in "Federalist No. 10" (Chapter 6), inevitably existed in a large republic. Equally important, added Jackson's ally Duff Green, it would put the "anti-slave party in the North . . . to sleep for twenty years to come."

Van Buren and the Jacksonians orchestrated a massive publicity campaign. In New York, fifty Democrat-funded newspapers declared their support for Jackson. Elsewhere, Jacksonians used mass meetings, torchlight parades, and barbecues to celebrate the candidate's frontier origin and rise to fame. They praised "Old Hickory" as a "natural" aristocrat, a self-made man.

The Jacksonians called themselves Democrats or "the Democracy" to convey their egalitarian message. As Thomas Morris told the Ohio legislature, Democrats were fighting for equality: the republic had been corrupted by legislative charters that gave "a few individuals rights and privileges not enjoyed by the citizens at large." Morris promised that the Democracy would destroy such "artificial distinction." Jackson himself declared that "equality among the people in the rights conferred by government" was the "great radical principle of freedom."

Jackson's message appealed to many social groups. His hostility to corporations and to Clay's American System won support from northeastern artisans and workers who felt threatened by industrialization. Jackson captured the votes of Pennsylvania ironworkers and New York farmers who had benefitted from the controversial Tariff of Abominations. Yet, by astutely declaring his support for a "judicious" tariff that would balance regional interests, Jackson remained popular in the South. In the Southeast and Midwest, Jackson's well-known hostility toward Native Americans reassured white farmers seeking Indian removal.

The Democrats' celebration of popular rule carried Jackson into office. In 1824, about one-quarter of the electorate had voted; in 1828, more than one-half went to the polls, and 56 percent voted for the Tennessee senator — the first president from a trans-Appalachian state (Figure 9.1 and Map 9.4). Jackson's popularity and sharp temper frightened men of wealth. Senator Daniel Webster of Massachusetts, a former Federalist and now a corporate lawyer, warned his clients that the new president would "bring a breeze with him. Which way it will blow, I cannot tell [but] . . . my fear is stronger than my hope." Supreme Court

Candidate	Electoral Vote	Popular Vote	Percent of Popular Vote
Andrew Jackson (Democratic Republican)	178	647,286	56
John Q. Adams (National Republican)	83	508,064	44

MAP 9.4 **The Presidential Election of 1828**
As in 1824, John Quincy Adams carried all of New England and some of the Mid-Atlantic states. However, Andrew Jackson swept the rest of the nation and won a resounding victory in the electoral college. Over 1.1 million American men cast ballots in 1828, more than three times the number who voted in 1824.

justice Joseph Story shared Webster's apprehensions. Watching an unruly Inauguration Day crowd climb over the elegant White House furniture to congratulate Jackson, Story lamented that "the reign of King 'Mob' seemed triumphant."

> **IN YOUR OWN WORDS**   How did Jackson and the new Democratic Party overcome sectional differences?

TRACE CHANGE OVER TIME
Jackson lost the presidential election of 1824 and won in 1828: what changes explain these different outcomes?

Jackson in Power, 1829–1837

American-style political democracy—a broad franchise, a disciplined political party, and policies favoring specific interests—ushered Andrew Jackson into office. Jackson used his popular mandate to transform the national government. During his two terms, he enhanced presidential authority, destroyed the mercantilist and nationalist American System, established a new ideology of limited government, and supported Indian removal. An Ohio supporter summed up Jackson's vision: "the Sovereignty of the People, the Rights of the States, and a Light and Simple Government."

Jackson's Agenda: Rotation and Decentralization

To make policy, Jackson relied primarily on his so-called Kitchen Cabinet. Its most influential members were two Kentuckians, Francis Preston Blair, who edited the *Washington Globe*, and Amos Kendall, who wrote Jackson's speeches; Roger B. Taney (pronounced "tawny") of Maryland, who became attorney general, treasury secretary, and then chief justice of the Supreme Court; and Martin Van Buren, whom Jackson named secretary of state.

Following Van Buren's example in New York, Jackson used patronage to create a disciplined national party. He rejected the idea of "property in office" (that a qualified official held a position permanently) and insisted on a rotation of officeholders when a new administration took power. Rotation would not lessen expertise, Jackson insisted, because public duties were "so plain and simple that men of intelligence may readily qualify themselves for their performance." William L. Marcy, a New York Jacksonian, offered a more realistic explanation for rotation: government jobs were like the spoils of war, and "to the victor belong the spoils of the enemy." Jackson used those spoils to reward his allies and win backing for his policies.

Jackson's highest priority was to destroy the American System. He believed that government-sponsored plans for national economic development were unconstitutional. Declaring that the "voice of the people" called for "economy in the expenditures of the Government," Jackson vetoed four internal improvement bills in 1830, including an extension of the National Road, arguing that they infringed on "the reserved powers of states." By eliminating expenses, these vetoes also undermined the case for protective tariffs. As Jacksonian senator William Smith of South Carolina pointed out, "Destroy internal improvements and you leave no motive for the tariff."

IDENTIFY CAUSES
Jackson cut the national budget and the national debt but increased the number of federal employees. How do you explain this paradox?

The Tariff and Nullification

The Tariff of 1828 had helped Jackson win the presidency, but it saddled him with a major political crisis. There was fierce opposition to high tariffs throughout the South and especially in South Carolina. That state was the only one with an African American majority—56 percent of the population in 1830—and its slave owners, like the white sugar planters in the West Indies, feared a black rebellion. Even more, they worried about the legal abolition of slavery. The British Parliament had declared that slavery in its West Indian colonies would end in 1833; South Carolina planters, vividly recalling northern efforts to end slavery in Missouri, worried that the U.S. Congress would follow the British lead. So they attacked the tariff, both to lower rates and to discourage the use of federal power to attack slavery.

The crisis began in 1832, when Congress reenacted the Tariff of Abominations. In response, leading South Carolinians called a state convention that boldly adopted an Ordinance of Nullification declaring the tariffs of 1828 and 1832 to be null and void. The ordinance prohibited the collection of those duties in South Carolina after February 1, 1833, and threatened secession if federal officials tried to collect them.

South Carolina's act of **nullification** — the argument that a state has the right to void, within its borders, a law passed by Congress — rested on the constitutional arguments developed in *The South Carolina Exposition and Protest* (1828). Written anonymously by Vice President John C. Calhoun, the *Exposition* contended that protective tariffs and other national legislation that operated unequally on the various states lacked fairness and legitimacy. "Constitutional government and the government of a majority," Calhoun concluded, "are utterly incompatible."

Calhoun's argument echoed the claims made by Jefferson and Madison in the Kentucky and Virginia Resolutions of 1798. Those resolutions asserted that, because state-based conventions had ratified the Constitution, sovereignty lay in the states, not in the people. Beginning from this premise, Calhoun argued that a state convention could declare a congressional law to be void within the state's borders. Replying to this **states' rights** interpretation of the Constitution, which had little support in the text of the document, Senator Daniel Webster of Massachusetts presented a nationalist interpretation that celebrated popular sovereignty and Congress's responsibility to secure the "general welfare."

Jackson hoped to find a middle path between Webster's strident nationalism and Calhoun's radical doctrine of localist federalism. Jackson declared that South Carolina's Ordinance of Nullification violated the letter of the Constitution and was "destructive of the great object for which it was formed." At his request, Congress in early 1833 passed a military Force Bill, authorizing the president to compel South Carolina's obedience to national laws. At the same time, Jackson addressed the South's objections to high import duties with a new tariff act that, over the course of a decade, reduced rates to the modest levels of 1816. Export-hungry midwestern wheat farmers joined southern planters in advocating low duties to avoid retaliatory tariffs by foreign nations. "Illinois wants a market for her agricultural products," declared Senator Sidney Breese in 1846. "[S]he wants the market of the world."

Having won the political battle by securing a tariff reduction, the South Carolina convention did not press its constitutional stance on nullification. Jackson was satisfied. He had assisted the South economically while upholding the constitutional principle of national authority — a principle that Abraham Lincoln would embrace to defend the Union during the secession crisis of 1861.

CONSIDER POINTS OF VIEW
How did South Carolina justify nullification on constitutional grounds?

The Bank War

In the midst of the tariff crisis, Jackson faced a major challenge from politicians who supported the **Second Bank of the United States**. Founded in Philadelphia in 1816 (Chapter 7), the bank was privately managed and operated under a twenty-year charter from the federal government, which owned 20 percent of its stock. The bank's most important role was to stabilize the nation's money supply, which consisted primarily of paper money issued by state-chartered banks. The state banks promised to redeem the notes on demand with "hard" money (or "specie") — that is, gold or silver coins minted by the U.S. or foreign governments — but there were few coins in circulation. By collecting those notes and regularly demanding specie, the Second Bank kept the state banks from issuing too much paper money and depreciating its value.

This cautious monetary policy pleased creditors — the bankers and entrepreneurs in Boston, New York, and Philadelphia, whose capital investments were underwriting economic development. However, expansion-minded bankers, including friends of Jackson's in Nashville, demanded an end to central oversight. Moreover, many ordinary Americans worried that the Second Bank would force weak banks to close, leaving them holding worthless paper notes. Many politicians resented the arrogance of the bank's president, Nicholas Biddle. "As to mere power," Biddle boasted, "I have been for years in the daily exercise of more personal authority than any President habitually enjoys."

Jackson's Bank Veto   Although the Second Bank had many enemies, a political miscalculation by its friends brought its downfall. In 1832, Henry Clay and Daniel Webster persuaded Biddle to seek an early extension of the bank's charter (which still had four years to run). They had the votes in Congress to enact the required legislation and hoped to lure Jackson into a veto that would split the Democrats just before the 1832 elections.

Jackson turned the tables on Clay and Webster. He vetoed the rechartering bill with a masterful message that blended constitutional arguments with class rhetoric and patriotic fervor. Adopting the position taken by Thomas Jefferson in 1793, Jackson declared that Congress had no constitutional authority to charter a national bank. He condemned the bank as "subversive of the rights of the States," "dangerous to the liberties of the people," and a privileged monopoly that promoted "the advancement of the few at the expense of . . . farmers, mechanics, and laborers." Finally, the president noted that British aristocrats owned much of the bank's stock. Such a powerful institution should be "purely American," Jackson declared with patriotic zeal.

Jackson's attack on the bank carried him to victory in 1832. Old Hickory and Martin Van Buren, his new running mate, overwhelmed Henry Clay, who headed the National Republican ticket, by 219 to 49 electoral votes. Jackson's most fervent supporters were eastern workers and western farmers, who blamed the Second Bank for high prices and stagnant farm income. Other Jackson supporters had prospered during a decade of strong economic growth. Thousands of middle-class Americans — lawyers, clerks, shopkeepers, and artisans — had used the opportunity to rise in the world and cheered Jackson's attack on privileged corporations.

The Bank Destroyed   Early in 1833, Jackson met their wishes by appointing Roger B. Taney, a strong opponent of corporate privilege, as head of the Treasury Department. Taney promptly transferred the federal government's gold and silver from the Second Bank to various state banks, which critics labeled Jackson's "pet banks." To justify this abrupt (and probably illegal) transfer, Jackson declared that his reelection represented "the decision of the people against the bank" and gave him a mandate to destroy it. This sweeping claim of presidential power was new and radical. Never before had a president claimed that victory at the polls allowed him to pursue a controversial policy or to act independently of Congress (Analyzing Voices).

The "bank war" escalated into an all-out political battle. In March 1834, Jackson's opponents in the Senate passed a resolution composed by Henry Clay that censured the president and warned of executive tyranny: "We are in the midst of a revolution, hitherto bloodless, but rapidly descending towards a total change of the pure republican character of the Government, and the concentration of all power in the hands of one man." The censure did not deter Jackson. "The Bank is trying to kill me but I will kill it," he vowed to Van Buren. And so he did. When the Second Bank's national charter expired in 1836, Jackson prevented its renewal.

Jackson had destroyed both national banking — the handiwork of Alexander Hamilton — and the American System of protective tariffs and public works created by Henry Clay and John Quincy Adams. The result was a profound check on economic activism and innovative policymaking by the national government. "All is gone," observed a Washington newspaper correspondent. "All is gone, which the General Government was instituted to create and preserve."

King Andrew the First, 1833   Jackson's decision to veto the rechartering of the Second Bank of the United States helped him win reelection, but for his opponents it confirmed the fear that he was an autocrat. This political cartoon portrays Jackson as a king. He wears a crown and holds a scepter in one hand and his veto power in the other. Underfoot lie a tattered copy of the Constitution, the bank charter, and an internal improvements bill. The cartoon appeared in the fall of 1833, after his treasury secretary, Roger B. Taney, removed federal deposits from the Bank of the United States. Library of Congress.

PLACE EVENTS IN CONTEXT
Why — and how — did Jackson destroy the Second National Bank?

The Character and Goals of Andrew Jackson

From the start of his career, Andrew Jackson was a controversial figure. "Hot-tempered," "Indian-hater," "military despot," said his critics, while his friends praised him as a forthright statesman. His contemporary biographer, the journalist James Parton, found him a man of many faces, an enigma. Others thought they understood his personality and policies: James Hamilton, a loyal Jacksonian congressman, recalled Jackson's volatile temper. Henry Clay, his archrival, warned that Jackson's quest for power threatened American republicanism, while wealthy New York Whig Philip Hone accused him of inciting class warfare. After talking with dozens of Americans, Frenchman Alexis de Tocqueville offered a balanced interpretation of the man and his goals.

JAMES PARTON
Preface to *The Life of Andrew Jackson* (1860)

SOURCE: James Parton, *The Life of Andrew Jackson. In Three Volumes* (New York: Mason Brothers, 1860), vol. 1, vii–viii.

❝ If any one . . . had asked what I had yet discovered respecting General Jackson, I might have answered thus: 'Andrew Jackson, I am given to understand, was a patriot and a traitor. He was one of the greatest of generals, and wholly ignorant of the art of war. . . . The first of statesmen, he never devised, he never framed a measure. He was the most candid of men, and was capable of the profoundest dissimulation. A most law-defying, law-obeying citizen. A stickler for discipline, he never hesitated to disobey his superior. A democratic autocrat. An urbane savage. An atrocious saint.' ❞

JAMES HAMILTON JR.
Recalling an Event in 1827, as Jackson Campaigns for the Presidency

SOURCE: Sean Wilentz, ed., *Major Problems in the Early Republic, 1787–1848* (Lexington, MA: D. C. Heath, 1991), 374.

❝ The steamer Pocahontas was chartered by citizens of New Orleans to convey the General and his party from Nashville to that city. She was fitted out in the most sumptuous manner. The party was General and Mrs. Jackson, . . . Governor Samuel Houston, Wm. B. Lewis, Robert Armstrong, and others. . . . The only freight was the General's cotton-crop. . . .

In the course of the voyage an event occurred, which I repeat, as it is suggestive of [his] character. A steamer of greater speed than ours, going in the same direction, passed us, crossed our bow; then stopped and let us pass her and then passed us again in triumph. This was repeated again and again, until the General, being excited by the offensive course, ordered a rifle to be brought to him; hailed the pilot of the other steamer, and swore that if he did the same thing again he would shoot him. ❞

PHILIP HONE
Ruminating in His Diary on the Jacksonians' Victory in the New York Elections of 1834

SOURCE: Sean Wilentz, ed., *Major Problems in the Early Republic, 1787–1848* (Lexington, MA: D. C. Heath, 1991), 392–393.

❝ I apprehend that Mr. Van Buren [Jackson's vice president] and his friends have no permanent cause of triumph in their victory. They . . . have mounted a vicious horse, who, taking the bit in his mouth, will run away with [them]. . . . This battle had been fought upon the ground of the poor against

---

Indian Removal

The status of Native American peoples posed an equally complex political problem. By the late 1820s, white voices throughout the South and Midwest demanded the resettlement of Indian peoples west of the Mississippi River. Many whites who were sympathetic to Native Americans also favored resettlement. Removal to the West seemed the only way to protect Indians from alcoholism, financial exploitation, and cultural decline (Interpretations).

However, most Indians did not want to leave their ancestral lands. For centuries, Cherokees and Creeks had lived in Georgia, Tennessee, and Alabama; Chickasaws and Choctaws in Mississippi and Alabama; and Seminoles in Florida. During the War of 1812, Andrew Jackson had forced the Creeks to relinquish millions of acres, but Indian nations still controlled vast tracts and wanted to keep them.

Cherokee Resistance But on what terms? Some Indians had adopted white ways. An 1825 census revealed that various Cherokees owned 33 gristmills, 13 sawmills, the rich, and this unworthy prejudice, this dangerous delusion, has been encouraged by the leaders of the triumphant party, and fanned into a flame by the polluted breath of the hireling press in their employ. . . .

The cry of 'Down with the aristocracy!' mingled with the shouts of victory. . . . They have succeeded in raising this dangerous spirit [of the mob], and have gladly availed themselves of its support to accomplish a temporary object; but can they allay it at pleasure? . . . Eighteen thousand men in New York have voted for the high-priest of the party whose professed design is to bring down the property, the talents, the industry, the steady habits of that class which constituted the real strength of the Commonwealth, to the common level of the idle, the worthless, and the unenlightened. Look to it, ye men of respectability in the Jackson party, are ye not afraid of the weapons ye have used in this warfare? 99

HENRY CLAY

Introducing a Senate Resolution Censuring Jackson, December 26, 1833

SOURCE: Calvin Colton, ed., *The Life . . . of Henry Clay*, 6 vols. (New York: A. Barnes, 1857), 576–580.

66 We are in the midst of a revolution, hitherto bloodless, but rapidly tending toward a total change of the pure republican character of the government, and to the concentration of all power in the hands of one man. The powers of Congress are paralyzed, except when exerted in conformity with his will, by frequent and an extraordinary exercise of the executive veto, not anticipated by the founders of our Constitution, and not practiced by any of the predecessors of the present chief magistrate. . . .

The judiciary has not been exempt from the prevailing rage for innovation. Decisions of the tribunals, deliberately pronounced, have been contemptuously disregarded. . . . Our Indian relations, coeval with the existence of the government, and recognized and established by numerous laws and treaties, have been subverted. . . . The system of protection of improvement lies crushed beneath the veto. The system of protection of American industry [will soon meet a similar fate]. . . . In a term of eight years, a little more than equal to that which was required to establish our liberties [as an independent republic between 1776 and 1783], the government will have been transformed into an elective monarchy — the worst of all forms of government. 99

ALEXIS DE TOCQUEVILLE

Analysis of Jackson in *Democracy in America* (1835)

SOURCE: Alexis de Tocqueville, *Democracy in America*, abr. by Thomas Bender (New York: Modern Library, 1981), 271–273.

66 We have been told that General Jackson has won battles; that he is an energetic man, prone by nature and habit to the use of force, covetous of power and a despot by inclination.

All this may be true; but the inferences which have been drawn from these truths are very erroneous. It has been imagined that General Jackson is bent on establishing a dictatorship in America, introducing a military spirit, and giving a degree of influence to the central authority that cannot but be dangerous to provincial [state] liberties. . . .

Far from wishing to extend the Federal power, the President belongs to the party which is desirous of limiting that power to the clear and precise letter of the Constitution and which never puts a construction upon that act favorable to the government of the Union; far from standing forth as the champion of centralization, General Jackson is the agent of the state jealousies; and he was placed in his lofty station by the passions that are most opposed to the central government. 99

QUESTIONS FOR ANALYSIS

1. Was Jackson a "democratic autocrat," as Parton puts it? Would the authors of the other excerpts agree? Did Jackson instigate class warfare, as Hone suggests?

2. In your judgment, which writer, Clay or Tocqueville, offers the more accurate assessment of Jackson and his policies?

3. Do you agree with Philip Hone's view that the Jacksonian Democrats mobilized "poor against the rich"? What evidence would support or contradict Hone's assertion?

2,400 spinning wheels, 760 looms, and 2,900 plows. Many of these owners were mixed-race, the offspring of white traders and Indian women. They had grown up in a bicultural world, knew the political and economic ways of whites, and often favored assimilation into white society. Indeed, some of these mixed-race people were indistinguishable from southern planters. At his death in 1809, Georgia Cherokee James Vann owned one hundred black slaves, two trading posts, and a gristmill. Three decades later, forty other mixed-blood Cherokee families each owned ten or more African American workers.

Prominent mixed-race Cherokees believed that integration into American life was the best way to protect their property and the lands of their people. In 1821, Sequoyah, a part-Cherokee silversmith, perfected a system of writing for the Cherokee language; six years later, mixed-race Cherokees devised a new charter of Cherokee government modeled directly on the U.S. Constitution. "You asked us to throw off the hunter and warrior state," Cherokee John Ridge told a Philadelphia audience in 1832. "We did so. You asked us to form a republican government: We did so. . . . You asked us to learn to

The Indian Removal Act, passed by Congress in 1830 at Andrew Jackson's request, has polarized historians' assessments of his presidency more than any other issue. Unlike some earlier presidents who encouraged the assimilation of Native groups, Jackson supported a policy of moving Native Americans from their lands in the American Southeast to unoccupied federal lands beyond the Mississippi River. The issue came to a head in the late 1820s, just as Jackson's presidency began, when the Cherokees, living within the borders of Georgia, declared themselves to be a sovereign nation. Neither the state, nor Jackson, nor the Supreme Court agreed with them. The 1830 Indian Removal Act granted Jackson authority to negotiate treaties with Native tribes to achieve his policy of removing them. Some tribes agreed to move. When others, like the Seminoles, Creeks, and Cherokees, resisted, the federal government used a forced removal policy. The result was great suffering as Indians died on the Trail of Tears.

Historians agree on the basic narrative of Jackson's Indian policy, but they debate his motivations. Robert V. Remini and Anthony F. C. Wallace interpret Jackson's policies regarding Native Americans in different ways. Was Jackson motivated by a humanitarian concern for Native Americans, or were his policies reflective of the era's racial discrimination against "savages"?

Was Indian Removal Humanitarian or Racist?

ROBERT V. REMINI

SOURCE: Robert V. Remini, *Andrew Jackson and the Course of American Freedom, 1822–1832* (New York: Harper & Row, 1981), 2: 221, 228.

There is no doubt that Jackson believed absolutely that he was pursuing a "just and humane policy towards the Indians." Given the greed of the white man and the certitude that the two races could not intermingle or live side by side, Jackson contended that only through removal could the Indians escape inevitable annihilation. Once relocated beyond the Mississippi the federal government might then exercise "parental control" over their interests and in that way "perpetuate their race." Most Americans probably agreed with this policy. As "hard and cruel as it was then thought," wrote one contemporary . . . it "is now universally felt to have been as kind as it was necessary." . . . [T]he only sane policy for a just government, Jackson declared, was to get the Indian to a place of safety, which he fervently believed existed west of the Mississippi River.

ANTHONY F. C. WALLACE

SOURCE: Anthony F. C. Wallace, *The Long Bitter Trail: Andrew Jackson and the Indians* (Hill & Wang, 1993), 56.

Jackson never proposed exterminating the Indians or at least in public rhetoric, removing by force of arms those who wished to remain. But he was adept at devising conditions that would make those who chose not to remove . . . miserable. . . . [H]e seems to have regarded as inevitable the ultimate extinction of the Native Americans. . . . [T]heir doom was not to be regretted, however. . . . But whatever were Jackson's private reasons for . . . Indian removal — . . . political ambition, financial greed, and philosophical rationalization — there remained the political forces that he mobilized under the banner of the Democratic Party. The exaltation of the common man . . . the sense of America as . . . destined for continental expansion, the open acceptance of racism — these were popular, politically powerful themes that would have driven any Democratic President to press for a policy of Indian removal.

QUESTIONS FOR ANALYSIS

1. Identify one key difference between Remini and Wallace in their interpretation of Jackson's attitude toward Native Americans.

2. To what extent does each of these historians believe Jackson's view of Native Americans was widely shared by white Americans at the time?

3. In considering these two excerpts and Chapter 9's discussion, why do you think Indian removal became a leading issue during Jackson's presidency?

---

read: We did so. You asked us to cast away our idols, and worship your God: We did so." Full-blood Cherokees, who made up 90 percent of the population, resisted many of these cultural and political innovations but were equally determined to retain their ancestral lands. "We would not receive money for land in which our fathers and friends are buried," one full-blood chief declared. "We love our land; it is our mother."

What the Cherokees did or wanted carried no weight with the Georgia legislature. In 1802, Georgia had given up its western land claims in return for a federal promise to extinguish Indian landholdings in the state. Now it demanded fulfillment of that pledge. Having spent his military career fighting Indians and seizing their lands, Andrew Jackson gave full support to Georgia. On assuming the presidency, he withdrew the federal troops that had protected Indian enclaves there and in Alabama and Mississippi. The states, he declared, were sovereign within their borders.

The Removal Act and Its Aftermath Jackson then pushed the **Indian Removal Act of 1830** through Congress over the determined opposition of evangelical Protestant men — and women. To block removal, Catharine Beecher and Lydia Sigourney composed a Ladies Circular that urged "benevolent ladies" to use "prayers and exertions to avert the calamity of removal." Women from across the nation flooded Congress with petitions. Nonetheless, Jackson's bill squeaked through the House of Representatives by a vote of 102 to 97.

The Removal Act created the Indian Territory on national lands acquired in the Louisiana Purchase and located in present-day Oklahoma and Kansas. It promised money and reserved land to Native American peoples who would give up their ancestral holdings east of the Mississippi River. Government officials promised the Indians that they could live on their new land, "they and all their children, as long as grass grows and water runs." However, as one Indian leader noted, on the Great Plains "water and

MAP 9.5 The Removal of Native Americans, 1820–1846
As white settlers moved west, the U.S. government forced scores of Native American communities to leave their ancestral lands. Andrew Jackson's Indian Removal Act of 1830 formalized this policy. Subsequently, many Indian peoples signed treaties that exchanged their lands in the East, Midwest, and Southeast for money and designated reservations in an Indian Territory west of the Mississippi River. When the Sauk, Fox, Cherokees, and Seminoles resisted resettlement, the government used the U.S. Army to enforce the removal policy.

Andrew Jackson as the Great Father, 1835 Jackson championed the Indian Removal Act of 1830, which created the Indian Territory on lands obtained in the Louisiana Purchase and forced dozens of Native American nations throughout the eastern United States to move across the Mississippi. Jackson professed a concern for Native American welfare, prompting this sarcastic portrayal as the "Great Father" tending to the needs of his diminutive Native American "children." Jackson is portrayed unflatteringly, with dark skin that seems to suggest his own racial ambiguity. William L. Clements Library, University of Michigan.

timber are scarcely to be seen." When Chief Black Hawk and his Sauk and Fox followers refused to leave rich, well-watered farmland in western Illinois in 1832, Jackson sent troops to expel them by force. Eventually, the U.S. Army pursued Black Hawk into the Wisconsin Territory and, in the brutal eight-hour Bad Axe Massacre, killed 850 of his 1,000 warriors. Over the next five years, American diplomatic pressure and military power forced seventy Indian peoples to sign treaties and move west of the Mississippi (Map 9.5).

In the meantime, the Cherokees had carried the defense of their lands to the Supreme Court, where they claimed the status of a "foreign nation." In *Cherokee Nation v. Georgia* (1831), Chief Justice John Marshall denied that claim and declared that Indian peoples were "domestic dependent nations." However, in *Worcester v. Georgia* (1832), Marshall and the Court sided with the Cherokees against Georgia. Voiding Georgia's extension of state law over the Cherokees, the Court held that Indian nations were "distinct political communities, having territorial boundaries, within which their authority is exclusive [and is] guaranteed by the United States."

Instead of guaranteeing the Cherokees' territory, the U.S. government took it from them. In 1835, American officials and a minority Cherokee faction negotiated the Treaty of New Echota, which specified that Cherokees would resettle in Indian Territory. When only 2,000 of 17,000 Cherokees had moved by the May 1838 deadline, President Martin Van Buren ordered General Winfield Scott to enforce the treaty. Scott's army rounded up 14,000 Cherokees (including mixed-race African Cherokees) and marched them 1,200 miles, an arduous journey that became known as the **Trail of Tears**. Along the way, 3,000 Indians died of starvation and exposure. Once in Oklahoma, the Cherokees excluded anyone of "negro or mulatto parentage" from governmental office, thereby affirming that full citizenship in their nation was racially defined. Just as the United States was a "white man's country," so Indian Territory would be a "red man's country."

Pressed by their white neighbors, the Creeks, Chickasaws, and Choctaws accepted grants of land west of the Mississippi, leaving the Seminoles in Florida as the only numerically significant Indian people remaining in the Southeast. Government pressure persuaded about half of the Seminoles to migrate to Indian Territory, but families whose ancestors had intermarried with runaway slaves feared the emphasis on "blood purity" there. During the 1840s, they fought a successful guerrilla war against the U.S. Army and retained their lands in central Florida. These Seminoles were the exception: the Jacksonians had forced the removal of most eastern Indian peoples.

Jackson's Impact

Jackson's legacy is complex. He expanded the authority of the nation's chief executive: as Jackson put it, "The President is the direct representative of the American people." Assuming that role during the nullification crisis, he upheld national authority by threatening the use of military force, laying the foundation for Lincoln's defense of the Union a generation later. At the same time (and somewhat contradictorily), Jackson curbed the reach of the national government. By undermining Henry Clay's American System of national banking, protective tariffs, and internal improvements, Jackson reinvigorated the Jeffersonian tradition of a limited and frugal central government.

The Taney Court Jackson also undermined the constitutional jurisprudence of John Marshall by appointing Roger B. Taney as his successor in 1835. During his long tenure as chief justice (1835–1864), Taney partially reversed the nationalist and vested-property-rights decisions of the Marshall Court and gave constitutional legitimacy to Jackson's policies of states' rights and free enterprise. In the landmark case *Charles River Bridge Co. v. Warren Bridge Co.* (1837), Taney declared that a legislative charter — in this case, to build and operate a toll bridge — did not necessarily bestow a monopoly, and that a legislature could charter a competing bridge to promote the general welfare: "While the rights of private property are sacredly guarded, we must not forget that the community also has rights." This decision directly challenged Marshall's interpretation of the contract clause of the Constitution in *Dartmouth College v. Woodward* (1819), which had stressed the binding nature of public charters and the sanctity of "vested rights" (Chapter 7). By limiting the property claims of existing canal and turnpike companies, Taney's decision allowed legislatures to charter competing railroads that would provide cheaper and more efficient transportation.

The Taney Court also limited Marshall's nationalistic interpretation of the commerce clause by enhancing the regulatory role of state governments. For example, in *Mayor of New York v. Miln* (1837), the Taney Court ruled that New York State could use its "police power" to inspect the health of arriving immigrants. The Court also restored to the states some of the economic powers they had exercised prior to the Constitution of 1787. In *Briscoe v. Bank of Kentucky* (1837), the justices allowed a bank owned by the state of Kentucky to issue currency, despite the wording of Article 1, Section 10 of the Constitution, which prohibits states from issuing "bills of credit."

States Revise Their Constitutions   Inspired by Jackson and Taney, Democrats in the various states mounted their own constitutional revolutions. Between 1830 and 1860, twenty states called conventions that furthered democratic principles by reapportioning state legislatures on the basis of population and giving the vote to all white men. Voters also had more power because the new documents mandated the election, rather than the appointment, of most public officials, including sheriffs, justices of the peace, and judges.

The new constitutions also embodied the principles of **classical liberalism, or laissez-faire**, by limiting the government's role in the economy. (Twenty-first-century social-welfare liberalism endorses the opposite principle: that government should intervene in economic and social life.) As president, Jackson had destroyed the American System, and his disciples now attacked the state-based Commonwealth System (see Chapter 8), which used chartered corporations and state funds to promote economic development. Most Jackson-era constitutions prohibited states from granting special charters to corporations and extending loans and credit guarantees to private businesses. "If there is any danger to be feared in . . . government," declared a New Jersey Democrat, "it is the danger of associated wealth, with special privileges." The revised constitutions also protected taxpayers by setting strict limits on state debt. Said New York reformer Michael Hoffman, "We will not trust the legislature with the power of creating indefinite mortgages on the people's property."

"The world is governed too much," the Jacksonians proclaimed as they embraced a small-government, laissez-faire outlook and celebrated the power of ordinary people to make decisions in the voting booth and the marketplace.

> **IN YOUR OWN WORDS**   What were the constitutional arguments for and against internal improvements, the tariff, and nullification?

Blackhawk   This portrait of Black Hawk (1767–1838), by George Catlin, shows the Indian leader holding his namesake, a black hawk and its feathers. When Congress approved Andrew Jackson's Indian Removal Act in 1830, Black Hawk mobilized Sauk and Fox warriors to protect their ancestral lands in Illinois. "It was here, that I was born — and here lie the bones of many friends and relatives," the aging chief declared. "I . . . never could consent to leave it." National Portrait Gallery, Smithsonian Institution, USA/Bridgeman Images.

> **COMPARE AND CONTRAST**
> How did the views of Jackson and John Marshall differ regarding the status and rights of Indian peoples?

> **EXPLAIN CONSEQUENCES**
> How did the Taney Court and the Jacksonian state constitutions alter the American legal and constitutional system?

Class, Culture, and the Second Party System

The rise of the Democracy and Jackson's tumultuous presidency sparked the creation in the mid-1830s of a second national party: the **Whigs**. For the next two decades, Whigs and Democrats competed fiercely for votes and appealed to different cultural groups. Many evangelical Protestants became Whigs, while most Catholic immigrants and traditional Protestants joined the Democrats. By debating issues of economic policy, class power, and moral reform, party politicians offered Americans a choice between competing programs and political leaders. The First Party System in United States politics, pitting Federalists against Jeffersonian Republicans, had ended with the collapse of the Federalist Party and the "era of good feeling." The Second Party System, pitting Whigs against Democrats, persisted until the Whig Party fractured in the 1850s.

The Whig Worldview

The Whig Party arose in 1834, when a group of congressmen contested Andrew Jackson's policies and his high-handed, "kinglike" conduct. They took the name *Whigs* to identify themselves with the pre-Revolutionary American and British parties—also called Whigs—that had opposed the arbitrary actions of British monarchs. The Whigs accused "King Andrew I" of violating the Constitution by creating a spoils system and undermining elected legislators, whom they saw as the true representatives of the sovereign people. One Whig accused Jackson of ruling in a manner "more absolute than that of any absolute monarchy of Europe."

Initially, the Whigs consisted of political factions with distinct points of view. However, guided by Senators Webster of Massachusetts, Clay of Kentucky, and Calhoun of South Carolina, they gradually coalesced into a party with a distinctive stance and coherent ideology. The Whigs celebrated the entrepreneur and the enterprising individual: "This is a country of self-made men," they boasted, pointing to the relative absence of permanent distinctions of class and status among white citizens. Embracing the Industrial Revolution, northern Whigs welcomed the investments of "moneyed capitalists," which provided workers with jobs and "bread, clothing and homes." Whig congressman Edward Everett championed a "holy alliance" among laborers, owners, and governments and called for a return to Henry Clay's American System. Many New England and Pennsylvania textile and iron workers shared Everett's vision because they benefitted directly from protective tariffs.

Calhoun's Dissent   Support for the Whigs in the South—less widespread than that in the North—rested on the appeal of specific policies and politicians. Some southern Whigs were wealthy planters who invested in railroads and banks or sold their cotton to New York merchants. But the majority were poorer whites who resented the power and policies of low-country planters, most of whom were Democrats.

Southern Whigs rejected their party's enthusiasm for high tariffs and social mobility, and John C. Calhoun was their spokesman. Extremely conscious of class divisions in society, Calhoun believed that northern Whigs' rhetoric of equal opportunity was contradicted not only by slavery, which he considered a fundamental American institution, but also by the wage-labor system of industrial capitalism. "There is and always has been in an advanced state of wealth and civilization a conflict between labor and capital," Calhoun declared in 1837. He urged slave owners and factory owners to unite against their common foe: the working class of enslaved blacks and propertyless whites.

Most northern Whigs denied Calhoun's class-conscious social ideology. "A clear and well-defined line between capital and labor" might fit the slave South or class-ridden Europe, Daniel Webster conceded, but in the North "this distinction grows less and less definite as commerce advances." Ignoring the ever-increasing numbers of propertyless immigrants and native-born wageworkers, Webster focused on the growing size of the middle class, whose members generally favored Whig candidates. In the election of 1834, the Whigs took control of the House of Representatives by appealing to evangelical Protestants and upwardly mobile families—prosperous farmers, small-town merchants, and skilled industrial workers in New England, New York, and the new communities along the Great Lakes.

Anti-Masons Become Whigs   Many Whig voters in 1834 had previously supported the Anti-Masons, a powerful but short-lived party that formed in the late 1820s. As its

John C. Calhoun (1782–1850) This daguerreotype, made close to the time of Calhoun's death, suggests his emotional intensity and thwarted ambition. The prime advocate of the doctrines of nullification and states' rights, a founder of the Whig Party, and a steadfast defender of slavery, Calhoun found his lifelong pursuit of the presidency frustrated by Martin Van Buren's political skills and sectional divisions over tariffs and slavery. Image courtesy of the Gibbes Museum of Art/Carolina Art Association.

name implies, Anti-Masons opposed the Order of Freemasonry. Freemasonry began in Europe as an organization of men seeking moral improvement by promoting the welfare and unity of humanity. Many Masons espoused republicanism, and the Order spread rapidly in America after the Revolution. Its ideology, mysterious symbols, and semisecret character gave the Order an air of exclusivity that attracted ambitious businessmen and political leaders, including George Washington, Henry Clay, and Andrew Jackson. In New York State alone by the mid-1820s, there were more than 20,000 Masons, organized into 450 local lodges. However, after the kidnapping and murder in 1826 of William Morgan, a New York Mason who had threatened to reveal the Order's secrets, the Freemasons fell into disrepute. Thurlow Weed, a newspaper editor in Rochester, New York, spearheaded an Anti-Masonic Party, which condemned the Order as a secret aristocratic fraternity. The new party quickly ousted Freemasons from local and state offices, and just as quickly ran out of political steam.

Because many Anti-Masons espoused temperance, equality of opportunity, and evangelical morality, they gravitated to the Whig Party. Throughout the Northeast and Midwest, Whig politicians won election by proposing legal curbs on the sale of alcohol and local ordinances that preserved Sunday as a day of worship. The Whigs also secured the votes of farmers, bankers, and shopkeepers, who favored Henry Clay's American System. For these citizens of the growing Midwest, the Whigs' program of government subsidies for roads, canals, and bridges was as important as their moral agenda.

In the election of 1836, the Whig Party faced Martin Van Buren, the architect of the Democratic Party and Jackson's handpicked successor. Like Jackson, Van Buren denounced the American System and warned that its revival would create a "consolidated government." Positioning himself as a defender of individual rights, Van Buren also condemned the efforts of Whigs and moral reformers to enact state laws imposing temperance and national laws abolishing slavery. "The government is best which governs least" became his motto in economic, cultural, and racial matters.

To oppose Van Buren, the Whigs ran four candidates, each with a strong regional reputation. They hoped to garner enough electoral votes to throw the contest into the House of Representatives. However, the Whig tally — 73 electoral votes collected by William Henry Harrison of Ohio, 26 by Hugh L. White of Tennessee, 14 by Daniel Webster of Massachusetts, and 11 by W. P. Mangum of Georgia — fell far short of Van Buren's 170 votes. Still, the four Whigs won 49 percent of the popular vote, showing that the party's message of economic and moral improvement had broad appeal.

COMPARE AND CONTRAST
How did the ideology of the Whigs differ from that of the Jacksonian Democrats?

Labor Politics and the Depression of 1837–1843

As the Democrats battled Whigs on the national level, they faced challenges from urban artisans and workers. Between 1828 and 1833, artisans and laborers in fifteen states formed Working Men's Parties. "Past experience teaches us that we have nothing to hope from the aristocratic orders of society," declared the New York Working Men's Party. It vowed "to send men of our own description, if we can, to the Legislature at Albany."

The new parties' agenda reflected the values and interests of ordinary urban workers. The Philadelphia Working Men's Party set out to secure "a just balance of power . . . between all the various classes." It called for the abolition of private banks, chartered monopolies, and debtors' prisons, and it demanded universal public education and a fair system of taxation (Thinking Like a Historian). It won some victories, electing a number of assemblymen and persuading the Pennsylvania legislature in 1834 to authorize tax-supported schools. Elsewhere, Working Men's candidates won office in many cities, but their parties' weakness in statewide contests soon took a toll. By the mid-1830s, most politically active workers had joined the Democratic Party.

The Working Men's Parties left a mixed legacy. They mobilized craft workers and gave political expression to their ideology of artisan republicanism. As labor intellectual

Becoming Literate: Public Education and Democracy

The struggle for a genuinely *democratic* polity — "government of the people, by the people, and for the people," as Lincoln put it — played out at the local and state level in battles over who should participate in the political arena. As legislators argued over extending the franchise, they considered the knowledge that citizens needed to participate responsibly in politics. Although primary education was publicly supported in most New England towns (giving that region nearly universal literacy), it received only spotty funding in the other northern states and almost none in the South (restricting literacy there to one-third of the white population). The following documents address the resulting debate over publicly supported education and citizenship.

1. **Editorial from the *Philadelphia National Gazette*, 1830.** *Pennsylvania was one of the first states to debate legislation regarding universal free public education.*

   The scheme of Universal Equal Education . . . is virtually "Agrarianism" [redistribution of land from rich to poor]. It would be a compulsory application of the means of the richer, for the direct use of the poorer classes. . . . One of the chief excitements to industry . . . is the hope of earning the means of educating their children respectably . . . that incentive would be removed, and the scheme of state and equal education be a premium for comparative idleness, to be taken out of the pockets of the laborious and conscientious.

2. **Thaddeus Stevens, speech before the Pennsylvania General Assembly, February 1835.** *Pennsylvania's Free Public School Act of 1834 was the handiwork of the Working Men's Party of Philadelphia (see p. 295). When over half of Pennsylvania's school districts refused to implement the law, the legislature threatened to repeal it. Thaddeus Stevens, later a leading antislavery advocate, turned back that threat through this speech to the Pennsylvania General Assembly.*

   It would seem to be humiliating to be under the necessity, in the nineteenth century, of entering into a formal argument to prove the utility, and to free governments, the absolute necessity of education. . . . Such necessity would be degrading to a Christian age and a free republic. If an elective republic is to endure for any great length of time, every elector must have sufficient information, not only to accumulate wealth and take care of his pecuniary concerns, but to direct wisely the Legislatures, the Ambassadors, and the Executive of the nation; for some part of all these things, some agency in

approving or disapproving of them, falls to every freeman. If, then, the permanency of our government depends upon such knowledge, it is the duty of government to see that the means of information be diffused to every citizen. This is a sufficient answer to those who deem education a private and not a public duty — who argue that they are willing to educate their own children, but not their neighbor's children.

3. **"Letter from a Teacher" in Catharine E. Beecher, *The True Remedy for the Wrongs of Women*, 1851.** *The public school movement created new opportunities not just for children of middle and lower classes but also for the young Protestant women who contributed to the "Benevolent Empire" as professional educators. Beecher's academy in Hartford, Connecticut, sent out dozens of young women to establish schools.*

   I am now located in this place, which is the county-town of a newly organized county [in a midwestern state]. . . . The Sabbath is little regarded, and is more a day for diversion than devotion. . . . My school embraces both sexes and all ages from five to seventeen, and not one can read intelligibly.

4. **"Popular Education," 1833.** *This piece appeared in the* North American Review, *the nation's first literary and cultural journal and the mouthpiece of New England's intellectual elite.*

   [T]he mind of a people, in proportion as it is educated, will not only feel its own value, but will also perceive its rights. We speak now of those palpable rights which are recognised by all free states. . . . [T]he palpable rights of men, those of personal security, of property and of the free and unembarrassed pursuit of individual welfare, it

Orestes Brownson defined their distinctive vision, "All men will be independent proprietors, working on their own capitals, on their own farms, or in their own shops." However, this emphasis on proprietorship inhibited alliances between the artisan-based Working Men's Parties and the rapidly increasing class of dependent wage earners. As Joseph Weydemeyer, a close friend of Karl Marx, reported from New York in the early 1850s, many American craft workers "are incipient bourgeois, and feel themselves to be such."

The **Panic of 1837** threw the American economy — and the workers' movement — into disarray. The panic began when the Bank of England tried to boost is obviously impossible to conceal from an educated and reading people. Such a people rises at once above the condition of feudal tenants. . . . It directs its attention to the laws and institutions that govern it. It compels public office to give an account of itself. It strips off the veil of secrecy from the machinery of power. . . . And when all this is spread abroad in newspaper details . . . of a people that can read; when the estimate is freely made, of what the government tax levies upon the daily hoard, and upon apparel, and upon every comfort of life, can it be doubted that such a people will demand and obtain an influence in affairs that so vitally concern it? This would be freedom.

5. Judge Baker, sentencing hearing in the court case against Mrs. Margaret Douglass of Norfolk, Virginia, January 10, 1854. *Southern whites considered the acquisition of literacy by blacks, whether slave or free, as a public danger, especially after the Nat Turner uprising in Southampton County, Virginia, in 1831 (Chapter 10). A Virginia court sent Mrs. Margaret Douglass to jail for a month "as an example to all others" for teaching free black children to read so they might have access to books on religion and morality.*

There are persons, I believe, in our community, opposed to the policy of the law in question. They profess to believe that universal intellectual culture is necessary to religious instruction and education, and that such culture is suitable to a state of slavery. . . .

Such opinions in the present state of our society I regard as manifestly mischievous. It is not true that our slaves cannot be taught religious and moral duty, without being able to read the Bible and use the pen. Intellectual and religious instruction often go hand in hand, but the latter may well be exist without the former; . . . among the whites one-fou[r]th or more are entirely without a knowledge of letters, [nonetheless,] respect for the law, and for moral and religious conduct and behavior, are justly and prope[r]ly appreciated and practiced. . . .

The first legislative provision upon this subject was introduced in the year 1831, immediately succeeding the bloody scenes of the memorable Southampton insurrection; and . . . was re-enacted with additional penalties in the year 1848. . . . After these several and repeated recognitions of the wisdom and propriety of the said act, it may well be said that bold and open opposition to it [must be condemned] . . . as a measure of self-preservation and protection.

6. Working Men's Party poster for immigrant voters, New York, 1830.

Source: Joshua R. Greenberg, Advocating the Man/Picture Research Consultants & Archives.

ANALYZING THE EVIDENCE

1. What arguments does the editorial in the *Philadelphia National Gazette* (source 1) advance? How does Stevens (source 2) reframe this argument?

2. What does the letter from a former student of Beecher's (source 3) tell us about the links between educational reform and other social movements, such as Sabbatarianism (p. 307)?

3. How is the argument of the author in source 4 similar to, or different from, that in sources 1 and 2?

4. How does Judge Baker (source 5) justify the denial of education to African Americans?

5. What do the occupations of the Working Men's Party candidates suggest about its definition of "worker" (source 6)?

PUTTING IT ALL TOGETHER

Using these documents and materials in this chapter, write an essay that discusses public education, responsible citizenship, and social reform in America between 1800 and 1854.

the faltering British economy by sharply curtailing the flow of money and credit to the United States. Since 1822, British manufacturers had extended credit to southern planters to expand cotton production, and British investors had purchased millions of dollars of the canal bonds from the northern states. Suddenly deprived of British funds, American planters, merchants, and canal corporations had to withdraw gold from domestic banks to pay their foreign debts. Moreover, British textile mills drastically reduced their purchases of raw cotton, causing its price to plummet from 20 cents a pound to 10 cents or less.

Hard Times The Panic of 1837 struck hard at Americans of all social ranks. This anti-Democratic cartoon shows unemployed workers turning to drink; women and children begging in the streets; and fearful depositors withdrawing funds as their banks collapse. As the plummeting hot-air balloon in the background symbolizes, the rising "Glory" of an independent America was crashing to earth. © Museum of the City of New York, USA/Bridgeman Images.

Falling cotton prices and the drain of specie to Britain set off a financial panic. On May 8, the Dry Dock Bank of New York City ran out of specie, prompting worried depositors to withdraw gold and silver coins from other banks. Within two weeks, every American bank had stopped trading specie and called in its loans, turning a financial panic into an economic crisis. "This sudden overthrow of the commercial credit" had a "stunning effect," observed Henry Fox, the British minister in Washington. "The conquest of the land by a foreign power could hardly have produced a more general sense of humiliation and grief."

To stimulate the economy, state governments increased their investments in canals and railroads. However, as governments issued (or guaranteed) more bonds to finance these ventures, they were unable to pay the interest charges, sparking a severe financial crisis on both sides of the Atlantic in 1839. Nine state governments defaulted on their debts, and hard-pressed European lenders cut the flow of new capital to the United States.

The American economy fell into a deep depression. By 1843, canal construction had dropped by 90 percent, prices and wages had fallen by 50 percent, and unemployment in seaports and industrial centers had reached 20 percent. Bumper crops drove down cotton prices, pushing hundreds of planters and merchants into bankruptcy. Minister Henry Ward Beecher described a land "filled with lamentation . . . its inhabitants wandering like bereaved citizens among the ruins of an earthquake, mourning for children, for houses crushed, and property buried forever."

By creating a surplus of unemployed workers, the depression finished off the union movement and the Working Men's Parties. In 1837, six thousand masons, carpenters, and other building-trades workers lost their jobs in New York City, destroying their unions' bargaining power. By 1843, most local unions, all the national labor organizations, and all the workers' parties had disappeared.

IDENTIFY CAUSES
What factors led to the demise of the Anti-Masonic and Working Men's political parties?

"Tippecanoe and Tyler Too!"

Many Americans blamed the Democrats for the depression of 1837–1843. They criticized Jackson for destroying the Second Bank and directing the Treasury Department in 1836 to issue the **Specie Circular**, an executive order that required the Treasury Department to accept only gold and silver in payment for lands in the national domain. Critics charged—mistakenly—that the Circular drained so much specie from the economy that it sparked the Panic of 1837.

The public turned its anger on Van Buren, who took office just before the panic struck. Ignoring the pleas of influential bankers, the new president refused to revoke the Specie Circular or take actions to stimulate the economy. Holding to his philosophy of limited government, Van Buren advised Congress that "the less government interferes with private pursuits the better for the general prosperity." As the depression deepened in 1839, this laissez-faire outlook commanded less and less political support. Worse, Van Buren's major piece of fiscal legislation, the Independent Treasury Act of 1840, delayed recovery by pulling federal specie out of Jackson's pet banks (where it had backed loans) and placing it in government vaults, where it had little economic impact.

The Log Cabin Campaign   The Whigs exploited Van Buren's weakness. In 1840, they organized their first national convention and nominated William Henry Harrison of Ohio for president and John Tyler of Virginia for vice president. A military hero of the Battle of Tippecanoe and the War of 1812, Harrison was well advanced in age (sixty-eight) and had little political experience. However, the Whig leaders in Congress, Henry Clay and Daniel Webster, wanted a president who would rubber-stamp their program for protective tariffs and a national bank. An unpretentious, amiable man, Harrison told voters that Whig policies were "the only means, under Heaven, by which a poor industrious man may become a rich man without bowing to colossal wealth."

The depression stacked the political cards against Van Buren, but the election turned as much on style as on substance. It became the great "log cabin campaign"—the first time two well-organized parties competed for votes through a new style of campaigning. Whig songfests, parades, and mass meetings drew new voters into politics. Whig speakers assailed "Martin Van Ruin" as a manipulative politician with aristocratic tastes—a devotee of fancy wines, elegant clothes, and polite refinement, as indeed he was. Less truthfully, they portrayed Harrison as a self-made man who lived contentedly in a log cabin and quaffed hard cider, a drink of the common people. In fact, Harrison's father was a wealthy Virginia planter who had signed the Declaration of Independence, and Harrison himself lived in a series of elegant mansions.

The Whigs boosted their electoral hopes by welcoming women to campaign festivities—a "first" for American politics. Many Jacksonian Democrats had long embraced an ideology of aggressive manhood, likening politically minded females to "public" women, prostitutes who plied their trade in theaters and other public places. Whigs took a more restrained view of masculinity and recognized that Christian women had already entered American public life through the temperance movement and other benevolent activities. In October 1840, Daniel Webster celebrated moral reform to an audience of twelve hundred women and urged them to back Whig candidates. "This way of making politicians of their women is something new under the sun," exclaimed one Democrat, worried that it would bring more Whig men to the polls. And it did: more than 80 percent of the eligible male voters cast ballots in 1840, up from

Harrison's Log Cabin and Cider Campaign   To boost the chances that William Henry Harrison would be elected president in 1840, Whig political strategists promoted him as the "log cabin and hard cider" candidate, in contrast to the aristocratic Martin Van Buren. On this patriotic cotton banner, Harrison, coming out the door of his cabin in shirtsleeves, greets a veteran who has lost a leg in service to his country. A third man bends down before a keg of hard cider, presumably intending to offer the visitor a drink. Despite Harrison's well-to-do background—the son of a prominent Virginia slaveowner, he had served as territorial governor of Indiana and in both the House and the Senate—the campaign presented him as a simple Ohio farmer. The populist appeal of the Whig campaign was misleading, but it succeeded in elevating Harrison to the White House. © Collection of the New-York Historical Society, USA/Bridgeman Images.

CONSIDER POINTS OF VIEW
How did Whigs and Democrats view women in politics, and why did they hold those views?

fewer than 60 percent in 1832 and 1836 (see Figure 9.1, p. 283). Heeding the Whigs' campaign slogan "Tippecanoe and Tyler Too," they voted Harrison into the White House with 53 percent of the popular vote and gave the party a majority in Congress.

Tyler Subverts the Whig Agenda   Led by Clay and Webster, the Whigs in Congress prepared to reverse the Jacksonian revolution. Their hopes were short-lived; barely a month after his inauguration in 1841, Harrison died of pneumonia, and the nation got "Tyler Too." But in what capacity: as acting president or as president? The Constitution was vague on the issue. Ignoring his Whig associates in Congress, who wanted a weak chief executive, Tyler took the presidential oath of office and declared his intention to govern as he pleased. As it turned out, that would not be like a Whig.

Tyler had served in the House and the Senate as a Jeffersonian Democrat, firmly committed to slavery and states' rights. He had joined the Whigs only to protest Jackson's stance against nullification. On economic issues, Tyler shared Jackson's hostility to the Second Bank and the American System. He therefore vetoed Whig bills that would have raised tariffs and created a new national bank. Outraged by this betrayal, most of Tyler's cabinet resigned in 1842, and the Whigs expelled Tyler from their party. "His Accidency," as he was called by his critics, was now a president without a party.

The split between Tyler and the Whigs allowed the Democrats to regroup. The party vigorously recruited small farmers in the North, smallholding planters in the South, and former members of the Working Men's Parties in the cities. It also won support among Irish and German Catholic immigrants — whose numbers had increased during the 1830s — by backing their demands for religious and cultural liberty, such as the freedom to drink beer and whiskey. A pattern of ethnocultural politics, as historians refer to the practice of voting along ethnic and religious lines, now became a prominent feature of American life. Thanks to these urban and rural recruits, the Democrats remained the majority party in most parts of the nation. Their program of equal rights, states' rights, and cultural liberty was attractive to more white Americans than the Whig platform of economic nationalism, moral reform, temperance laws, and individual mobility.

IN YOUR OWN WORDS   What principles united the Whig Party, and why did the Tyler presidency fail to fulfill its leaders' wishes?

SUMMARY

In this chapter, we examined the causes and the consequences of the democratic political revolution. We saw that the expansion of the franchise weakened the political system run by notables of high status and encouraged the transfer of power to professional politicians — men like Martin Van Buren, who were mostly of middle-class origin.

We also witnessed a revolution in government policy, as Andrew Jackson and his Democratic Party dismantled the mercantilist economic system of government-supported economic development. On the national level, Jackson destroyed Henry Clay's American System; on the state level, Democrats wrote new constitutions that ended the Commonwealth System of government charters and subsidies to private businesses. Jackson's treatment of Native Americans was equally revolutionary; the Removal Act of 1830 forcefully resettled eastern Indian peoples west of the Mississippi River, opening their ancestral lands to white settlement.

Finally, we watched the emergence of the Second Party System. Following the split in the Republican Party during the election of 1824, two new parties — the Democrats and the Whigs — developed on the national level and eventually absorbed the members of the Anti-Masonic and Working Men's Parties. The new party system established universal suffrage for white men and a mode of representative government that was responsive to ordinary citizens. In their scope and significance, these political innovations matched the economic advances of both the Industrial Revolution and the Market Revolution.

TERMS TO KNOW

Identify and explain the significance of each term below.

Key Concepts and Events

franchise (p. 274)

notables (p. 274)

political machine (p. 276)

spoils system (p. 277)

caucus (p. 277)

demographic transition (p. 278)

republican motherhood (p. 278)

American Colonization Society (p. 280)

Missouri Compromise (p. 281)

American System (p. 281)

internal improvements (p. 282)

corrupt bargain (p. 282)

Tariff of Abominations (p. 283)

nullification (p. 286)

states' rights (p. 286)

Second Bank of the United States (p. 286)

Indian Removal Act of 1830 (p. 291)

Trail of Tears (p. 292)

classical liberalism, or laissez-faire (p. 293)

Whigs (p. 293)

Panic of 1837 (p. 296)

Specie Circular (p. 299)

Key People

Martin Van Buren (p. 276)

Mary Wollstonecraft (p. 278)

Richard Allen (p. 280)

John Quincy Adams (p. 281)

Henry Clay (p. 281)

Andrew Jackson (p. 281)

John C. Calhoun (p. 281)

Roger B. Taney (p. 285)

John Tyler (p. 299)

REVIEW QUESTIONS

Answer these questions to demonstrate your understanding of the chapter's main ideas.

1. How did Jackson and the new Democratic Party overcome sectional differences?

2. What were the constitutional arguments for and against internal improvements, the tariff, and nullification?

3. What principles united the Whig Party, and why did the Tyler presidency fail to fulfill its leaders' wishes?

4. Review the events listed under "Politics and Power" on the thematic timeline on page 236. As the timeline indicates, the Working Men's and Anti-Masonic Parties rose and declined between 1827 and 1834, and then the Whig Party emerged. How do you explain the timing of these events?

MAKING CONNECTIONS

Recognize the larger developments and continuities within and across chapters by answering these questions.

1. The chapter argues that a democratic revolution swept America in the decades after 1820 and uprooted the old system of politics. After reviewing the discussions of politics in Chapters 6 and 7, explain how party systems and political alignments changed over time and then assess the strength of this argument.

2. Look again at the cartoon depictions of Andrew Jackson, as King Andrew (p. 287) and the Great Father (p. 292). What point of view does each cartoonist support, and how effective are the cartoons in championing that view? How are today's negative political advertisements on television similar or different?

KEY TURNING POINTS

Refer to the chapter chronology on page 274 for help in answering the question below.

Based on the events in the chronology (and your reading of this chapter), which five-year period brought more significant changes to American political and economic life: 1829–1833, Andrew Jackson's first term as president, or 1837–1842, the years of panic and depression? Explain and defend your choice.

Religion, Reform, and Culture
1820–1848

CHAPTER

IDENTIFY THE BIG IDEA

What changes and conflicts emerged as Americans developed a national culture?

Amid a wild thunderstorm in the summer of 1830, an African American seamstress in Philadelphia woke to hear God speaking. "I rose up and walked the floor wringing my hands and crying under great fear," Rebecca Cox Jackson wrote later. She prayed for hours, plunged in "the chamber of death." Suddenly she felt ecstasy: "my spirit was light, my heart filled with love for God and all mankind. . . . I ran downstairs and opened the door to let the lightning in the house, for it was like sheets of glory to my soul." God had told her, Jackson believed, that sexual relations caused sin: she should leave her husband. Sharing this news with her astonished spouse, Jackson was reportedly so full of spiritual power that she placed her hands on a hot stove over and over and removed them unhurt.

Jackson left home and became a traveling preacher. In upstate New York she discovered the communal movement of Shakers, or United Society of Believers in Christ's Second Appearing, whose popular nickname came from their ecstatic dances in worship. Like Jackson, Shakers practiced sexual abstinence. They also recognized women as religious and community leaders. Inspired by visions of a "mother spirit," Jackson returned to Philadelphia and built her own African American Shaker community, which endured for decades after her death in 1871.

Like Rebecca Cox Jackson, many Americans of the 1830s and 1840s discovered new identities and callings. Influenced by the era's economic and political transformations, they believed they could perfect their lives and society as a whole. Mainstream reformers, especially in the emerging northeastern middle class, advocated church attendance and a strict moral code. Their efforts were driven in part by growing fears of disorder, as they watched the rise of urban saloons, prostitution, and a boisterous working-class street culture. Soon, more radical reformers promoted a bewildering assortment of ideas: rejection of church institutions, common ownership of property, immediate emancipation of slaves, and sexual equality. These activists challenged social hierarchies and provoked horrified opposition. As one fearful southerner argued, radicals favored a world with "No-Marriage, No-Religion, No-Private Property, No-Law and No-Government."

Such fears were not exaggerated. Rapid economic growth and geographical expansion had weakened traditional institutions, forcing individuals to fend for themselves. In 1835, Alexis de Tocqueville coined the word *individualism* to describe the result. Native-born white Americans were "no longer attached to each other by any tie of caste, class, association, or family," the French aristocrat lamented, and so lived in social isolation. But while Tocqueville mourned the loss of social ties, Americans built new movements for community, worship, and reform.

Great American Revivals   As shown in this painting of an 1819 Methodist camp meeting, the Second Great Awakening attracted large crowds of men, women, and children to revivals in outdoor venues. In the South, many African Americans also attended. In an atmosphere of intense excitement, some people (like the man in the foreground) were helped by friends and family members after being overcome with awareness of their sins and the spiritual power of redemption and grace. The tents in the background show that participants camped for the duration of the meeting as preaching, prayer, and conversions continued for several days. Library of Congress.

CHAPTER CHRONOLOGY

As you read, ask yourself why this chapter begins and ends with these dates and identify the links among related events.

1816	▶ African Methodist Episcopal Church founded		**1836**	▶ House of Representatives adopts gag rule barring antislavery petitions
1821	▶ Emma Willard founds Troy Female Seminary for young women		**1837**	▶ Horace Mann begins public school expansion in Massachusetts
1823	▶ Charles Grandison Finney begins Protestant revival campaigns			▶ Grimké sisters defend public roles for women
				▶ Abolitionist Elijah Lovejoy killed by a mob in Illinois
1827	▶ *Freedom's Journal,* first African American newspaper, published in New York		**1839–1845**	▶ First wave of married women's property laws
1829	▶ Violence drives over a thousand African Americans out of Cincinnati		**1840**	▶ Liberty Party first runs James G. Birney for president
	▶ David Walker's *Appeal . . . to the Colored Citizens of the World*		**1840s**	▶ Fourierist communities arise in Midwest
1830	▶ Joseph Smith publishes *The Book of Mormon*		**1841**	▶ Dorothea Dix promotes hospitals for mentally ill
1830s	▶ Emergence of minstrel shows			▶ Catharine Beecher publishes *Treatise on Domestic Economy*
	▶ Peak membership of Shaker communities		**1844**	▶ Margaret Fuller publishes *Woman in the Nineteenth Century*
1831	▶ William Lloyd Garrison founds *The Liberator*		**1845**	▶ Henry David Thoreau goes to Walden Pond
	▶ Nat Turner's uprising in Virginia		**1846**	▶ Brigham Young leads Mormons to Salt Lake
1832	▶ Ralph Waldo Emerson turns to transcendentalism		**1848**	▶ Seneca Falls Convention proposes women's equality
	▶ American Temperance Society founded			▶ John Humphrey Noyes establishes cooperative experiment at Oneida
	▶ Charles Knowlton publishes first American birth control guide		**1851**	▶ Herman Melville publishes *Moby-Dick*
1833	▶ American Anti-Slavery Society founded		**1855**	▶ Dr. William Sanger surveys sex trade in New York City
1834	▶ New York activists create Female Moral Reform Society			▶ Walt Whitman publishes *Leaves of Grass*
1835	▶ James Gordon Bennett founds *New York Herald*			
	▶ Abolitionists launch great postal campaign			

Spiritual Awakenings

At the time of the American Revolution, every state except Pennsylvania and Rhode Island had a legally established church that claimed everyone as a member and collected compulsory religious taxes. In the years that followed, the combined pressure of Enlightenment principles and religious dissent eliminated most state support for religion and allowed voluntary church membership. Americans in large numbers joined evangelical Methodist and Baptist churches that preached spiritual equality and developed egalitarian cultures marked by communal singing and emotional services.

From the 1790s through the 1830s, the country experienced powerful waves of religious revival. One of the largest frontier camp meetings, at Cane Ridge in Kentucky in 1801, lasted for nine electrifying days and attracted almost 20,000 people. Similar religious excitement swept all regions of the country. Known to historians as the **Second Great Awakening**, this upheaval stimulated an array of long-lasting reform movements. By the time the Awakening subsided, New England intellectuals led by Ralph Waldo Emerson were developing a radical individualist theology known as transcendentalism. Other spiritual seekers, like Rebecca Cox Jackson, joined utopian communities to remake the world.

The Second Great Awakening

In the South, evangelical religion was initially a disruptive force because many ministers spoke of spiritual equality and criticized slavery. Husbands and planters grew angry when wives became more assertive and blacks joined evangelical congregations. To retain white men in their churches, Methodist and Baptist preachers gradually adapted their religious message to justify the authority of yeomen patriarchs and slave-owning planters. Man was naturally at "the head of the woman," declared one Baptist minister, while a Methodist conference told Christian slaves to be "submissive, faithful, and obedient." African Americans, both free and enslaved, developed a theology of their own (see Chapter 11).

The Second Great Awakening in the North

Many New Englanders rejected Calvinists' emphasis on human depravity and celebrated reason and free will. A new sect of Universalists, who preached universal salvation, gained tens of thousands of converts. Congregationalists discarded the concept of the Trinity—Father, Son, and Holy Spirit—and, taking the name *Unitarians*, emphasized reason. "The ultimate reliance of a human being is, and must be, on his own mind," argued William Ellery Channing, a famous Unitarian minister. A children's catechism conveyed the denomination's optimistic message: "If I am good, God will love me, and make me happy." Reflecting this optimism, ministers and popular writers linked individual salvation to religious benevolence. The mark of a true church, declared Christian social reformer Lydia Maria Child, is when members' "heads and hearts unite in working for the welfare of the human race."

African American Worship in the South After the 1831 revolt led by enslaved preacher Nat Turner, few southern African Americans were permitted to worship by themselves without whites' presence and supervision. In this rare sketch of a South Carolina church service, published in London in 1863, the plantation owners preside over the meeting, sharing the religious message while also making sure that the preacher's words don't challenge the hierarchies of slavery. Hulton Archive/Getty Images.

By the 1820s, many Protestant Christians embraced that goal. Unlike the First Great Awakening, which split churches into warring factions, the second fostered cooperation among denominations. Between 1815 and 1826, religious leaders founded five interdenominational societies: the American Education Society, Bible Society, Sunday School Union, Tract Society, and Home Missionary Society. Based in northeastern cities, these societies dispatched hundreds of missionaries to the West and distributed thousands of Bibles and religious pamphlets.

One of the Awakening's most successful leaders was Presbyterian minister Charles Grandison Finney. Born into a poor farming family in Connecticut, Finney planned to become a lawyer before he underwent an intense religious experience in 1823 and chose the ministry. Beginning in towns along the Erie Canal, the young minister conducted emotional revival meetings. Finney's central message was that "God has made man a moral free agent" who could choose salvation. This doctrine of free will was particularly attractive to members of the new middle class, who emphasized self-discipline, sought to improve their material condition, and welcomed Finney's assurance that heaven was also in their grasp.

Finney's greatest triumph came in 1830, when he moved his revivals to Rochester, New York, a new commercial city on the Erie Canal. Preaching every day for six months and promoting group prayer in family homes, Finney converted influential merchants and manufacturers of Rochester. They promised to attend church, give up intoxicating beverages, and work hard. To encourage their employees to do the same, wealthy businessmen founded a Free Presbyterian Church—"free" because members did not have to pay for pew space. Other evangelicals founded churches to serve transient canal laborers, while pious businessmen set up a savings bank to encourage thrift among workers. Finney's wife, Lydia, and other middle-class women carried the evangelical message to the wives of the unconverted, set up Sunday schools for poor children, and formed the Female Charitable Society to assist the unemployed.

Finney's efforts were not completely successful. Skilled workers in strong craft organizations—boot makers, carpenters, stonemasons, and boatbuilders—protested that they needed higher wages and better schools more urgently than sermons and prayers. Most poor people ignored Finney's revival, as did Irish Catholic immigrants, many of whom hated Protestants as religious heretics and political oppressors.

Nonetheless, revivalists from New England to the Midwest copied Finney's message and techniques. In New York City, wealthy silk merchants Arthur and Lewis Tappan founded the *Journal of Commerce* to promote business enterprise while advocating Finney's evangelical and reform ideas. Revivals swept through Pennsylvania, North Carolina, Tennessee, and Indiana, where, a convert reported, "you could not go upon the street and hear any conversation, except upon religion." The success of the revivals "has been so general and thorough," concluded a Presbyterian general assembly, "that the whole customs of society have changed."

EXPLAIN CONSEQUENCES
What was Charles Finney's central message, and how did it change the "customs of society"?

The Benevolent Empire   The reform impulse sweeping through Protestant denominations found fertile ground in America's growing cities. Members of the rising middle classes wanted to save the world; they also wanted safe cities and a disciplined workforce (Interpretations). By the 1820s, led by Congregational and Presbyterian ministers, upwardly mobile reformers created a network of organizations that historians call the **Benevolent Empire**. Their goal was to restore "the moral government of God" by reducing consumption of alcohol and other vices that they believed resulted in poverty. Reform-minded individuals had regulated their own behavior; now they tried to control the lives of working people — by persuasion if possible, by law if necessary.

The Benevolent Empire targeted age-old evils such as drunkenness, adultery, prostitution, and crime, but its methods were new. Instead of relying on church sermons, reformers created large-scale organizations such as the Prison Discipline Society and the General Union for Promoting the Observance of the Christian Sabbath. Each organization had a managing staff, a network of hundreds of chapters, thousands of volunteer members, and a newspaper. Often acting in concert, these groups encouraged people to exercise self-control and acquire "regular habits." They persuaded local governments to ban public carnivals of drink and dancing, such as Negro Election Day (festivities in which African Americans symbolically took control of the government), which had been enjoyed by whites as well as blacks. Reformers created homes for abandoned children and asylums for the insane, who previously had often been confined by their families in attics and cellars.

Temperance advocates built the most successful movement. Beer and rum had long been a standard part of American holidays and everyday life. Grogshops dotted almost every block in working-class districts and became centers of disorder. During the 1820s and 1830s, alcohol consumption reached new heights, even among the elite; alcoholism, for example, killed Daniel Tompkins, vice president under James Monroe. Heavy drinking was devastating for wage earners, who could ill afford its costs. Though Methodist artisans and ambitious craftsmen swore off liquor to protect their skills, health, and finances, other workers drank heavily on the job — and not just during the traditional 11 a.m. and 4 p.m. "refreshers." A baker recalled how "one man was stationed at the window to watch, while the rest drank."

The evangelical Protestants who took over the American Temperance Society in 1832 set out to curb consumption of alcohol. The society grew quickly to two thousand chapters and more than 200,000 members. Its campaigns relied on revivalist methods — group confession and prayer, and using women as

Taking the "Cold Water" Pledge   This 1841 pledge sheet, published in Philadelphia, illustrates the interlinked appeals of domesticity and temperance. As the man on the right signs a pledge to abstain from all liquor, his wife and adoring child look on with satisfaction. Signed copies of such illustrated pledges, celebrating family bonds and women's influence, hung in the parlors of many homes to remind husbands and fathers of their temperance promise. The men on the left, however, show that control over the antebellum movement against the "liquor evil" lay squarely in the hands of men. Library of Congress.

Historians identify an early-nineteenth-century Market Revolution (Chapter 8) that changed the ways people worked, lived, and related to one another. Manufacturing shifted work from household to factory. Workers no longer lived within the households of their employers and were less influenced by them. European romanticism and expanded democratic participation encouraged individualism. Importantly, an evangelical movement of religious revivals also cast doubt on older Calvinist ideas of predestination, giving hope to believers that they and their communities could achieve Christ-like perfection.

What Motivated Antebellum Reformers?

For the large group of antebellum reformers who participated in missionary, temperance, health, Sabbath protection, and education movements—as well as smaller groups struggling for abolitionism and women's rights—these changes created problems and opportunities. With society changing rapidly and new problems arising, what could be done to make it better? Historians, including Paul E. Johnson and Steven Mintz, have debated the factors motivating antebellum reformers. Were these reformers asserting control in areas where they felt they had lost power and influence, or were they inspired by the chance to perfect humans and society?

PAUL E. JOHNSON

Source: Paul E. Johnson, *A Shopkeeper's Millennium: Society and Revivals in Rochester, New York, 1815–1837* (New York: Hill and Wang, 1978), 138.

Evangelicalism was a middle-class solution to problems . . . generated in the early stages of manufacturing. Revivals provided entrepreneurs with a means of imposing new standards of work discipline and personal comportment upon themselves and the men who worked for them, and thus they functioned as powerful social controls. . . . A significant minority of workingmen participated willingly in that process. And that, of course, is the most total and effective social control of all.

STEVEN MINTZ

Source: Steven Mintz, *Moralists & Modernizers: America's Pre-Civil War Reformers* (Baltimore: Johns Hopkins University Press, 1995), xiv.

[A] growing number of Americans believed that the only way to stabilize the social order was to internalize self-restraints within the depths of individual character through religion and moral reform. But the roots of reform did not lie exclusively in fear and anxiety. Reform also arose out of a millennialist sense of possibilities that was both secular and religious in its origins. . . . [A] new "middle-class" reform gospel . . . sought simultaneously to free individuals from various forms of bondage; to eradicate such "relics of barbarism" as chattel slavery and corporal punishment; and to create a sober, educated, self-disciplined citizenry.

QUESTIONS FOR ANALYSIS

1. How does each historian describe the motivations of antebellum reformers?
2. How do these historians differ in their understanding of evangelicalism's role in antebellum reform?
3. How does this chapter's discussion of the economic transformation help you to understand why both historians put the middle class at the center of antebellum reform efforts?

---

spiritual guides—and were a stunning success (Analyzing Voices). On one day in New York City in 1841, more than 4,000 people took the temperance pledge. Annual consumption of spirits fell dramatically, from an average of 5 gallons per person in 1830 to 2 gallons in 1845.

Despite this trend, temperance advocates were frustrated that thousands of Americans—especially working-class men—refused to join the cause. By the early 1850s they turned from the goal of individual persuasion toward prohibition—laws to forbid the manufacture and sale of alcohol. In 1851, the Maine legislature passed a statute outlawing sale of alcoholic beverages in the state. The Maine Supreme Court upheld the statute, arguing that the legislature had the "right to regulate by law the sale of any article, the use of which would be detrimental of the morals of the people." The success of this **Maine Law** shaped the reformers' goals for decades to come (Chapter 17).

Saving the Nation from Drink

The temperance crusade was the most successful antebellum reform movement. It mobilized more than a million supporters in all sections of the nation and significantly lowered the consumption of alcoholic beverages. Nonetheless, like other reform efforts, the antidrinking crusade divided over questions of strategy and tactics. The following passages, taken from the writings of leading temperance advocates, show that some reformers favored legal regulation while others preferred persuasion and voluntary abstinence.

LYMAN BEECHER
"Intemperance Is the Sin of Our Land"

A leading Protestant minister and spokesman for the Benevolent Empire, Lyman Beecher regarded drunkenness as a sin. His *Six Sermons on . . . Intemperance* (1829) condemned the recklessness of working-class drunkards and called on responsible members of the middle class to lead the way to a temperate society.

❝ Intemperance is the sin of our land, and, with our boundless prosperity, is coming in upon us like a flood; and if anything shall defeat the hopes of the world, which hang upon our experiment of civil liberty, it is that river of fire. . . .

In every city and town the poor-tax, created chiefly by intemperance, is [increasing the burden on taxpaying citizens]. . . . The frequency of going upon the town [relying on public welfare] has taken away the reluctance of pride, and destroyed the motives to providence which the fear of poverty and suffering once supplied. The prospect of a destitute old age, or of a suffering family, no longer troubles the vicious portion of our community. They drink up their daily earnings, and bless God for the poorhouse, and begin to look upon it as, of right, the drunkard's home. . . . Every intemperate and idle man, whom you behold tottering about the streets and steeping himself at the stores, regards your houses and lands as pledged to take care of him, puts his hands deep, annually, into your pockets. . . .

What then is this universal, natural, and national remedy for intemperance? IT IS THE BANISHMENT OF ARDENT SPIRITS FROM THE LIST OF LAWFUL ARTICLES OF COMMERCE, BY A CORRECT AND EFFICIENT PUBLIC SENTIMENT; SUCH AS HAS TURNED SLAVERY OUT OF HALF OUR LAND, AND WILL YET EXPEL IT FROM THE WORLD.

We are not therefore to come down in wrath upon the distillers, and importers, and venders of ardent spirits. None of us are enough without sin to cast the first stone. . . . It is the buyers who have created the demand for ardent spirits, and made distillation and importation a gainful traffic. . . . Let the temperate cease to buy — and the demand for ardent spirits will fall in the market three fourths, and ultimately will fail wholly. . . .

This however cannot be done effectually so long as the traffic in ardent spirits is regarded as lawful, and is patronized by men of reputation and moral worth in every part of the land. Like slavery, it must be regarded as sinful, impolitic, and dishonorable. That no measures will avail short of rendering ardent spirits a contraband of trade, is nearly self-evident. ❞

ABRAHAM LINCOLN
"A New Class of Champions"

In Baltimore in 1840, a group of reformed alcoholics formed the Washington Temperance Society, which turned the antidrinking movement in a new direction. By talking publicly about their personal experiences of alcoholic decline and spiritual recovery, they inspired thousands to "sign the pledge" of total abstinence. (Its philosophy exists today in the organization Alcoholics Anonymous.) In 1842, Lincoln, an ambitious lawyer and Illinois legislator who did not drink, praised such "moral suasion" in an address to the Washingtonians of Springfield, Illinois.

❝ Although the temperance cause has been in progress for near twenty years, it is apparent to all that it is just now being crowned with a degree of success hitherto unparalleled. The

---

Temperance met resistance among workers who enjoyed their "refreshers" and Sunday beer. Even more controversial was Sabbatarianism, a movement to require business closings on the Christian Sabbath. As the Market Revolution spread, merchants and storekeepers conducted business on Sundays. Sabbatarians pressured state legislatures to halt such practices and urged Congress to repeal an 1810 law allowing mail to be transported — though not delivered — on Sundays. Members boycotted shipping companies that did business on the Sabbath and campaigned for municipal laws forbidding games and festivals on the Lord's day.

Provoking opposition from workers and freethinkers, these efforts had limited success. Men who labored twelve to fourteen hours a day, six days a week, wanted the freedom to spend their one day of leisure as they wished. To keep goods moving, shipping company managers demanded that the Erie Canal provide lockkeepers on list of its friends is daily swelled by the additions of fifties, of hundreds, and of thousands.

The warfare heretofore waged against the demon intemperance has somehow or other been erroneous. . . . [Its] champions for the most part have been preachers [such as Beecher], lawyers, and hired agents. Between these and the mass of mankind there is a want of approachability. . . .

But when one who has long been known as a victim of intemperance bursts the fetters that have bound him, and appears before his neighbors 'clothed and in his right mind,' . . . to tell of the miseries once endured, now to be endured no more . . . there is a logic and an eloquence in it that few with human feelings can resist. . . .

In my judgment, it is to the battles of this new class of champions that our late success is greatly, perhaps chiefly, owing. . . . [Previously,] too much denunciation against dram-sellers and dram-drinkers was indulged in. This I think was both impolitic and unjust. . . . When the dram-seller and drinker were incessantly [condemned] . . . as moral pestilences . . . they were slow [to] . . . join the ranks of their denouncers in a hue and cry against themselves.

By the Washingtonians this system of consigning the habitual drunkard to hopeless ruin is repudiated. . . . They teach hope to all — despair to none. As applying to their cause, they deny the doctrine of unpardonable sin. . . .

If the relative grandeur of revolutions shall be estimated by the great amount of human misery they alleviate, and the small amount they inflict, then indeed will this be the grandest the world shall ever have seen. Of our political revolution of '76 we are all justly proud. It has given us a degree of political freedom far exceeding that of any other nation of the earth. . . . But, with all these glorious results, past, present, and to come, [this freedom] had its evils too. It [was abused by drunken husbands and thereby] breathed forth famine, swam in blood, and rode in fire; and long, long after, the orphan's cry and the widow's wail continued to break the sad silence that ensued. These were the price, the inevitable price, paid for the blessings it brought. . . .

Turn now to the temperance revolution. In it we shall find a stronger bondage broken, a viler slavery manumitted, a greater tyrant deposed; in it, more of want supplied, more disease healed, more sorrow assuaged. By it no orphans starving, no widows weeping.

Glorious consummation! Hail, fall of fury! Reign of reason, all hail! 99

AMERICAN TEMPERANCE MAGAZINE
"You Shall Not Sell"

The *American Temperance Magazine*, like other antiliquor advocates, moved beyond the goal of moral suasion to work for legal prohibition of alcohol. Here the editor explains why.

SOURCE: David Brion Davis, *Antebellum American Culture: An Interpretive Anthology* (University Park: Pennsylvania State University Press, 1997), 395–398, 403–409.

66 This is a utilitarian age. The speculative has in all things yielded to the practical. Words are mere noise unless they are things [and result in action].

In this sense, moral suasion is moral balderdash. 'Words, my lord, words' . . . are a delusion. . . . The drunkard's mental and physical condition pronounces them an absurdity. He is ever in one or other extreme — under the excitement of drink, or in a state of morbid collapse. . . . Reason with a man when all reason has fled, and it is doubtful whether he or you is the greater fool. . . . Moral suasion! Bah!

Place this man we have been describing out of the reach of temptation. He will have time to ponder. His mind and frame recover their native vigor. The public-house does not beset his path. . . . Thus, and thus only, will reformation and temperance be secured. And how is this accomplished? Never except through the instrumentality of the law. If it were possible to reason the drunkard into sobriety, it would not be possible to make the rumseller forego his filthy gains. Try your moral suasion on him. . . . The only logic he will comprehend, is some such ordinance as this, coming to him in the shape and with the voice of law — you shall not sell. 99

QUESTIONS FOR ANALYSIS

1. What does Lincoln's address suggest about his general political philosophy?
2. Compare Beecher's position to Lincoln's. In what ways are they similar? How are they different?
3. What positions do these selections take with respect to the appropriate role of government in regulating morality and personal behavior?

Sundays. Using laws to enforce a particular set of moral beliefs, they said, was "contrary to the free spirit of our institutions."

Ralph Waldo Emerson and Transcendentalism

Influential New England philosopher Ralph Waldo Emerson ranged far beyond benevolent reform. He celebrated the overthrow of old hierarchies and the spiritual power of individuals, influencing thousands of ordinary Americans and a generation of writers in the **American Renaissance**, a mid-nineteenth-century flourishing of literature and philosophy. Its roots lay with Unitarian ministers from well-to-do New England families who questioned the constraints of their Puritan heritage. For inspiration, they turned to European **romanticism**, a new conception of self and society. Romantic

IDENTIFY CAUSES
What was the Benevolent Empire, and why did it emerge at this historical moment?

The Founder of Transcendentalism
As this painting of Ralph Waldo Emerson by an unknown artist indicates, the young philosopher was an attractive man, his face brimming with confidence and optimism. With his radiant personality and incisive intellect, Emerson deeply influenced dozens of influential writers, artists, and scholars and enjoyed great success as a lecturer to the emerging middle class. Stock Montage/Getty Images.

thinkers, such as German philosopher Immanuel Kant and English poet Samuel Taylor Coleridge, rejected the ordered, rational world of the eighteenth-century Enlightenment. They embraced human passion and sought deeper insight into the mysteries of existence. Through spiritual quest and self-knowledge, young Unitarians believed, each individual could experience the infinite and eternal.

Emerson's Individualism. As a Unitarian, Emerson already stood outside the mainstream of American Protestantism. In 1832, Emerson took a more radical step by resigning his Boston pulpit and rejecting organized religion. He moved to Concord, Massachusetts, and wrote influential essays probing what he called "the infinitude of the private man," the radically free person. In doing so, Emerson was launching the intellectual movement of **transcendentalism**. He argued that people needed to shake off inherited customs and institutions and discover their "original relation with Nature," in order to enter a mystical union with the "currents of Universal Being."

Transcendentalists' message of self-realization reached hundreds of thousands of people through Emerson's writings and lectures. Beginning in 1826, the lyceum movement — modeled on the public forum of the ancient Greek philosopher Aristotle — arranged speaking tours by poets, preachers, scientists, and reformers. The lyceum became an important cultural institution in the North and Midwest, though not in the South, where the middle class was smaller and popular education had a lower priority. Emerson became the most popular speaker in America, eventually delivering fifteen hundred lectures in more than three hundred towns in twenty states.

Emerson's individualistic ethos spoke to the experiences of many middle-class Americans, who had left family farms to make their way in the urban world. His pantheistic, nature-centered view of God encouraged Unitarians in Boston to create Mount Auburn Cemetery, a beautiful landscape with burial markers for the dead of all faiths. Despite his own rejection of organized religion, Emerson's optimism also inspired many Protestant leaders of the Second Great Awakening, such as Finney, who urged believers to reject old doctrines and seek direct experiences of God's power.

Thoreau, Fuller, and Whitman New England intellectual Henry David Thoreau heeded Emerson's call to seek inspiration from the natural world. In 1845, depressed by his beloved brother's death, Thoreau built a cabin near Walden Pond in Concord, Massachusetts, and lived alone there for two years. In 1854, he published *Walden, or Life in the Woods*, an account of his search for meaning beyond the artificiality of civilized society:

> I went to the woods because I wished to live deliberately, to front only the essential facts of life, and see if I could not learn what it had to teach, and not, when I came to die, discover that I had not lived.

Walden's most famous metaphor provides an enduring justification for independent thinking: "If a man does not keep pace with his companions, perhaps it is because he hears a different drummer." Beginning from this premise, Thoreau urged readers to avoid unthinking conformity and peacefully resist unjust laws.

As Thoreau sought self-realization for men, Margaret Fuller explored the possibilities of freedom for women. Born into a wealthy Boston family, Fuller mastered six languages and read broadly. Embracing Emerson's ideas, she started a transcendental discussion group for educated Boston women in 1839. While editing *The Dial*, the leading transcendentalist journal, Fuller also published *Woman in the Nineteenth Century* (1844). In it, Fuller endorsed the transcendental principle that all people could develop a life-affirming mystical relationship with God. Every woman therefore deserved psychological and social independence: the ability "to grow, as an intellect to discern, as a soul to live freely and unimpeded." She also called for equality in education and work: "We would have every arbitrary barrier thrown down [and] every path laid open to Woman as freely as to Man." Fuller traveled to Italy to report on the Revolution of 1848,

To see a longer excerpt of *Woman in the Nineteenth Century*, along with other primary sources from this period, see *Sources for America's History*.

only to drown in a shipwreck on her way home to the United States. Her life and writings inspired a rising generation of women writers and reformers.

Emerson issued a declaration of literary independence, urging American authors to reject European influences and find inspiration in everyday life: "the ballad in the street; the news of the boat; the glance of the eye; the form and gait of the body." No one responded to that call more vibrantly than poet Walt Whitman. While working as a printer, teacher, journalist, and publicist for the Democratic Party, Whitman recalled that he had been "simmering, simmering"; Emerson "brought me to a boil." Poetry was the "direction of his dreams." In *Leaves of Grass*, a collection of wild, exuberant poems first published in 1855 and constantly revised and expanded, Whitman recorded in verse his efforts to transcend various "invisible boundaries": between solitude and community, between prose and poetry, even between the living and the dead. At the center of *Leaves of Grass* is the individual: "I celebrate myself, and sing myself." Through his Emersonian "original relation" with nature, Whitman claims perfect communion with others: "Every atom belonging to me as good belongs to you." For Emerson, Thoreau, and Fuller, the individual had a divine spark; for Whitman, America's collective democracy assumed a sacred character.

Margaret Fuller, 1848 At the age of thirty-eight, American transcendentalist author Margaret Fuller moved to Italy, where she reported on the Revolution of 1848 for the *New York Tribune*. There she fell in love with Thomas Hicks (1823–1890), a much younger American artist. Hicks rebuffed Fuller's romantic advances but painted this flattering portrait, softening her features and giving her a pensive look. Fuller took as a lover a petty noble and republican revolutionary, Giovanni Angelo, Marchese d'Ossoli, and gave birth to a son in September 1848. Two years later, the entire family died in a shipwreck while en route to the United States. Niday Picture Library/Alamy Stock Photo.

Limits of Transcendentalism Like many others, transcendentalists worried that the new market society—focused on work, profits, and consumption—was debasing Americans' spiritual lives. "Things are in the saddle," Emerson wrote, "and ride mankind." Seeking to revive intellectual life, transcendentalists created communal experiments. The most important was Brook Farm, just outside Boston, where Emerson, Thoreau, and Fuller were residents or frequent visitors. Members recalled that they "inspired the young with a passion for study, and the middle-aged with deference and admiration." But Brook Farm was an economic failure. The residents planned to produce their own food and exchange surplus milk, vegetables, and hay for manufactures. However, most members had few farming skills; only cash from affluent residents kept the enterprise afloat for five years. After a devastating fire in 1846, the community disbanded and sold the farm. With this failure, transcendentalists abandoned their quest for new social institutions. They accepted the emerging commercial order but tried to reform it, especially through the education of workers and the movement to abolish slavery.

In the meantime, Emerson's writings influenced two great novelists, Nathaniel Hawthorne and Herman Melville, with more pessimistic worldviews. Both sounded powerful warnings about the dangers of individualism when it became unfettered egoism. The main characters of Hawthorne's novel *The Scarlet Letter* (1850), Hester Prynne and Arthur Dimmesdale, blatantly challenge their seventeenth-century New England community by committing adultery and producing a child. Their decision to ignore social restraints results not in liberation but in degradation: a profound sense of guilt and condemnation by the community.

Melville explored the limits of individualism in even more extreme and tragic terms and became a scathing critic of transcendentalism. His most powerful work, *Moby-Dick* (1851), tells the story of Captain Ahab's obsessive hunt for a mysterious white whale, which ends in the destruction of Ahab and almost his entire crew. Here, the quest for spiritual meaning in nature brings death, not transcendence, because Ahab lacks discipline and self-restraint. *Moby-Dick* was a commercial failure. Middle-class readers who devoured sentimental American fiction refused to follow Melville into the dark, dangerous realm of individualism gone mad. They emphatically preferred the optimistic views of Emerson or Finney.

CONSIDER POINTS OF VIEW
What were the main principles of transcendentalism, and how did they differ from the beliefs of most Protestant Christians?

MAP 10.1 Major Communal Experiments Before 1860
Some experimental communities settled along the frontier, but the vast majority chose rural areas in settled regions of the North and Midwest. Because they opposed slavery, communalists usually avoided the South. Most secular experiments failed within a few decades, as conflicts arose within the communities, or as founders lost their reformist enthusiasm or died off; some tightly knit religious communities, such as the Shakers and the Mormons, were longer-lived.

Utopian Experiments

Like the founders of Brook Farm, thousands of less affluent Americans rejected life in America's emerging market society and sought to create ideal communities, or **utopias**, in rural parts of the Northeast and Midwest (Map 10.1). They hoped to build models for different ways of living. Many rural communalists were farmers and artisans seeking refuge from the economic depression of 1837–1843. Others were religious idealists. By advocating common ownership of property (socialism) and unconventional forms of family life, communalists challenged traditional property rights and gender roles.

The first successful American communal movement was the one that attracted Rebecca Cox Jackson: Shakerism. In 1770, Ann Lee Stanley (Mother Ann Lee), a young cook in Manchester, England, had a vision that she was an incarnation of Christ. Four years later, she led a few disciples to America and established a church near Albany, New York. After her death in 1784, her followers formed disciplined religious communities. Members embraced common ownership of property; accepted strict oversight by church leaders; and pledged to abstain from alcohol, tobacco, politics, and war. Shakers' repudiation of sexual pleasure and marriage followed Mother Ann's teaching that "lustful gratifications of the flesh" were "the foundation of human corruption." Holding that God was "a dual person, male and female," Shakers placed community governance in the hands of both women and men — Elderesses and Elders.

Shakers founded twenty communities, mostly in New England, New York, and Ohio. Their agriculture and crafts, especially furniture making, acquired a reputation for quality that made them self-sustaining and even comfortable. Because the Shakers disdained sexual intercourse, they relied on conversions and the adoption of thousands of young orphans to increase their numbers. During the 1830s, three thousand adults, mostly women, joined the Shakers, attracted by their communal intimacy and sexual equality. However, as the Benevolent Empire expanded public and private orphanages during the 1840s and 1850s, Shaker communities began to decline and, by 1900, virtually disappeared.

Other Americans championed the ideas of French reformer Charles Fourier, who devised an eight-stage theory of social evolution that predicted the imminent decline of individual property rights and capitalism, through the creation of cooperative communities whose members shared work and property. Fourier's leading disciple in America, Albert Brisbane, argued that **Fourierist socialism** would liberate workers from low wages and servitude to capitalist employers. Fourierists also called for "associated households" in which both sexes shared domestic labor, emancipating women from "slavish domestic duties."

Following the Panic of 1837, Fourierism found a receptive audience among educated farmers and craftsmen who yearned for economic stability and communal solidarity. In the 1840s, Fourierists started nearly one hundred cooperative communities,

Shakers at Prayer Most Americans viewed the Shakers with a mixture of fascination and suspicion. They feared the sect's radical aspects, such as a commitment to celibacy and communal property, and considered the Shakers' dancing more an invitation to debauchery than a form of prayer. Those apprehensions surface in this engraving, *The Shakers of New Lebanon* (New York), which expresses both the powerful intensity and the collective character of this Shaker spiritual ritual. The work of the journalist-engraver Joseph Becker, the picture appeared in Frank Leslie's *Illustrated Newspaper* in 1873. Bettmann/Getty Images.

mostly in western New York and the Midwest. Members worked in cooperative groups and owned property in common, including stores, banks, schools, and libraries. Most communities quickly collapsed as members fought over work responsibilities and social policies. Fourierism's rapid decline revealed the difficulty of maintaining a utopian community in the absence of a charismatic leader or a compelling religious vision.

John Humphrey Noyes ascribed the Fourierists' failure to their secular outlook and praised Shakers as the true "pioneers of modern Socialism." Noyes was a well-to-do graduate of Dartmouth College who joined the ministry after hearing a sermon by Charles Grandison Finney. Dismissed as a pastor for holding unorthodox beliefs, Noyes turned to perfectionism, an evangelical Protestant movement of the 1830s that attracted thousands of New Englanders who had migrated to New York and Ohio. Perfectionists believed Christ had already returned to earth (the Second Coming) and therefore people could aspire to sinless perfection. Unlike most perfectionists, who lived conventional personal lives, Noyes rejected marriage. But instead of Shaker-style celibacy, Noyes embraced "complex marriage," in which all members of the community married one another. He rejected monogamy partly to free women from their status as the property of their husbands.

In 1839, Noyes set up a perfectionist community near his hometown of Putney, Vermont. Local outrage, however, forced Noyes to relocate in 1848 to an isolated site near Oneida, New York. To give women time and energy to participate fully in community affairs, Noyes urged them to avoid multiple pregnancies. He instructed men to help by avoiding orgasm during intercourse. Less positively, he encouraged sexual relations at a very early age and used his position of power to manipulate the sexual lives of his followers. Eventually dissenters reported on such practices to outsiders. When Noyes fled to Canada in 1879 to avoid prosecution for adultery, the community abandoned complex marriage but remained a successful cooperative silverware venture until the mid-twentieth century.

The historical significance of the Shaker, Fourierist, and Oneida projects does not lie in their numbers, which were small, or in their fine crafts. Rather, it stems from their radical questioning of traditional sexual norms and of the capitalist values and class divisions of the emerging market society. Their utopian communities stood as countercultural blueprints for a more egalitarian social and economic order.

Joseph Smith and Mormonism   The era's most successful religious utopian movement emerged, like several others, from religious ferment among families of Puritan descent who lived along the Erie Canal — heirs to religious beliefs in supernatural powers and visions of the divine. The founder of Mormonism, Joseph Smith, was born in Vermont to a poor farming and shop-keeping family who migrated to Palmyra in central New York. In 1820, Smith began to have religious experiences: "A pillar of light above the brightness of the sun at noonday came down from above and rested upon me and I was filled with the spirit of God." Smith believed God had singled him out for special revelations. In 1830, he published *The Book of Mormon*, which he claimed to have translated from ancient hieroglyphics on gold plates shown to him by an angel

BURNING OF MORMON TEMPLE AT NAUVOO.

The Burning of Nauvoo Temple   After the lynching of founding prophet Joseph Smith in 1844, and facing ongoing hostility and violence, Mormons were forced to flee Nauvoo, Illinois. Most fled to Utah in 1846 under the leadership of Brigham Young. They left behind not only homes and businesses but also the 53,000-square-foot Nauvoo Temple, built over six years at an immense price in building materials and human labor. With no ready non-Mormon buyers, church leaders were forced to sell the Temple for $500, a tiny fraction of the cost. On the night of October 8–9, 1848, as shown in this dramatic lithograph, arsonists burned the temple to the ground. Everett Collection.

UNDERSTAND CAUSES
Name three communal utopias of the 1830s and 1840s. Who joined each group and why?

named Moroni. *The Book of Mormon* told the story of ancient Jews from the Middle East who had migrated to the Western Hemisphere and were visited by Jesus Christ soon after his Resurrection. Smith's account explained the presence of Native peoples in the Americas and integrated the New World into the Judeo-Christian tradition.

Smith organized the **Church of Jesus Christ of Latter-day Saints, or Mormons**. Seeing himself as a prophet in a sinful, excessively individualistic society, he emphasized the family as the heart of religious and social life. Like many Protestants, Smith encouraged practices that led to individual success in the age of capitalist markets and factories: frugality, hard work, and enterprise. But Smith also stressed communal discipline. His goal was a church-directed society that would restore primitive Christianity and encourage moral perfection.

Constantly harassed by violent threats, Smith struggled to find a secure place to settle. At one point he identified Jackson County in Missouri as the site of the "City of Zion," and his followers began to move there. But they met extreme hostility: Mormons were "enemies of mankind and ought to be destroyed," said one cleric, and Missouri's governor agreed, issuing an order for Mormons to be "exterminated or driven out." Smith and his growing congregation eventually settled in Nauvoo, Illinois, a town they founded on the Mississippi River. By the early 1840s Nauvoo had 30,000 residents. Mormons' prosperity and their secret rituals and rigid discipline — including bloc voting in Illinois elections — fueled resentment among their neighbors. Antagonism increased when Smith asked Congress to make Nauvoo a separate federal territory and declared himself a candidate for president of the United States.

In secret, Smith also preached a new revelation justifying polygamy, the practice of a man having multiple wives. Smith pointed to biblical precedent for this practice of patriarchal or **plural marriage**. The revelation caused some of Smith's followers to break with him; when word got out, polygamy enraged church enemies. In 1844, Illinois officials arrested Smith and charged him with treason for allegedly conspiring to create a Mormon colony in Mexican territory. An anti-Mormon mob stormed the jail in Carthage, Illinois, where Smith and his brother Hyrum were being held and murdered them.

Some Mormons who rejected polygamy remained in the Midwest, led by Smith's son, Joseph Smith III. About 6,500 Mormons, however, fled the United States under the guidance of Brigham Young, Smith's leading disciple. Beginning in 1846, they crossed the Great Plains into Mexican territory and settled the Great Salt Lake Valley in present-day Utah (Map 10.2). Using cooperative labor and an irrigation system based on communal water rights, Mormon pioneers quickly built successful agricultural communities.

MAP 10.2 The Mormon Trek, 1830–1848
Because of their unorthodox religious views and communal solidarity, Mormons faced hostility first in New York and then in Missouri and Illinois. After the murder of church founder Joseph Smith in 1844, Brigham Young led the majority of Latter-day Saints from Illinois westward to Omaha, Nebraska. From Omaha the migrants followed the path of the Oregon Trail to Fort Bridger and then struck off to the southwest to settle in the basin of the Great Salt Lake, along the Wasatch Range in what is now Utah. At the time, this land was part of northern Mexico and was occupied by Utes, Paiutes, and Shoshones. The United States's victory in the U.S.-Mexico War (Chapter 11) turned Deseret into U.S. territory only two years later.

> **IN YOUR OWN WORDS** To what extent did antebellum intellectual and religious movements draw on the values of individualism, on the one hand, and of communal cooperation, on the other?

> **COMPARE AND CONTRAST**
> In what ways was Mormonism similar to, and different from, other utopian movements of the era?

Urban Cultures and Conflicts

As utopians organized communities in the countryside, rural migrants and foreign immigrants plunged into the exciting and risky world of the growing cities. In 1800, American cities had been overgrown towns: New York had only 60,000 residents; Philadelphia, 41,000. Then urban growth accelerated as a huge in-migration outweighed the high death rates that persisted for city dwellers (especially infants and children). By 1850, New York's population had ballooned to over half a million. Five other cities — Baltimore, Boston, Philadelphia, New Orleans, and Cincinnati — had more than 100,000 each. In the Northeast, by this time, the arrival of thousands of desperate immigrants fleeing the Irish famine (Chapter 12) made the working class seem even more alien and threatening. Cities generated new cultural practices that drew newcomers while also scandalizing middle-class reformers.

Sex in the City

Thousands of young men and women flocked to the city searching for adventure and fortune, but many found only a hard life. Young men labored for meager wages building tenements, warehouses, and workshops. Others worked as low-paid clerks or operatives in mercantile and manufacturing firms. Young women had an even harder time. Thousands toiled as live-in domestic servants, ordered about by the mistress of the household and often sexually exploited by the master. Others scraped out a bare living as needlewomen in New York City's booming ready-made clothes industry. Unwilling to endure domestic service or subsistence wages, many young girls turned to prostitution. Dr. William Sanger's careful survey, commissioned in 1855 by worried city officials, found that six thousand women engaged in commercial sex. Three-fifths were native-born whites; the rest were foreign immigrants; most were between fifteen and twenty years old. Half were or had been domestic servants, half had children, and half were infected with syphilis.

Commercialized sex — and sex in general — became one of the allures of urban life for men. "Sporting men" boasted of their sexual conquests in racy journals like *Flash*. Otherwise respectable husbands kept mistresses in handy apartments, and working men frequented bawdy houses. New York City had two hundred brothels in the 1820s and five hundred by the 1850s. Prostitutes — so-called public women — openly advertised their wares on Broadway, the city's most fashionable thoroughfare, and welcomed clients on the infamous third tier of theaters. Many men considered illicit sex a right. "Man is endowed by nature with passions that must be gratified," declared *Sporting Whip*. Even Reverend William Berrian, pastor of the ultra-respectable Trinity Episcopal Church, admitted from the pulpit that he had resorted ten times to "a house of ill-fame."

Not all urban sex was commercial. Freed from family oversight, men formed homoerotic relationships; as early as 1800, the homosexual "fop" was an acknowledged character in Philadelphia. Heterosexual young people moved from partner to partner until they chanced on an ideal mate. Middle-class youth strolled Broadway in the latest fashions: elaborate bonnets and silk dresses for young women; flowing capes, leather boots, and silver-plated walking sticks for young men. Rivaling the elegance on Broadway were the colorful costumes of the working-class Bowery, the broad avenue that ran along the east side of lower Manhattan. By day, Bowery Boys worked as apprentices or journeymen. By night, they prowled the streets as "dandies," hair cropped at the back of the head "as close as scissors could cut," with long front locks "matted by a lavish application of *bear's grease*, the ends tucked under so as to form a roll and brushed until they shone like glass bottles." The "B'hoy," as he was called, cut a dashing figure as he walked along with a "Bowery Gal" in a bright dress and shawl. To some shocked observers, however, such couples represented disorder and disrespect for middle-class values of respectability and piety.

Popular Fiction and the Penny Press

Fostered by high literacy rates and advances in technology, publishing became one of the American city's most lucrative industries. By 1850 the United States had over six hundred magazines in publication. Boston and Philadelphia specialized in religious devotionals, sentimental and reform literature, and magazines for the growing middle class. Most Protestant denominations communicated with followers through monthly publications, as did homeopathic doctors, leaders of the Sunday School movement, and temperance advocates. For affluent women, *Godey's Lady's Book* depicted the latest Paris fashions and offered uplifting stories, poems, and advice on wifely and motherly duties. By publishing novels in serial form, magazines became an important springboard for popular fiction. America's expanding print culture also provided a forum for newly arrived groups to assert their American identities. Jewish authors included poet Penina Moïse of Charleston,

A Violent Death Imagined in the Penny Press This cover of an 1843 New York almanac shows the commercial appeal of the sensational case of Mary Rogers, who is depicted here being abducted and thrown over a cliff by two sinister gentlemen. After it was discovered that Rogers, whose body was found floating in the East River, had likely died of a botched abortion, sympathy turned against the former "cigar girl." Even as the narrative of her death changed, her fate continued to suggest the risks of sexual danger and violence that faced young women in the growing cities. © Collection of the New-York Historical Society, USA/Bridgeman Images.

South Carolina, and Reform Rabbi Isaac Mayer Wise, editor of *The Israelite* and author of historical novels such as *The Jewish Heroine* (1855).

Print culture helped Americans navigate the chaotic, unstable world of the market economy. Advice books told aspiring young men how to dress and comport themselves and how to recognize deception and fraud. Other guidebooks counseled women and men on how to choose marriage partners and manage their domestic lives, by limiting family size, for example, to provide more nurture and education for each child. Despite repeated indictments for "obscenity," Massachusetts physician Charles Knowlton sold thousands of copies of *The Fruits of Philosophy* (1832), the first American guide to contraceptive practices.

Knowlton's sales were modest, however, in comparison with urban newspapers, which won huge audiences as the cost of printing fell and entrepreneurs developed new models for marketing and delivery. By the 1830s, young boys in New York hawked daily newspapers on the streets; four major **penny papers** had a combined circulation of 50,000, reaching many more readers as copies passed from hand to hand in tenements, workshops, and saloons. Within two years of its first issue in 1835, the *New York Herald* was selling 11,500 copies a day, the largest circulation of any American newspaper.

The *Herald*'s editor was colorful and controversial James Gordon Bennett, a brilliant businessman adept at attracting advertising revenue. Bennett pitched his paper to "the great masses of the community — the merchant, mechanic, working people — the private family as well as the public hotel — the journeyman and his employer." Unabashedly racist and strongly proslavery, Bennett won loyalty through his ardent support for building an "Empire in the West." The *Herald* also featured gossip, exposés, and above all, lurid and sensational accounts of violent crime, often falsified for dramatic effect. Disgusted, Walt Whitman denounced Bennett as a "reptile marking his path with slime wherever he goes.... A midnight ghoul, preying on rottenness and repulsive filth." Undeterred, Bennett built the *Herald* into a political force that exerted national influence by the time of the Civil War.

Fascinated by the urban underworld of crime, author Edgar Allan Poe drew on such sensational journalism to develop a new genre of popular fiction. Deserted by his father and orphaned at age three, Poe had a tumultuous relationship with the Richmond, Virginia, family who adopted him. He found a position at *The Southern Literary Messenger* before moving north to edit a series of gentlemen's magazines in Philadelphia and New York, quarreling all the time with owners and coworkers. Disdaining those who wrote for small literary audiences, Poe sought to represent and reach what he called "the popular mind." Despite his tormented career and early death from complications of alcoholism, Poe's dark stories of supernatural terror and secret crime, like "The Murders in the Rue Morgue," helped establish the genres of mystery and detective fiction.

Urban Entertainments

City pastimes extended far beyond the printed page. In New York, working men could partake of traditional rural blood sports — rat and terrier fights, boxing matches — at Sportsmen's Hall, or they could seek drink and fun in billiard and bowling saloons. Other workers crowded the pit of the Bowery Theatre to see the "Mad Tragedian," Junius Brutus Booth, perform Shakespeare's *Richard III*.

Rampant Racism Minstrel shows and their music were just two facets of the racist culture of mid-nineteenth-century America. Exploiting the market for almanacs among farmers and city folk alike, the publishing firm of Fisher and Brother produced the *Black Joke Al-Ma-Nig* for 1852. Like other almanacs, it provided astrological charts, weather predictions, and a detailed calendar of events. Such racist caricatures of black faces and language influenced white views of African Americans well into the twentieth century. Courtesy: The Library Company of Philadelphia, www .librarycompany.org.

Dance and Social Identity in Antebellum America

Styles of dance and attitudes toward them tell us a great deal about cultural and social norms. When nineteenth-century Americans took to partying, their dances — regardless of the class or ethnic identity of the dancers — focused more on individual couples and allowed more room for improvisation and intimacy than the dance forms of the previous century.

1. **William Sidney Mount, *Rustic Dance After a Sleigh Ride*, 1830.** *In the eighteenth century, wealthy, fashionable Americans danced the French minuet, a ceremonious and graceful dance in which couples executed prescribed steps while barely touching. Ordinary white folks preferred the country dances brought by their ancestors from Europe, which also involved intricate steps, line formations, and limited physical contact. Mount (1807–1868) was self-taught, lived in rural Long Island, and depicted scenes of everyday life. This painting, replete with amorous pursuits, depicts a traditional contra dance in which the lead couple advances a few steps and then sashays to the back of the line, as another couple takes its place.*

Source: Museum of Fine Arts, Boston, Massachusetts, USA/Bequest of Martha C. Karolik for the M. and M. Karolik Collection of American Paintings, 1815–1865/Bridgeman Images.

2. **"The Polka Fashions," from *Godey's Lady's Book*, 1845.** *"A magazine of elegant literature," according to its publisher, Louis A. Godey, the* Lady's Book *was the most widely circulated American periodical prior to the Civil War and an arbiter of good taste among the aspiring middle classes. Each issue contained a sheet of music for the latest dance craze. The* Lady's Book *cautiously endorsed the waltz, a sensuous dance that required a close embrace, but enthusiastically welcomed its cousin, the polka, whose lively tempo and rapid spinning had a wholesome and joyful quality. Introduced from Bohemia, the polka dominated the ballrooms of America's upper and middle classes in the 1840s and 1850s.*

Source: Private Collection/Bridgeman Images.

3. **George Templeton Strong, diary entry, December 23, 1845.**

Well, last night I spent at Mrs. Mary Jones's great ball. Very splendid affair — "the Ball of the Season." . . . Two houses open, standing supper table, "dazzling array of beauty and fashion." "Polka" for the first time brought under my inspection. It's a kind of insane Tartar jig performed to disagreeable music of an uncivilized character.

Reform-minded couples enjoyed evenings at the huge Broadway Tabernacle, where they could hear an abolitionist lecture or see the renowned Hutchinson Family Singers lead a roof-raising rendition of their antislavery anthem, "Get Off the Track." Families could visit the museum of oddities (and hoaxes) created by P. T. Barnum, the great cultural entrepreneur and founder of Barnum & Bailey Circus.

The most popular theatrical entertainments were **minstrel shows**, which featured white actors in blackface presenting comic routines that combined racist caricature and social criticism. Minstrelsy began around 1830, when a few actors put on blackface and

4. **Description of juba dancing from Charles Dickens, *American Notes for General Circulation*, 1842.** *In New York's Five Points slum in 1842, Charles Dickens described a challenge dance featuring William Henry Lane, or Master Juba, a young African American who created juba dancing, a blend of Irish jig and African dance moves.*

The corpulent black fiddler, and his friend who plays the tambourine, stamp upon the boarding of the small raised orchestra in which they sit, and play a lively measure. Five or six couples come upon the floor, marshalled by a lively young negro, who is the wit of the assembly, and the greatest dancer known. . . . Instantly the fiddler grins, and goes at it tooth and nail; there is new energy in the tambourine. . . . Single shuffle, double shuffle, cut and cross-cut; snapping his fingers, rolling his eyes, turning in his knees, presenting the backs of his legs in front, spinning about on his toes and heels like nothing but the man's fingers on the tambourine; dancing with two left legs, two right legs, two wooden legs, two wire legs, two spring legs — all sorts of legs and no legs — . . . having danced his partner off her feet, and himself too, he finishes by leaping gloriously on the bar-counter, and calling for something to drink.

5. **Poster advertising Barlow, Wilson, Primrose, and West's "Mammoth Minstrels' Colored Masquerade."** *Unlike slavery, minstrelsy survived the Civil War and remained popular until the early twentieth century, when it evolved into vaudeville.*

Barlow, Wilson, Primrose, and West's Mammoth Minstrels toured the United States, Europe, and Australia between 1877 and 1882, thrilling audiences with the clog dances that had devolved out of juba.

SOURCES: (3) Luther S. Harris, *Around Washington Square: An Illustrated History of Greenwich Village* (Baltimore, 2003), 41; (4) Charles Dickens, *American Notes and Pictures from Italy* (C. Scribner: New York, 1868), 107.

ANALYZING THE EVIDENCE

1. What do sources 1 and 2 suggest about sexual manners among rural folk and genteel urbanites?

2. What does the polka (sources 3 and 4) reveal about changing cultural practices among the social elite?

3. Compare the juba and minstrelsy dances described above (sources 4 and 5) with the polka and contra dance forms (sources 1 and 2). How do each of the images reflect broader social developments?

4. The waltz, polka, and juba dances were popular during the Second Great Awakening, when (and long after) preachers often complained that "dance is destructive to Christian life." Why might ministers (and priests) take such a view?

PUTTING IT ALL TOGETHER

Using the material on class, religion, and culture in Chapters 9 and 11, and the insights you have gathered by a careful inspection of these sources, write an essay showing how dance and other entertainments reflect or reveal differences among American social groups.

SOURCE: Private Collection/Photo © Barbara Singer/Bridgeman Images.

performed song-and-dance routines (Thinking Like a Historian). The most famous was John Dartmouth Rice, whose "Jim Crow" blended a shuffle-dance-and-jump with unintelligible lyrics delivered in "Negro dialect." By the 1840s hundreds of minstrel troupes toured the country. Minstrel players used African musical instruments, including banjos and castanets.

At least one traveling group, Gavitt's Original Ethiopian Serenaders, was actually composed of black musicians. But in the vast majority of shows, white performers used rambling lyrics and vicious stereotypes to depict African Americans as lazy, sensual, and

Paul Cuffee The life of merchant Paul Cuffee (1759–1817) illustrates how African Americans who achieved business success could use their newfound prosperity for community building and political activism. Born in Massachusetts, Cuffee was the son of a freed slave and a Wampanoag Indian woman. Like his parents and nine brothers and sisters, he was a devout Quaker. Cuffee became a boatbuilder and trader along the Massachusetts coast. After working on a whaling ship, he captained a blockade-running vessel during the American Revolution and spent several months in a British prison in New York. By the 1810s Cuffee had built a transatlantic merchant fleet crewed by black and Indian sailors. One of the wealthiest men of color in the United States, Cuffee built an interracial school for his children and those of white, black, and Native American neighbors. He also helped persuade the Massachusetts legislature to grant voting rights to black men. Library of Congress.

irresponsible. Minstrel singers simultaneously criticized white society: their songs ridiculed the alleged drunkenness of Irishmen, parodied the halting English of German immigrants, denounced women's demands for political rights, and mocked the arrogance of upper-class men. Still, minstrelsy declared white supremacy most of all. The racial stereotypes of minstrelsy — which can be traced up through the era of radio and television and beyond — had an immense and enduring impact on American popular culture.

> **IN YOUR OWN WORDS** What new working-class cultural practices emerged in large antebellum cities, and why?

African Americans and the Struggle for Freedom

Between 1820 and 1840, in northern states that abolished slavery, free African American communities found their political voice. Chief among their goals was abolition of slavery. By the 1830s they began to work with white allies, who like other reformers drew on the religious enthusiasm of the Second Great Awakening. After the American Revolution, white antislavery activists had assailed human bondage as contrary to republicanism and liberty, but most had called for gradual emancipation with compensation to slave owners. Three decades later, white and black abolitionists built the nation's first interracial movement for justice, demanding immediate, uncompensated emancipation: an uncompromising stance that met with fierce denunciations and violence.

Free Black Communities, North and South

The free black population in the slave states lived primarily in coastal cities — Mobile, Memphis, New Orleans — and in the Upper South. Partly because skilled Europeans avoided the South, free blacks formed the backbone of the urban artisan workforce, laboring as carpenters, blacksmiths, barbers, butchers, and shopkeepers. Whatever their skills, free blacks faced many dangers. White officials often denied jury trials to free blacks accused of crimes; sometimes they forced people charged with vagrancy back into slavery. Some free blacks were simply kidnapped and sold.

Seeking opportunity and protection, some free blacks distanced themselves from plantation slaves and assimilated white culture and values. Indeed, mixed-race individuals sometimes joined the planter class. David Barland, one of twelve children born to a white Mississippi planter and his black slave Elizabeth, himself owned no fewer than eighteen slaves. But such men and women were rare. Most free African Americans identified with the great mass of slaves, some of whom were their relatives. Calls by white planters in the 1840s to re-enslave free African Americans reinforced black unity.

Almost half of free blacks in the United States in 1840 (some 170,000) lived in the free states of the North. However, few enjoyed unfettered freedom. In rural areas, blacks worked as farm laborers or tenant farmers; in towns and cities, they toiled as domestic servants, laundresses, or day laborers. Only a small number owned land. "You do not see one out of a hundred . . . that can make a comfortable living, own a cow, or a horse," a traveler in New Jersey noted. In most states, law or custom prohibited northern blacks from voting or attending public schools. They could testify in court against whites only in Massachusetts. The federal government did not allow African Americans to work for the postal service, claim public lands, or hold a passport. Furthermore, the Fugitive Slave Law (1793) allowed owners and hired slave catchers to seize suspected runaways and return them to bondage. As black activist Martin Delaney remarked in 1852: "We are slaves in the midst of freedom."

Of the few African Americans able to make full use of their talents, several achieved great distinction. Mathematician and surveyor Benjamin Banneker published an almanac and helped lay out the new capital in the District of Columbia; Joshua Johnston won praise for his portraiture. More impressive and enduring were the community institutions created by free blacks. Throughout the North, largely unknown men and women founded schools, mutual-benefit organizations, and fellowship groups, often called **Free African Societies**. Discriminated against by white Protestants, they formed their own congregations and a new religious denomination — the **African Methodist Episcopal Church**. Founded in 1816, it spread across the Northeast and Midwest and even founded a few congregations in the slave states of Missouri, Kentucky, Louisiana, and South Carolina.

Leading African Americans in the North advocated a strategy of social uplift, encouraging free blacks to "elevate" themselves through education, temperance, and hard work. By securing "respectability," they argued, blacks could become the social equals of whites. To promote that goal, black businessmen and ministers founded an array of churches, schools, and self-help associations. Capping this effort, John Russwurm and Samuel D. Cornish of New York published the first African American newspaper, *Freedom's Journal*, in 1827.

> **COMPARE AND CONTRAST**
> How were the lives of free African Americans different in the northern and southern states?

The Rise of Abolitionism

Free blacks' quest for respectability elicited a violent response in Boston, Pittsburgh, and other northern cities among whites who refused to accept African Americans as social equals. Motivated by racial contempt, white mobs terrorized black communities. White workers in northern towns laid waste to taverns and brothels where blacks and whites mixed and vandalized African American churches, temperance halls, and orphanages.

Responding to such attacks, David Walker published a stirring pamphlet, *An Appeal . . . to the Colored Citizens of the World* (1829), protesting black "wretchedness in this Republican Land of Liberty!!!!!" Walker was a free black from North Carolina who had moved to Boston, where he sold secondhand clothes and copies of *Freedom's Journal.* Self-educated, Walker ridiculed the religious pretensions of slaveholders and in biblical language warned of a slave revolt if justice were delayed. "We must and shall be free," he told white Americans. "And woe, woe, will be it to you if we have to obtain our freedom by fighting." Walker's call represented a radical challenge to the beliefs of white citizens, both North and South, including those who led the American Colonization Society (Chapter 9). Walker's *Appeal* quickly went through three printings and, carried by black merchant seamen, reached free African Americans in the South.

Nat Turner's Revolt While David Walker called for a violent rebellion, Nat Turner, a slave in Southampton County, Virginia, staged one — a chronological coincidence that had far-reaching consequences. As a child, Turner had taught himself to read and hoped for emancipation, but one master forced him into the fields, while another separated him from his wife. Becoming deeply spiritual, Turner had a religious vision in which "the Spirit" explained that "Christ had laid down the yoke he had borne for the sins of men, and that I should take it on and fight against the Serpent,

A Call for Revolution David Walker, who ran a used clothing shop in Boston, spent his hard-earned savings to publish *An Appeal . . . to the Colored Citizens of the World* (1829), a learned and passionate attack on racial slavery. Walker depicted Christ as an avenging "God of justice and of armies" and raised the banner of slave rebellion. A year later, a passerby found Walker in the doorway of his shop, dead from unknown causes. Library of Congress.

for the time was fast approaching when the first should be last and the last should be first." In August 1831, Turner and a group of relatives and friends rose in rebellion and killed at least 55 white men, women, and children. Turner, apparently seeking to seize weapons from a nearby armory and take up a defensive position in the Great Dismal Swamp, hoped hundreds of slaves would rally to his cause, but he mustered only 60. The white militia quickly dispersed his poorly armed force and took their revenge. One company of cavalry killed 40 blacks in two days. They put 15 of the severed heads on poles to warn "all those who should undertake a similar plot." Turner died by hanging, still identifying his mission with that of his Savior. "Was not Christ crucified?" he asked.

Turner's Rebellion sowed terror across the South. For a brief moment, the American Colonization Society became wildly popular as Americans debated remedies for the violence inherent in the slave system. Deeply shaken, Virginia's legislature debated a law providing for gradual emancipation and colonization abroad. When the bill failed by a vote of 73 to 58, the possibility that southern planters would voluntarily end slavery ended forever. Instead, the southern states toughened their slave codes, limited black movement, banned independent slave preaching, and prohibited anyone from teaching slaves to read. Blaming northern "agitation," they met Walker's radical *Appeal* with radical measures of their own.

The American Anti-Slavery Society Rejecting Turner's and Walker's strategy of armed rebellion, a cadre of northern white Protestants launched a moral crusade to abolish the slave regime by pacifist means. If planters did not allow blacks their God-given status as free moral agents, these radicals warned, they faced eternal damnation at the hands of a just God. The most determined white advocate of **abolitionism** was William Lloyd Garrison. A Massachusetts-born printer, Garrison had worked during the 1820s in Baltimore on an antislavery newspaper, the *Genius of Universal Emancipation*. In 1830 he went to jail, convicted of libeling a New England merchant engaged in the domestic slave trade. After his release Garrison moved to Boston and started his own weekly, *The Liberator* (1831–1865). Inspired by a bold pamphlet written by English Quaker Elizabeth Coltman Heyrick, Garrison demanded immediate abolition without compensation to slaveholders. "I will not retreat a single inch," he declared, "AND I WILL BE HEARD."

Garrison accused the American Colonization Society of perpetuating slavery. He assailed the U.S. Constitution as "a covenant with death and an agreement with Hell" because it implicitly accepted racial bondage. In 1833, Garrison and sixty other religious abolitionists, black and white, established the **American Anti-Slavery Society** (AA-SS). It won financial support from the influential New York merchants and editors Arthur and Lewis Tappan. Women abolitionists established separate groups, including the Philadelphia Female Anti-Slavery Society, founded by Lucretia Mott in 1833.

AA-SS leaders launched a three-pronged attack. Using new steam-powered presses to print a million pamphlets, they first carried out a "great postal campaign" in 1835, flooding the nation, including the South, with antislavery literature. More publications followed, including Theodore Weld's *The Bible Against Slavery* (1837). Two years later, Weld teamed up with the Grimké sisters — Angelina, whom he married, and Sarah. The Grimkés had left their father's plantation in South Carolina, converted to Quakerism, and taken up the abolitionist cause. In *American Slavery as It Is: Testimony of a Thousand Witnesses* (1839), Weld and the Grimkés addressed a simple question: "What is the actual condition of the slaves in the United States?" Using evidence from southern newspapers and firsthand testimony, they showed slavery's inherent violence. Angelina Grimké told of a whipping house used by South Carolina slave owners: "One poor girl, [who was] sent there to be flogged, and who was accordingly stripped naked and whipped, showed me the deep gashes on her back — I might have laid my whole finger in them — large pieces of flesh had actually been cut out by the torturing lash."

Filled with such images of suffering, the book sold more than 100,000 copies in a single year.

Abolitionists' second tactic was to aid fugitive slaves. They provided lodging and jobs for escaped blacks in free states and helped build the **Underground Railroad**, an informal network of blacks and whites who assisted fugitives. In Baltimore, a free African American sailor loaned his identification papers to future abolitionist Frederick Douglass, who used them to escape to New York. Harriet Tubman and other runaways risked re-enslavement or death by returning repeatedly to the South to help others escape. "I should fight for . . . liberty as long as my strength lasted," Tubman explained, "and when the time come for me to go, the Lord let them take me." Thanks to the Railroad, about a thousand African Americans reached freedom in the North each year.

A petition campaign was the final element of abolitionists' program. Between 1835 and 1838, the AA-SS bombarded Congress with nearly 500,000 signatures of citizens demanding abolition of slavery in the District of Columbia, an end to the interstate slave trade, and a ban on admission of new slave states. Along with many free blacks, thousands of deeply religious white farmers and small-town proprietors supported these efforts. The number of local abolitionist societies grew from two hundred in 1835 to two thousand by 1840, with nearly 200,000 members. The transcendentalist thinker Emerson condemned Americans for supporting slavery, while Thoreau, viewing the U.S.-Mexico War as a naked scheme to extend slavery, refused to pay taxes and submitted to arrest. In 1848, he published "Resistance to Civil Government," a foundational text for later advocates of civil disobedience. African American minister Henry Highland Garnet went further; his *Address to the Slaves of the United States of America* (1841) urged "Resistance! Resistance!" Still, abolitionists remained a small minority in the North, at most perhaps 10 percent of northerners and midwesterners.

COMPARE AND CONTRAST
How did the ideology and tactics of the Garrisonian abolitionists differ from those of the American Colonization Society?

Hostility to Abolitionism   The rhetoric of Walker and the AA-SS, combined with the shock of Turner's Rebellion, alarmed white Americans. Abolitionist agitation, ministers warned, risked "setting friend against friend" and "embittering one portion of the land against the other." Northern merchants and textile manufacturers supported southern planters who supplied them with cotton, as did hog farmers in Ohio, Indiana, and Illinois and pork packers in Cincinnati and Chicago who profited from lucrative sales in the South. Wealthy men feared that attacks on slave property might become an assault on all property rights. Conservative clergymen condemned the public roles assumed by abolitionist women. Northern working men feared freed blacks would work for lower wages and take their jobs. Finally, whites almost universally opposed "amalgamation," the racial mixing and intermarriage that Garrison seemed to support by holding meetings of blacks and whites of both sexes together.

Racial fears and hatreds led to violent mob actions. In 1829, working-class whites in Cincinnati drove over a thousand African Americans from the city — enforcing, through vigilantism, an 1807 law that had banned all blacks from Ohio. Four years later, a mob of 1,500 New Yorkers stormed a church in search of Garrison and Arthur Tappan. Another white mob swept through Philadelphia's African American neighborhoods, clubbing and stoning residents and destroying homes and churches. In 1835, "gentlemen of property and standing" — lawyers, merchants, and bankers — broke up an abolitionist convention in Utica, New York. Two years later, a mob in Alton, Illinois, shot and killed Elijah P. Lovejoy, editor of the abolitionist *Alton Observer*. By pressing for emancipation and equality, abolitionists had revealed the extent of racial prejudice.

In the South, racial solidarity increased and whites banned all abolitionist writings, sermons, and lectures. Georgia's legislature offered a $5,000 reward to anyone who would kidnap Garrison and bring him to the South to be tried (or lynched) for inciting rebellion. In Nashville, vigilantes whipped a northern college student for distributing abolitionist pamphlets; in Charleston, a mob attacked the post office and destroyed

AN AFFECTING SCENE IN KENTUCKY.

The Complexities of Race This cartoon takes aim at Richard Mentor Johnson of Kentucky, the distraught man being comforted by abolitionists Frederick Douglass and William Lloyd Garrison. A longtime congressman and senator, Johnson was the Democrats' vice-presidential candidate in 1836. Although the party stood for the South and slavery — and condemned mixed-race unions — Johnson lived openly with an African American woman, Julia Chinn, whose daughters hold her portrait. Future Supreme Court justice John Catron noted with disgust that Johnson tried "to force his daughters into society" and that they and their mother "claimed equality." Racial prejudice cost Johnson some votes, but he won a plurality in the electoral college, and, on a party-line vote, Democrats in the Senate elected him Martin Van Buren's vice president. Library of Congress.

UNDERSTAND CAUSATION
What factors caused radical abolitionism to emerge in the 1830s and 1840s?

sacks of abolitionist mail. After 1835, southern postmasters simply refused to deliver mail suspected to be of abolitionist origin. By that time, politicians joined the fray. President Andrew Jackson, a longtime slave owner, asked Congress to restrict use of the mails by abolitionist groups. Congress refused, but in 1836, the House of Representatives adopted the so-called **gag rule**. Under this informal agreement, which remained in force until 1844, the House automatically tabled abolitionist petitions, refusing even to discuss the explosive issue of slavery.

Assailed from the outside, abolitionists also divided internally over gender issues and political strategy. Many antislavery clergymen opposed public roles for women, but Garrison championed women's rights: "Our object is universal emancipation, to redeem women as well as men from a servile to an equal condition." In 1840, this issue split the movement. Women's rights advocates remained in the AA-SS, while opponents founded a new organization, the American and Foreign Anti-Slavery Society.

At the same time, dissenters from Garrison's strategy of "moral suasion" focused their energies on electoral politics. Led by key African Americans who had escaped from slavery, this group broke with Garrison and argued that slavery would never end except through electoral action. They organized the **Liberty Party**, the first antislavery political party. In 1840, they nominated James G. Birney, a former Alabama slave owner, for president. Birney won few votes, but his campaign began to open the way for further electoral action against slavery. In 1844, Birney's second run for president would have a far-ranging impact (Chapter 11). Political abolitionists would, over the next two decades, transform the political system.

CONSIDER POINTS OF VIEW
Which groups of Americans opposed the abolitionists, and why?

IN YOUR OWN WORDS How did free African American communities shape American life and culture, and how did black civic leadership transform debates over slavery and race?

The Women's Rights Movement

The controversial role of abolitionist women reflected a broad shift in American culture. The post-Revolutionary ideal of republican motherhood (Chapter 9) recognized a limited civic role for women. By the 1830s and 1840s, republican motherhood was shaped by religious revivals and rapid expansion of the middle class. The result was **domesticity**, a set of ideals that emerged first among middle-class and elite families in the Northeast. Advocates of domesticity hailed "Woman's Sphere of Influence," celebrating women's special role as mothers and homemakers. Some even praised women's charitable efforts — as long as they didn't go too far. Almost all Americans believed married women should remain under their husbands' authority and that women should stay in the "separate sphere" of the home, away from politics. As one minister put it, women had no place in "the markets of trade, the scenes of politics and popular agitation, the courts of justice and the halls of legislation." But women's education and reform work raised questions about these long-standing norms of marriage and family authority. By the 1840s, a small group of northern women began to advocate women's equal rights.

Origins of the Women's Rights Movement

Women formed a crucial part of the Second Great Awakening and the Benevolent Empire. After 1800, more than 70 percent of the members of New England Congregational churches were women. The predominance of women prompted Congregational ministers to end traditional gender-segregated prayer meetings, and evangelical Methodist and Baptist preachers actively promoted mixed-sex praying. "Our prayer meetings have been one of the greatest means of the conversion of souls," a minister in central New York reported in the 1820s, "especially those in which brothers and sisters have prayed together."

Far from leading to sexual promiscuity, as critics feared, mixing men and women in religious activities promoted greater self-discipline. Believing in female virtue, young women and the men who courted them postponed sexual intercourse until after marriage — previously a much rarer form of self-restraint. In many New England towns, more than 30 percent of the women who married between 1750 and 1800 bore a child within eight months of their wedding day; by the 1820s, the rate had dropped to 15 percent.

As women claimed spiritual authority, men tried to curb their power. In both the North and the South, evangelical Baptist churches that had once advocated spiritual equality now prevented women from voting on church matters or offering public testimonies of faith. Testimonies by women, one layman declared, were "directly opposite to the apostolic command in [Corinthians] xiv, 34, 35, 'Let your women learn to keep silence in the churches.'" Such injunctions merely changed the focus of women's religious activism. Embracing the ideal of republican motherhood, Christian women throughout the United States founded maternal associations to encourage proper child rearing. By the 1820s, journals such as *Mother's Magazine*, widely read in hundreds of towns and villages, gave women a sense of shared identity and purpose. Women also undertook missionary

Women's Education Even in education-conscious New England, before 1800 few girls attended free public primary schools for more than a few years. Subsequently, as this detail from *Scenes from a Seminary for Young Ladies* (c. 1810–1820) indicates, some girls stayed in school into their teenage years and studied a wide variety of subjects, including geography. Many graduates of these female academies became teachers, a new field of employment for women. Saint Louis Art Museum, Missouri, USA/Bridgeman Images.

fund-raising, Sunday School teaching, and other religious activities. The ideal of domesticity justified such work, since it celebrated women as more pious, caring, patient, and self-sacrificing than men could be. In towns and on prosperous farms in the Northeast and Midwest, women drew on domesticity to claim new roles.

Domesticity and Education Outside the South — where literacy lagged for white women and was banned altogether for enslaved women — a post-Revolutionary surge in women's education gave the rising generation tools and confidence to pursue reform. Religious activism also advanced female education, as churches sponsored academies for girls from the middling classes. Emma Willard, the first American advocate of higher education for women, opened the Middlebury Female Seminary in Vermont in 1814 and later founded girls' academies in Waterford and famously at Troy, New York, in 1821.

The intellectual leader of the new women educators was Catharine Beecher, whose *Treatise on Domestic Economy* (1841) advised women on how to make their homes examples of middle-class efficiency and domesticity. Though Beecher largely upheld woman's "separate sphere," she made an exception for teaching, arguing that "energetic and benevolent women" were better qualified than men to instruct the young.

By the 1820s, women educated in the nation's growing female seminaries and academies participated in a remarkable expansion of public education. From Maine to Wisconsin, women vigorously supported the movement led by reformer Horace Mann to increase elementary schooling and improve the quality of instruction. As secretary of the Massachusetts Board of Education from 1837 to 1848, Mann lengthened the school year, established standards in key subjects, and recruited well-educated women as teachers. By the 1850s, a majority of teachers were women, both because local school boards heeded Beecher's arguments and because they discovered they could hire women at much lower wages than men. A female teacher earned $12 to $14 a month with room and board — less than a male farm laborer. But among the employments open to women, teaching became a respectable and relatively well-paid option, as well as a route into public life.

Moral Reform Keenly aware of the dangers around them, women in the growing cities made particularly bold efforts at reform. In 1834, middle-class women in New York City founded the **Female Moral Reform Society** and elected Lydia Finney, wife of revivalist Charles Grandison Finney, as its president. Rejecting the sexual double standard, its members demanded chaste behavior by men. Employing only women as agents, society members provided moral guidance for young female factory operatives, seamstresses, and servants. They visited brothels, where they sang hymns, searched for runaway girls, and pointedly recorded the names of clients. By 1840, the society had blossomed into a national association with 555 chapters and 40,000 members throughout the North and Midwest. Many local chapters founded homes of refuge for prostitutes; in New York and Massachusetts they won passage of laws that made seduction a crime.

Dorothea Dix became a model for women who set out to improve public institutions. Dix's paternal grandparents were prominent Bostonians, but her father, a Methodist minister, ended up an impoverished alcoholic. Emotionally abused as a child, Dix grew into a compassionate young woman with a strong sense of moral purpose. She used money from her grandparents to set up charity schools to "rescue some of America's miserable children from vice." By 1832, she had published seven popular books, including *Conversations on Common Things* (1824), an enormously successful treatise on natural science and moral improvement.

In 1841, Dix took up a new cause. Discovering that insane women were jailed alongside male criminals, she persuaded Massachusetts lawmakers to enlarge the state hospital to house indigent mental patients. Exhilarated by that success, Dix began a national movement to establish public asylums for the mentally ill. By 1854, she had traveled more than 30,000 miles and had visited eighteen state penitentiaries, three hundred county jails, and more than five hundred almshouses and hospitals. Dix's reports and agitation prompted many states to improve their prisons and public hospitals. Like women's entry into education, Dix's career showed that ideas about women's "natural" maternalism and self-sacrifice did not necessarily confine them at home.

> **TRACE CHANGE OVER TIME**
> How did the ideal of domesticity limit the lives of middle-class women, and what new opportunities did it offer?

From Antislavery to Women's Rights

Women joined the antislavery movement, in part, because they understood the special horrors of slavery for women. In her autobiography, *Incidents in the Life of a Slave Girl*, former slave Harriet Jacobs described how enslaved women were sexually coerced and raped by masters. "I cannot tell how much I suffered in the presence of these wrongs," she wrote. She reported that such sexual assaults incited additional cruelty by slave owners' wives, who were enraged by their husbands' promiscuity. Jacobs and others made pointed gender-based appeals to northern women. Angelina Grimké denounced the slave system in which "women are degraded and brutalized, . . . forcibly plundered of their virtue and their offspring." "*They are our sisters*," she wrote, "and to us, as women, they have a right to look for sympathy with their sorrows, and effort and prayer for their rescue."

As Garrisonian women attacked slavery, they frequently violated social taboos by speaking publicly. Maria W. Stewart, an African American, spoke to mixed crowds in Boston in the early 1830s. Soon scores of women were delivering lectures condemning slavery. When Congregationalist clergymen in New England assailed Angelina and Sarah Grimké for such activism in a pastoral letter in 1837, Sarah Grimké turned to the Bible for justification: "The Lord Jesus defines the duties of his followers . . . without any reference to sex or condition," she observed. "Men and women were created equal; both are moral and accountable beings."

In a pamphlet debate with Catharine Beecher, Angelina Grimké pushed the argument beyond religion by invoking Enlightenment principles to claim equal civic rights: "It is a woman's right to have a voice in all the laws and regulations by which she is governed, whether in Church or State." By 1840, female abolitionists were asserting that traditional gender roles resulted in the domestic slavery of women. They focused particularly on the laws of coverture (Chapter 4), which gave husbands all rights of property and child custody and even declared a wife's body to belong to her husband. Having acquired a public voice and political skills in the crusade for African American freedom, thousands of northern women now advocated greater rights for themselves.

Unlike radical utopians, women's rights advocates of the 1840s did not reject the institution of marriage or conventional divisions of labor within the family. Instead, they tried to strengthen the legal rights of married women by seeking legislation that permitted them to own property (America in Global Context). This initiative won crucial support from affluent men, who feared bankruptcy in the volatile market economy and wanted to protect family assets by putting them in their wives' names. Fathers also desired their married daughters to have property rights to shield them (and their paternal inheritances) from financially irresponsible husbands. Such motives prompted legislatures in three states — Mississippi, Maine, and Massachusetts — to enact **married women's property laws** between 1839 and 1845. Then, in 1848, women activists in New York won a comprehensive statute that gave women full legal control over any

Women's Rights in France and the United States, 1848

During the political uprising in France in 1848, Pauline Roland and Jeanne Deroine unsuccessfully sought voting rights and an equal civil status for French women. However, the two women won election to the Central Committee of the Associative Unions, the umbrella organization of French trade unions. Imprisoned for their activism, they dispatched a letter to the Second Woman's Rights Convention, which met in Worcester, Massachusetts, in 1851.

When their letter was read to the Convention, Ernestine Potowsky Rose (1810–1892) offered the following response, which indicated the different perspective and political strategy of the American women's movement.

PAULINE ROLAND AND JEANNE DEROINE

Letter to the Convention of the Women of America

Dear Sisters: Your courageous declaration of Woman's Rights has resounded even to our prison and has filled our souls with inexpressible joy. In France the [conservative] reaction [to the uprising of 1848] has suppressed the cry of liberty of the women of the future. . . . The Assembly kept silence in regard to the right of one half of humanity. . . . No mention was made of the right of woman in a Constitution framed in the name of Liberty, Equality, and Fraternity. . . .

[However,] the right of woman has been recognized by the laborers and they have consecrated that right by the election of those who had claimed it in vain for both sexes. . . . It is by labor; it is by entering resolutely into the ranks of the working people that women will conquer the civil and political equality on which depends the happiness of the world. . . . Sisters of America! your socialist sisters of France are united with you in the vindication of the right of woman to civil and political equality. . . . [Only] by the union of the working classes of both sexes [can we achieve] . . . the civil and political equality of woman.

ERNESTINE ROSE

Speech to the Second Woman's Rights Convention

SOURCE: *History of Woman Suffrage*, ed. Elizabeth Cady Stanton, Susan B. Anthony, and Matilda Joslyn Gage (New York: Fowler & Wells, 1887), 1: 234–242.

After having heard the letter read from our poor incarcerated sisters of France, well might we exclaim, Alas poor France! Where is thy glory?

. . . But need we wonder that France, governed as she is by Russian and Austrian despotism, does not recognize . . . the Rights of Woman, when even here, in this far-famed land of freedom . . . woman, the mockingly so-called "better half" of man, has yet to plead for her rights. . . . In the laws of the land, she has no rights; in government she has no voice. . . . From the cradle to the grave she is subject to the power and control of man. Father, guardian, or husband, one conveys her like some piece of merchandise over to the other.

. . . Carry out the republican principle of universal suffrage, or strike it from your banners and substitute "Freedom and Power to one half of society, and Submission and Slavery to the other." Give women the elective franchise. Let married women have the same right to property that their husbands have. . . .

There is no reason against woman's elevation, but . . . prejudices. The main cause is a pernicious falsehood propagated against her being, namely that she is inferior by her nature. Inferior in what? What has man ever done that woman, under the same advantages could not do?

QUESTIONS FOR ANALYSIS

1. What strategy to achieve women's rights do Roland and Deroine advocate? What strategy can be detected in Rose's remarks? In what ways are their perspectives similar to or different from one another?

2. What does this French-American comparison, along with your reading of this chapter, suggest about the nature and values of the American women's rights movement?

property they brought to a marriage. This law became the model for similar laws in fourteen other states.

Also in 1848, Elizabeth Cady Stanton and Lucretia Mott organized a gathering of women's rights activists in the small New York town of Seneca Falls. Seventy women and thirty men attended the **Seneca Falls Convention**, which issued a rousing manifesto extending to women the egalitarian republican ideology of the Declaration of Independence. "All men and women are created equal," the Declaration of Sentiments declared. It denounced coverture and asserted that no man had the right to tell a woman what her "sphere" should be—a decision that belonged to "her conscience and her God." The Declaration called for women's higher education, access to property rights and the professions, rights of divorce, and an end to the sexual double standard. It also claimed women's "right to the elective franchise." The authors acknowledged that their struggle would be difficult, because society worked to "destroy [woman's] confidence in her own powers, to lessen her self-respect." But they called Americans to work for gender equality.

Most Americans—both male and female—dismissed the Seneca Falls declaration as nonsense. In her diary, one small-town mother lashed out at the female reformer who "talks of her wrongs in harsh tone, who struts and strides, and thinks that she proves herself superior to the rest of her sex." Still, the women's rights movement grew. In 1850, delegates to the first national women's rights convention in Worcester, Massachusetts, called on churches to eliminate theological notions of female inferiority. Addressing state legislatures, they proposed laws to allow married women to institute lawsuits and testify in court. After 1850 the movement held annual national conventions—though few southern-born women attended. Women's rights continued to have a strong abolitionist bent. Passionate speeches by African American women, in particular, reminded convention delegates of the continued plight of women in slavery.

Legislative campaigns for women's rights required talented organizers and speakers. The most prominent was Susan B. Anthony, a Quaker who had acquired political skills in the temperance and antislavery movements. Those experiences, Anthony reflected, taught her "the great evil of woman's utter dependence on man." Joining the women's rights movement, she worked closely with Elizabeth Cady Stanton, an elite New Yorker who wrote some of the movement's most eloquent manifestos. Anthony created an activist network of political "captains," all women, who relentlessly lobbied state legislatures. In 1860, her efforts secured a New York law granting women the right to control their own wages; to own property acquired by "trade, business, labors, or services"; and, if widowed, to assume sole guardianship of her children. Genuine individual equality for women, the dream of transcendentalist Margaret Fuller, had advanced a small step closer to reality. In ways large and small, new thinkers and reform movements had altered the character of American culture.

No. VI.—SOMETHING MORE OF BLOOMERISM.
(BEHIND THE COUNTER THERE IS ONE OF THE "INFERIOR ANIMALS.")

Attacking the Women's Rights Movement Amelia Jenks Bloomer (1818–1894) wrote for her husband's newspaper, the *County Courier* of Seneca Falls, New York. In 1848 she attended the women's convention there and began her own biweekly newspaper, *The Lily*, focusing on temperance and women's rights. In 1851, Bloomer enthusiastically promoted—and serendipitously gave her name to—the comfortable women's costume devised by another temperance activist: loose trousers gathered at the ankles topped by a short skirt. Fearing women's quest for equal dress and equal rights, humorists such as John Leech ridiculed the new female attire. Here, bloomer-attired women smoke away and belittle the male proprietor as "one of the 'inferior animals,'" a thinly veiled effort by Leech to reassert men's "natural" claim as the dominant sex. From *Punch*, 1851, John Leech Archive/Picture Research Consultants & Archives.

> **PLACE EVENTS IN CONTEXT**
> What was the relationship between the abolitionist and women's rights movements?

> **IN YOUR OWN WORDS** What new rights did women gain in the early nineteenth century, and which women most benefitted from these changes? What rights remained out of reach?

SUMMARY

Between the 1820s and the 1840s, Americans developed new republican ideas and practices. A sweeping series of Protestant revivals, known to historians as the Second Great Awakening, inspired thousands of Americans to evangelize and reform the world. In doing so they built movements to shelter orphans, reform prisons, combat prostitution, discourage alcohol consumption, and close businesses on the Christian Sabbath. Many of these efforts were aimed at the urban working classes, whom middle-class reformers viewed as undisciplined and sinful. Urban workers, however, often ignored reformers and built their own vibrant cultures of leisure and entertainment, including such enduring institutions as minstrel shows and the penny press.

Some reformers took more radical directions. Critics of the emerging market economy, ranging from pious Shakers to Fourierist socialists, founded utopian communities to experiment with different ways of organizing labor and family life. The most successful of these, the Mormons, met such hostility and violence from non-Mormons that they eventually trekked west to resettle in what is now Utah. New England intellectuals, led by Ralph Waldo Emerson, articulated transcendentalism, a romantic movement that emphasized spiritual connections with nature and the individual autonomy of each human soul. Transcendentalist thinkers joined the growing movement for immediate abolition of slavery, which originated in free African American communities in the North and also found support among some white northern evangelicals and Quakers. Some whites responded to abolitionist ideas — and to African American business success and political activism — with threats and riots. But the antislavery movement survived external pressures and internal disagreements. By the 1840s a small group of northern abolitionist women, inspired by ideals of equality and by the growth of women's education and reform activism, argued for women's rights.

CHAPTER 10 REVIEW

TERMS TO KNOW   *Identify and explain the significance of each term below.*

Key Concepts and Events

individualism (p. 302)

Second Great Awakening (p. 304)

Benevolent Empire (p. 306)

Maine Law (p. 307)

American Renaissance (p. 309)

romanticism (p. 309)

transcendentalism (p. 310)

utopias (p. 312)

Fourierist socialism (p. 312)

Church of Jesus Christ of Latter-day Saints, or Mormons (p. 314)

plural marriage (p. 315)

penny papers (p. 317)

minstrel shows (p. 318)

Free African Societies (p. 321)

African Methodist Episcopal Church (p. 321)

abolitionism (p. 322)

American Anti-Slavery Society (p. 322)

Underground Railroad (p. 323)

gag rule (p. 324)

Liberty Party (p. 324)

domesticity (p. 325)

Female Moral Reform Society (p. 326)

married women's property laws (p. 327)

Seneca Falls Convention (p. 328)

Key People

Rebecca Cox Jackson (p. 302)

Charles Grandison Finney (p. 305)

Ralph Waldo Emerson (p. 309)

Henry David Thoreau (p. 310)

Margaret Fuller (p. 310)

Walt Whitman (p. 311)

Mother Ann Lee (p. 312)

Joseph Smith (p. 314)

David Walker (p. 321)

Nat Turner (p. 321)

William Lloyd Garrison (p. 322)

Angelina and Sarah Grimké (p. 322)

Dorothea Dix (p. 326)

Susan B. Anthony (p. 329)

Elizabeth Cady Stanton (p. 329)

REVIEW QUESTIONS

Answer these questions to demonstrate your understanding of the chapter's main ideas.

1. To what extent did antebellum intellectual and religious movements draw on the values of individualism, on the one hand, and of communal cooperation, on the other?

2. What new working-class cultural practices emerged in large antebellum cities, and why?

3. How did free African American communities shape American life and culture, and how did black civic leadership transform debates over slavery and race?

4. What new rights did women gain in the early nineteenth century, and which women most benefitted from these changes? What rights remained out of reach?

5. Review the events listed under "Culture and Society" on the thematic timeline on page 237, paying particular attention to the entries related to individualism and rights on the one hand and to various communal and religious movements on the other. What was the relationship between these somewhat contradictory cultural impulses? How were these two movements related to the social and economic changes in America in the decades after 1800?

MAKING CONNECTIONS

Recognize the larger developments and continuities within and across chapters by answering these questions.

1. How did Americans begin to define themselves, in this period, as members of the middle class or urban working class? How did each group expect men and women to behave, dress, and spend their time? What tensions and conflicts did these differences provoke?

2. Historians often refer to the decades between 1820 and 1850 as the era of "white men's democracy." To what extent do you think that name is appropriate for American intellectual and religious life during this

period? What tools and strategies did African Americans use to seek inclusion in the "white men's democracy"? How did women, white and black, seek inclusion?

3. In what ways did the era of reform (1820–1848) increase the social and cultural freedoms that existed during the Revolutionary era (1770–1820), and for whom? Do you see any ways in which such freedoms diminished? If so, how and for whom?

KEY TURNING POINTS

Refer to the chapter chronology on page 304 for help in answering the question below.

Transformative social and political movements that arose in the United States between 1820 and 1848 included temperance, antislavery, and women's emancipation. What events in

the chronology were landmark moments for each of these reform efforts? To what extent did each succeed or meet resistance to its demands, and why?

Imperial Ambitions
1820–1848

IDENTIFY THE BIG IDEA

How did the ideology of Manifest Destiny shape U.S. government policies and the experiences of ordinary people?

Since the nation's founding in 1776, visionaries believed that it would become both a republic and an empire, predicting a glorious expansion across the continent. "It belongs of right to the United States to regulate the future destiny of North America," declared the *New-York Evening Post* in 1803. Politicians soon took up the refrain. "Our natural boundary is the Pacific Ocean," asserted Massachusetts congressman Francis Baylies in 1823. "The swelling tide of our population must and will roll on until that mighty ocean interposes its waters." Missouri senator Thomas Hart Benton concurred. "All obey the same impulse — *that of going to the West*," he wrote, "which, from the beginning of time has been the course of heavenly bodies, of the human race, and of science, civilization, and national power following in their train." Northerners and southerners alike viewed westward expansion as the durable foundation of American identity.

But in the 1820s, the United States was only one of the imperial powers vying for control of western North America. Mexico, which gained its independence from Spain in 1821, claimed a broad swath of the Southwest that stretched from Coahuila y Tejas on the Gulf coast to Alta California on the Pacific, and France, Mexico's principal creditor, had an interest in helping it to defend that claim. North of Alta California, Great Britain and the United States competed for control of a vast region known as the Oregon Country. Still farther north, Russia laid claim to a coastal strip stretching north to the arctic circle and west to the Bering Strait. And throughout these lands, Native American groups controlled access to resources. In particular, U.S. expansion directly threatened the sovereignty and independence of the Plains Indians, many of whom were formidable and well armed. Despite the confidence of politicians, U.S. control of the North American West was far from assured (Map 11.1).

President James Polk, an ardent imperialist, willingly assumed the risks associated with expansion. "I would meet the war which either England or France . . . might wage and fight until the last man," he told Secretary of State James Buchanan in 1846. Polk's aggressive expansionism sparked conflict. A war with Mexico intended to be "brief, cheap, and bloodless" became "long, costly, and sanguinary," complained Senator Benton. Polk oversaw massive territorial acquisitions — New Mexico, California, and the Oregon Country — but, in so doing, set the stage for a bitter debate over slavery.

John Gast, *American Progress* In 1845, journalist John O'Sullivan coined the term *Manifest Destiny* to describe Americans' suddenly urgent longing to extend the boundaries of the republic to the Pacific Ocean. More than a quarter century later, John Gast's *American Progress* (1872) gave visual form to that aspiration in an allegorical painting that was widely distributed through color lithographs. The goddess Liberty floats westward, holding a "School Book" in one hand and telegraph lines trailing from the other as symbols of the advance of Anglo-American civilization across the continent. Library of Congress.

As you read, ask yourself why this chapter begins and ends with these dates and then identify the links among related events.

1810s ▶ Africans from Congo region influence black culture for decades	**1835** ▶ Mexico creates stronger central government, outlaws slavery
1818 ▶ United States and Great Britain agree to joint control of Oregon Country	**1836** ▶ Texas declares its independence from Mexico
1820s ▶ Mexican government encourages migration to Coahuila y Tejas ▶ African Americans increasingly adopt Christian beliefs	**1842–1843** ▶ Immigration to the Oregon Country increases dramatically
	1844 ▶ James K. Polk elected president
1820 ▶ Major Stephen H. Long labels the Great Plains the "Great American Desert"	**1845** ▶ John L. O'Sullivan coins the phrase *Manifest Destiny* ▶ Texas admitted into Union
1821 ▶ Mexico gains independence from Spain	**1846** ▶ United States declares war on Mexico ▶ Treaty with Britain divides Oregon Country ▶ California's "Bear Flag Republic" declares independence
1830s ▶ Percentage of slave-owning white families falls ▶ Yeoman farm families retreat to hill country ▶ Lawyers become influential in southern politics	
	1847 ▶ American troops capture Mexico City

MAP 11.1 Nonnative Claims to North America, 1821

In 1821, North America was a complex patchwork. Louisiana and Missouri were the first two states west of the Mississippi. Beyond the states' borders, the Michigan, Missouri, Arkansas, and East and West Florida Territories extended U.S. claims. To the south, the newly independent nation of Mexico claimed nearly as much territory as the United States did, while British Canada included a vast landscape to the north. Russia controlled the northern Pacific coast, while Mexico claimed Alta and Baja California. In between, Great Britain and the United States vied for the Oregon Country, which held the key to each nation's desire for an outlet to the Pacific. Underlying all these claims, a large and diverse population of Native Americans considered their own claims to be sovereign.

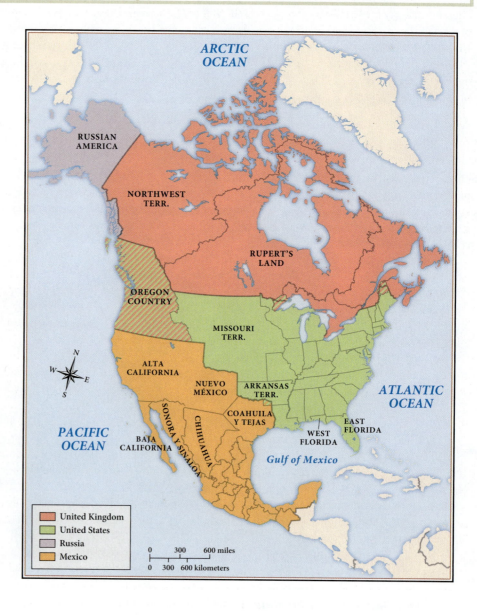

The Expanding South

For southerners, imperial ambitions meant territorial expansion and a commitment to the slave plantation system. With slavery's resurgence in the early nineteenth century, the social and political order of the South settled into new patterns. A small minority of planter elites came to dominate southern society, while a larger number of middling planters and aspiring slaveholders supported their ambitions. But the growing number of propertyless whites separated themselves from the plantation economy by moving onto marginal lands. Southern expansionists pushed into east Texas in the 1820s, while the planters of the Cotton South who dominated state legislatures adapted their aristocratic ideals to the demands of a democratic political order.

Planters, Small Freeholders, and Poor Freemen

Although the South was a **slave society**—a society in which the institution of slavery affected all aspects of life—most white southerners did not own slaves. The percentage of white families who held blacks in bondage steadily decreased—from 36 percent in 1830, to 31 percent in 1850, to about 25 percent a decade later. However, slave ownership varied by region. In some cotton-rich counties, 40 percent of the white families owned slaves; in the hill country near the Appalachian Mountains, the proportion dropped to 10 percent.

Planter Elites   A privileged minority of 395,000 southern families owned slaves in 1860, their ranks divided into a strict hierarchy. The top one-fifth of these families owned twenty or more slaves. This elite—just 5 percent of the South's white population—dominated the economy, owning over 50 percent of the entire slave population of 4 million and growing 50 percent of the South's cotton crop (Map 11.2). The average wealth of these planters was $56,000 (about $1.6 million in purchasing power today); by contrast, a prosperous southern yeoman or northern farmer owned property worth a mere $3,200.

Wealthy southerners cast themselves as a **republican aristocracy**. "The planters here are essentially what the nobility are in other countries," declared James Henry Hammond of South Carolina. "They stand at the head of society & politics . . . [and form] an aristocracy of talents, of virtue, of generosity and courage." Wealthy planters feared federal government interference with their slave property, while on the state level, they worried about populist politicians who would mobilize poorer whites.

Many southern leaders criticized the growth of middle-class democracy in the Northeast and Midwest. "Inequality is the fundamental law of the universe," declared one planter. Others condemned professional politicians as "a set of demagogues" and questioned the legitimacy of universal suffrage. "Times are sadly different now to what they were when I was a boy," lamented David Gavin, a prosperous South Carolinian. Then, the "Sovereign people, alias mob" had little influence; now they vied for power with the elite. "[How can] I rejoice for a freedom," Gavin thundered, "which allows every bankrupt, swindler, thief, and scoundrel, traitor and seller of his vote to be placed on an equality with myself?"

Substantial proprietors, another fifth of the slave-owning population, held title to six to twenty bondsmen and -women. These middling planters owned almost 40 percent of the enslaved laborers and produced more than 30 percent of the cotton. Often they pursued dual careers as skilled artisans or professional men. Thus some of the fifteen slaves owned by Georgian Samuel L. Moore worked in his brick factory, while others labored on his farm. Dr. Thomas Gale used the income from his medical practice to buy a Mississippi plantation that annually produced 150 bales of cotton. In Alabama, lawyer Benjamin Fitzpatrick used his legal fees to buy ten slaves.

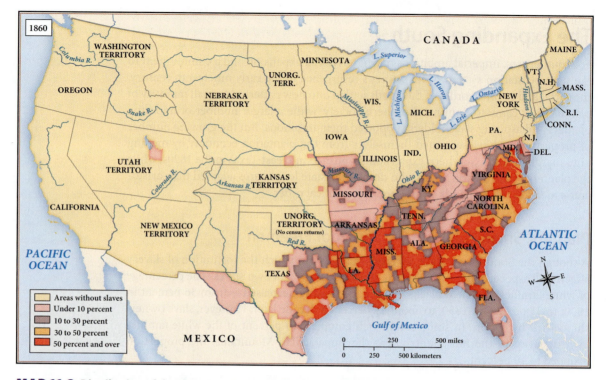

MAP 11.2 Distribution of the Slave Population in 1860
The center of the African American population shifted steadily westward, following the cotton boom. By 1860 the slave plantation system had pushed into east Texas, while the majority of blacks lived and worked along the Mississippi River and in an arc of fertile cotton lands — the "black belt" — sweeping from Mississippi through South Carolina.

Like Fitzpatrick, lawyers acquired wealth by managing the affairs of the slave-owning elite, representing planters and merchants in suits for debt, and helping smallholders and tenants register their deeds and contracts. Standing at the legal crossroads of their small towns, they rose to prominence and regularly won election to public office. Less than 1 percent of the male population, in 1828 lawyers made up 16 percent of the Alabama legislature and an astounding 26 percent in 1849.

Small Freeholders Smallholding slave owners were much less visible than the wealthy grandees and the middling lawyer-planters. These planters held from one to five black laborers in bondage and owned a few hundred acres of land. Some smallholders were well-connected young men who would rise to wealth when their father's death blessed them with more land and slaves. Others were poor but ambitious men trying to pull themselves up by their bootstraps, often encouraged by elite planters and proslavery advocates. "Ours is a proslavery form of Government, and the proslavery element should be increased," declared a Georgia newspaper. "We would like to see every white man at the South the owner of a family of negroes." Some aspiring planters achieved modest prosperity. A German settler reported from Alabama in 1855 that "nearly all his countrymen" who emigrated with him were slaveholders. "They were poor on their arrival in the country; but no sooner did they realize a little money than they invested it in slaves."

Bolstered by the patriarchal ideology of the planter class, middling farmers ruled with a firm hand. The male head of the household had legal authority over all the dependents — wives, children, and slaves — and, according to one South Carolina judge, the right on his property "to be as churlish as he pleases." Their wives had little power; like women in the North, under the laws of coverture, they lost their legal identity when they married (Chapter 10). To express their concerns, many southern women joined churches, where they usually outnumbered men by a margin of two to one. Women especially welcomed the message of spiritual equality preached in evangelical Baptist and Methodist churches, and they hoped that the church community would hold their husbands to the same standards of Christian behavior to which they conformed. However, most churches supported patriarchal rule and told female members to remain in "wifely obedience" to their husbands.

Whatever their authority within the household, most southern freeholders lived and died as hardscrabble farmers. They worked alongside their slaves in the fields, struggled to make ends meet as their families grew, and moved regularly in search of opportunity. In 1847, James Buckner Barry left North Carolina with his new wife and two slaves to settle in Bosque County, Texas. There he worked part-time as an Indian fighter while his slaves toiled on a drought-ridden farm that barely kept the family in food. In South Carolina, W. J. Simpson struggled for years as a smallholding cotton planter and then gave up. He hired out one of his two slaves and went to work as an overseer on his father's farm.

Poor Freemen   Less fortunate smallholders fell from the privileged ranks of the slave-owning classes. Selling their land and slaves to pay off debts, they joined the mass of propertyless tenants who farmed the estates of wealthy landlords. In 1860, in Hancock County, Georgia, there were 56 slave-owning planters and 300 propertyless white farm laborers and factory workers; in nearby Hart County, 25 percent of the white farmers were tenants. Across the South, about 40 percent of the white population worked as tenants or farm laborers. As the *Southern Cultivator* observed, they had "no legal right nor interest in the soil [and] no homes of their own."

Propertyless whites suffered the ill consequences of living in a slave society that accorded little respect to hardworking white laborers. Nor could they hope for a better life for their children, because slave owners refused to pay taxes to fund public schools. Moreover, wealthy planters bid up the price of slaves, depriving white laborers and tenants of easy access to the labor required to accumulate wealth. Finally, planter-dominated legislatures forced all white men, whether they owned slaves or not, to serve in the patrols and militias that deterred black uprisings. After touring the South, the future architect of New York's Central Park, Frederick Law Olmsted, concluded that the majority of white southerners "are poor. They . . . have little — very little — of the common comforts and consolations of civilized life. Their destitution is not material only; it is intellectual and it is moral."

Marking this moral destitution, poor whites enjoyed the psychological satisfaction that they ranked above blacks. As Alfred Iverson, a U.S. senator from Georgia, explained: a white man "walks erect in the dignity of his color and race, and feels that he is a superior being, with the more exalted powers and privileges than others." To reinforce that sense of racial superiority, planter James Henry Hammond told his poor white neighbors, "In a slave country every freeman is an aristocrat."

Rejecting that half-truth, many southern whites fled planter-dominated counties in the 1830s and sought farms in the Appalachian hill country and beyond — in western Virginia, Kentucky, Tennessee, the southern regions of Illinois and Indiana, and Missouri. Living as small farmers, they used family labor to grow foodstuffs for sustenance. To obtain cash or store credit to buy agricultural implements, cloth, shoes, salt, and other necessities, farm families sold their surplus crops, raised hogs for market sale, and — when the price of

North Carolina Emigrants: *Poor White Folks*   Completed in 1845, James Henry Beard's (1811–1893) painting depicts a family moving north to Ohio. Unlike many optimistic scenes of emigration, the picture conveys a sense of resigned despair. The family members, led by a sullen, disheveled father, pause at a water trough while their cow drinks and their dog chews a bone. The mother looks apprehensively toward the future as she cradles a child; two barefoot older children listlessly await their father's command. New York writer Charles Briggs interpreted the painting as an "eloquent sermon on Anti-Slavery . . . , the blight of Slavery has paralyzed the strong arm of the man and destroyed the spirit of the woman." Although primarily a portrait painter, Beard questioned the ethics and optimism of American culture in *Ohio Land Speculator* (1840) and *The Last Victim of the Deluge* (1849), as well as in *Poor White Folks.* Cincinnati Art Museum, Ohio, USA/Gift of the Proctor & Gamble Company/Bridgeman Images.

cotton rose sharply — grew a few bales. Their goals were modest: on the family level, they wanted to preserve their holdings and buy enough land to set up their children as small-scale farmers. As citizens, smallholders wanted to control their local government and elect men of their own kind to public office. But most understood that the slave-based cotton economy sentenced family farmers to a subordinate place in the social order. They could hope for a life of independence and dignity only by moving north or farther west, where labor was "free" and hard work was respected.

By the 1830s, settlers from the South had carried both small farming and plantation slavery into Arkansas and Missouri. Between those states and the Rocky Mountains stretched great grasslands. An army explorer, Major Stephen H. Long, thought the plains region "almost wholly unfit for cultivation" and in 1820 labeled it the **Great American Desert**. The label stuck. Americans looking for land turned south, to Mexican territory. At the same time, elite planters struggled to control state governments in the Cotton South.

CONSIDER POINTS OF VIEW
What social groups made up white southern society, and how did they interact?

The Settlement of Texas

After winning independence from Spain in 1821, the Mexican government pursued an activist settlement policy. To encourage migration to the newly reconfigured state of Coahuila y Tejas, it offered sizable land grants both to its own citizens and to American emigrants. Moses Austin, an American land speculator, settled smallholding farmers on his large grant, and his son, Stephen F. Austin, acquired even more land — some 180,000 acres — which he sold to newcomers. By 1835, about 27,000 white Americans and their 3,000 African American slaves were raising cotton and cattle in the well-watered plains and hills of eastern and central Texas. They far outnumbered the 3,000 Mexican residents, who lived primarily near the southwestern Texas towns of Goliad and San Antonio.

Houston, Capital of Texas, c. 1845–1850 This German lithograph by an unknown artist depicts the town of Houston, Texas, during one of the brief periods (1837–1839 and again in 1842) when it served as capital of the Republic of Texas. Though Houston was a small, boisterous port town surrounded by bayous on the Gulf Coast, this scene, bathed in moonlight, makes it look like a bucolic German village. The rolling hills bear little resemblance to Houston's flatter, more open topography. The neat, snug homes surrounding a church steeple suggest an orderly, peaceful community steeped in tradition. In fact, Houston — founded only a decade earlier — had grown rapidly and haphazardly, developed a reputation for drunkenness and brawling, and suffered in its early years from repeated yellow fever outbreaks. After the failed revolutions of 1848, German immigrants began arriving in the United States in large numbers. This lithograph was probably printed as part of a promotional campaign to lure them to Houston. Museum of Fine Arts, Houston, Texas, USA/The Bayou Bend Collection. Gift of the Estate of Miss Ima Hogg/Bridgeman Images.

When Mexico in 1835 adopted a new constitution creating a stronger central government and dissolving state legislatures, the Americans split into two groups. The "war party," led by Sam Houston and recent migrants from Georgia, demanded independence for Texas. Members of the "peace party," led by Stephen Austin, negotiated with the central government in Mexico City for greater political autonomy. They believed Texas could flourish within a decentralized Mexican republic, a "federal" constitutional system favored by the Liberal Party in Mexico (and advocated in the United States by Jacksonian Democrats). Austin won significant concessions for the Texans, including an exemption from a law ending slavery, but in 1835 Mexico's president, General Antonio López de Santa Anna, nullified them. Santa Anna wanted to impose national authority throughout Mexico. Fearing central control, the war party provoked a rebellion that most of the American settlers ultimately supported. On March 2, 1836, the American rebels proclaimed the independence of Texas and adopted a constitution legalizing slavery.

To put down the rebellion, President Santa Anna led an army that wiped out the Texan garrison defending the **Alamo** in San Antonio and then captured Goliad, executing about 350 prisoners of war (see Map 11.3). Santa Anna thought that he had crushed the rebellion, but New Orleans and New York newspapers romanticized the deaths at the Alamo of folk heroes Davy Crockett and Jim Bowie. Drawing on anti-Catholic sentiment aroused by Irish immigration and the massacre at Goliad, they urged Americans to "Remember the Alamo" and depicted the Mexicans as tyrannical butchers in the service of the pope. American adventurers, lured by offers of land grants, flocked to Texas to join the rebel forces. Commanded by General Sam Houston, the Texans routed Santa Anna's overconfident army in the Battle of San Jacinto in April 1836, winning de facto independence. The Mexican government refused to recognize the Texas Republic but, for the moment, did not seek to conquer it.

The Texans voted for annexation by the United States, but President Martin Van Buren refused to bring the issue before Congress. As a Texas diplomat reported, the cautious Van Buren and other party politicians feared that annexation would spark a war with Mexico and, beyond that, a "desperate death-struggle . . . between the North and the South [over the extension of slavery]; a struggle involving the probability of a dissolution of the Union."

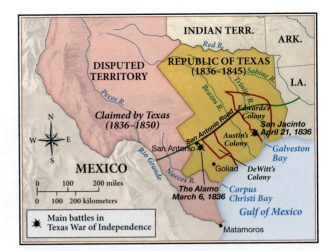

MAP 11.3 American Settlements, Texas War of Independence, and Boundary Disputes
During the 1820s the Mexican government encouraged Americans to settle in the sparsely populated state of Coahuila y Tejas. By 1835 the nearly 30,000 Americans far outnumbered Mexican residents. To put down an American-led revolt, General Santa Anna led 6,000 soldiers into Tejas in 1836. After overwhelming the rebels at the Alamo in March, Santa Anna set out to capture the Texas Provisional Government, which had fled to Galveston. But the Texans' victory at San Jacinto in April ended the war and secured de facto independence for the Republic of Texas (1836–1845). However, the annexation of Texas to the United States sparked a war with Mexico in 1846, and the state's boundaries remained in dispute until the Compromise of 1850.

The Politics of Democracy

As national leaders refused admission to Texas, elite planters faced political challenges in the Cotton South. Unlike the planter-aristocrats who ruled the colonial world, they lived in a republican society with a democratic ethos. The Alabama Constitution of 1819 granted suffrage to all white men; it also provided for a **secret ballot** (rather than voice-voting); apportionment of legislative seats based on population; and the election of county supervisors, sheriffs, and clerks of court. Given these democratic provisions, political factions in Alabama had to compete for votes. When a Whig newspaper sarcastically asked whether the state's policies should "be governed and controlled by the whim and caprice of the majority of the people," Democrats hailed the power of the common folk. They called on "Farmers, Mechanics, laboring men" to repudiate Whig "aristocrats . . . the soft handed and soft headed gentry."

CONSIDER POINTS OF VIEW
What issues divided the Mexican government and the Americans in Texas, and what proposals sought to resolve them?

Taxation Policy   Whatever the electioneering rhetoric, most Whig and Democrat political candidates were men of means. In the early 1840s, nearly 90 percent of Alabama's legislators owned slaves, testimony to the political power of the slave-owning minority. Still, relatively few lawmakers — only about 10 percent — were rich planters, a group voters by and large distrusted. "A rich man cannot sympathize with the poor," declared one candidate. Consequently, the majority of state and county officials in the Cotton South came from the ranks of middle-level planters and planter-lawyers. Astute politicians, they refrained from laying "oppressive" taxes on the people, particularly the white majority who owned no slaves. Between 1830 and 1860, the Alabama legislature obtained about 70 percent of the state's revenue from taxes on slaves and land. Another 10 to 15 percent came from levies on carriages, gold watches, and other luxury goods and on the capital invested in banks, transportation companies, and manufacturing enterprises.

To win the votes of taxpaying slave owners, Alabama Democrats advocated limited government and low taxes. They attacked their Whig opponents for favoring higher taxes and for providing government subsidies for banks, canals, railroads, and other

Colonel and Mrs. James A. Whiteside, Son Charles and Servants   James A. Whiteside (1803–1861) was a Tennessee lawyer, politician, land speculator, and entrepreneur, with investments in iron manufacturing, banking, steamboats, and railroads. In 1857, he became vice president of the Nashville, Chattanooga, and St. Louis Railroad. The following year, Whiteside persuaded the Scottish-born painter James Cameron (1817–1882) to move to Chattanooga, where Cameron completed this ambitious portrait of the colonel; his second wife, Harriet; their youngest child, Charles; and two enslaved "servants." The painting shows the family at home, with a view of Chattanooga and of Lookout Mountain, where the colonel had built a hotel. Whiteside died from pneumonia in 1861 after returning home from Virginia with his son James, who had fallen ill while serving in the Confederate army.   Hunter Museum of American Art, Chattanooga, Tennessee. Oil on canvas, c. 1858–1859. Gift of Mr. & Mrs. Thomas B. Whiteside, 1975.7.

internal improvements. "Voting against appropriations is the safe and popular side," one Democratic legislator declared, and his colleagues agreed; until the 1850s, they rejected most of the bills that would have granted subsidies to transportation companies or banks.

If tax policy in Alabama had a democratic thrust, elsewhere in the South it did not. In some states, wealthy planters used their political muscle to exempt slave property from taxation. Or they shifted the burden to backcountry freeholders, who owned low-quality pasturelands, by taxing farms according to acreage rather than value. Planter-legislators also spared themselves the cost of building fences around their fields by requiring small farmers to "fence in" their livestock. And, during the 1850s, wealthy legislators throughout the South used public funds to subsidize the canals and railroads in which they had invested, ignoring the protests of yeoman-backed legislators.

The Paradox of Southern Prosperity

Even without these internal improvements, the South had a strong economy. Indeed, it ranked fourth in the world in 1860, with a per capita income among whites higher than that of France and Germany. As a contributor to a Georgia newspaper argued in the 1850s, planters and yeomen should not complain about "tariffs, and merchants, and manufacturers" because "the most highly prosperous people now on earth, are to be found in these very [slave] States." Such arguments tell only part of the story. Nearly all African Americans — 40 percent of the population — lived in dire and permanent poverty. And, although the average southern white man was 80 percent richer than the average northerner in 1860, the southerner's *nonslave* wealth was only 60 percent of the northern average. Moreover, the wealth of the industrializing Northeast was increasing at a faster pace than that of the South. Between 1820 and 1860, slave-related trade across the Atlantic declined from 12.6 percent of world trade to 5.3 percent.

Influential southerners blamed the shortcomings of their plantation-based economy on outsiders: "Purely agricultural people," intoned slave-owning planter-politician James Henry Hammond, "have been in all ages the victims of rapacious tyrants grinding them down." And they steadfastly defended their way of life. "We have no cities — we don't want them," boasted U.S. senator Louis Wigfall of Texas in 1861. "We want no manufactures: we desire no trading, no mechanical or manufacturing classes. . . . As long as we have our rice, our sugar, our tobacco, and our cotton, we can command wealth to purchase all we want." So wealthy southerners continued to buy land and slaves, a strategy that neglected investments in the great technological innovations of the nineteenth century — water- and steam-powered factories, machine tools, steel plows, and crushed-gravel roads — that would have raised the South's productivity and wealth.

Urban growth, the key to prosperity in Europe and the North, occurred primarily in the commercial cities around the periphery of the South: New Orleans, St. Louis, and Baltimore. Factories — often staffed by slave labor — appeared primarily in the

Chesapeake region, which had a diverse agricultural economy and a surplus of enslaved workers. Within the Cotton South, wealthy planters invested in railroads primarily to grow and sell more cotton; when the Western & Atlantic Railroad reached the Georgia upcountry, the cotton crop there quickly doubled. Cotton and agriculture remained king.

Slavery also deterred Europeans from migrating to the South, because they feared competition from bound labor. Their absence deprived the region of skilled artisans and of hardworking laborers to drain swamps, dig canals, smelt iron, and work on railroads. When entrepreneurs tried to hire slaves for these dangerous tasks, planters replied that "a negro's life is too valuable to be risked." Slave owners also feared that hiring out would make their slaves too independent. As a planter told Frederick Law Olmsted, such workers "had too much liberty . . . and got a habit of roaming about and taking care of themselves."

Thus, despite its increasing size and booming exports, the South remained an economic colony: Great Britain and the North bought its staple crops and provided its manufactures, financial services, and shipping facilities. In 1860, some 84 percent of southerners — more than double the percentage in the northern states — still worked in agriculture, and southern factories turned out only 10 percent of the nation's manufactures. The South's fixation on an "exclusive and exhausting" system of cotton monoculture and slave labor filled South Carolina textile entrepreneur William Gregg with "dark forebodings": "It has produced us such an abundant supply of all the luxuries and elegances of life, with so little exertion on our part, that we have become enervated, unfitted for other and more laborious pursuits."

> **EXPLAIN CONSEQUENCES**
> How did the political power of slave owners affect tax policy and economic development in the southern states?

> **IN YOUR OWN WORDS** What were the strengths and limitations of the South's economy and social structure?

The African American World

By the 1820s, the cultural life of most slaves reflected both the values and customs of their West African ancestors and the language, laws, and religious beliefs of the South's white population. This mix of African- and European-derived cultural values persisted for decades because whites discouraged blacks from assimilating and because slaves prized their diverse African heritages.

Evangelical Black Protestantism

The emergence of black Christianity illustrated the synthesis of African and European cultures. From the 1790s to the 1840s, the Second Great Awakening swept over the South, and evangelical Baptist and Methodist preachers converted thousands of white families and hundreds of enslaved blacks. Until that time, African-born blacks, often identifiable by their ritual scars, had maintained the religious practices of their homelands.

African Religions and Christian Conversion   Africans carried their traditional religious practices to the United States. Some practiced Islam, but the majority relied on African gods and spirits. As late as 1842, Charles C. Jones, a Presbyterian minister, noted that the blacks on his family's plantation in Georgia believed "in second-sight, in apparitions, charms, witchcraft . . . [and other] superstitions brought from Africa." Fearing for their own souls if they withheld "the means of salvation" from African Americans, Jones and other zealous Protestant preachers and planters set out to convert slaves.

Other Protestant crusaders came from the ranks of pious black men and women who had become Christians in the Chesapeake. Swept to the Cotton South by the domestic slave trade, they carried with them the evangelical message of emotional conversion, ritual baptism, and communal spirituality. Equally important, these crusaders adapted Protestant doctrines to black needs. Enslaved Christians pointed out that blacks as well as whites were "children of God" and should be treated accordingly. **Black Protestantism** generally ignored the doctrines of original sin and predestination, and preachers didn't use biblical passages that encouraged unthinking obedience to authority. A white minister in Liberty County, Georgia, reported that when he urged slaves to obey their masters, "one half of my audience deliberately rose up and walked off."

Black Worship   Indeed, some African American converts envisioned the deity as the Old Testament warrior who had liberated the Jews and so would liberate them. Inspired by a vision of Christ, Nat Turner led his bloody rebellion against slavery in Virginia (see Chapter 10). Other black Christians saw themselves as Chosen People: "de people dat is born of God." Charles Davenport, a Mississippi slave, recalled black preachers "exhort[ing] us dat us was de chillun o' Israel in de wilderness an' de Lawd done sont us to take dis lan' o' milk an' honey."

Black Kitchen Ball   In this 1838 painting, *Kitchen Ball at White Sulphur Springs Virginia*, African American slaves dance to the music of a fiddle and a fife (on the right). These men and women were not field hands, but the household slaves of well-to-do plantation families vacationing at a mountain resort. Note the light complexions and Europeanized features of the most prominent figures, the result of either racial mixing or the cultural perspective of the artist. The painter, Christian Mayr, was born in Germany in 1805 and migrated to the United States in 1833. After working for years as a traveling portrait painter, Mayr settled in New York City in 1845 and died there in 1850. DeAgostini/Getty Images.

Still, African Americans expressed their Christianity in distinctive ways. The thousands of blacks who joined the Methodist Church respected its ban on profane dancing but praised the Lord in what minister Henry George Spaulding called the "religious dance of the Negroes." Spaulding described the African-derived "ring shout" this way: "Three or four, standing still, clapping their hands and beating time with their feet, commence singing in unison one of the peculiar shout melodies, while the others walk around in a ring, in single file, joining also in the song." The songs themselves were usually collective creations, devised spontaneously from bits of old hymns and tunes. Recalled an ex-slave:

> We'd all be at the "prayer house" de Lord's day, and de white preacher he'd splain de word and read whar Esekial done say — Dry bones gwine ter lib ergin. And, honey, de Lord would come a-shinin' thoo dem pages and revive dis ole nigger's heart, and I'd jump up dar and den and holler and shout and sing and pat, and dey would all cotch de words and I'd sing it to some ole shout song I'd heard 'em sing from Africa, and dey'd all take it up and keep at it, and keep a-addin' to it, and den it would be a spiritual.

By such African-influenced means, black congregations devised a distinctive and joyous brand of Protestant worship to sustain them on the long journey to emancipation and the Promised Land. "O my Lord delivered Daniel," the slaves sang. "O why not deliver me too?"

> To read more about slave songs in the South, along with other primary sources from this period, see *Sources for America's History*.

> **PLACE EVENTS IN CONTEXT**
> How did the Second Great Awakening affect the development of black religion?

Forging Families and Communities

Black Protestantism was one facet of an increasingly homogeneous African American culture in the rural South. Even in South Carolina — a major point of entry for imported slaves — only 20 percent of the black residents in 1820 had been born in Africa. The domestic slave trade mingled blacks from many states, erased regional differences, and prompted the emergence of a core culture in the Lower Mississippi Valley. A prime example was the fate of the **Gullah dialect**, which combined words from English and a variety of African languages in an African grammatical structure. Spoken by blacks in the Carolina lowcountry well into the twentieth century, Gullah did not take root on the cotton plantations of Alabama and Mississippi. There, slaves from Carolina were far outnumbered by migrants from the Chesapeake, who spoke black English. Like Gullah, black English used double negatives and other African grammatical forms, but it consisted primarily of English words rendered with West African pronunciation (for example, with *th* pronounced as *d* — "de preacher").

Nonetheless, African influences remained significant. At least one-third of the slaves who entered the United States between 1776 and 1809 came from the Congo region of West-Central Africa, and they brought their cultures with them. As traveler Isaac Holmes reported in 1821: "In Louisiana, and the state of Mississippi, the slaves . . . dance for several hours during Sunday afternoon. The general movement is in what they call the Congo dance." Similar descriptions of blacks who "danced the Congo and sang a purely African song to the accompaniment of . . . a drum" appeared as late as 1890.

African Americans also continued to respect African incest taboos by shunning marriages between cousins. On the Good Hope Plantation in South Carolina, nearly half of the slave children born between 1800 and 1857 were related by blood to one another; yet when they married, only one of every forty-one unions took place between cousins. White planters were not the source of this taboo: cousin marriages were frequent among the 440 South Carolina men and women who owned at least one hundred slaves in 1860, in part because such unions kept wealth within an extended family (Thinking Like a Historian).

Childhood in Black and White

A major theme of Harriet Beecher Stowe's powerful antislavery novel *Uncle Tom's Cabin* is the sin of separating black families and denying parental rights to enslaved mothers and fathers. The following documents reveal the dynamics of plantation family life, and particularly mother-child relations.

1. **Ex-slave Josephine Smith, interviewed at age ninety-four by Mary A. Hicks, Raleigh, North Carolina, 1930s.** *Slave children had loving but limited relationships with their mothers, who worked long hours in the fields and were sometimes sold away from their children.*

I 'members seein' a heap o' slave sales, wid de niggers in chains, an' de spec'ulators sellin' an' buyin' dem off. I also 'members seein' a drove of slaves wid nothin' on but a rag 'twixt dere legs bein' galloped roun' 'fore de buyers. 'Bout de wust thing dat eber I seed do' wuz a slave woman at Louisburg who had been sold off from her three weeks old baby, an wuz bein' marched ter New Orleans.

She had walked till she quz give out, an' she wuz weak enough ter fall in de middle o' de road. . . . As I pass by dis 'oman begs me in God's name fer a drink o' water, an' I gives it ter her. I ain't neber be so sorry fer nobody. . . . Dey walk fer a little piece an' dis 'oman fall out. She dies dar side o' de road, an' right dar dey buries her, cussin', dey tells me, 'bout losin' money on her.

2. **"Narrative of James Curry, a Fugitive Slave,"** *The Liberator*, **January 10, 1840.** *The abolitionist newspaper* The Liberator *published heartrending accounts of death and separation in slave families and how "fictive kinship" assisted the survivors.*

My mother's labor was very hard. She would go to the house in the morning, take her pail upon her head, and go away to the cow-pen, and milk fourteen cows. She then put on the bread for the family breakfast, and got the cream ready for churning, and set a little child to churn it, she having the care of from ten to fifteen children, whose mothers worked in the field. . . . Among the slave children, were three little orphans, whose mothers, at their death, committed them to the care of my mother. One of them was a babe. She took them and treated them as her own. The master took no care about them. She always took a share of the cloth she had provided for her own children, to cover these little friendless ones.

3. **Former slave Barney Alford, interview for the Works Progress Administration in Mississippi, 1930s.**

Ole mammy 'Lit' wus mity ole en she lived in one corner of de big yard en she keered fur all de black chilluns while de old folks wurk in de field. Mammy Lit wus good to all de chilluns en I had ter help her wid dem chilluns en keep dem babies on de pallet. Mammy Lit smoked a pipe, en sum times I wuld hide dat pipe, en she wuld slap me fur it, den sum times I wuld run way en go ter de kitchen whar my mammy wus at wurk en mammy Lit wuld hafter cum fur me en den she wuld whip me er gin. She sed I wus bad.

4. **"Mrs. Meriwether Administering Bitters," illustration from John Pendleton Kennedy,** *Swallow Barn, Or, A Sojourn in the Old Dominion*, **1851.** *Bitters — strong alcoholic beverages flavored with bitter herbs — were administered as medicine in the nineteenth century, as in this depiction of a planter's wife tending to enslaved children. Kennedy's cheerful depictions of Virginia plantation life in this popular book, first published in 1832, reinforced the notion of slavery as a "positive good."*

SOURCE: Picture Research Consultants & Archives.

5. G. M. J., "Early Culture of Children," 1855. *This excerpt from a Christian advice manual for mothers reflects the values of the mid-nineteenth-century white Protestant middle class.*

"Train up a child in the way he should go," is a law as imperative in the 19th century, as when first uttered by the lips of the wise man. Mothers are the natural executors of this law to their daughters. Nothing but the most unavoidable and pressing force of circumstances, should wrench this power from their hands. Who will guard with a mother's jealous eye the health, habits, morals, and religion of this most delicate part of creation. . . . How often I have been pained to see mothers place those delicate plants in the nursery with servants, whose tastes, feelings, morals, manners, and language are but a little removed from the lower animals of creation; there to receive impressions, and imbibe habits, which will grow with their growth, and strengthen with their strength, until like the branches of the giant oak, they shall expand and deepen into a shade that will forever conceal the parent stock.

6. Visiting Cards Created by Philadelphia Portrait Painter and Photographer Peregrine F. Cooper, As We Found Them (left), As They Are Now (right), 1864. *One of the ways to "train up a child in the way he should go" was to inculcate abolitionist sentiments early and often.*

AS WE FOUND THEM.

These children were owned by Thomas White, of Mathews Co., Va., until Feb. 20th, when Capt. Riley, 6th U.S. C. I., took them and gave them to the Society of Friends to educate at the Orphan's Shelter, Philadelphia.

Profits from sale, for the benefit of the children.

AS THEY ARE NOW.

The Mother of these children was beaten, branded and sold at auction because she was kind to Union Soldiers. As she left for Richmond, Va., Feb. 15th, 1864, bound down in a cart, she prayed "O! God send the Yankees to take my children away."

Profits from sale, for the benefit of the children.

SOURCE: Peregrine F. Cooper/George Eastman House/Getty Images (both photos).

SOURCES: (1) WPA Slave Narrative Project, 1936–38, learnnc.org; (2) "Narrative of James Curry, a Fugitive Slave," *The Liberator*, January 10, 1840, learnnc.org; (3) The MS Gen Web Project, msgw.org/slaves/alford-xslave.htm; (5) *Home Garner; or the Intellectual and Moral Store House*, ed. Mary G. Clarke (Philadelphia: J. P. Lippincott & Co., 1855), 115.

ANALYZING THE EVIDENCE

1. What do these sources reveal about slave communities? About the extent to which the ideology of "benevolent paternalism" governed the behavior of slave owners?

2. How does the engraving (source 4) compare to the descriptions of the care of slave children (sources 1–3)? What biases, if any, can you detect in these sources?

3. How would a person holding the beliefs described in source 5 react to the engraving of Mrs. Meriwether? To images showing slave "mammies" raising the master's children?

4. How do the images of enslaved children in source 6 pertain to "train[ing] up a child in the way he should go"? How effective are they? What emotions do they play upon?

PUTTING IT ALL TOGETHER

Write an essay that assesses the economic, legal, and political arguments over slavery in light of the experiences of enslaved mothers and children.

Unlike white marriages, slave unions were not legally binding. According to a Louisiana judge, "slaves have no legal capacity to assent to any contract . . . because slaves are deprived of all civil rights." Nonetheless, many African Americans took marriage vows before Christian ministers or publicly marked their union in ceremonies that included the West African custom of jumping over a broomstick together. Once married, newly arrived young people in the Cotton South often chose older people in their new communities as fictive "aunts" and "uncles." The slave trade had destroyed their family but not their family values.

The creation of fictive kinship ties was part of a community-building process, a partial substitute for the family ties that sustained whites during periods of crisis. Naming children was another. Recently imported slaves frequently gave their children African names. Males born on Friday, for example, were often called Cuffee—the name of that day in several West African languages. Many American-born parents chose names of British origin, but they usually named sons after fathers, uncles, or grandfathers and daughters after grandmothers. Those transported to the Cotton South often named their children for relatives left behind. Like incest rules and marriage rituals, this intergenerational sharing of names evoked memories of a lost world and bolstered kin ties in the new one.

CONSIDER POINTS OF VIEW
How did African cultural practices affect the lives of enslaved African Americans?

Negotiating Rights

By forming stable families and communities, African Americans gradually created a sense of order in the harsh and arbitrary world of slavery. In a few regions, slaves won substantial control over their lives.

Working Lives   During the Revolutionary era, blacks in the rice-growing lowlands of South Carolina successfully asserted the right to labor by the "task." Under the **task system**, workers had to complete a precisely defined job each day—for example, digging up a quarter-acre of land, hoeing half an acre, or pounding seven mortars of rice. By working hard, many finished their tasks by early afternoon, a Methodist preacher reported, and had "the rest of the day for themselves, which they spend in working their own private fields . . . planting rice, corn, potatoes, tobacco &c. for their own use and profit."

Slaves on sugar and cotton plantations led more regimented lives, thanks to the gang-labor system. As one field hand put it, there was "no time off [between] de change of de seasons. . . . Dey was allus clearin' mo' lan' or sump'." Many slaves faced bans on growing crops on their own. "It gives an excuse for trading," explained one owner, and that encouraged roaming and independence. Still, many masters hired out surplus workers as teamsters, drovers, steamboat workers, turpentine gatherers, and railroad builders; in 1856, no fewer than 435 hired slaves laid track for the Virginia & Tennessee Railroad. Many owners regretted the result. As an overseer remarked about a slave named John, "He is not as good a hand as he was before he went to Alabamy."

Antebellum Slave Quarters   During the colonial period, owners often housed their slaves by gender in communal barracks. In the nineteenth century, slaves usually lived in family units in separate cabins. The slave huts on this South Carolina plantation were sturdily built but had few windows. Inside, they were sparsely furnished. From The New York Public Library.

The planters' greatest fear was that enslaved African Americans — a majority of the population in most cotton-growing counties — would rise in rebellion. Legally speaking, owners had virtually unlimited power over their slaves. "The power of the master must be absolute," intoned Justice Thomas Ruffin of the North Carolina Supreme Court in 1829. But absolute power required brutal coercion, and only hardened or sadistic masters had the stomach for such violence. "These poor negroes, receiving none of the fruits of their labor, do not love work," explained one woman who worked her own farm; "if we had slaves, we should have to . . . beat them to make use of them."

Moreover, passive resistance by African Americans seriously limited their owners' power. Slaves slowed the pace of work by feigning illness and losing or breaking tools. One Maryland slave, faced with transport to Mississippi and separation from his wife, flatly refused "to accompany my people, or to be exchanged or sold," his owner reported. Masters ignored such feelings at their peril. A slave (or a relative) might retaliate by setting fire to the master's house and barns, poisoning his food, or destroying his crops. Fear of resistance, as well as critical scrutiny by abolitionists, prompted many masters to reduce their reliance on the lash and use positive incentives such as food and special privileges. Noted Frederick Law Olmsted: "Men of sense have discovered that it was better to offer them rewards than to whip them." Nonetheless, owners could always resort to violence, and countless masters regularly asserted their power by demanding sex from their female slaves. As ex-slave Bethany Veney lamented in her autobiography, from "the unbridled lust of the slave-owner . . . the law holds . . . no protecting arm" over black women.

Survival Strategies Slavery remained an exploitative system grounded in fear and coercion. Over the decades, hundreds of individual slaves responded by attacking their masters and overseers. But only a few blacks — among them Gabriel and Martin Prosser (1800) and Nat Turner (1831) (Chapter 10) — plotted mass uprisings. Most slaves recognized that revolt would be futile. The tasks of planning, organizing, and assembling weapons for such an action were all but impossible under the constraints of slavery. Whites, by contrast, were readily mobilized, well armed, and determined to maintain their position of racial superiority.

Escape was equally problematic. Blacks in the Upper South could flee to the North, but only by leaving their families and kin. Slaves in the Lower South escaped to sparsely settled regions of Florida, where some intermarried with the Seminole Indians. Elsewhere in the South, escaped slaves eked out a meager existence in inhospitable marshy areas or mountain valleys. Consequently, most African Americans remained on plantations; as Frederick Douglass put it, they were "pegged down to one single spot, and must take root there or die."

"Taking root" meant building the best possible lives for themselves. Over time, enslaved African Americans pressed their owners for a greater share of the product of their labor, much like unionized workers in the North were doing. Thus slaves insisted on getting paid for "overwork" and on the right to cultivate a garden and sell its produce. "De menfolks tend to de gardens round dey own house," recalled a Louisiana slave. "Dey raise some cotton and sell it to massa and git li'l money dat way." Enslaved women raised poultry and sold chickens and eggs. An Alabama slave remembered buying "Sunday clothes with dat money, sech as hats and pants and shoes and dresses." By the 1850s, thousands of African Americans were reaping the small rewards of this underground economy, and some accumulated sizable

CLASS No. 1.

Comprises those prisoners who were found guilty and executed.

Prisoners Names.	Owners' Names.	Time of Commit.	How Disposed of.
Peter	James Poyas	June 18	Hanged on Tuesday the 2d July, 1822, on Blake's lands, near Charleston.
Ned	Gov. T. Bennett,	do.	
Rolla	do.	do	
Batteau	do.	do.	
Denmark Vesey	A free black man	22	
Jessy	Thos. Blackwood	23	
John	Elias Horry	July 5	Do. on the Lines near Ch.; Friday July 12.
Gullah Jack	Paul Pritchard	do.	
Mingo	Wm. Harth	June 21	
Lot	Forrester	27	
Joe	P. L. Jore	July 6	
Julius	Thos. Forrest	8	
Tom	Mrs. Russell	10	
Smart	Robt. Anderson	do.	
John	John Robertson	11	
Robert	do.	do.	
Adam	do.	do.	
Polydore	Mrs. Faber	do.	Hanged on the Lines near Charleston, on Friday, 26th July.
Bacchus	Benj. Hammet	do.	
Dick	Wm. Sims	13	
Pharaoh	— Thompson	do.	
Jemmy	Mrs. Clement	18	
Mauidore	Mordecai Cohen	19	
Dean	— Mitchell	do.	
Jack	Mrs. Purcell	12	
Bellisle	Est. of Jos. Yates	18	
Naphur	do.	do.	
Adam	do.	do.	
Jacob	John S. Glen	16	
Charles	John Billings	18	
Jack	N. McNeill	22	
Cæsar	Miss Smith	do.	
Jacob Stagg	Jacob Lankester	23	Do. Tues. July 30.
Tom	Wm. M. Scott	24	
William	Mrs. Garner	Aug. 2	Do. Friday, Aug. 9.

"An Account of the Late Intended Insurrection, Charleston, South Carolina" In 1820, Charleston had a free black population of 1,500 and an array of African American institutions, including the Brown Fellowship Society (for those of mixed racial ancestry) and an African Methodist Episcopal (AME) church. In 1822, Charleston authorities accused a free black, Denmark Vesey, of organizing a revolt to free the city's slaves. Although historians long accepted the truth of that charge, recent scholarship suggests that Vesey's only offense was antagonizing some whites by claiming his rights as a free man and that fearful slave owners conjured up the plot. Regardless, South Carolina officials hanged Vesey and thirty-four alleged co-conspirators and tore down the AME church where they allegedly plotted the uprising. David M. Rubenstein Rare Book & Manuscript Library, Duke University.

PLACE EVENTS IN CONTEXT
Identify five responses that enslaved people could make to the demands placed upon them. What were the benefits and limitations of each?

property. Enslaved Georgia carpenter Alexander Steele owned four horses, a mule, a silver watch, two cows, a wagon, and large quantities of fodder, hay, and corn.

Whatever their material circumstances, few slaves accepted the legitimacy of their status. Although he was fed well and never whipped, a former slave told an English traveler, "I was cruelly treated because I was kept in slavery." In an address to a white audience on the Fourth of July, the escaped slave and abolitionist Frederick Douglass asked, "What, to the American slave, is your Fourth of July? I answer: a day that reveals to him, more than all other days in the year, the gross injustice and cruelty to which he is the constant victim."

IN YOUR OWN WORDS What resources and strategies gave African American slaves a measure of control over their lives?

Manifest Destiny, North and South

The institution of slavery cast a pall over national politics. The Missouri crisis of 1819–1821 (Chapter 9) frightened the nation's leaders. For the next two decades, the professional politicians who ran the Second Party System avoided policies, such as the annexation of the slaveholding Republic of Texas, that would prompt regional strife. Then, during the 1840s, many citizens embraced an ideology of expansion and proclaimed a God-given duty to extend American republicanism to the Pacific Ocean. But whose republican institutions: the hierarchical slave system of the South or the more egalitarian, reform-minded, capitalist-managed society of the North and Midwest? Or both? Ultimately, the failure to find a political solution to this question would rip the nation apart.

The Push to the Pacific

As expansionists developed continental ambitions, the term *Manifest Destiny* captured those dreams. John L. O'Sullivan, editor of the *Democratic Review*, coined the phrase in 1845: "Our manifest destiny is to overspread the continent allotted by Providence for the free development of our yearly multiplying millions." Underlying the rhetoric of Manifest Destiny was a sense of Anglo-American cultural and racial superiority: the "inferior" peoples who lived in the Far West—Native Americans and Mexicans—would be subjected to American dominion, taught republicanism, and converted to Protestantism (Interpretations).

Long before American politicians became interested in the Far West, however, the region was enmeshed in trade systems that connected Pacific coast settlements with Asia, Europe, and eastern North America. Russian traders made contact with Aleut and Tlingit communities in Alaska in the late eighteenth century and developed a lucrative trade in sea otter pelts, which was controlled after 1799 by the Russian-American Company. British explorer James Cook mapped the Pacific coast in 1778 and learned of the great demand for sea otter pelts in China, prompting a series of British trading voyages to the Pacific Northwest. Between 1788 and 1814, American traders based in Boston overtook their British rivals and dominated the region's maritime trade. Then, in the nineteenth century, overland traders from the Pacific Fur Company of John Jacob Astor, the North West Company based in Montreal, and the Hudson's Bay Company all pushed westward to establish footholds in the region. Thus, the Native peoples of the Pacific Northwest had had sustained contact with Europeans for two generations before the United States became interested in settlement there.

INTERPRETATIONS

What Explains American Enthusiasm for Manifest Destiny?

John O'Sullivan first used the term *Manifest Destiny* in an 1845 article in the *United States Magazine and Democratic Review*. He was writing in favor of the annexation of Texas, a politically divisive issue that had been at the center of the 1844 presidential election. Democrats especially embraced the article's call to "overspread and to possess the whole of the continent." This pro-expansionist sentiment rallied advocates of war with Mexico and emboldened others to challenge Great Britain for the Oregon Territory in the Pacific Northwest. Ultimately, champions of Manifest Destiny scored victories in the 1840s and 1850s that created the American empire they chased. But what motivated their enthusiasm? Reginald Horsman and Amy S. Greenberg take up this question but reach different conclusions.

REGINALD HORSMAN

SOURCE: Reginald Horsman, *Race and Manifest Destiny: The Origins of American Racial Anglo-Saxonism* (Cambridge: Harvard University Press, 1981), 5–6.

By 1850 . . . Americans had evidence plain before them that they were a chosen people; from the English they had learned that the Anglo-Saxons had always been peculiarly gifted in the arts of government; from the scientists and ethnologists they were learning that they were of a distinct Caucasian race, innately endowed with abilities that placed them above other races; from the philologists . . . they were learning that they were the descendants of those Aryans who followed the sun to carry civilization to the whole world. . . . [M]any Americans found comfort in the strength and status of a distinguished racial heritage. The new racial ideology could be used to force new immigrants to conform to the prevailing political, economic, and social system, and it could also be used to justify the sufferings or deaths of blacks, Indians, or Mexicans. Feelings of guilt could be assuaged by assumptions of historical and scientific inevitability. . . . Agrarian and commercial desires and the search for national and personal wealth and security were at the heart of mid-nineteenth-century expansion, but the racial ideology that accompanied and permeated these drives helped determine the nature of America's specific relationships with other peoples encountered in the surge to world power.

AMY S. GREENBERG

SOURCE: Amy S. Greenberg, *Manifest Manhood and the Antebellum American Empire* (New York: Cambridge University Press, 2005), 6, 11, 14, 17.

[T]he American encounter with potential new territories in the antebellum period was shaped by concerns at home, especially evolving gendered ideals and practices. . . . [B]y 1848 . . . two preeminent and dueling . . . masculinities [had emerged]: *restrained manhood* and *martial manhood*. . . . [T]hese two masculinities . . . competed for [dominance]. Territorial expansionism provided one important stage on which this battle was waged. . . . [A]ggressive expansionism, defined here as support for the use of war to gain new American territory . . . was supported by martial men, and . . . debates over Manifest Destiny also were debates over the meaning of American manhood and womanhood. . . . The restrained men who opposed aggressive expansionism also believed that America's Manifest Destiny was yet to be fulfilled, but they envisioned it unfolding . . . through trade and the spread of American social and religious institutions. . . . But in the 1850s the discourse of aggressive expansionism dominated the discussion of America's proper role in the world . . . and . . . led to an unintended victory for martial manhood. It ended up exacerbating the growing sectional conflict by promoting violence as a solution to discord.

QUESTIONS FOR ANALYSIS

1. Describe one major difference between Horsman's and Greenberg's explanations of Manifest Destiny in the antebellum period.
2. To what extent do Horsman and Greenberg agree on the consequences of Manifest Destiny?
3. From Chapter 11's discussion of the expanding American empire, identify two pieces of evidence supporting either Horsman's or Greenberg's interpretation of Manifest Destiny.

Oregon As a result of their overlapping trading activities, Britain and the United States agreed in 1818 to joint control of the Oregon Country, which allowed settlement by people from both nations. Under its terms, the British-run Hudson's Bay Company developed a lucrative fur business and oversaw Indian relations north of the Columbia River, while Methodist missionaries and a few hundred American farmers settled to the south, in the Willamette Valley (Map 11.4).

MAP 11.4 Territorial Conflict in Oregon, 1819–1846
As thousands of American settlers poured into the Oregon Country in the early 1840s, British authorities tried to keep them south of the Columbia River. However, the migrants—and fervent expansionists—asserted that Americans could settle anywhere in the territory, raising the prospect of armed conflict. In 1846, British and American diplomats resolved the dispute by dividing most of the region at the forty-ninth parallel while giving both nations access to fine harbors (Vancouver and Seattle) through the Strait of Juan de Fuca.

Oregon City on the Willamette River, 1850-1852 Americans quickly populated the Far West and re-created there the small-town life of the eastern states. This painting by John Mix Stanley, completed in 1850–1852, captures Oregon City in an early stage of development, when the ground along the river was little more than cleared dirt. On the south bank are a church, several large merchandise warehouses, and numerous houses. On the riverbank opposite, a few smaller structures have begun to appear. In the foreground are two Native Americans, who had a very different way of life and would be steadily pushed off the lands of their ancestors. Library of Congress.

In 1842, American interest in Oregon increased dramatically. The U.S. Navy published a glowing report of fine harbors in the Puget Sound, which New England merchants trading with China were already using. Simultaneously, a party of one hundred farmers journeyed along the Oregon Trail, which fur traders and explorers had blazed from Independence, Missouri, across the Great Plains and the Rocky Mountains (Map 11.5). Their letters from Oregon told of a mild climate and rich soil.

"Oregon fever" suddenly raged. A thousand men, women, and children—with a hundred wagons and five thousand oxen and cattle—gathered in Independence in April 1843. As the spring mud dried, they began their six-month trek, hoping to miss the winter snows. Another 5,000 settlers, mostly farm families from the southern border states (Missouri, Kentucky, and Tennessee), set out over the next two years. These pioneers overcame floods, dust storms, livestock deaths, and a few armed encounters with Native peoples before reaching Oregon, a journey of 2,000 miles.

By 1860, about 250,000 Americans had braved the **Oregon Trail**, with 65,000 heading for Oregon, 185,000 to California, and others staying in Wyoming, Idaho, and Montana. More than 34,000 migrants died, mostly from disease and exposure; fewer than 500 deaths resulted from Indian attacks. The walking migrants wore paths 3 feet deep, and their wagons carved 5-foot ruts across sandstone formations in southern Wyoming—tracks that are visible today. Women found the trail especially difficult; in addition to their usual chores and the new work of driving wagons and animals, they lacked the support of female kin and the security of their domestic space. About 2,500 women endured pregnancy or gave birth during the long journey, and some did not survive. "There was a woman died in this train yesterday," Jane Gould Tortillott noted in her diary. "She left six children, one of them only two days old."

The 10,000 migrants who made it to Oregon in the 1840s mostly settled in the Willamette Valley. Many families squatted on 640 acres and hoped Congress would legalize their claims so that they could sell surplus acreage to new migrants. The settlers quickly created a race- and gender-defined polity by restricting voting to a "free male descendant of a white man."

California About 3,000 other early migrants ended up in the Mexican province of California. They left the Oregon Trail along the Snake River, trudged down the California Trail, and mostly settled in the interior along the Sacramento River, where there were few Mexicans. A remote outpost of Spain's American empire, California had few non-native residents until the 1770s, when Spanish authorities built a chain of forts and

MAP 11.5   The Great Plains: Settler Trails, Indian Raiders, and Traders

By the 1850s, the Mormon, Oregon, and Santa Fe trails ran across "Indian Country," the semiarid, bison-filled Great Plains west of the ninety-fifth meridian, and then through the Rocky Mountains. Tens of thousands of Americans set out on these trails to found new communities in Utah, Oregon, New Mexico, and California. This mass migration exposed sedentary Indian peoples to American diseases, guns, and manufactures. However, raids by Comanches and Sioux affected their lives even more significantly, as did the Euro-American traders who provided a ready market for Indian horses and mules, dried meat, and bison skins.

religious missions along the Pacific coast. When Mexico achieved independence in 1821, its government took over the Franciscan-run missions and freed the 20,000 Indians whom the monks had persuaded or coerced into working on them. Some mission Indians rejoined their tribes, but many intermarried with mestizos (Mexicans of mixed Spanish and Indian ancestry). They worked on huge ranches—the 450 estates created by Mexican officials and bestowed primarily on their families and political allies. The owners of these vast properties (averaging 19,000 acres) mostly raised Spanish cattle, prized for their hides and tallow.

William Henry Jackson, *California Crossing, South Platte River,* **detail, 1867** The South Platte River was wide (stretching from the foreground to the low bluff in the middle of the picture) but shallow, allowing relatively easy passage for the migrants' cattle and covered wagons. Wagon trains followed the course of the various branches of the Platte River for more than 300 miles across the Great Plains. During the late spring and early summer, wagons often stretched as far as the eye could see. National Park Service/Picture Research Consultants & Archives.

The ranches soon linked California to the American economy. New England merchants dispatched dozens of agents to buy leather for the booming Massachusetts boot and shoe industry and tallow to make soap and candles. Many agents married the daughters of the elite Mexican ranchers — the **Californios** — and adopted their manners, attitudes, and Catholic religion. A crucial exception was Thomas Oliver Larkin, a successful merchant in the coastal town of Monterey. Although Larkin worked closely with Mexican politicians and landowners, he remained strongly American in outlook.

Like Larkin, the American migrants in the Sacramento River Valley did not assimilate into Mexican society. Some hoped to emulate the Americans in Texas by colonizing the country and then seeking annexation. However, in the early 1840s, these settlers numbered only about 1,000, far outnumbered by the 7,000 Mexicans who lived along the coast.

> **IDENTIFY CAUSES**
> What developments prompted thousands of Americans to follow the Oregon Trail to the Pacific coast?

The Plains Indians

As the Pacific-bound wagon trains rumbled across Nebraska along the broad Platte River, the migrants encountered the unique ecology of the Great Plains. A vast sea of wild grasses stretched from Texas to Saskatchewan in Canada, and west from the Missouri River to the Rocky Mountains. Tall grasses flourished in the eastern regions of the future states of Kansas, Nebraska, and the Dakotas, where there was moderate rainfall. To the west, in the semiarid region beyond the ninety-fifth meridian, the migrants found short grasses that sustained a rich wildlife dominated by buffalo and grazing antelopes. Nomadic buffalo-hunting Indian peoples roamed the western plains, while the eastern river valleys were home to semisedentary tribes and, since the 1830s, the Indian peoples whom Andrew Jackson had "removed" to the west. A line of military forts — stretching from Fort Jesup in Louisiana to Fort Snelling, then in the Wisconsin Territory — policed the boundary between white settlements and what Congress in 1834 designated as Permanent Indian Territory.

For centuries, the Indians who lived on the eastern edge of the plains, such as the Pawnees and the Mandans on the Upper Missouri River, subsisted primarily on corn and beans, supplemented by buffalo meat. They hunted buffalo on foot, driving them over cliffs or into canyons for the kill. To the south, the nomadic Apaches acquired horses from Spanish settlers in New Mexico and ranged widely across the plains. The Comanches, who migrated down the Arkansas River from the Rocky Mountains around 1750, developed both a horse-based culture and imperial ambitions. Skilled buffalo hunters and fierce warriors, the Comanches slowly pushed the Apaches to the southern edge of the plains. They also raided Spanish settlements in New Mexico, incorporating captured women and children into their society.

After 1800, the Comanches gradually built up a pastoral economy, raising horses and mules and selling them to northern Indian peoples and to Euro-American farmers in Missouri and Arkansas. Many Comanche families owned thirty to thirty-five horses or mules, far more than the five or six required for hunting buffalo and fighting neighboring peoples. The Comanches also exchanged goods with merchants and travelers along the Santa Fe Trail, which cut through their territory as it connected Missouri and New Mexico. By the early 1840s, goods worth nearly $1 million moved along the trail each year.

George Catlin, *Comanche Feats of Horsemanship*, 1834 When artist George Catlin accompanied the dragoons of the U.S. Army into Indian Territory in the 1830s, the Comanches were masters of the southern plains. They hunted buffalo, raised horses and mules for sale, and used their skills as horsemen to dominate other Indian peoples and control the passage of Americans along the Santa Fe Trail. Smithsonian American Art Museum, Washington, DC/Art Resource, NY.

By the 1830s, the Kiowas, Cheyennes, and Arapahos had also adopted this horse culture and, allied with the Comanches, dominated the plains between the Arkansas and Red rivers. The new culture brought sharper social divisions. Some Kiowa men owned hundreds of horses and had several "chore wives" and captive children who worked for them. Poor men, who owned only a few horses, had difficulty finding marriage partners and often had to work for their wealthy kinsmen.

While European horses made Plains Indians wealthier and more mobile, European diseases and guns thinned their ranks. A devastating smallpox epidemic spread northward from New Spain in 1779–1781 and killed half of the Plains peoples. Twenty years later, another smallpox outbreak left dozens of deserted villages along the Missouri River. Smallpox struck the northern plains again from 1837 to 1840, killing half of the Assiniboines and Blackfeet and nearly a third of the Crows, Pawnees, and Cheyennes. "If I could see this thing, if I knew where it came from, I would go there and fight it," exclaimed a distressed Cheyenne warrior.

European weapons also altered the geography of Native peoples. Around 1750, the Crees and Assiniboines, who lived on the far northern plains, acquired guns by trading wolf pelts and beaver skins to the British-run Hudson's Bay Company. Once armed, they drove the Blackfoot peoples westward into the Rocky Mountains and took control of the Saskatchewan and Upper Missouri River basins. When the Blackfeet obtained guns and horses around 1800, they emerged from the mountains and pushed the Shoshones and Crows to the south. Because horses could not easily find winter forage in the snow-filled plains north of the Platte River, Blackfoot families kept only five to ten horses and remained hunters rather than pastoralists.

The powerful Lakota Sioux, who acquired guns and ammunition from French, Spanish, and American traders along the Missouri River, also remained buffalo hunters. A nomadic war-prone people who lived in small groups, the Lakotas largely avoided major epidemics. They kept some sedentary peoples, such as the Arikaras, in subjection and raided others for their crops and horses. By the 1830s, the Lakotas were the dominant tribe on the central as well as the northern plains. "Those lands once belonged to the Kiowas and the Crows," boasted the Oglala Sioux chief Black Hawk, "but we whipped those nations out of them, and in this we did what the white men do when they want the lands of the Indians."

The Sioux's prosperity also came at the expense of the bison, which provided them with a diet rich in protein and with hides and robes to sell. The number of hides and robes shipped down the Missouri River each year by the American Fur Company and the Missouri Fur Company increased from 3,000 in the 1820s, to 45,000 in the 1830s, and to 90,000 annually after 1840. North of the Missouri, the story was much the same. The 24,000 Indians of that region — Blackfeet, Crees, and Assiniboines — annually killed about 160,000 bison. The women dried the meat to feed their people and to sell to white traders and soldiers. The women also undertook the arduous work of skinning and tanning the hides, which they fashioned into tepees, robes, and sleeping covers. Over time, Indian hunters increased the kill and traded surplus hides and robes — about 40,000 annually by the 1840s — for pots, knives, guns, and other Euro-American manufactures. As among the Kiowas, trade increased social divisions. "It is a fine sight," a traveler noted around 1850, "to see one of those big men among the Blackfeet, who has two or three lodges, five or six wives, twenty or thirty children, fifty to a hundred head of horses; for his trade amounts to upward of $2,000 per year."

Although the Blackfeet, Kiowas, and Lakotas contributed bison hides to the national economy, they did not fully grasp their market value as winter clothes, leather accessories, and industrial drive belts. Consequently, they could not demand the best price. Moreover, the increasing size of the kill diminished the bison herds. Between 1820 and 1870, the northern herd shrank from 5 million to less than 2 million. When the Assiniboines' cultural hero Inkton'mi had taught his people how to kill the bison, he told them that the animals "will live as long as your people. There will be no end of them until the end of time." Meant as a perpetual guarantee, by the 1860s Inkton'mi's words prefigured the end of time — the demise of traditional bison hunting and, perhaps, of the Assiniboines as well.

The Fateful Election of 1844

The election of 1844 changed the American government's policy toward the Great Plains, the Far West, and Texas. Since 1836, southern leaders had supported the annexation of Texas, but cautious party politicians, pressured by northerners who opposed the expansion of slavery, had rebuffed them. Now rumors swirled that Great Britain was encouraging Texas to remain independent; wanted California as payment for the Mexican debts owed to British investors; and had designs on Spanish Cuba, which some slave owners wanted to add to the United States. To thwart such imagined schemes, southern expansionists demanded the immediate annexation of Texas.

At this crucial juncture, Oregon fever altered the political landscape in the North. In 1843, Americans in the Ohio River Valley and the Great Lakes states organized "Oregon conventions," and Democratic and Whig politicians alike called for American sovereignty over the entire Oregon Country, from Spanish California to Russian Alaska (which began at 54°40′ north latitude). With northerners demanding Oregon, President John Tyler, a proslavery zealot, called for the annexation of Texas. Disowned by the Whigs because he thwarted Henry Clay's nationalist economic program, Tyler hoped to win reelection in 1844 as a Democrat. To curry favor among northern expansionists, Tyler supported claims to all of Oregon.

In April 1844, Tyler and John C. Calhoun, his proslavery, expansionist-minded secretary of state, sent the Senate a treaty to bring Texas into the Union. However, the two major presidential hopefuls, Democrat Martin Van Buren and Whig Henry Clay, opposed Tyler's initiative. Fearful of raising the issue of slavery, they persuaded the Senate to reject the treaty.

Nonetheless, expansion into Texas and Oregon became the central issue in the election of 1844. Most southern Democrats favored Texas annexation and refused to support Van Buren's candidacy. The party also passed over Tyler, whom they did not trust. Instead, the Democrats selected Governor James K. Polk of Tennessee, a slave owner and an avowed expansionist. Known as "Young Hickory" because he was a protégé of Andrew Jackson, Polk shared his mentor's iron will, boundless ambition, and determination to open up lands for American settlement. Accepting the false claim in the Democratic Party platform that both areas already belonged to the United States, Polk campaigned for the "Re-occupation of Oregon and the Re-annexation of Texas." He insisted that the United States defy British claims and occupy "the whole of the territory of Oregon" to the Alaskan border. **"Fifty-four forty or fight!"** became his jingoistic cry.

The Whigs nominated Henry Clay, who again advocated his American System of high tariffs, internal improvements, and national banking. Clay initially dodged the issue of Texas but, seeking southern votes, ultimately supported annexation. Northern Whigs who opposed the admission of a new slave state refused to vote for Clay and cast their ballots for James G. Birney of the Liberty Party (Chapter 10). Birney garnered less than 3 percent of the national vote but took enough Whig votes in New York to cost Clay that state — and the presidency.

Following Polk's narrow victory, congressional Democrats called for immediate Texas statehood. However, they lacked the two-thirds majority in the Senate needed to ratify a treaty of annexation. So the Democrats admitted Texas using a joint resolution of Congress, which required just a majority vote in each house, and Texas became the twenty-eighth state in December 1845. Polk's strategy of linking Texas and Oregon had put him in the White House and Texas in the Union. Shortly, it would make the expansion of the South — and its system of slavery — the central topic of American politics (Analyzing Voices).

TRACE CHANGE OVER TIME
Why did some Great Plains peoples flourish between 1750 and 1860 while others did not?

CONSIDER POINTS OF VIEW
Why did party politicians initially oppose the annexation of Texas, and how did this view change during the election of 1844?

IN YOUR OWN WORDS Did the idea of Manifest Destiny cause westward migration and political support for territorial expansion, or did it only justify actions taken for other reasons?

The U.S.-Mexico War: Expansion and Slavery

Conflict with Mexico prompted debates over the Polk administration's aggressive efforts to acquire territory and spread slavery. Here, Polk's critics face off against the expansionists.

JOHN L. O'SULLIVAN, EDITOR

"Manifest Destiny," from *United States Magazine and Democratic Review*, July 1845

SOURCE: Sean Wilentz, ed., *Major Problems in the Early Republic, 1787–1848* (Lexington, MA: D. C. Heath, 1991), 525–528.

66 Texas is now ours . . . [Britain and France tried] to intrude themselves [into Texas affairs] . . . for the avowed object of thwarting our policy and hampering our power, limiting our greatness and checking the fulfillment of our manifest destiny to overspread the continent allotted by Providence for the free development of our yearly multiplying millions. . . .

The independence of Texas was complete and absolute. It was an independence, not only in fact, but of right. . . . What then can be more preposterous than all this clamor by Mexico and the Mexican interest, against Annexation, as a violation of any rights of hers . . . ?

Nor is there any just foundation for the charge that Annexation is a great pro-slavery measure — calculated to increase and perpetuate that institution. Slavery had nothing to do with it. . . . That it will tend to facilitate and hasten the disappearance of Slavery from all the northern tier of the present Slave States, cannot surely admit of serious question. The greater value in Texas of the slave labor now employed in those States, must soon produce the effect of draining off that labor southwardly. . . .

California will, probably, next fall away. . . . Already the advance guard of the irresistible army of Anglo-Saxon emigration has begun to pour down upon it, armed with the plough and the rifle, and marking its trail with schools and colleges, courts and representative halls, mills and meeting-houses. A population will soon be in actual occupation of California. . . . And they will have a right to independence — to self-government . . . a better and a truer right than the artificial title of sovereignty in Mexico, a thousand miles distant, inheriting from Spain a title good only against those who have none better. 99

JAMES BUCHANAN, U.S. SECRETARY OF STATE

Letter to John Slidell, Minister Plenipotentiary to Mexico, November 1845

SOURCE: Victoria Bissell Brown and Timothy J. Shannon, eds., *Going to the Source: The Bedford Reader in American History* (Boston: Bedford/St. Martin's, 2004), 1: 260–262.

66 In your negotiations with Mexico, the independence of Texas must be considered a settled fact, and is not to be called in question. . . .

It may, however, be contended on the part of Mexico, that the Nueces and not the Rio del Norte [Rio Grande], is the true western boundary of Texas. I need not furnish you arguments to controvert this position. . . . The jurisdiction of Texas has been extended beyond that river [the Nueces] and . . . representatives from the country between it and the Del Norte have participated in the deliberations both of her Congress and her Convention. . . .

The case is different in regard to New Mexico. Santa Fe, its capital, was settled by the Spaniards more than two centuries ago; and that province has been ever since in their possession and that of the Republic of Mexico. The Texans never have conquered or taken possession of it. . . . [However,] a great portion of New Mexico being on this side of the Rio Grande and included within the limits already claimed by Texas, it may hereafter, should it remain a Mexican province, become a subject of dispute. . . . It would seem to be equally

---

The U.S.-Mexico War, 1846–1848

In the Southwest, as in the Oregon Country, dramatic change came quickly in the 1840s. Comanches, Kiowas, Apaches, and Navajos who had traded peacefully with northern Mexicans for decades began, instead, to make war on their ranches and towns, ruining the region's economy and devastating many of its settlements. The Mexican government proved unable to suppress these attacks. Recognizing an opportunity to gain even more territory, Polk determined to go to war if necessary to acquire all the Mexican lands between Texas and the Pacific Ocean. What he and many Democrats the interest of both Powers, that New Mexico should belong to the United States. . . .

It is to be seriously apprehended that both Great Britain and France have designs upon California. . . . This Government . . . would vigorously interpose to prevent the latter from becoming either a British or a French Colony. . . . The possession of the Bay and harbor of San Francisco, is all important to the United States. . . . Money would be no object. **99**

CHARLES SUMNER, CONSCIENCE WHIG AND FUTURE REPUBLICAN SENATOR FROM MASSACHUSETTS

Letter to Robert Winthrop, Whig Congressman from Massachusetts, October 25, 1846

SOURCE: Sean Wilentz, ed., *Major Problems in the Early Republic, 1787–1848* (Lexington, MA: D. C. Heath, 1991), 541.

66 If we regard Texas as a province of Mexico, its boundaries must be sought in the geography of that republic. If we regard it as an independent State, they must be determined by the extent of jurisdiction which the State was able to maintain. Now it seems clear that the river Nueces was always recognized by Mexico as the western boundary; and it is undisputed that the State of Texas, since its Declaration of Independence, never exercised any jurisdiction beyond the Nueces. . . .

In the month of January, 1846, the President of the United States directed the troops under General Taylor, called the Army of Occupation, to take possession of this region [west of the Nueces River]. Here was an act of aggression. As might have been expected, it produced collision. The Mexicans, aroused in self-defence, sought to repel the invaders. . . .

Here the question occurs, What was the duty of Congress in this emergency? Clearly to withhold all sanction to unjust war, — to aggression upon a neighboring Republic. . . . The American forces should have been directed to retreat, not from any human force, but from wrongdoing; and this would have been a true victory.

Alas! This was not the mood of Congress. With wicked speed a bill was introduced, furnishing large and unusual supplies of men and money. . . . This was adopted by a vote of 123 to 67; and the bill then leaped forth, fully armed, as a measure of open and active hostility against Mexico. **99**

WALT WHITMAN, POET AND EDITOR OF THE *BROOKLYN EAGLE*

Editorial, September 1, 1847

SOURCE: Sean Wilentz, ed., *Major Problems in the Early Republic, 1787–1848* (Lexington, MA: D. C. Heath, 1991), 543.

66 The question whether or no there shall be slavery in the new territories . . . is a question between the grand body of white workingmen, the millions of mechanics, farmers, and operatives of our country, with their interests on the one side — and the interests of the few thousand rich, 'polished,' and aristocratic owners of slaves at the South, on the other side.

Experience has proved . . . that a stalwart mass of respectable workingmen, cannot exist, much less flourish, in a thorough slave State. Let any one think for a moment what a different appearance New York, Pennsylvania, or Ohio, would present — how much less sturdy independence and family happiness there would be — were slaves the workmen there, instead of each man as a general thing being his own workman. . . .

Slavery is a good thing enough . . . to the rich — the one out of thousands; but it is destructive to the dignity and independence of all who work, and to labor itself. . . . All practice and theory . . . are strongly arrayed in favor of limiting slavery to where it already exists. **99**

QUESTIONS FOR ANALYSIS

1. What arguments do Buchanan and Sumner make about the boundaries of Texas, the issue that sparked the fighting? Whose argument is more persuasive and why?
2. Do O'Sullivan's and Buchanan's assertions support or undercut the claim that the U.S.-Mexico War was an aggressive act of imperialism?
3. Why does Whitman oppose the expansion of slavery? Given Whitman's views, who might have gotten his vote in the election of 1848? Why?
4. Two of the sources are newspaper editorials; two are letters written by or addressed to public officials. How does the nature of each of these sources influence its content?

---

consciously ignored was the domestic crisis that a war of conquest to expand slavery would unleash.

The "War of a Thousand Deserts"

Since gaining independence in 1821, Mexico had not prospered. Its federal system of government tended to serve the northern frontier states poorly, while two decades of political instability resulted in a stagnant economy and modest tax revenues, which debt payments to European bankers quickly devoured. In the 1830s and 1840s, Comanche warriors conducted dozens of campaigns against the settlements of the Mexican north.

Mexico's central government lacked the resources to respond effectively, and the northern territories were devastated. Always sparsely settled—California and New Mexico had a Spanish-speaking population of only 75,000 in 1840—many northern ranches and communities were abandoned in what one historian has called the "War of a Thousand Deserts." Nevertheless, Mexican officials vowed to preserve their nation's historic boundaries. When its breakaway province of Texas prepared to join the American Union, Mexico suspended diplomatic relations with the United States.

Polk's Expansionist Program

President Polk moved quickly to acquire Mexico's other northern provinces. He hoped to foment a revolution in California that, like the 1836 rebellion in Texas, would lead to annexation. In October 1845, Secretary of State James Buchanan told merchant Thomas Oliver Larkin, now the U.S. consul for the Mexican province, to encourage influential Californios to seek independence and union with the United States. To add military muscle to this scheme, Polk ordered American naval commanders to seize San Francisco Bay and California's coastal towns in case of war with Mexico. The president also instructed the War Department to dispatch Captain John C. Frémont and an "exploring" party of soldiers into Mexican territory. By December 1845, Frémont's force had reached California's Sacramento River Valley.

With these preparations in place, Polk launched a secret diplomatic initiative: he sent Louisiana congressman John Slidell to Mexico, telling him to secure the Rio Grande boundary for Texas and to buy the provinces of California and New Mexico for $30 million. Insulted by U.S. disregard for Mexico's sovereignty, government officials refused to meet with Slidell (America in Global Context).

Events now moved quickly toward war. Polk ordered General Zachary Taylor and an American army of 2,000 soldiers to occupy disputed lands between the Nueces River (the historic southern boundary of Spanish Texas) and the Rio Grande, which the Republic of Texas had claimed as its border with Mexico. "We were sent to provoke a fight," recalled Ulysses S. Grant, then a young officer serving with Taylor, "but it was essential that Mexico should commence it." When the armies clashed near the Rio Grande in May 1846, Polk delivered the war message he had drafted long before. Taking liberties with the truth, the president declared that Mexico "has passed the boundary of the United States, has invaded our territory, and shed American blood upon the American soil." Ignoring pleas by some Whigs for a negotiated settlement, an overwhelming majority in Congress voted for war—a decision greeted with great popular acclaim. To avoid a simultaneous war with Britain, Polk

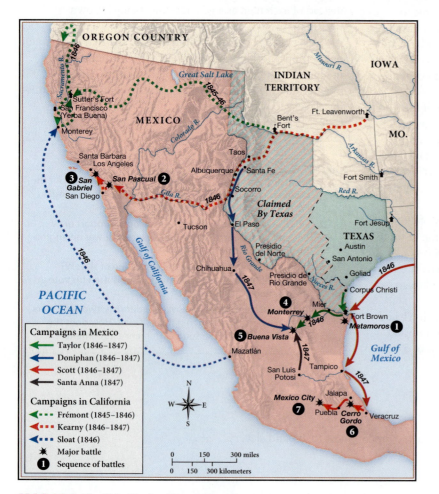

MAP 11.6 The U.S.-Mexico War, 1846–1848

After moving west from Fort Leavenworth in present-day Kansas, American forces commanded by Captain John C. Frémont and General Stephen Kearny defeated Mexican armies in California in 1846 and early 1847. Simultaneously, U.S. troops under General Zachary Taylor and Colonel Alfred A. Doniphan won victories over General Santa Anna's forces south of the Rio Grande. In mid-1847, General Winfield Scott mounted a successful seaborne attack on Veracruz and Mexico City, ending the war.

Financing War

To explain the outcome of war, we usually focus on the combatants' military assets, but a nation's finances also play a crucial role. In the U.S.-Mexico War, the United States benefitted from low federal expenditures and a reliable tax system. Mexico, though it had been one of Spain's most valuable colonies, struggled financially after it gained independence in 1821. Higher expenses and widespread tax evasion caused large deficits, making it difficult to borrow the funds it needed to fight. The United States kept expenses low, nearly eliminated the federal debt, and ran small deficits, which made it easier to finance the war effort. The following tables illustrate this comparison.

Mexico: Tax Revenues, 1790–1844	
1790	$10,466,831
1808	$58,829,740
1816	$47,920,070
1840	$15,452,919
1844	$20,592,058

United States: Tax Revenues, 1790–1844	
1792	$3,670,000
1808	$17,061,000
1816	$47,678,000
1840	$19,480,000
1844	$29,321,000

Mexico: Revenues and Expenses, 1840–1844			
	Revenues	Expenses	Deficit
1840	$15,452,919	$21,255,097	$5,802,173
1841	$14,724,788	$22,997,219	$8,272,431
1842	$15,968,774	$30,639,711	$14,670,937
1843	$19,602,180	$34,035,277	$14,433,097
1844	$20,592,058	$31,304,102	$10,712,044

United States: Revenues and Expenses, 1840–1844			
	Revenues	Expenses	Deficit
1840	$19,480,000	$24,318,000	$4,837,000
1841	$16,860,000	$26,566,000	$9,706,000
1842	$19,976,000	$25,206,000	$5,230,000
1843	$ 8,303,000	$11,858,000	$3,555,000
1844	$29,321,000	$22,338,000	($6,984,000)

SOURCES: Barbara A. Tenenbaum, *The Politics of Penury: Debts and Taxes in Mexico, 1821–1856* (Albuquerque: University of New Mexico Press, 1986); *Historical Statistics of the United States: Millennial Edition Online* (New York: Cambridge University Press).

QUESTIONS FOR ANALYSIS

1. Why do you think Mexico's tax collection system might have been more effective when it was a colony of Spain than it was once the nation gained independence? Why did the United States have a different experience?

2. Compare the nations' revenues, expenses, and deficits in the years 1840–1844. What are the most significant differences?

---

retreated from his demand for "fifty-four forty or fight" and in June 1846 accepted British terms that divided the Oregon Country at the forty-ninth parallel.

American Military Successes

American forces in Texas quickly established their military superiority. Zachary Taylor's army crossed the Rio Grande; occupied the Mexican city of Matamoros; and, after a fierce six-day battle in September 1846, took the interior Mexican town of Monterrey. Two months later, a U.S. naval squadron in the Gulf of Mexico seized Tampico, Mexico's second most important port. By the end of 1846, the United States controlled much of northeastern Mexico (Map 11.6).

Street Fighting in the Calle de Iturbide, 1846 Monterrey, which had resisted Spanish troops during Mexico's war for independence (1820–1821), was captured by the Americans only after bloody house-to-house fighting in the U.S.-Mexico War (1846–1848). Protected by thick walls and shuttered windows, Mexican defenders pour a withering fire on the dark-uniformed American troops and buckskin-clad frontier fighters. A large Catholic cathedral looms in the background, its foundations obscured by the smoke from the Mexicans' cannons. West Point Museum, United States Military Academy, West Point, NY.

COMPARE AND CONTRAST
How was the American acquisition of California similar to, and different from, the American-led creation of the Texas Republic?

Fighting also broke out in California. In June 1846, naval commander John Sloat landed 250 marines in Monterey and declared that California "henceforward will be a portion of the United States." Simultaneously, American settlers in the Sacramento River Valley staged a revolt and, supported by Frémont's force, captured the town of Sonoma, where they proclaimed the independence of the "**Bear Flag Republic**." To cement these victories, Polk ordered army units to capture Santa Fe in New Mexico and then march to southern California. Despite stiff Mexican resistance, American forces secured control of California early in 1847.

Polk expected these victories to end the war, but he underestimated the Mexicans' national pride and the determination of President Santa Anna. In February 1847 in the Battle of Buena Vista, Santa Anna nearly defeated Taylor's army in northeastern Mexico. With most Mexican troops deployed in the north, Polk approved General Winfield Scott's plan to capture the port of Veracruz and march 260 miles to Mexico City. An American army of 14,000 seized the Mexican capital in September 1847. That American victory cost Santa Anna his presidency, and a new Mexican government made a forced peace with the United States.

IN YOUR OWN WORDS What were the roles of Plains Indians, Anglo-American immigrants to Texas, the Mexican government, the U.S. government, and the American public in sparking the U.S.-Mexico War?

SUMMARY

This chapter explored the imperial ambitions of the United States and the competition among nations for control of western North America. It began by tracing the contours of the southern social order that emerged with the expansion of slave plantation agriculture. It followed the migration of ambitious slaveholders into the Mexican state of Coahuila y Tejas, considered the challenges that aristocratic planters faced in a democratic political order, and analyzed the patterns of work, family, community life, and culture that structured African American experience.

The American ideology of Manifest Destiny, which held that God intended that the dominion of the United States should extend across the entire North American continent, informed U.S. efforts to claim the Oregon Country and California and shaped the country's interactions with the independent Plains Indians, many of whom were formidable powers in their own right. Finally, the chapter examined the aftermath of the presidential election of 1844, which brought James K. Polk to power and set the nation's course toward war with Mexico. In Chapter 12, we will consider the effects of that war on American society and politics.

TERMS TO KNOW

Identify and explain the significance of each term below.

Key Concepts and Events

slave society (p. 335)

republican aristocracy (p. 335)

Great American Desert (p. 338)

Alamo (p. 339)

secret ballot (p. 339)

black Protestantism (p. 342)

Gullah dialect (p. 343)

task system (p. 346)

Manifest Destiny (p. 348)

Oregon Trail (p. 350)

Californios (p. 352)

"Fifty-four forty or fight!" (p. 355)

Bear Flag Republic (p. 360)

Key People

Sam Houston (p. 338)

Stephen Austin (p. 338)

Antonio López de Santa Anna (p. 338)

James K. Polk (p. 355)

Zachary Taylor (p. 358)

John C. Frémont (p. 358)

REVIEW QUESTIONS

Answer these questions to demonstrate your understanding of the chapter's main ideas.

1. What were the strengths and limitations of the South's economy and social structure?

2. What resources and strategies gave African American slaves a measure of control over their lives?

3. Did the idea of Manifest Destiny cause westward migration and political support for territorial expansion, or did it only justify actions taken for other reasons?

4. What were the roles of Plains Indians, Anglo-American immigrants to Texas, the Mexican government, the U.S. government, and the American public in sparking the U.S.-Mexico War?

5. Review the events listed under "Migration and Settlement" on the thematic timeline on page 237, and then discuss how southern expansion, the end of the Atlantic slave trade in 1808, and the subsequent rise of the internal slave trade affected the experiences and identities of the African American population.

MAKING CONNECTIONS

Recognize the larger developments and continuities within and across chapters by answering these questions.

1. How were the American territorial acquisitions of the 1840s similar to, and/or different from, those of the Treaty of Paris of 1783 and the Louisiana Purchase (discussed in Chapters 6 and 7)?

2. In the painting *American Progress* (p. 333), why does John Gast choose Liberty to lead the republic westward? How does he interpret the American experience, and what stories does he tell in the image's foreground, middle ground, and background? How does the evidence in the chapter challenge Gast's interpretation of westward expansion?

KEY TURNING POINTS

Refer to the chapter chronology on page 334 for help in answering the question below.

Focusing on developments in the 1830s and 1840s, what were the similarities and differences between the outcomes of Manifest Destiny in the North and the South?

5
PART

Consolidating a Continental Union
1844–1877

Should historians of the United States call the mid-nineteenth century the Civil War era? Many do, but in *America's History* we choose a slightly different emphasis. Like other scholars, we argue that the Civil War and the end of slavery brought extraordinary changes in U.S. politics, law, society, and culture. We devote a full chapter to the political crisis of the 1850s; one to the Civil War itself; one to the turmoil of Reconstruction, the postwar struggle over power and policy in the ex-Confederacy and nationwide; and one to the consolidation of the West, a process that began before the Civil War and continued after the end of Reconstruction.

The first Republican president, Abraham Lincoln, engineered the triumph of the Union, but on terms few expected when the war began. Instead of a short, heroic conflict between white northerners and southerners, the Civil War turned into an agonizing "hard war" that lasted four weary years. Emancipation, which few white Unionists expected at the start, proved essential to winning the war, as did the participation and sacrifice of African Americans, 180,000 of whom served in the U.S. Army for the first time.

Union victory ended slavery—a momentous achievement. It did not, however, resolve the bitter disagreements that had caused the war in the first place. In fact, conflicting points of view only multiplied in the decades after Confederate defeat. That's why, in Part 5, we place the Civil War in broader context. In one of history's astonishing upsets, the Republican Party—which did not exist until 1854—not only won national power by 1860 but, because of the South's secession, wielded it freely to remake federal policies. Those policies increased U.S. control over the trans-Mississippi West, transformed economic and political relationships among the nation's regions, and set the stage for U.S. global power. ▶

Sectional Conflict and Civil War

The U.S.-Mexico War prompted a decade-long debate over whether slavery should expand into the newly conquered lands. The Compromise of 1850, a complex legislative agreement designed to solve the conflict, won little support in either North or South, and the Kansas-Nebraska Act of 1854 precipitated even further conflict. Southern Whigs abandoned their party for the Democrats, while northern Whigs became Republicans or anti-immigrant Know-Nothings. By 1860 Democrats also split on sectional lines, enabling the election of Republican president Abraham Lincoln.

Starting with South Carolina, eleven southern states seceded in response to Lincoln's election and created the Confederate States of America. Elsewhere, citizens rallied to preserve the Union. In the long Civil War that followed, the military forces of the Union and Confederacy were at first evenly matched. However, as neither side proved able to crush the other, the North's superior financial and industrial resources gradually gave it the advantage, as did Lincoln's proclamation of emancipation in 1863. Linking Union victory to the end of slavery undermined European support for the Confederacy and added thousands of African Americans to the northern armies, helping Union forces sweep across the South and end the war.

Alabama Department of Archives and History.

Expanding Federal Power

The Civil War created a powerful American state, as the Union government mobilized millions of men and billions of dollars. Republicans created an elaborate network of national banks and — for the first time in U.S. history — a significant federal bureaucracy. Congress intervened forcefully to integrate the national economy and promote industrialization. These policies, along with the nation's dynamic postwar economy, set the nation on a course toward global power.

The Civil War increased federal authority in other ways. Three Republican-sponsored constitutional amendments limited the powers of the states and imposed new definitions of citizenship — prohibiting slavery, enfranchising black men, and forbidding state actions that denied people equal protection under the law. The U.S. Army, which occupied parts of the ex-Confederacy as late as 1877, also suppressed Indian resistance and extended national control in the West.

Library of Congress.

A Continental Empire

The United States claimed large swaths of western territory in the 1840s, through victory in the U.S.-Mexico War and the California gold rush that followed. But it was post–Civil War railroad building and economic expansion that truly brought the West into the orbit of federal authority. This expansion intensified conflicts between Native peoples, Mexican Americans, and Anglo newcomers. By 1890, most Native peoples had been forced onto reservations, while thousands of Mexicans also found themselves dispossessed. The legacies of the Civil War, therefore, were as significant in the West as in the former Confederacy. Western minerals, lumber, cattle, wheat, and oil proved essential to the transformation we will discuss in Part 6: the United States's economic transformation and rise to global economic power.

Denver Public Library, Western History Collection/ Bridgeman Images.

Consolidating a Continental Union 1844–1877

The Granger Collection, New York.

Thematic Understanding

This timeline arranges some of the important events of this period into themes. Which events reflect the causes and consequences of the Civil War, as well as Union and Confederate actions during the war itself? Which events show how the United States asserted control over the trans-Mississippi West, and who resisted that process and why? Which events in each set of conflicts were military, economic, or legal and constitutional? How would you compare and contrast these different modes of nation-building? ▶

	AMERICAN AND NATIONAL IDENTITY	POLITICS AND POWER	WORK, EXCHANGE, AND TECHNOLOGY	
1840	• Free Soil Party forms (1848) • Foreign Miner's Tax enacted in California (1850)	• James K. Polk elected president (1844) • Wilmot Proviso approved by House but not by Senate (1846)	• Gold discovered in California (1848)	
1850	• American (Know-Nothing) Party forms (1851) • *Dred Scott v. Sandford* allows slavery in all U.S. territories (1857) • John Brown raids federal arsenal at Harpers Ferry (1859)	• Compromise of 1850 • Kansas-Nebraska Act tests popular sovereignty (1854) • Republican Party forms (1854) • Rep. Preston Brooks canes Sen. Charles Sumner on Senate floor (1856)	• Comstock silver lode discovered in Nevada (1859)	
1860	• General Butler declares refugee slaves "contraband of war" (1861) • Dakota Sioux uprising in Minnesota (1862) • Lincoln issues preliminary emancipation proclamation (Sept. 1862) • Union initiates draft, sparking riots in New York City (1863) • Lincoln delivers Gettysburg Address (1863) • Ex-Confederate states pass Black Codes to limit freedpeople's rights (1865) • Civil Rights Act passed over President Johnson's veto (1866) • Wyoming Territory grants women suffrage (1869)	• Lincoln elected president (1860) • Deep South states secede (1860–1861) • Confederate forces fire on Fort Sumter (April 1861) • Upper South secedes (1861) • Confederates win First Battle of Bull Run (July 1861) • Union wins battles of Gettysburg and Vicksburg (July 1863) • Lincoln reelected (1864) • Robert E. Lee surrenders to Grant (April 1865) • Lincoln assassinated (1865) • Reconstruction Act (1867) • Impeachment of Andrew Johnson (1868) • Fourteenth Amendment (1868) • Ulysses S. Grant elected president (1868)	• Legal Tender Act authorizes greenback currency (1862) • Explosion kills munitions workers in Pittsburgh (1862) • Long Drive of Texas longhorns begins (1865) • Transcontinental railroad completed (1869)	
1870	• Utah Territory grants women suffrage (1870) • *Minor v. Happersett*: Supreme Court rules that Fourteenth Amendment does not extend national voting rights to women (1875) • Sioux, Cheyennes, and Arapahos win Battle of Little Big Horn (1876)	• Congress passes Enforcement Laws to suppress Klan (1870) • Fifteenth Amendment (1870) • Grant reelected; Crédit Mobilier scandal (1872) • *Slaughterhouse Cases* (1873) • Sweeping Democratic gains in congressional elections (1874) • *Munn v. Illinois* (1877)	• Panic of 1873 ushers in severe economic depression (1873) • United States begins to move to gold standard (1873)	
1880	• Rise of the Ghost Dance movement • Dawes Severalty Act (1887)			
1890	• Massacre of Sioux Ghost Dancers at Wounded Knee, South Dakota (1890)			

	CULTURE AND SOCIETY	MIGRATION AND SETTLEMENT	GEOGRAPHY AND THE ENVIRONMENT	AMERICA IN THE WORLD	
		• Great Irish famine prompts mass immigration to United States (1845–1851) • "Forty-niners" seek gold in California (1849)		• Congress supports Polk's recommendation and declares war on Mexico (1846) • Treaty of Guadalupe Hidalgo transfers Mexican lands to United States (1848)	**1840**
	• Harriet Beecher Stowe publishes *Uncle Tom's Cabin* (1852)			• Treaty of Kanagawa opens U.S. coaling stations in Japan (1854) • Ostend Manifesto urges U.S. seizure of Cuba (1854) • William Walker deposes Nicaraguan government, sets up "filibuster" regime (1856) • President Buchanan seeks to buy and annex Cuba as a slave state (1858)	**1850**
	• U.S. Sanitary Commission formed (1861) • Morrill Act funds public state universities (1862) • Louisa May Alcott publishes *Hospital Sketches* (1863) • Women's rights advocates form Woman's Loyal National League (1863)	• African Americans escape slavery and become "contrabands" behind Union lines (1861–1865)	• Homestead Act passed (1862) • Yosemite Valley reserved as public park (1864) • Sherman's army devastates Georgia and South Carolina (1864–1865)	• Britain and France refuse recognition to the Confederacy; Britain impounds Confederate ships being built in British shipyards (1863) • Burlingame Treaty with China (1868)	**1860**
	• Ku Klux Klan at peak of power (1870) • Victoria Woodhull declares support for "free love" (1871) • Beecher-Tilton scandal dominates headlines (1875)	• Nez Perce forcibly removed from homelands in Northwest (1877) • Exoduster migration to Kansas (1879)	• General Mining Act (1872) • Yellowstone National Park created (1872) • John Wesley Powell presents *Report on . . . Arid Region of the United States* (1879)		**1870**
	• Sitting Bull tours with Buffalo Bill's Wild West (1885)	• Chiricahua Apache leader Geronimo surrenders (1886)	• Dry cycle begins on the Great Plains (1886)		**1880**
					1890

12 CHAPTER

Sectional Conflict and Crisis
1844–1861

The U.S.-Mexico War was immensely popular with millions of Americans. Those who opposed it took big risks, as young Abraham Lincoln discovered to his dismay. In December 1847, as a freshman Whig congressman from Illinois, Lincoln introduced a bill demanding that President Polk identify the exact geographical spot where the war had begun, which Polk claimed had been in U.S. territory. Lincoln, like other critics, believed U.S. troops had been trespassing on Mexican soil. But Lincoln's "spot resolution" went nowhere. Ridiculing the young congressman, a newspaper in his home state nicknamed him "Spotty Lincoln" and a Democrat defeated him in the next election. Lincoln went back to his law practice in Springfield.

Soon afterward, in 1849, tales of California gold generated great excitement over the riches waiting in newly won territories. Thousands of American men rushed west, joining counterparts from Mexico, Chile, Hawaii, Britain, and elsewhere to gather gold from the beds of California's rivers and streams. San Francisco became an overnight boomtown. Alas, few struck it rich, and the chaotic quest for gold led to vigilantism, ugly racial conflicts, and the deliberate near-extermination of California's Native peoples.

Like the lure of California gold, U.S. dreams of territorial expansion gave way to harsher truths in the 1850s. The process of incorporating the **Mexican cession** — lands the United States had acquired in the war — reignited fierce debates over the expansion of slavery. Though only a small minority of white northerners were abolitionists, by the 1850s many feared the "slave power" of southern interests and wanted western territories reserved as "free soil" for white farmers. Rising politicians — among them Lincoln, who returned to politics to help found the Illinois Republican Party — vowed to block the expansion of slavery, pointing out that the Northwest Ordinance of 1787 barred slavery in the Midwest. Southerners, in turn, insisted that the Constitution protected slaveholders' property rights throughout the nation. As early as 1850, some radicals called for secession while others launched military expeditions into Latin America to add territory to slavery's empire. As conflict accelerated, violence erupted in California, Kansas, Virginia, and even on the Senate floor. The dispute shattered old alliances, ultimately fragmenting both major parties. By 1861 it ignited a political firestorm that engulfed the Union.

IDENTIFY THE BIG IDEA

What caused the political turmoil that led to the rise of the Republican Party, Democratic division, and southern secession?

Fugitive Slave Law Convention in Cazenovia, New York, 1850 This daguerreotype, a detail from the only known photograph of an abolitionist meeting before the Civil War, shows the movement's diversity and determination. Over 2,000 abolitionists gathered in upstate New York for the convention, including about 50 fugitive slaves. Frederick Douglass, center left, presided. The group denounced the federal Fugitive Slave Act, which Congress was then debating; issued a letter of solidarity with those still enslaved; and raised money to free William Chaplin, a Washington, D.C., man who was imprisoned for helping a slave escape. Though the convention did not stop passage of the Fugitive Slave Act, it showed the growing militancy and political ambition of those who denounced the cruelty of slavery. Artokoloro Quint Lox Limited/Alamy Stock Photo.

As you read, ask yourself why this chapter begins and ends with these dates and identify the links among related events.

1844	▶ James K. Polk elected president
1845–1851	▶ Great Irish famine prompts mass immigration to United States
1846	▶ Congress supports Polk's recommendation and declares war against Mexico
1846	▶ Wilmot Proviso approved by House but not by Senate
1848	▶ Gold found in California; gold rush begins ▶ Treaty of Guadalupe Hidalgo transfers Mexican lands to United States ▶ Free Soil Party forms
1850	▶ Compromise of 1850 passes, including Fugitive Slave Act ▶ Foreign Miner's Tax enacted in California
1851	▶ American (Know-Nothing) Party forms
1852	▶ Harriet Beecher Stowe publishes *Uncle Tom's Cabin*
1854	▶ Treaty of Kanagawa opens U.S. coaling stations in Japan ▶ Ostend Manifesto urges U.S. seizure of Cuba ▶ Kansas-Nebraska Act tests policy of popular sovereignty ▶ Republican Party forms
1856	▶ Rep. Preston Brooks canes Sen. Charles Sumner on Senate floor ▶ William Walker deposes Nicaraguan government, sets up "filibuster" regime

1857	▶ *Dred Scott v. Sandford* allows slavery in all U.S. territories
1858	▶ President James Buchanan urges Congress to admit Kansas under the proslavery Lecompton constitution ▶ Buchanan seeks to buy and annex Cuba as a slave state ▶ United States fights brief "Mormon War" for federal control of Utah
1859	▶ John Brown raids federal arsenal at Harpers Ferry
1860	▶ Abraham Lincoln elected president in four-way contest ▶ South Carolina secedes (December)
1861	▶ Mississippi, Florida, Alabama, Georgia, Louisiana, and Texas secede before February 1 ▶ Confederate States of America formed (February) ▶ Lincoln inaugurated (March) ▶ Confederate forces fire on Fort Sumter when Lincoln administration directs an attempted food resupply (April) ▶ Lincoln calls for three-month volunteer troops to suppress ▶ rebellion Four Upper South states (Virginia, Arkansas, North Carolina, Tennessee) secede

A Divisive War, 1844–1850

"The United States will conquer Mexico," Ralph Waldo Emerson had predicted as the war began, but "Mexico will poison us." He was right. The U.S.-Mexico War roused bitter sectional conflict, even while it was being fought. Some northern Whigs — among them Charles Francis Adams of Massachusetts (son of John Quincy Adams) and Chancellor James Kent of New York — opposed the war on moral grounds, calling it "causeless & wicked & unjust." These **conscience Whigs** accused Polk of waging the war to add new slave states and increase slave-owning Democrats' control of the federal government. Swayed by such arguments, troops deserted in droves (leading to the highest desertion rate of any American war), and antiwar activists denounced enlistees as "murderers and robbers."

"Free Soil" in Politics

When voters repudiated Polk's war policy in the election of 1846, Whigs took control of the House. They called for a congressional pledge that the United States would not seek any land from the Mexican republic. Polk's expansionist policies also split the Democrats. As early as 1839, Ohio Democrat Thomas Morris had warned that "the power of slavery is aiming to govern the country." In 1846, David Wilmot, an antislavery Democratic congressman from Pennsylvania, took up that refrain and proposed the **Wilmot Proviso**, a ban on slavery in any territories gained from the war with Mexico. Whigs and antislavery Democrats in the House of Representatives quickly passed the bill, dividing Congress along sectional lines. Fearful that southern voters would heed radical calls for secession, a few proslavery northern senators joined their southern colleagues to kill the proviso. But the dispute had just begun.

Slavery in the Mexican Cession   At the war's end, President Polk, Secretary of State Buchanan, and Senators Stephen A. Douglas of Illinois and Jefferson Davis of Mississippi called for annexation of a huge swath of Mexican territory south of the Rio Grande. John C. Calhoun and others, however, feared this would require the assimilation of many mixed-race people. They favored only annexation of sparsely settled New Mexico and California. "Ours is a government of the white man," proclaimed Calhoun; it should never welcome "any but the Caucasian race." To unify the Democratic Party, Polk and Buchanan accepted Calhoun's policy. In 1848, Polk signed, and the Senate ratified, the Treaty of Guadalupe Hidalgo, in which the United States agreed to pay Mexico $15 million in return for more than one-third of its territory (Map 12.1).

Congress also created the Oregon Territory in 1848 and, two years later, passed the Oregon Donation Land Claim Act, which granted farm-sized plots of land to settlers who took up residence before 1854. Soon, treaties with Native peoples erased Indian titles to much of the new territory. With the claiming of Oregon, New Mexico, and California, American conquest of the Far West rapidly advanced.

Commentators debated whether the arid lands of the Southwest were suitable for slavery or cotton culture. Debates over expansion dominated the election of 1848. The Senate's rejection of the Wilmot Proviso revived charges that southern politicians were leading a **"slave power" conspiracy** to dominate the federal government. They pointed out that the Constitution allowed slaveholding states to count each slave as three-fifths of a person for purposes of electoral representation, though of course slaves did not vote; thus, whites in areas with large numbers of slaves had disproportionate political

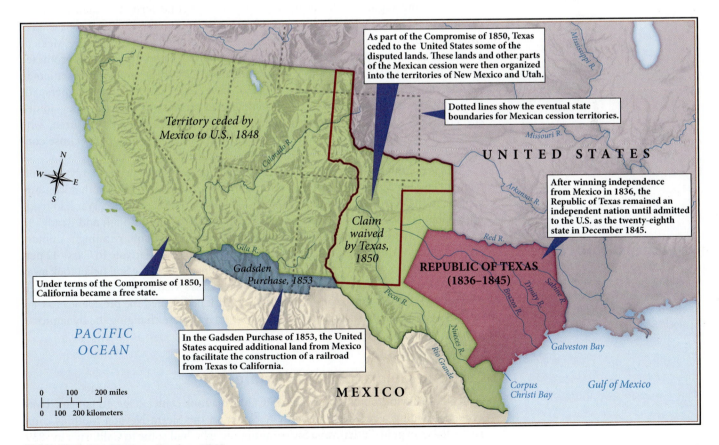

As part of the Compromise of 1850, Texas ceded to the United States some of the disputed lands. These lands and other parts of the Mexican cession were then organized into the territories of New Mexico and Utah.

Dotted lines show the eventual state boundaries for Mexican cession territories.

Territory ceded by Mexico to U.S., 1848

UNITED STATES

After winning independence from Mexico in 1836, the Republic of Texas remained an independent nation until admitted to the U.S. as the twenty-eighth state in December 1845.

Claim waived by Texas, 1850

REPUBLIC OF TEXAS (1836–1845)

Gadsden Purchase, 1853

Under terms of the Compromise of 1850, California became a free state.

PACIFIC OCEAN

In the Gadsden Purchase of 1853, the United States acquired additional land from Mexico to facilitate the construction of a railroad from Texas to California.

Galveston Bay

Corpus Christi Bay   Gulf of Mexico

MEXICO

0   100   200 miles
0   100   200 kilometers

MAP 12.1 The Mexican Cession, 1848
In the Treaty of Guadalupe Hidalgo (1848), Mexico ceded to the United States its vast northern territories — the present-day states of California, Nevada, Utah, Arizona, New Mexico, and half of Colorado. These new territories, President Polk boasted to Congress, "constitute of themselves a country large enough for a great empire, and the acquisition is second in importance only to that of Louisiana in 1803."

power. Northerners also argued that Democrats were favoring southern interests in their appointments and policies.

To protest this perceived bias, thousands of ordinary northerners, such as farmer Abijah Beckwith of Herkimer County, New York, joined the **free soil movement**. Slavery, Beckwith wrote in his diary, was an "aristocratic" institution, a danger to "the great mass of the people [because it] . . . threatens the general and equal distribution of our lands into convenient family farms." Free soil ideas drew on a popular movement for access to public lands that had been growing since the 1820s. Increasingly, frontier congressmen pressured the U.S. government to give land to poor farmers — a demand ultimately fulfilled by the Homestead Act of 1862 (Interpretations).

Free soilers quickly organized for the election of 1848. Compared with abolitionists, the new Free Soil Party placed less emphasis on slavery as a sin. Instead, like Beckwith, the new party's leaders depicted slavery as a threat to republicanism and the Jeffersonian ideal of a freeholder society, arguments that won broad support among aspiring white farmers. Hundreds of men and women in the Great Lakes states joined free soil organizations formed by the American and Foreign Anti-Slavery Society. So, too, did Frederick Douglass, the foremost black abolitionist, who attended the first Free Soil Party convention in the summer of 1848 and endorsed its strategy. Douglass believed Free Soilers could achieve far more political clout than abolitionists could, ultimately undermining slavery. William Lloyd Garrison and other abolitionists, however, condemned the new party's stress on the rights of freeholders as racist "whitemanism."

The Election of 1848   The conflict over slavery took a toll on Polk and the Democratic Party. Scorned by Whigs and Free Soilers and exhausted by his rigorous dawn-to-midnight work regime, Polk declined to run for a second term and died just three months after leaving office. In his place, Democrats nominated Senator Lewis Cass of Michigan, an avid expansionist who had advocated buying Cuba, annexing Mexico's Yucatán Peninsula, and taking all of Oregon. To maintain party unity, Cass promoted a new idea — squatter sovereignty. Under this plan, Congress would allow settlers in each territory to determine its status as free or slave. Cass's doctrine failed to persuade those northern Democrats who opposed any expansion of slavery. They joined the Free Soil Party, as did former Democratic president Martin Van Buren, who became its candidate for president. To attract Whig votes, the new party chose conscience Whig Charles Francis Adams for vice president.

Whigs nominated General Zachary Taylor, a Louisiana slave owner firmly committed to defending slavery in the South but not in the territories, a position that won him support in the North. The general's military exploits in the U.S.-Mexico War had made him a popular hero, known affectionately to his troops as "Old Rough and Ready." In 1848, as in 1840 with the candidacy of William Henry Harrison, running a military hero worked for the Whigs. Taylor took 47 percent of the popular vote to Cass's 42 percent. However, Taylor won in part because Van Buren and the Free Soil ticket took away enough Democratic votes in New York to block Cass's victory there. Although their numbers were small, antislavery voters in New York had denied the presidency to Clay in 1844 and to Cass in 1848. Bitter debates over slavery were changing the dynamics of national politics.

PLACE EVENTS IN CONTEXT
What did conscience Whigs, David Wilmot, and free soilers have in common, and why did they all rise to prominence between 1846 and 1848?

California Gold and Racial Warfare

Even before Taylor took office, events in California took center stage. In January 1848, workers building a milldam for John A. Sutter in the Sierra Nevada foothills came across flakes of gold. Sutter was a Swiss immigrant who had come to California in 1839, become a Mexican citizen, and accumulated land in the Sacramento Valley. He tried to hide the discovery, but by mid-1848 indigenous Californians, Mexican Californios, and Anglo-Americans from Monterey and San Francisco poured into the foothills, along with scores of Mexicans and Chileans. By January 1849, sixty-one crowded ships had

During the antebellum period, the cotton complex pushed west into the Mississippi Valley as planters expanded onto the region's more fertile soil. This demographic and economic shift west fueled antislavery anxieties that slavery would spread across the continent. Abraham Lincoln's Republican Party responded to this fear by rejecting popular sovereignty in the territories and decrying the infamous *Dred Scott* decision. To slavery's supporters, the movement west kindled hopes of economic and political survival in the face of mounting abolitionist attacks. While slavery's enemies and defenders clashed over the legitimacy of its expansion into the territories, many on both sides accepted the idea that slavery *could* expand even into areas such as the Great Plains, the Southwest, and California. But did slavery have a future in the West? And, if so, what was it? Two scholars, Charles W. Ramsdell and Stacey L. Smith, offer different assessments regarding the limits of slavery's expansion.

Did Slavery Have a Future in the West?

CHARLES W. RAMSDELL

SOURCE: Charles W. Ramsdell, "The Natural Limits of Slavery Expansion," *Mississippi Valley Historical Review* 16 (September 1929): 157. Reprinted by permission of *The Journal of American History*/The Organization of American Historians, Oxford University Press via Copyright Clearance Center.

It took more than twenty years of experimentation and adaptation with wind mills, dry-farming, and new drought-resisting feed crops for the cotton farmer to conquer the plains. There is little reason to believe that the conquest could have been effected earlier [than the 1880s]; there is even less basis for belief that the region would ever have been filled with plantations and slaves . . . it is likely that the institution of slavery would have declined toward extinction in the Old South before the cotton conquest of the plains could have been accomplished, even had there been no Civil War.

STACEY L. SMITH

SOURCE: Stacey L. Smith, *Freedom's Frontier: California and the Struggle over Unfree Labor, Emancipation, and Reconstruction* (Chapel Hill: University of North Carolina Press, 2013), 5–6.

[Scholars have] done much to dispel the myth that the West was a landscape of liberty. . . . [They have] demonstrated how the region's vast geography and seemingly limitless opportunities restricted rather than enhanced workers' freedom. Reliant on employers and labor contractors to move them to and across the West's wide-open spaces, immigrant workers often became enmeshed in debt peonage and contract labor. . . . [Historians] have documented the journeys of slaves to the goldfields, California's systems of forced Indian labor, the lives of Chinese women bound in the sex trade, and the debates over imagined Chinese "coolie" slavery on the Pacific coast. . . . [T]he idea that western environments, economies, or social structures were somehow incompatible with bound labor is gradually losing its force.

QUESTIONS FOR ANALYSIS

1. Name two ways that these two historians differ in their assessment of the West as a potential site for slavery's expansion.

2. To what extent does each historian emphasize factors such as geography and environment in assessing slavery's future in the West?

3. Why is this debate over the potential for slavery in the West important to historians seeking to understand the sectional crisis described in this chapter?

---

left New York and other northeastern ports to sail around Cape Horn to San Francisco; by May, twelve thousand wagons had crossed the Missouri River bound for the goldfields. Forty-niners from South America, Europe, China, and Australia also converged on California to seek their fortunes (America in Global Context).

Forty-Niners The mining prospectors — almost all men — lived in crowded, chaotic towns and camps amid gamblers, saloonkeepers, and prostitutes. They set up "claims clubs" to settle mining disputes and cobbled together a system of legal rules based on practice "back East." Anglo-American miners usually treated alien whites fairly, but they ruthlessly expelled Indians, Mexicans, and Chileans from the goldfields or

The Gold Rush: California and Australia

In 1849, hundreds of Australian men booked passage for San Francisco, hoping to make their fortune in the California goldfields. A mere two years later, thousands more Australian "diggers" flocked to the colony of Victoria in Australia itself, drawn by a gold strike that yielded one-third of the world's gold output during the 1850s.

In California and Victoria, miners lived mostly in canvas tents and flimsy wood shanties and found gold initially in stream beds. In both territories, the huge migration virtually wiped out the Aboriginal peoples. Similarly, both rushes attracted about 40,000 Chinese miners, an influx that, in the race-conscious, English-speaking world of the nineteenth century, prompted riots and legislation in both regions to restrict Asian migrants. Finally, only a few California "forty-niners" or Australian "diggers" made a fortune.

There were differences as well. Upon a gold strike in California, the prospectors would stake their claims and collectively protect them — a rough system of democratic self-rule. In Victoria, the British crown owned much of the land, and gold commissioners and police administered the diggings, selling licenses to dig for 30 shillings (about $200 in present-day U.S. dollars) a month. Distressed by license fees and corrupt local officials, 10,000 miners at Ballarat voted to create a Reform League, which demanded abolition of fees and universal male suffrage. When authorities ignored their demands, 500 miners seized a rich mine at Eureka. In the ensuing struggle, British troops killed 22 miners, ending the armed uprising.

Despite these differences — as well as a significant disparity in the proportion of women — California and Victoria were both transformed by the nearly simultaneous discovery of gold. Within a few decades a mining boom vastly increased their wealth and boosted their populations, as the following chart indicates:

TABLE 12.1

Nonnative Population Increases from Gold Rush in United States and Australia

California, United States				Victoria, Australia			
	Total	Women		Nonwhite		Total	Women		Nonwhite
1845	11,000							
1850	93,000	7,000	7%	1%	1851	97,000	39,000	40%	0%
1860	380,000	120,000	31%	15%	1861	540,000	219,000	40%	5%
1870	560,000	211,000	37%	11%	1871	746,000	339,000	45%	4%

QUESTIONS FOR ANALYSIS

1. How would you account for the relative numbers of women in Victoria and California and how those proportions changed over time? How might the percentage of women affect the character of the two societies?

2. Why were there no equivalents of the Ballarat Reform League and the Eureka Stockade in California, given that the two rushes were similar in so many ways and fostered similar anti-Chinese violence and legislation?

confined them to marginal diggings. When substantial numbers of Chinese miners arrived in 1850, often in the employ of Chinese companies, whites called for laws to expel them from California. Chilean immigrant Vicente Pérez Rosales reported sardonically on affairs in San Francisco: the leading official was "a Yankee, more or less drunk"; in disputes "between a Yankee and someone who speaks Spanish, his job is to declare the Spaniard guilty and make him pay the court costs." A **Foreign Miner's Tax**, implemented in 1850, charged a prohibitive fee that drove out many Latino and Asian miners.

The first miners to exploit a site often met success, scooping up easily reached deposits and leaving small pickings for later arrivals. "High hopes" wrecked, one late-comer saw himself and most other forty-niners as little better than "convicts condemned to exile and hard labor." They faced disease and death as well: "Diarrhea was so general during the fall and winter months" and so often fatal, a Sacramento doctor remarked, that it was called "the disease of California."

By the mid-1850s almost as many people were sailing from San Francisco each year as were arriving to seek their fortune. But thousands of disillusioned forty-niners were too ashamed, exhausted, broke, or ambitious to go home. Some became wageworkers for companies that engaged in hydraulic or underground mining; others turned to farming. "Instead of going to the mines where fortune hangs upon the merest chance," one frustrated miner advised emigrants, "commence the cultivation of the soil."

Racial Warfare and Land Rights Farming required arable land, and Mexican grantees and Native peoples occupied much of it. American migrants brushed aside both groups, brutally eliminating the Indians and wearing down Mexican claimants with legal tactics and political pressure.

Subjugation of Native peoples came first. When the gold rush began in 1848, California Indians numbered about 150,000; by 1861, there were only 30,000. As elsewhere in the Americas, European diseases took the lives of thousands. Some miners sexually assaulted Native women and forced them into virtual slavery as domestic workers. White settlers also undertook systematic campaigns of extermination, which local leaders did little to stop. "A war of extermination will continue to be waged . . . until the Indian race becomes extinct," predicted Governor Peter Burnett in 1851.

Congress abetted these assaults. At the bidding of white Californians, it repudiated treaties that federal agents had negotiated with 119 tribes and that had allotted the state's Indians 7 million acres of land. Instead, in 1853, Congress authorized five reservations of only 25,000 acres each and refused to provide Indians with military protection. Consequently, some settlers simply murdered Indians to push them off nonreservation lands.

The Yuki people, who lived in the Round Valley in northern California, were one target. As the *Petaluma Journal* reported nonchalantly in April 1857: "Within the past three weeks, from 300 to 400 bucks, squaws and children have been killed by whites." Other white Californians turned to slave trading: "Hundreds of Indians have been stolen and carried into the settlements and sold," the state's Indian Affairs superintendent reported in 1856. Labor-hungry farmers quickly put them to work. Expelled from their lands and widely dispersed, many Indian peoples could no longer sustain distinct communities. Those tribal communities that survived were devastated by population loss. In 1854, at least 5,000 Yukis lived in the Round Valley; a decade later, only 85 men and 215 women remained.

Mexicans and Californios who held grants to thousands of acres were harder to dislodge. The Treaty of Guadalupe Hidalgo guaranteed that property owned by Mexicans would be "inviolably respected." Though many of the eight hundred grants made by Spanish and Mexican authorities in California were poorly documented or in some cases fraudulent, a Land Claims Commission created by Congress eventually upheld the validity of 75 percent of them. In the meantime, however, hundreds of Anglo-Americans set up farms on the sparsely settled grants. Having come of age in the antimonopoly Jacksonian era, these squatters rejected the legitimacy of Californios' claims to "unimproved" land and successfully pressured local land commissioners and judges to void or reduce the size of many grants. Indeed, Anglos' clamor for land was so intense and their numbers so large that many Californio claimants gave up and sold off their properties at bargain prices.

In northern California, farmers found that they could grow most eastern crops: corn and oats to feed work horses, pigs, and chickens; potatoes, beans, and peas for the farm table; and refreshing grapes, apples, and peaches. Ranchers gradually replaced

EXPLAIN CONSEQUENCES
By 1870, what were the main results in California of the discovery of gold?

Spanish cattle with American breeds that yielded more milk and meat, which found a ready market as California's population shot up to 380,000 by 1860 and 560,000 by 1870. Using the latest agricultural machinery and scores of hired workers, California farmers produced huge crops of wheat and barley, which San Francisco merchants exported to Europe at high prices. The gold rush turned into a wheat boom.

1850: Crisis and Compromise

When British miner William Shaw arrived in California in 1849, he brought a Chinese carpenter and a young Malaysian man as his employees. He reported that a posse of armed Anglo-Americans immediately confronted him, demanding to know whether the workers were "in a state of slavery or vassalage to us." Shaw assured them that his men were paid, but he found his group shunned and denied medical care because it included Asians. The Chinese and Malaysian men ended up dying of fever.

As this group's experience suggested, Americans carried the burning issue of slavery with them to the Pacific coast. Recognizing these tensions and hoping to avoid an extended debate over slavery, President Taylor advised Californians to skip the territorial phase and immediately apply for statehood. Early in the gold rush, in November 1849, voters ratified a state constitution prohibiting slavery; Taylor urged Congress to admit California as a free state.

Constitutional Conflict   California's bid for admission produced passionate debate in Congress and four distinct responses. On the verge of death, John C. Calhoun reiterated his deep resentment of the North's "long-continued agitation of the slavery question." He proposed a constitutional amendment to create a dual presidency, permanently dividing executive power between North and South. Calhoun also advanced the radical argument that Congress had no constitutional authority to regulate slavery in the territories. Slaves were property, Calhoun insisted, and the Constitution restricted Congress's power to abrogate or limit property rights. That argument ran counter to a half century of practice: Congress had prohibited slavery in the Northwest Territory in 1787 and had extended that ban to most of the Louisiana Purchase in the Missouri Compromise of 1820. But Calhoun's position — that planters could by right take slave property into new territories — won growing support in the Deep South.

Other southerners favored a more moderate proposal to extend the Missouri Compromise line to the Pacific Ocean. This plan won the backing of Pennsylvanian James Buchanan and other influential northern Democrats. It would guarantee slave owners access to some western territory, including a separate state in southern California.

A third alternative was Lewis Cass's idea of squatter sovereignty — allowing newcomers in a territory to decide the status of slavery. Democratic senator Stephen Douglas of Illinois now championed this approach, renaming it **popular sovereignty** to link it to republican ideology, which placed ultimate power in the hands of voters. Douglas's idea had considerable appeal. Politicians hoped it would relieve Congress from having to make explosive decisions about slavery, and men on the frontier welcomed the power it would give them. However, popular sovereignty was a slippery concept. Could residents accept or ban slavery when a territory was first organized, or must they delay their decision until a territory had enough people to frame a constitution and apply for statehood? Douglas did not say.

For their part, free soilers and opponents of slavery refused to accept any proposal for California or other territories that allowed slavery. Senator Salmon P. Chase of Ohio, elected by a Democratic–Free Soil coalition, and Senator William H. Seward, a New York Whig, urged a fourth plan: federal laws to restrict slavery within its existing boundaries and eventually end it completely. Condemning slavery as "morally unjust, politically unwise, and socially pernicious" and invoking "a higher law than the

Resolving the Crisis of 1850 By 1850, Whig Henry Clay had been in Congress for nearly four decades. Now in partnership with fellow Whig Daniel Webster and Democrat Stephen Douglas, Clay fashioned a complex—and controversial—compromise that preserved the Union. In this engraving, he addresses a crowded Senate chamber, with Webster sitting immediately to his left. Clay addresses his remarks to his prime antagonist, southern advocate John C. Calhoun, the man with the long white hair at the far right of the picture. Library of Congress.

Constitution," Seward demanded bold action to advance freedom, "the common heritage of mankind."

A Complex Compromise Faced with bitter and potentially disastrous political divisions, senior Whig and Democratic politicians worked desperately to draft bills that could pass Congress. Aided by Millard Fillmore, who became president in 1850 after Zachary Taylor's sudden death, Whig leaders Henry Clay and Daniel Webster and Democrat Stephen A. Douglas managed to win passage of five separate laws known collectively as the **Compromise of 1850**. To mollify southern planters, the compromise included a new Fugitive Slave Act strengthening federal aid to slave catchers. To satisfy various groups of northerners, the legislation admitted California as a free state, resolved a boundary dispute between New Mexico and Texas in favor of New Mexico, and abolished the slave trade (but not slavery) in the District of Columbia. Finally, the compromise organized the rest of the conquered Mexican lands into the territories of New Mexico and Utah and, invoking popular sovereignty, left the issue of slavery in the hands of their residents (Map 12.2).

The Compromise of 1850 preserved national unity by accepting once again the stipulation advanced by the South since 1787: no Union without slavery. Still, southerners feared for the future and threatened secession. Militant activists (or "fire-eaters") in South Carolina, Georgia, Mississippi, and Alabama organized a special convention to safeguard "southern rights." Georgia congressman Alexander H. Stephens called on delegates to this Nashville Convention to prepare "men and money, arms and munitions, etc. to meet the emergency." Passage of the compromise deflated the secessionist bubble, however: when the convention reconvened for a second meeting, only a small

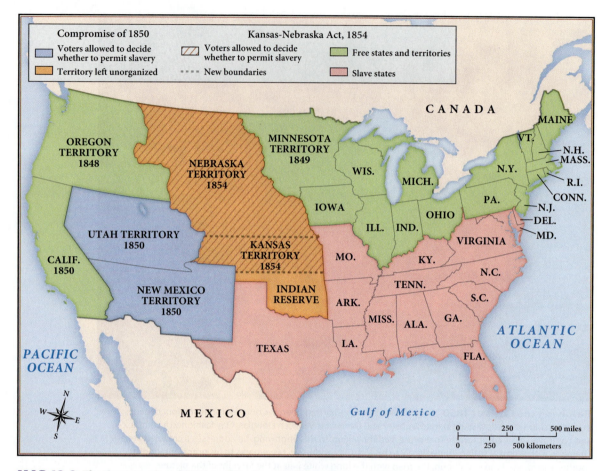

MAP 12.2 The Compromise of 1850 and the Kansas-Nebraska Act of 1854
The contest over the expansion of slavery involved vast territories. The Compromise of 1850 peacefully resolved the status of the Far West: California would be a free state, and settlers in the Utah and New Mexico territories would vote for or against slavery (the doctrine of popular sovereignty). However, the Kansas-Nebraska Act of 1854 voided the Missouri Compromise (1820) and instituted popular sovereignty in those territories. That decision sparked a bitter local war and revealed a fatal flaw in the doctrine.

group showed up. Most southerners continued to support the Union, but the convention had spelled out conditions for that support: Congress must protect slavery where it existed and grant statehood to any territory that ratified a proslavery constitution.

> **IN YOUR OWN WORDS** What political conflicts were triggered by U.S. acquisition of lands in the U.S.-Mexico War?

The End of the Second Party System, 1850–1858

The Missouri Compromise had endured for a generation, and architects of the Compromise of 1850 hoped their agreement would have an even longer life. Religious leaders, businessmen, and leading judges called on citizens to support the compromise to preserve "government and civil society." Their hopes quickly faded. Demanding freedom for fugitive slaves and free soil in the West, antislavery northerners refused to accept the legitimacy of the compromise, while proslavery southerners plotted to extend slavery into the West, the Caribbean, northern Mexico, and Central America. At the same time, the arrival of millions of Irish and German immigrants triggered another set of political upheavals. The resulting disputes fragmented both parties and precipitated a crisis.

The Abolitionist Movement Grows

The Fugitive Slave Act of 1850 proved the most controversial element of the compromise. To mollify slaveholders, who found it increasingly difficult to capture escaped fugitives in the North, the act set up special federal courts to determine the legal status of alleged runaways. An owner's sworn affidavit was considered proof, while defendants could not receive a jury trial or even the right to testify. U.S. marshals and clerks were paid $10 for each person remanded to slavery and only $5 when they set a captive free.

Under the act's provisions, southern owners located and re-enslaved about 200 fugitives, as well as some free blacks. The plight of runaways and the presence of slave catchers aroused popular hostility in the North and Midwest, broadening support for the abolitionist cause. Ignoring the threat of prison sentences and $1,000 fines, free blacks and white abolitionists protected fugitives. In October 1850, Boston abolitionists helped two slaves escape from Georgia slave catchers. Rioters in Syracuse, New York, broke into a courthouse, freed a fugitive and spirited him to Canada, and then tried to charge the U.S. marshal with kidnapping. Abandoning non-violence, Frederick Douglass declared that "the only way to make a Fugitive Slave Law a dead letter is to make half a dozen or more dead kidnappers." Precisely such a deadly result occurred in Christiana, Pennsylvania, in September 1851, when twenty African Americans exchanged gunfire with Maryland slave catchers, killing two of them. Federal authorities indicted thirty-six blacks and four whites for treason and other crimes, but a Pennsylvania jury acquitted one defendant, and the government dropped charges against the rest.

The following year, an electrifying novel helped strengthen abolitionist sentiment in the North. Harriet Beecher Stowe's *Uncle Tom's Cabin* (1852) conveyed the moral principles of abolitionism by depicting heart-rending personal situations: the barbarity of whippings and sexual abuse; the cruel separation of enslaved husbands and wives, mothers and children; and the sin and guilt of white Christian men and women who could not escape the slave system. Touching a nerve, Stowe's book quickly sold 310,000 copies in the United States and double that number in Britain, where it prompted an antislavery petition signed by 560,000 English women.

Promoters soon created theatrical versions of *Uncle Tom's Cabin* — including, improbably, a musical that drew on some of the tropes of minstrel shows. These introduced broad popular audiences to characters such as Uncle Tom, who endures unspeakable cruelties with Christian patience and hope, and Little Eva, an angelic slaveholder's child who, on her deathbed, begs in vain for Tom's freedom. When white southerners indignantly challenged Stowe's portrayal of slavery, she published a *Key to Uncle Tom's Cabin* presenting the evidence she had used, including autobiographies and other testimony from those who had escaped slavery.

As Stowe's novel sparked outrage, northern legislators protested that the Fugitive Slave Act violated state sovereignty. Many states passed **personal liberty laws** that guaranteed to all residents, including alleged escapees from slavery, the right to a jury trial. In 1857, the Wisconsin Supreme Court went further, ruling in *Ableman v. Booth* that the Fugitive Slave Act was unconstitutional because it violated the rights of Wisconsin's citizens. Taking a states' rights stance — traditionally a southern position — the Wisconsin court denied the federal judiciary's authority to review its decision. In 1859, Chief Justice Roger B. Taney led a unanimous Supreme

"Eliza's Flight," 1852 The popularity of Harriet Beecher Stowe's *Uncle Tom's Cabin* prompted the quick marketing of stage productions, board games, music, and even china and wallpaper. This sheet-music cover illustrates the dramatic escape of the enslaved heroine Eliza, who clutches her baby Harry as she jumps from ice floe to ice floe across the Ohio River. Pursuers in the background watch disappointed. The circulation of such images suggests how effectively Stowe appealed to domesticity, urging white readers (and singers) to oppose slavery because it separated loving husbands and wives and parents and children from one another. Eliza's escape and reunion with her husband George provided readers with one of the book's few happy subplots. Courtesy of the Lester S. Levy Collection of Sheet Music, The Sheridan Libraries, The Johns Hopkins University.

Court in affirming the supremacy of federal courts — a position that has withstood the test of time — and upholding the constitutionality of the Fugitive Slave Act.

But popular opposition made the law difficult to enforce. Some African Americans fled temporarily to Canada. Others formed vigilance committees, vowing to defend themselves and their families to the death. Even in far-off San Francisco, networks of abolitionists organized to help local freedom seekers after an 1852 California law authorized southerners who had arrived before statehood, bringing their slaves, to take them back in bondage when they departed the state. The resulting Underground Railroad activity showed the complexity of U.S. racial identities: under the law, an African American named Charlotte Gomez was arrested for having rescued an indigenous nine-year-old Yuki girl who had been forced into servitude in a white family. The slavery question now touched every corner of the country.

> **IDENTIFY CAUSES**
> How did the Fugitive Slave Act increase sectional conflict?

The Whig Party's Demise

Hoping to unify their party in 1852, Whigs ran yet another war hero, General Winfield Scott, as their presidential candidate. Among Democrats, southerners demanded a candidate who embraced Calhoun's constitutional argument that all territories were open to slavery. However, northern and midwestern Democrats stood behind the three leading candidates — Lewis Cass of Michigan, Stephen Douglas of Illinois, and James Buchanan of Pennsylvania — who advocated popular sovereignty. Ultimately, the party settled on Franklin Pierce of New Hampshire, a congenial man who was sympathetic to the South. The Whigs floundered: as the Free Soil Party ran another spirited campaign, many northerners demanded that Whigs take a stronger stand against slavery expansion, while Democrats strengthened their base in the South by arguing that the Whigs were not doing enough to protect slavery. Pierce swept to victory.

Proslavery Initiatives   As president, Pierce pursued an expansionist foreign policy. With California and Oregon now firmly in U.S. hands, northern merchants wanted a trans-Pacific commercial empire, and Pierce moved to support them. For centuries, since unpleasant encounters with Portuguese traders in the 1600s, Japan's leaders had adhered to a policy of strict isolation. Americans, who wanted coal stations in Japan, argued that trade would extend what one missionary called "commerce, knowledge, and Christianity, with their multiplied blessings." Whether or not Japan wanted these blessings was irrelevant. In 1854, Commodore Matthew Perry succeeded in getting Japanese officials to sign the **Treaty of Kanagawa**, allowing U.S. ships to refuel at two ports. The Pierce administration rejected Perry's bid to annex more Pacific territories, including Formosa (now Taiwan). But by 1858 the United States and Japan had commenced trade, and a U.S. consul took up residence in Japan's capital, Edo (now known as Tokyo).

Pierce did far more to satisfy southern expansionists. The president and his aggressive secretary of state, William Marcy, first sought to buy extensive Mexican lands south of the Rio Grande. Ultimately, Pierce settled for a smaller slice of territory — the Gadsden Purchase of 1853, now part of Arizona and New Mexico — that opened the way for his negotiator, James Gadsden, to build a transcontinental rail line from New Orleans to Los Angeles.

Pierce's most controversial initiatives came in the Caribbean and Central America. Southern expansionists had long urged Cuban slave owners to declare independence from Spain and join the United States. To assist the expansionists and American traders who still supplied enslaved Africans to Cuba, Pierce threatened war with Spain and covertly supported **filibustering** (private military) expeditions. In 1853 John Quitman, a fabulously wealthy cotton planter and former governor of Mississippi, organized a not-so-secret expedition to take Cuba. Volunteers and offers of aid poured in from across the South. A Texan hailed Quitman's plan as the "paramount enterprise of the age," while a Mississippian reported that in his area "the desire that Cuba should be acquired as a Southern conquest is almost unanimous."

An American Merchant Ship in Yokohama Harbor, 1861 After the United States forcibly "opened" Japan to foreign trade in 1854, American and European ships and visitors became a familiar sight in the port of Yokohama. In these 1861 prints — two panels of a five-panel series — artist Hashimoto Sadahide meticulously details activity in Yokohama Harbor. On the left, goods are carried onto an American merchant ship; on the right, two women dressed in Western style watch the arrival of another boat. In the background, a steamship flies the Dutch flag; a rowboat heading to or from another (unseen) ship carries the flag of France. Library of Congress.

In 1854, Marcy arranged for American diplomats in Europe to compose the **Ostend Manifesto**, urging Pierce to seize Cuba by force. When the document was exposed, however, Whigs, northern Democrats, and Free Soilers all denounced it, calling it new evidence of southern "slave power" machinations. Pierce saw the political risks of supporting filibusters and withdrew his support for Quitman, who eventually cancelled his plan.

That did not stop William Walker, a Tennessee-born adventurer who had failed as a California forty-niner. Gathering other disappointed gold-seekers, Walker first tried to capture Sonora, in northern Mexico. After that failed, he organized three separate expeditions to Central America between 1855 and 1860. In 1856, after being hired as mercenaries to help a faction in a civil war in Nicaragua, Walker and 300 men overthrew the country's government and established their own (with some help from New York shipping magnate Cornelius Vanderbilt, who operated a U.S.-Nicaragua steamship line). Walker's new government declared slavery legal in Nicaragua and received immediate recognition from the United States. But Walker could not hold on to power. He fled Nicaragua and then returned to Central America twice more before being captured and shot and killed, apparently by Honduran forces, in 1860. Combined with the expeditions of other filibusters, Walker's exploits confirmed many northerners' belief that the "slave power" would stop at nothing to expand.

Immigrants and Know-Nothings

While conflict over slavery intensified, another issue vied for center stage in politics. Outside the South, where the slave-labor system discouraged poor immigrants from settling, foreign immigration rose sharply in the 1840s and 1850s. Newcomers arrived almost entirely from northern Europe — England, Ireland, the German states, and Scandinavia — and their circumstances varied widely. German-speaking migrants were a mix of Protestants, Catholics, and Jews, and they included many skilled workers who came in family groups. Often bringing funds they had saved, more than half settled on farms or in small towns. Not so Irish Catholics, who came from an overwhelmingly rural island that was not an independent nation but a colony of Britain. Thus when a catastrophe hit Ireland in the late 1840s, it forced millions to flee or die.

The Irish Famine   Ireland's population had grown rapidly during the Napoleonic Wars. Most Irish farmers, working as tenants for English landlords, were required to send their grain crops to England. The poorest third of households ate little but potatoes. Ireland was thus terribly vulnerable to a potato blight in 1845 that destroyed almost the whole crop the following year. Forced to eat their seed potatoes to avoid starvation, and with very little aid offered by the British government, millions of Irish were soon desperate. *An Gorta Mór* — Celtic for "The Great Hunger" — had descended.

The results were horrific. Between 1845 and 1851 over one million people died of malnutrition or diseases that preyed on the hungry, including dysentery and cholera. "Famine and pestilence are sweeping away hundreds," reported a journalist from Bantry on the southwest coast. "The number of deaths is beyond counting." Those who could gathered their meager possessions and took passage: over 1.5 million — one-sixth of Ireland's people — emigrated, mostly to the United States.

In the 1820s and 1830s, Irish immigrants had largely been poor, unskilled men who came alone and found "heavy, rough work" in northeastern cities and towns, repairing streets or digging canals. The famine refugees came, instead, largely in family groups. Since the famine struck hardest against children and the elderly, the refugees tended to be young, healthy adults — tenant farmers, although not the very poorest. But the Atlantic voyage held new dangers: shipboard conditions in cheap steerage berths were terrible, and typhus and other diseases turned many vessels into "coffin ships." In 1853, when a cholera epidemic raged, 10 percent of Irish immigrants died at sea.

Those Irish who landed in the United States made up more than a third of all American immigrants in the 1850s. Unable to afford land, they clustered in urban areas. By 1860, a third of Irish-born Americans lived in just ten cities. Finding employment as laborers, factory workers, and domestic servants, the new arrivals faced great hardship. Some, however, through thrift and determination, managed to find their way into the ranks of shopkeepers, policemen, or farmers. Many formed mutual aid groups to support their communities. They also found support through the American Catholic Church, which soon became an Irish-dominated institution.

As early as the 1850s, some Irish began to send positive reports to kin back home (Thinking Like a Historian). Like many later groups, the Irish developed a pattern of **chain migration**. Once a newcomer settled in, he or she saved carefully and arranged to send for neighbors and family members. As a result, steady streams of immigrants arrived long

Immigrants and Nativists Clash in New York, 1857 This engraving shows how a backlash against Irish immigration led to gang violence that alarmed Americans. In this street fight, raucous July 4 celebrations escalated into raids and counter-raids between a nativist gang known as the "Bowery Boys" and their Irish immigrant rivals, known popularly as the "Dead Rabbits" (their name for themselves was the "Roach Guards"). Lasting two days, the riot involved hundreds of men and ended with looting and property destruction. Only with help of the New York State militia was order restored. Sarin Images/Granger, NYC.

after the famine had passed. Between 1860 and 1910, more than 2.6 million Irish would arrive — far more than during the famine itself.

Hostility Toward Immigrants

Already by 1850, immigrants were a major presence throughout the Northeast (Figure 12.1). Like other immigrant groups, Irish and Germans boosted the American economy. Factories expanded on low-wage Irish labor. Thousands of elite and middle-class women hired "Bridgets" — Irishwomen — for domestic labor. German-language shop signs filled entire neighborhoods; Irish pubs sprang up all over Boston, while German foods (sausages, hamburgers, sauerkraut) became part of New York culture.

But the scale of immigration prompted a political backlash. Native-born Americans looked with dismay on the crowded tenement districts that sprang up to house low-paid Irish factory workers. They feared the erosion of wages — with some justification, since employers repeatedly used immigrants to break strikes and reduce pay. Advocates of the growing temperance movement condemned Irishmen's tendency to frequent the neighborhood saloon and German families' Sunday afternoons at the *biergarten*. One German observer complained that everywhere three Germans settled together, "one opened a saloon so that the other two might have a place to argue." Some English-speakers also resented the tendency of proud Germans to continue speaking their own language and patronize their own newspapers, businesses, and clubs.

Perhaps the most significant factor in this era's **nativism** — hostility toward immigrants — was anti-Catholicism. Almost all the newly arrived Irish and perhaps a third of Germans were Catholics. Viewing the pope as authoritarian, some Protestants argued that Catholics could not develop the independent judgment that would make them good citizens. They would instead expect the pope to tell them how to vote. Northerners who mistrusted the "slave power" made such arguments with particular forcefulness. "Slavery and priestcraft," declared one Republican leader in 1854, "have a common purpose: they seek [to add to the United States] Cuba and Hayti and the Mexican States together, because they will be Catholic and Slave. I say they are in alliance by the necessity of their nature — for one denies the right of a man to his body, and the other the right of a man to his soul." Other nativists, believing vows of celibacy were unnatural, provoked hysteria over the alleged secret crimes of Catholic priests and nuns. *The Awful Disclosures of Maria Monk*, a popular exposé originally published in 1836, alleged that sexual debauchery and infanticide went on behind the closed doors of a Montreal convent. Though its claims were debunked, the book circulated for decades, stoking anti-Catholic prejudice.

The actions of some working-class Irish immigrants intensified these fears. In urban areas, groups of Irish men became notorious for organizing mob violence against African Americans, temperance parades, and abolitionist meetings. A much larger number devoted themselves to electoral politics. Most urban Irish forged loyalties with the Democratic Party, which gave them a foothold in the political process. This fueled, in turn, allegations that Irish voters and politicians were corrupt and clannish.

A small number of German immigrants provoked anger in the opposite direction. As radicals who were fleeing oppressive governments after the failed European

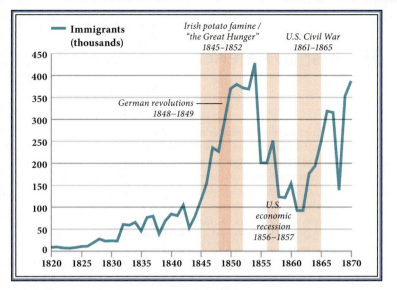

FIGURE 12.1 The Surge in Immigration, 1845–1855

In 1845, failure of the potato crop in Ireland prompted wholesale migration to the United States of peasants from the overcrowded farms of its western counties. Population growth and limited economic prospects likewise spurred the migration of tens of thousands of German peasants, while the failure of the liberal republican political revolution of 1848 prompted hundreds of prominent German politicians and intellectuals to follow them. An American economic recession cut the flow of immigrants, but the booming northern economy during the Civil War again persuaded Europeans to set sail for the United States.

The Irish in America

Hardship and hostility accompanied the surge of Irish immigration to the United States, especially when millions began to arrive during the famine. The documents below provide different perspectives on the forms of discrimination and hardship that Irish men and women faced, their reflections on opportunity in America, and the ways they adapted to life in an industrializing economy.

1. **Mary Anne Sadlier, *The Blakes and the Flanagans*, 1855.** *Through her domestic novels, Irish-born author Mary Ann Sadlier defended the respectability of her fellow immigrants. To assert Irish Catholics' readiness to claim equal citizenship, she appealed to the values of American middle-class women: motherhood, piety, hard work, thrift, and selfless community service. This frontispiece from Sadlier's novel* The Blakes and the Flanagans: A Tale, Illustrative of Irish Life in the United States *depicts two Irish-born sisters with pupils from their school.*

Source: Courtesy of the University of Iowa Libraries.

2. **Account by a visiting Scotsman, LaSalle County, Illinois (1840).** *After passing through the town of Utica, Illinois, this traveler commented on a nearby camp along the construction line of the Illinois & Michigan Canal.*

We had scarcely got beyond the edge of town before we came to a colony of Irish laborers employed on the Illinois Canal, and a more repulsive scene we had not for a long time beheld. The number congregated here were about 200, including men, women and children, and these were crowded together in 14 or 15 log huts, temporarily erected for their shelter. I had never been in the south of Ireland and cannot say how far the appearance of this colony differed from that of villages there, but certainly in the north of Ireland, over which I have traveled from Dublin to Londonderry, I never saw anything approaching the scene before us in dirtiness and disorder.

. . . Poverty could be no excuse, as the men were all paid at the rate of a dollar a day for their labor, had houses rent free, and provisions of every kind abundantly cheap. But whiskey and tobacco seemed the chief delights of the men. Of the women and children, no language would give an adequate idea of their filthy condition, in garments and person. It required only a little industry to preserve both in a state of cleanliness, for water was abundant in the river close at hand, and soap abundant and cheaper than in England. It is not to be wondered that Americans conceive a very low estimate of the Irish people generally, when they have such unfavorable specimens of the nation, as these almost constantly before their eyes. Unhappily, of the immigrants who land at New York, the large majority are not merely ignorant and poor . . . but drunken, dirty, indolent, and riotous.

3. **Margaret McCarthy to her family (1850).** *McCarthy, age 23, had emigrated alone from County Cork to New York City the previous year.*

I write these few lines to you hopeing [they] may find you all in as good State of health as I am at present thank God I received your welcome letter To me Dated 22nd. of May . . . My D[ea]r Father I must only say that this is a good place and A good Country for if one place does not Suit A man he can go to Another . . . [But] the Emmigrants has not money enough to Take them to the Interior of the Country which obliges them to Remain here in New York and the like places for which Reason Causes the less demand for Labour and also the great Reduction in wages for this Reason I would advise no one to Come to America that would not have Some Money after landing here that Enable them to go west in case they would get no work to do here but any man or woman without a family are fools that would not venture and Come to this plentyful Country where no man or woman ever Hungerd or ever will. There are Dangers upon Dangers Attending Comeing here but my Friends . . . Fortune will favour the brave have Courage and prepare yourself. . . . This will be my last remittance until I see you all here. . . . I will have for [Mary] A Silk

Dress A Bonnet and Viel . . . Tell my D[ea]r Mother to Bring all her bed Close and also to bring the Kittle and an oven and have handles on them and do not forget the Smoothing Irons. . . .

4. Advertisement, *Philadelphia Public Record* (1852)

WANTED — In a private family, a WOMAN, to do general Housework; she must understand plain Cooking, Washing, Ironing, and give the best recent [recom]mendations for honesty, sobriety, cleanliness and smartness. No Irish need apply. Address H.L.D., Ledger Office.

5. Letter from William Lloyd Garrison to a friend in Dublin, Ireland, July 2, 1852. *The Boston abolitionist expresses frustration at the failure of Irish immigrants to join his cause, even though an antislavery movement was thriving in Ireland.*

It is now quite apparent that [Irish American voters] will go en masse with Southern men-stealers, and in opposition to the antislavery movement. This will not be done intelligently by them, but will be effectually controlled by a crafty priesthood and unprincipled political demagogues. When we had our great meeting in Faneuil Hall, we took all parties by surprise. Our Irish fellow-citizens, who were then present, acted out their natural love of liberty, to the life; for at that time, they had not been instructed how to act by their leaders, and the Pilot and Diary, and other Irish papers here, had not opened their batteries. Since that time, however, they have kept wholly aloof from us, and it is impracticable to get them to listen. . . .

6. Advertisements from the *Catholic Herald*, Philadelphia. *These notices suggest the plight of many families separated by emigration.*

May 20, 1841. Information Wanted — Of John Early of the County Mayo, Ireland. Any person knowing any thing of the said John Early, will oblige his distressed wife by sending information to the office of this paper or to the Clergy of St. John's Church, 13th St., Phila.

July 17, 1844. Information Wanted — of Patrick Lynch, a native of the Parish of Kilberry, County Meath, Ireland. He was in Carthage, N. Y. about a year ago, which place he left for Philadelphia. His wife, Jane Lynch, has arrived in Philadelphia and stops at the house of his nephew, Christopher Nevin, Pearl street above 13th st., where she would be glad to hear from him.

7. *The Know-Nothing and American Crusader*, 29 July 1854. *This pamphlet circulated in various Eastern cities at the height of anti-immigrant agitation.*

We must not let this fact go-by — the Roman Catholics are bound to serve their Church before their Country. What is the practical and inevitable result of such a system in this country? Why, that every Catholic stands committed as an enemy to the Republic. . . .

Not an office in this whole land should be filled by any but Americans. There is a full supply. They are all capable. They are intelligent, patriotic and all that. Then where is the logic, justice, even decency, of permitting foreigners to hold these places. Many of the best offices

[in Washington] . . . are filled by foreigners. And two-thirds of those are IRISH.

8. Cartoon from *Harper's Weekly*, 1859. *This caricature illustrates prejudices against the Irish Catholic men who found rapid success in urban politics.*

OUR EDUCATORS.

American School Commissioner: "But, my good Sir, we have always read the Bible in our American Schools." . . . Irish School Commissioner: "Worse luck, thin; ye'll rade it no more! Father O'Flaherty says it interfares wid our holy religion, an' by the Vargin it won't and it shan't be read!" Source: The Granger Collection, New York.

Sources: (2) John Lamb, "Old Canal Days," *Lockport Free Press*, 15 June 1978; (3) Nancy F. Cott et al, *Root of Bitterness: Documents of the Social History of American Women*, 2nd ed. (Boston: Northeastern University Press, 1992), 152-5; (4) Philadelphia Public Record, Oct. 12, 1852; (5) Quoted in Noel Ignatieff, *How the Irish Became White* (New York: Routledge, 1995), 22; (6 & 7) Historical Society of Pennsylvania.

ANALYZING THE EVIDENCE

1. What hardships did Irish immigrants face after their arrival in the United States, and how did those differ for men and for women?

2. What arguments or assumptions did native-born Americans make, in rejecting Irish newcomers? How might immigrants such as Mary Anne Sadlier and Margaret McCarthy have responded to the criticisms of Garrison, the *Know-Nothing and American Crusader*, and *Harper's Weekly*?

3. What explanations do these documents provide as to why immigrant voters might have chosen to vote for political candidates who shared their ethnic background?

PUTTING IT ALL TOGETHER

Using these documents and what you have learned from Chapter 12, explain how the arrival of large numbers of Irish Americans shaped the U.S. economy and society. What allies and opponents did they find in society and politics, and why?

revolutions of 1848, they brought socialist ideals, and some enrolled in the abolitionist cause. Abraham Lincoln, resuming his political career in the 1850s after his early defeat as a Whig, discovered that many German Americans in Illinois were eager to prevent slavery's expansion onto "free soil." Lincoln greeted one group in Chicago as "*German Fellow-Citizens*" who were "true to Liberty, not *selfishly*, but upon *principle*." Among whites who supported slavery, though — including many Irish immigrants — the antislavery views of these German immigrants made them politically suspect.

As early as the mid-1830s, nativists called for a halt to immigration and mounted a cultural and political assault on foreign-born residents. Gangs of nativists assaulted Irish youths in the streets. In 1844, a new group called the American Republican Party won the endorsement of local Whigs and swept New York City's elections by stressing temperance, anti-Catholicism, and nativism. Rather than trying to stop immigration, they sought to deny voting and office-holding rights to noncitizens, especially by delaying the waiting period before immigrants could naturalize.

By 1850, with immigration swelling, various local nativist societies banded together as the Order of the Star-Spangled Banner. The following year they formed the **American, or Know-Nothing, Party**. When questioned, the party's secrecy-conscious members often replied, "I know nothing" — hence the nickname given by their opponents. The American Party's program was far from secret, however; supporters wanted to mobilize native-born Protestants against the "alien menace" of Irish and German Catholics, discourage further immigration, and institute literacy tests for voting. The new party drew primarily from former Whigs in the South, and about equally from Whigs and Democrats in the North. Many northern Know-Nothings had an antislavery or free soil outlook. By the mid-1850s, it was clear that these voters were hostile both to immigrants and to the expansion of slavery. What was unclear, yet, was whether a new national party would take up both of these issues, or which one party leaders would prioritize.

In 1854, voters elected dozens of American Party candidates to the House of Representatives and gave the party control of the state governments of Massachusetts and Pennsylvania. The emergence of a Protestant-based nativist party to replace the Whigs became a real possibility. At that same moment, Illinois Democrat Stephen Douglas proposed a new application of his idea of popular sovereignty, furthering the Whig Party's collapse and sending the Union spinning toward disaster.

The West and the Fate of the Union

Since the Missouri Compromise prohibited new slave states in the Louisiana Purchase north of 36°30′, southern senators had long prevented the creation of new territories there. It remained Permanent Indian Territory. But Douglas wanted to open it up to allow a transcontinental railroad to link Chicago to California. In 1854 he proposed to extinguish Native American rights on the Great Plains and create a large free territory called Nebraska.

Southern politicians opposed Douglas's initiative. They hoped to extend slavery throughout the Louisiana Purchase and have a southern city — New Orleans, Memphis, or St. Louis — serve as the eastern terminus of a transcontinental railroad. To win their support, Douglas amended his bill so that it explicitly repealed the Missouri Compromise, potentially enabling slavery to extend farther west in new areas. He also agreed to the formation of two territories, Nebraska and Kansas, raising the prospect that settlers in the southern one, Kansas, would choose slavery. Knowing the revised bill would "raise a hell of a storm," Douglas insisted to northerners that Kansas, even though it lay next door to the slave state of Missouri, was not suited to plantation agriculture and would become a free state. After weeks of bitter debate, the Senate passed the **Kansas-Nebraska Act** (see Map 12.2, p. 376). With petitions opposed to the bill flooding the House of Representatives, the measure barely squeaked through.

Emergence of the Republican Party The Kansas-Nebraska Act of 1854 jolted the political system. It galvanized thousands of northerners, especially Whigs, to stand up against the "slave power." Cotton textile magnate Amos Lawrence lamented, "We went to bed one night old fashioned, conservative Union Whigs and waked up stark mad abolitionists." In northeastern cities where nativism had been strong, renewed controversy over slavery's expansion in the West deflected attention from immigration. The Kansas-Nebraska Act also crippled the Democratic Party, with northern "anti-Nebraska Democrats" denouncing it as "part of a great scheme for extending and perpetuating supremacy of the slave power." In 1854, these former Democrats joined ex-Whigs and Free Soil supporters to form the Republican Party.

The new party was a coalition of "strange, discordant and even hostile elements," one Republican observed. Many abolitionists refused to join, arguing that the Republicans compromised too much on the need for immediate abolition. However, almost all Republicans disliked and wished to limit slavery, which, they argued, drove down the wages of free workers and degraded the dignity of manual labor. Like Thomas Jefferson, Republicans praised a society based on "the middling classes who own the soil and work it with their own hands." Abraham Lincoln, now a Republican, conveyed the new party's vision of social mobility. "There is no permanent class of hired laborers among us," he declared, ignoring growing economic and social divisions in the industrializing North and Midwest. Lincoln and his fellow Republicans envisioned a society of independent farmers, artisans, and proprietors, and they celebrated middle-class values: domesticity and respectability, religious commitment, and capitalist enterprise.

Meanwhile, thousands of settlers rushed into the Kansas Territory, putting Douglas's concept of popular sovereignty to the test. On the side of slavery, Missouri senator David R. Atchison encouraged residents of his state to cross temporarily into Kansas to vote in crucial elections there. Opposing Atchison was the abolitionist New England Emigrant Aid Society, which dispatched its supporters to Kansas. Adding to the tension, in 1855 the Pierce administration accepted the legitimacy of a proslavery legislature in Lecompton, Kansas, that had been elected with aid from border-crossing Missourians. The majority of Kansas residents favored free soil and refused allegiance to the Lecompton government.

In 1856, both sides turned to violence, prompting Horace Greeley of the *New York Tribune* to label the territory "Bleeding Kansas." A proslavery force, seven hundred strong, looted and burned the antislavery town of Lawrence. The attack enraged John Brown, a fifty-six-year-old abolitionist from New York who commanded a free-state militia. Brown was a complex man with a record of failed businesses, but his intellectual and moral intensity won the trust of influential people. Avenging the sack of Lawrence, Brown and his followers murdered five proslavery settlers at Pottawatomie. Abolitionists must "fight fire with fire" and "strike terror in the hearts of the proslavery people," Brown declared. The attack on Lawrence and the Pottawatomie killings started a guerrilla war in Kansas that took nearly two hundred lives.

In Washington, leaders of the new Republican Party distanced themselves from Brown and from radical abolitionists but took the lead in denouncing proslavery maneuvers. In May 1856, in a speech called "The Crime Against Kansas," Massachusetts Republican senator Charles Sumner accused his South

Armed Abolitionists in Kansas, 1859 The confrontation between North and South in Kansas took many forms. In the spring of 1859, Dr. John Doy (seated) slipped across the border into Missouri and tried to lead thirteen escaped slaves to freedom in Kansas, only to be captured and jailed in St. Joseph, Missouri. The serious-looking men standing behind Doy, well armed with guns and Bowie knives, attacked the jail and carried Doy back to Kansas. The photograph celebrated and memorialized their successful exploit. Kansas State Historical Society.

Carolina colleague Andrew P. Butler of having taken "the harlot slavery" as his mistress. Butler's cousin Preston Brooks, also a southern congressman, decided to avenge his kinsman, but he disdained to fight a gentleman's duel with any "Black Republican." Instead, he found Sumner working at his desk on the Senate floor and beat him unconscious with a walking cane. Sumner, gravely injured, did not resume his seat for many months. The attack shocked northerners, providing further evidence of the arrogance and outrageousness of proslavery political leaders. Massachusetts voters reelected Sumner even while he remained disabled and could not serve. Brooks, at the same time, resigned his seat as a matter of honor but was reelected by a large margin. He received replacement canes and notes of congratulation from allies across the South.

Buchanan's Failed Presidency   The violence in Kansas dominated the presidential election of 1856. The new Republican Party stoked anger over Bleeding Kansas. Its platform denounced the Kansas-Nebraska Act and demanded that the federal government prohibit slavery in all the territories. Linking Mormon plural marriage with slavery, it used the language of domesticity and civilization to denounce "those twin relics of barbarism, polygamy and slavery." Republicans also called for federal subsidies to build transcontinental railroads, reviving a Whig economic proposal popular among midwestern Democrats. For president, the Republicans nominated Colonel John C. Frémont, a free soiler who had won fame in the conquest of Mexican California.

The American Party entered the election with equally high hopes, but like the Whigs, it split along sectional lines over slavery. The party's southern faction nominated former Whig president Millard Fillmore, while the northern contingent endorsed Frémont. During the campaign, Republicans won the votes of many northern Know-Nothings by demanding legislation banning foreign immigrants and imposing high tariffs on foreign manufactures. As a Pennsylvania Republican put it, "Let our motto be, protection to everything American, against everything foreign." In New York, Republicans campaigned on a reform platform designed to unite "all of the Anti-Slavery, Anti-Popery, and Anti-Whiskey" voters.

Democrats reaffirmed their support for popular sovereignty and the Kansas-Nebraska Act and nominated James Buchanan of Pennsylvania. A tall, dignified, and experienced politician, Buchanan was staunchly prosouthern. He won the three-way race with 1.8 million popular votes (45.3 percent) and 174 electoral votes. A dramatic restructuring of politics was becoming apparent: with the splintering of the American Party, Republicans replaced the Whigs as the second major party (see Map 12.3, p. 391). However, Frémont had not won a single vote in the South; had he triumphed, a North Carolina newspaper warned, the result would have been "a separation of the states." The fate of the republic hinged on President Buchanan's ability to quiet the passions of the past decade and hold the Democratic Party—the only remaining national party—together. In the end, he could not.

Dred Scott: Petitioner for Freedom   Events—and his own values and weaknesses—conspired against Buchanan. Early in 1857, the Supreme Court handed down the **Dred Scott** decision, which sought to clarify Congress's constitutional authority over slavery. Dred Scott was an enslaved African American who had lived for almost five years with his owner, an army surgeon, in the free state of Illinois and in Wisconsin Territory, both places where the Missouri Compromise (1820) prohibited slavery. Scott argued that residence in a free state and territory had made him free. Buchanan opposed Scott's appeal and, hoping to resolve the slavery controversy, secretly pressured two justices from Pennsylvania to side with their southern colleagues.

Seven of the nine justices declared that Scott was still a slave, but they disagreed on the legal rationale. Chief Justice Roger B. Taney of Maryland, a slave owner himself, wrote the most influential opinion. He declared that Negroes, whether enslaved or free, could not be citizens of the United States; he added, notoriously, that they had "no rights that a white man was bound to respect." Therefore, no African American could sue in federal court—a controversial argument, given that free blacks were citizens in many northern states. Taney then made two even more radical claims. First, he endorsed John C. Calhoun's argument that the Fifth Amendment, which prohibited "taking" of property without due process, meant that Congress could not prevent southern citizens from moving slave property into the territories. Consequently, the chief justice concluded, the provisions of the Northwest Ordinance and Missouri Compromise that prohibited slavery had *never* been constitutional. Second, Taney declared that Congress could not give to territorial governments any powers that it did not possess, such as the authority to prohibit slavery. Taney thereby endorsed Calhoun's interpretation of popular sovereignty: only when settlers wrote a constitution and requested statehood could they prohibit slavery.

In a single stroke, Taney had declared Republicans' proposals to restrict the expansion of slavery through legislation to be unconstitutional. Republicans could never accept the legitimacy of Taney's constitutional arguments, which indeed had significant flaws. Led by Senator Seward of New York, they accused the chief justice and President Buchanan of participating in the slave power conspiracy.

Buchanan then added fuel to the raging constitutional fire. Ignoring pleas from his advisers, who saw that antislavery residents held a clear majority in Kansas, he refused to allow a popular vote on the proslavery Lecompton constitution and in 1858 strongly urged Congress to admit Kansas as a slave state. Angered by Buchanan's machinations, Stephen Douglas, the most influential Democratic senator and architect of the Kansas-Nebraska Act, broke with the president and persuaded Congress to deny Kansas statehood. (Kansas would enter the Union as a free state in 1861.) Still determined to aid the South, Buchanan resumed negotiations to buy Cuba in December 1858. By pursuing an open proslavery agenda — first in *Dred Scott* and then in Kansas and Cuba — Buchanan widened the split in his party and the nation.

The Mormon War   The president's policies in the West did nothing to stem the growing controversy. When the United States had acquired Mexico's northern territories in 1848, Salt Lake Mormons had petitioned Congress to create a vast new state, Deseret, stretching from Utah to the Pacific coast. Instead, grudgingly, Congress set up the much smaller Utah Territory in 1850, and President Pierce appointed Mormon leader Brigham Young as governor. Tensions between Mormons and federal authorities simmered in the early 1850s. Pressured by Protestant leaders to end polygamy and angered by Mormons' threat to nullify federal laws, Buchanan dispatched a small army to Utah in 1858. He and other Democrats apparently sought to deflect attention from the slavery question. "I believe," one of the president's advisers wrote him privately, "we can supersede the Negro-Mania with the almost universal excitements of an Anti-Mormon Crusade." Buchanan backed down, however; he decided that forced abolition of polygamy might be a risky precedent for ending slavery, and he offered a pardon to Utah citizens who acknowledged federal authority. The Mormon War ended quietly, turning the nation's attention once again to the question of slavery's expansion.

> **PLACE EVENTS IN CONTEXT**
> Why did northern Democratic presidents, such as Pierce and Buchanan, adopt prosouthern policies?

> **IN YOUR OWN WORDS**   Why did Democrats and Whigs fail in their attempts to keep the issue of slavery in the federal territories from creating a sectional rift?

Abraham Lincoln and the Republican Triumph, 1858–1860

While Democrats divided along sectional lines, Republicans gained support in the North and Midwest, and Abraham Lincoln emerged as one of the party's most eloquent and politically astute candidates. However, few southerners trusted Lincoln, and his presidential candidacy in 1860 revived secessionist agitation.

Lincoln's Political Career

The middle-class world of storekeepers, lawyers, and entrepreneurs in the small towns of the Ohio River Valley shaped Lincoln's early career. He came from a hardscrabble yeoman farm family that was continually on the move — from Kentucky, where Lincoln was born in 1809, to Indiana and then Illinois. In 1831, Lincoln rejected his father's life as a subsistence farmer and became a store clerk in New Salem, Illinois. Socially ambitious, he won entry to the middle class by mastering its culture; he joined the New Salem Debating Society, read Shakespeare, and studied law. Admitted to the bar in 1837, Lincoln moved to Springfield, the new state capital. There he met Mary Todd, the cultured daughter of a Kentucky banker; they married in 1842. Her tastes were aristocratic; his were humble. She was volatile; he was easygoing but suffered bouts of depression that tried her patience and tested his character.

An Ambitious Politician Lincoln became a dexterous party politician, adept in the use of patronage and passage of legislation. As a Whig in the Illinois legislature, he promoted education, banks, canals, and railroads. During his single term in Congress during the U.S.-Mexico War, he took a middle ground by voting for military appropriations but also endorsing the Wilmot Proviso's ban on slavery in any acquired territories. Lincoln also introduced legislation that would require the gradual, compensated emancipation of slaves in the District of Columbia. To avoid future racial strife, he favored the colonization of freed blacks in Africa or South America.

After his defeat in 1848, Lincoln returned to Illinois and focused on his growing law practice representing railroads and manufacturers. The Kansas-Nebraska Act propelled him back into politics as a Republican. Shocked by the act's repeal of the Missouri Compromise and Senator Douglas's advocacy of popular sovereignty, Lincoln reaffirmed his opposition to slavery in the territories. Although he believed Congress had no power under the Constitution to interfere with slavery in states where it already existed, he likened slavery to a cancer that had to be cut out if the nation's republican ideals and moral principles were to endure.

The Lincoln-Douglas Debates In 1858, Lincoln ran for the U.S. Senate seat held by Douglas. Lincoln claimed that the proslavery Supreme Court might soon declare that the Constitution "does not permit a state to exclude slavery," just as it had decided in *Dred Scott* that "neither Congress nor the territorial legislature" could ban slavery in a territory. In that event, he warned, "we shall awake to the reality . . . that the Supreme Court has made Illinois a slave state." This prospect informed Lincoln's famous House Divided speech. Quoting the biblical adage "A house divided against itself cannot stand," he predicted that American society "cannot endure permanently half slave and half free. . . . It will become all one thing, or all the other."

The Senate race in Illinois attracted national interest because of Douglas's prominence and Lincoln's reputation as a formidable speaker. During a series of seven debates, Douglas declared his support for white supremacy: "This government was made by our fathers, by white men for the benefit of white men," he said, attacking Lincoln for supporting "negro equality." Lincoln parried Douglas's racist attacks by arguing that free blacks should have equal economic opportunities but not equal political rights. Taking the offensive, he asked how Douglas could accept the *Dred Scott* decision (which protected slave property in the territories) yet advocate popular sovereignty (which allowed settlers to exclude slavery). Douglas responded that a territory's residents

Abraham Lincoln, 1859 Lincoln was not a handsome man, and he photographed poorly. His campaign managers had this photo — and many others — retouched to soften Lincoln's features. However, no photograph, no matter how realistic, captured Lincoln's complex personality and wit or the intensity of his spirit and intellect. To grasp Lincoln, it is necessary to read his words. Library of Congress.

could exclude slavery by not adopting laws to protect it. That position pleased neither proslavery nor antislavery advocates. Nonetheless, when Democrats won a narrow majority in the state legislature, they reelected Douglas to the U.S. Senate.

The Union Under Siege

The debates with Douglas gave Lincoln a national reputation, and in the election of 1858, the Republican Party won control of the U.S. House of Representatives. Shaken by Republicans' advance, southern Democrats divided again. Moderates, who included Senator Jefferson Davis of Mississippi, strongly defended "southern rights" and demanded ironclad political or constitutional protections for slavery. The so-called fire-eaters — powerful orators such as Robert Barnwell Rhett of South Carolina and William Lowndes Yancey of Alabama — repudiated the Union and actively promoted secession. President Buchanan's secessionist secretary of war, John B. Floyd, quietly sold ten thousand federal muskets to South Carolina.

Antislavery northerners likewise took a strong stance. Senator Seward of New York declared that freedom and slavery were locked in "an irrepressible conflict." Ruthless abolitionist John Brown, who had perpetrated the Pottawatomie massacre, showed what that might mean. In October 1859, Brown led eighteen heavily armed black and white men in a raid on the federal arsenal at Harpers Ferry, Virginia. Brown hoped to arm slaves with the arsenal's weapons and mount a major rebellion to end slavery.

The raid was a failure, and Brown was quickly captured. But though he was a poor military strategist, Brown made an excellent martyr. As Virginia rushed to convict and execute him, the wounded Brown came to the courtroom on a stretcher. From the gallows he declared that the New Testament

> teaches me that all things whatsoever I would that men should do to me, I should do even so to them. It teaches me, further, to remember them that are in bonds as bound with them. I endeavored to act up to that instruction. . . . If it is deemed necessary that I should forfeit my life for the furtherance of the ends of justice, and mingle my blood further with the blood of my children and with the blood of millions in this slave country . . . I say, let it be done.

As had happened after the caning of Senator Sumner, onlookers' reactions divided the nation even more than the acts of Brown himself. Southerners were shocked to find that a group of abolitionists — the "Secret Six" — had funded Brown's raid. They were equally outraged to read that northern churchbells tolled on the day of Brown's hanging. "The lesson of the hour is insurrection," thundered abolitionist Wendell Phillips. In Virginia, the *Richmond Enquirer* reported that "the Harpers Ferry invasion has advanced the cause of disunion more than any other event." Republican leaders denounced Brown's plot, but Democrats called it "a natural, logical, inevitable result of the doctrines and teachings of the Republican party." One southern Democratic paper warned that Republicans planned to "put the torch to our dwellings and the knife to our throats."

The Election of 1860

Within months, southern Democrats decided they could no longer count on their northern allies. At the party's convention in April 1860, northern Democrats rejected Jefferson Davis's proposal to protect slavery in the territories. Delegates from eight southern states quit the meeting. At a second Democratic convention, northern and midwestern delegates nominated Stephen Douglas for president. Meeting separately, southern Democrats nominated the sitting vice president, John C. Breckinridge of Kentucky. Democrats — the only remaining party with strong bases in both North and South — had split in half.

With Democrats divided, Republicans sensed victory. They courted white voters with a free soil platform that opposed both slavery and racial equality: "Missouri for

CONSIDER POINTS OF VIEW
Why did Lincoln argue the United States could no longer endure "half slave and half free" when it had already done so for several decades?

THE NATIONAL GAME. THREE "OUTS" AND ONE "RUN".
ABRAHAM WINNING THE BALL.

Lincoln on Home Base Beginning in the 1820s and 1830s, the language and imagery of sports saturated politics, cutting across the lines of class and party. Wielding a long, bat-like rail labeled "Equal Rights and Free Territory," Abraham Lincoln holds a baseball and appears ready to score a victory in the election. His three opponents—from left to right, John Bell (the candidate of a new Constitutional Union Party), Stephen A. Douglas, and John C. Breckinridge— will soon be "out." Indeed, according to the pro-Lincoln cartoonist, they were about to be "skunk'd." As Douglas laments, their attempt to put a "short stop" to Lincoln's presidential ambitions had failed. Library of Congress.

white men and white men for Missouri," declared that state's Republican platform. The national Republican convention chose Lincoln as its presidential candidate because he was more moderate on slavery than the best-known Republicans, Senators William Seward of New York and Salmon Chase of Ohio. Lincoln also conveyed a compelling egalitarian image that appealed to smallholding farmers, wage earners, and midwestern voters.

The Republican strategy worked. Although Lincoln was not on the ballot in any Deep South state, and though he received less than 1 percent of the popular vote in the South and only 40 percent of the national vote, he won every northern and western state except New Jersey, giving him 180 (of 303) electoral votes and thus a majority in the electoral college. Breckinridge took 72 electoral votes by sweeping the Deep South and picking up Delaware, Maryland, and North Carolina. Douglas won 30 percent of the popular ballot but secured only 51 electoral votes, winning in Missouri and New Jersey. Republicans had united voters in the Northeast and Midwest behind free soil. To his surprise, Lincoln also won California and Oregon by the barest of margins, apparently due in part to public outrage over a duel in which a proslavery California Democrat killed an antislavery rival (Map 12.3).

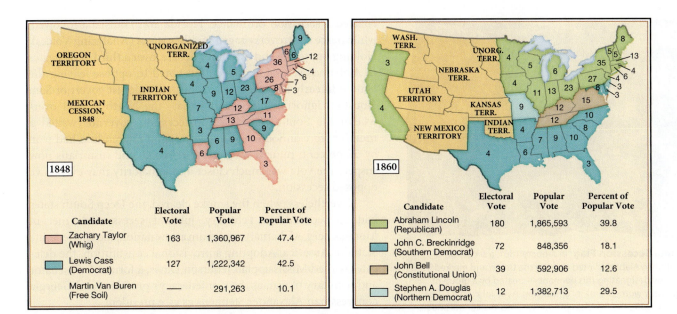

MAP 12.3 Political Realignment, 1848 and 1860

In the presidential election of 1848, both the Whig and Democratic candidates won electoral votes throughout the nation. Subsequently, the political conflict over slavery and the Compromise of 1850 destroyed the Whig Party in the South. As the only nationwide party, the Democrats won easily over the Whigs in 1852 and, with the opposition split between the Republican and American parties, triumphed in 1856 as well. However, a new region-based party system appeared by 1860 and persisted for the next seventy years — with Democrats dominant in the South and Republicans usually controlling the Northeast, Midwest, and Far West.

A revolution was in the making. "Oh My God!!! This morning heard that Lincoln was elected," Keziah Brevard, a widowed South Carolina plantation mistress and owner of two hundred slaves, scribbled in her diary. "Lord save us." Slavery had long been part of the American constitutional order — an order many southerners now believed was under siege. Fearful of a massive slave uprising, Chief Justice Taney recalled "the horrors of St. Domingo [Haiti]." At the very least, warned John Townsend of South Carolina, a Republican administration in Washington would suppress "the inter-State slave trade" and thereby "cripple this vital Southern institution of slavery." To many slaveholders, it seemed time to think carefully about Lincoln's 1858 statement that the Union must "become all one thing, or all the other."

> **IN YOUR OWN WORDS** What factors led to the rise of the Republican Party and Lincoln's election in 1860?

To see a longer excerpt of Keziah Brevard's diary, along with other primary sources from this period, see *Sources for America's History*.

PLACE EVENTS IN CONTEXT
What was the relationship between the collapse of the Second Party System and the Republican victory in the election of 1860?

Secession Winter, 1860–1861

Following Lincoln's election, secessionist fervor swept through the Deep South. The Union collapsed first in South Carolina, home of John C. Calhoun and nullification. Robert Barnwell Rhett and other fire-eaters had demanded secession since the Compromise of 1850, and their goal was now within reach. "Our enemies are about to take possession of the Government," warned one South Carolinian. Frightened by that prospect, a state convention voted unanimously on December 20, 1860, to dissolve "the union now subsisting between South Carolina and other States."

Fire-eaters elsewhere in the Deep South quickly called similar conventions and organized mobs to attack local Union supporters. In early January, white Mississippians

Alabama Secession Flag In January 1861, a secession convention in Alabama voted to leave the Union and marked its decision by designating this pennant — created by a group of Montgomery women — as its official flag. As in John Gast's *American Progress* (p. 333), the Goddess of Liberty forms the central image. Here she holds a sword and a flag with a single star, symbolizing Alabama's new status as an independent republic. Alabama Department of Archives and History.

enacted a secession ordinance. Florida and Louisiana followed, while fierce controversy raged in other states (Analyzing Voices). Holding out to the end of a bitter debate, over a third of delegates to Alabama's secession convention voted to oppose leaving the Union. In early February, Texans ousted Unionist governor Sam Houston, ignoring his warning that "the North . . . will overwhelm the South." Georgia's prosecession governor waited a month before announcing that a secession referendum had won by 57 percent; returns were never released, and historians now suspect the vote was much closer and a majority may even have opposed secession.

Nevertheless, when the smoke cleared, the Deep South states had all seceded. In February, jubilant secessionists met in Montgomery, Alabama, to proclaim a new nation, the Confederate States of America. Adopting a provisional constitution, the delegates named Mississippian Jefferson Davis, a former U.S. senator and secretary of war, as the Confederacy's president and Georgia congressman Alexander Stephens as vice president.

Secessionist fervor was less intense in four states of the Upper South (Virginia, North Carolina, Tennessee, and Arkansas), where there were fewer slaves. White opinion was especially divided in the four border slave states (Maryland, Delaware, Kentucky, and Missouri), where yeomen farmers held greater political power, and over whose ground any resulting civil war would likely be fought. The legislatures of Virginia and Tennessee refused to join the secessionist movement and urged a compromise.

Meanwhile, President Buchanan's administration floundered. Buchanan declared secession illegal but, in line with his states' rights outlook, claimed that the federal government lacked authority to restore the Union by force. Buchanan's timidity prompted South Carolina's new government to demand the surrender of Fort Sumter (a federal garrison in Charleston Harbor) and to cut off its supplies. The president again backed down, refusing to use the navy to supply the fort.

Instead, the outgoing president urged Congress to find a compromise. The plan proposed by Senator John J. Crittenden of Kentucky received the most support. His proposal had two parts. The first, which Congress approved, called for a constitutional amendment to protect slavery from federal interference in any state where it already existed. Crittenden's second provision called for the westward extension of the Missouri Compromise line (36°30′ north latitude) to the California border. The provision would have banned slavery north of the line and allowed it to the south, including any territories "hereafter acquired," raising the prospect of expansion into Cuba or Central America.

Congressional Republicans rejected Crittenden's second proposal on strict instructions from president-elect Lincoln. With good reason, Lincoln feared it would unleash new imperialist adventures. "On the territorial question, I am inflexible," he wrote; restoring the Missouri Compromise line would simply invite southerners to keep "filibustering to expand slavery." In 1787, 1821, and 1850, the North and South had resolved their differences over slavery. In 1861, there would be no compromise.

In his March 1861 inaugural address, Lincoln carefully outlined his positions. He promised to safeguard slavery where it existed but vowed to prevent its expansion. Equally important, the Republican president declared that the Union was "perpetual"; consequently, the secession of the Confederate states was illegal. Lincoln asserted his intention to "hold, occupy, and possess" federal property in the seceded states and "to collect duties and imposts" there. If military force was necessary to preserve the Union, Lincoln — like Democrat Andrew Jackson during the nullification crisis — would use it. The choice was the South's: return to the Union or face war.

The South's decision came quickly (Map 12.4). When Lincoln dispatched an unarmed ship to resupply Fort Sumter, Jefferson Davis and his associates in the Provisional Government of the Confederate States decided to seize the fort. Their forces opened fire on April 12, with ardent fire-eater Edmund Ruffin supposedly firing the first cannon. Two days later, the Union defenders capitulated. On April 15, Lincoln called 75,000 state militiamen into federal service for ninety days to put down an insurrection "too powerful to be suppressed by the ordinary course of judicial proceedings."

Northerners responded to Lincoln's call to arms with wild enthusiasm. In western Pennsylvania, a group of lumbermen organized themselves into a regiment, built rafts, and floated down to Harrisburg before the state governor had even requested volunteers. Asked to provide thirteen regiments, Republican governor William Dennison of Ohio sent twenty. Most northern Democrats lent their support. Despite his past differences with Lincoln, Stephen Douglas toured the North urging citizens to support the government. "Every man must be for the United States or against it," he declared. "There can be no neutrals in this war, only patriots — or traitors."

Voters in the Middle and Border South now faced a new situation: war was imminent. Those eight states accounted for two-thirds of whites in the slaveholding states, three-fourths of their industrial production, and well over half of their food. They were home to many of the nation's best military leaders, including Colonel Robert E. Lee of Virginia, a career officer whom veteran General Winfield Scott recommended to Lincoln to lead the new Union army. Those states were also geographically strategic. Kentucky, with its 500-mile border on the Ohio River, was essential to the movement of troops and supplies. Maryland was vital to the Union's security because it bordered the nation's capital on three sides.

The weight of its history as a slave-owning society decided the outcome in Virginia. On April 17, 1861, a convention approved secession by a vote of 88 to 55, with dissenters concentrated in the state's yeoman-dominated northwestern counties. Elsewhere, Virginia whites embraced the Confederate cause. "The North was the aggressor," declared Richmond lawyer William Poague as he enlisted. "The South resisted her invaders." Refusing General Scott's offer of the Union command, Robert E. Lee resigned from the U.S. Army. "Save in defense of my native state," Lee told Scott, "I never desire again to draw my sword." Arkansas, Tennessee, and North Carolina quickly joined Virginia in the Confederacy.

Whatever their prior views, the citizens of eleven southern states now committed to separate nationhood on a basis already determined by the Deep South. Two weeks after Lincoln's inauguration, the Confederacy's new vice president, Alexander Stephens of Georgia, outlined its goals in his famous "cornerstone" speech. Jefferson and other founders, he wrote, had considered slavery an "evil" — an institution they inherited and

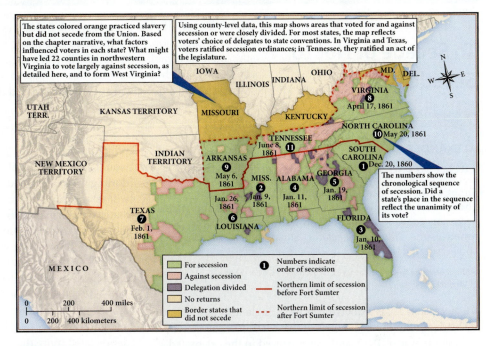

MAP 12.4 The Process of Secession, 1860–1861
The states of the Lower South had the highest concentration of slaves, and they led the secessionist movement. After the attack on Fort Sumter in April 1861, the states of the Upper South joined the Confederacy. Yeomen farmers in Tennessee and the backcountry of Alabama, Georgia, and Virginia opposed secession but, except in the future state of West Virginia, initially rallied to the Confederate cause. Consequently, the South entered the Civil War with its white population relatively united.

To Secede or Not to Secede?

Across the South, between November 1860 and April 1861, legislators and citizens debated secession. They weighed economic interests and property rights, cultural ties, political loyalties, patriotism, and of course touching on all of these, the question of slavery. In these excerpts three political leaders—a Virginian, Georgian, and Mississippian—explained their positions and tried to influence voters or legislators to heed their warnings.

ALEXANDER STUART

Letter to the *Staunton* (VA) *Spectator*, 1860

Stuart, a Whig from strongly Unionist Augusta County in Virginia's Shenandoah Valley, won election as a delegate to the state's secession convention. In an open letter to constituents, published in the *Staunton Spectator*, Stuart argued that Virginia should stay in the Union.

SOURCE: *Staunton Spectator*, January 22, 1861, from "Valley of the Shadow," University of Virginia, http://valley.lib.virginia.edu/.

66 Secession . . . is a doctrine of New England origin. It had its birth among the Federalists of that section of the Union, during the war of 1812, and was nurtured in the celebrated Hartford Convention. . . . In my judgment, it is at war with the whole theory of our institutions. . . .

There is no natural antagonism between the Northern and Southern States. On the contrary, each is necessary to the other. They are the complements of each other, and together constitute the most perfect social, industrial and political systems, that the world has ever seen. . . . The South produces what the North wants, but cannot produce; and the North furnishes what the South needs, but cannot supply for itself. . . . The present condition of antagonism and alienation is unnatural. It is not the legitimate result of any conflict of the social and industrial systems of the two sections, but is the work of those 'DESIGNING MEN,' both North and South, against whom Washington so impressively warned us in his farewell address.

It is true that the Northern States, under the lead of such men, have been guilty of gross outrages on the rights of the South, [but] . . . I believe that all our rights can be secured, and all our wrongs most effectually redressed in the Union, and under the Constitution. . . . I have not been able to perceive how we could add to the security of our slave property by surrendering the guarantees of the Constitution, and substantially bringing down the Canada frontier to the borders of Virginia. It would lead to emancipation and

probably to emancipation in blood. Nor can I see how we would secure our rights in the [federal] territories by abandoning them. I am equally at a loss to understand how we will establish any of our demands against the Northern States on a firmer basis, by severing our connection with them, and thereby from us, the million and a half of friends we had in those States at the last election. . . .

Should war follow the dissolution, the consequences must be of the most frightful character. Brother would be arrayed against brother, and the whole land would be drenched with blood. The border country would be ravaged and laid waste with fire and sword. . . . Real estate would be depreciated more than 50 per cent; business in all its departments would be paralyzed; credit destroyed; personal property of all kinds impressed for public use; our slaves incited to insurrection; and ruin and desolation would overwhelm the whole country.

. . . The people should weigh these matters well before they decide to embark on the unknown and tempestuous sea of convulsion and revolution. . . . 99

ALEXANDER STEPHENS

Address to the Georgia Legislature, 1860

The Georgia legislature undertook a vigorous debate over secession in December 1860. The Unionist address given by prominent Whig congressman Alexander Stephens was noted throughout the South. When Georgia seceded, Stephens nonetheless went with his state and became vice president of the Confederacy.

SOURCE: William W. Freehling and Craig M. Simpson, eds., *Secession Debated: Georgia's Showdown in 1860* (New York: Oxford University Press, 1992), 51–80.

66 It is said that Mr. Lincoln's policy and principles are against the Constitution, and that, if he carries them out, it will be destructive of our rights. Let us not anticipate a threatened evil. If he violates the Constitution, then will come our time to act. Do not let *us* break it, because, forsooth, *he* may. . . . Mr. Lincoln . . . is bound by the

practiced reluctantly, believing it "wrong in principle, socially, morally, and politically." The new Confederacy, Stephens declared, "is founded upon exactly the opposite idea; its foundations are laid, its corner-stone rests, upon the great truth that the negro is not equal to the white man; that subordination to the superior race is his natural and normal condition. This, our new government, is the first, in the history of the world, based upon this great physical, philosophical, and moral truth."

constitutional checks which are thrown around him, which at this time render him powerless to do any great mischief. This shows the wisdom of our system. The President of the United States is no emperor, no dictator, — he is clothed with no absolute power. He can do nothing unless he is backed by power in Congress. . . . The gains in the Democratic party in Pennsylvania, Ohio, New Jersey, New York, Indiana, and other states . . . have been enough to make a majority of nearly thirty in the next House [of Representatives] against Mr. Lincoln. . . . In the Senate he will also be powerless. There will be a majority of four against him. . . .

When I look around and see our prosperity in everything, — agriculture, commerce, art, science, and every department of progress, physical, moral, and mental, — certainly, in the face of such an exhibition, if we can, without the loss of power, or any essential right or interest, remain in the Union, it is our duty to ourselves and to posterity to do so. Let us not unwisely yield to this temptation. . . .

If the policy of Mr. Lincoln and his Republican associates shall be carried out, or attempted to be carried out, no man in Georgia will be more willing or ready than myself to defend our rights, interest, and honor at every hazard and to the last extremity. What is this policy? It is, in the first place, to exclude us, by an act of Congress, from the Territories, with our slave property. . . .

It is the duty of the States to deliver fugitive slaves, as well as it is the duty of the General Government to see that it is done. The Northern States, on entering into the Federal compact, pledged themselves to surrender such fugitives. . . . They have violated their plighted faith. What ought we to do in view of this? . . . We are . . . bound, before proceeding to violent measure, to set forth our grievances, . . . to give them an opportunity to redress the wrong. Has our State yet done this? I think not. . . . 99

WILLIAM HARRIS
Address to the Georgia Legislature, 1860

After seceding, several Deep South states appointed "secession commissioners," whose job was to travel to other slaveholding states to encourage them to join the new Confederacy. In the midst of Georgia's debate, William Harris, one of Mississippi's commissioners, made this impassioned plea to the Georgia legislature.

SOURCE: William L. Harris, commissioner from Mississippi, address to the Georgia legislature, December 17, 1860, in Charles B. Dew, *Apostles of Disunion: Southern Secession Commissioners and the Causes of the Civil War* (Charlottesville: University of Virginia Press, 2001), 83–89.

66 Our fathers made this a government for the white man, rejecting the negro, as an ignorant, inferior, barbarian race, incapable of self-government, and not, therefore, entitled to be associated with the white man upon terms of civil, political, or social equality. This new administration comes into power, under the solemn pledge to overturn and strike down this great feature of our Union . . . and to substitute in its stead their new theory of the universal equality of the black and white races.

Our fathers secured to us, by our Constitutional Union, now being overturned by this Black Republican rule, protection to life, liberty, and property, *all over the Union.* . . . Our Constitution, in unmistakable language, guarantees the return of our fugitive slaves. Congress has recognized her duty in this respect, by enacting proper laws for the enforcement of this right. And yet these laws have been continually nullified. . . .

Mississippi is firmly convinced that there is but one alternative: This *new union* with Lincoln Black Republicans and free negroes, without slavery; or slavery under our old constitutional bond of union, without Lincoln Black Republicans, or free negroes either, to molest us. . . . [For] the latter, then *secession* is inevitable.

. . . Sink or swim, live or die, survive or perish, the part of Mississippi is chosen. She will never submit to the principles and policy of this Black Republican Administration. She had rather see the last of her race, men, women and children, immolated in one common funeral pyre, than see them subjected to the degradation of civil, political and social equality with the negro race. 99

QUESTIONS FOR ANALYSIS

1. All of the authors quoted here were well-to-do southern men who owned slaves. Based on their arguments, what appeared to motivate some of them to advocate secession while others did not?

2. Who was the intended audience for each of these documents? How might that have affected each document's argument, language, and tone?

3. Stuart and Stevens both suggest that, through further negotiations with the Lincoln administration and Congress, a compromise might be reached that would avoid armed conflict. What specific guarantees from Lincoln and Congress does each demand? Based on your reading of this chapter, what might have been the outcome of such negotiations?

For millions of loyal Unionists outside the South, secession and the Confederate attack on Fort Sumter automatically meant war. Yet on both sides, few Americans understood what the next four years would bring. At first many thought the South would back down and return to the Union if Republicans stood firm. Republican congressman Thaddeus Stevens scoffed, "They have tried it fifty times, and fifty times they have found weak and recreant tremblers in the north." If war came, northerners were confident of their superior numbers and power. For their part, southerners argued that cotton was "King" and would give them extraordinary economic and political leverage, including likely aid from Britain and France. Many southerners also claimed that "the Yankees are cowards and will not fight," as one put it. A South Carolina congressman promised to drink all the blood that would be shed as a result of the Confederacy's founding.

But others expected something different. When Fort Sumter fell, a former army officer and banker named William Tecumseh Sherman was serving as superintendent of a military school in Louisiana. Upon hearing that Lincoln had called up 75,000 troops for three months, Sherman was sure it would not be enough: "You might as well attempt to put out the flames of a burning house with a squirt-gun." He left Louisiana and rejoined the U.S. Army. As volunteers began to mobilize, an enslaved woman in Mississippi named Dora Franks overheard a conversation between her master and his wife: "He feared all the slaves 'ud be took away. She say if dat was true she feel lak jumpin' in de well." Franks added, "I hate to hear her say dat, but from dat minute I started prayin' for freedom."

> **IN YOUR OWN WORDS**   After South Carolina's secession, why were Unionists and Confederates unable to avoid war?

SUMMARY

U.S. victory in the U.S.-Mexico War set off bitter political conflicts over whether Congress could or should allow slavery in lands taken from Mexico. Some northerners, both Democrats and Whigs, opposed slavery in the new territories. Southern Democrats responded angrily, claiming the constitutional right to carry slave property into all U.S. territories. Senior congressmen engineered the Compromise of 1850, hoping to placate all sides. But this series of bills, which included a controversial new Fugitive Slave Act, settled little.

The discovery of gold led to rapid settlement of California; though few got rich, an array of gold-seekers pushed out Mexican landholders and waged a war of extermination on Native peoples. Abolitionist sentiment grew; even more broadly popular was the free soil movement, which by 1848 became a political party advocating that western lands be reserved for free white families. As antislavery activists protested the injustice of the Fugitive Slave Act, and with evidence emerging that southerners were working to annex slave Cuba, abolitionists began to warn that southern Democrats' "slave power" conspiracy controlled federal power. In response, some radical southerners began to advocate secession.

Northern Democratic efforts to implement popular sovereignty in the territories, through the Kansas-Nebraska Act, proved disastrous: increasing violence in Kansas led coalitions of former Democrats, Whigs, and Free Soilers in the North to form the Republican Party. Amid massive immigration from Ireland, it appeared for a while that nativism might eclipse slavery as a key national issue. But by 1856 the Republican Party emerged as the main challenger to Democrats in the North. In 1860 the Democratic Party also fragmented on sectional lines, leading to a four-way race in which Republican Abraham Lincoln emerged victorious. South Carolina seceded almost immediately, arguing that southern slavery could no longer be protected in the Union. Though thousands of white southerners opposed secession, majorities in the Deep South voted to leave the Union. After Confederate forces fired on federal Fort Sumter, Lincoln called up troops to suppress rebellion. Four more states in the Upper South then seceded, leading by April 1861 to civil war.

TERMS TO KNOW

Identify and explain the significance of each term below.

Key Concepts and Events

Mexican cession (p. 366)

conscience Whigs (p. 368)

Wilmot Proviso (p. 368)

"slave power" conspiracy (p. 369)

free soil movement (p. 370)

Foreign Miner's Tax (p. 372)

popular sovereignty (p. 374)

Compromise of 1850 (p. 375)

personal liberty laws (p. 377)

Treaty of Kanagawa (p. 378)

filibustering (p. 378)

Ostend Manifesto (p. 379)

chain migration (p. 380)

nativism (p. 381)

American, or Know-Nothing, Party (p. 384)

Kansas-Nebraska Act (p. 384)

Dred Scott decision (p. 386)

Key People

Lewis Cass (p. 370)

Stephen Douglas (p. 374)

Harriet Beecher Stowe (p. 377)

Justice Roger B. Taney (p. 377)

William Walker (p. 379)

Abraham Lincoln (p. 384)

John Brown (p. 385)

REVIEW QUESTIONS

Answer these questions to demonstrate your understanding of the chapter's main ideas.

1. What political conflicts were triggered by U.S. acquisition of lands in the U.S.-Mexico War?

2. Why did Democrats and Whigs fail in their attempts to keep the issue of slavery in the federal territories from creating a sectional rift?

3. What factors led to the rise of the Republican Party and Lincoln's election in 1860?

4. After South Carolina's secession, why were Unionists and Confederates unable to avoid war?

5. Chapter 12 revisits the years between 1844 and 1848, which have already been explored in earlier chapters. Review the timelines in Part 4 (pp. 236–237) and Part 5 (pp. 364–365), and consider what events occurred in those years. Why do you think they were included in both Parts 4 and 5? If you were making your own timeline of the events and trends that led to the Civil War, would you begin in 1844, 1848, or another date? What causes of sectional crisis would your timeline emphasize?

MAKING CONNECTIONS

Recognize the larger developments and continuities within and across chapters by answering these questions.

1. Compare the political realignment of the 1850s with the decline of the Federalists and the first emergence of mass political parties in the 1820s (Chapter 9). Why did well-established parties fragment and disappear, and how did new ones capture the support of millions of voters?

2. The United States had been a nation of immigrants since its founding—and long before. In comparison with earlier periods you have studied, what new factors caused a strong nativist movement to emerge suddenly in the 1850s?

KEY TURNING POINTS

Refer to the chapter chronology on page 368 for help in answering the questions below.

1. At the beginning of the 1850s, despite sectional tensions, almost no one in the United States expected a civil war between the North and South to result. What events in the 1850s made southern secession and civil war more likely? Which may have constituted a "tipping point" after which secession and war were difficult, if not impossible, to avoid?

2. Some historians view the Civil War as a crisis brewed in Washington, D.C., by politicians who made provocative or dangerous decisions. Others argue that the war's causes emerged from broader conflicts in American economy, society, and culture. In the Chapter Chronology, what evidence do you see for each of these views?

13

CHAPTER

Bloody Ground: The Civil War
1861–1865

In February 1865, as U.S. troops under General William Tecumseh Sherman completed their destructive march through Georgia and crossed into South Carolina, their pace quickened. They were approaching the state capital, Columbia, where four years earlier South Carolina legislators had passed the ordinance of secession. "Hail Columbia, happy land," some of the soldiers sang, "If we don't burn you, I'll be damned." "The whole army," wrote Sherman, "is burning with an insatiable desire to wreak vengeance upon South Carolina. I almost tremble at her fate, but feel that she deserves all that seems in store for her."

As the Union army approached, many white residents of Columbia fled. Terrified of slave revolt, others set up a new whipping post in town, where one enslaved man received a hundred lashes for communicating with federal prisoners held nearby. Local officials dithered: one wanted to defend Columbia house by house, but at the last moment Confederate commanders abandoned the city. Even before Sherman arrived, looting began. Things got worse when arriving Union soldiers discovered 120 barrels of whiskey. One regiment entered the capitol building, voted to revoke secession, and plundered trophies from the senate chamber. More sober soldiers remembered being greeted with glares and curses from whites and shouts of "God bless you" from African Americans. One woman, freed from slavery, gave birth three days later to a son she named Liberty Sherman.

The Union army destroyed all targets of military importance in the city — warehouses, rail stations, machinery. Stacks of cotton bales left on the streets caught fire, and a stiff breeze carried the flames from house to house. One well-dressed southern lady managed to locate Lt. Col. Jeremiah Jenkins, the Union provost marshal, as he hurried around trying to stamp out fires. She begged him to protect her home, but Jenkins replied, "The women of the South kept the war alive — and it is only by making them suffer that we can subdue the men."

The burning of Columbia showed that the Civil War unfolded in ways no one expected at the start. In 1861 both Unionists and Confederates had believed they were embarking on a quick and limited conflict. Each side argued they would quickly win. Both proved wrong. Such is often the case at the outset of wars that become long, agonizing, and terrible, and the Civil War was no exception. As each side hung on fiercely, determined to win, the scale of conflict escalated on battlefields and home fronts. The result, in President Lincoln's words, was "fundamental and astounding": unprecedented political and civilian mobilization; hundreds of thousands dead; the Confederacy's crushing defeat; and the end of slavery.

IDENTIFY THE BIG IDEA

How and why did the Union win the Civil War?

Ruins of Richmond   A street scene in Richmond, Virginia, capital of the Confederacy, in 1865. The women's black dresses indicate that they have recently lost husbands, sons, or other close relatives. On the left, the camera's long exposure caught the ghostly image of a man walking by — possibly a veteran in Confederate gray.   The Granger Collection, New York.

CHAPTER CHRONOLOGY

As you read, ask yourself why this chapter begins and ends with these dates and identify the links among related events.

1861
▶ General Butler declares refugee slaves "contraband of war" (May)
▶ Confederates win First Battle of Bull Run (July 21)
▶ First Confiscation Act (August)
▶ West Virginia created and remains with the Union (October)
▶ U.S. Sanitary Commission formed

1862
▶ Legal Tender Act authorizes greenbacks (February)
▶ Confederate Far West campaign turned back at Glorieta Pass (March)
▶ Union victory at Pea Ridge, Arkansas (March)
▶ Union victory at Shiloh (April 6–7)
▶ Confederacy introduces military draft (April)
▶ Union halts Confederates at Antietam (September 17)
▶ Explosion kills munitions workers in Pittsburgh (September 17)
▶ Lincoln issues preliminary emancipation proclamation (September 22)

1863
▶ Britain and France refuse recognition to the Confederacy; Britain impounds Confederate ships being built in British shipyards
▶ Lincoln signs final Emancipation Proclamation (January 1)
▶ Union wins battles at Gettysburg (July 1–3) and Vicksburg (July 4)
▶ Union initiates draft (March), sparking riots in New York City (July)
▶ Women's rights activists form Woman's Loyal National League
▶ Lincoln delivers Gettysburg Address (November)

1864
▶ Ulysses S. Grant named commander of all Union forces (March)
▶ William Tecumseh Sherman takes Atlanta (September 2)
▶ Lincoln reelected (November 8)
▶ Sherman's army devastates Georgia and South Carolina

1865
▶ Robert E. Lee surrenders to Grant (April 9)
▶ Lincoln assassinated (April 14)
▶ Thirteenth Amendment ratified (December 6)

War Begins, 1861–1862

With hindsight we know that the Civil War lasted four years, the Union won, and the war abolished slavery. But if any of these outcomes had been apparent in 1861, the South would not likely have seceded. Southern leaders banked on cotton's centrality to the national and world economy in achieving Confederate independence. They viewed slavery as an asset to the war effort and argued that southern soldiers would be braver and more effective than northern immigrants and urban workers, whom one disdainfully referred to as "mongrel hordes of Yankees." Events on the battlefield, however, proved neither quick nor decisive. By fall 1862, both the Union and the Confederacy were forced to adopt new military and political strategies.

Early Expectations

In 1861, patriotic fervor filled both Union and Confederate armies with eager young volunteers. One Union recruit wrote that "if a fellow wants to go with a girl now he had better enlist. The girls sing 'I am bound to be a Soldier's Wife or Die an Old Maid.'" Even men of sober minds joined up. "I don't think a young man ever went over all the considerations more carefully than I did," reflected William Saxton of Cincinnatus, New York. "It might mean sickness, wounds, loss of limb, and even life itself. . . . But my country was in danger." The southern call for volunteers was even more successful, thanks to the region's strong military tradition and culture of masculine honor. Confederate soldiers emphasized their duty to protect hearth and home as well as northerners' opposition to slavery. If it had not been for "Psalm singing 'brethren' and 'sistern' . . . preaching abolitionism from every northern pulpit," one Alabama infantryman wrote to his wife, "I would never have been soldiering."

Speaking as provisional president of the Confederacy in April 1861, Jefferson Davis identified the Confederate cause with that of Patriots in 1776: like their grandfathers, white southerners were fighting for the "sacred right of self-government." That right included slaveholding. Secessionists did not believe Lincoln when he promised not to interfere "directly or indirectly . . . with the institution of slavery in the States where it exists." Soon, one southern senator warned, "cohorts of Federal office-holders,

Abolitionists, may be sent into [our] midst" to encourage slave revolts of the kind John Brown had attempted. Slave rebellion raised the prospect of racial mixture, or amalgamation — by which, of course, white southerners meant sexual relations between white *women* and black *men*, given that white masters had already fathered untold thousands of children by enslaved black women. "Better, far better! [to] endure all horrors of civil war," insisted a Confederate recruit, "than to see the dusky sons of Ham leading the fair daughters of the South to the altar." To preserve black subordination and white supremacy, radical southerners chose the dangerous enterprise of secession.

Lincoln responded in a speech to Congress on July 4, 1861, portraying secession as an attack on representative government, America's great contribution to world history. The issue, Lincoln declared, was "whether a constitutional republic" had the will and means to "maintain its territorial integrity against a domestic foe." Living in a world still ruled by monarchies, northern leaders believed that the collapse of the American Union would destroy the possibility of republican governments.

Officers of the 57th Georgia Infantry, CSA, and Their Cook These Confederate officers posed for their portrait while serving with the Army of Tennessee in 1863. First Lieutenant Archibald McKinley and Captain John Richard Bonner smoke pipes and display their swords; Second Lieutenant William S. Stetson holds up his cup. Scott, who is serving Stetson from a flask, was enslaved. Thousands of African American slaves went with Confederate troops to dig trenches, cook, and otherwise help with the hard work of war. Many were eager to go — in some cases because service at the front provided opportunities for escape to Union lines. GCSU Library Special Collections.

Campaigns East and West

Confederates had the advantage of defense: they only needed to preserve their new national boundaries to achieve independence. Moreover, with 9 million people, the Confederacy could mobilize enormous armies. Enslaved blacks, one-third of the population, produced food for the army and raw cotton for export. Southerners counted on sales of **King Cotton** — the leading American export and an essential global commodity — to purchase clothes, boots, blankets, and weapons from abroad. Confederate leaders believed Britain and France, with their large textile industries, were too dependent on cotton not to recognize and assist the Confederacy. Their hopes were boosted in November 1861 when a hot-headed U.S. naval captain intercepted a British steamer, the *Trent*, to seize and detain two Confederate diplomats en route from Cuba to London. The incident nearly precipitated war between the United States and Britain, until the Lincoln administration wisely released the prisoners and the crisis subsided.

In contrast to the Confederacy's defensive stance, the Union had the more difficult job of bringing the rebels back into the Union. U.S. commanding general Winfield Scott proposed a strategy of peaceful persuasion through economic sanctions, combined with a naval blockade of southern ports. Lincoln agreed to the blockade, which was organized with impressive efficiency through the navy's purchase and charter of merchant vessels. By the start of 1862, over 260 ships were on blockade duty and another 100 under construction. But Lincoln, determined to crush the rebellion, insisted also on an aggressive military campaign to restore the Union.

Failed Attempts to Take Richmond and Washington Lincoln hoped a quick strike against the Confederate capital of Richmond, Virginia, would end the rebellion. Many northerners were equally optimistic. "What a picnic," thought one New York volunteer, "to go down South for three months and clean up the whole business." In July 1861, Lincoln ordered General Irvin McDowell's army of 30,000 men to attack General P. G. T. Beauregard's force of 20,000 troops at Manassas (Bull Run), a Virginia rail junction 30 miles southwest of Washington. McDowell launched a strong assault near Bull Run, but panic swept his troops when the Confederate soldiers counterattacked, shouting the hair-raising "rebel yell." McDowell's troops — and many civilians who had come to observe the battle — retreated in disarray. Suddenly, Washington, D.C., seemed threatened, the first of several times during the war that federal officials and residents made preparations to flee.

The Confederate victory at Bull Run showed the rebellion's strength. Lincoln replaced McDowell with General George McClellan and enlisted a million men to serve for three years in the new Army of the Potomac. A cautious military engineer, McClellan spent the winter of 1861–1862 training the recruits and launched his first major offensive in March 1862. With great logistical skill, the Union general ferried 100,000 troops down the Potomac River to the Chesapeake Bay and landed them on the peninsula between the York and James Rivers (Map 13.1). Ignoring Lincoln's advice to "strike a blow" quickly, McClellan advanced slowly toward Richmond, allowing Confederates to mount a counterstrike. Thomas J. "Stonewall" Jackson marched a Confederate force rapidly northward through the Shenandoah Valley in western Virginia and threatened Washington. When Lincoln recalled 30,000 troops from McClellan's army to protect the Union capital, Jackson returned quickly to Richmond to bolster General Robert E. Lee's army. In late June, Lee launched a ferocious six-day attack that cost 20,000 casualties to the Union's 10,000. When McClellan failed to exploit the Confederates' losses, Lincoln ordered a withdrawal. Richmond remained secure.

Border Wars   In addition to taking the Confederate capital, Lincoln's second major goal was to hold on to strategic border areas where relatively few whites owned slaves. To secure the railroad connecting Washington to the Ohio River Valley, Lincoln ordered General McClellan to take control of northwestern Virginia. In October 1861, Unionist-leaning voters in that area chose overwhelmingly to create a breakaway territory, West Virginia. Unwilling to "cut our own throats merely to sustain . . . a most unwarrantable rebellion," as one put it, West Virginians formed their own state in 1863. Unionists also carried the day in Delaware.

In Maryland, where slavery remained entrenched, a pro-Confederate mob attacked Massachusetts troops traveling through Baltimore in late April 1861, causing some of the war's first combat deaths: three soldiers and nine civilians. When Maryland secessionists destroyed railroad bridges and telegraph lines, Lincoln ordered Union troops to occupy the state and arrest Confederate sympathizers, including legislators, releasing them only in November 1861, after Unionists had secured control of Maryland's government. Lincoln's actions provoked bitter debate over this suspension of **habeas corpus** — a legal instrument that protects citizens from arbitrary arrest. The president's opponents pointed to Article I, Section 9 of the U.S. Constitution, which states that "the privilege of the Writ of Habeas Corpus shall not be suspended"; Lincoln argued that the same clause continues, "unless when in Cases of Rebellion or Invasion the public Safety may require it." To ardent Unionists, a rebellion was clearly under way. Lincoln continued to use occasional habeas corpus suspensions throughout the war when he deemed them essential; Republicans and Democrats continued to disagree bitterly over his actions.

In Kentucky, where secessionist and Unionist sentiment was evenly balanced, Lincoln moved cautiously. He allowed Kentucky's thriving trade with the Confederacy to continue until August 1861, when Unionists took over the state government. After the Confederacy unwisely responded to the trade cutoff by invading Kentucky in September, Illinois volunteers commanded by Ulysses S. Grant drove them out, and Kentucky public opinion swung against the Confederacy. Mixing military force with political persuasion, Lincoln had kept three border states (Delaware, Maryland, and Kentucky) and the northwestern portion of Virginia in the Union.

But how far west did "border regions" extend? As the territorial conflicts of the 1850s had revealed, the answer was not clear. Lincoln's election roused deep suspicion among many westerners, from Utah Mormons — whom Republicans had alienated by seeking to abolish polygamy — to gold-rush Californians, nearly 40 percent of whom were southern-born. In Oregon, a former U.S. senator praised the "gallant South" and

In September 1862, Union forces halted the Confederate invasion of Maryland with victories at South Mountain and Antietam (11 and 12).

South Mountain Sept. 14, 1862

Antietam Sept. 17, 1862

Frederick

Harpers Ferry

MARYLAND

Baltimore

Winchester May 25, 1862

WEST VIRGINIA (1863)

Potomac R.

Shenandoah R.

To relieve pressure on Richmond, Confederate troops under General Stonewall Jackson made a run up the Shenandoah Valley, threatening Washington (4, 5, and 7).

Washington, D.C.

The only major battle of 1861 — Bull Run — took place about 30 miles southwest of the Union's capital. It left both armies in disarray.

Bull Run July 21, 1861 Aug. 29–30, 1862

B L U E   R I D G E   M T S.

McDowell May 8, 1862

Cross Keys June 8, 1862

Cedar Mt. Aug. 9, 1862

Fredericksburg Dec. 13, 1862

N W E S

At Fredericksburg (13) in December 1862, Confederate forces repulsed another Union thrust into the heart of Virginia.

The Peninsular Campaign (2 and 3; 6 and 8) began in May 1862 as an attempt by the Union armies to take Richmond by moving up the peninsula between the James and York rivers.

Rappahannock R.

0   20   40 miles
0   20   40 kilometers

Assisted by Jackson's attacks, Lee repulsed the Union assault on Richmond and then advanced toward Washington. After another Confederate victory in the Second Battle of Bull Run (10) in August 1862, Lee's army moved into Maryland.

Fair Oaks May 31–June 1, 1862

Chesapeake Bay

VIRGINIA

Richmond

Seven Days June 25–July 1, 1862

York R.

Siege of Yorktown Apr. 5–May 4, 1862

James R.

Williamsburg May 5, 1862

Union Movements

McDowell
McClellan
Frémont
Banks
Shields
Pope
Burnside
Union victory

Confederate Movements

Johnston
Holmes
Jackson
Lee
Confederate victory
Railroad
Sequence of battles

To help you to follow the sequence of the major battles of the eastern campaigns of 1862, each battle is dated and its place in the chronology denoted by a number in a circle.

Ft. Monroe

MAP 13.1 The Eastern Campaigns of 1862

Many of the great battles of the Civil War took place in the 125 miles separating the Union capital, Washington, D.C., and the Confederate capital, Richmond, Virginia. During 1862, Confederate generals Thomas Jonathan "Stonewall" Jackson and Robert E. Lee won battles that defended the Confederate capital (3, 6, 8, and 13) and launched offensive strikes against Union forces guarding Washington (1, 4, 5, 7, 9, and 10). They also suffered a defeat — at Antietam (12), in Maryland — that was almost fatal to the Confederate cause. As was often the case in the Civil War, the victors in these battles were either too bloodied or too timid to exploit their advantage.

claimed that "the Republican Party will have war enough at home." In Indian Territory (now Oklahoma), many slave-owning Choctaws, Chickasaws, and Cherokees cast their lot with the Confederacy, hoping to secure more autonomy than the Union had allowed them. Thus, the war bitterly divided Native peoples in Indian Territory. It was a Confederate Cherokee, General Stand Watie, who became the war's highest-ranking Native American.

Meanwhile, Texas coveted New Mexico, and enterprising Confederates argued that they could bolster their economy if they captured the gold mines of Colorado,

MAP 13.2 **The Western Campaigns, 1861–1862**

As the Civil War intensified in 1862, Union and Confederate military and naval forces sought control of the great valleys of the Ohio, Tennessee, and Mississippi rivers, as well as the trans-Mississippi west. In fall 1861, a Confederate force marched west from Texas, hoping to seize the rich mining areas of Nevada and Colorado, but they were turned back in March 1862 at the Battle of Glorieta Pass. From February through April 1862, Union armies moved south through western Tennessee. By the end of June, Union naval forces controlled the Mississippi River north of Memphis and from the Gulf of Mexico to Vicksburg. These military and naval victories gave the Union control of crucial transportation routes, kept Missouri in the Union, and carried the war to the borders of the states of the Lower South.

seized Nevada's fabulously rich Comstock silver lode, and perhaps even took San Francisco. In autumn 1861, therefore, an expedition of 3,500 Texans marched west and succeeded in capturing Albuquerque and Santa Fe. But the following March, as the Confederates headed north, Union forces turned them back at the Battle of Glorieta Pass (Map 13.2). Henceforth Union control of the Far West remained secure. Among the victorious troops were Colorado volunteers whose massacre of friendly Cheyennes at Sand Creek, soon after, embroiled the West in a new round of Indian wars (Chapter 15).

The Struggle to Control the Mississippi Union commanders in Tennessee also won key victories, dividing the Confederacy and reducing the mobility of its armies. Because Kentucky did not join the rebellion, the Union already dominated the Ohio River Valley. In February 1862, the Union army used an innovative tactic to extend control to the south and west. General Grant used riverboats clad with iron plates to capture Fort Donelson on the Cumberland River and Fort Henry on the Tennessee River. When Grant moved south to seize critical railroad lines, Confederate troops led by Albert Sidney Johnston and P. G. T. Beauregard caught his army by surprise near a small log church at Shiloh, Tennessee. However, Grant relentlessly committed troops and forced a Confederate withdrawal.

When it ended on April 7, the Battle of Shiloh left 20,000 men dead or wounded—a shocking total, larger than most of the war's prior battles combined. A Tennessee private wrote of hearing the cries of "the wounded begging piteously for help," while Grant's

Union Gunboats on the Mississippi Steam-powered ironclad gunboats played a key role in the Union war effort, as in the scene depicted here, of the bombardment and capture of Island Number 10, near the far northwest corner of Tennessee, in April 1862. By July 1863 the Union controlled the entire Mississippi River, dividing the Confederacy in two. The Confederate government also built gunboats and eventually deployed a tiny submarine, pointing toward ominous new developments in the technology of destruction. This Currier & Ives lithograph enabled supporters of the Union effort to follow the war's progress. Everett Collection/Alamy.

second in command, General William Tecumseh Sherman, described "piles of dead soldiers' mangled bodies . . . without heads or legs." Grant surveyed a large field "so covered with dead that it would have been possible to walk over the clearing in any direction, stepping on dead bodies, without a foot touching the ground." Ambrose Bierce, an Indiana sergeant, was haunted afterward by the hideous sight of charred bodies of Illinois men, too wounded to flee the battlefield, who had burned to death when the woodland caught fire. Some lay in "postures of agony that told of the tormenting flame." Those who survived Shiloh had few illusions about the war's supposed romance and glory.

Farther north and west, the Union barely maintained control of the crucial border slave state of Missouri. At the war's start Lincoln had mobilized the state's German American militia, most of whom strongly opposed slavery. In July 1861 they defeated a force of Confederate sympathizers commanded by the state's governor. In March 1862, at the battle of Pea Ridge, Arkansas, a small Union army defeated a Confederate force that had hoped to capture St. Louis and attack Grant from behind. The Union victory at Pea Ridge secured Missouri for the Union, though it did not end violent local conflicts that continued through the war.

Meanwhile, Union naval forces commanded by David G. Farragut struck the Confederacy from the Gulf of Mexico. They captured New Orleans, the Deep South's financial center and largest city. The Union army also took control of fifteen hundred plantations and 50,000 slaves in the surrounding region, striking a strong blow against slavery. Workers on some plantations looted their owners' mansions; in order to harvest cotton and sugar, planters were forced to pay wages. "[Slavery there] is forever destroyed and worthless," declared a northern reporter. The taking of New Orleans, combined with other Union victories, had significantly undermined Confederate strength in the Mississippi River Valley.

Antietam and Its Consequences

In the east, hoping for victories that would humiliate Lincoln's government, Lee went on the offensive. Joining with Jackson in northern Virginia, he routed Union troops in August 1862, in the Second Battle of Bull Run, and then struck north through western Maryland. There, he nearly met disaster. When the Confederate commander divided his force, sending Jackson to capture Harpers Ferry in West Virginia, a copy of Lee's orders fell into McClellan's hands. But the Union general again failed to exploit his advantage, delaying an attack against Lee's depleted army and thereby allowing it to secure a strong defensive position west of Antietam Creek, near Sharpsburg, Maryland. Outnumbered 87,000 to 50,000, Lee desperately fought off McClellan's attacks until Jackson's troops arrived and saved the Confederates from a major defeat. Appalled by the Union casualties, McClellan allowed Lee to retreat to Virginia.

The fighting at Antietam was savage. A Wisconsin officer described his men "loading and firing with demoniacal fury." A sunken road—nicknamed Bloody Lane—was filled with Confederate bodies two and three deep, and the advancing Union troops knelt on this "ghastly flooring" to shoot at retreating Confederates. The day of the battle, September 17, 1862, remains the bloodiest single day in U.S. military history. Together, the Confederate and Union dead numbered 4,800 and the wounded 18,500, of whom 3,000 soon died. (By comparison, American troops suffered 6,000 casualties on D-Day, which began the invasion of Nazi-occupied France in World War II.)

In public, Lincoln claimed Antietam as a Union victory; privately, he criticized McClellan for not pursuing Lee to seek a full Confederate surrender. A masterful organizer of men and supplies, McClellan refused to risk his troops, fearing heavy casualties would undermine public support for the war. Lincoln worried more about the danger of a lengthy war. He dismissed McClellan and began a long search for an aggressive

To see a longer excerpt from Ambrose Bierce's account of Shiloh, along with other primary sources from this period, see *Sources for America's History*.

Antietam These Confederate soldiers, from General William Starke's Louisiana infantry, died on September 17, 1862, while attacking Union troops along the Hagerstown Pike. This and many other photographs by Alexander Gardner were exhibited in New York by Matthew Brady. Northern commentators were shocked by their immediacy, which brought home the violence of war to civilians far from the battlefield. Frustrated by Brady's failure to recognize the photographers who worked for him, Gardner soon broke with his employer and began to work on his own, becoming one of the war's leading photographers. Library of Congress.

commanding general. At the same time, he began laying the groundwork for ending slavery.

Calls for Emancipation From the war's beginning, northern abolitionists called for slavery's end. Because slave-grown crops sustained the Confederacy, activists justified black emancipation on military grounds. As Frederick Douglass put it, "Arrest that hoe in the hands of the Negro, and you smite the rebellion in the very seat of its life."

In the South, enslaved African Americans exploited wartime chaos to seize freedom for themselves. When three slaves reached the camp of Union general Benjamin Butler in Virginia in May 1861, he labeled them "contraband of war" (enemy property that can be legitimately seized, according to international law) and refused to return them. Butler's term captured the imagination of northerners. Soon thousands of so-called **"contrabands"** were camping with Union armies. Near Fredericksburg, Virginia, an average of 200 blacks appeared every day, "with their packs on their backs and handkerchiefs tied over their heads — men, women, little children, and babies." The influx created a humanitarian crisis. Abolitionist Harriet Jacobs reported that hundreds of refugees were "packed together in the most miserable quarters," where many died from smallpox and dysentery. To provide legal status to the refugees — some 400,000 by war's end — in August 1861 Congress passed the Confiscation Act, which authorized the seizure of all property, including slave property, used to support the rebellion.

With the Confiscation Act, **Radical Republicans** — members of the party who had bitterly opposed the "slave power" since the mid-1850s — began to use wartime legislation to destroy slavery. Their leaders were Treasury Secretary Salmon Chase, Senator Charles Sumner of Massachusetts, and Representative Thaddeus Stevens of Pennsylvania. A longtime member of Congress, Stevens was skilled at fashioning legislation that could win majority support. In April 1862, Radicals persuaded Congress to end slavery in the District of Columbia by providing compensation for owners; in June, Congress outlawed slavery in the federal territories (finally enacting the Wilmot Proviso of 1846); in July, it passed a second Confiscation Act, which declared "forever free" the thousands of refugee slaves and all slaves captured by the Union army. Emancipation had become an instrument of war.

The Emancipation Proclamation Initially, Lincoln rejected emancipation as a war aim. In August 1861, when Union general John C. Frémont (who had been the Republican presidential candidate in 1856) issued a field order freeing the slaves of Missouri Confederates, Lincoln promptly revoked it. But he faced rising Radical Republican pressure and, from his field commanders, reports of overwhelming throngs of African American refugees, most of whom risked their lives to reach Union lines and expressed strong support for the Union. Secretly, the president drafted a general proclamation of emancipation in July 1862. He began to test the waters in his public statements. "If I could save the Union without freeing any slave, I would do it," he wrote to Horace Greeley of the *New York Tribune,* "and if I could save it by freeing all the slaves, I would do it." With this statement Lincoln reassured white Americans, fearful of Radical goals, that his paramount goal was to save the Union — while also planting the idea that emancipation might be the best way to accomplish that aim.

Secretary of State William Seward, fearful that the Union would look desperate if it threatened emancipation after a string of military losses, advised Lincoln to wait for a Union victory. Lincoln took his advice. Considering the Battle of Antietam "an indication of the Divine Will," Lincoln issued a preliminary proclamation of emancipation on September 22, 1862, basing its legal authority on his duty as commander in chief to suppress rebellion. The proclamation warned that the president would abolish slavery in all states that remained out of the Union on January 1, 1863. Rebel states could preserve slavery by renouncing secession. None chose to do so.

Eastman Johnson, *A Ride for Freedom — The Fugitive Slaves*, c. 1862 At the second battle of Manassas in September 1862, American genre painter Eastman Johnson (1824–1906) witnessed this "veritable incident" of an African American family fleeing slavery — and then painted it. A powerful, split-second image of the riders' silhouettes, Johnson's painting captures the father looking forward toward freedom, while the mother cradles a young child and looks back apprehensively for possible pursuers. By "freeing themselves," this family and thousands of blacks set the stage for Lincoln's Emancipation Proclamation.   Brooklyn Museum of Art, New York, USA/Gift of Gwendolyn O. L. Conkling/Bridgeman Images.

The proclamation was politically astute. Lincoln conciliated slave owners in the Union-controlled border states, such as Maryland and Missouri, by leaving slavery intact there. He also permitted slavery to continue in areas occupied by Union armies: western and central Tennessee, western Virginia, and southern Louisiana. Consequently, the **Emancipation Proclamation** did not immediately free a single slave. Yet, as abolitionist Wendell Phillips argued, Lincoln's proclamation had moved slavery to "the edge of Niagara," ready to sweep it over the brink. Advancing Union troops became agents of slavery's destruction. "I became free in 1863, in the summer, when the yankees come by and said I could go work for myself," recalled Jackson Daniel of Maysville, Alabama. On South Carolina's Sea Islands, which were under Union control and largely abandoned by Confederate land owners, an idealistic group of northern abolitionists arrived to bring aid to freedpeople, open schools, and recruit the First South Carolina U.S. Regiment (Colored). As Lincoln now saw it, "the old South is to be destroyed and replaced by new propositions and ideas."

Hailed by reformers in Europe, emancipation helped persuade Britain and France to refrain from recognizing the Confederacy, in a war now being fought between slavery and freedom. Though Britain never recognized the Confederacy as an independent nation, it treated the rebel government as a belligerent power, with the right under international law to borrow money and purchase weapons. However, British manufacturers had stockpiled cotton and began to develop new sources of the commodity in Egypt and India.

Confederate president Jefferson Davis labeled the Emancipation Proclamation the "most execrable measure recorded in the history of guilty man." In the Union, the measure was hardly less controversial. In the 1862 midterm elections, Democrats denounced emancipation as unconstitutional, warned of slave uprisings, and predicted that freed blacks would take white jobs. Every freed slave, suggested one nativist New Yorker, should "shoulder an Irishman and leave the Continent." Such sentiments propelled Democrat Horatio Seymour into the governor's office in New York; if abolition was a war goal, Seymour argued, the South should not be conquered. In the election, Democrats swept to victory in Pennsylvania, Ohio, and Illinois and gained 34 seats in Congress. However, Republicans still held a 25-seat majority in the House and gained 5 seats in the Senate. Lincoln refused to retreat. Calling emancipation an "act of justice," he signed the final proclamation on New Year's Day 1863. "If my name ever goes into history," he said, "it was for this act."

CONSIDER POINTS OF VIEW
Explain the roles played by at least five individuals and groups in bringing about the Emancipation Proclamation.

The proclamation meant little, however, without victory on the battlefield to enforce it. Lincoln's first choice to replace McClellan, Ambrose E. Burnside, proved to be more daring but woefully incompetent. In December, after heavy losses in futile attacks against well-entrenched Confederate forces at Fredericksburg, Virginia, Burnside resigned his command, and Lincoln replaced him with Joseph "Fighting Joe" Hooker. As 1862 ended, Confederates were optimistic: the outcome at Fredericksburg demonstrated that the Union still lacked effective generals, and the South had won a stalemate in the East.

IN YOUR OWN WORDS What early political and military strategies did Confederate and Union leaders adopt, and which were most successful?

Toward "Hard War," 1863

The military carnage in 1862 made clear that the war would be long and costly. Grant later remarked that, after Shiloh, he "gave up all idea of saving the Union except by complete conquest." Lincoln committed the Union to mobilizing all its resources — economic, political, and cultural — in support of the North's military effort and to end slavery in the South. Aided by the Republican Party and a talented cabinet, Lincoln gradually organized an effective central government that adopted new strategies to pursue victory. In the Confederacy, despite the doctrine of states' rights, Jefferson Davis also exerted centralized authority to harness resources for the fight. Both North and South implemented military drafts — a dramatic change from the all-volunteer forces of 1861. The Union availed itself, also, of a fresh and determined body of volunteers: African American soldiers. What emerged from these developments, and out of the logic of the struggle itself, was a far more ruthless and systemic war.

Politics North and South

With nearly two-thirds of the nation's population, the North was far better equipped than the South to sustain the prolonged, large-scale conflict that the Civil War became by 1863. Its economy also lent itself better to wartime needs — largely because of recent innovations. In 1852, canals carried twice as much tonnage as the nation's newly emerging railroads. But by 1860, after capitalists in Boston, New York, and London secured state charters and invested heavily, railroads had become the major carriers of wheat and freight from the Midwest to northeastern Atlantic ports, returning with machine tools, hardware, and furniture manufactured in the Northeast. Served by a vast network of locomotive and freight-car repair shops, railroads also hauled lumber from Michigan to the prairie states and livestock to Chicago's rapidly growing slaughterhouses.

The Union was thus investing in a state-of-the-art transportation system, and entrepreneurs were also modernizing agricultural technology. After 1847, John Deere operated a steel plow factory in Moline, Illinois. Far better than older cast-iron plows manufactured in New York, Deere plows enabled farmers to cut through deep, tough roots of prairie grasses and open new regions for farming. Other midwestern companies, such as McCormick and Hussey, mass-produced self-raking reapers that harvested 12 acres of grain a day, rather than the 2 acres an adult worker could cut by hand. Such innovations proved to be substantial advantages when the Civil War became long and resource-intensive. Without "reapers, mowers, separators, sowers, drills &c," wrote the *Cincinnati Gazette*, "the wheat, oats, and hay of Ohio, in 1862, could not have been got in safely." "We have seen," one journalist reported in the 1863 harvest season, "a stout matron whose sons are in the army, with her team cutting hay at seventy-five cents per acre, and she cut seven acres with ease in a day, riding leisurely upon her cutter. . . . War occupations, even on a most gigantic scale, do not seem to check the supply of food."

Republican Economic and Fiscal Policies To mobilize northern resources, the Republican-dominated Congress enacted a program of government-assisted economic development. It imposed high tariffs, averaging nearly 40 percent, on various foreign goods, thereby encouraging domestic industries. To boost agricultural output, it offered free land to farmers through the Homestead Act of 1862. Republicans also created an integrated network of national banks and implemented Clay's program for a nationally financed transportation system, chartering the Union Pacific and Central Pacific companies to build a transcontinental railroad and granting them substantial land subsidies to complete the difficult work (see Chapter 15). This economic program won the allegiance of farmers, workers, and entrepreneurs while bolstering the Union's ability to fight a long war.

Trestle Bridge at Whiteside This 1864 image from *Photographic Views of Sherman's Campaign* shows a celebrated 780-foot railroad trestle bridge, built by Union engineers (and carefully guarded) after the original bridge was destroyed by Confederate forces seeking to stop a Union advance. Engineering feats such as this one, including pontoon bridges and other innovations, played a central role in supplying troops and enabling them to conquer territory. Confederates, for example, were incredulous when General William T. Sherman launched his march across South Carolina's low country swamps. "When I learned that Sherman's army was marching through the Salk swamps," wrote General Joseph Johnston, "making its own [plank] roads at the rate of a dozen miles a day, I made up my mind that there had been no such army in existence since the days of Julius Caesar." Digital image courtesy of the Getty's Open Content Program.

New industries sprang up to provide the Union's 1.5 million soldiers with guns, clothes, and food. Over the course of the war, soldiers consumed more than half a billion pounds of pork and other packed meats. To meet this demand, Chicago railroads built new lines to carry thousands of hogs and cattle to the city's stockyards and slaughterhouses. By 1862, Chicago had passed Cincinnati as the meatpacking capital of the nation, bringing prosperity to thousands of midwestern farmers and great wealth to Philip D. Armour and other meatpacking entrepreneurs.

Bankers and financiers likewise found themselves pulled into the war effort. Annual U.S. government spending shot up from $63 million in 1860 to more than $865 million in 1864. To raise that enormous sum, Republicans created a modern system of public finance that raised money in three ways. First, the government raised money directly by increasing tariffs, placing high duties on alcohol and tobacco, and imposing taxes on business corporations, large inheritances, and the incomes of wealthy citizens. These levies paid about 20 percent of the war's cost. Interest-paying bonds issued by the U.S. Treasury financed another 65 percent. The National Banking Acts of 1863 and 1864 forced most banks to buy those bonds, and Philadelphia banker and Treasury Department agent Jay Cooke used newspaper ads and 2,500 subagents to persuade a million northern families to buy them.

The Union paid the remaining 15 percent by printing paper money. The Legal Tender Act of 1862 authorized $150 million in paper currency—soon known as **greenbacks**—and required the public to accept them as legal tender. Like the Continental currency of the Revolutionary era, greenbacks could not be exchanged for specie; however, the Treasury issued a limited amount of paper money, so it lost only a small part of its face value.

By 1863, the Lincoln administration had created an efficient war machine and a set of strategic priorities. Henry Adams, the grandson of John Quincy Adams and a future novelist and historian, noted the change from his diplomatic post in London: "Little by little, one began to feel that, behind the chaos in Washington power was taking shape; that it was massed and guided as it had not been before." The short-term results

TRACE CHANGE OVER TIME
How did the wartime policies of the Republican-controlled Congress redefine the character of the federal government?

contributed substantially to Union victory. In the longer term, immense concentrations of capital in many industries — meatpacking, steel, coal, railroads, textiles, shoes — gave a few men "command of millions of money," setting up new political conflicts in the postwar era.

Confederate Policies and Conflicts   Economic demands on the South were equally great, but, true to its states' rights philosophy, the Confederacy initially left most matters to the state governments. However, as the scale and length of the conflict became clear, Jefferson Davis's administration took extraordinary measures. It built and operated shipyards, armories, foundries, and textile mills; commandeered food and scarce raw materials such as coal, iron, copper, and lead; set prices; requisitioned slaves to work on fortifications; and directly controlled foreign trade.

The Confederate Congress, dominated by slaveholders, opposed many of Davis's initiatives, particularly taxes. It refused to tax cotton exports and slaves, the most valuable property held by wealthy planters. Consequently, the Confederacy covered less than 10 percent of its expenditures through taxation. The government paid another 30 percent by borrowing, but as Union forces secured control of more and more southern territory, wealthy planters and foreign bankers grew reluctant to provide loans, fearing they would never be repaid. Consequently, the Confederacy paid 60 percent of its war costs by printing paper money. This flood of currency created spectacular inflation: by 1865, prices had risen to ninety-two times their 1861 level.

Conflicts over government impressment, or borrowing, of slaves also revealed weaknesses in the Confederacy. Many planters were reluctant to lend their slaves to work on military fortifications, rightly fearing that if these enslaved men found themselves near the battlefront, they would try to flee to Union lines. As a result, wealthy southerners used their political pull to keep slaves in private use. "The planter," wrote the *Mobile Register* angrily in 1863, "is more ready to contribute his sons than his slaves to the war."

Poor whites had no such luxury. The Confederate **one-tenth tax**, adopted in April 1863, required all farmers to turn over a tenth of their crops and livestock to the government for military use. Applied to poor families with husbands and fathers in the army, the policy pushed thousands of civilians to the brink of starvation. In letters and petitions to state officials, women pleaded desperately for help, designating themselves proudly as "S.W.," Soldiers' Wives. "The rich is all at home making great fortunes," wrote an outraged group of Georgia women, "and don't care what becomes of the poor class of people [as long as] they can save there neggroes."

As food prices soared, riots erupted in more than a dozen southern cities and towns. In Richmond, several hundred women broke into bakeries, crying, "our children are starving." In Randolph County, Alabama, women confiscated grain from a government warehouse "to prevent starvation of themselves and their families." As inflation spiraled upward, many southerners refused to accept paper money. When South Carolina storekeeper Jim Harris refused the depreciated currency presented by Confederate soldiers, they raided his storehouse and, he claimed, "robbed it of about five thousand dollars worth of goods." Army supply officers likewise seized goods from merchants and offered payment in worthless IOUs. Facing a public that feared strong government and high taxation, the Confederacy could sustain the war effort only by seizing its citizens' property.

Still, after two years of war, the Confederate position was far from weak. Virginia, North Carolina, and Tennessee deployed their substantial industrial capacity. Richmond, with its Tredegar Iron Works, served as an important manufacturing center. The purchase of Enfield rifles from Britain and the capture of 100,000 Union guns at Harpers Ferry near the start of the war helped the Confederacy provide every infantryman with a modern rifle-musket by 1863. Even though life had become difficult, the Confederate military was hardly ready to surrender.

COMPARE AND CONTRAST
How did Union and Confederate civilians' experiences of their wartime governments differ?

INTERPRETATIONS

How Divided Was the Confederate Public?

Did the Union army (the North) win the Civil War, or did the Confederate army (the South) lose it? Questions like these have kept historians busy. To explain the outcome of that war, historians have looked at a wide variety of factors, seizing upon one or another as the decisive tipping point. Many have argued that the North's material resources of capital, industry, and population gave it the edge. Others have wondered how the South lasted so long and have pointed to its superior military commanders and its "home field" advantages as well as ideological commitments. Many southerners, for example, believed they were fighting to save their homes and way of life from northern abolitionist aggression. Historians Gary W. Gallagher and Drew Gilpin Faust focus on the Confederacy itself. Did southerners imagine themselves to be a separate nation? Was their nationalism strong enough to sustain a terrible and costly war?

GARY W. GALLAGHER

Source: Gary W. Gallagher, *The Confederate War* (Cambridge: Harvard University Press, 1997), 63.

Strong feelings of national identity helped spawn the impressive will Confederates exhibited during their war for independence. With the goal of mounting the broad military effort necessary to establish nationhood, soldiers and civilians of the Confederacy tolerated severe intrusions on personal freedom, accepted the erosion of states' rights as the central government sought to equip and feed its armies, and, toward the end, debated openly the possibility of arming and freeing slaves to win the war.

DREW GILPIN FAUST

Source: From Drew Gilpin Faust, "Altars of Sacrifice: Confederate Women and the Narratives of War," *The Journal of American History* by Mississippi Valley Historical Association; Organization of American Historians. Reproduced with permission of Organization of American Historians in the format Book via Copyright Clearance Center.

Countless women of all classes had in effect deserted the ranks. . . . Refusing to accept the economic deprivation further military struggle would have required, resisting additional military service by their husbands and sons . . . Southern women undermined both objective and ideological foundations for the Confederate effort; they directly subverted the South's military and economic effectiveness as well as civilian morale. . . . It may well have been because of its women that the South lost the Civil War.

QUESTIONS FOR ANALYSIS

1. How do these two historians differ in their assessment of Confederate wartime unity?
2. What factor does Faust emphasize that might explain the limits of Confederate nationalism?

3. From this chapter's discussion of the Confederacy, identify two factors that support or challenge the argument for Confederate nationalism during the war.

Conscription With battles proving more and more deadly and no end in sight, the supply of volunteers for the armies soon dried up. Still, both the Union and the Confederacy needed more men. The South acted first. In April 1862, following the bloodshed at Shiloh, the Confederate Congress imposed the first legally binding **draft (conscription)** in American history. New laws required existing soldiers to serve for the duration of the war and mandated three years of military service from all men between the ages of eighteen and thirty-five. In September 1862, after heavy casualties at Antietam, the age limit jumped to forty-five.

The Confederate draft had two loopholes, both controversial. First, it exempted one white man — the planter, a son, or an overseer — for each twenty slaves, allowing some whites on large plantations to avoid military service. This **twenty-Negro rule**, a Mississippi legislator warned Jefferson Davis, "has aroused a spirit of rebellion in some places." Second, wealthier draftees could hire substitutes. By the time the Confederate Congress closed this loophole in 1864, the price of a substitute had soared to $300 in gold, three times the annual wage of a skilled worker. Laborers and poor farmers angrily complained that both these measures made the war a "poor man's fight" (Interpretations).

SOUTHERN "VOLUNTEERS".

Military Conscription This Currier & Ives print was likely published soon after the Confederacy instituted a military draft in April 1862. It depicts a "Union man," two wealthy planters, and a barefoot backwoodsman. The Union did not have long to satirize the Confederates' reliance on conscripted troops: within a few months, Lincoln and the Republican Congress instituted a comprehensive military draft for the Union. Library of Congress.

Some southerners refused to serve. Because the Confederate constitution vested sovereignty in individual states, the government in Richmond could not compel military service. Independent-minded governors such as Joseph Brown of Georgia and Zebulon Vance of North Carolina simply ignored President Davis's first draft call in early 1862. Elsewhere, state judges issued writs of habeas corpus and ordered the Confederate army to release reluctant draftees. The Confederate Congress, however, overrode judges' authority to free conscripted men, keeping substantial armies in the field well into 1864. Confederate militia also scoured areas that harbored large groups of deserters, like Jones County and surrounding areas of southeast Mississippi, using bloodhounds to track resisters and hanging those they could catch.

The Union's draft or Enrollment Act, introduced in March 1863, provoked equally dramatic opposition. Some recent German and Irish immigrants refused to serve; it was not their war, they said. Northern Democrats used the furor to bolster support for their party, which increasingly criticized Lincoln's policies. They accused Lincoln of drafting poor whites to liberate enslaved blacks, who would then flood northern cities. In July 1863, as conscription went into effect, immigrants' hostility toward the draft and toward blacks sparked virulent **draft riots** in New York City. For five days working-class men ran rampant, burned draft offices, sacked the homes of influential Republicans, and attacked the police. The rioters lynched and mutilated a dozen African Americans, drove hundreds of black families from their homes, and burned down the Colored Orphan Asylum. To suppress the mobs, Lincoln rushed in Union troops who had just fought at Gettysburg; they killed more than a hundred rioters. The war on the battlefield was eroding peace at home.

In contested areas, the Union government treated draft resisters and enemy sympathizers ruthlessly. Union commanders in Missouri and other border states levied special taxes on southern supporters. Lincoln went further, suspending habeas corpus and, over the course of the war, temporarily imprisoning about 15,000 southern sympathizers without trial. He also gave military courts jurisdiction over civilians who discouraged enlistments or resisted the draft, preventing acquittals by sympathetic local juries. However, most Union states used incentives to lure recruits. To meet local quotas set by the Militia Act of 1862, towns, counties, and states offered cash bounties of as much as $600 (about $11,000 today) and signed up nearly a million men.

CONSIDER POINTS OF VIEW
What made military conscription so controversial in both the Confederacy and the Union?

The Impact of Emancipation

Facing controversy and violent resistance, the Lincoln administration pursued a novel strategy: enlisting African American soldiers. As early as 1861, free African Americans and fugitive slaves had volunteered, hoping to end slavery and secure citizenship rights. Yet many northern whites refused to serve with blacks. "I am as much opposed to slavery as any of them," a New York soldier told his local newspaper, "but I am not willing to be put on a level with the negro and fight with them." Union generals also opposed military service by African Americans, doubting they would make good soldiers. Nonetheless, as the war unfolded, free and contraband blacks formed volunteer regiments in New England, South Carolina, Louisiana, and Kansas.

The Emancipation Proclamation changed military policy and popular sentiment. It invited former slaves to serve in the Union army. Northern whites, having suffered thousands of casualties, now accepted that African Americans should share in the fighting and dying. A heroic and costly attack by the black troops of the 54th Massachusetts Infantry on Fort Wagner, South Carolina, in 1863 convinced Union officers that African American soldiers could fight bravely. Commentators observed that black soldiers from the seceded states could have a triple impact: in addition to strengthening the Union army, their liberation demoralized white southerners and robbed the Confederacy of much-needed labor.

Military service did not end racial discrimination. Black Union soldiers initially earned less than white soldiers ($10 a month versus $13). They served in segregated regiments under white commissioned officers and they died, mostly from disease, at higher rates than white soldiers. Nonetheless, over 180,000 African Americans volunteered by 1865, fighting for emancipation and often their own freedom. "Hello, Massa," said one black soldier to his former master, who had been taken prisoner, "bottom rail on top dis time." Raiding a South Carolina town for supplies, a Union colonel took pleasure in introducing a plantation mistress to Corporal Robert Sutton of his regiment, saying he believed they had been "previously acquainted." When the woman recognized the corporal, her former slave, she "drew herself up, and dropped out the monosyllables of her answer as if they were so many drops of nitric acid: . . . '*we* called him Bob!' " The worst fears of secessionists had come true. Through the disciplined agency of the Union army, African Americans had risen in a successful rebellion against slavery.

Lincoln, among others, believed the Union could not have won the war without black troops. At the same time, southern responses to the new soldiers upped the stakes in the conflict. Furious Confederate officials vowed to treat black Union prisoners as runaway slaves and execute their officers for inciting slave rebellion. Colonel Thomas Wentworth Higginson, an abolitionist who went south to lead the First South Carolina Regiment (Colored), wrote that his men "fought with ropes round their necks." Confederate threats gave them "grim satisfaction . . . [and] a peculiar sense of self-respect. . . . The First South Carolina must fight it out or be re-enslaved." Faced with southern intransigence, General Grant suggested that the Union retaliate by shooting Confederate prisoners, man for man. Lincoln declined to carry out this policy, but race warfare nonetheless erupted on the battlefield. At Fort Pillow in Tennessee, in April 1864, Confederate cavalry under Nathan Bedford Forrest (future founder of the Ku Klux Klan) gunned down African American troops as they tried to surrender. After a subsequent battle in Mississippi, one Union lieutenant wrote, "We did not take many prisoners. The Negroes remembered 'Fort Pillow.' "

Confederates' refusal to exchange African American prisoners precipitated a new Union policy: suspending prisoner exchanges, which had taken place regularly since the war's start. As a result, by late 1863 both sides accumulated large numbers of prisoners of war, who suffered horrific conditions in crowded prison camps. Particularly notorious was the Confederacy's prison at Andersonville, Georgia, where over 13,000 of 45,000 Union prisoners died of disease or malnutrition. Amid public outrage, both Lee and Grant tried to reopen prisoner exchanges, but they could not agree on the treatment of black Union troops. Lee warned that "negroes belonging to our citizens" could not be "considered subjects of exchange." Grant responded that his government had a duty "to secure to all persons received into her armies the rights due to soldiers." The effort to renew exchanges failed.

Grant was guided in these discussions by the Union's **Lieber Code**, an innovative statement of the laws of war drafted by German immigrant law professor Francis Lieber, who had sons serving in both the Union and Confederate armies. Issued in April 1863,

African American Soldiers Strengthen the Union Army Determined to end racial slavery, tens of thousands of African Americans volunteered for service in the Union army in 1864 and 1865, boosting the northern war effort at a critical moment. This unknown soldier posed for his studio portrait at Benton Barracks, Saint Louis, Missouri, proudly displaying his weapons while backed by the American flag. Library of Congress.

the code declared that the "law of nations and of nature" had never recognized slavery and knew "no distinction of color." Anyone who escaped a slaveholding locality was therefore free, and African American soldiers must be treated exactly as whites were. Arguing that the most humane war was one that ended quickly, Lieber defined "military necessity" liberally, permitting many military actions, from shooting spies to starving civilians, if they would "hasten surrender." At the same time, Lieber's code spelled out protections for prisoners of war, outlawed use of torture for any reason, and forbade "the infliction of suffering for the sake of suffering or for revenge." Widely admired in Europe, the code provided a foundation for later international agreements on the laws of war, including the Geneva Conventions.

Citizens and the Work of War

Lieber was among tens of thousands of civilians who contributed in distinctive ways to the Union war effort, from buying bonds to sewing banners. Unlike the rural Confederacy, northern states had an increasingly urban population and stronger infrastructure of schools, press, and reform groups that provided a base for innovative forms of civilian mobilization. On both sides, however, the conflict was a "people's war" marked by intensive citizen participation.

Medicine and Nursing   In 1861, prominent New Yorkers established the **U.S. Sanitary Commission** to provide Union troops with clothing, food, and medical services. While paid agents and spokesmen were male, over 200,000 women supported the commission as volunteers, working through seven thousand local auxiliaries. "I almost weep," reported one agent, "when these plain rural people come to send their simple offerings to absent sons and brothers." The commission also recruited battlefield nurses and doctors for the Union army.

Despite these efforts, dysentery, typhoid, and malaria spread through the camps, as did mumps and measles, viruses that were often deadly to rural recruits. Diseases and infections killed about 250,000 Union soldiers, nearly twice the 135,000 who died in combat. These numbers would have been far higher if the Sanitary Commission had not, for example, persuaded key military leaders that their troops should dig latrines for proper waste disposal. The internationally acclaimed U.S. ambulance corps, authorized by Congress in 1864, developed efficient procedures to evacuate wounded soldiers from the battlefield. As a result of such efforts, one historian estimates that 25 percent of wounded Union soldiers died in 1861 but only 10 percent by 1864 (Thinking Like a Historian).

Confederate troops were less fortunate because the Confederate army's health system was poorly organized. Scurvy was a special problem for southern soldiers; lacking vitamin C in their diets, they suffered muscle ailments and had low resistance to camp diseases. Confederate women created dozens of local or state-level relief societies, and thousands volunteered as nurses. "The war is certainly ours as well as that of the men," wrote Kate Cumming, a Scottish-born immigrant to Alabama who served for four years at Confederate hospitals in Georgia. In her diary Cumming recorded the horrors of hospital service, with wounded soldiers groaning in agony among piles of amputated limbs. "I daily witness the same sad scenes — men dying all around me. I do not know who they are, nor have I time to learn."

Women and the War   Far more than Cumming and her fellow Confederate nurses, northern women had a strong base of antebellum public and reform activism on which to build. Freedmen's aid societies, which sent supplies and teachers to black refugees in the South, attracted the energies of religious congregations and of African American abolitionists such as Harriet Tubman and Sojourner Truth. In 1863, women's rights advocates founded the **Woman's Loyal National League**, hoping energetic war service would bring recognition and voting rights.

The war also drew women into the wage-earning workforce as clerks and factory operatives. Thousands of educated Union women became government clerks in offices such as the Treasury Department—the first women hired to work for the U.S. government. White southern women staffed the efficient Confederate postal service. In both North and South, millions of women took over farm tasks, filled jobs in hospitals and schools, and worked in factories.

Working-class women did some of the war's most grueling, dangerous work in munitions factories, where gunpowder caused over thirty explosions during the war. One of the most horrific occurred in Pittsburgh, Pennsylvania, on September 17, 1862, the same day as the battle of Antietam. With the Allegheny Arsenal's largely female, Irish immigrant employees under pressure to increase production of rifle cartridges, a spark triggered a series of explosions that destroyed the building and left seventy-eight dead. The arsenal grounds became an outdoor morgue. One Pittsburgh paper described the "agonizing screams of relatives and friends upon discovering the remains of some loved one whose humble earnings contributed to their comfort." Most were burned beyond recognition.

Emma Edmonds, *Nurse and Spy in the Union Army* Civilians in both the Union and Confederacy had an insatiable appetite for heroic and romantic war stories—an enthusiasm that outlasted the far less romantic experiences of men on the actual battlefield. Sarah Emma Edmonds, a Canadian-born nurse, wrote a sensational postwar autobiography in which she celebrated (and exaggerated) her exploits as a spy. Here she is depicted in disguise as a Union soldier, riding swiftly away from the enemy firing at her from the woods. In other scenes, she infiltrated a Confederate force and defended herself with a pistol. The war helped create a national market for inexpensive, action-packed "dime novels" and adventure stories. The Granger Collection, New York.

A few daring women worked as spies and scouts, and at least five hundred disguised themselves as men in order to serve in the Union or Confederate armies. Those who made it through the trauma of battle without being discovered were often accepted afterward by fellow soldiers who kept their secret. More frequently, women who adhered to the rules of domesticity contributed as writers, penning patriotic songs, poems, editorials, and fiction. Eventually, even the most reluctant Unionist and Confederate men were forced to recognize women's value to the cause. As Union nurse Clara Barton, who later founded the American Red Cross, recalled, "At the war's end, woman was at least fifty years in advance of the normal position which continued peace would have assigned her."

The War at Home In contested border regions such as Tennessee, North Carolina, and Missouri, few boundaries existed between home and battlefield. There, civilians found themselves trapped between ruthless guerrilla or irregular bands of soldiers, such as William Quantrill's notorious Confederate raiders. Operating often as near-bandits, such guerrillas on both sides raided, plundered, tortured civilians for information, and carried out revenge killings. In 1863, after a Union commander detained a group of wives and sisters of Quantrill's men, five of the women were killed in a federal building collapse. In retaliation, Quantrill and his men burned the "Free State" town of Lawrence, Kansas, and summarily executed 183 men and boys. The Union responded by evacuating ten thousand people from four Missouri counties that bordered Kansas—while Quantrill continued to wreak destruction in other parts of the state.

As casualties mounted to shocking levels, civilians in both North and South became more and more familiar with the rituals of mourning. The rising tide of death created new industries: embalmers, for example, devised a zinc chloride fluid to preserve soldiers' bodies, allowing them to be shipped home for burial, an innovation that began modern funeral practices. Military cemeteries with hundreds of crosses in neat rows replaced the landscaped "rural cemeteries" that had been in vogue in American cities

Military Deaths — and Lives Saved — During the Civil War

The Civil War, like all wars before and since, encouraged innovation in both the destruction and the saving of human life. More than 620,000 soldiers — 360,000 on the Union side and 260,000 Confederates — died during the war, about 20 percent of those who served. However, thanks to advances in camp hygiene and battlefield treatment, the Union death rate was about 54–58 per 1,000 soldiers per year, less than half the level for British and French troops during the Crimean War of 1854–1855.

1. **Report by surgeon Charles S. Tipler, medical director of the Army of the Potomac, January 4, 1862.** *Most Civil War deaths came from disease. The major killers were bacterial intestinal diseases — typhoid fever, diarrhea, and dysentery — which spread because of unsanitary conditions in the camps.*

   The aggregate strength of the forces from which I have received reports is 142,577. Of these, 47,836 have been under treatment in the field and general hospitals, 35,915 of whom have been returned to duty, and 281 have died; 9,281 remained under treatment at the end of the month; . . .

   The diseases from which our men have suffered most have been continued remittent and typhoid fevers, measles, diarrhea, dysentery, and the various forms of catarrh [heavy discharge of mucus from the nose]. Of all the scourges incident to armies in the field I suppose that chronic diarrheas and dysenteries have always been the most prevalent and the most fatal. I am happy to say that in this army they are almost unknown. We have but 280 cases of chronic diarrhea and 69 of chronic dysentery reported in the month of November.

2. **Minié ball wounds: femur shot by Springfield 1862 rifle and Private George W. Lemon, 1867.** *Ninety percent of battle casualties were the victims of a new technology: musket-rifles that fired lethal soft-lead bullets called minié balls (after their inventor, Claude-Étienne Minié). The rifle-musket revolutionized military strategy by enormously strengthening defensive forces. Infantrymen could now kill reliably at 300 yards — triple the previous range of muskets. Initially, the new technology baffled commanders, who continued to use the tactics perfected during the heyday of the musket and bayonet charge, sending waves of infantrymen against enemy positions.*

SOURCE: National Museum of Health and Medicine, Armed Forces Institute of Pathology, Washington, D.C.

3. **Private Ludwig Kohn, his wound and its treatment.** *Overwhelmed by the scale of battlefield casualties and the small number of doctors qualified to treat them, surgeons struggled to share effective methods. Photography proved convenient for this purpose. Dr. Reed Bontecou, a Union army surgeon, took this photograph of Private Ludwig Kohn, 214th Pennsylvania Volunteers, treating him for a bullet wound in the right side of the chest, received at Gettysburg on July 1, 1863. "Exit below scapula" Bontecou explained in his notes accompanying the photo, on which he sketched the minié ball's path. Bontecou took dozens of such photographs, hoping to improve medical treatment for future soldiers and civilians. He did not record the opinions of his subjects — some of whom were photographed with horrific wounds, open amputations, and exposed genitals. Private Kohn, unlike most photograph subjects, jauntily wore his Union soldier's cap, suggesting his pride in fighting for the Union cause. Bontecou recorded that Kohn recovered fully.*

SOURCE: U.S. National Library of Medicine.

4. **Kate Cumming, April 23, 1862, journal entry on treating a Confederate victim after the Battle of Shiloh.** *Union surgeons performed 29,980 battlefield amputations during the Civil War. Confederate records are less complete, but surgeons apparently undertook about 28,000 amputations. They quickly removed limbs too shattered to mend, which increased the chances of survival. According to one witness, "surgeons and their assistants, stripped to the waist and bespattered with blood, stood around, some holding the poor fellows while others, armed with long, bloody knives and saws, cut and sawed away with frightful rapidity, throwing the mangled limbs on a pile nearby as soon as removed." This journal entry from a young Confederate nurse in Corinth, Mississippi, describes the plight of one such victim after the Battle of Shiloh.*

A young man whom I have been attending is going to have his arm cut off. Poor fellow! I am doing all I can to cheer him. He says that he knows that he will die, as all who have had limbs amputated in this hospital have died. . . . He lived only a few hours after his amputation.

5. **William Williams Keen, MD, "Surgical Reminiscences of the Civil War," 1905.** *Although 73 percent of the Union amputees survived the war, infected wounds — deadly gangrene — took the lives of most soldiers who suffered certain gunshot injuries in this pre-antibiotic, pre-antiseptic era. Keen, who later became the first brain surgeon in the United States, served as a surgeon in the Union army.*

Not more than one incontestable example of recovery from a gunshot wound of the stomach and not a single incontestable case of wound of the small intestines are recorded during the entire war among the almost 250,000 wounded. . . .

Of 852 amputations of the shoulder-joint, 236 died, a mortality of 28.5 per cent. Of 66 cases of amputation of the hip-joint, 55, or 83.3 per cent died. Of 155 cases of trephining [cutting a hole in the skull to relieve pressure], 60 recovered and 95 died, a mortality of over 61 per cent. Of 374 ligations of the femoral artery, 93 recovered and 281 died, a mortality of over 75 per cent.

These figures afford a striking evidence of the dreadful mortality of military surgery in the days before antisepsis and first-aid packages. Happily such death-rates can never again be seen, at least in civilized warfare.

6. **U.S. Surgeon Jonathan Letterman, Report on Medical Care after Antietam, 1863.** *Letterman introduced several effective innovations, including an ambulance corps and a triage system in which soldiers received immediate first aid and then, as needed, were moved to stabilization centers and long-term care. Here Letterman describes medical efforts after the battle of Antietam on September 17, 1862. Later surgeons hailed him as "The Father of Battlefield Medicine."*

The troops on our left were those among whom no ambulance system existed, but here, owing to the exertions of the medical officers, the wounded were removed by the evening of the day following the battle. . . . Two large camps of hospital tents were formed on the outskirts of [Frederick, Maryland], capable of containing one thousand beds each. . . . All the available buildings in this city (six in number) were taken at once for hospitals [and] fitted up with great rapidity, particularly so when it is considered that the enemy was in possession of the city the day before; . . . the buildings [were] selected and prepared, beds, bedding, dressings, stores, food, cooking arrangements made, surgeons, stewards, cooks, and nurses detailed. . . . [By] the 30th of September these hospitals contained 2,321 patients.

SOURCES: (1) The War of the Rebellion: *A Compilation of the Official Records of the Union and Confederate Armies* (Washington, DC: Government Printing Office, 1889), Series 1, Vol. 5 (Part V), 111–112; (4) Kate Cumming, *A Journal of Hospital Life in the Confederate Army of Tennessee* (Louisville, KY: John P. Morton & Company, 1866), 19; (5) William Williams Keen, "Surgical Reminiscences of the Civil War," in Addresses and Other Papers (Philadelphia: W. B. Saunders, 1905), 433–434; (6) US War Department, The War of the Rebellion (Washington DC: US Government Printing Office, 1880–1901), Vol. 19, 106–117, courtesy Antietam on the Web, antietam.aotw.org/exhibit.php?exhibit_id=73.

ANALYZING THE EVIDENCE

1. Based on Tipler's report (source 1), would you say the Union army was healthy or unhealthy? Ready for battle or not?

2. Consider sources 2–5. How do you think the reentry of tens of thousands of maimed veterans into civil society affected American culture?

3. What do sources 4–6 suggest about the successes and limitations of battlefield medicine during the Civil War?

4. Consider the Civil War in the context of the Industrial Revolution. What was the impact of factory production and technological advances on the number of weapons and their killing power? And how might the organizational innovations of the Industrial Revolution pertain to the conflict? In this regard, what do you make of the new method of battlefield triage pioneered by Union doctor Jonathan Letterman (source 6)?

PUTTING IT ALL TOGETHER

As a "total war" the Civil War involved the citizenry as well as the military, marshaling all of the two societies' resources and ingenuity. Using your understanding of these documents and the textbook, write an essay that discusses the relation of the war to technology, medicine, public finance, and the lives of women on the battle lines and the home front.

PLACE EVENTS IN CONTEXT
How did the Union and Confederacy mobilize their populations, and how effective were these methods in influencing the course of the war?

before the Civil War. As thousands of mothers, wives, and sisters mourned the deaths of fallen soldiers, they faced changed lives. Even the poorest bereaved women often dyed a dress black so they could mark the loss of a husband, son, or father. Middle-class women, with greater financial resources, might purchase black-bordered stationery, onyx jewelry, or other tokens of grief. The destructive war, in concert with America's emerging consumer culture and ethic of domesticity, produced a new "cult of mourning" among the middle and upper classes.

Vicksburg and Gettysburg

Confederate hopes ran high in the spring of 1863. In the Union, Democrats had made significant gains in 1862, and popular support was growing for a negotiated peace. Two brilliant victories in Virginia by General Robert E. Lee, at Fredericksburg (December 1862) and Chancellorsville (May 1863), further eroded northern support for the war. At this critical juncture, General Ulysses Grant mounted a major offensive to split the Confederacy in two. Grant drove south along the west bank of the Mississippi in Arkansas and then crossed the river near Vicksburg, Mississippi. There, he defeated two Confederate armies and laid siege to the city. After repelling Union assaults for six weeks, the exhausted and starving Vicksburg garrison surrendered on July 4, 1863.

Five days later, Union forces took Port Hudson, Louisiana, near Baton Rouge, and seized control of the entire Mississippi River. Grant had cut off Louisiana, Arkansas, and Texas from the rest of the Confederacy and prompted thousands of slaves to desert their plantations. Confederate troops responded by targeting refugees for re-enslavement and massacre. "The battlefield was sickening," a Confederate officer reported from Arkansas, "no orders, threats or commands could restrain the men from vengeance on the negroes, and they were piled in great heaps about the wagons, in the tangled brushwood, and upon the muddy and trampled road." Partly due to the undercounting of civilian casualties on occasions such as this, historians have revised upward their reckoning of the war's total deaths: not 620,000, as was previously thought, but over 750,000.

As Grant had advanced toward Vicksburg in May, Confederate leaders had argued over the best strategic response. President Davis and other politicians wanted to send an army to Tennessee to relieve the Union pressure along the Mississippi River. General Lee, buoyed by his recent victories, favored a new invasion of the North. That strategy, Lee suggested, would either draw Grant's forces to the east or give the Confederacy a major victory that would destroy the North's will to fight.

Lee won out. In June 1863, he maneuvered his army north through Maryland into Pennsylvania. The Army of the Potomac moved along with him, positioning itself between Lee and Washington, D.C. On July 1, the two great armies met by accident at Gettysburg, Pennsylvania, in what became a decisive confrontation (Map 13.3). On the first day of battle, Lee drove the Union's advance guard to the south of town. There, Union commander George G. Meade placed his troops in well-defended hilltop positions and called for reinforcements. By the morning of July 2, Meade had 90,000 troops to Lee's 75,000. Lee knew he was outnumbered but was determined not to give up; he ordered assaults on Meade's flanks, which failed.

On July 3, Lee decided on a dangerous frontal assault against the center of the Union line. After the heaviest artillery barrage of the war, Lee sent General George E. Pickett and his 14,000 men to take Cemetery Ridge. When Pickett's men charged across a mile of open terrain, they faced deadly fire from artillery and massed riflemen. Thousands suffered death, wounds, or capture. As the three-day battle ended, the Confederates counted 28,000 casualties—one-third of Lee's Army of Northern Virginia—while 23,000 of Meade's soldiers lay killed or wounded. Shocked by the bloodletting, Meade allowed the Confederate units to escape. Lincoln was furious at Meade's caution, perceiving that "the war will be prolonged indefinitely."

Still, Gettysburg was a major Union victory and, together with the simultaneous triumph at Vicksburg, marked a military and political turning point. In his

MAP 13.3 Lee Invades the North, 1863

After Lee's victories at Chancellorsville (1) in May and Brandy Station (2) in June, the Confederate forces moved northward, constantly shadowed by the Union army. On July 1, the two armies met accidentally near Gettysburg, Pennsylvania. In the ensuing battle (3), the Union army, commanded by General George Meade, emerged victorious, primarily because it was much larger than the Confederate force and held well-fortified positions along Cemetery Ridge, which gave its units a major tactical advantage.

Gettysburg Address, dedicating a national cemetery at the battlefield, Lincoln dared to hope that the Union might win. Such a victory, he argued, would extend the promise of the Declaration of Independence that "all men are created equal." Without mentioning slavery by name, Lincoln suggested that Americans could draw "from these honored dead" the determination not only to preserve the Union, but also to bring about "a new birth of freedom" in the United States (Analyzing Voices).

As southern citizens grew increasingly critical of their government, Confederate elections of 1863 went sharply against politicians who supported Jefferson Davis. Meanwhile, northern citizens rallied to the Union, and Republicans swept state elections in Pennsylvania, Ohio, and New York. In Europe, the victories boosted the leverage of the Union's diplomats. Since 1862, a British-built ironclad cruiser, the CSS *Alabama,* had sunk or captured more than a hundred Union merchant ships, and the Confederacy was about to accept delivery of two more ironclads. With a Union victory increasingly likely, the British government decided to impound the warships. British workers and reformers had long condemned slavery and praised emancipation. Moreover, because of poor grain harvests, Britain depended on imports of wheat and flour from the American Midwest. King Cotton diplomacy had failed and King Wheat stood triumphant. "Rest not your hopes in foreign nations," President Jefferson Davis advised his people. "This war is ours; we must fight it ourselves."

EXPLAIN CONSEQUENCES
How did the battles at Vicksburg and Gettysburg alter Unionists' and Confederates' goals?

IN YOUR OWN WORDS In what ways did the scope and direction of the Civil War change in 1863, and why?

These Honored Dead

The Civil War brought death to the young and healthy, and mourning to those who loved them, on an unprecedented scale. In the documents below — a letter, a poem, a work of fiction, and a famous presidential address — four Americans reckoned with the meaning of soldiers' sacrifice.

JAMES R. MONTGOMERY
A Last Letter Home, 1864

Private James R. Montgomery of Camden, Mississippi, age twenty five, was mortally wounded at the battle of Spotsylvania Courthouse. This letter, covered with bloodstains, remains in the collections of the Museum of the Confederacy, Richmond, Virginia. Montgomery died four days later. His family was never able to locate his grave.

SOURCE: James Robert Montgomery letter, written May 10, 1864 at Spotsylvania Court House, Civil War Voices, Soldier Studies, http://www.soldierstudies.org/index.php?action=view_letter&Letter=1503.

66 Dear Father,
This is my last letter to you. I went into battle this evening as courier for Genl. Heth. I have been struck by a piece of shell and my right shoulder is horribly mangled & I know death is inevitable. I am very weak but I write to you because I know you would be delighted to read a word from your dying son. I know death is near, that I will die far from home and friends of my early youth but I have friends here too who are kind to me. My friend Fairfax will write you at my request and give you the particulars of my death. My grave will be marked so that you may visit it if you desire to do so, but it is optionary with you whether you let my remains rest here or in Miss. I would like to rest in the grave yard with my dear mother and brothers but it's a matter of minor importance. Let us all try to reunite in heaven. I pray my God to forgive my sins and I feel that his promises are true that he will forgive me and save me. Give my love to all my friends. My strength fails me. My horse and my equipments will be left for you. Again, a long farewell to you. May we meet in heaven. Your dying son, J. R. Montgomery 99

WALT WHITMAN
Excerpt from "Come Up from the Fields Father," 1865

In this poem, Walt Whitman imagines an Ohio family receiving news of their son.

SOURCE: Walt Whitman, excerpt from "Come Up from the Fields Father," *Civil War Poetry and Prose* (New York: Dover, 1995), 12–14.

Come up from the fields father, here's a letter from our Pete,
And come to the front door mother, here's a letter from thy dear son.

Lo, 'tis autumn, . . . Where apples ripe in the orchards hang and grapes on the trellis'd vines,

(Smell you the smell of the grapes on the vines?
Smell you the buckwheat where the bees were lately buzzing?). . . .

Down in the fields all prospers well,
But now from the fields come father, come at the daughter's call,
And come to the entry mother, to the front door come right away.

Fast as she can she hurries, something ominous, her steps trembling,
She does not tarry to smooth her hair nor adjust her cap.

Open the envelope quickly,
O this is not our son's writing, yet his name is sign'd,
O a strange hand writes for our dear son, O stricken mother's soul!
All swims before her eyes, flashes with black, she catches the main words only,
Sentences broken, gunshot wound in the breast, cavalry skirmish, taken to hospital,
At present low, but will soon be better.
 . . . Grieve not so, dear mother, (the just-grown daughter speaks through her sobs,
The little sisters huddle around speechless and dismay'd,)
See, dearest mother, the letter says Pete will soon be better.
Alas poor boy, he will never be better, (nor may-be needs to be better, that brave and simple soul,)
While they stand at home at the door he is dead already,
The only son is dead. . . .

LOUISA MAY ALCOTT
"A Night," from *Hospital Sketches*, 1863

Louisa May Alcott, future author of *Little Women*, launched her career with her immensely popular *Hospital Sketches*, a fictionalized account of her own experiences. Alcott contracted typhoid fever while nursing in a Union hospital and suffered the effects for the rest of her life. In this passage, Nurse Tribulation Periwinkle describes the death of a wounded Virginia blacksmith who fought for the Union.

SOURCE: Louisa May Alcott, *Hospital Sketches* (Boston: James Redpath, 1863), 55–66, University of Pennsylvania Digital Library of Women Writers, http://digital.library.upenn.edu/women/alcott/sketches/sketches.html.

66 I had been summoned to many death beds in my life, but to none that made my heart ache as it did then. . . . As I went in, John stretched out both hands:
    'I knew you'd come! I guess I'm moving on, ma'am.'

He was; and so rapidly that, even while he spoke, over his face I saw the grey veil falling that no human hand can lift. I sat down by him, wiped the drops from his forehead, stirred the air about him with the slow wave of a fan, and waited to help him die. He stood in sore need of help — and I could do so little; for, as the doctor had foretold, the strong body rebelled against death, and fought every inch of the way. . . . For hours he suffered dumbly, without a moment's respite, or a moment's murmuring; his limbs grew cold, his face damp, his lips white, and, again and again, he tore the covering off his breast, as if the lightest weight added to his agony; yet through it all, his eyes never lost their perfect serenity, and the man's soul seemed to sit therein, undaunted by the ills that vexed his flesh.

One by one, the men woke, and round the room appeared a circle of pale faces and watchful eyes, full of awe and pity; for, though a stranger, John was beloved by all. Each man there had wondered at his patience, respected his piety, admired his fortitude, and now lamented his hard death. . . .

For a little while, there was no sound in the room but the drip of water, from a stump or two, and John's distressful gasps, as he slowly breathed his life away. I thought him nearly gone, and had just laid down the fan, believing its help to be no longer needed, when suddenly he rose up in his bed, and cried out with a bitter cry that broke the silence, sharply startling everyone with its agonized appeal:

'For God's sake, give me air!'

It was the only cry pain or death had wrung from him. . . . Dan flung up the window. The first red streak of dawn was warming the grey east, a herald of the coming sun; John saw it, and with the love of light which lingers in us to the end, seemed to read in it a sign of hope of help, for, over his whole face there broke that mysterious expression, brighter than any smile, which often comes to eyes that look their last. He laid himself gently down; and, stretching out his strong right arm, as if to grasp and bring the blessed air to his lips in a fuller flow, lapsed into a merciful uncon- sciousness, which assured us that for him suffering was for- ever past. He died then; for, though the heavy breaths still tore their way up for a little longer, they were but the waves of an ebbing tide that beat unfelt against the wreck, which an immortal voyager had deserted with a smile. He never spoke again.

. . . The lovely expression which so often beautifies dead faces, soon replaced the marks of pain, and I longed for those who loved him best to see him when half an hour's acquaintance with Death had made them friends. . . . I kissed this good son for [his mother's] sake, and laid [an unopened letter from his mother, which had just arrived] in his hand, . . . making myself happy with the thought that, even in his solitary place in the 'Government Lot,' he would not be without some token of the love which makes life beautiful and outlives death. 99

ABRAHAM LINCOLN
Gettysburg Address, 1863

Abraham Lincoln gave this speech four and a half months after the Battle of Gettysburg, at dedication ceremonies for the national cemetery for U.S. soldiers killed in the battle.

SOURCE: Abraham Lincoln, "Gettysburg Address" (Hay Copy), Gettysburg, Pennsylvania, November 19, 1863, Gettysburg Foundation, http://www .gettysburgfoundation.org/41.

66 Four score and seven years ago our fathers brought forth, upon this continent, a new nation, conceived in Liberty, and dedicated to the proposition that all men are created equal.

Now we are engaged in a great civil war, testing whether that nation, or any nation so conceived, and so dedicated, can long endure. We are met here on a great battlefield of that war. We have come to dedicate a portion of it, as a final resting place for those who here gave their lives that that nation might live. It is altogether fitting and proper that we should do this.

But, in a larger sense, we can not dedicate — we can not consecrate — we can not hallow — this ground. The brave men, living and dead, who struggled here, have consecrated it far above our poor power to add or detract. The world will little note, nor long remember, what we say here, but can never forget what they did here.

It is for us, the living, rather, to be dedicated here to the unfinished work which they who fought here have, thus far, so nobly carried on. It is rather for us to be here dedicated to the great task remaining before us — that from these hon- ored dead we take increased devotion to that cause for which they gave the last full measure of devotion — that we here highly resolve that these dead shall not have died in vain; that this nation, under God, shall have a new birth of freedom; and that this government of the people, by the people, for the people, shall not perish from the earth. 99

QUESTIONS FOR ANALYSIS

1. What do these documents tell us about the ways in which religious faith helped Americans cope with wartime death and loss?

2. Historians have argued that nineteenth-century Americans shared an ideal of "a good death": one in which the dying person demonstrated strong character, maintained hope of salvation through his final sufferings, and spoke mean- ingful last words to the loved ones gathered around. How do these authors, interpreting violent deaths that took place far from home, seek to preserve elements of a "good death"?

3. Which of these authors describe a larger political purpose in soldiers' deaths, and what meanings do they suggest for those sacrifices?

The Road to Union Victory, 1864–1865

The Union victories of 1863 made it less and less likely that the South would win independence through a decisive military triumph. Confederate leaders, however, still hoped for a battlefield stalemate and a negotiated peace. To keep the Union in Republican hands, Lincoln faced the daunting task of conquering the South. By the time his new generals finally succeeded, the war's impact had devastated the South.

Grant and Sherman Take Command

Lincoln finally found a ruthless commanding general in March 1864, when he placed Ulysses S. Grant in charge of all Union armies. From then on, the president determined overall strategy and Grant implemented it. Lincoln wanted a simultaneous advance against the major Confederate armies, a strategy Grant had long favored, in order to achieve a decisive victory before the election of 1864.

Grant knew how to fight a war that relied on industrial technology and targeted the enemy's infrastructure. At Vicksburg in July 1863, he had besieged the whole city and forced its surrender. Then, in November, he had used railroads to rescue an endangered Union army near Chattanooga, Tennessee. Grant believed the cautious tactics of previous Union commanders had prolonged the war. He was willing to accept heavy casualties, a stance that earned him a reputation as a butcher. But he followed the tenets of Lieber's code: whatever "military necessity" he might need to invoke, Grant would bring the war to its end.

Grant Planning a Strategic Maneuver On May 21, 1864, the day this photograph was taken, Grant pulled his forces from Spotsylvania Court House, where a bitter two-week battle (May 8–21) resulted in 18,000 Union and 10,000 Confederate casualties. He moved his army to the southeast, seeking to outflank Lee's forces. Photographer Timothy H. O'Sullivan caught up to the Union army's high command at Massaponax Church, Virginia, and captured this image of Grant (to the left) leaning over a pew and reading a map held by General George H. Meade. As Grant plots the army's movement, his officers smoke their pipes and read reports of the war in newspapers that had just arrived from New York City. Intercepting Grant's forces, Lee took up fortified positions first at the North Anna River and then at Cold Harbor, where the Confederates scored their last major victory of the war (May 31–June 3). Library of Congress.

In May 1864, Grant ordered two major offensives. Personally taking charge of the 115,000-man Army of the Potomac, he set out to destroy Lee's force of 75,000 troops in Virginia. Grant instructed General William Tecumseh Sherman, who shared his harsh outlook, to invade Georgia and take Atlanta. "All that has gone before is mere skirmish," Sherman wrote as he prepared for battle. "The war now begins." As a young military officer stationed in the South, Sherman had sympathized with the planter class and felt that slavery upheld social stability. However, secession meant "anarchy," he told his southern friends in early 1861: "If war comes . . . I must fight your people whom I best love." Sherman, more than anyone else, developed the philosophy and tactics of **hard war**. When Confederate guerrillas fired on a boat carrying Unionist civilians near Randolph, Tennessee, Sherman had sent a regiment to destroy the town, asserting, "We are justified in treating all inhabitants as combatants."

Grant advanced toward Richmond, hoping to force Lee to fight in open fields, where the Union's superior manpower and artillery would prevail.

Remembering his tactical errors at Gettysburg, Lee remained in strong defensive positions and attacked only when he held an advantage. The Confederate general seized such opportunities twice in May 1864, winning costly victories at the battles of the Wilderness and Spotsylvania Court House. At Spotsylvania, troops fought at point-blank range; an Iowa recruit recalled "lines of blue and grey [firing] into each other's faces; for an hour and a half." Despite heavy losses in these battles and then at Cold Harbor, Grant drove on (Map 13.4). His attacks severely eroded Lee's forces, which suffered 31,000 casualties, but Union losses were even higher: 55,000 killed or wounded.

Stalemate The fighting took a heavy psychological toll. "Many a man has gone crazy since this campaign began from the terrible pressure on mind and body," observed a Union captain. In June 1864, Grant laid siege to Petersburg, an important railroad center near Richmond. As the siege continued, Union and Confederate soldiers built complex networks of trenches, tunnels, and artillery emplacements stretching 40 miles along the eastern edge of Richmond and Petersburg, foreshadowing the devastating trench warfare that would emerge in France during World War I. Invoking the intense imagery of the Bible, an officer described the continuous artillery barrages and sniping as "living night and day within the 'valley of the shadow of death.'" The stress was especially great for the outnumbered Confederates, who spent months in the muddy, hellish trenches without rotation to the rear.

As time passed, Lincoln and Grant felt pressures of their own. The enormous casualties and military stalemate threatened Lincoln with defeat in the November election. Republicans' outlook worsened in July, when a body of almost 3,000 Confederate cavalry raided and burned the town of Chambersburg, in southern Pennsylvania, and threatened Washington. To punish farmers in the Shenandoah Valley who had aided the Confederate raiders, Grant ordered General Philip H. Sheridan to turn the region into "a barren waste." Sheridan's troops conducted a scorched-earth campaign, destroying grain, barns, and gristmills and any other resource useful to the Confederates. Hard war had become hard indeed.

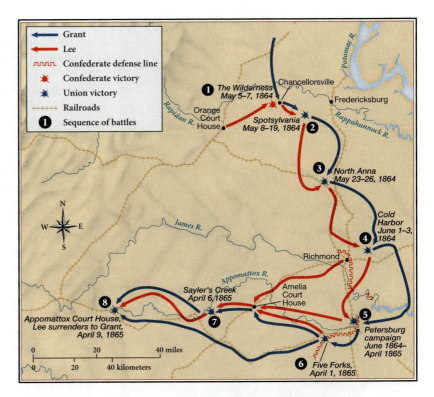

MAP 13.4 The Closing Virginia Campaign, 1864–1865
Beginning in May 1864, General Ulysses S. Grant launched an all-out campaign against Richmond, trying to lure General Robert E. Lee into open battle. Lee avoided a major test of strength. Instead, he retreated to defensive positions and inflicted heavy casualties on Union attackers at the Wilderness, Spotsylvania Court House, North Anna, and Cold Harbor (1–4). From June 1864 to April 1865, the two armies faced each other across defensive fortifications outside Richmond and Petersburg (5). Grant finally broke this ten-month siege by a flanking maneuver at Five Forks (6). Lee's surrender followed shortly.

EXPLAIN CONSEQUENCES
How did Grant's appointment as general in chief affect the course of the war?

The Election of 1864 and Sherman's March

As the siege at Petersburg dragged on, General William Tecumseh Sherman's 90,000 Union men moved methodically toward Atlanta, a railway hub at the heart of the Confederacy. General Joseph E. Johnson's Confederate army of 60,000 stood in Sherman's way and, in June 1864, inflicted heavy casualties on his forces near Kennesaw Mountain, Georgia. By late July, the Union army was poised on the northern outskirts of Atlanta, but the next month brought little gain. Like Grant, Sherman seemed bogged down in a hopeless campaign.

Both Unionists and Confederates pinned their hopes on the election of 1864. In June, the Republican convention rebuffed attempts to prevent Lincoln's renomination. It endorsed the president's war strategy, demanded unconditional Confederate

William Tecumseh Sherman A man of nervous energy, Sherman smoked cigars and talked continuously. When seated, he crossed and uncrossed his legs incessantly, and a journalist described his fingers as constantly "twitching his red whiskers — his coat buttons — playing a tattoo on the table — or running through his hair." On the battlefield Sherman was a decisive general who commanded the loyalty of his troops. A photographer captured this image of Sherman in 1865, following his devastating march through Georgia and the Carolinas. National Archives.

surrender, and called for a constitutional amendment to abolish slavery. Delegates likewise embraced Lincoln's political strategy. To attract border-state and Democratic voters, the Republicans took a new name, the National Union Party, and chose Andrew Johnson, a Tennessee slave owner and Unionist Democrat, as Lincoln's running mate.

The Democratic Party met in August and nominated George McClellan for president. Lincoln had twice removed McClellan from military commands: first for an excess of caution and then for his opposition to emancipation. Like McClellan, Democratic delegates rejected emancipation and condemned Lincoln's repression of domestic dissent, particularly his suspension of habeas corpus and use of military courts to prosecute civilians. However, they split into two camps over war policy. War Democrats vowed to continue fighting until the rebellion ended, while Peace Democrats called for a "cessation of hostilities" and a constitutional convention to negotiate a peace settlement. Although personally a War Democrat, McClellan promised if elected to recommend to Congress an immediate armistice and a peace convention. Hearing this news, Confederate vice president Alexander Stephens celebrated "the first ray of real light I have seen since the war began." He predicted that if Atlanta and Richmond held out, Lincoln would be defeated and McClellan would eventually accept an independent Confederacy.

The Fall of Atlanta and Lincoln's Victory Stephens's hopes collapsed on September 2, 1864, as Atlanta fell to Sherman's army. In a stunning move, the Union general pulled his troops from the trenches, swept around the city, and destroyed its rail links to the south. Fearing that Sherman would encircle his army, Confederate general John B. Hood abandoned the city. "Atlanta is ours, and fairly won," Sherman telegraphed Lincoln, sparking hundred-gun salutes and wild Republican celebration. "We are gaining strength," Lincoln warned Confederate leaders, "and may, if need be, maintain the contest indefinitely."

A deep pessimism settled over the Confederacy. Mary Chesnut, a South Carolina plantation mistress and general's wife, wrote in her diary, "I felt as if all were dead within me, forever," and foresaw the end of the Confederacy: "We are going to be wiped off the earth." Recognizing the dramatically changed military situation, McClellan repudiated the Democratic peace platform. Democrats' fall campaign focused heavily instead on the alleged dangers of emancipation. Cartoonists caricatured Lincoln as an ape; parade floats featured "Negroes" — white men in blackface makeup — dancing with white women. An anonymous Democratic pamphlet warned of the dangers of race mixing, coining the term **miscegenation** to denounce interracial marriage and claim that it would result from Republican policies.

The National Union Party went on the offensive, attacking McClellan's inconsistency and attacking Peace Democrats as traitors. Boosted by Sherman's victories in Georgia, Lincoln won a clear-cut victory in November. He received 55 percent of the popular vote and won 212 of 233 electoral votes. Republicans and National Unionists captured 145 of the 185 seats in the House of Representatives and increased their Senate majority to 42 of 52 seats. Republicans owed their victory in part to the votes of Union troops.

Legal emancipation was already underway at the edges of the South. In 1864, Maryland and Missouri amended their constitutions to end slavery, and the three Confederate states occupied by the Union army — Tennessee, Arkansas, and

Louisiana—followed suit. Still, abolitionists worried that the Emancipation Proclamation, based legally on the president's wartime powers, would lose its force at the end of the war. It took three attempts, but urged on by Lincoln and the National Equal Rights League, Congress finally approved the Thirteenth Amendment in January 1865 (Table 13.1). Once ratified by two-thirds of the states, in December 1865, the amendment officially ended slavery in the United States.

Sherman Crosses Georgia Thanks to Sherman, the Confederacy was also reaching its end. After capturing Atlanta, Sherman advocated a bold strategy. Instead of pursuing a retreating Confederate army northward into Tennessee, he proposed to move south, live off the land, and "cut a swath through to the sea." To persuade Lincoln and Grant to approve his unconventional plan, Sherman argued that his march would be "a demonstration to the world, foreign and domestic, that we have a power [Jefferson] Davis cannot resist." The general lived up to his pledge (Map 13.5). "We are not only fighting hostile armies," Sherman wrote, "but a hostile people, and must make old and young, rich and poor, feel the hard hand of war." He left Atlanta in flames, and during his 300-mile March to the Sea his army consumed or demolished everything in its path. Though Sherman's army focused on damaging property, not murdering civilians, the havoc so demoralized Confederate soldiers that many deserted their units and returned home. When Sherman reached Savannah in mid-December, the city's 10,000 defenders left without a fight.

Georgia's African Americans treated Sherman as a savior. "They flock to me, old and young," he wrote. "They pray and shout and mix up my name with Moses . . . as

TABLE 13.1

The Challenge of Passing the Thirteenth Amendment

This table shows the results of votes in the House of Representatives on amending the Constitution to abolish slavery throughout the United States. The measure needed a 2/3 vote to pass. In 1864, well after Lincoln issued the Emancipation Proclamation as a war measure, Confederate hopes were fading and 180,000 African American troops had fought for the Union. Why did a constitutional amendment abolishing slavery prove, nevertheless, so difficult to pass in Congress? What military and political events happened between June 1864 and January 1865 that made passage possible at last?

	Republican	Democrat	Union	Uncond. Union	Total
Feb. 15, 1864 (trial vote)					
Yea	66	1	1	10	78
Nay	2	52	7	1	62
Absent	17	20	2	3	42
Abstain	1	0	0	0	1
June 15, 1864 (on Senate bill)					
Yea	78	4	0	11	93
Nay	1	58	6	0	65
Absent	6	10	4	3	23
Abstain	1	0	0	0	1
Jan. 31, 1865 (on Senate bill)					
Yea	86	15	4	14	119
Nay	0	50	6	0	56
Absent	0	8	0	0	8
Abstain	0	0	0	0	0

SOURCE: Michael Vorenberg, *Final Freedom: The Civil War, the Abolition of Slavery, and the Thirteenth Amendment* (New York: Cambridge University Press, 2001), 252.

MAP 13.5 Sherman's March Through the Confederacy, 1864–1865
The Union victory in November 1863 at Chattanooga, Tennessee was almost as critical as the victories in July at Gettysburg and Vicksburg, because it opened up a route of attack into the heart of the Confederacy. In mid-1864, General William Tecumseh Sherman advanced on the railway hub of Atlanta. After taking the city in September 1864, Sherman relied on other Union armies to stem an invasion of Tennessee by Confederate General John Bell Hood, while Sherman began a devastating march across Georgia. By December Sherman's army reached Savannah, and from there they cut a swath through the Carolinas. Note how Sherman's march followed key rail lines: his troops ripped up, heated, and twisted sections of track to disrupt Confederate transport and communications.

well as 'Abram Linkom,' the Great Messiah of 'Dis Jubilee.'" To provide for the hundreds of African American families now following his army, Sherman issued **Special Field Order No. 15**, which set aside 400,000 acres of prime rice-growing land for the exclusive use of freedpeople. By June 1865, about 40,000 African Americans were cultivating "Sherman lands." Many expected the lands were to be theirs forever, a form of payment for generations of unpaid labor: "All the land belongs to the Yankees now and they gwine divide it out among de coloured people." By March, after his destructive march through South Carolina, Sherman was ready to link up with Grant and crush Lee's army.

The Confederacy Collapses

Grant's war of attrition in Virginia had already exposed a weakness in the Confederacy: rising class resentment among poor whites. Angered by slave owners' exemptions from military service and fearing that the Confederacy was doomed, ordinary southern farmers now repudiated the draft. "All they want is to git you . . . to fight for their infurnal negroes," grumbled an Alabama hill farmer. More and more soldiers fled their units. "I am now going to work instead of to the war," vowed David Harris, another backcountry yeoman. By 1865, at least 100,000 men had deserted from Confederate armies, prompting reluctant Confederate leaders to approve the enlistment of black soldiers

A Southern Refugee Family   As Union and Confederate armies swept back and forth across northern Virginia and other war zones, the civilian population feared for its property and personal security. Here, two southern women—their husbands presumably away at war—have hitched up their mules and piled their goods and children on a farm wagon in order to flee the fighting. Lucky refugees had relatives in safe areas; others had to rely on the goodwill of strangers.   National Archives.

and promising them freedom. It was a hollow offer: tens of thousands were already proving excellent soldiers for the Union.

The symbolic end of the war took place in Virginia. In April 1865, Grant finally gained control of the crucial railroad junction at Petersburg and forced Lee to abandon Richmond. As Lincoln visited the ruins of the Confederate capital, greeted by joyful freedmen and women, Grant cut off Lee's escape route to North Carolina. It was one of Lincoln's last acts: on April 14, a pro-Confederate actor named John Wilkes Booth assassinated the president, shouting "Sic semper tyrannis"—Virginia's state motto, *thus always to tyrants*. Lincoln's murder plunged the Union into mourning and opened disturbing questions about the postwar political order (Chapter 14).

Before his death Lincoln had received, with weary satisfaction, news that the Union had won. On April 9, almost four years to the day after the attack on Fort Sumter, Lee had surrendered at Appomattox Court House, Virginia. In return for their promise not to fight again, Grant allowed Confederate officers and men to take their horses and personal weapons and go home. By late May, all the secessionist armies and governments had surrendered or melted away.

> **PLACE EVENTS IN CONTEXT**
> To what extent were Grant and Sherman's military strategy and tactics responsible for the Confederacy's defeat?

The World the War Made

The brutal conflict was finally over. The North had won, to a large degree, because the Confederacy had not won quickly. Southern leaders' hopes for European aid, based on the power of King Cotton, turned out to be misplaced, and the Union proved far better equipped to fight a grueling four-year war of attrition. The Union could not have won, however, without impressive wartime innovations in policy, strategy, and technology. These ranged from the adoption of greenback dollars and steam-powered gunboats to the Lieber Code and the hard war tactics of Grant and Sherman. The Confederacy had innovated, also, exerting strong centralized powers to marshal men and resources for the conflict. But the Union had ultimately proven bolder and stronger. "As our case is new," Lincoln had told Congress in 1863, "so we must think anew, and act anew." Northerners had done so, most notably by abolishing slavery and recruiting African American soldiers, and had persevered to maintain the Union.

Over 700,000 people were dead. Delivering his second inaugural address in March 1865, Lincoln sought to explain the carnage by eloquently suggesting that the war's purpose had not been to preserve the Union but to end slavery. That purpose, however ignored or disavowed by Union leaders, had been a divine plan. "If we shall suppose," Lincoln said,

> that American slavery is one of those offenses which, in the providence of God, must needs come, but which, having continued through His appointed time, He now wills to remove, and that He gives to both North and South this terrible war as the woe due to those by whom the offense came, shall we discern therein any departure from those divine attributes which the believers in a living God always ascribe to Him? Fondly do we hope, fervently do we pray, that this mighty scourge of war may speedily pass away. Yet, if God wills that it continue until all the wealth piled by the bondsman's two hundred and fifty years of unrequited toil shall be sunk, and until every drop of blood drawn with the lash shall be paid by another drawn with the sword, as was said three thousand years ago, so still it must be said, "the judgments of the Lord are true and righteous altogether.

For the first time, Lincoln had named the sin of slavery as the central cause of the war — and proposed, remarkably, that both the Union and Confederacy shared guilt for that sin. Abolitionist Frederick Douglass, who heard the address, told Lincoln afterward that it was a "sacred effort." Yet at the same time, Lincoln's second inaugural depicted the catastrophe of war as visited only on *whites* — as if enslaved African Americans had been passive victims and bystanders, rather than participants in the war who, as "contra-bands," scouts, soldiers, and refugees, had suffered terribly as well, and had played decisive roles in the Union victory. Even Lincoln's most powerful antislavery speech, then, revealed unresolved political problems that would arise with peace. As southern states returned to the Union, what kind of nation would emerge? Former Confederates wanted a "reunion" of the white North and South, a nation adhering as nearly as possible to prewar principles. African Americans and Radical Republicans wanted revolution — a complete transformation of the South. Neither would get their wish.

As for the future of the United States, an optimistic New York census-taker suggested that the conflict had had an "equalizing effect." In some ways he was right. Slavery was dead: in a transformation of immense significance, no American could ever again legally claim to own another human being. The official also reflected that, in the North, "military men from the so called 'lower classes' now lead society, having been elevated by real merit and valor." However perceptive these remarks, they ignored the wartime emergence of the new financial aristocracy that soon presided over what Mark Twain labeled the Gilded Age. As early as 1863, a journalist warned that when the war was over, "there will be the same wealth in the country, but it will be in fewer hands; we shall have . . . more merchant princes and princely bankers."

Astonishing its European rivals, the United States did emerge from the Civil War with the "same wealth," and relatively unscathed. High tariffs put in place by Republicans, for example, paid off the nation's war debt with remarkable speed (America in Global Context). And however devastated the South's economy might be, the United States had started on the path to global economic power. In the postwar period, Republicans would wrestle with the limits of that power at home and on the world stage.

> **IN YOUR OWN WORDS**   How did Union objectives appear different to Lincoln at the end of the Civil War than they had at the beginning?

War Debt: Britain and the United States, 1830–1900

Wars cost money, sometimes a lot of money, and nations often pay for them by issuing bonds and expanding the national debt. The British national debt grew enormously between 1750 and 1815 as it fought a long series of wars, all of which involved either its American colonies or the United States: the Great War for Empire (1754–1763), the War of American Independence (1776–1783), and the Wars of the French Revolution and Napoleon (1793–1815). Consequently, Britain's national debt peaked in 1815 at 260 percent of its gross domestic product (GDP). Even in 1830, after years of high taxation and economic growth, the debt amounted to 180 percent of British GDP.

By comparison, the United States in 1830 was virtually debt-free, as the policies of Jeffersonian Republicans reduced its debt from about 27 percent of GDP in 1790 to less than 5 percent. Ample tariff revenues and the frugal policies of Presidents Andrew Jackson and Martin Van Buren then cut the debt nearly to zero by the early 1840s. Even the war with Mexico barely raised the level of debt, thanks to the return of prosperity and growth of GDP between 1844 and 1857.

Then came the Civil War, which boosted the Union debt from $62 million in 1860 to $2.2 billion at the end of 1865, a 1,500 percent increase. (The Fourteenth Amendment, ratified in 1868, declared "illegal and void" all debts incurred by the Confederacy.) In relation to GDP, the U.S. national debt shot up to 27 percent, the same level as 1790, and then—thanks again to tariff revenue—decreased gradually to about 10 percent of GDP by 1900. By then, the British national debt had fallen to about 40 percent of its GDP, as the British—the world's strongest power—mostly avoided new wars and built a prosperous commercial and industrial economy. The cost of war, civil or international, may well be a high national debt.

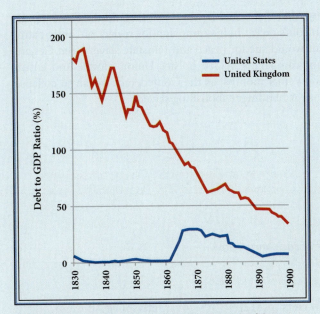

FIGURE 13.1 **War Debt: Britain and the United States, 1830–1900**

QUESTIONS FOR ANALYSIS

1. In 1864, President Lincoln lamented: "This war of ours, in its magnitude and in its duration, is one of the most terrible. It has produced a national debt and taxation unprecedented, at least in this country." Given the relative size of the Union debt in relation to that of Britain, were Lincoln's worries exaggerated?

2. In 2012, the national debt of the United States—now the world's premier economic and military power—was nearly 100 percent of GDP and, since 1940, has averaged about 60 percent of GDP. Given those facts, and the evidence in this chart, is it fair to conclude that one of the costs of global power is a high national debt?

SUMMARY

As the Civil War began, both the Union and the Confederacy hoped for a quick, decisive victory, but none was forthcoming. Union commander George B. McClellan proved unable to crush his daring southern equivalent, Robert E. Lee, but as attempts to invade the West and North failed, Confederates proved unable to move the theater of war outside their own territory. From the beginning, also, thousands of African Americans fled to Union lines, undermining Confederates' war effort. Congress soon authorized use of these "contrabands" as scouts, spies, and paid workers.

By 1862 and 1863, new strategies were needed. First the Confederacy and then the Union instituted military conscription. This unprecedented move, along with new taxes and inflation, caused considerable civilian unrest, especially in the South, as Union forces made inroads into occupying Confederate land and resources. Even more important was the Emancipation Proclamation, which Lincoln issued after the Union victory at Antietam and put into effect on January 1, 1863. African American troops soon enlisted for the Union, hardening Confederate attitudes but playing a crucial role in Union victory. Two decisive battles in the summer of 1863, Gettysburg and Vicksburg, began to turn the tide toward Union victory. Lincoln then chose an effective commander, Ulysses Grant, to lead U.S. forces, but it took almost two years of grueling, brutal campaigns to defeat the South.

In the fall of 1864, exhausted and shocked by the war's magnitude, Confederates pinned their last hopes on Lincoln's defeat in his campaign for reelection, anticipating that his Democratic opponent would sue for peace and reinstate slavery. But General William T. Sherman's brilliant campaigns helped bolster Union morale and ensure Lincoln's reelection. In the war's final months, as the Confederacy began to collapse, Congress passed the Thirteenth Amendment abolishing slavery.

CHAPTER 13 REVIEW

TERMS TO KNOW
Identify and explain the significance of each term below.

Key Concepts and Events

King Cotton (p. 401)

habeas corpus (p. 402)

"contrabands" (p. 406)

Radical Republicans (p. 406)

Emancipation Proclamation (p. 407)

greenbacks (p. 409)

one-tenth tax (p. 410)

draft (conscription) (p. 411)

twenty-Negro rule (p. 411)

draft riots (p. 412)

Lieber Code (p. 413)

U.S. Sanitary Commission (p. 414)

Woman's Loyal National League (p. 414)

Gettysburg Address (p. 419)

hard war (p. 422)

miscegenation (p. 424)

Special Field Order No. 15 (p. 426)

Key People

Abraham Lincoln (p. 400)

Jefferson Davis (p. 400)

George McClellan (p. 402)

Robert E. Lee (p. 402)

Ulysses S. Grant (p. 402)

William Tecumseh Sherman (p. 405)

REVIEW QUESTIONS
Answer these questions to demonstrate your understanding of the chapter's main ideas.

1. What early political and military strategies did Confederate and Union leaders adopt, and which were most successful?

2. In what ways did the scope and direction of the Civil War change in 1863, and why?

3. How did Union objectives appear different to Lincoln at the end of the Civil War than they had at the beginning?

4. The thematic timeline for Part 5 (pp. 364–365) lists events or developments in the 1860s relating directly to the South's secession and the Civil War. Does that list capture the war's overwhelming importance to the history of nineteenth-century America? If not, is this deficiency inherent to timelines, or does it reflect a faulty construction of this specific timeline? How would you address this problem?

Celebrating the Fifteenth Amendment, 1870   This lithograph depicts a celebration in Baltimore on May 15, 1870. With perhaps 200,000 people attending, the grand parade and orations marked passage of the Fifteenth Amendment, which enfranchised men irrespective of "race, color, or previous condition of servitude." The heroes depicted at the top are Martin Delany, the first black man to become an officer in the U.S. Army; abolitionist Frederick Douglass, born in slavery on Maryland's Eastern Shore; and Mississippi senator Hiram Rhodes Revels. The images at the bottom carried the following captions: "Liberty Protects the Marriage Altar," "The Ballot Box is open to us," and "Our Representative Sits in the National Legislature." Such lithographs, widely printed and sold, capture the pride, hope, and optimism of Reconstruction — but the optimism was not to last.   Library of Congress.

As you read, ask yourself why this chapter begins and ends with these dates and try to identify the links among related events.

1864 ▶ Wade-Davis Bill passed by Congress but killed by Lincoln's pocket veto

1865 ▶ Freedmen's Bureau established
▶ Lincoln assassinated; Andrew Johnson succeeds him as president
▶ Johnson implements restoration plan
▶ Ex-Confederate states pass Black Codes to limit freedpeople's rights

1866 ▶ Civil Rights Act passes over Johnson's veto
▶ Major Republican gains in congressional elections

1867 ▶ Reconstruction Act

1868 ▶ Impeachment of Andrew Johnson
▶ Fourteenth Amendment ratified
▶ Ulysses S. Grant elected president

1870 ▶ Ku Klux Klan at peak of power
▶ Congress passes Enforcement Laws to suppress Klan
▶ Fifteenth Amendment ratified
▶ Victoria Woodhull declares her support for "free love"

1872 ▶ Grant reelected; Crédit Mobilier scandal emerges

1873 ▶ Panic of 1873 ushers in severe economic depression
▶ Supreme Court severely curtails Reconstruction in *Slaughter-House Cases*

1874 ▶ Sweeping Democratic gains in congressional elections

1875 ▶ Whiskey Ring and other scandals undermine Grant administration
▶ *Minor v. Happersett*: Supreme Court rules that Fourteenth Amendment does not extend voting rights to women
▶ Beecher-Tilton scandal dominates headlines

1877 ▶ Rutherford B. Hayes becomes president
▶ Federal Reconstruction ends

The Struggle for National Reconstruction

Congress clashed with President Johnson, in part, because the framers of the Constitution did not anticipate a civil war or provide for its aftermath. Had Confederate states legally left the Union when they seceded? If so, then their reentry required action by Congress. If not — if even during secession they had retained U.S. statehood — then restoring them might be an administrative matter, best left to the president. Lack of clarity on this fundamental question made for explosive politics.

Presidential Approaches: From Lincoln to Johnson

As wartime president, Lincoln had offered a plan similar to Johnson's. It granted amnesty to most ex-Confederates and allowed each rebellious state to return to the Union as soon as 10 percent of its voters had taken a loyalty oath and the state had approved the Thirteenth Amendment, abolishing slavery. But even amid defeat, Confederate states rejected this **Ten Percent Plan** — an ominous sign for the future. In July 1864, Congress proposed a tougher substitute, the **Wade-Davis Bill**, that required an oath of allegiance by a majority of each state's adult white men, new governments formed only by those who had never taken up arms against the Union, and permanent disenfranchisement of Confederate leaders. Lincoln defeated the Wade-Davis Bill with a pocket veto, leaving it unsigned when Congress adjourned. At the same time, he opened talks with key congressmen, aiming for a compromise.

On April 14, 1865, Lincoln was shot by John Wilkes Booth while watching a play at Ford's Theatre. We will never know what would have happened had Lincoln lived. His death precipitated grief and political turmoil. As a special train bore the president's flag-draped coffin home to Illinois, thousands of Americans lined the railroad tracks in mourning. Furious and grief-stricken, many Unionists blamed all Confederates for the acts of southern sympathizer John Wilkes Booth and his accomplices in the murder. At the same time, Lincoln's death left the presidency in the hands of Andrew Johnson, a man utterly lacking in Lincoln's moral sense and political judgment.

Johnson was a self-styled "common man" from the hills of eastern Tennessee. Trained as a tailor, he built his political career on the support of farmers and laborers. Loyal to the Union, Johnson had refused to leave the U.S. Senate when Tennessee seceded. After federal forces captured Nashville in 1862, Lincoln appointed Johnson as Tennessee's military governor. In the election of 1864, placing Lincoln and this War Democrat on the ticket together had seemed a smart move, designed to promote unity. But after Lincoln's death, Johnson's disagreement with Republicans, combined with his belligerent and contradictory actions, wreaked political havoc.

The new president and Congress confronted a set of problems that would have challenged even Lincoln. During the war, Unionists had insisted that rebel leaders were a small minority and most white southerners wanted to rejoin the Union. With even greater optimism, Republicans hoped the defeated South would accept postwar reforms. Ex-Confederates, however, contested that plan through both violence and political action. New southern state legislatures, created under Johnson's limited Reconstruction plan, moved to restore slavery in all but name. In 1865, they enacted **Black Codes**, designed to force former slaves back to plantation labor. Like similar laws passed in other places after slavery ended, the codes reflected plantation owners' economic interests (America in Global Context). They imposed severe penalties on blacks who did not hold full-year labor contracts and also set up procedures for taking black children from their parents and apprenticing them to former slave masters.

Faced with these developments, Johnson gave all the wrong signals. He had long talked tough against southern planters. But in practice, Johnson allied himself with ex-Confederate leaders, forgiving them when they appealed for pardons. White southern leaders were delighted. "By this wise and noble statesmanship," wrote a Confederate legislator, "you have become the benefactor of the Southern people." Northerners and freedmen were disgusted. The president had left Reconstruction "to the tender mercies of the rebels," wrote one Republican. An angry Union veteran in Missouri called Johnson "a traitor to the loyal people of the Union." Emboldened by Johnson's indulgence, ex-Confederates began to filter back into the halls of power. When Georgians elected Alexander Stephens, former vice president of the Confederacy, to represent them in Congress, many outraged Republicans saw this as the last straw.

Congress Versus the President

Under the Constitution, Congress is "the judge of the Elections, Returns and Qualifications of its own Members" (Article 1, Section 5). Using this power, Republican majorities in both houses had refused to admit southern delegations when Congress convened in December 1865, effectively blocking Johnson's program. Hoping to mollify Congress, some southern states dropped the most objectionable provisions from their Black Codes. But at the same time, antiblack violence erupted in various parts of the South.

Congressional Republicans concluded that the federal government had to intervene. Back in March 1865, Congress had established the **Freedmen's Bureau** to aid displaced blacks and other war refugees. In early 1866, Congress voted to extend the bureau, gave it direct funding for the first time, and authorized its agents to investigate southern abuses. Even more extraordinary was the **Civil Rights Act of 1866**, which declared formerly enslaved people to be citizens and granted them equal protection and rights of contract, with full access to the courts.

These bills provoked bitter conflict with Johnson, who vetoed them both. Johnson's racism, hitherto publicly muted, now blazed forth: "This is a country for white men, and by God, as long as I am president, it shall be a government for white men." Galvanized, Republicans in Congress gathered two-thirds majorities and overrode both vetoes, passing the Civil Rights Act in April 1866 and the Freedmen's Bureau law four months later. Their resolve was reinforced by continued upheaval in the

COMPARE AND CONTRAST
How did Lincoln and Johnson approach Reconstruction differently?

Violence in New Orleans, Louisiana, 1866 Violence against freedmen revealed the lengths that some whites would go to maintain the South's prewar social and political order. In New Orleans, white and African American delegates gathered at the Mechanics Institute on July 30, 1866, to develop a new state constitution. John T. Monroe, a former New Orleans mayor and vocal white supremacist, led a mob of white men — including city police and ex-Confederate soldiers — to attack the convention. Shooting into the windows and then rushing into the building to beat and kill delegates, the mob massacred the largely unarmed delegates. In this image, delegates are shot as they try to flee at the back of the building. By the end of the day, 238 people were killed, including 40 delegates to the convention and at least 200 black Union veterans. The massacre provoked outrage in the North and contributed to the election of a more strongly Republican Congress, in November, which imposed military Reconstruction on the South. The New York Public Library/Art Resource, NY.

Labor Laws After Emancipation: Haiti and the United States

Many government officials agreed with former masters on the need to control rural workers. Often planters themselves or allied with the planter class, they believed that economic strength and public revenue depended on plantation export crops and that workers would not produce those without legal coercion.

This was true in the British Caribbean and also Haiti, which eventually, after a successful slave revolt ending in 1803, became an independent republic led by former slaves and, in particular, by propertied free men of color. In the passage below, a British observer describes a rural labor code adopted by Haiti's government in 1826. Despite the law, Haiti's large plantations did not revive; the island's economy, even more than that of the U.S. South, came to be dominated by small-scale, impoverished farmers.

The Code of Laws before us is one that could only have been framed by a legislature composed of proprietors of land, having at their command a considerable military power, of which they themselves were the leaders; for a population whom it was necessary to compel to labour. . . .

The choice of a master, altho' expressly reserved to the labourer, is greatly modified by the clauses which restrain the labourer from quitting the section of country to which he belongs; and from the absence of any clause compelling proprietors to engage him; so that the cultivator must consent to bind himself to whomsoever may be willing to engage him, or remain in prison, to be employed among convicts. . . .

The Code begins (Article 1) by declaring Agriculture to be the foundation of national prosperity; and then decrees (Article 3), That all persons, excepting soldiers, and civil servants of the State, professional persons, artizans, and domestic servants, shall cultivate the soil. The next clause (Article 4), forbids the inhabitants of the country quitting it to dwell in towns or villages; and every kind of wholesale or retail trade

is forbidden (Article 7) to be exercised by persons dwelling in the country.

Further articles stipulate that any person dwelling in the country, not being the owner or occupier of land, and not having bound himself in the manner directed, . . . shall be considered a vagabond, be arrested, and taken before a Justice, who, after reading the Law to him, shall commit him to jail, until he consent to bind himself according to law.

. . . Those who are hired from a job-master [labor agent], . . . are entitled to receive half the produce, after deducting the expences of cultivation; [those who are bound to the proprietor directly], one-fourth of the gross produce of their labour. . . . Out of their miserable pittance, these Haitian labourers are to provide themselves and their children with almost every thing, and to lay by a provision for old age. . . .

These, with the regulations already detailed, clearly shew what is intended to be the condition of the labouring population of Haiti. I must not call it slavery; the word is objectionable; but few of the ingredients of slavery seem to be wanting.

QUESTIONS FOR ANALYSIS

1. Compare this Haitian law with the Black Codes briefly adopted by ex-Confederate states, and with the sharecropping system that evolved in the United States during Reconstruction (p. 444). What did these labor systems — or proposed systems — have in common? How did they differ?

2. Why would the Haitian government, led by men of color, enact such laws? What considerations other than race might have shaped their views, and why?

South. In addition to the violence in Memphis, twenty-four black political leaders and their allies in Arkansas were murdered and their homes burned.

Anxious to protect freedpeople and reassert Republican power in the South, Congress took further measures to sustain civil rights. In what became the **Fourteenth Amendment** (1868), it declared that "all persons born or naturalized in the United States" were citizens. No state could abridge "the privileges or immunities of citizens of the United States"; deprive "any person of life, liberty, or property, without due process of law"; or deny anyone "equal protection." In a stunning increase of federal power, the Fourteenth Amendment declared that when people's essential rights were at stake, national citizenship henceforth took priority over citizenship in a state.

Johnson opposed ratification, but public opinion had swung against him. In the 1866 congressional elections, voters gave Republicans a 3-to-1 majority in Congress.

Power shifted to the so-called Radical Republicans, who sought sweeping transformations in the defeated South. The Radicals' leader in the Senate was Charles Sumner of Massachusetts, the fiery abolitionist who in 1856 had been nearly beaten to death by South Carolina congressman Preston Brooks. Radicals in the House followed Thaddeus Stevens of Pennsylvania, a passionate advocate of freedmen's political and economic rights. With such men at the fore, and with congressional Republicans now numerous and united enough to override Johnson's vetoes on many questions, Congress proceeded to remake Reconstruction.

PLACE EVENTS IN CONTEXT
Under what circumstances did the Fourteenth Amendment win passage, and what problems did its authors seek to address?

Radical Reconstruction

The **Reconstruction Act of 1867**, enacted in March, divided the conquered South into five military districts, each under the command of a U.S. general (Map 14.1). To reenter the Union, former Confederate states had to grant the vote to freedmen and deny it to leading ex-Confederates. Each military commander was required to register all eligible adult males, black as well as white; supervise state constitutional conventions; and ensure that new constitutions guaranteed black suffrage. Congress would readmit a state to the Union once these conditions were met and the new state legislature ratified the Fourteenth Amendment. Johnson vetoed the Reconstruction Act, but Congress overrode his veto (Table 14.1).

The Impeachment of Andrew Johnson   In August 1867, Johnson fought back by "suspending" Secretary of War Edwin M. Stanton, a Radical, and replacing him with Union general Ulysses S. Grant, believing Grant would be a good soldier and follow

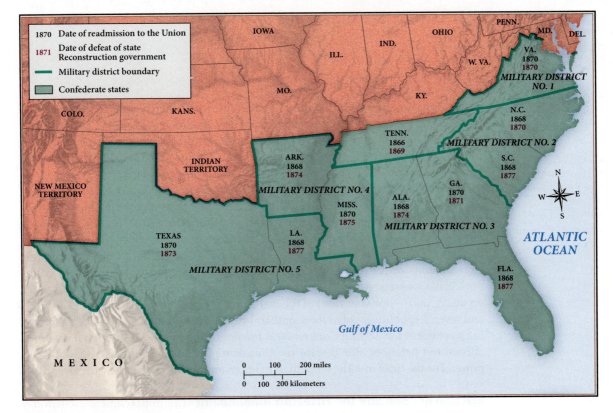

MAP 14.1 Reconstruction
The federal government organized the Confederate states into five military districts during congressional Reconstruction. For the states shown in this map, the first date indicates when that state was readmitted to the Union; the second date shows when Republicans lost control of the state government. All the ex-Confederate states rejoined the Union between 1868 and 1870, but the periods of Radical government varied widely. Republicans lasted only a few months in Virginia; they held on until the end of Reconstruction in Louisiana, Florida, and South Carolina.

TABLE 14.1

Primary Reconstruction Laws and Constitutional Amendments	
Law (Date of Congressional Passage)	**Key Provisions**
Thirteenth Amendment (December 1865*)	Prohibited slavery
Civil Rights Act of 1866 (April 1866)	Defined citizenship rights of freedmen
	Authorized federal authorities to bring suit against those who violated those rights
Fourteenth Amendment (June 1866†)	Established national citizenship for persons born or naturalized in the United States
	Prohibited the states from depriving citizens of their civil rights or equal protection under the law
	Reduced state representation in House of Representatives by the percentage of adult male citizens denied the vote
Reconstruction Act of 1867 (March 1867)	Divided the South into five military districts, each under the command of a Union general
	Established requirements for readmission of ex-Confederate states to the Union
Tenure of Office Act (March 1867)	Required Senate consent for removal of any federal official whose appointment had required Senate confirmation
Fifteenth Amendment (February 1869‡)	Forbade states to deny citizens the right to vote on the grounds of race, color, or "previous condition of servitude"
Ku Klux Klan Act (April 1871)	Authorized the president to use federal prosecutions and military force to suppress conspiracies to deprive citizens of the right to vote and enjoy the equal protection of the law

* Ratified by three-fourths of all states in December 1865.

† Ratified by three-fourths of all states in July 1868.

‡ Ratified by three-fourths of all states in March 1870.

orders. Johnson, however, had misjudged Grant, who publicly objected to the president's machinations. When the Senate overruled Stanton's suspension, Grant — now an open enemy of Johnson — resigned so Stanton could resume his place as secretary of war. On February 21, 1868, Johnson formally dismissed Stanton. The feisty secretary of war responded by barricading himself in his office, precipitating a crisis.

Three days later, for the first time in U.S. history, legislators in the House of Representatives introduced articles of impeachment against the president, employing their constitutional power to charge high federal officials with "Treason, Bribery, or other high Crimes and Misdemeanors." The House serves, in effect, as the prosecutor in such cases, and the Senate serves as the court. The Republican majority brought eleven counts of misconduct against Johnson, most relating to infringement of the powers of Congress. After an eleven-week trial in the Senate, thirty-five senators voted for conviction — one vote short of the two-thirds majority required. Twelve Democrats and seven Republicans voted for acquittal. The dissenting Republicans felt that removing a president for defying Congress was too damaging to the constitutional system of checks and balances. But despite the president's acquittal, Congress had shown its power. For the brief months remaining in his term, Johnson was largely irrelevant.

Election of 1868 and the Fifteenth Amendment The impeachment controversy made Grant, already the Union's greatest war hero, a Republican idol as well. He easily won the party's presidential nomination in 1868. Although he supported congressional Reconstruction, Grant also urged sectional reconciliation. His Democratic opponent, former New York governor Horatio Seymour, almost declined the nomination because he understood that Democrats could not yet overcome the stain of disloyalty.

Grant won by an overwhelming margin, receiving 214 out of 294 electoral votes. Republicans retained two-thirds majorities in both houses of Congress.

In February 1869, following this smashing victory, Republicans produced the era's last constitutional amendment, the Fifteenth. It protected male citizens' right to vote irrespective of race, color, or "previous condition of servitude." Despite Radical Republicans' protests, the amendment left room for a poll tax (paid for the privilege of voting) and literacy requirements. Both were concessions to northern and western states that sought such provisions to keep immigrants and the "unworthy" poor from the polls. Congress required the four states remaining under federal control to ratify the measure as a condition for readmission to the Union. A year later, the **Fifteenth Amendment** became law.

Passage of the Fifteenth Amendment, despite its limitations, was an astonishing feat. Elsewhere in the Western Hemisphere, lawmakers had left emancipated slaves in a condition

"We Accept the Situation" This 1867 *Harper's Weekly* cartoon refers to the Military Reconstruction Act of 1867, which instructed ex-Confederate states to hold constitutional conventions and stipulated that the resulting constitutions must provide voting rights for black men. The two images here suggest white northerners' views of both ex-Confederates and emancipated slaves. How is each depicted? What does this suggest about the troubles that lay ahead for Reconstruction policy? The cartoonist was Thomas Nast (1840–1902), one of the most influential artists of his era. Nast first drew "Santa Claus" in his modern form, and it was he who began depicting the Democratic Party as a kicking donkey and Republicans as an elephant — suggesting (since elephants are supposed to have good memories) their long remembrance of the Civil War and emancipation. Library of Congress.

of semi-citizenship, with no voting rights. But, like almost all Americans, congressional Republicans had extraordinary faith in the power of the vote. Many African Americans agreed. "The colored people of these Southern states have cast their lot with the Government," declared a delegate to Arkansas's constitutional convention, "and with the great Republican Party. . . . The ballot is our only means of protection." In the election of 1870, hundreds of thousands of African Americans voted across the South, in an atmosphere of collective pride and celebration.

> **TRACE CHANGE OVER TIME**
> How and why did federal Reconstruction policies evolve between 1865 and 1870?

Women's Rights Denied

Passage of the Fifteenth Amendment was a bittersweet victory for national women's rights leaders, who had campaigned for the ballot since the Seneca Falls Convention of 1848. They hoped to secure voting rights for women and African American men at the same time. As Elizabeth Cady Stanton put it, women could "avail ourselves of the strong arm and the blue uniform of the black soldier to walk in by his side." The protected categories for voting in the Fifteenth Amendment could have read "race, color, *sex*, or previous condition of servitude." But that word proved impossible to obtain.

Enfranchising black men had clear benefits for the authors of Reconstruction. It punished ex-Confederates and ensured Republican support in the South. But women's party loyalties were more divided, and a substantial majority of northern voters—all men, of course—opposed women's enfranchisement. Even Radicals feared that this "side issue" would overburden their program. Influential abolitionists such as Wendell Philips refused to campaign for women's suffrage, fearing it would detract from the focus on black men. Philips criticized women's leaders for being "selfish." "Do you believe," Stanton hotly replied, "the African race is entirely composed of males?"

By May 1869, the former allies were at an impasse. At a convention of the Equal Rights Association, black abolitionist and women's rights advocate Frederick Douglass

OUT IN THE COLD.

"Out in the Cold" Though many women, including African American activists in the South, went to the polls in the early 1870s to test whether the new Fourteenth Amendment had given them the vote, federal courts subsequently rejected women's voting rights. Only Wyoming and Utah territories fully enfranchised women. At the same time, revised naturalization laws allowed immigrant men of African descent — though not of Asian descent — to become citizens. With its crude Irish, African, and Chinese racial caricatures, this 1884 cartoon from the humor magazine *The Judge* echoes the arguments of some white suffragists: though men of races stereotyped as inferior had been enfranchised, white women were not. The woman knocking on the door is also a caricature, with her harsh appearance and masculine hat. Library of Congress.

pleaded for white women to consider the situation in the South and allow black male suffrage to take priority. "When women, because they are women, are hunted down, . . . dragged from their homes and hung upon lamp posts," Douglass said, "then they will have an urgency to obtain the ballot equal to our own." Some women's suffrage leaders joined Douglass in backing the Fifteenth Amendment without the word *sex*. But many, especially white women, rejected Douglass's plea. One African American woman remarked that they "all go for sex, letting race occupy a minor position." Embittered, Elizabeth Cady Stanton lashed out against "Patrick and Sambo and Hans and Ung Tung," maligning uneducated freedmen and immigrants who could vote while educated white women could not. Douglass's resolution in support of the Fifteenth Amendment failed, and the convention broke up.

A rift thus opened in the women's movement. The majority, led by Lucy Stone, reconciled themselves to disappointment. Organized into the **American Woman Suffrage Association**, they remained loyal to the Republican Party in hopes that once Reconstruction had been settled, it would be women's turn. A group led by Elizabeth Cady Stanton and Susan B. Anthony struck out in a new direction. They saw that, once the Reconstruction amendments had passed, women's suffrage was unlikely in the near future. Stanton declared that woman "must not put her trust in man." The new organization she headed, the **National Woman Suffrage Association** (NWSA), focused exclusively on women's rights and took up the battle for a federal suffrage amendment.

In 1873, NWSA members decided to test the new constitutional amendments. Suffragists all over the United States, including some black women in the South, tried to register and vote. Most were turned away. In an ensuing lawsuit, suffrage advocate Virginia Minor of Missouri argued that the registrar who denied her a ballot had violated her rights under the Fourteenth Amendment. In *Minor v. Happersett* (1875), the Supreme Court dashed such hopes. It ruled that suffrage rights were not inherent in citizenship; women were citizens, but state legislatures could deny women the vote if they wished.

Women's rights advocates began to focus narrowly on suffrage as their movement suffered backlash from controversies over sexual freedom. After Victoria Woodhull, a flamboyant young woman from Ohio, became the nation's first female stockbroker on Wall Street, she won notoriety by denouncing marriage as a form of tyranny. She urged that women be "trained like men," for independent thought and economic self-sufficiency. Particularly sensational was Woodhull's insistence, in a speech in New York in 1871, that "I am a free lover. I have an inalienable, constitutional, and natural right to love whom I may, to love as long or as short a period as I can; to change that love every day if I please."

Woodhull helped trigger the **Beecher-Tilton scandal**, a sensational trial that dominated headlines in the mid-1870s. She accused Brooklyn Congregationalist minister Henry Ward Beecher, a staunch Republican and abolitionist from a famous reform family, of secretly being a free lover himself. For making allegations of adultery, Woodhull was tried on obscenity charges, briefly jailed, and released. Beecher was then sued by the husband of a congregant with whom he had allegedly had an affair. The results of the trial were inconclusive, but the relentless publicity, including the publication of intimate letters, damaged the reputation of everyone involved. Many Americans concluded that Radical Republicans wanted to go too far, and that, in private, former abolitionists like Beecher and his congregants were behaving immorally. Social conservatives, including ex-Confederates in the South, gleefully watched leading abolitionists get their come-uppance. Women's rights advocates, who had welcomed Victoria Woodhull as an ally, soon distanced themselves from her free love proclamations. Leaders such as Susan B. Anthony decided that the only way to win the vote was to practice and advocate strict sexual respectability.

Despite these defeats and embarrassments, Radical Reconstruction had created the conditions for a nationwide women's rights movement. Some argued for suffrage as part of a broader expansion of democracy. Others, on the contrary, saw white women's votes as a possible counterweight to the votes of African American or Chinese men (while opponents pointed out that black and immigrant women would likely be enfranchised, too). When Wyoming Territory gave women full voting rights in 1869, its governor received telegrams of congratulation from around the world.

Victoria Woodhull Free-love advocate Victoria Woodhull became a controversial figure in the 1870s as she campaigned for universal voting rights, denounced marriage laws for enslaving women, and urged women to work for economic independence. Here, Woodhull and her sister Tennessee Claflin attempt to vote in New York in 1875 — seeking, like other women's rights advocates, to trigger legal challenges over their right to do so. Like others, Woodhull and Claflin were turned away from the polls. In 1872 Woodhull had run as the first woman candidate for president on the Equal Rights ticket. Kean Collection/Hulton Archive/Getty Images.

Afterward, contrary to dire predictions, female voters in Wyoming did not appear to neglect their homes, abandon their children, or otherwise "unsex" themselves. Women's suffrage could no longer be dismissed as the absurd notion of a tiny minority. It had become a serious issue for national debate.

> **IN YOUR OWN WORDS**   What factors explain how Reconstruction policies unfolded between 1865 and 1870, and what was the impact on different groups of Americans?

> **CONSIDER POINTS OF VIEW**
> Abolitionists and women's suffrage advocates were generally close allies before 1865. What divisions emerged during Reconstruction and why?

The Meaning of Freedom

While political leaders wrangled in Washington, emancipated slaves acted on their own ideas about freedom. Emancipation meant many things: the end of punishment by the lash; the ability to move around; reunion of families; and opportunities to build schools and churches and to publish and read newspapers. Foremost among freedpeople's demands were voting rights and economic autonomy. Former Confederates opposed these goals. Most southern whites believed the proper place for blacks was as "servants and inferiors," as a Virginia planter testified to Congress. Mississippi's governor, elected under President Johnson's plan, vowed that "ours is and it shall ever be, a government of white men." Meanwhile, as Reconstruction unfolded, it became clear that on economic questions, southern blacks and northern Republican policymakers did not see eye to eye.

The Quest for Land

During the Civil War, wherever Union forces had conquered portions of the South, rural black workers had formed associations that agreed on common goals and even practiced military drills. After the war, when resettlement became the responsibility of the Freedmen's Bureau, thousands of rural blacks hoped for land distributions. But Johnson's amnesty plan, which allowed pardoned Confederates to recover property seized during the war, blasted such hopes. In October 1865, for example, Johnson ordered General Oliver O. Howard, head of the Freedmen's Bureau, to restore plantations on South Carolina's Sea Islands to white property holders. Dispossessed blacks protested: "Why do you take away our lands? You take them from us who have always been true, always true to the Government! You give them to our all-time enemies! That is not right!" Former slaves resisted efforts to evict them. Led by black Union veterans, they fought pitched battles with former slaveholders and bands of ex-Confederate soldiers. But white landowners, sometimes aided by federal troops, generally prevailed.

Freed Slaves and Northerners: Conflicting Goals

On questions of land and labor, freedmen in the South and Republicans in Washington seriously differed. The economic revolution of the antebellum period had transformed New England and the Mid-Atlantic states. Believing similar development could revolutionize the South, most congressional leaders sought to restore cotton as the country's leading export, and they envisioned former slaves as wageworkers on cash-crop plantations, not independent farmers. Only a handful of Republican leaders, like Thaddeus Stevens, argued that freed slaves had earned a right to land grants, through what Lincoln had referred to as "four hundred years of unrequited toil." Stevens proposed that southern plantations be treated as "forfeited estates of the enemy" and broken up into small farms for former slaves. "Nothing will make men so industrious and moral," Stevens declared, "as to let them feel that they are above want and are the owners of the soil which they till."

Today, most historians of Reconstruction agree with Stevens: policymakers did not do enough to ensure freedpeople's economic security. Without land, former slaves were left poor and vulnerable. At the time, though, Stevens had few allies. A deep veneration for private property lay at the heart of his vision, but others interpreted the same principle differently: they defined ownership by legal title, not by labor invested. Though often accused of harshness toward the defeated Confederacy, most Republicans — even Radicals — could not imagine "giving" land to former slaves. The same congressmen, of course, had no difficulty giving away homesteads on the frontier that had been taken from Indians. But they were deeply reluctant to confiscate white-owned plantations.

Some southern Republican state governments did try, without much success, to use tax policy to break up large landholdings and get them into the hands of poorer whites and blacks. In 1869, South Carolina established a land commission to buy property and resell it on easy terms to the landless; about 14,000 black families acquired farms through the program. But such initiatives were the exception, not the rule. Over time, some rural blacks did succeed in becoming small-scale landowners, especially in Upper South states such as Virginia, North Carolina, and Tennessee. But it was an uphill fight, and policymakers provided little aid.

Wage Labor and Sharecropping

Without land, most freedpeople had few options but to work for former slave owners. Landowners wanted to retain the old gang-labor system, with wages replacing the food, clothing, and shelter that slaves had once received. Southern planters — who had recently scorned the North for the cruelties of wage labor — now embraced waged work with apparent satisfaction. Maliciously comparing black workers to free-roaming pigs, landowners told them to "root, hog, or die." Former slaves found themselves with rock-bottom wages; it was a shock to find that emancipation and "free labor" did not prevent a hardworking family from nearly starving.

African American workers used a variety of tactics to fight back. As early as 1865, alarmed whites across the South reported that former slaves were holding mass meetings to agree on "plans and terms for labor." Such meetings continued through the Reconstruction years. Facing limited prospects at home, some workers left the fields and traveled long distances to seek better-paying jobs on the railroads or in turpentine and lumber camps. Others — from rice cultivators to laundry workers — organized strikes.

What did the Thirteenth Amendment really accomplish? The answer may seem self-evident: it abolished slavery. But how free were newly emancipated slaves during the years immediately following the war, in comparison to earlier and later decades? For historians who measure change over time, it is a question worth asking.

Formerly enslaved people sought out and reunited with family members they could find who had been sold to other regions during slavery. They also founded businesses, churches, and schools and worked to secure economic stability and political rights. The ideological, political, and economic system that had sustained slavery prior to the Civil War, however, did not entirely disappear. Gender made a difference: as they had under slavery, the experiences of women differed from those of men. Historians Tera W. Hunter and Jacqueline Jones focus on the postwar experiences of freedwomen to understand what changes emancipation brought to their lives and to assess how much freedom they were able to secure.

How Free Were Freedwomen in Reconstruction?

TERA W. HUNTER

SOURCE: Tera W. Hunter, *To Joy My Freedom: Southern Black Women's Lives and Labors After the Civil War* (Cambridge: Harvard University Press, 1997), 28.

African-American women decided to quit work over such grievances as low wages, long hours, and unpleasant tasks. . . . [I]t was an effective strategy to deprive employers of complete power over their labor. . . . Occasional refusals to sell their labor or self-imposed limits enabled working-class women to conduct their own family and community affairs in ways that mitigated the demands of white supremacy and the market economy.

JACQUELINE JONES

SOURCE: Jacqueline Jones, *Labor of Love, Labor of Sorrow: Black Women, Work and the Family from Slavery to the Present* (New York: Vintage Books, 1986), 7.

[B]lack working women . . . lacked the control over their own productive energies and material resources. . . . Though perhaps "freed" or "liberated" from narrow sex-role conventions, they remained tied to overwhelming wage-earning and child-rearing responsibilities. . . . [W]hen measured against traditional standards of power — usually defined in terms of wealth; personal autonomy; and control over workers, votes, or inheritances — black wives and mothers had little leverage with which to manipulate the behavior of their kinfolk.

QUESTIONS FOR ANALYSIS

1. How does each historian assess the impact of the Reconstruction era on freedwomen?
2. Name two factors that each historian considers when evaluating freedom for freedwomen during Reconstruction.
3. What evidence from the chapter supports or refutes the interpretation that emancipation empowered freedwomen in the years following the Civil War?

At the same time, struggles raged between employers and freedpeople over women's work. In slavery, African American women's bodies had been the sexual property of white men. Protecting black women from such abuse, as much as possible, was a crucial priority for freedpeople. When planters demanded that black women go back into the fields, African Americans resisted resolutely. "I seen on some plantations," one freedman recounted, "where the white men would . . . tell colored men that their wives and children could not live on their places unless they work in the fields. The colored men [answered that] whenever they wanted their wives to work they would tell them themselves."

There was a profound irony in this man's definition of freedom: it designated a wife's labor as her husband's property. Some black women asserted their independence and headed their own households, though this was often a matter of necessity rather than choice. For many freedpeople, the opportunity for a stable family life was one of the greatest achievements of emancipation. Many enthusiastically accepted the northern ideal of domesticity. Missionaries, teachers, and editors of black newspapers urged men to work diligently and support their families, and they told women (though many worked for wages) to devote themselves to motherhood and the home (Interpretations).

Even in rural areas, former slaves refused to work under conditions that recalled slavery. There would be no gang work, they vowed: no overseers, no whippings, no regulation of their private lives. Across the South, planters who needed labor were forced to yield to what one planter termed the "prejudices of the freedmen, who desire to be masters of their own time." In a few areas, waged work became the norm — for example, on the giant sugar plantations of Louisiana financed by northern capital. But cotton planters lacked money to pay wages, and sometimes, in lieu of a wage, they offered a share of the crop. Freedmen, in turn, paid their rent in shares of the harvest.

Thus the Reconstruction years gave rise to a distinctive system of cotton agriculture known as **sharecropping**, in which freedmen worked as renters, exchanging their labor for the use of land, house, implements, and sometimes seed and fertilizer. Sharecroppers typically turned over half of their crops to the landlord (Map 14.2). In a credit-starved agricultural region that grew crops for a world economy, sharecropping was an effective strategy, enabling laborers and landowners to share risks and returns. But it was a very unequal relationship. Starting out penniless, sharecroppers had no way to make it through the first growing season without borrowing for food and supplies.

Country storekeepers stepped in. Bankrolled by northern suppliers, they furnished sharecroppers with provisions and took as collateral a lien on the crop, effectively assuming ownership of croppers' shares and leaving them only what remained after debts had been paid. Crop-lien laws enforced lenders' ownership rights to the crop share. Once indebted at a store, sharecroppers became easy targets for exorbitant prices, unfair interest rates, and crooked bookkeeping. As cotton prices declined in the 1870s, more and more sharecroppers fell into permanent debt. If the merchant was also the

MAP 14.2 The Barrow Plantation, 1860 and 1881
This map is a modern redrawing of one that first appeared in the popular magazine *Scribner's Monthly* in April 1881, accompanying an article about the Barrow plantation. Comparing the 1860 map of this central Georgia plantation with the 1881 map reveals the impact of sharecropping on patterns of black residence. In 1860, the slave quarters were clustered near the planter's house. In contrast, by 1881 the sharecroppers were scattered across the plantation's 2,000 acres, having built cabins on the ridges between the low-lying streams. The surname *Barrow* was common among the sharecropping families, which means almost certainly that they had been slaves who, years after emancipation, still had not moved on. For sharecroppers, freedom meant not only their individual lots and cabins but also the school and church shown on the map.

landowner or conspired with the landowner, debt became a pretext for forced labor, or peonage.

Sharecropping arose in part because it was a good fit for cotton agriculture. Cotton, unlike sugarcane, could be raised efficiently by small farmers (provided they had the lash of indebtedness always on their backs). We can see this in the experience of other regions that became major producers in response to the global cotton shortage set off by the Civil War. In India, Egypt, Brazil, and West Africa, variants of the sharecropping system emerged. Everywhere international merchants and bankers, who put up capital, insisted on passage of crop-lien laws. Indian and Egyptian villagers ended up, like their American counterparts, permanently under the thumb of furnishing merchants.

By 1890, three out of every four black farmers in the South were tenants or sharecroppers; among white farmers, the ratio was one in three. For freedmen, sharecropping was not the worst choice, in a world where former masters threatened to impose labor conditions that were close to slavery. But the costs were devastating. With farms leased on a year-to-year basis, neither tenant nor owner had much incentive to improve the property. The crop-lien system rested on expensive interest payments — money that might otherwise have gone into agricultural improvements or to meet human needs. And sharecropping committed the South inflexibly to cotton, a crop that generated the cash required by landlords and furnishing merchants. The result was a stagnant farm economy that blighted the South's future. As Republican governments tried to remake the region, they confronted not only wartime destruction but also the failure of their hopes that free labor would create a modern, prosperous South, built in the image of the industrializing North. Instead, the South's rural economy remained mired in widespread poverty and based on an uneasy compromise between landowners and laborers.

Picking Cotton in Mississippi After emancipation most African Americans in the South, lacking land or capital, continued to work in agriculture. Through sharecropping and other arrangements, they sought as much autonomy and control over their work as they could obtain. Many families made it a priority for women to work in the home and children to attend school. At harvest time, however, everyone was needed in the fields. The Granger Collection, New York.

IDENTIFY CAUSES
Why did sharecropping emerge, and how did it affect freedpeople and the southern economy?

Republican Governments in the South

Between 1868 and 1871, all the former Confederate states met congressional stipulations and rejoined the Union. Protected by federal troops, Republican administrations in these states retained power for periods ranging from a few months in Virginia to nine years in South Carolina, Louisiana, and Florida. These governments remain some of the most misunderstood institutions in all U.S. history. Ex-Confederates never accepted their legitimacy. Many other whites agreed, focusing particularly on the role of African Americans who began to serve in public office. "It is strange, abnormal, and unfit," declared one British visitor to Louisiana, "that a *negro* Legislature should deal . . . with the gravest commercial and financial interests." During much of the twentieth century, historians echoed such critics, condemning Reconstruction leaders as ignorant and corrupt. These historians shared the racial prejudices of the British observer: black men were simply unfit to govern.

In fact, Reconstruction governments were ambitious. They were hated, in part, because they undertook impressive reforms in public education, family law, social services, commerce, and transportation. Like their northern allies, southern Republicans admired the economic and social transformations that had occurred in the North before the Civil War and worked energetically to import them.

The southern Republican Party included former Whigs, a few former Democrats, black and white newcomers from the North, and southern African Americans. From the start, its leaders faced the dilemma of racial prejudice. In the upcountry, white

Cotton Farmers, Marietta, Georgia, c. 1880 Before the Civil War, the South had proudly called itself the "Cotton Kingdom." After the war, cotton was still king, but few southerners got rich on cotton profits. Instead, thousands of small-scale farmers, white and black, struggled with plunging crop prices, debt, and taxes on land to support an array of ambitious Reconstruction programs. The farmers here have baled their cotton for market and pose with their wagons in Marietta's courthouse square. Courtesy Georgia Archives, Vanishing Georgia Collection, cob262.

Unionists were eager to join the party but sometimes reluctant to work with black allies. In most areas, the Republicans also desperately needed African Americans, who constituted a majority of registered voters in Alabama, Florida, South Carolina, and Mississippi.

For a brief moment in the late 1860s, black and white Republicans joined forces through the Union League, a secret fraternal order. Formed in border states and northern cities during the Civil War, the league became a powerful political association that spread through the former Confederacy. Functioning as a grassroots wing of Radical Republicanism, it pressured Congress to uphold justice for freedmen. After blacks won voting rights, the league organized meetings at churches and schoolhouses to instruct freedmen on political issues and voting procedures. League clubs held parades and military drills, giving a public face to the new political order.

The Freedmen's Bureau also supported grassroots Reconstruction efforts. Though some bureau officials sympathized with planters, most were dedicated, idealistic men who tried valiantly to reconcile opposing interests. Bureau men kept a sharp eye out for unfair labor contracts and often forced landowners to bargain with workers and tenants. They advised freedmen on economic matters; provided direct payments to desperate families, especially women and children; and helped establish schools. In cooperation with northern aid societies, the bureau played a key role in founding African American colleges and universities such as Fisk, Tougaloo, and the Hampton Institute. These institutions, in turn, focused on training teachers. By 1869, there were more than three thousand teachers instructing freedpeople in the South. More than half were themselves African Americans.

Ex-Confederates viewed the Union League, Freedmen's Bureau, and Republican Party as illegitimate forces in southern affairs, and they resented the political education of freedpeople. They referred to southern whites who supported Reconstruction as scalawags—an ancient Scots-Irish term for worthless animals—and denounced northern whites as carpetbaggers, self-seeking interlopers who carried all their property in cheap suitcases called carpetbags. Such labels glossed over the actual diversity of white Republicans. Many arrivals from the North, while motivated by personal profit, also brought capital and skills. Interspersed with ambitious schemers were reformers hoping to advance freedmen's rights. So-called scalawags were even more varied. Some southern Republicans were former slave owners; others were ex-Whigs or even ex-Democrats who hoped to attract northern capital. But most hailed from the backcountry and wanted to rid the South of its slaveholding aristocracy, believing slavery had victimized whites as well as blacks.

Southern Democrats' contempt for black politicians, whom they regarded as ignorant field hands, was just as misguided as their stereotypes about white Republicans. Many African American leaders in the South came from the ranks of antebellum free blacks. Others were skilled men like Robert Smalls of South Carolina, who as a slave had worked for wages that he turned over to his master. Smalls, a steamer pilot in Charleston harbor, had become a war hero when he escaped with his family and other slaves and brought his ship to the Union navy. Buying property in Beaufort after the war, Smalls became a state legislator and later a congressman. Blanche K. Bruce, another former slave, had been tutored on a Virginia plantation by his white father; during the war, he escaped and established a school for freedmen in Missouri. In 1869, he moved to Mississippi and became, five years later, Mississippi's second black U.S. senator. Political leaders such as Smalls and Bruce were joined by northern blacks—including ministers, teachers, and Union veterans—who moved south to support Reconstruction.

During radical Reconstruction, such men fanned out into plantation districts and recruited former slaves to participate in politics. Literacy helped freedman Thomas Allen, a Baptist minister and shoemaker, win election to the Georgia legislature. "The colored people came to me," Allen recalled, "and I gave them the best instructions I could. I took the *New York Tribune* and other papers, and in that way I found out a great deal, and I told them whatever I thought was right." Though never proportionate to their numbers in the population, blacks became officeholders across the South. In South Carolina, African Americans constituted a majority in the lower house of the legislature in 1868. Over the course of Reconstruction, twenty African Americans served in state administrations as governor, lieutenant governor, secretary of state, or lesser offices. More than six hundred became state legislators, and sixteen were congressmen.

Both white and black Republicans had big plans. Their southern Reconstruction governments eliminated property qualifications for the vote and abolished Black Codes. Their new state constitutions expanded the rights of married women, enabling them to own their own property and wages—"a wonderful reform," one white woman in Georgia wrote, for "the cause of Women's Rights." Like their counterparts in the North, southern Republicans also believed in using government to foster economic growth. Seeking to diversify the economy beyond cotton agriculture, they poured money into railroads and other projects.

In myriad ways, Republicans brought southern state and city governments up to date. They outlawed corporal punishments such as whipping and branding. They established hospitals and

Hiram R. Revels In 1870, Hiram Rhodes Revels (1827–1901) was elected to the U.S. Senate from Mississippi to fill Jefferson Davis's former seat. Revels was a free black from North Carolina who had moved to the North and attended Knox College in Illinois. During the Civil War he had recruited African Americans for the Union army and, as an ordained Methodist minister, served as chaplain of a black regiment in Mississippi, where he settled after the war. The Granger Collection, New York.

asylums for orphans and the disabled. South Carolina offered free public health services, while Alabama provided free legal representation for defendants who could not pay. Some municipal governments paved streets and installed streetlights. Petersburg, Virginia, established a board of health that offered free medical care during the smallpox epidemic of 1873. Nashville, Tennessee, created soup kitchens for the poor.

Most impressive of all were achievements in public education, where the South had lagged woefully. Republicans viewed education as the foundation of a true democratic order. By 1875, over half of black children were attending school in Mississippi, Florida, and South Carolina. African Americans of all ages rushed to the newly established schools, even when they had to pay tuition. They understood why slaveholders had criminalized slave literacy: the practice of freedom rested on the ability to read newspapers, labor contracts, history books, and the Bible. A school official in Virginia reported that freedpeople were "*crazy* to learn." One Louisiana man explained why he was sending his children to school, even though he needed their help in the field. It was "better than leaving them a fortune; because if you left them even five hundred dollars, some man having more education than they had would come along and cheat them out of it all." Thousands of white children, particularly girls and the sons of poor farmers and laborers, also benefitted from new public education systems. Young white women's graduation from high school, an unheard-of occurrence before the Civil War, became a celebrated event in southern cities and towns.

Southern Reconstruction governments also had their flaws — flaws that would become more apparent as the 1870s unfolded. In the race for economic development, for example, state officials allowed private companies to hire out prisoners to labor in mines and other industries, in a notorious system known as **convict leasing**. Corruption was rife and conditions horrific. In 1866, Alabama's governor leased 200 state convicts to a railroad construction company for the grand total of $5. While they labored to build state-subsidized lines such as the Alabama and Chattanooga, prisoners were housed at night in open, rolling cages. Physical abuse was common and medical care nonexistent. At the start of 1869, Alabama counted 263 prisoners available for leasing; by the end of the year, a staggering 92 of them had died. While convict leasing expanded in later decades, it began during Reconstruction, supported by both Republicans and Democrats.

PLACE EVENTS IN CONTEXT
What policies did southern Reconstruction legislators pursue, and what needs of the postwar South did they seek to serve?

Freedmen's School, Petersburg, Virginia, 1870s A Union veteran, returning to Virginia in the 1870s to photograph battlefields, captured this image of an African American teacher and her students at a freedmen's school. Note the difficult conditions in which they study: many are barefoot, and there are gaps in the walls and floor of the school building. Nonetheless, the students have a few books. Despite poverty and relentless hostility from many whites, freedpeople across the South were determined to get a basic education for themselves and their children. William L. Clements Library, University of Michigan.

Building Black Communities

Enslaved African Americans had built networks of religious worship and mutual aid, but these operated largely in secret. After emancipation, southern blacks could engage in open community building. In doing so, they cooperated with northern missionaries and teachers, both black and white, who came to help in the great work of freedom. "Ignorant though they may be, on account of long years of oppression, they exhibit a desire to hear and to learn, that I never imagined," reported African American minister Reverend James Lynch, who traveled from Maryland to the Deep South. "Every word you say while preaching, they drink down and respond to, with an earnestness that sets your heart all on fire."

Independent churches quickly became central community institutions, as blacks across the South left white-dominated congregations, where they had sat in segregated balconies, and built churches of their own. These churches joined their counterparts in the North to become national denominations, including, most prominently, the National Baptist Convention and the African Methodist Episcopal Church. Black churches served not only as sites of worship but also as schools, social centers, and meeting halls. Ministers were often political spokesmen as well. As Charles H. Pearce, a black Methodist pastor in Florida, declared, "A man in this State cannot do his whole duty as a minister except he looks out for the political interests of his people." Religious leaders articulated the special destiny of freedpeople as the new "Children of Israel."

The flowering of black churches, schools, newspapers, and civic groups was one of the most enduring initiatives of the Reconstruction era. Dedicated teachers and charity leaders embarked on a project of "race uplift" that never ceased thereafter, while black entrepreneurs were proud to build businesses that served their communities. The issue of desegregation — sharing public facilities with whites — was a trickier one. Though some black leaders pressed for desegregation, they were keenly aware of the backlash this was likely to provoke. Others made it clear that they preferred their children to attend all-black schools, especially if they encountered hostile or condescending white teachers and classmates. Many had pragmatic concerns. Asked whether she wanted her boys to attend an integrated school, one woman in New Orleans said no: "I don't want my children to be pounded by . . . white boys. I don't send them to school to fight, I send them to learn."

At the national level, congressmen wrestled with similar issues as they debated an ambitious civil rights bill championed by Radical Republican senator Charles Sumner. Sumner first introduced his bill in 1870, seeking to enforce, among other things, equal access to schools, public transportation, hotels, and churches. Due to a series of defeats and delays, the bill remained on Capitol Hill for five years. Opponents charged that shared public spaces would lead to race mixing and intermarriage. Some sympathetic Republicans feared a backlash, while others

COMPARE AND CONTRAST
Compare the results of African Americans' community building with their struggles to obtain better working conditions. What links do you see between these efforts?

Fisk Jubilee Singers, 1873 Fisk University in Nashville, Tennessee, was established in 1865 to provide higher education for African Americans from across the South. When funds ran short in 1871, enterprising students formed the Jubilee Singers choral group (bottom) and toured to raise money for the school. They performed African American spirituals and folk songs, such as "Swing Low, Sweet Chariot," arranged in ways that appealed to white audiences, making this music nationally popular for the first time. In 1872, the group performed for President Grant at the White House. Money raised by this acclaimed group saved Fisk from bankruptcy and built the university's imposing Jubilee Hall (top). Private Collection/© Look and Learn/Illustrated Papers Collection/Bridgeman Images.

To see a call for passage of the Civil Rights Act from an African American Congress, along with other primary sources from this period, see *Sources for America's History*.

questioned whether, because of the First Amendment, the federal government had the right to regulate churches. On his deathbed in 1874, Sumner exhorted a visitor to remember the civil rights bill: "Don't let it fail." In the end, the Senate removed Sumner's provision for integrated churches, and the House removed the clause requiring integrated schools. But to honor the great Massachusetts abolitionist, Congress passed the **Civil Rights Act of 1875**. The law required "full and equal" access to jury service and to transportation and public accommodations, irrespective of race. It was the last such act for almost a hundred years — until the Civil Rights Act of 1964.

> **IN YOUR OWN WORDS** What goals were southern freedmen and freedwomen able to achieve in the post–Civil War years, and why? What goals were they not able to achieve, and why not?

The Undoing of Reconstruction

Sumner's death marked the waning of Radical Reconstruction. That movement had accomplished more than anyone dreamed a few years earlier. But a chasm had opened between the goals of freedmen, who wanted autonomy, and policymakers, whose first priorities were to reincorporate ex-Confederates into the nation and build a powerful national economy. Meanwhile, the North was flooded with one-sided, racist reports such as James M. Pike's influential book *The Prostrate State* (1873), which claimed South Carolina was in the grip of "black barbarism." Events of the 1870s deepened the northern public's disillusionment. Scandals rocked the Grant administration, and an economic depression curbed both private investment and public spending. At the same time, northern resolve was worn down by continued ex-Confederate resistance and violence. Only full-scale military intervention could reverse the situation in the South, and by the mid-1870s the North had no political willpower to renew the occupation.

The Republicans Unravel

Republicans had banked on economic growth to underpin their ambitious program, but their hopes were dashed in 1873 by the sudden onset of a severe worldwide depression. In the United States, the initial panic was triggered by the bankruptcy of the Northern Pacific Railroad, backed by leading financier Jay Cooke. Cooke's supervision of Union finances during the Civil War had made him a national hero; his downfall was a shock, and since Cooke was so well connected in Washington, it raised suspicions that Republican financial manipulation had caused the depression. Officials in the Grant administration deepened public resentment toward their party when they rejected pleas to increase the money supply and provide relief from debt and unemployment.

The impact of the depression varied in different parts of the United States. Farmers suffered a terrible plight as crop prices plunged, while industrial workers faced layoffs and sharp wage reductions. Within a year, 50 percent of American iron manufacturing had stopped. By 1877, half the nation's railroad companies had filed for bankruptcy. Rail construction halted. With hundreds of thousands thrown out of work, people took to the road. Wandering "tramps," who camped by railroad tracks and knocked on doors to beg for work and food, terrified prosperous Americans.

In addition to discrediting Republicans, the depression directly undercut their policies, most dramatically in the South. The ex-Confederacy was still recovering from the ravages of war, and its new economic and social order remained fragile. The bold policies of southern Republicans — for education, public health, and grants to railroad builders — cost a great deal of money. Federal support, through programs like the Freedmen's Bureau, had begun to fade even before 1873. Republicans had banked on major infusions of northern and foreign investment capital; for the most part, these failed to materialize. Investors who had sunk money into Confederate bonds, only to have those repudiated, were especially wary. The South's economy grew more slowly than Republicans had hoped, and after 1873, growth screeched to a halt. State debts mounted rapidly, and as crushing interest on bonds fell due, public credit collapsed.

Not only had Republican officials failed to anticipate a severe depression; during the era of generous spending, considerable funds had also been wasted or had ended up in the pockets of corrupt officials. Two swindlers in North Carolina, one of them a former Union general, were found to have distributed more than $200,000 in bribes and loans to legislators to gain millions in state funds for rail construction. Instead of building railroads, they used the money to travel to Europe and speculate in stocks and bonds. Not only Republicans were on the take. "You are mistaken," wrote one southern Democrat to a northern friend, "if you suppose that all the evils . . . result from the carpetbaggers and negroes. The Democrats are leagued with them when anything is proposed that promises to pay." In South Carolina, when African American congressman Robert Smalls was convicted of taking a bribe, the Democratic governor pardoned him in exchange for an agreement that federal officials would drop an investigation of Democratic election fraud.

One of the depression's most tragic results was the failure of the Freedman's Savings and Trust Company. This private bank, founded in 1865, had worked closely with the Freedmen's Bureau and Union army across the South. Former slaves associated it with the party of Lincoln, and thousands responded to northerners' call for thrift and savings by bringing their small deposits to the nearest branch. African American farmers, entrepreneurs, churches, and charitable groups opened accounts at the bank. But in the early 1870s, the bank's directors sank their money into risky loans and speculative investments. In June 1874, the bank failed.

Some Republicans believed that, because the bank had been so closely associated with the U.S. Army and federal agencies, Congress had a duty to step in. Even one southern Democrat argued that the government was "morally bound to see to it that not a dollar is lost." But in the end, Congress refused to compensate the 61,000 depositors. About half recovered small amounts — averaging $18.51 — but the others received nothing. The party of Reconstruction was losing its moral gloss.

"Grantism" During his second term of office, President Grant was lampooned for the problems of his scandal-ridden administration. Here, the humor magazine *Puck* shows Grant barely defying gravity to keep himself and his corrupt subordinates aloft and out of jail. He hangs from a "third term" bar because many predicted that the Republican party would nominate him yet again in 1876. Due in large part to the administration's scandals, this did not happen, but the Union war hero nonetheless remained personally popular. Library of Congress.

The Disillusioned Liberals

As a result of the depression and rising criticism of postwar activist government, a revolt emerged in the Republican Party. It was led by influential intellectuals, journalists, and businessmen who believed in **classical liberalism**: free trade, small government, low property taxes, and limitation of voting rights to men of education and property. Liberals responded to the massive increase in federal power, during the Civil War and Reconstruction, by urging a policy of *laissez faire*, in which government "let alone" business and the economy. In the postwar decades, laissez faire advocates never succeeded in ending federal policies such as the protective tariff and national banking system (Chapter 16), but their arguments helped roll back Reconstruction. Unable to block Grant's renomination for the presidency in 1872, the dissidents broke away and formed a new party under the name Liberal Republican. Their candidate was Horace Greeley, longtime publisher of the *New York Tribune* and veteran reformer and abolitionist. The Democrats, still in disarray, also nominated Greeley, notwithstanding his editorial diatribes against them. A poor campaigner, Greeley was assailed so severely that, as he said, "I hardly knew whether I was running for the Presidency or the penitentiary."

Grant won reelection overwhelmingly, capturing 56 percent of the popular vote and every electoral vote. Yet Liberal Republicans had shifted the terms of debate. The agenda they advanced — smaller government, restricted voting rights, and reconciliation with ex-Confederates — resonated with Democrats, who had long advocated limited government and were working to reclaim their status as a legitimate national party. Liberalism thus crossed party lines, uniting disillusioned conservative Republicans with Democrats who denounced government activism. E. L. Godkin of *The Nation* and other classical liberal editors played key roles in turning northern public opinion against Reconstruction. With unabashed elitism, Godkin and others claimed that freedmen were unfit to vote. They denounced universal suffrage, which "can only mean in plain English the government of ignorance and vice."

The second Grant administration gave liberals plenty of ammunition. The most notorious scandal involved **Crédit Mobilier**, a sham corporation set up by shareholders in the Union Pacific Railroad to secure government grants at an enormous profit. Organizers of the scheme protected it from investigation by providing gifts of Crédit Mobilier stock to powerful members of Congress. Controversy over this railroad scandal arose even before Grant's reelection; by 1875 another scandal emerged involving the so-called "Whiskey Ring," a network of liquor distillers and treasury agents who defrauded the government of millions of dollars of excise taxes on whiskey. The ringleader was Grant's private secretary, Orville Babcock. Others went to prison, but Grant stood by Babcock, possibly perjuring himself to save his secretary from jail. The stench of scandal permeated the White House.

Counterrevolution in the South

While northerners became preoccupied with scandals and the shock of economic depression, ex-Confederates seized power in the South. Most believed (as northern liberals had also begun to argue) that southern Reconstruction governments were illegitimate "regimes." Led by the planters, ex-Confederates staged a massive insurgency to take back the South.

When they could win at the ballot box, southern Democrats took that route. They got ex-Confederate voting rights restored and campaigned against "negro rule." But when force was necessary, southern Democrats used it. Present-day Americans, witnessing political violence in other countries, seldom remember that our own history includes the overthrow of elected governments by paramilitary groups. But this is exactly how Reconstruction ended in many parts of the South. Ex-Confederates terrorized Republicans, especially in districts with large proportions of black voters. Black political leaders were shot, hanged, beaten to death, and in one case even beheaded (Analyzing Voices). Many Republicans, both black and white, went into hiding or fled for their lives. Southern Democrats called this violent process "Redemption" — a heroic name that still lingers today, even though this seizure of power was murderous and undemocratic.

No one looms larger in this bloody story than Nathan Bedford Forrest, a decorated Confederate general. Born in poverty in 1821, Forrest had risen to become a big-time slave trader and Mississippi planter. A fiery secessionist, Forrest had formed a Tennessee Confederate cavalry regiment, fought bravely at the battle of Shiloh, and won fame as a daring raider. On April 12, 1864, his troops perpetrated one of the war's worst atrocities, the massacre at Fort Pillow, Tennessee, of black Union soldiers who were trying to surrender.

After the Civil War, Forrest's determination to uphold white supremacy altered the course of Reconstruction. William G. Brownlow, elected as Tennessee's Republican governor in 1865, was a tough man, a former prisoner of the Confederates who was not shy about calling his enemies to account. Ex-Confederates struck back with a campaign of terror, targeting especially Brownlow's black supporters. Amid the mayhem, ex-Confederates formed the first **Ku Klux Klan** group in late 1865 or early 1866. As it proliferated across the state, the Klan turned to Forrest, who had been trying, unsuccessfully, to rebuild his prewar fortune. Late in 1866, at a secret meeting in Nashville, Forrest donned the robes of Grand Wizard. His activities are mostly cloaked in mystery, but there is no mistake about his goals: the Klan would strike blows against the despised Republican government of Tennessee.

In many towns, the Klan became virtually identical to the Democratic Party. Klan members—including Forrest—dominated Tennessee's delegation to the Democratic national convention of 1868. At home, the Klan unleashed a murderous campaign of terror, and though Governor Brownlow responded resolutely, in the end Republicans cracked. The Klan and similar groups—organized under such names as the White League and Knights of the White Camelia—arose in other states. Vigilantes burned freedmen's schools, beat teachers, attacked Republican gatherings, and murdered political opponents. By 1870, Democrats had seized power in Georgia and North Carolina and were making headway across the South. Once they took power, they slashed property taxes and passed other laws favorable to landowners. They terminated Reconstruction programs and cut funding for schools, especially those teaching black students.

Ku Klux Klan Mask White supremacists of the 1870s organized under many names and wore many costumes, not simply (or often) the white cone-shaped hats that were made famous later, in the 1920s, when the Klan underwent a nationwide resurgence. Few masks from the 1870s have survived. The horns and fangs on this one, from North Carolina, suggest how Klan members sought to strike terror in their victims, while also hiding their own identities. North Carolina Museum of History.

In responding to the Klan between 1869 and 1871, the federal government showed it could still exert power effectively in the South. Determined to end Klan violence, Congress held extensive hearings and in 1870 passed laws designed to protect freedmen's rights under the Fourteenth and Fifteenth Amendments. These so-called **Enforcement Laws** authorized federal prosecutions, military intervention, and martial law to suppress terrorist activity. Grant's administration made full use of these new powers. In South Carolina, where the Klan was deeply entrenched, U.S. troops occupied nine counties, made hundreds of arrests, and drove as many as 2,000 Klansmen from the state.

This assault on the Klan, while raising the spirits of southern Republicans, revealed how dependent they were on Washington. "No such law could be enforced by state authority," one Mississippi Republican observed, "the local power being too weak." But northern Republicans were growing disillusioned with Reconstruction, while in the South, prosecuting Klansmen was an uphill battle against all-white juries and unsympathetic federal judges. After 1872, prosecutions dropped off. Meanwhile, the Texas government fell to the Democrats in 1873 and Alabama and Arkansas fell in 1874.

> **CONSIDER POINTS OF VIEW**
> How did ex-Confederates, freedpeople, Republicans, and classical liberals view the end of Reconstruction?

Reconstruction Rolled Back

As divided Republicans debated how to respond, voters in the congressional election of 1874 handed them one of the most stunning defeats of the nineteenth century. Responding especially to the severe depression that gripped the nation, they removed almost half of the party's 199 representatives in the House. Democrats, who had held 88 seats, now commanded an overwhelming majority of 182. "The election is not merely a victory but a revolution," exulted a Democratic newspaper in New York.

After 1874, with Democrats in control of the House, Republicans who tried to shore up their southern wing had limited options. Bowing to election results, the Grant administration began to reject southern Republicans' appeals for aid. Events in Mississippi showed the outcome. As state elections neared there in 1875, paramilitary

The Impact of Terror

In 1871, thousands of southerners testified before a congressional committee investigating white vigilantism and Ku Klux Klan night-riding in former Confederate states. Their testimony provides a window into the local operations of violence and intimidation. Here, William Coleman, formerly of Winston County, Mississippi, testified to the impact of Klan violence on himself, his family, and his neighbors.

WILLIAM COLEMAN

Testimony on Klan Violence

Source: *Testimony Taken by the Joint Select Committee to Inquire into the Condition of Affairs in the Late Insurrectionary States, Mississippi* (Washington, DC: Government Printing Office, 1872), 1: 482–488.

Macon, Mississippi, November 6, 1871.
William Coleman (colored) sworn and examined.

Q. Where do you live?

A. I live in Macon.

Q. How long have you lived here?

A. I came here about the last of April.

Q. Where did you come from?

A. I came from Winston County.

Q. — What occasioned your coming here?

A. I got run by the Ku-Klux.

Q. Give the particulars to the committee.

A. Give the particulars?

Q. Tell how it occurred. . . .

A. Well, I don't know anything that I had said or done that injured any one, further than being a radical, . . . I had done bought my land and paid for it, and I had . . . — eighteen head of hogs to kill this fall. I had twelve head of sheep, and one good milk-cow, and a yearling, and the cow had a right young calf again, and I had my mule and my filly, and all of it was paid for but my mule. . . . The mule cost me $65, and I had him hired out to pay for him. . . .

Q. Did any of the Ku-Klux come to your house?

A. They did.

Q. In the night-time?

A. They came about a half hour or more before day, as nigh as I can recollect. . . . When they busted the door open, coming in shooting, I was frightened, and I can only tell you as nigh as my recollection will afford. . . .

I jumped up and said, "Hallo." Then one at the door said, "Raise a light in there." "What for; who is you?" I said. . . . He says, "God damn you, we didn't come to tell you who we are." I was peeping through the little crack in the door. . . . I saw men out there standing with horns and faces [masks] on all of them, and they all had great, long white cow-tails way down the breast. . . . They told me they rode from Shiloh in two hours, and came to kill me. . . . They shot right smart in that house before they got in, but how many times I don't know, they shot so fast outside; but when they come in, they didn't have but three loads to shoot. . . . I dashed about among them, but they knocked me down several times. Every time I would get up, they would knock me down again. I saw they were going to kill me. . . . I grabbed my ax-handle, and commenced fighting, and then they just took and cut me with knives. They surrounded me in the floor and took my shirt off. They got me out on the floor; some had me by the legs and some by the arms and the neck and anywhere, just like dogs string out a coon, and they took me out to the big road before my gate and whipped me until I couldn't move or holler or do nothing, but just lay there. . . . They left me there for dead, and what it was done for was because I was a radical, and I didn't deny my profession anywhere and I never will. I never will vote that conservative ticket if I die.

Q. Did they tell you they whipped you because you were a radical?

A. They told me, "God damn you, when you meet a white man in the road lift your hat; I'll learn you, God damn you, that you are a nigger, and not to be going about like you thought yourself a white man. . . ." [I believe it was] because I had my filly; I had bought her to ride, not to stay in the stable, but to ride when I got ready, like you would do with your property. When I bought her I bought her for $75; she was not nigh grown; a little thing, with flaxen mane and tail, and light cream-color. . . .

Q. Were you working on your own land?

A. Yes sir; that I bought and paid for; $473 for it.

Q. How many men were concerned in beating you?

A. Eight men.

Q. Were they all disguised?

A. Yes sir; every one of them. . . .

Q. Did you know any one that night?

A. Of course I did. I ought to know them, my neighbors; and I knocked off the faces [masks] and horns fighting . . . [and saw one without his mask]; of course I knowed him. I would know him again except it was his ashes. . . .

Q. They said they came from Shiloh? . . . Did they say they were the spirits of the confederate dead?

A. They didn't tell me nothing about spirits. . . .

Q. When was Nathan Cannon whipped?

A. He was whipped last year. . . . I went one night to stay with him to go to church [but came late and saw night-riders] stripping him and beating him and knocking him about with pistols. . . . They whipped him about an hour before he started to holler, and when he started to holler "murder, murder" — every word was murder — I just jumped on my filly and started for home. . . . I wouldn't tell my wife about it, for fear she would get so uneasy and be tore up in mind, and I didn't tell it, but somebody told it. . . .

Q. Was he badly whipped?

A. He never worked none, to my recollection, in five weeks. . . .

Q. Have you known any teachers of colored schools to be interfered with?

A. Peter Cooper was run from there a short time after I was. He is down here making shoes.

Q. Was he a teacher of a colored school?

A. Yes, sir; they burned up his books and took several dollars of money from him. I know they got $23 from him that night. . . .

Q. Do you know of any colored churches or schools being burned down?

A. There was only one school-house that I ever knew burned down. They teached in it about a week.

Q. Was it a school for colored children?

A. Yes, sir. . . .

Q. Did you ever hear of any colored people sleeping out of their houses in that county?

A. I have heard it and done it myself.

Q. Why?

A. Because I was afraid to stay in my own house. . . . I have left my house and told my wife to stay in there, for they don't hurt women unless some of the women is sassy to some of their wives, or speak like a white woman, and they call that sass; then they go and whip them nearly to death; but I knew my wife wouldn't say nothing. . . .

Q. Do you think that colored people feel afraid of personal harm and violence in that country?

A. Yes, sir, they do . . . and you would, too, if you were most devoured with devils like that. . . . Here is a knot on my head they did to me that night, [indicating,] and here is one in the edge of my ear, the whole width of the stick, and a long hole over here, in the back of my head. When they took me out of the house I was as bloody as a hog that had been knocked down and stuck in a hog-pen and wallered in his own blood. . . . They meant to beat me to death. . . .

Q. Are you afraid to go back there?

A. . . . My life is better to me than anything there. I would not go back there if there was gold there higher than one of these pines.

QUESTIONS FOR ANALYSIS

1. In this testimony, what achievements does Coleman describe in his life and work in the six years since emancipation? What does this tell us about African Americans' priorities and strategies when freedom came?

2. What does his testimony reveal about the tactics and motivations of night-riders?

3. How does Coleman describe the impact of the riders' violence on his life and those of his neighbors and community? How do you think Winston County was different after the vigilantes had done their work?

4. Coleman and his wife adopted different strategies for dealing with Klan violence. Imagine a conversation between them about how to respond when night-riders came to the door. What were the advantages and dangers of each approach?

groups such as the Red Shirts operated openly. Mississippi's Republican governor, Adelbert Ames, a Union veteran from Maine, appealed for U.S. troops, but Grant refused. "The whole public are tired out with these annual autumnal outbreaks in the South," complained a Grant official, who told southern Republicans that they were responsible for their own fate. Facing a rising tide of brutal murders, Governor Ames — realizing that only further bloodshed could result — urged his allies to give up the fight. Brandishing guns and stuffing ballot boxes, Democratic "Redeemers" swept the 1875 elections and took control of Mississippi. By 1876, Reconstruction was largely over. Republican governments, backed by token U.S. military units, remained in only three southern states: Louisiana, South Carolina, and Florida. Elsewhere, former Confederates and their allies took power.

The Supreme Court Rejects Equal Rights   Though ex-Confederates seized power in southern states, new landmark constitutional amendments and federal laws remained in force. If the Supreme Court had left these intact, subsequent generations of civil rights advocates could have used the federal courts to combat racial discrimination and violence. Instead, the Court closed off this avenue for the pursuit of justice, just as it dashed the hopes of women's rights advocates.

As early as 1873, in a group of decisions known collectively as the ***Slaughter-House Cases***, the Court began to undercut the power of the Fourteenth Amendment. In *Slaughter-House* and a related ruling, *U.S. v. Cruikshank* (1876), the justices argued that the Fourteenth Amendment offered only a few, rather trivial federal protections to citizens (such as access to navigable waterways). In *Cruikshank* — a case that emerged from a gruesome killing of African American farmers by ex-Confederates in Colfax, Louisiana, followed by a Democratic political coup — the Court ruled that voting rights remained a state matter unless the state itself violated those rights. If former slaves' rights were violated by individuals or private groups (including the Klan), that lay beyond federal jurisdiction. The Fourteenth Amendment did not protect citizens from armed vigilantes, even when those vigilantes seized political power. The Court thus gutted the Fourteenth Amendment. In the ***Civil Rights Cases*** (1883), the justices also struck down the Civil Rights Act of 1875, paving the way for later decisions that sanctioned segregation. The impact of these decisions endured well into the twentieth century.

The Political Crisis of 1877

After the grim election results of 1874, Republicans faced a major battle in the presidential election of 1876. Abandoning Grant, they nominated Rutherford B. Hayes, a former Union general who was untainted by corruption and — even more important — hailed from the key swing state of Ohio. Hayes's Democratic opponent was New York governor Samuel J. Tilden, a Wall Street lawyer with a reform reputation. Tilden favored home rule for the South, but so, more discreetly, did Hayes. With enforcement on the wane, Reconstruction did not figure prominently in the campaign, and little was said about the states still led by Reconstruction governments: Florida, South Carolina, and Louisiana.

Once returns started coming in on election night, however, those states loomed large. Tilden led in the popular vote and seemed headed for victory until sleepless politicians at Republican headquarters realized that the electoral vote stood at 184 to 165, with the 20 votes from Florida, South Carolina, and Louisiana still uncertain. If Hayes took those votes, he would win by a margin of 1. Citing ample evidence of Democratic fraud and intimidation, Republican officials certified all three states for Hayes. "Redeemer" Democrats who had taken over the states' governments submitted their own electoral votes for Tilden. When Congress met in early 1877, it confronted two sets of electoral votes from those states.

The Constitution does not provide for such a contingency. All it says is that the president of the Senate (in 1877, a Republican) opens the electoral certificates before the House (Democratic) and the Senate (Republican) and "the Votes shall then be counted" (Article 2, Section 1). Suspense gripped the country. There was talk of inside deals or a new election — even a violent coup. Finally, Congress appointed an electoral commission to settle the question. The commission included seven Republicans, seven Democrats, and, as the deciding member, David Davis, a Supreme Court justice not known to have fixed party loyalties. Davis, however, disqualified himself by accepting an Illinois Senate seat. He was replaced by Republican justice Joseph P. Bradley, and by a vote of 8 to 7, on party lines, the commission awarded the election to Hayes.

In the House of Representatives, outraged Democrats vowed to stall the final count of electoral votes so as to prevent Hayes's inauguration on March 4. But in the end, they went along, partly because Tilden himself urged that they do so. Hayes had publicly indicated his desire to offer substantial patronage to the South, including federal funds for education and internal improvements. He promised "a complete change of men and policy," naively hoping he could count on support from old-line southern Whigs and protect black voting rights. Hayes was inaugurated on schedule. He expressed hope in his inaugural address that the federal government could serve "the interests of both races carefully and equally." But, setting aside the U.S. troops who were serving on border duty in Texas, only 3,000 Union soldiers remained in the South. As soon as the new president ordered them back to their barracks, the last Republican administrations in the South collapsed. Reconstruction had ended.

Lasting Legacies

In the short run, the political events of 1877 had little impact on most southerners. Much of the work of "Redemption" had already been done. What mattered was the long, slow decline of Radical Republican power and the corresponding rise of Democrats in the South and nationally. It was obvious that so-called Redeemers in the South had assumed power through violence. But many Americans, including prominent classical liberals who shaped public opinion, believed the Democrats had overthrown corrupt, illegitimate governments. Thus the end justified the means. After 1874, those who deplored the results had little political traction. The only remaining question was how far Reconstruction would be rolled back.

The South never went back to the antebellum status quo. Sharecropping, for all its flaws and injustices, was not slavery. Freedmen and freedwomen managed to resist gang labor and work on their own terms. They also established their right to marry, read and write, worship as they pleased, and travel in search of a better life — rights that were not easily revoked. Across the South, black farmers overcame great odds to buy and work their own land. African American businessmen built thriving enterprises. Black churches and community groups sustained networks of mutual aid. Parents sacrificed to send their children to school, and a few proudly watched their sons and daughters graduate from college.

Reconstruction had also shaken, if not fully overturned, the legal and political framework that had made the United States a white man's country. This was a stunning achievement, and though hostile courts and political opponents undercut it, no one ever repealed the Thirteenth, Fourteenth, or Fifteenth Amendments. They remained in the Constitution, and the civil rights movement of the twentieth century would return and build on this framework (Chapter 26).

Still, in the final reckoning, Reconstruction failed. The majority of freedpeople remained in poverty, and by the late 1870s their political rights were also eroding. Vocal advocates of smaller government argued that Reconstruction had been a mistake; pressured by economic hardship, northern voters abandoned their southern Unionist allies.

The South's "Lost Cause"

After Reconstruction ended, many white southerners celebrated the Confederacy as a heroic "Lost Cause." Through organizations such as the Sons of Confederate Veterans and United Daughters of the Confederacy, they profoundly influenced the nation's memories of slavery, the Civil War, and Reconstruction.

1. **Commemorative postcard of living Confederate flag, Robert E. Lee Monument, Richmond, Virginia, 1907.** *An estimated 150,000 people gathered in 1890 to dedicate this statue — ten times more than had attended earlier memorial events.*

Source: The Library of Virginia.

2. **From the United Daughters of the Confederacy Constitution, 1894.** *The United Daughters of the Confederacy (UDC), founded in 1894, grew in three years to 136 chapters and by the late 1910s counted a membership of 100,000.*

The objects of this association are historical, educational, memorial, benevolent, and social: To fulfill the duties of sacred charity to the survivors of the war and those dependent on them; to collect and preserve material for a truthful history of the war; to protect historic places of the Confederacy; to record the part taken by the Southern women . . . in patient endurance of hardship and patriotic devotion during the struggle; to perpetuate the memory of our Confederate heroes and the glorious cause for which they fought; to cherish the ties of friendship among members of this Association; to endeavor to have used in all Southern schools only such histories as are just and true.

3. **McNeel Marble Co. advertisement in *Confederate Veteran* magazine, 1905.**

To the Daughters of the Confederacy: In regard to that Confederate monument which your Chapter has been talking about and planning for since you first got organized. Why not buy it NOW and have it erected before all the old veterans have answered the final roll call? Why wait and worry about raising funds? Our terms to U.D.C. Chapters are so liberal and our plans for raising funds are so effective as to obviate the necessity of either waiting or worrying. During the last three or four years we have sold Confederate monuments to thirty-seven of your sister Chapters. . . . Our designs, our prices, our work, our business methods have pleased them, and we can please you. What your sister Chapters have done, you can do. . . . WRITE TO-DAY.

4. **Confederate veteran's letter, *Confederate Veteran* magazine, 1910.** *An anonymous Georgian who had served in Lee's army sent the following letter to the veterans' magazine after attending a reunion in Memphis.*

Reunion gatherings are supposed to be for the benefit of the old veterans; but will you show us where the privates, the men who stood the hardships and did the fighting, have any consideration when they get to the city that is expected to entertain them? . . . [In Memphis, I] stopped at the school building, where there were at least twenty-five or thirty old veterans lying on the ground, and had been there all night. All this while the officers were being banqueted, wined, dined, and quartered in the very best hotels; but the private must shift for himself, stand

One of the enduring legacies of this process was the way later Americans remembered Reconstruction itself. After "Redemption," generations of schoolchildren were taught that ignorant, lazy blacks and corrupt whites had imposed illegitimate Reconstruction "regimes" on the South. White southerners won national support for their celebration of a heroic Confederacy (Thinking Like a Historian).

One of the first historians to challenge these views was the great African American intellectual W. E. B. Du Bois. In *Black Reconstruction in America* (1935), Du Bois meticulously documented the history of African American struggle, white vigilante violence, and national policy failure. If Reconstruction, he wrote, "had been conceived as a major national program . . . whose accomplishment at any price was well worth the effort, we should be living today in a different world." His words still ring true, but around on the street, or sit on the curbstone. He must march if he is able, but the officers ride in fine carriages. Pay more attention to the men of the ranks — men who did service! I always go prepared to pay my way; but I do not like to be ignored.

5. **Matthew Page Andrews, *The Women of the South in War Times*, 1923.** *Matthew Page Andrews's* The Women of the South in War Times, *approved by the UDC, was a popular textbook for decades in schools throughout the South.*

The Southern people of the "old regime" have been pictured as engaged primarily in a protracted struggle for the maintenance of negro slavery. . . . Fighting on behalf of slavery was as far from the minds of these Americans as going to war in order to free the slaves was from the purpose of Abraham Lincoln, whose sole object, frequently expressed by him, was to "preserve the Union." . . .

That, in the midst of war, there were almost no instances of arson, murder, or outrage committed by the negroes of the South is an everlasting tribute to the splendid character of the dominant race and their moral uplift of a weaker one. . . . When these negroes were landed on American shores, almost all were savages taken from the lowest forms of jungle life. It was largely the women of the South who trained these heathen people, molded their characters, and, in the second and third generations, lifted them up a thousand years in the scale of civilization.

6. **Susie King Taylor, *Reminiscences of My Life in Camp with the 33d United States Colored Troops, Late 1st S.C. Volunteers*, 1902.** *Susie King Taylor, born in slavery in Georgia in 1848, fled with her uncle during the Civil War and served as a nurse in the Union army.*

I read an article, which said the ex-Confederate Daughters had sent a petition to the managers of the local theatres in Tennessee to prohibit the performance of "Uncle Tom's Cabin," claiming it was exaggerated (that is, the treatment of the slaves), and would have a very bad effect on the children who might see the drama. I paused and thought back a few years of the heartrending scenes I have witnessed. . . . I remember, as if it were yesterday, seeing droves of negroes going to be sold,

and I often went to look at them, and I could hear the auctioneer very plainly from my house, auctioning these poor people off.

Do these Confederate Daughters ever send petitions to prohibit the atrocious lynchings and wholesale murdering and torture of the negro? Do you ever hear of them fearing this would have a bad effect on the children? Which of these two, the drama or the present state of affairs, makes a degrading impression upon the minds of our young generation? In my opinion it is not "Uncle Tom's Cabin." . . . It does not seem as if our land is yet civilized.

SOURCES: (2) *Minutes of the Seventh Annual Meeting of the United Daughters of the Confederacy* (Nashville, TN: Press of Foster & Webb, Printers, 1901), 235; (3) *Confederate Veteran*, 1905; (4) *Confederate Veteran*, Vol. XVIII (Nashville, TN: S. A. Cunningham, 1910); (5) Matthew Page Andrews, ed., *The Women of the South in War Times* (Baltimore: The Norman, Remington Co., 1923), 3–4, 9–10; (6) Susie King Taylor, *Reminiscences of My Life in Camp* (Boston: Published by the author, 1902), 65–66.

ANALYZING THE EVIDENCE

1. What do sources 2 and 3 tell us about the work of local UDC chapters? What does the advertisement suggest about the economy of the postwar South?

2. What can you infer from these sources about the situation in the South after the Civil War? Why might women have played a particularly important role in memorial associations?

3. Compare and contrast sources 4 and 6. Who did "Lost Cause" associations serve, and how is this connected to issues of class and race?

4. How does source 5 depict slaves? Slaveholders? Is this an accurate account of the history of the South, and how does this compare to source 4? What do these different interpretations suggest about the legacy of "Redemption"?

PUTTING IT ALL TOGETHER

"Lost Cause" advocates often stated that their work was not political. To what extent was this true, based on the evidence here? What do these documents suggest about the influence of the Lost Cause, and also the limitations and challenges it faced? What do they tell us about the legacies of Reconstruction more broadly?

in 1935 historians ignored him. Not a single scholarly journal reviewed Du Bois's important book. Ex-Confederates had lost the war, but they won control over the nation's memory of Reconstruction.

Meanwhile, though their programs failed in the South, Republicans carried their nation-building project into the West, where their policies helped consolidate a continental empire. There, the federal power that had secured emancipation created the conditions for the United States to become an industrial power and a major leader on the world stage.

IN YOUR OWN WORDS Why and how did federal Reconstruction policies falter in the South?

SUMMARY

Postwar Republicans faced two tasks: restoring rebellious states to the Union and defining the role of emancipated slaves. After Lincoln's assassination, his successor, Andrew Johnson, hostile to Congress, unilaterally offered the South easy terms for reentering the Union. Exploiting this opportunity, southerners adopted oppressive Black Codes and put ex-Confederates back in power. Congress impeached Johnson and, though failing to convict him, seized the initiative and placed the South under military rule. In this second, or radical, phase of Reconstruction, Republican state governments tried to transform the South's economic and social institutions. Congress passed innovative civil rights acts and funded new agencies like the Freedmen's Bureau. The Fourteenth Amendment defined U.S. citizenship and asserted that states could no longer supersede it, and the Fifteenth Amendment gave voting rights to formerly enslaved men. Debate over this amendment precipitated a split among women's rights advocates, since women did not win inclusion.

Freedmen found that their goals conflicted with those of Republican leaders, who counted on cotton to fuel economic growth. Like southern landowners, national lawmakers envisioned former slaves as wageworkers, while freedmen wanted their own land. Sharecropping, which satisfied no one completely, emerged as a compromise suited to the needs of the cotton market and an impoverished, credit-starved region.

Nothing could reconcile ex-Confederates to Republican government, and they staged a violent counterrevolution in the name of white supremacy and "Redemption." Meanwhile, struck by a massive economic depression, northern voters handed Republicans a crushing defeat in the election of 1874. By 1876, Reconstruction was dead. Rutherford B. Hayes's narrow victory in the presidential election of that year resulted in withdrawal of the last Union troops from the South. A series of Supreme Court decisions also undermined the Fourteenth Amendment and civil rights laws, setting up legal parameters through which, over the long term, disenfranchisement and segregation would flourish.

CHAPTER 14 REVIEW

TERMS TO KNOW   *Identify and explain the significance of each term below.*

Key Concepts and Events

Ten Percent Plan (p. 434)

Wade-Davis Bill (p. 434)

Black Codes (p. 435)

Freedmen's Bureau (p. 435)

Civil Rights Act of 1866 (p. 435)

Fourteenth Amendment (p. 436)

Reconstruction Act of 1867 (p. 437)

Fifteenth Amendment (p. 439)

American Woman Suffrage Association (p. 440)

National Woman Suffrage Association (p. 440)

Minor v. Happersett (p. 440)

Beecher-Tilton scandal (p. 440)

sharecropping (p. 444)

convict leasing (p. 448)

Civil Rights Act of 1875 (p. 450)

classical liberalism (p. 451)

Crédit Mobilier (p. 452)

Ku Klux Klan (p. 453)

Enforcement Laws (p. 453)

Slaughter-House Cases (p. 456)

Civil Rights Cases (p. 456)

Key People

Andrew Johnson (p. 434)

Charles Sumner (p. 437)

Thaddeus Stevens (p. 437)

Ulysses S. Grant (p. 437)

Elizabeth Cady Stanton (p. 439)

Victoria Woodhull (p. 440)

Robert Smalls (p. 447)

Blanche K. Bruce (p. 447)

Nathan Bedford Forrest (p. 452)

REVIEW QUESTIONS

Answer these questions to demonstrate your understanding of the chapter's main ideas.

1. What factors explain how Reconstruction policies unfolded between 1865 and 1870, and what was the impact on different groups of Americans?

2. What goals were southern freedmen and freedwomen able to achieve in the post–Civil War years, and why? What goals were they not able to achieve, and why not?

3. Why and how did federal Reconstruction policies falter in the South?

4. Look again at the events listed under "American and National Identity" on the thematic timeline on page 364. Some historians have argued that, during this era, the United States moved, politically and socially, from being a loose union of states to being a more unified and inclusive *nation*. To what extent do you agree? Use the events of Reconstruction as evidence in making your case.

MAKING CONNECTIONS

Recognize the larger developments and continuities within and across chapters by answering these questions.

1. Ex-Confederates were not the first Americans to engage in violent protest against what they saw as tyrannical government power. Imagine, for example, a conversation between a participant in Shays's Rebellion (Chapter 6) and a southern Democrat who participated in the overthrow of a Republican government in his state. How would each describe his grievances? Whom would he name as enemies? Compare and contrast the tactics of these and other violent protests against government power in the United States. To what extent did these groups succeed?

2. Return to the image at the start of this chapter (p. 433), which shows a celebration in Baltimore after ratification of the Fifteenth Amendment. Note the various activities depicted as representations of the impact of emancipation and voting rights for black men. How might an African American family at the time have understood the image? What about a southern white family opposed to the Fifteenth Amendment?

KEY TURNING POINTS

Refer to the chapter chronology on page 434 for help in answering the question below.

Identify two crucial turning points in the course of Reconstruction. What caused those shifts in direction, and what were the results?

15

Conquering a Continent
1860–1890

On May 10, 1869, Americans poured into the streets for a giant party. In big cities, the racket was incredible. Cannons boomed and train whistles shrilled. New York fired a hundred-gun salute at City Hall. Congregations sang anthems, while the less religious gathered in saloons to celebrate with whiskey. Philadelphia's joyful throngs reminded an observer of the day, four years earlier, when news had arrived of Lee's surrender. The festivities were prompted by a long-awaited telegraph message: executives of the Union Pacific and Central Pacific railroads had driven a golden spike at Promontory Point, Utah, linking up their lines. Unbroken track now stretched from the Atlantic to the Pacific. A journey across North America could be made in less than a week.

The first **transcontinental railroad** meant jobs and money. San Francisco residents got right to business: after firing a salute, they loaded Japanese tea on a train bound for St. Louis, marking California's first overland delivery to the East. In coming decades, trade and tourism fueled tremendous growth west of the Mississippi. San Francisco, which in 1860 had handled $7.4 million in imports, increased that figure to $49 million over thirty years. The new railroad would, as one speaker predicted in 1869, "populate our vast territory" and make America "the highway of nations."

The railroad was also a political triumph. Victorious in the Civil War, Republicans saw themselves as heirs to the American System envisioned by antebellum Whigs. They believed government intervention in the economy was the key to nation building. But unlike Whigs, whose plans had met stiff Democratic opposition, Republicans enjoyed a decade of unparalleled federal power. They used it vigorously: U.S. government spending per person, after skyrocketing in the Civil War, remained well above earlier levels. Republicans believed that national economic integration was the best guarantor of lasting peace. As a New York minister declared, the federally supported transcontinental railroad would "preserve the Union."

The minister was wrong on one point. He claimed the railroad was a peaceful achievement, in contrast to military battles that had brought "devastation, misery, and woe." In fact, creating a continental empire caused plenty of woe. Regions west of the Mississippi could only be incorporated if the United States subdued Native peoples and established favorable conditions for international investors — often at great domestic cost. And while conquering the West helped make the United States into an industrial power, it also deepened America's rivalry with European empires and created new patterns of exploitation.

> ## IDENTIFY THE BIG IDEA
>
> **How did U.S. policymakers seek to stimulate the economy and integrate the trans-Mississippi west into the nation, and how did this affect people living there?**

The Great West In the wake of the Civil War, Americans looked westward. Republicans implemented an array of policies to foster economic development in the "Great West." Ranchers, farmers, and lumbermen cast hungry eyes on the remaining lands held by Native Americans. Steamboats and railroads, both visible in the background of this image, became celebrated as symbols of the expanding reach of U.S. economic might. This 1881 promotional poster illustrates the bountiful natural resources to be found out west, as well as the land available for ranching, farming, and commerce. The men in the lower left corner are surveying land for sale. Library of Congress.

CHAPTER CHRONOLOGY

As you read, ask yourself why this chapter begins and ends with these dates and identify the links among related events.

1859	▶ Comstock silver lode discovered in Nevada		1873	▶ United States begins to move to gold standard
1862	▶ Homestead Act		1876	▶ Battle of Little Big Horn
	▶ Dakota Sioux uprising in Minnesota		1877	▶ Nez Perce forcibly removed from ancestral homelands in Northwest
	▶ Morrill Act funds public state universities			▶ *Munn v. Illinois* Supreme Court decision
1864	▶ Sand Creek massacre of Cheyennes in Colorado		1879	▶ Exoduster migration to Kansas
	▶ Yosemite Valley reserved as public park			▶ John Wesley Powell presents *Report on the Lands of the Arid Region of the United States*
1865	▶ Long Drive of Texas longhorns begins		1880s	▶ Rise of the Ghost Dance movement
1866	▶ Fetterman massacre		1885	▶ Sitting Bull tours with Buffalo Bill's Wild West
1868	▶ Burlingame Treaty with China		1886	▶ Dry cycle begins on the plains
1869	▶ Transcontinental railroad completed			▶ Chiricahua Apache leader Geronimo surrenders
	▶ Wyoming women's suffrage		1887	▶ Dawes Severalty Act
1870	▶ Utah women's suffrage		1890	▶ Massacre of Sioux Ghost Dancers at Wounded Knee, South Dakota
1872	▶ General Mining Act			
	▶ Yellowstone National Park created			

The Republican Vision

Reshaping the former Confederacy was only part of Republicans' plan for a reconstructed nation. They remembered the era after Andrew Jackson's destruction of the Second National Bank as one of economic chaos, when the United States had become vulnerable to international creditors and market fluctuations. Land speculation on the frontier had provoked extreme cycles of boom and bust. Failure to fund a transcontinental railroad had left different regions of the country disconnected. This, Republicans believed, had helped trigger the Civil War, and they were determined to set a new direction.

Even while the war raged, Congress made vigorous use of federal power, launching the transcontinental rail project and a new national banking system. Congress also raised the **protective tariff** on a range of manufactured goods, from textiles to steel, and on some agricultural products, like wool and sugar. At federal customhouses in each port, foreign manufacturers who brought merchandise into the United States had to pay import fees. These tariff revenues gave U.S. manufacturers, who did not pay the fees, a competitive advantage in America's vast domestic market.

The economic depression that began in 1873 set limits on Republicans' economic ambitions, just as it hindered their Reconstruction plans in the South. But their policies continued to shape the economy. Though some historians argue that the late nineteenth century was an era of *laissez faire* or unrestrained capitalism, in which government sat passively by, the industrial United States was actually the product of a massive public-private partnership in which government played critical roles.

EXPLAIN CONSEQUENCES

In what ways did Republicans use federal power on the world stage, and in what ways did they continue policies from the pre–Civil War era?

The New Union and the World

The United States emerged from the Civil War with new leverage in its negotiation with European countries, especially Great Britain, whose navy dominated the seas. Britain, which had allowed Confederate raiding ships such as CSS *Alabama* to be built in its shipyards, submitted afterward to arbitration and paid the United States $15.5 million in damages. Flush with victory, many Americans expected more British and Spanish territories to drop into the Union's lap. Senator Charles Sumner proposed, in fact, that Britain settle the *Alabama* claims by handing over Canada.

Such dreams were a logical extension of pre–Civil War conquests, especially in the U.S.-Mexico War. With the coasts now linked by rail, merchants and manufacturers looked across the Pacific, hungry for trade with Asia.

Union victory also increased U.S. economic influence in Latin America. While the United States was preoccupied with its internal war, France had deposed Mexico's government and installed an emperor. On May 5, 1867, Mexico overthrew the French invaders and executed Emperor Maximilian. But while Mexico regained independence, it lay open to the economic designs of its increasingly powerful northern neighbor.

A new model emerged for asserting U.S. power in Latin America and Asia: not by direct conquest, but through trade. The architect of this vision was William Seward, secretary of state from 1861 to 1869 under presidents Abraham Lincoln and Andrew Johnson. A New Yorker of grand ambition and ego, Seward believed, like many contemporaries, that Asia would become "the chief theatre of [world] events" and that commerce there was key to America's prosperity. He urged the Senate to purchase sites in both the Pacific and the Caribbean for naval bases and refueling stations. When Japan changed policy and tried to close its ports to foreigners, Seward dispatched U.S. naval vessels to join those of Britain, France, and the Netherlands in reopening trade by force. At the same time, Seward urged annexation of Hawaii. He also predicted that the United States would one day claim the Philippines and build a Panama canal.

Seward's short-term achievements were modest. Exhausted by civil war, Americans had little enthusiasm for further military exploits. Seward achieved only two significant victories. In 1868, he secured congressional approval for the **Burlingame Treaty** with China, which guaranteed the rights of U.S. missionaries in China and set official terms for the emigration of Chinese laborers, some of whom were already clearing farmland and building railroads in the West. That same year, Seward negotiated the purchase of Alaska from Russia. After the Senate approved the deal, Seward waxed poetic:

Our nation with united interests blest
Not now content to poise, shall sway the rest;
Abroad our empire shall no limits know,
But like the sea in endless circles flow.

Many Americans scoffed at the purchase of Alaska, a frigid arctic tract that skeptics nicknamed "Seward's Icebox." But the secretary of state mapped out a path his Republican successors would follow thirty years later in an aggressive bid for global power.

CHRISTMAS AT WASHINGTON.

Christmas in Washington, 1883 Because high tariffs paid off the Union's Civil War debts with astonishing speed, and because the federal government provided no social services or safety net for workers in the booming economy, politicians in Washington faced a happy problem by the mid-1880s: a surplus. Here, *Puck* depicts congressional leaders dancing around a Christmas tree loaded with the treats they can buy with the extra money — while the taxpayer stands out in the cold. The Granger Collection, New York.

Integrating the National Economy

Closer to home, Republicans focused on transportation infrastructure. Railroad development in the United States began well before the Civil War, with the first locomotives arriving from Britain in the early 1830s. Unlike canals or roads, railroads offered the promise of year-round, all-weather service. Locomotives could run in the dark and never needed to rest, except to take on coal and water. Steam engines crossed high mountains and rocky gorges where pack animals could find no fodder and canals could never reach. West of the Mississippi, railroads opened vast regions for farming, trade, and tourism. A transcontinental railroad executive was only half-joking when he said, "The West is purely a railroad enterprise."

Governments could choose to build and operate railroads themselves or promote construction by private companies. Unlike most European countries, the United States chose the private approach. The federal government, however, provided essential loans, subsidies, and grants of public land. States and localities also lured railroads with offers of financial aid, mainly by buying railroad bonds. Without this aid, rail networks would have grown much more slowly and would probably have concentrated in urban regions. With it, railroads enjoyed an enormous — and reckless — boom. By 1900, virtually no corner of the country lacked rail service (Map 15.1). At the same time, U.S. railroads built across the border into Mexico (America in Global Context).

Railroad companies transformed American capitalism. They adopted a legal form of organization, the corporation, that enabled them to raise private capital in prodigious amounts. In earlier decades, state legislatures had chartered corporations for specific public purposes, binding these creations to government goals and oversight. But over the course of the nineteenth century, legislatures gradually began to allow any business to become a corporation by simply applying for a state charter. Among the first corporations to become large interstate enterprises, private railroads were much freer than earlier companies to do as they pleased. After the Civil War, they received lavish public aid with few strings attached. Their position was like that of American banks in late 2008 after the big federal bailout: even critics acknowledged that public aid to these giant companies was good for the economy, but they observed that it also lent government support to fabulous accumulations of private wealth.

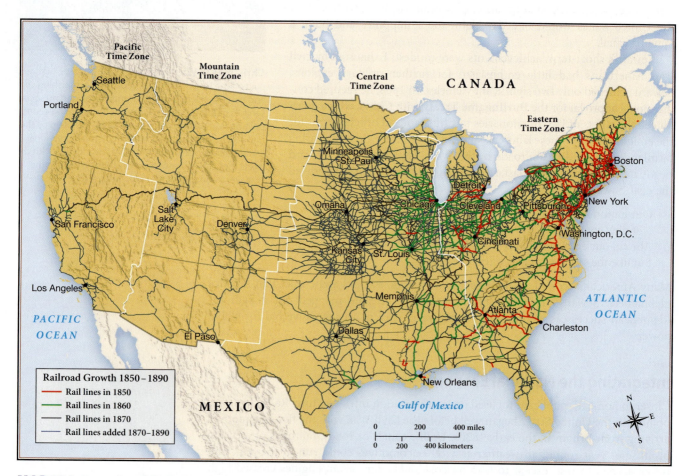

MAP 15.1 Expansion of the Railroad System, 1850–1890

In 1850, the United States had 9,000 miles of rail track; by 1890, it had 167,000 miles, including transcontinental lines terminating in San Francisco, Los Angeles, and Seattle. The tremendous burst of construction during the last twenty years of that period essentially completed the nation's rail network, although there would be additional expansion for the next two decades. The main areas of growth were in the South and in lands west of the Mississippi. Time zones — an innovation introduced not by government entities, but by railroad corporations in 1883 — are marked by the white lines.

Tariffs and Economic Growth   Along with the transformative power of railroads, Republicans' protective tariffs helped build other U.S. industries, including textiles and steel in the Northeast and Midwest and, through tariffs on imported sugar and wool, sugar beet farming and sheep ranching in the West. Tariffs also funded government itself. In an era when the United States did not levy income taxes, tariffs provided the bulk of treasury revenue. The Civil War had left the Union with a staggering debt of $2.8 billion. Tariff income erased that debt and by the 1880s generated huge budget *surpluses*—a circumstance hard to imagine today.

As Reconstruction faltered, tariffs came under political fire. Democrats argued that tariffs taxed American consumers by denying them access to low-cost imported goods and forcing them to pay subsidies to U.S. manufacturers. Republicans claimed, conversely, that tariffs benefitted workers because they created jobs, blocked low-wage foreign competition, and safeguarded America from the kind of industrial poverty that had arisen in Europe. According to this argument, tariffs helped American men earn enough to support their families; wives could devote themselves to homemaking, and children could go to school, not the factory. For protectionist Republicans, high tariffs were akin to the abolition of slavery: they protected and uplifted the most vulnerable workers.

In these fierce debates, both sides were partly right. Protective tariffs did play a powerful role in economic growth. They helped transform the United States into a global industrial power. Eventually, though, even protectionist Republicans had to admit that Democrats had a point: tariffs had not prevented industrial poverty in the United States. Corporations accumulated massive benefits from tariffs but failed to pass them along to workers, who often toiled long hours for low wages. Furthermore, tariffs helped foster trusts, corporations that dominated whole sectors of the economy and wielded near-monopoly power. The rise of large private corporations and trusts generated enduring political problems.

Building the Central Pacific Railroad   In 1865, Chinese workers had labored to build the 1,100-foot-long, 90-foot-high trestle over the divide between the American and Bear rivers at Secret Town in the Sierra Nevada Mountains. In 1877, the Chinese workers shown in this photograph by Carleton Watkins were again at work on the site, burying the trestle to avoid replacement of the aging timbers, which had become a fire hazard. Copyright © Phoebe A. Hearst Museum of Anthropology and the Regents of the University of California, Photography by unknown (Catalog No. 13-1304ee).

The Role of Courts   While fostering growth, most historians agree, Republicans did not give government enough regulatory power over the new corporations. State legislatures did pass hundreds of regulatory laws after the Civil War, but interstate companies challenged them in federal courts. In ***Munn v. Illinois*** (1877), the Supreme Court affirmed that states could regulate key businesses, such as railroads and grain elevators, that were "clothed in the public interest." However, the justices feared that too many state and local regulations would impede business and fragment the national marketplace. Starting in the 1870s, they interpreted the "due process" clause of the new Fourteenth Amendment—which dictated that no state could "deprive any person of life, liberty, or property, without due process of law"—as shielding corporations from excessive regulation. Ironically, the Court refused to use the same amendment to protect the rights of African Americans.

In the Southwest as well, federal courts promoted economic development at the expense of racial justice. Though the United States had taken control of New Mexico and Arizona after the U.S.-Mexico War, much land remained afterward in the hands of Mexican farmers and ranchers. Many lived as *peónes*, under long-standing agreements with landowners who held large tracts originally granted by the Spanish crown. The post–Civil War years brought railroads and an influx of land-hungry Anglos. New Mexico's governor reported indignantly that Mexican shepherds were often "asked" to leave their ranges "by a cowboy or cattle herder with a brace of pistols at his belt and a Winchester in his hands."

The Santa Fe Railroad in Mexico and the United States

This map, based on an 1885 traveler's guide published by the Atchison, Topeka, and Santa Fe Railroad, includes the company's U.S. lines and also those of its Mexican Central Railroad, an ATSF subsidiary that crossed the border and terminated at Guaymas and Mexico City, Mexico. The dots represent the many stops that the trains made along the routes between major cities. Most Mexican railroads in this era were built and operated by U.S. companies. As you analyze this map, consider the significance of imported Mexican raw materials and agricultural products to the U.S. economy.

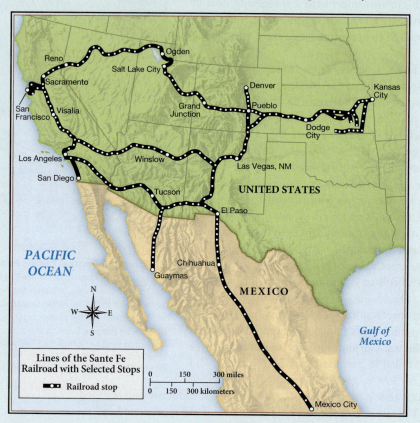

MAP 15.2 The Santa Fe Railroad System, 1885

QUESTIONS FOR ANALYSIS

1. In what directions could passengers and freight travel on ATSF lines in each country? What does this suggest about the objectives of railroad companies like this one?

2. Based on this evidence, how might Mexicans have experienced the arrival of railroads differently from residents of the western United States?

Existing land claims were so complex that Congress eventually set up a special court to rule on land titles. Between 1891 and 1904, the court invalidated most traditional claims, including those of many New Mexico *ejidos*, or villages owned collectively by their communities. Mexican Americans lost about 64 percent of the contested lands. In addition, much land was sold or appropriated through legal machinations like those of a notorious cabal of politicians and lawyers known as the Santa Fe Ring. The result was displacement of thousands of Mexican American villagers and farmers. Some found work as railroad builders or mine workers; others, moving into the sparse high country of the Sierras and Rockies where cattle could not survive, developed sheep raising into a major enterprise.

Silver and Gold In an era of nation building, U.S. and European policymakers sought new ways to rationalize markets. Industrializing nations, for example, tried to develop an international system of standard measurements and even a unified currency. Though these proposals failed as each nation succumbed to self-interest, governments did increasingly agree that, for "scientific" reasons, money should be based on gold, which was thought to have an intrinsic worth above other metals. Great Britain had long held to the **gold standard**, meaning that paper notes from the Bank of England could be backed by gold held in the bank's vaults. During the 1870s and 1880s, the United States, Germany, France, and other countries also converted to gold.

Beforehand, these nations had been on a bimetallic standard: they issued both gold and silver coins, with respective weights fixed at a relative value. The United States switched to the gold standard in part because treasury officials and financiers were watching developments out west. Geologists accurately predicted the discovery of immense silver deposits, such as Nevada's Comstock Lode, without comparable new gold strikes. A massive influx of silver would clearly upset the long-standing ratio. Thus, with a law that became infamous to later critics as the **"Crime of 1873,"** Congress chose gold. It directed the U.S. Treasury to cease minting silver dollars and, over a six-year period, retire Civil War–era greenbacks (paper dollars) and replace them with notes from an expanded system of national banks. After this process was complete in 1879, the treasury exchanged these notes for gold on request. (Advocates of bimetallism did achieve one small victory: the Bland-Allison Act of 1878 required the U.S. Mint to coin a modest amount of silver.)

By adopting the gold standard, Republican policymakers sharply limited the nation's money supply, to the level of available gold. The amount of money circulating in the United States had been $30.35 per person in 1865; by 1880, it fell to only $19.36 per person. Today, few economists would sanction such a plan, especially for an economy growing at breakneck speed. They would recommend, instead, increasing money supplies to keep pace with development. But at the time, policymakers remembered rampant antebellum speculation and the hardships of inflation during the Civil War. The United States, as a developing country, also needed to attract investment capital from Britain, Belgium, and other European nations that were on the gold standard. Making it easy to exchange U.S. bonds and currency for gold encouraged European investors to send their money to the United States.

Republican policies fostered exuberant growth and a breathtakingly rapid integration of the economy. Railroads and telegraphs tied the nation together. U.S. manufacturers amassed staggering amounts of capital and built corporations of national and even global scope. With its immense, integrated marketplace of workers, consumers, raw materials, and finished products, the United States was poised to become a mighty industrial power.

IN YOUR OWN WORDS What federal policies contributed to the rise of America's industrial economy, and what were their results?

Incorporating the West

Republicans wanted farms as well as factories. As early as 1860, popular lyrics hailed the advent of "Uncle Sam's Farm":

> A welcome, warm and hearty, do we give the sons of toil,
> To come west and settle and labor on Free Soil;
> We've room enough and land enough, they needn't feel alarmed —
> Oh! Come to the land of Freedom and vote yourself a farm.

The **Homestead Act** (1862) gave 160 acres of federal land to any applicant who occupied and improved the property. Republicans hoped the bill would help build up the interior West, which was inhabited by Indian peoples but remained "empty" on U.S. government survey maps.

Implementing this plan required innovative policies. The same year it passed the Homestead Act, Congress also created the federal Department of Agriculture and, through the Morrill Act, set aside 140 million federal acres that states could sell to raise money for public universities. The goal of these **land-grant colleges** was to broaden educational opportunities and foster technical and scientific expertise. After the Civil War, Congress also funded a series of geological surveys, dispatching U.S. Army officers, scientists, and photographers to chart unknown western terrain and catalog resources.

To a large extent, these policies succeeded in incorporating lands west of the Mississippi. The United States began to exploit its western empire for minerals, lumber, and other raw materials. But for ordinary Americans who went west, dreams often outran reality. Well-financed corporations, not individual prospectors, reaped most of the profits from western mines, while the Great Plains environment proved resistant to ranching and farming.

MAP 15.3 Mining Frontiers, 1848–1890
The Far West was America's gold country because of its geological history. Veins of gold and silver form when molten material from the earth's core is forced up into fissures caused by the tectonic movements that create mountain ranges, such as the ones that dominate the far western landscape. It was these veins, the product of mountain-forming activity many thousands of years earlier, that prospectors began to discover after 1848 and furiously exploit. Although widely dispersed across the Far West, the lodes that they found followed the mountain ranges bisecting the region and bypassing the great plateaus not shaped by the ancient tectonic activity.

Mining Empires

In the late 1850s, as easy pickings in the California gold rush diminished, prospectors scattered in hopes of finding riches elsewhere. They found gold at many sites, including Nevada, the Colorado Rockies, and South Dakota's Black Hills (Map 15.3). As news of each strike spread, remote areas turned overnight into mob scenes of prospectors, traders, prostitutes, and saloon keepers. At community meetings, white prospectors made their own laws, often using them as an instrument for excluding Mexicans, Chinese, and blacks.

The silver from Nevada's **Comstock Lode**, discovered in 1859, built the boomtown of Virginia City, which soon acquired fancy hotels, a Shakespearean theater, and even its own stock exchange. In 1870, a hundred saloons operated in Virginia City, brothels lined D Street, and men outnumbered women 2 to 1. In the 1880s, however, as the Comstock ore gave out, Virginia City suffered the fate of many mining camps: it became a ghost town. What remained was a ravaged landscape with mountains of debris, poisoned water sources, and surrounding lands stripped of timber.

In hopes of encouraging development of western resources, Congress passed the General Mining Act of 1872, which allowed those who discovered minerals on federally owned land to work the claim and keep all the proceeds. (The law — including the $5-per-acre fee for filing a claim — remains in force today.) Americans idealized the notion of the lone, hardy mining prospector with his pan and his mule, but digging into deep veins of deep ore required big money. Consortiums of powerful investors, bringing engineers and advanced equipment, generally extracted the most wealth. This was the case for the New York trading firm Phelps Dodge, which invested in massive copper mines and smelting operations on both sides of the U.S.-Mexico border. The mines created jobs in new towns like Bisbee and Morenci, Arizona — but with dangerous conditions and low pay, especially for those who received the segregated "Mexican wage." Anglos, testified one Mexican mine worker, "occupied decorous residences . . . and had large amounts of money," while "the Mexican population and its economic condition offered a pathetic contrast." He protested this affront to "the most elemental principles of justice."

The rise of western mining created an insatiable market for timber and produce from the Pacific Northwest. Seattle and Portland grew rapidly as supply centers, especially during the great gold rushes of California (after 1848) and the Klondike in Canada's Yukon Territory (after 1897). Residents of Tacoma, Washington, claimed theirs was the "City of Destiny" when it became the Pacific terminus for the Northern Pacific, the nation's third transcontinental railroad, in 1887. But rival businessmen in Seattle succeeded in promoting their city as the gateway to Alaska and the Klondike. Seattle, a town with 1,000 residents in 1870, grew over the next forty years to a population of a quarter million.

Cattlemen on the Plains

While boomtowns arose across the West, hunters began transforming the plains. As late as the Civil War years, great herds of bison still roamed this region. But overhunting and the introduction of European animal afflictions, like the bacterial disease brucellosis, were already decimating the herds. In the 1870s, hide hunters finished them off so thoroughly that at one point fewer than two hundred bison remained in U.S. territory. Hunters hidden downwind, under the right conditions, could kill four dozen at a time without moving from the spot. They took hides but left the meat to rot, an act of vast wastefulness that shocked Native peoples.

Removal of the bison opened opportunities for cattle ranchers. South Texas provided an early model for their ambitious plans. By the end of the Civil War, about five million head of longhorn cattle grazed on Anglo ranches there. In 1865, the Missouri Pacific Railroad reached Sedalia, Missouri, far enough west to be accessible as Texas reentered the Union. A longhorn worth $3 in Texas might command $40 at Sedalia. With this incentive, ranchers inaugurated the Long Drive, hiring cowboys to herd cattle hundreds of miles north to the new rail lines, which soon extended into Kansas. At Abilene and Dodge City, Kansas, ranchers sold their longhorns and trail-weary cowboys crowded into saloons. These cow towns captured the nation's imagination as symbols of the Wild West, but the reality was much less exciting. Cowboys, many of them African Americans and Latinos, were really farmhands on horseback who worked long, harsh hours for low pay.

North of Texas, public grazing lands drew investors and adventurers eager for a taste of the West. By the early 1880s, as many as 7.5 million cattle were overgrazing the plains' native grasses. A cycle of good weather postponed disaster, which arrived in 1886: record blizzards and bitter cold. An awful scene of rotting carcasses greeted cowboys as they rode onto the range that spring. Further hit by a severe drought the following summer, the cattle boom collapsed.

Thanks to new strategies, however, cattle ranching survived and became part of the integrated national economy. As railroads reached Texas and ranchers there abandoned the Long Drive, the invention of barbed wire — which

Hydraulic Mining, New Dutch Flat, California, 1868   When surface veins of gold played out, miners turned to hydraulic mining, the modern form of which was invented in California in 1853. The technology was simple, using high-pressure streams of water to wash away hillsides of gold-bearing soil. Although building the reservoirs, piping systems, and sluices cost money, the profits from hydraulic mining helped transform western mining into big business. But, as this photograph suggests, extensive hydraulic mining wreaked large-scale havoc on the environment. Library of Congress.

Bison Skulls on the Plain, 1892   After hunters slaughtered millions of bison and left the carcasses to rot, pioneers gathered the skulls and sold them for processing. The destruction of the great bison herds, then, occurred as part of the broad process of industrialization: buffalo leather was converted into belts that operated industrial machinery, while the skulls were ground up for fertilizer or other uses, such as charcoal for sugar manufacture. The Granger Collection, New York.

Cowboys, Real and Mythic As early as the 1860s, popular dime novels such as this one (right) celebrated the alleged ruggedness, individual freedoms, and gun-slinging capabilities of western cowboys. (Note that this 1888 story, like most dime novels, was published in New York.) Generations of young Americans grew up on stories of frontier valor and "Cowboys versus Indians." In fact, cowboys like the ones depicted in the photograph were really wageworkers on horseback. An ethnically diverse group, including many blacks and Hispanics, they earned perhaps $25 a month, plus meals and a bed in the bunkhouse, in return for long hours of grueling, lonesome work. Left: Getty Images. Right: Denver Public Library, Western History Collection/Bridgeman Images.

enabled ranchers and farmers to fence large areas cheaply and easily on the plains, where wood was scarce and expensive — made it easier for northern cattlemen to fence small areas and feed animals on hay. Stockyards appeared beside the rapidly extending railroad tracks, and trains took these gathered cattle to giant slaughterhouses in cities like Chicago, which turned them into cheap beef for customers back east.

Homesteaders

Republicans envisioned the Great Plains dotted with small farms, but farmers had to be persuaded that crops would grow there. Powerful interests worked hard to overcome the popular idea that the grassland was the Great American Desert. Railroads, eager to sell land the government had granted them, advertised aggressively. Land speculators, transatlantic steamship lines, and western states and territories joined the campaign.

Newcomers found the soil beneath the native prairie grasses deep and fertile. Steel plows enabled them to break through the tough roots, while barbed wire provided cheap, effective fencing against roaming cattle. European immigrants brought strains of hard-kernel wheat that tolerated the extreme temperatures of the plains. As if to confirm promoters' optimism, a wet cycle occurred between 1878 and 1886, increasing rainfall in the arid regions east of the Rockies. Americans decided that **"rain follows the plow"**: settlement and farming of the plains was increasing rainfall. Some attributed the rain to soil cultivation and tree planting, while others credited God. One Harvard professor proposed that steel railroad tracks attracted moisture. Such optimists would soon learn their mistake.

The motivation for most settlers, American or immigrant, was to better themselves economically. Union veterans, who received favorable terms in staking homestead claims, played a major role in settling Kansas and other plains states. When severe depression hit northern Europe in the 1870s, Norwegians and Swedes joined German emigrants in large numbers. At the peak of "American fever" in 1882, more than 105,000 Scandinavians left for the United States. Swedish and Norwegian became the primary languages in parts of Minnesota and the Dakotas.

For some African Americans, the plains represented a promised land of freedom. In 1879, a group of black communities left Mississippi and Louisiana in a quest to escape poverty and white violence. Some 6,000 blacks departed together, most carrying little but the clothes on their backs and faith in God. They called themselves **Exodusters**, participants in a great exodus to Kansas. The 1880 census reported 40,000 blacks there, by far the largest African American concentration in the West aside from Texas, where the expanding cotton frontier attracted hundreds of thousands of black migrants.

For newcomers, taming the plains differed from pioneering in antebellum Iowa or Oregon. Dealers sold big new machines to help with plowing and harvesting. Western wheat traveled by rail to giant grain elevators and traded immediately on world markets. Hoping frontier land values would appreciate rapidly, many farmers planned to profit from selling acres as much as (or more than) from their crops. In boom times, many rushed into debt to acquire more land and better equipment. All these enthusiasms — for cash crops, land speculation, borrowed money, and new technology — bore witness to the conviction that farming was, as one agricultural journal remarked, a business "like all other business."

Women in the West Early miners, lumbermen, and cowboys were overwhelmingly male, but homesteading was a family affair. The success of a farm depended on the work of wives and children who tended the garden and animals, preserved food, and helped out at harvest time. Some women struck out on their own: a study of North Dakota found between 5 and 20 percent of homestead claims filed by single women, often working land adjacent to that of sisters, brothers, and parents. Family members thus supported one another in the difficult work of farming, while easing the loneliness many newcomers felt. Looking back with pride on her homesteading days, one Dakota woman said simply, "It was a place to stay and it was mine."

While promoting farms in the West, Republicans clashed with the distinctive religious group that had already settled Utah: Mormons, or members of the Church of Jesus Christ of Latter-day Saints (LDS). After suffering persecution in Missouri and Illinois, Mormons had moved west to Utah in the 1840s, attracting many working-class converts from England as well. Most Americans at the time were deeply hostile to Mormonism, especially the LDS practice of plural marriage — sanctioned by church founder Joseph Smith — through which some Mormon men married more than one wife.

Mormons had their own complex view of women's role, illustrated by the career of Mormon leader Emmeline Wells. Born Emmeline Woodward in New Hampshire, Wells converted to Mormonism at age thirteen along with her mother and joined the exodus to Utah in 1848. After her first husband abandoned her when he left the church, Wells became the seventh wife of church elder Daniel Wells. In 1870, due in part to organized pressure from Wells and other Mormon women, the Utah legislature granted full voting rights to women, becoming the second U.S. territory to do so (after Wyoming, in 1869). The measure increased LDS control, since most Utah women were Mormons, while non-Mormons in mining camps were predominantly male. It also recognized the central role of women in Mormon life.

Amid the constitutional debates of Reconstruction, polygamy and women's voting rights became intertwined issues (Analyzing Voices). Encouraged by other plural wives, Wells began in 1877 to write for a Salt Lake City newspaper, the *Woman's Exponent*. She served as editor for forty years and led local women's rights groups. At first, Utah's

ANALYZING VOICES

Women's Rights in the West

In 1870, Utah's territorial legislature granted voting rights to women. The decision was a shock to advocates of women's suffrage in the East: they expected their first big victories would come in New England. Furthermore, Utah was overwhelmingly peopled by Mormons — members of the Church of Jesus Christ of Latter-day Saints (LDS). Critics saw Mormonism as a harshly patriarchal religion. They especially loathed the Mormon practice of "plural marriage," in which some Mormon men took more than one wife. Most easterners thought this practice was barbaric and demeaning to women. Over the next two decades, Republicans pressured Mormons to abolish plural marriage. They also disenfranchised Mormon women and required men to take an antipolygamy oath; Congress refused to admit Utah as a state. Only after 1890, when the LDS church officially abolished plural marriage, was Utah statehood possible. In 1896, when Utah became a state, women's voting rights were finally reinstated.

FANNY STENHOUSE

Exposé of Polygamy: A Lady's Life Among the Mormons (1872)

An Englishwoman who converted to the faith and moved to Utah, Stenhouse became disillusioned and published her book to criticize the practice of Mormon polygamy.

SOURCE: *Exposé of Polygamy: A Lady's Life Among the Mormons*, ed. Linda Wilcox DeSimone (Logan: Utah State University Press, 2008), 72–73, 155.

❝ How little do the Mormon men of Utah know what it is, in the truest sense, to have a wife, though they have so many 'wives,' after their own fashion. Almost imperceptibly to the husband, and even the wife herself, a barrier rises between them the very day that he marries another woman. It matters not how much she believes in the doctrine of plural marriages, or how willing she may be to submit to it; the fact remains the same. The estrangement begins by her trying to hide from him all secret sorrow; for she feels that what has been can not be undone now, and she says, 'I cannot change it; neither would I if I could, because it is the will of God, and I must bear it; besides, what good will it do to worry my husband with all my feelings?'

. . . A man may have a dozen wives; but from the whole of them combined he will not receive as much real love and devotion as he might from one alone, if he had made her feel that she had his undivided affection and confidence. How terribly these men deceive themselves! When peace, or rather quiet, reigns in their homes, they think that the spirit of God is there. But it is not so! It is a calm, not like the gentle silence of sleep, but as the horrible stillness of death — the death of the heart's best affections, and all that is worth calling love. All true love has fled, and indifference has taken its place. The very children feel it. What do they — what can they care about their fathers? They seldom see them.

Whatever, in the providence of God, may be the action of Congress toward Utah, if the word of a feeble woman can be listened to, let me respectfully ask the Honorable Senators and Representatives of the United States that, in the abolition of Polygamy, if such should be the decree of the nation, let no compromise be made where subtlety can bind the woman now living in Polygamy to remain in that condition. ❞

ELIZA SNOW, HARRIET COOK YOUNG, PHOEBE WOODRUFF

A Defense of Plural Marriage

The vast majority of Mormon women defended their faith and the practice of plural marriage. The statements by Eliza Snow, Harriet Cook Young, and Phoebe Woodruff, below, were made at a public protest meeting in Salt Lake City in 1870. LDS women pointed proudly to their new suffrage rights as proof of their religion's just treatment of women. Why did Mormons, who dominated the Utah legislature, give women full voting rights? In part, they sought to protect their church by increasing Mormon voting power: most of the non-Mormons were single men who worked on ranches or in mining camps. But the LDS Church also celebrated women's central role in the family and community.

legislature blocked Wells's candidacy in a local election, based on her sex. But when Utah won statehood in 1896, Wells had the pleasure of watching several women win seats in the new legislature, including Dr. Martha Hughes Cannon, a physician and Mormon plural wife who became the first American woman to serve in a state senate. Like their counterparts in other western states, Utah's women experienced a combination of severe frontier hardships and striking new opportunities.

Environmental Challenges Homesteaders faced a host of challenges, particularly the natural environment of the Great Plains. Clouds of grasshoppers could descend and destroy a crop in a day; a prairie fire or hailstorm could do the job in an hour. In

474

Some women achieved prominence as midwives, teachers, and professionals.

Source: Edward W. Tullidge, *Women of Mormondom* (New York: Tullidge & Crandall, 1877), 390–391, 396, 400.

66 *Eliza Snow:* Our enemies pretend that, in Utah, woman is held in a state of vassalage — that she does not act from choice, but by coercion — that we would even prefer life elsewhere, were it possible for us to make our escape. What nonsense! We all know that if we wished we could leave at any time — either go singly, or to rise en masse, and there is no power here that could, or would wish to, prevent us. I will now ask this assemblage of intelligent ladies, do you know of anyplace on the face of the earth, where woman has more liberty, and where she enjoys such high and glorious privileges as she does here, as a latter-day saint? No! The very idea of woman here in a state of slavery is a burlesque on good common sense.

Harriet Cook Young: Wherever monogamy reigns, adultery, prostitution and foeticide, directly or indirectly, are its concomitants. . . . The women of Utah comprehend this; and they see, in the principle of plurality of wives, the only safeguard against adultery, prostitution, and the reckless waste of pre-natal life, practiced throughout the land.

Phoebe Woodruff: God has revealed unto us the law of the patriarchal order of marriage, and commanded us to obey it. We are sealed to our husbands for time and eternity, that we may dwell with them and our children in the world to come; which guarantees unto us the greatest blessing for which we are created. If the rulers of the nation will so far depart from the spirit and letter of our glorious constitution as to deprive our prophets, apostles and elders of citizenship, and imprison them for obeying this law, let them grant this, our last request, to make their prisons large enough to hold their wives, for where they go we will go also. 99

SUSAN B. ANTHONY
Letter to *The Revolution*, July 5, 1871

National women's suffrage leaders responded awkwardly to the Utah suffrage victory. Being associated with Mormons, they understood, damaged their fragile new movement in the eyes of most Americans. But they tried tentatively to forge alliances with Mormon women they viewed as progressive, as well as dissidents in the church. Suffrage leader Susan B. Anthony traveled to Salt Lake City in 1871 to try to forge alliances with Mormon women,

especially dissidents such as Fanny Stenhouse. Anthony expressed strong disapproval of polygamy, but she also tried to change the debate to focus on the vulnerability of all married women to exploitation by their husbands. Her report from Utah, published in her journal *The Revolution*, is below.

Source: *The Revolution*, July 20, 1871.

66 Woman's work in monogamy and polygamy is essentially one and the same — that of planting her feet on the solid ground of self-support; . . . there is and can be no salvation for womanhood but in the possession of power over her own subsistence.

The saddest feature here is that there really is nothing by which these women can earn an independent livelihood for themselves and children. No manufacturing establishments; no free schools to teach. Women here, as everywhere, must be able to live honestly and honorably without men, before it can be possible to save the masses of them from entering into polygamy or prostitution, legal or illegal. Whichever way I turn, whatever phase of social life presents itself, the same conclusion comes — independent bread alone can redeem woman from her sure subjection to man. . . .

Here is missionary ground. Not for 'thus saith the Lord,' divine rights, canting priests, or echoing priestesses of any sect whatsoever; but for great, god-like, humanitarian men and women, who 'feel for them in bonds as bound with them,' . . . a simple, loving, sisterly clasp of hands with these struggling women, and an earnest work with them. Not to modify nor ameliorate, but to ABOLISH the whole system of woman's subjection to man in both polygamy and monogamy. 99

QUESTIONS FOR ANALYSIS

1. What arguments did the Mormon women make in defense of plural marriage? On what grounds did Stenhouse argue for its abolition?

2. Susan B. Anthony's letter was published in Boston. How might Mormon women have reacted to it? How might non-Mormon women have reacted to the statements by Snow, Young, and Woodruff?

3. Compare the experiences of plural marriage described by Stenhouse, on the one hand, and Snow, Young, and Woodruff, on the other. How do you account for these very different perspectives?

---

spring, homesteaders faced sudden, terrifying tornados, while their winter experiences in the 1870s added the word *blizzard* to America's vocabulary. On the plains, also, water and lumber were hard to find. Newly arrived families often cut dugouts into hillsides and then, after a season or two, erected houses made of turf cut from the ground.

Over the long term, homesteaders discovered that the western grasslands did not receive enough rain to grow wheat and other grains. As the cycle of rainfall shifted from wet to dry, farmers as well as ranchers suffered. "A wind hot as an oven's fury . . . raged like a pestilence," reported one Nebraskan, leaving "farmers helpless, with no weapon against this terrible and inscrutable wrath of nature." By the late 1880s, some recently

Family on the L. W. Hall Farm, Buffalo County, Nebraska, 1903 This family has moved from its original sod house into a new frame house. Perhaps they asked the photographer to include in his image the windmill, a key to their prosperity. Other photographs on this property, some taken in 1907, show thriving young trees and a woman proudly posed with her new hand-cranked washing machine. How might this family have responded to the argument, made in this textbook chapter and by some critics at the time, that farming was a failure on the arid Great Plains? What different story might they tell about their hardships and successes? Nebraska State Historical Society RG2608-3267. Image cropped slightly from original to remove border.

settled lands emptied as homesteaders fled in defeat — 50,000 from the Dakotas alone. It became obvious that farming in the arid West required methods other than those used east of the Mississippi.

Clearly, 160-acre homesteads were the wrong size for the West: farmers needed either small irrigated plots or immense tracts for dry farming, which involved deep planting to bring subsoil moisture to the roots and quick harrowing after rainfalls to slow evaporation. Dry farming developed most fully on huge corporate farms in the Red River Valley of North Dakota. But even family farms, the norm elsewhere, could not survive on less than 300 acres of grain. Crop prices were too low, and the climate too unpredictable, to allow farmers to get by on less.

In this struggle, settlers regarded themselves as nature's conquerors, striving, as one pioneer remarked, "to get the land subdued and the wilde nature out of it." Much about its "wilde nature" was hidden to the newcomers. They did not know that destroying biodiversity, which was what farming the plains really meant, opened pathways for exotic, destructive pests and weeds, and that removing native grasses left the soil vulnerable to erosion. By the turn of the twentieth century, about half the nation's cattle and sheep, one-third of its cereal crops, and nearly three-fifths of its wheat came from the Great Plains. But in the drier parts of the region, it was not a sustainable achievement. This renowned breadbasket was later revealed to be, in the words of one historian, "the largest, longest-run agricultural and environmental miscalculation in American history."

John Wesley Powell, a one-armed Union veteran, predicted the catastrophe from an early date. Powell, employed by the new U.S. Geological Survey, led a famous expedition in the West in which his team navigated the rapids of the Colorado River through the Grand Canyon in wooden boats. In his *Report on the Lands of the Arid Region of the United States* (1879), Powell told Congress bluntly that 160-acre homesteads would not work in dry regions. Impressed with the success of Mormon irrigation projects in Utah,

Powell urged the United States to follow their model. He proposed that the government develop the West's water resources, building dams and canals and organizing landowners into local districts to operate them. Doubting that rugged individualism would succeed in the West, Powell proposed massive cooperation under government control.

After heated debate, Congress rejected Powell's plan. Critics accused him of playing into the hands of large ranching corporations; boosters were not yet willing to give up the dream of small homesteads. But Powell turned out to be right. Though environmental historians do not always agree with Powell's proposed solutions, they point to his *Report on Arid Lands* as a cogent critique of what went wrong on the Great Plains. Later, federal funding paid for dams and canals that supported intensive agriculture in many parts of the West.

> **COMPARE AND CONTRAST**
> Compare the development of mining, ranching, and farming in the West. How did their environmental consequences differ?

The First National Park

Powell was not the only one rethinking land use. The West's incorporation into the national marketplace occurred with such speed that some Americans began to fear rampant overdevelopment. Perhaps the federal government should not sell off all its public land, but instead hold and manage some of it. Amid the heady initiatives of Reconstruction, Congress began to preserve sites of unusual natural splendor. As early as 1864, Congress gave 10 square miles of the Yosemite Valley to California for "public use, resort, and recreation." (In 1890, Yosemite reverted to federal control.) In 1872, Congress set aside 2 million acres of Wyoming's Yellowstone Valley as the world's first national park: preserved as a public holding, it would serve as "a public park or pleasuring ground for the benefit and enjoyment of the people."

Railroad tourism, which developed side by side with other western industries, was an important motive for the creation of **Yellowstone National Park**. The Northern Pacific Railroad lobbied Congress vigorously to get the park established. Soon, luxury

Thomas Moran, *Grand Canyon of the Yellowstone,* **1872**   In 1871, English-born artist Thomas Moran joined Ferdinand Hayden's expedition to the Yellowstone Valley on behalf of the U.S. Geological Survey, an important new federal agency dedicated to mapping and exploring the West, as well as undertaking scientific investigations of flora, fauna, and potential mineral and timber resources. Moran's painting, along with photographs by William Henry Jackson and other eyewitness testimony to Yellowstone's uniqueness and beauty, helped introduce the American public to their first new national park. The painting remains property of the federal government, who commissioned Hayden's expedition, and hangs in the Smithsonian American Art Museum. Smithsonian American Art Museum, Washington, D.C./Art Resource, NY.

Pullman cars ushered visitors to Yellowstone's hotel, operated by the railroad itself. But creation of the park was fraught with complications. Since no one knew exactly what a "national park" was or how to operate it, the U.S. Army was dispatched to take charge; only in the early 1900s, when Congress established many more parks in the West, did consistent management policies emerge. In the meantime, soldiers spent much of their time arresting Native peoples who sought to hunt on Yellowstone lands.

The creation of Yellowstone was an important step toward an ethic of respect for land and wildlife. So was the 1871 creation of a **U.S. Fisheries Commission**, which made recommendations to stem the decline in wild fish; by the 1930s, it merged with other federal wildlife bureaus to become the U.S. Fish and Wildlife Service. At the same time, eviction of Indians showed that defining small preserves of "uninhabited wilderness" was part of conquest itself. In 1877, for example, the federal government forcibly removed the Nez Perce tribe from their ancestral land in what is now Idaho, Washington, and Oregon. Under the leadership of young Chief Joseph, the Nez Perce tried to flee to Canada. After a journey of 1,100 miles, they were forced to surrender just short of the border. During their trek, five bands crossed Yellowstone; as a Nez Perce named Yellow Wolf recalled, they "knew that country well." For thirteen days, Nez Perce men raided the valley for supplies, waylaying several groups of tourists. The conflict made national headlines. Easterners, proud of their new "pleasuring ground," were startled to find that it remained a site of Native resistance. Americans were not settling an empty West. They were *un*settling it by taking it from Native peoples who already lived there.

IDENTIFY CAUSES
What factors led to the creation of the first national parks?

> **IN YOUR OWN WORDS** What factors led to transformation of the trans-Mississippi west after the Civil War?

A Harvest of Blood: Native Peoples Dispossessed

Before the Civil War, when most Americans believed the prairie could not be farmed, Congress reserved the Great Plains for Indian peoples. But in the era of steel plows and railroads, policymakers suddenly had the power and desire to incorporate the whole region. The U.S. Army fought against the loosely federated Sioux — the major power on the northern grasslands — as well as other peoples who had agreed to live on reservations but found conditions so desperate that they fled (Map 15.4). These "reservation wars," caused largely by local violence and confused federal policies, were messy and bitter. Pointing to failed military campaigns, army atrocities, and egregious corruption in the Indian Bureau, reformers called for new policies that would destroy Native peoples' traditional lifeways and "civilize" them — or, as one reformer put it, "kill the Indian and save the man."

The Civil War and Indians on the Plains

In August 1862, the attention of most Unionists and Confederates was riveted on General George McClellan's failing campaign in Virginia. But in Minnesota, the Dakota Sioux were increasingly frustrated. In 1858, the year Minnesota secured statehood, they had agreed to settle on a strip of land reserved by the government, in exchange for receiving regular payments and supplies. But Indian agents, contractors, and even Minnesota's territorial governor pocketed most of the funds. When the Dakotas protested that their children were starving, state officials dismissed their appeals. Corruption was so egregious that one leading Minnesotan, Episcopal bishop Henry Whipple, wrote an urgent appeal to President James Buchanan. "A nation which sows robbery," he warned, "will reap a harvest of blood."

MAP 15.4 Indian Country in the West, to 1890
As settlement pushed onto the Great Plains after the Civil War, Native peoples put up bitter resistance but ultimately to no avail. Over a period of decades, they ceded most of their lands to the federal government, and by 1890 they were confined to scattered reservations.

Whipple's prediction proved correct. During the summer of 1862, a decade of anger boiled over. In a surprise attack, Dakota fighters fanned out through the Minnesota countryside, killing immigrants and burning farms. They planned to sweep eastward to St. Paul but were stopped at Fort Ridgely. In the end, more than four hundred whites lay dead, including women and children from farms and small towns. Thousands fled; panicked officials telegraphed for aid, spreading hysteria from Wisconsin to Colorado.

Minnesotans' ferocious response to the uprising set the stage for further conflict. A hastily appointed military court, bent on revenge, sentenced 307 Dakotas to death, making it clear that rebellious Indians would be treated as criminals rather than warriors. President Abraham Lincoln reviewed the trial records and commuted most of the sentences but authorized the deaths of 38 Dakota men. They were hanged just after Christmas 1862 in the largest mass execution in U.S. history. Two months later, Congress canceled all treaties with the Dakotas, revoked their annuities, and expelled them from Minnesota. The scattered bands fled west to join nonreservation allies.

As the uprising showed, the Civil War created two dangerous conditions in the West, compounding the problems already caused by corruption. With the Union army fighting the Confederacy, western whites felt vulnerable to Indian attacks. They also

Enclosed Dakota Camp at Fort Snelling, Minnesota, 1862 During the trial of Dakota warriors involved in the 1862 rebellion, and through the harsh Minnesota winter that followed, more than a thousand Dakota people were imprisoned in an enormous enclosure on Pike Island, near St. Paul. A measles epidemic broke out in the crowded camp and dozens died, especially children. Though U.S. soldiers were often unfriendly toward their captives, local sentiment was even more hostile; troops regularly marched through the camp, in part to protect the Dakotas from vigilante violence. In 1863 all members of the tribe were forcibly removed from the state. In November 1862, photographer Benjamin Franklin Upton captured this image of Dakota tents in the Pike Island enclosure. Minnesota Historical Society.

discovered they could fight Indians with minimal federal oversight. In the wake of the Dakota uprising, worried Coloradans favored a military campaign against the Cheyennes — allies of the Sioux — even though the Cheyennes had shown little evidence of hostility. Colorado militia leader John M. Chivington, an aspiring politician, determined to quell public anxiety and make his career.

In May 1864, Cheyenne chief Black Kettle, fearing his band would be attacked, consulted with U.S. agents, who instructed him to settle along Sand Creek in eastern Colorado until a treaty could be signed. On November 29, 1864, Chivington's Colorado militia attacked the camp while most of the men were out hunting, slaughtering more than a hundred women and children. "I killed all I could," one officer testified later. "I think and earnestly believe the Indian to be an obstacle to civilization and should be exterminated." Captain Silas Soule, who served under Chivington but refused to give his men the order to fire, dissented. "It was hard to see little children on their knees," he wrote later, "having their brains beat out by men professing to be civilized." Chivington's men rode back for a celebration in Denver, where they hung Cheyenne scalps (and women's genitals) from the rafters of the Apollo Theater.

The northern plains exploded in conflict. Infuriated by the **Sand Creek massacre**, Cheyennes carried war pipes to the Arapahos and Sioux, who attacked and burned white settlements along the South Platte River. Ordered to subdue these peoples, the U.S. Army failed miserably: officers could not even locate the enemy, who traveled rapidly in small bands and knew the country well. A further shock occurred in December 1866 when 1,500 Sioux warriors executed a perfect ambush, luring Captain William Fetterman and 80 soldiers from a Wyoming fort and wiping them out. With the **Fetterman massacre**, the Sioux succeeded in closing the Bozeman Trail, a private road under army protection that had served as the main route into Montana.

General William Tecumseh Sherman, now commanding the army in the West, swore to defeat defiant Indians. But the Union hero met his match on the plains.

Red Cloud's Bedroom, 1891 Taken on the Pine Ridge Reservation in South Dakota by photographer C. G. Morledge, this photograph shows the bedroom of Red Cloud, a distinguished Oglala Lakota leader. Red Cloud had won a war against the U.S. Army just after the Civil War. He negotiated so tenaciously and shrewdly, afterward, with what he saw as meddlesome Indian agents, that his people nicknamed Pine Ridge "The Place Where Everything Is Disputed." Some of the contents of Red Cloud's bedroom may surprise you. How do you interpret the presence of five American flags? The visual images on the walls? What strategies and ways of life, blending old and new, does the photograph suggest? Compare it to Edward S. Curtis, "Little Plume and Yellow Kidney" (p. 487). In what ways did Morledge and Curtis craft different representations of Indian life? Denver Public Library, Western History Collection/Bridgeman Images.

Another year of fighting proved expensive and inconclusive. In 1868, the Sioux, led by the Oglala band under Chief Red Cloud, told a peace commission they would not sign any treaty unless the United States pledged to abandon all its forts along the Bozeman Trail. The commission agreed. Red Cloud had won.

In the wake of these events, eastern public opinion turned against the Indian wars, which seemed at best ineffective, at worst brutal. Congress held hearings on the slaughter at Sand Creek. Though Chivington, now a civilian, was never prosecuted, the massacre became an infamous example of western vigilantism. By the time Ulysses Grant entered the White House in 1869, the authors of Reconstruction in the South also began to seek solutions to what they called the "Indian problem."

> **IDENTIFY CAUSES**
> What factors led to warfare between whites and Native peoples on the plains?

Grant's Peace Policy

Grant inherited an Indian policy in disarray. Federal incompetence was highlighted by yet another mass killing of friendly Indians in January 1870, this time on the Marias River in Montana, by an army detachment that shot and burned to death 173 Piegans (Blackfeet). Having run out of other options, Grant introduced a peace policy, based on recommendations from Christian advisors. He offered selected appointments to the reformers — including many former abolitionists — who had created such groups as the Indian Rights Association and the Women's National Indian Association (Interpretations).

Rejecting the virulent anti-Indian stance of many westerners, reformers argued that Native peoples had the innate capacity to become equal with whites. They believed, however, that Indians could achieve this only if they embraced Christianity and white ways. Reformers thus aimed to destroy indigenous languages, cultures, and religions. Despite humane intentions, their condescension was obvious. They ignored dissenters like Dr. Thomas Bland of the National Indian Defense Association, who suggested that

What Factors Motivated America's Indian Policies?

In the latter nineteenth century, the U.S. government adopted a number of policies designed to eliminate the "Indian problem" by eliminating the Indian: first through military engagement, then through a program of assimilation. The Dawes Severalty Act of 1887, for example, distributed tribal lands among individual Native Americans to break apart reservations and tribal identities. Indian children were often placed in boarding schools under white supervision, where they learned English and were introduced to Christianity.

Scholars have not always agreed on how to explain the motivations of late-nineteenth-century reformers. Two historians, Francis Paul Prucha and Margaret D. Jacobs, interpret this period and America's Indian policies in different ways.

FRANCIS PAUL PRUCHA

SOURCE: Francis Paul Prucha, *The Indian in American Society: From the Revolutionary War to the Present* (Berkeley: University of California Press, 1985), 19.

The treaty system ended in 1871, when Congress decided that no more treaties would be made with Indian tribes . . . but the paternalism of the federal government toward the Indians continued . . . [under the] Board of Indian Commissioners . . . [which included] a remarkable collection of high-minded Christian philanthropists, suffused with a spirit of benevolence, who epitomized the evangelical religious atmosphere of the nineteenth century. For better or for worse, the American Indians fell into the hands of this group and their successors.

MARGARET D. JACOBS

SOURCE: Margaret D. Jacobs, *White Mother to a Dark Race: Settler Colonialism, Maternalism, and the Removal of Indigenous Children in the American West and Australia, 1880–1940* (Lincoln: University of Nebraska Press, 2009), 25, 88.

[O]fficials often proclaimed that they were ushering in a new age of dealing fairly and kindly with . . . indigenous inhabitants. Yet these new policies actually entailed one of the most draconian measures possible: the removal of indigenous children from their kin . . . to be raised in distant institutions. . . . [I]nstead of watching from the sidelines as male government officials designed and carried out policies of indigenous child removal, many white women reformers campaigned for a greater role in setting public policy for indigenous peoples and became deeply implicated in this phase of settler colonialism.

QUESTIONS FOR ANALYSIS

1. Identify two ways these two historians differ in their description of America's Indian policies.

2. According to these two historians, what role did gender play in shaping policies toward Native Americans?

3. To what extent does this chapter support one or the other of these historians' interpretations of America's Indian policies?

---

instead of an "Indian problem" there might be a "white problem" — refusal to permit Indians to follow their own lifeways. To most nineteenth-century Americans, such a notion was shocking and uncivilized. Increasingly dismissive of blacks' capacity for citizenship and hostile toward "heathen" Chinese immigrants, white Americans were even less willing to understand and respect Indian cultures. They believed that in the modern world, Native peoples were fated for extinction (Thinking Like a Historian).

Indian Boarding Schools Reformers focused their greatest energy on educating the next generation. Realizing that acculturation — adoption of white ways — was difficult when children lived at home, agents and missionaries created off-reservation schools. Native families were exhorted, bullied, and bribed into sending their children to these schools, where, in addition to school lessons, boys learned farming skills and girls practiced housekeeping. "English only" was the rule; students were punished if they spoke their own languages. Mourning Dove, a Salish girl from what is now Washington State, remembered that her school "ran strictly. We never talked during meals without permission, given only on Sunday or special holidays. Otherwise there was silence — a terrible silent silence. I was used to the freedom of the forest, and it was hard to learn this strict discipline. I was punished many times before I learned." The Lakota boy Plenty Kill, who at boarding school received the new name Luther, remembered his loneliness and fear upon arrival: "The big boys would sing brave songs, and that would start the girls to crying. . . . The girls' quarters were about a hundred and fifty yards from ours, so we could hear them." After having his hair cut short, Plenty Kill felt a profound change in his identity. "None of us slept well that night," he recalled. "I felt that I was no more Indian, but would be an imitation of a white man."

Even in the first flush of reform zeal, Grant's policies faced major hurdles. Most Indians had been pushed off traditional lands and assigned to barren ground that would have defeated the most enterprising farmer. Poverty and dislocation left Indians especially vulnerable to the ravages of infectious diseases like measles and scarlet fever. At the same time, Quaker, Presbyterian, and Methodist reformers fought turf battles among themselves and with Catholic missionaries. Many traders and agents also continued to steal money and supplies from people they were supposed to protect. In the late 1870s, Rutherford B. Hayes's administration undertook more housecleaning at the Bureau of Indian Affairs, but corruption lingered.

From the Indians' point of view, reformers often became just another interest group in a crowded field of whites sending hopelessly mixed messages. The attitudes of individual army representatives, agents, and missionaries ranged from courageous and sympathetic to utterly ruthless. Many times, after chiefs thought they had reached a face-to-face agreement, they found it drastically altered by Congress or Washington bureaucrats. Nez Perce leader Joseph observed that "white people have too many chiefs. They do not understand each other. . . . I cannot understand why so many chiefs are allowed to talk so many different ways, and promise so many different things." A Kiowa chief agreed: "We make but few contracts, and them we remember well. The whites make so many they are liable to forget them. The white chief seems not to be able to govern his braves."

Native peoples were nonetheless forced to accommodate, as independent tribal governance and treaty making came to an end. Back in the 1830s, the U.S. Supreme Court had declared Indians no longer sovereign but rather "domestic dependent nations." On a practical basis, however, both the U.S. Senate and agents in the field continued to negotiate treaties as late as 1869. Two years later, the House of Representatives, jealous of Senate privileges, passed a bill to abolish all treaty making with Indians. The Senate agreed, provided that existing treaties remained in force. It was one more step in a long, torturous erosion of Native rights. Eventually, the U.S. Supreme Court ruled in ***Lone Wolf v. Hitchcock*** (1903) that Congress could make whatever Indian policies it chose, ignoring all existing treaties. That same year, in *Ex Parte Crow Dog*, the Court ruled that no Indian was a citizen unless Congress designated him so. Indians were henceforth wards of the government. These rulings remained in force until the New Deal of the 1930s.

Breaking Up Tribal Lands Reformers' most sweeping effort to assimilate Indians was the **Dawes Severalty Act** (1887), the dream of Senator Henry L. Dawes of Massachusetts, a leader in the Indian Rights Association. Dawes saw the reservation system as an ugly relic of the past. Through severalty — division of tribal lands — he hoped to force Indians onto individual landholdings, partitioning reservations into homesteads, just like those of white farmers. Supporters of the plan believed that land-ownership would encourage Indians to assimilate. It would lead, as Dawes wrote, to "a personal sense of independence." Individual property, echoed another reformer, would make the Indian man "intelligently selfish, . . . with a *pocket that aches to be filled with dollars!*"

The Dawes Act was a disaster. It played into the hands of whites who coveted Indian land and who persuaded the government to sell them land that was not needed for individual allotments. In this and other ways, the Bureau of Indian Affairs (BIA)

To see a longer excerpt of Mourning Dove's autobiography, along with other primary sources from this period, see *Sources for America's History*.

Representing Indians

The documents below, designed for white audiences, all depict American Indians in the West.

1. **Buffalo Bill Cody's Wild West advertisement, 1899.** *Cody never called the Wild West a "show," placing tremendous emphasis on its allegedly authentic reenactments of events.*

SOURCE: Library of Congress.

2. **Lewis Henry Morgan, *Ancient Society*, 1877.** *Morgan, a leading American anthropologist, studied the Iroquois and other Native peoples. In 1877 he published an influential theory of human development, ranking various peoples in their "progress" from the "lowest stage of savagery" through the pinnacle of "civilization" — northern Europeans.*

Some tribes and families have been left in geographical isolation to work out the problems of progress. . . . [Others] have been adulterated through external influence. Thus, while Africa was and is an ethnical chaos of savagery and barbarism, Australia and Polynesia were in savagery, pure and simple. . . . The Indian family of America, unlike any other existing family, exemplified the condition of mankind in three successive ethnical periods. . . . The far northern Indians and some of the coast tribes of North and South America were in the Upper Status of savagery; the partially Village Indians east of the Mississippi were in the Lower Status of

Status of Civilization (from Morgan, *Ancient Society*, 1877)	
I. Lower Status of Savagery	From the Infancy of the Human Race to the commencement of the next Period.
II. Middle Status of Savagery	From the acquisition of a fish subsistence and a knowledge of the use of fire . . .
III. Upper Status of Savagery	From the Invention of the Bow and Arrow . . .
IV. Lower Status of Barbarism	From the Invention of the Art of Pottery . . .
V. Middle Status of Barbarism	From the Domestication of animals on the Eastern hemisphere, and in the Western from the cultivation of maize and plants by Irrigation . . .
VI. Upper Status of Barbarism	From the Invention of the process of Smelting Iron Ore, with the use of iron tools . . .
VII. Civilization	From the Invention of writing, to the present time.

barbarism, and the Village Indians of North and South America were in the Middle Status. . . .

Commencing, then, with the Australians and Polynesians, following with the American Indian tribes, and concluding with the Roman and Grecian, who afford the highest exemplifications respectively of the six great stages of human progress, the sum of their united experiences may be supposed fairly to represent that of the human family. . . . We are dealing substantially, with the ancient history and condition of our own remote ancestors.

3. **Touring Indian Country, 1888 and 1894.** *Hoping to lure eastern tourists, the Northern Pacific Railroad published an annual journal,* Wonderland, *describing the natural splendors and economic progress of the West, as seen from its rail lines.*

We are now in the far-famed Yellowstone Valley. . . . There are but few Indians now to be seen along the line of the railroad, and those are engaged in agricultural and industrial pursuits. The extinction of the buffalo has rendered the Indian much more amenable to the civilizing influences brought to bear upon him than he formerly was, and very fair crops of grain are being raised at some of the agencies. At the Devil's Lake agency, for example, 60,000 bushels of wheat have been raised by the [Sioux and Chippewa] Indians in a single season. . . .

[The Crows'] great reservation is probably the garden spot of Montana, and the throwing open of a large portion of it to [white] settlement, which cannot long be delayed, will assuredly give an immense impetus to the agricultural interests of the Territory. . . .

The Flatheads have probably 10,000 or more horses and 5,000 or 6,000 cattle. . . . As ranchers and farmers the Flatheads are a success. It would be a matter of surprise to some people who think that the only good Indian is a dead Indian, to see the way some of the women handle sewing machines.

SOURCES: (2) Lewis H. Morgan, *Ancient Society* (New York: Henry Holt and Company, 1878), 12–13, 16–18; (3) John Hyde, *Wonderland* (St. Paul, 1888), 21, and (1894), 27.

4. **Gertrude Käsebier, photograph of Joe Black Fox, 1898.** *One of the first women to become a professional photographer, Käsebier here depicts Joe Black Fox relaxing with a cigarette. Black Fox, an Oglala Sioux, toured with Buffalo Bill's Wild West in 1900.*

SOURCE: Photographic History Collection, National Museum of American History, Smithsonian Institution.

ANALYZING THE EVIDENCE

1. Compare the depiction of the Plains Indians and Buffalo Bill Cody in source 1. How does source 4 differ from source 1? From Edward Curtis's depiction of Little Plume and Yellow Kidney (p. 487), in which all traces of modern life were erased? How might these depictions of "actual life" have shaped their audience's understanding of the West?

2. What bases did Morgan use for his rankings in source 2? How did he define the relationship between American Indians and whites (whom he refers to, in this passage, as "we")? Why did he suggest that Indians offered a unique opportunity for study?

3. Imagine that you were a wealthy, well-educated tourist preparing to travel west in 1900. Which of these documents would you most likely have encountered in advance? How might they have shaped your expectations and experiences?

4. These documents had different creators: an artist, a scholar, and two sets of entrepreneurs. What audiences did they have in mind? How do you think this affected their messages?

PUTTING IT ALL TOGETHER

Using these sources and your knowledge of the period, analyze the myths and realities of Native American life in the late nineteenth century.

CONSIDER POINTS OF VIEW
How did post–Civil War reformers believe they were improving U.S. Indian policies, and in what ways did that prove to be true and untrue?

implemented the law carelessly, to the outrage of Dawes. In Indian Territory, a commission seized more than 15 million "surplus" acres from Native tribes by 1894, opening the way for whites to convert the last federal territory set aside for Native peoples into the state of Oklahoma. In addition to catastrophic losses of collectively held property, Native peoples lost 66 percent of their individually allotted lands between the 1880s and the 1930s, through fraud, BIA mismanagement, and pressure to sell to whites.

The End of Armed Resistance

As the nation consolidated control of the West in the 1870s, Americans hoped that Grant's peace policy was solving the "Indian problem." In the Southwest, such formidable peoples as the Kiowas and Comanches had been forced onto reservations. The Diné or Navajo nation, exiled under horrific conditions during the Civil War but permitted to reoccupy their traditional land, gave up further military resistance. An outbreak among California's Modoc people in 1873 — again, humiliating to the army — was at last subdued. Only Sitting Bull, a leader of the powerful Lakota Sioux on the northern plains, openly refused to go to a reservation. When pressured by U.S. troops, he repeatedly crossed into Canada, where he told reporters that "the life of white men is slavery. . . . I have seen nothing that a white man has, houses or railways or clothing or food, that is as good as the right to move in open country and live in our own fashion."

In 1874, the Lakotas faced direct provocation. Lieutenant Colonel George Armstrong Custer, a brash self-promoter who had graduated last in his class at West Point, led an expedition into South Dakota's Black Hills and loudly proclaimed the discovery of gold. Amid the severe depression of the 1870s, prospectors rushed in. The United States, wavering on its 1868 treaty, pressured Sioux leaders to sell the Black Hills. The chiefs said no. Ignoring this answer, the government demanded in 1876 that all Sioux gather at the federal agencies. The policy backfired: not only did Sitting Bull refuse to report, but other Sioux, Cheyennes, and Arapahos slipped away from reservations to join him. Knowing they might face military attack, they agreed to live together for the summer in one great village numbering over seven thousand people. By June, they were camped on the Little Big Horn River in what is now southeastern Montana. Some of the young men wanted to organize raiding parties, but elders counseled against it. "We [are] within our treaty rights as hunters," they argued. "We must keep ourselves so."

The U.S. Army dispatched a thousand cavalry and infantrymen to drive the Indians back to the reservation. Despite warnings from experienced scouts — including Crow Indian allies — most officers thought the job would be easy. Their greatest fear was that the Indians would manage to slip away. But amid the nation's centennial celebration on the Fourth of July 1876, Americans received dreadful news. On June 26 and 27, Lieutenant Colonel Custer, leading the 7th Cavalry as part of a three-pronged effort to surround the Indians, had led 210 men in an ill-considered assault on Sitting Bull's camp. The Sioux and their allies had killed the attackers to the last man. "The Indians," one Oglala woman remembered, "acted just like they were driving buffalo to a good place where they could be easily slaughtered."

As retold by the press in sensational (and often fictionalized) accounts, the story of Custer's "last stand" quickly served to justify American conquest of Indian "savages." Long after Americans forgot the massacres of Cheyenne women and children at Sand Creek and of Piegan people on the Marias River, prints of the **Battle of Little Big Horn** hung in barrooms across the country. William F. "Buffalo Bill" Cody, in his traveling Wild West performances, enacted a revenge killing of a Cheyenne man named Yellow Hand in a tableau Cody called "first scalp for Custer." Notwithstanding that the tableau featured a white man scalping a Cheyenne, Cody depicted it as a triumph for civilization.

Little Big Horn proved to be the last military victory of Plains Indians against the U.S. Army. Pursued relentlessly after Custer's death and finding fewer and fewer bison to sustain them, Sioux parents watched their children starve through a bitter

Little Plume and Yellow Kidney Photographer Edward S. Curtis took this photograph of the Piegan (Blackfeet) leader Little Plume and his son Yellow Kidney. Curtis's extensive collection of photographs of Native Americans remains a valuable resource for historians. However, Curtis altered his images to make his Native subjects seem more "authentic": though Indians made widespread use of nonnative furniture, clothes, and other consumer goods (such as Singer sewing machines), Curtis removed those from the frame. He also retouched photographs to remove items such as belts and watches. Note the circular "shadow" here, against the lodge wall, near Little Plume's right arm: the original photograph included a clock. Library of Congress.

winter. Slowly, families trickled into the agencies and accommodated themselves to reservation life (Map 15.5). The next year, the Nez Perces, fleeing for the Canadian border, also surrendered. The final holdouts fought in the Southwest with Chiricahua Apache leader Geronimo. Like many others, Geronimo had accepted reservation life but found conditions unendurable. Describing the desolate land the tribe had been allotted, one Apache said it had "nothing but cactus, rattlesnakes, heat, rocks, and insects. . . . Many, many of our people died of starvation." When Geronimo took up arms in protest, the army recruited other Apaches to track him and his band into the hills; in September 1886, he surrendered for the last time. The Chiricahua Apaches never returned to their homeland. The United States had completed its military conquest of the West.

> **EXPLAIN CONSEQUENCES**
> How did Grant's peace policy fail to consider the needs of Native Americans in the West, and what were its results?

Strategies of Survival

Though the warpath closed, many Native peoples continued secretly to practice traditional customs. Away from the disapproving eyes of agents and teachers, they passed on their languages, histories, and traditional arts and medicine to younger generations. Frustrated missionaries often concluded that little could be accomplished because bonds of kinship and custom were so strong. Parents also hated to relinquish their children to off-reservation boarding schools. Thus more and more Indian schools ended up on or near reservations; white teachers had to accept their pupils' continued participation in the rhythms of Indian community life.

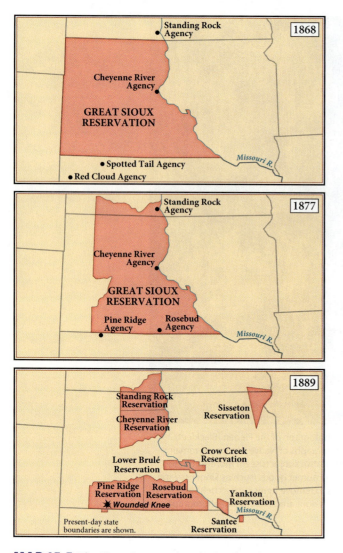

MAP 15.5 The Sioux Reservations in South Dakota, 1868–1889

In 1868, when they bent to the demand that they move onto the reservation, the Sioux thought they had gained secure rights to a substantial part of their ancestral hunting grounds. But harsh conditions on reservations led to continuing military conflicts. Land-hungry whites exerted continuous local pressure, and officials in Washington repeatedly changed the terms of Sioux landholdings — always eroding Native claims.

Selectively, most indigenous peoples adopted some white ways. Many parents urged their sons and daughters to study hard, learn English, and develop skills to help them succeed in the new world they confronted. Even Sitting Bull announced in 1885 that he wanted his children "to be educated like the white children are." Some Indian students grew up to be lawyers, doctors, and advocates for their people, including writers and artists who interpreted Native experiences for national audiences. One of the most famous was a Santee Sioux boy named Ohiyesa, who became Dr. Charles Eastman. Posted to the Pine Ridge Reservation in South Dakota, Eastman practiced medicine side by side with traditional healers, whom he respected, and wrote popular books under his Sioux name. He remembered that when he left for boarding school, his father had said, "We have now entered upon this life, and there is no going back. . . . Remember, my boy, it is the same as if I sent you on your first war-path. I shall expect you to conquer."

Nothing exemplified this syncretism, or cultural blending, better than the **Ghost Dance movement** of the late 1880s and early 1890s, which fostered American Indian peoples' hope that they could, through sacred dances, resurrect the bison and call a great storm to drive whites back across the Atlantic. The Ghost Dance drew on Christian elements as well as Native ones. As the movement spread from reservation to reservation — Paiutes, Arapahos, Sioux — indigenous peoples developed new forms of pan-Indian identity and cooperation.

White responses to the Ghost Dance showed continued misunderstanding and lethal exertion of authority. In 1890, when a group of Lakota Sioux Ghost Dancers left their South Dakota reservation, they were pursued by the U.S. Army, who feared that further spread of the religion would provoke war. On December 29, at **Wounded Knee**, the 7th Cavalry caught up with fleeing Lakotas and killed at least 150 — perhaps as many as 300. Like other massacres, this one could have been avoided. The deaths at Wounded Knee stand as a final indictment of decades of relentless U.S. expansion, white ignorance and greed, chaotic and conflicting policies, and bloody mistakes.

Western Myths and Realities

The post–Civil War frontier produced mythic figures who have played starring roles in America's national folklore ever since: "savage" Indians, brave pioneers, rugged cowboys, and gun-slinging sheriffs. Far from being invented by Hollywood in the twentieth century, these oversimplified characters emerged in the era when the nation incorporated the West. Pioneers helped develop the mythic ideal. As one Montana woman claimed, they had come west "at peril of their lives" and faced down "scalp dances" and other terrors; in the end, they "conquered the wilderness and transformed it into a land of peace and plenty." Some former cowboys, capitalizing on the popularity of dime novel Westerns, spiced up their memoirs for sale. Eastern readers were eager for stories like *The Life and Adventures of Nat Love* (1907), written by a Texas cowhand who had been born in slavery in Tennessee and who, as a rodeo star in the 1870s, had won the nickname "Deadwood Dick."

No myth-maker proved more influential than Buffalo Bill Cody. Unlike those who saw the West as free or empty, Bill understood that the United States had taken it by conquest. Ironically, his famous Wild West, which he insisted was not a "show" but an authentic representation of frontier experience, provided one of the few employment options for Plains Indians. To escape harsh reservation conditions, Sioux and Cheyenne men signed on with Bill and demonstrated their riding skills for cheering audiences across the United States and Europe, chasing buffalo and attacking U.S. soldiers and pioneer wagons in the arena. Buffalo Bill proved to be a good employer to Native men, including Lakota Sioux leader Sitting Bull, who toured with Bill's Wild West in 1885. Black Elk, another Lakota Sioux man who joined Cody's operation, recalled that Bill was generous and "had a strong heart." But Black Elk had a mixed reaction to the Wild West. "I liked the part of the show we made," he told an interviewer, "but not the part the Wasichus [white people] made." As he observed, the Wild West of the 1880s was at its heart a celebration of U.S. military conquest.

At this same moment of transition, a young historian named Frederick Jackson Turner reviewed recent census data and proclaimed the end of the frontier. Up to 1890, he wrote, a clear, westward-moving line had existed between "civilization and savagery." The frontier experience, Turner argued, shaped Americans' national character. It left them a heritage of "coarseness and strength, combined with acuteness and inquisitiveness," as well as "restless, nervous energy."

Today, historians reject Turner's depiction of Indian "savagery" — and his contradictory idea that white pioneers in the West claimed empty "free land." Many scholars have noted that frontier conquest was both violent and incomplete. The Dust Bowl of the 1930s, as well as more recent cycles of drought, have repeated late-nineteenth-century patterns of hardship and depopulation on the plains. During the 1950s and 1960s, also, uranium mining rushes in the West mimicked earlier patterns of boom and bust, leaving ghost towns in their wake. Turner himself acknowledged that the frontier had both good and evil elements. He noted that in the West, "frontier liberty was sometimes confused with absence of all effective government." But in 1893, when Turner first published "The Significance of the Frontier in American History," eager listeners heard only the positives. They saw pioneering in the West as evidence of American exceptionalism: of the nation's unique history and destiny. They claimed that "peaceful" American expansion was the opposite of European empires — ignoring the many military and economic similarities. Although politically the American West became a set of states rather than a colony, historians today emphasize the legacy of conquest that is central to its (and America's) history.

Less than two months after the massacre at Wounded Knee, General William T. Sherman died in New York. As the nation marked his passing with pomp and oratory, commentators noted that his career reflected a great era of conquest and consolidation of national power. Known primarily for his role in defeating the Confederacy, Sherman's first military exploits had been against Seminoles in Florida. Later, during the U.S.-Mexico War, he had gone west with the U.S. Army to help claim California. After the Civil War, the general went west again, supervising the forced removal of Sioux and Cheyennes to reservations.

When Sherman graduated from West Point in 1840, the United States had counted twenty-six states, none of them west of Missouri. At his death in 1891, the nation boasted forty-four states, stretching to the Pacific coast. The United States now rivaled Britain and Germany as an industrial giant, and its dynamic economy was drawing immigrants from around the world. Over the span of Sherman's career, the United States had become a major player on the world stage. It had done so through the kind of fierce military conquest that Sherman made famous, as well as through bold expansions of federal authority to foster economic expansion. From the wars and policies of Sherman's lifetime, the children and grandchildren of Civil War heroes inherited a vast empire. In the coming decades, it would be up to them to decide how they would use the nation's new power.

IN YOUR OWN WORDS In the late nineteenth century, what strategies did Native peoples in the West pursue in response to dispossession of their lands and efforts to assimilate them?

SUMMARY

Between 1861 and 1877, the United States completed its conquest of the continent. After the Civil War, expansion of railroads fostered integration of the national economy. Republican policymakers promoted this integration through protective tariffs, while federal court rulings facilitated economic growth and strengthened corporations. To attract foreign investment, Congress placed the nation on the gold standard. Federal officials also pursued a vigorous foreign policy, acquiring Alaska and asserting U.S. power indirectly through control of international trade in Latin America and Asia.

An important result of economic integration was incorporation of the Great Plains. Cattlemen built an industry linked to the integrated economy, in the process nearly driving the native bison to extinction. Homesteaders confronted harsh environmental conditions as they converted the grasslands for agriculture. Republicans championed homesteader families as representatives of domesticity, an ideal opposed to Mormon plural marriage in Utah. Homesteading accelerated the rapid, often violent, transformation of western environments. Perceiving this transformation, federal officials began setting aside natural preserves such as Yellowstone, often clashing with Native Americans who wished to hunt there.

Conflicts led to the dispossession of Native American lands. During the Civil War, whites clashed with the Sioux and their allies. Grant's peace policy sought to end this conflict by forcing Native Americans to acculturate to European-style practices. Indian armed resistance continued through the 1880s, ending with Geronimo's surrender in 1886. Thereafter, Native Americans survived by secretly continuing their traditions and selectively adopting white ways. Due in part to the determined military conquest of this period, the United States claimed a major role on the world stage. Frontier myths shaped Americans' view of themselves as rugged individualists with a unique national destiny.

CHAPTER 15 REVIEW

TERMS TO KNOW   *Identify and explain the significance of each term below.*

Key Concepts and Events

transcontinental railroad (p. 462)

protective tariff (p. 464)

Burlingame Treaty (p. 465)

Munn v. Illinois (p. 467)

gold standard (p. 469)

"Crime of 1873" (p. 469)

Homestead Act (p. 470)

land-grant colleges (p. 470)

Comstock Lode (p. 470)

"rain follows the plow" (p. 472)

Exodusters (p. 473)

Yellowstone National Park (p. 477)

U.S. Fisheries Commission (p. 478)

Sand Creek massacre (p. 480)

Fetterman massacre (p. 480)

Lone Wolf v. Hitchcock (p. 483)

Dawes Severalty Act (p. 483)

Battle of Little Big Horn (p. 486)

Ghost Dance movement (p. 488)

Wounded Knee (p. 488)

Key People

William Seward (p. 465)

Emmeline Wells (p. 473)

John Wesley Powell (p. 476)

Chief Joseph (p. 478)

Sitting Bull (p. 486)

George Armstrong Custer (p. 486)

William F. "Buffalo Bill" Cody (p. 486)

Geronimo (p. 487)

Ohiyesa (Dr. Charles Eastman) (p. 488)

Frederick Jackson Turner (p. 489)

REVIEW QUESTIONS

Answer these questions to demonstrate your understanding of the chapter's main ideas.

1. What federal policies contributed to the rise of America's industrial economy, and what were their results?

2. What factors led to transformation of the trans-Mississippi west after the Civil War?

3. In the late nineteenth century, what strategies did Native peoples in the West pursue in response to dispossession of their lands and efforts to assimilate them?

4. Review the events listed under "American and National Identity" and "Migration and Settlement" on the thematic timeline on pages 364–365. Between the 1840s and the 1870s, what distinctive patterns of racial and ethnic conflict occurred in the West? What were the results for different ethnic and racial groups?

MAKING CONNECTIONS

Recognize the larger developments and continuities within and across chapters by answering these questions.

1. During the Reconstruction years, Republican policymakers made sweeping policy decisions — especially having to do with land rights, voting rights, and education — that shaped the future of African Americans in the South and American Indians in the West. In an essay, compare U.S. policies toward the two groups. What assumptions and goals underlay each effort to incorporate racial minorities into the United States? To what extent did each effort succeed or fail, and why? How did the actions of powerful whites in each region shape the results?

2. Consider the image at the start of this chapter, "The Great West" (p. 463), which depicts how many Americans of the era thought the West *ought* to look when settlement was complete. Identify at least two other images in Chapter 15 that show what the natural and built environments of the West *really* looked like. What do you conclude from this comparison about the impact or the limits of U.S. policies in the West?

KEY TURNING POINTS

Refer to the chapter chronology on page 464 for help in answering the question below.

The military, political, and economic events of the Civil War years (1861–1865) are often treated as largely occurring in the Northeast and South — at places such as Shiloh, Gettysburg, and Washington, D.C. What impact did these developments have on the West, and what were their legacies?

Documents

The Declaration of Independence

In Congress, July 4, 1776,
The Unanimous Declaration of the Thirteen United States of America

When in the Course of human events, it becomes necessary for one people to dissolve the political bands which have connected them with another, and to assume among the Powers of the earth, the separate and equal station to which the Laws of Nature and of Nature's God entitle them, a decent respect to the opinions of mankind requires that they should declare the causes which impel them to the separation.

We hold these truths to be self-evident, that all men are created equal, that they are endowed by their Creator with certain unalienable rights, that among these are Life, Liberty, and the pursuit of Happiness. That to secure these rights, Governments are instituted among Men, deriving their just powers from the consent of the governed. That whenever any Form of Government becomes destructive of these ends, it is the Right of the People to alter or to abolish it, and to institute new Government, laying its foundation on such principles and organizing its powers in such form, as to them shall seem most likely to effect their Safety and Happiness. Prudence, indeed, will dictate that Governments long established should not be changed for light and transient causes; and accordingly all experience hath shown, that mankind are more disposed to suffer, while evils are sufferable, than to right themselves by abolishing the forms to which they are accustomed. But when a long train of abuses and usurpations, pursuing invariably the same Object evinces a design to reduce them under absolute Despotism, it is their right, it is their duty, to throw off such Government, and to provide new Guards for their future security. — Such has been the patient sufferance of these Colonies; and such is now the necessity which constrains them to alter their former Systems of Government. The history of the present King of Great Britain is a history of repeated injuries and usurpations, all having in direct object the establishment of an absolute Tyranny over these States. To prove this, let Facts be submitted to a candid world.

He has refused his Assent to Laws, the most wholesome and necessary for the public good.

He has forbidden his Governors to pass Laws of immediate and pressing importance, unless suspended in their operation till his Assent should be obtained; and, when so suspended, he has utterly neglected to attend to them.

He has refused to pass other Laws for the accommodation of large districts of people, unless those people would relinquish the right of Representation in the Legislature, a right inestimable to them and formidable to tyrants only.

He has called together legislative bodies at places unusual, uncomfortable, and distant from the depository of their public Records, for the sole purpose of fatiguing them into compliance with his measures.

He has dissolved Representative Houses repeatedly, for opposing with manly firmness his invasions on the rights of the people.

He has refused for a long time, after such dissolutions, to cause others to be elected; whereby the Legislative powers, incapable of Annihilation, have returned to the People at large for their exercise; the State remaining in the mean time exposed to all the dangers of invasion from without and convulsions within.

He has endeavoured to prevent the population of these States; for that purpose obstructing the Laws of Naturalization of Foreigners; refusing to pass others to encourage their migrations hither, and raising the conditions of new Appropriations of Lands.

He has obstructed the Administration of Justice, by refusing his Assent to Laws for establishing Judiciary powers.

He has made Judges dependent on his Will alone, for the tenure of their offices, and the amount and payment of their salaries.

He has erected a multitude of New Offices, and sent hither swarms of Officers to harass our People, and eat out their substance.

He has kept among us, in times of peace, Standing Armies without the Consent of our legislature.

He has affected to render the Military independent of and superior to the Civil Power.

He has combined with others to subject us to a jurisdiction foreign to our constitution, and unacknowledged by our laws; giving his Assent to their Acts of pretended Legislation:

For quartering large bodies of armed troops among us:

For protecting them, by a mock Trial, from Punishment for any Murders which they should commit on the Inhabitants of these States:

For cutting off our Trade with all parts of the world:

For imposing taxes on us without our Consent:

For depriving us, in many cases, of the benefits of Trial by jury:

For transporting us beyond Seas to be tried for pretended offences:

For abolishing the free System of English Laws in a neighbouring Province, establishing therein an Arbitrary government, and enlarging its Boundaries so as to render it at once an example and fit instrument for introducing the same absolute rule into these Colonies:

For taking away our Charters, abolishing our most valuable Laws, and altering fundamentally the Forms of our Governments:

For suspending our own Legislatures, and declaring themselves invested with Power to legislate for us in all cases whatsoever.

He has abdicated Government here, by declaring us out of his Protection and waging War against us.

He has plundered our seas, ravaged our Coasts, burnt our towns, and destroyed the lives of our people.

He is at this time transporting large armies of foreign mercenaries to compleat the works of death, desolation, and tyranny, already begun with circumstances of Cruelty & perfidy scarcely paralleled in the most barbarous ages, and totally unworthy the Head of a civilized nation.

He has constrained our fellow Citizens taken Captive on the high Seas to bear Arms against their Country, to become the executioners of their friends and Brethren, or to fall themselves by their Hands.

He has excited domestic insurrections amongst us, and has endeavoured to bring on the inhabitants of our frontiers, the merciless Indian Savages, whose known rule of warfare, is an undistinguished destruction of all ages, sexes, and conditions.

In every stage of these Oppressions We have Petitioned for Redress in the most humble terms: Our repeated Petitions have been answered only by repeated injury. A Prince, whose character is thus marked by every act which may define a Tyrant, is unfit to be the ruler of a free people.

Nor have We been wanting in attention to our British brethren. We have warned them from time to time of attempts by their legislature to extend an unwarrantable jurisdiction over us. We have reminded them of the circumstances of our emigration and settlement here. We have appealed to their native justice and magnanimity, and we have conjured them by the ties of our common kindred to disavow these usurpations, which would inevitably interrupt our connections and correspondence. They too have been deaf to the voice of justice and of consanguinity. We must, therefore, acquiesce in the necessity, which denounces our Separation, and hold them, as we hold the rest of mankind, Enemies in War, in Peace Friends.

We, therefore, the Representatives of the United States of America, in General Congress, Assembled, appealing to the Supreme Judge of the world for the rectitude of our intentions, do, in the Name, and by Authority of the good People of these Colonies, solemnly publish and declare, That these United Colonies are, and of Right ought to be FREE AND INDEPENDENT STATES; that they are Absolved from all Allegiance to the British Crown, and that all political connection between them and the State of Great Britain, is and ought to be totally dissolved; and that as Free and Independent States, they have full Power to levy War, conclude Peace, contract Alliances, establish Commerce, and to do all other Acts and Things which Independent States may of right do. And for the support of this Declaration, with a firm reliance on the Protection of Divine Providence, we mutually pledge to each other our Lives, our Fortunes, and our sacred Honor.

John Hancock

Button Gwinnett	George Wythe	James Wilson	Josiah Bartlett
Lyman Hall	Richard Henry Lee	Geo. Ross	Wm. Whipple
Geo. Walton	Th. Jefferson	Caesar Rodney	Matthew Thornton
Wm. Hooper	Benja. Harrison	Geo. Read	Saml. Adams
Joseph Hewes	Thos. Nelson, Jr.	Thos. M'Kean	John Adams
John Penn	Francis Lightfoot Lee	Wm. Floyd	Robt. Treat Paine
Edward Rutledge	Carter Braxton	Phil. Livingston	Elbridge Gerry
Thos. Heyward, Junr.	Robt. Morris	Frans. Lewis	Step. Hopkins
Thomas Lynch, Junr.	Benjamin Rush	Lewis Morris	William Ellery
Arthur Middleton	Benja. Franklin	Richd. Stockton	Roger Sherman
Samuel Chase	John Morton	John Witherspoon	Sam'el Huntington
Wm. Paca	Geo. Clymer	Fras. Hopkinson	Wm. Williams
Thos. Stone	Jas. Smith	John Hart	Oliver Wolcott
Charles Carroll of Carrollton	Geo. Taylor	Abra. Clark	

The Constitution of the United States of America

Agreed to by Philadelphia Convention, September 17, 1787
Implemented March 4, 1789

We the People of the United States, in Order to form a more perfect Union, establish Justice, insure domestic Tranquility, provide for the common defence, promote the general Welfare, and secure the Blessings of Liberty to ourselves and our Posterity, do ordain and establish this Constitution for the United States of America.

Article I

Section 1. All legislative Powers herein granted shall be vested in a Congress of the United States, which shall consist of a Senate and a House of Representatives.

Section 2. The House of Representatives shall be composed of Members chosen every second Year by the People of the several States, and the Electors in each State shall have the Qualifications requisite for Electors of the most numerous Branch of the State Legislature.

No Person shall be a Representative who shall not have attained to the Age of twenty-five Years, and been seven Years a Citizen of the United States, and who shall not, when elected, be an Inhabitant of that State in which he shall be chosen.

Representatives and direct Taxes shall be apportioned among the several States which may be included within this Union, according to their respective Numbers, *which shall be determined by adding to the whole Number of free Persons, including those bound to Service for a Term of Years, and excluding Indians not taxed, three fifths of all other Persons.** The actual Enumeration shall be made within three Years after the first Meeting of the Congress of the United States, and within every subsequent Term of ten Years, in such Manner as they shall by Law direct. The Number of Representatives shall not exceed one for every thirty Thousand, but each State shall have at Least one Representative; and *until such enumeration shall be made, the State of New Hampshire shall be entitled to chuse three, Massachusetts eight, Rhode Island and Providence Plantations one, Connecticut five, New York six, New Jersey four, Pennsylvania eight, Delaware one, Maryland six, Virginia ten, North Carolina five, South Carolina five, and Georgia three.*

When vacancies happen in the Representation from any State, the Executive Authority thereof shall issue Writs of Election to fill such Vacancies.

The House of Representatives shall chuse their Speaker and other Officers; and shall have the sole Power of Impeachment.

Section 3. The Senate of the United States shall be composed of two Senators from each State, *chosen by the Legislature thereof,*† for six Years; and each Senator shall have one Vote.

Immediately after they shall be assembled in Consequence of the first Election, they shall be divided as equally as may be into three Classes. The Seats of the Senators of the first Class shall be vacated at the Expiration of the second Year, of the second Class at the Expiration of the fourth Year, and of the third Class at the Expiration of the sixth Year, so that one-third may be chosen every second Year; and if Vacancies happen by Resignation, or otherwise, during the Recess of the Legislature of any State, the Executive thereof may make temporary Appointments until the next Meeting of the Legislature, which shall then fill such Vacancies.‡

No person shall be a Senator who shall not have attained to the Age of thirty Years, and been nine Years a Citizen of the United States, and who shall not, when elected, be an Inhabitant of that State for which he shall be chosen.

The Vice President of the United States shall be President of the Senate, but shall have no Vote, unless they be equally divided.

The Senate shall chuse their other Officers, and also a President pro tempore, in the absence of the Vice President, or when he shall exercise the Office of President of the United States.

The Senate shall have the sole Power to try all Impeachments. When sitting for that Purpose, they shall be on Oath or Affirmation. When the President of the United States is tried, the Chief Justice shall preside: And no Person shall be convicted without the Concurrence of two-thirds of the Members present.

Judgment in Cases of Impeachment shall not extend further than to removal from Office, and disqualification to hold and enjoy any Office of honor, Trust or Profit under the United States: but the Party convicted shall nevertheless be liable and subject to Indictment, Trial, Judgment and Punishment, according to Law.

Section 4. The Times, Places and Manner of holding Elections for Senators and Representatives, shall be prescribed in each State by the Legislature thereof; but the Congress may at any time by Law make or alter such Regulations, except as to the Places of Chusing Senators.

Note: The Constitution became effective March 4, 1789. Provisions in italics are no longer relevant or have been changed by constitutional amendment.
*Changed by Section 2 of the Fourteenth Amendment.

†Changed by Section 1 of the Seventeenth Amendment.
‡Changed by Clause 2 of the Seventeenth Amendment.

The Congress shall assemble at least once in every Year, and such Meeting *shall be on the first Monday in December, unless they shall by Law appoint a different Day.* *

Section 5. Each House shall be the Judge of the Elections, Returns and Qualifications of its own Members, and a Majority of each shall constitute a Quorum to do Business; but a smaller number may adjourn from day to day, and may be authorized to compel the Attendance of absent Members, in such Manner, and under such Penalties, as each House may provide.

Each House may determine the Rules of its Proceedings, punish its Members for disorderly Behavior, and, with the Concurrence of two-thirds, expel a Member.

Each House shall keep a Journal of its Proceedings, and from time to time publish the same, excepting such Parts as may in their Judgment require Secrecy; and the Yeas and Nays of the Members of either House on any question shall, at the Desire of one-fifth of those Present, be entered on the Journal.

Neither House, during the Session of Congress, shall, without the Consent of the other, adjourn for more than three days, nor to any other Place than that in which the two Houses shall be sitting.

Section 6. The Senators and Representatives shall receive a Compensation for their Services, to be ascertained by Law, and paid out of the Treasury of the United States. They shall in all Cases, except Treason, Felony and Breach of the Peace, be privileged from Arrest during their Attendance at the Session of their respective Houses, and in going to and returning from the same; and for any Speech or Debate in either House, they shall not be questioned in any other Place.

No Senator or Representative shall, during the Time for which he was elected, be appointed to any civil Office under the Authority of the United States, which shall have been created, or the Emoluments whereof shall have been increased, during such time; and no Person holding any Office under the United States, shall be a Member of either House during his Continuance in Office.

Section 7. All Bills for raising Revenue shall originate in the House of Representatives; but the Senate may propose or concur with Amendments as on other Bills.

Every Bill which shall have passed the House of Representatives and the Senate, shall, before it becomes a Law, be presented to the President of the United States; If he approve he shall sign it, but if not he shall return it, with his Objections to that House in which it shall have originated, who shall enter the Objections at large on their Journal, and proceed to reconsider it. If after such Reconsideration two-thirds of that House shall agree to pass the Bill, it shall be sent, together with the Objections, to the other House, by which it shall likewise be reconsidered, and if approved by two-thirds of that House, it shall become a Law. But in all such Cases the Votes of both Houses shall be determined by

Yeas and Nays, and the Names of the Persons voting for and against the Bill shall be entered on the Journal of each House respectively. If any Bill shall not be returned by the President within ten Days (Sundays excepted) after it shall have been presented to him, the Same shall be a Law, in like Manner as if he had signed it, unless the Congress by their Adjournment prevent its Return, in which Case it shall not be a Law.

Every Order, Resolution, or Vote to which the Concurrence of the Senate and the House of Representatives may be necessary (except on a question of Adjournment) shall be presented to the President of the United States; and before the Same shall take Effect, shall be approved by him, or being disapproved by him, shall be repassed by two-thirds of the Senate and House of Representatives, according to the Rules and Limitations prescribed in the Case of a Bill.

Section 8. The Congress shall have Power To lay and collect Taxes, Duties, Imposts and Excises, to pay the Debts and provide for the common Defence and general Welfare of the United States; but all Duties, Imposts and Excises shall be uniform throughout the United States;

To borrow Money on the credit of the United States;

To regulate Commerce with foreign Nations, and among the several States, and with the Indian Tribes;

To establish an uniform Rule of Naturalization, and uniform Laws on the subject of Bankruptcies throughout the United States;

To coin Money, regulate the Value thereof, and of foreign Coin, and fix the Standard of Weights and Measures;

To provide for the Punishment of counterfeiting the Securities and current Coin of the United States;

To establish Post Offices and post Roads;

To promote the Progress of Science and useful Arts, by securing for limited Times to Authors and Inventors the exclusive Right to their respective Writings and Discoveries;

To constitute Tribunals inferior to the supreme Court;

To define and punish Piracies and Felonies committed on the high Seas, and Offenses against the Law of Nations;

To declare War, grant Letters of Marque and Reprisal, and make Rules concerning Captures on Land and Water;

To raise and support Armies, but no Appropriation of Money to that Use shall be for a longer Term than two Years;

To provide and maintain a Navy;

To make Rules for the Government and Regulation of the land and naval Forces;

To provide for calling forth the Militia to execute the Laws of the Union, suppress Insurrections and repel Invasions;

To provide for organizing, arming, and disciplining the Militia, and for governing such Part of them as may be employed in the Service of the United States, reserving to the States respectively, the Appointment of the Officers, and the Authority of training the Militia according to the discipline prescribed by Congress;

To exercise exclusive Legislation in all Cases whatsoever, over such District (not exceeding ten Miles square) as may,

*Changed by Section 2 of the Twentieth Amendment.

by Cession of particular States, and the acceptance of Congress, become the Seat of Government of the United States, and to exercise like Authority over all Places purchased by the Consent of the Legislature of the State in which the Same shall be, for the Erection of Forts, Magazines, Arsenals, dock-Yards, and other needful Buildings; — And

To make all Laws which shall be necessary and proper for carrying into Execution the foregoing Powers, and all other Powers vested by this Constitution in the Government of the United States, or in any Department or Officer thereof.

Section 9. The Migration or Importation of such Persons as any of the States now existing shall think proper to admit, shall not be prohibited by the Congress prior to the Year one thousand eight hundred and eight but a tax or duty may be imposed on such Importation, not exceeding ten dollars for each Person.

The privilege of the Writ of Habeas Corpus shall not be suspended, unless when in Cases of Rebellion or Invasion the public Safety may require it.

No Bill of Attainder or ex post facto Law shall be passed.

*No capitation, or other direct, Tax shall be laid, unless in Proportion to the Census or Enumeration herein before directed to be taken.**

No Tax or Duty shall be laid on Articles exported from any State.

No Preference shall be given by any Regulation of Commerce or Revenue to the Ports of one State over those of another: nor shall Vessels bound to, or from, one State, be obliged to enter, clear, or pay Duties in another.

No Money shall be drawn from the Treasury, but in Consequence of Appropriations made by law; and a regular Statement and Account of the Receipts and Expenditures of all public Money shall be published from time to time.

No Title of Nobility shall be granted by the United States: And no Person holding any Office of Profit or Trust under them, shall, without the Consent of the Congress, accept of any present, Emolument, Office, or Title, of any kind whatever, from any King, Prince, or foreign State.

Section 10. No State shall enter into any Treaty, Alliance, or Confederation; grant Letters of Marque and Reprisal; coin Money; emit Bills of Credit; make any Thing but gold and silver Coin a Tender in Payment of Debts; pass any Bill of Attainder, ex post facto Law, or Law impairing the Obligation of Contracts, or grant any Title of Nobility.

No State shall, without the Consent of the Congress, lay any Imposts or Duties on Imports or Exports, except what may be absolutely necessary for executing its inspection Laws: and the net Produce of all Duties and Imposts, laid by any State on Imports or Exports, shall be for the Use of the Treasury of the United States; and all such Laws shall be subject to the Revision and Control of the Congress.

No State shall, without the Consent of the Congress, lay any duty of Tonnage, keep Troops, or Ships of War in time of Peace, enter into any Agreement or Compact with another State, or with a foreign Power, or engage in War, unless actually invaded, or in such imminent Danger as will not admit of delay.

Article II

Section 1. The executive Power shall be vested in a President of the United States of America. He shall hold his Office during the Term of four Years, and, together with the Vice President, chosen for the same Term, be elected, as follows:

Each State shall appoint, in such Manner as the Legislature thereof may direct, a Number of Electors, equal to the whole Number of Senators and Representatives to which the State may be entitled in the Congress; but no Senator or Representative, or Person holding an Office of Trust or Profit under the United States, shall be appointed an Elector.

The Electors shall meet in their respective States, and vote by Ballot for two Persons, of whom one at least shall not be an Inhabitant of the same State with themselves. And they shall make a List of all the Persons voted for, and of the Number of Votes for each; which List they shall sign and certify, and transmit sealed to the Seat of the Government of the United States, directed to the President of the Senate. The President of the Senate shall, in the Presence of the Senate and House of Representatives, open all the Certificates, and the Votes shall then be counted. The Person having the greatest Number of Votes shall be the President, if such Number be a Majority of the whole Number of Electors appointed; and if there be more than one who have such Majority, and have an equal Number of Votes, then the House of Representatives shall immediately chuse by Ballot one of them for President; and if no Person have a Majority, then from the five highest on the List the said House shall in like Manner chuse the President. But in chusing the President, the Votes shall be taken by States, the Representation from each State having one Vote; a quorum for this Purpose shall consist of a Member or Members from two thirds of the States, and a Majority of all the States shall be necessary to a Choice. In every Case, after the Choice of the President, the Person having the greatest Number of Votes of the Electors shall be the Vice President. But if there should remain two or more who have equal Votes, the Senate shall chuse from them by Ballot the Vice President.†

The Congress may determine the Time of chusing the Electors, and the Day on which they shall give their Votes; which Day shall be the same throughout the United States.

No Person except a natural born Citizen, or a Citizen of the United States, at the time of the Adoption of this Constitution, shall be eligible to the Office of President; neither shall any Person be eligible to that Office who shall not have attained to the Age of thirty five Years, and been fourteen Years a Resident within the United States.

In Case of the Removal of the President from Office, or of his Death, Resignation, or Inability to discharge the Powers

---

*Changed by the Sixteenth Amendment.

†Superseded by the Twelfth Amendment.

and Duties of the said Office, the same shall devolve on the Vice President, *and the Congress may by Law provide for the Case of Removal, Death, Resignation, or Inability, both of the President and Vice President, declaring what Officer shall then act as President, and such Officer shall act accordingly, until the Disability be removed, or a President shall be elected.**

The President shall, at stated Times, receive for his Services a Compensation, which shall neither be increased nor diminished during the Period for which he shall have been elected, and he shall not receive within that Period any other Emolument from the United States, or any of them.

Before he enter on the Execution of his Office, he shall take the following Oath or Affirmation:—"I do solemnly swear (or affirm) that I will faithfully execute the Office of President of the United States, and will to the best of my Ability, preserve, protect and defend the Constitution of the United States."

Section 2. The President shall be Commander in Chief of the Army and Navy of the United States, and of the Militia of the several States, when called into the actual Service of the United States; he may require the Opinion, in writing, of the principal Officer in each of the executive Departments, upon any Subject relating to the Duties of their respective Offices, and he shall have Power to Grant Reprieves and Pardons for Offences against the United States, except in Cases of Impeachment.

He shall have Power, by and with the Advice and Consent of the Senate, to make Treaties, provided two thirds of the Senators present concur; and he shall nominate, and by and with the Advice and Consent of the Senate, shall appoint Ambassadors, other public Ministers and Consuls, Judges of the supreme Court, and all other Officers of the United States, whose Appointments are not herein otherwise provided for, and which shall be established by Law: but the Congress may by Law vest the Appointment of such inferior Officers, as they think proper, in the President alone, in the Courts of Law, or in the Heads of Departments.

The President shall have Power to fill up all Vacancies that may happen during the Recess of the Senate, by granting Commissions which shall expire at the End of their next Session.

Section 3. He shall from time to time give to the Congress Information of the State of the Union, and recommend to their Consideration such Measures as he shall judge necessary and expedient; he may, on extraordinary Occasions, convene both Houses, or either of them, and in Case of Disagreement between them, with Respect to the Time of Adjournment, he may adjourn them to such Time as he shall think proper; he shall receive Ambassadors and other public Ministers; he shall take Care that the Laws be faithfully executed, and shall Commission all the Officers of the United States.

Section 4. The President, Vice President and all civil Officers of the United States, shall be removed from Office on Impeachment for, and Conviction of, Treason, Bribery, or other high Crimes and Misdemeanors.

Article III

Section 1. The judicial Power of the United States, shall be vested in one supreme Court, and in such inferior Courts as the Congress may from time to time ordain and establish. The Judges, both of the supreme and inferior Courts, shall hold their Offices during good Behaviour, and shall, at stated Times, receive for their Services a Compensation, which shall not be diminished during their Continuance in Office.

Section 2. The judicial Power shall extend to all Cases, in Law and Equity, arising under this Constitution, the Laws of the United States, and Treaties made, or which shall be made, under their Authority;—to all Cases affecting Ambassadors, other public Ministers and Consuls;—to all Cases of admiralty and maritime Jurisdiction;—to Controversies to which the United States shall be a Party;—to Controversies between two or more States;—*between a State and Citizens of another State;*†—between Citizens of different States;—between Citizens of the same State claiming Lands under Grants of different States, and between a State, or the Citizens thereof, and foreign States, Citizens or Subjects.

In all Cases affecting Ambassadors, other public Ministers and Consuls, and those in which a State shall be Party, the supreme Court shall have original Jurisdiction. In all the other Cases before mentioned, the supreme Court shall have appellate Jurisdiction, both as to Law and Fact, with such Exceptions, and under such Regulations as the Congress shall make.

The trial of all Crimes, except in Cases of Impeachment, shall be by Jury; and such Trial shall be held in the State where said Crimes shall have been committed; but when not committed within any State, the Trial shall be at such Place or Places as the Congress may by Law have directed.

Section 3. Treason against the United States, shall consist only in levying War against them, or in adhering to their Enemies, giving them Aid and Comfort. No Person shall be convicted of Treason unless on the Testimony of two Witnesses to the same overt Act, or on Confession in open Court.

The Congress shall have Power to declare the Punishment of Treason, but no Attainder of Treason shall work Corruption of Blood, or Forfeiture except during the Life of the Person attainted.

Article IV

Section 1. Full Faith and Credit shall be given in each State to the public Acts, Records, and judicial Proceedings of every other State. And the Congress may by general Laws prescribe the Manner in which such Acts, Records, and Proceedings shall be proved, and the Effect thereof.

*Modified by the Twenty-Fifth Amendment.

†Restricted by the Eleventh Amendment.

Section 2. The Citizens of each State shall be entitled to all Privileges and Immunities of Citizens in the several States.

A Person charged in any State with Treason, Felony, or other Crime, who shall flee from Justice, and be found in another State, shall on demand of the executive Authority of the State from which he fled, be delivered up, to be removed to the State having Jurisdiction of the Crime.

No Person held to Service or Labour in one State, under the Laws thereof, escaping into another, shall, in Consequence of any Law or Regulation therein, be discharged from such Service or Labour, but shall be delivered up on Claim of the Party to whom such Service or Labour may be due.*

Section 3. New States may be admitted by the Congress into this Union; but no new State shall be formed or erected within the Jurisdiction of any other State; nor any State be formed by the Junction of two or more States, or parts of States, without the Consent of the Legislatures of the States concerned as well as of the Congress.

The Congress shall have Power to dispose of and make all needful Rules and Regulations respecting the Territory or other Property belonging to the United States; and nothing in this Constitution shall be so construed as to Prejudice any Claims of the United States, or of any particular State.

Section 4. The United States shall guarantee to every State in this Union a Republican Form of Government, and shall protect each of them against Invasion; and on Application of the Legislature, or of the Executive (when the Legislature cannot be convened) against domestic Violence.

Article V

The Congress, whenever two-thirds of both Houses shall deem it necessary, shall propose Amendments to this Constitution, or, on the Application of the Legislatures of two-thirds of the several States, shall call a Convention for proposing Amendments, which, in either Case, shall be valid to all Intents and Purposes, as Part of this Constitution, when ratified by the Legislatures of three-fourths of the several States, or by Conventions in three-fourths thereof, as the one or the other Mode of Ratification may be proposed by the Congress; *Provided that no Amendment which may be made prior to the Year One thousand eight hundred and eight shall in any Manner affect the first and fourth Clauses in the Ninth Section of the first Article; and* that no State, without its Consent, shall be deprived of its equal Suffrage in the Senate.

Article VI

All Debts contracted and Engagements entered into, before the Adoption of this Constitution, shall be as valid against the United States under this Constitution, as under the Confederation.

This Constitution, and the Laws of the United States which shall be made in Pursuance thereof; and all Treaties made, or which shall be made, under the Authority of the United States, shall be the supreme Law of the Land; and the Judges in every State shall be bound thereby, any Thing in the Constitution or Laws of any State to the Contrary notwithstanding.

The Senators and Representatives before mentioned, and the Members of the several State Legislatures, and all executive and judicial Officers, both of the United States and of the several States, shall be bound by Oath or Affirmation, to support this Constitution; but no religious Test shall ever be required as a Qualification to any Office or public Trust under the United States.

Article VII

The Ratification of the Conventions of nine States shall be sufficient for the Establishment of this Constitution between the States so ratifying the Same.

Done in Convention by the Unanimous Consent of the States present the Seventeenth Day of September in the Year of our Lord one thousand seven hundred and Eighty seven and of the Independence of the United States of America the Twelfth. In Witness whereof We have hereunto subscribed our Names.

Go. Washington
President and deputy from Virginia

New Hampshire	*Connecticut*	*New Jersey*	*Pennsylvania*
John Langdon	**Wm. Saml. Johnson**	**Wil. Livingston**	**B. Franklin**
Nicholas Gilman	**Roger Sherman**	**David Brearley**	**Thomas Mifflin**
		Wm. Paterson	**Robt. Morris**
		Jona. Dayton	**Geo. Clymer**
			Thos. FitzSimons

*Superseded by the Thirteenth Amendment.

Massachusetts
Nathaniel Gorham
Rufus King
Jared Ingersoll
James Wilson
Gouv. Morris

Delaware
Geo. Read
Gunning Bedford jun
John Dickinson

New York
Alexander Hamilton
Richard Bassett
Jaco. Broom

Maryland
James McHenry
Dan. of St. Thos. Jenifer
Danl. Carroll

Virginia
John Blair
James Madison, Jr.

North Carolina
Wm. Blount
Richd. Dobbs Spaight
Hu Williamson

South Carolina
J. Rutledge

Charles Cotesworth Pinckney
Charles Pinckney
Pierce Butler

Georgia
William Few
Abr. Baldwin

Amendments to the Constitution (Including the Six Unratified Amendments)

Amendment I [1791]*

Congress shall make no law respecting an establishment of religion, or prohibiting the free exercise thereof; or abridging the freedom of speech, or of the press; or the right of the people peaceably to assemble, and to petition the Government for a redress of grievances.

Amendment II [1791]

A well regulated Militia, being necessary to the security of a free State, the right of the people to keep and bear Arms shall not be infringed.

Amendment III [1791]

No Soldier shall, in time of peace, be quartered in any house, without the consent of the Owner, nor in time of war, but in a manner to be prescribed by law.

Amendment IV [1791]

The right of the people to be secure in their persons, houses, papers, and effects, against unreasonable searches and seizures, shall not be violated, and no Warrants shall issue, but upon probable cause, supported by Oath or affirmation, and particularly describing the place to be searched, and the persons or things to be seized.

Amendment V [1791]

No person shall be held to answer for a capital or otherwise infamous crime, unless on a presentment or indictment of a Grand Jury, except in cases arising in the land or naval forces, or in the Militia, when in actual service in time of War or public danger; nor shall any person be subject for the same offence to be twice put in jeopardy of life or limb; nor shall be compelled in any criminal case to be a witness against himself, nor be deprived of life, liberty, or property, without due process of law; nor shall private property be taken for public use, without just compensation.

Amendment VI [1791]

In all criminal prosecutions, the accused shall enjoy the right to a speedy and public trial, by an impartial jury of the State and district wherein the crime shall have been committed, which district shall have been previously ascertained by law, and to be informed of the nature and cause of the accusation; to be confronted with the witnesses against him; to have compulsory process for obtaining witnesses in his favor, and to have the Assistance of Counsel for his defence.

Amendment VII [1791]

In suits at common law, where the value in controversy shall exceed twenty dollars, the right of trial by jury shall be preserved, and no fact tried by a jury, shall be otherwise reexamined in any Court of the United States, than according to the Rules of the common law.

Amendment VIII [1791]

Excessive bail shall not be required, nor excessive fines imposed, nor cruel and unusual punishments inflicted.

Amendment IX [1791]

The enumeration in the Constitution, of certain rights, shall not be construed to deny or disparage others retained by the people.

Amendment X [1791]

The powers not delegated to the United States by the Constitution, nor prohibited by it to the States, are reserved to the States respectively, or to the people.

Unratified Amendment

Reapportionment Amendment (proposed by Congress September 25, 1789, along with the Bill of Rights)

After the first enumeration required by the first article of the Constitution, there shall be one Representative for every thirty thousand, until the number shall amount to one hundred, after which the proportion shall be so regulated by Congress, that there shall be not less than one hundred Representatives, nor less than one Representative for every forty thousand persons, until the number of Representatives shall amount to two hundred; after which the proportion shall be so regulated by Congress, that there shall not be less than two hundred Representatives, nor more than one Representative for every fifty thousand persons.

Amendment XI [1795]

The Judicial power of the United States shall not be construed to extend to any suit in law or equity, commenced or prosecuted against one of the United States by Citizens of another State, or by Citizens or subjects of any foreign state.

*The dates in brackets indicate when the amendment was ratified.

Amendment XII [1804]

The Electors shall meet in their respective States and vote by ballot for President and Vice-President, one of whom, at least, shall not be an inhabitant of the same State with themselves; they shall name in their ballots the person voted for as President, and in distinct ballots the person voted for as Vice-President, and they shall make distinct lists of all persons voted for as President, and of all persons voted for as Vice-President, and of the number of votes for each, which lists they shall sign and certify, and transmit sealed to the seat of government of the United States, directed to the President of the Senate; — the President of the Senate shall, in the presence of the Senate and House of Representatives, open all the certificates and the votes shall then be counted; — The person having the greatest number of votes for President, shall be the President, if such number be a majority of the whole number of Electors appointed; and if no person have such majority, then from the persons having the highest numbers not exceeding three on the list of those voted for as President, the House of Representatives shall choose immediately, by ballot, the President. But in choosing the President, the votes shall be taken by States, the representation from each State having one vote; a quorum for this purpose shall consist of a member or members from two-thirds of the States, and a majority of all the States shall be necessary to a choice. And if the House of Representatives shall not choose a President whenever the right of choice shall devolve upon them, before *the fourth day of March* next following, then the Vice-President shall act as President, as in the case of the death or other constitutional disability of the President.* — The person having the greatest number of votes as Vice-President, shall be the Vice-President, if such number be a majority of the whole number of Electors appointed; and if no person have a majority, then from the two highest numbers on the list, the Senate shall choose the Vice-President; a quorum for the purpose shall consist of two-thirds of the whole number of Senators, and a majority of the whole number shall be necessary to a choice. But no person constitutionally ineligible to the office of President shall be eligible to that of Vice-President of the United States.

Unratified Amendment

Titles of Nobility Amendment (proposed by Congress May 1, 1810)

If any citizen of the United States shall accept, claim, receive or retain any title of nobility or honor or shall, without the consent of Congress, accept and retain any present, pension, office or emolument of any kind whatever, from any emperor, king, prince or foreign power, such person shall cease to be a citizen of the United States, and shall be incapable of holding any office of trust or profit under them, or either of them.

*Superseded by Section 3 of the Twentieth Amendment.

Unratified Amendment

Corwin Amendment (proposed by Congress March 2, 1861)

No amendment shall be made to the Constitution which will authorize or give to Congress the power to abolish or interfere, within any State, with the domestic institutions thereof, including that of persons held to labor or service by the laws of said State.

Amendment XIII [1865]

Section 1. Neither slavery nor involuntary servitude, except as a punishment for crime whereof the party shall have been duly convicted, shall exist within the United States, or any place subject to their jurisdiction.

Section 2. Congress shall have power to enforce this article by appropriate legislation.

Amendment XIV [1868]

Section 1. All persons born or naturalized in the United States, and subject to the jurisdiction thereof, are citizens of the United States and of the State wherein they reside. No State shall make or enforce any law which shall abridge the privileges or immunities of citizens of the United States; nor shall any State deprive any person of life, liberty, or property, without due process of law; nor deny to any person within its jurisdiction the equal protection of the laws.

Section 2. Representatives shall be apportioned among the several States according to their respective numbers, counting the whole number of persons in each State, excluding Indians not taxed. But when the right to vote at any election for the choice of electors for President and Vice-President of the United States, Representatives in Congress, the Executive and Judicial officers of a State, or the members of the Legislature thereof, is denied to any of the *male* inhabitants of such State, being *twenty-one* years of age and citizens of the United States, or in any way abridged, except for participation in rebellion, or other crime, the basis of representation therein shall be reduced in the proportion which the number of such *male* citizens shall bear to the whole number of *male* citizens *twenty-one* years of age in such State.

Section 3. No person shall be a Senator or Representative in Congress, or Elector of President and Vice-President, or hold any office, civil or military, under the United States, or under any State, who, having previously taken an oath, as a member of Congress, or as an officer of the United States, or as a member of any State legislature, or as an executive or judicial officer of any State, to support the Constitution of the United States, shall have engaged in insurrection or rebellion against the same, or given aid or comfort to the enemies thereof. Congress may, by a vote of two-thirds of each house, remove such disability.

Section 4. The validity of the public debt of the United States, authorized by law, including debts incurred for payment of pensions and bounties for services in suppressing insurrection or rebellion, shall not be questioned. But neither the United States nor any State shall assume or pay any debt or obligation incurred in aid of insurrection or rebellion against the United States, or any claim for the loss or emancipation of any slave; but all such debts, obligations, and claims shall be held illegal and void.

Section 5. The Congress shall have power to enforce, by appropriate legislation, the provisions of this article.

Amendment XV [1870]

Section 1. The right of citizens of the United States to vote shall not be denied or abridged by the United States or by any State on account of race, color, or previous condition of servitude —

Section 2. The Congress shall have power to enforce this article by appropriate legislation.

Amendment XVI [1913]

The Congress shall have power to lay and collect taxes on incomes, from whatever source derived, without apportionment among the several States, and without regard to any census or enumeration.

Amendment XVII [1913]

Section 1. The Senate of the United States shall be composed of two Senators from each State, elected by the people thereof, for six years; and each Senator shall have one vote. The electors in each State shall have the qualifications requisite for electors of [voters for] the most numerous branch of the State legislatures.

Section 2. When vacancies happen in the representation of any State in the Senate, the executive authority of such State shall issue writs of election to fill such vacancies: Provided, that the Legislature of any State may empower the executive thereof to make temporary appointments until the people fill the vacancies by election as the Legislature may direct.

Section 3. *This amendment shall not be so construed as to affect the election or term of any Senator chosen before it becomes valid as part of the Constitution.*

Amendment XVIII [1919; repealed 1933 by Amendment XXI]

Section 1. *After one year from the ratification of this article the manufacture, sale, or transportation of intoxicating liquors within, the importation thereof into, or the exportation thereof from the United States and all territory subject to the jurisdiction thereof, for beverage purposes, is hereby prohibited.*

Section 2. *The Congress and the several States shall have concurrent power to enforce this article by appropriate legislation.*

Section 3. *This article shall be inoperative unless it shall have been ratified as an amendment to the Constitution by the legislatures of the several States, as provided by the Constitution,* within seven years from the date of the submission thereof to the States by the Congress.

Amendment XIX [1920]

Section 1. The right of citizens of the United States to vote shall not be denied or abridged by the United States or by any State on account of sex.

Section 2. Congress shall have the power to enforce this article by appropriate legislation.

Unratified Amendment
Child Labor Amendment
(proposed by Congress June 2, 1924)

Section 1. *The Congress shall have power to limit, regulate, and prohibit the labor of persons under eighteen years of age.*

Section 2. *The power of the several States is unimpaired by this article except that the operation of State laws shall be suspended to the extent necessary to give effect to legislation enacted by Congress.*

Amendment XX [1933]

Section 1. The terms of the President and Vice-President shall end at noon on the 20th day of January, and the terms of Senators and Representatives at noon on the 3rd day of January, of the years in which such terms would have ended if this article had not been ratified; and the terms of their successors shall then begin.

Section 2. The Congress shall assemble at least once in every year, and such meeting shall begin at noon on the 3rd day of January, unless they shall by law appoint a different day.

Section 3. If, at the time fixed for the beginning of the term of the President, the President-elect shall have died, the Vice-President-elect shall become President. If a President shall not have been chosen before the time fixed for the beginning of his term, or if the President-elect shall have failed to qualify, then the Vice-President-elect shall act as President until a President shall have qualified; and the Congress may by law provide for the case wherein neither a President-elect nor a Vice-President-elect shall have qualified, declaring who shall then act as President, or the manner in which one who is to act shall be selected, and such person shall act accordingly until a President or Vice-President shall have qualified.

Section 4. The Congress may by law provide for the case of the death of any of the persons from whom the House of Representatives may choose a President whenever the right of choice shall have devolved upon them, and for the case of the death of any of the persons from whom the Senate may choose a Vice-President whenever the right of choice shall have devolved upon them.

Section 5. Sections 1 and 2 shall take effect on the 15th day of October following the ratification of this article.

Section 6. This article shall be inoperative unless it shall have been ratified as an amendment to the Constitution by the Legislatures of three-fourths of the several States within seven years from the date of its submission.

Amendment XXI [1933]

Section 1. The eighteenth article of amendment to the Constitution of the United States is hereby repealed.

Section 2. The transportation or importation into any State, Territory, or Possession of the United States for delivery or use therein of intoxicating liquors, in violation of the laws thereof, is hereby prohibited.

Section 3. This article shall be inoperative unless it shall have been ratified as an amendment to the Constitution by conventions in the several States, as provided in the Constitution, within seven years from the date of the submission thereof to the States by the Congress.

Amendment XXII [1951]

Section 1. No person shall be elected to the office of the President more than twice, and no person who has held the office of President, or acted as President, for more than two years of a term to which some other person was elected President shall be elected to the office of President more than once. But this article shall not apply to any person holding the office of President when this Article was proposed by the Congress, and shall not prevent any person who may be holding the office of President, or acting as President, during the term within which this Article becomes operative from holding the office of President or acting as President during the remainder of such term.

Section 2. This article shall be inoperative unless it shall have been ratified as an amendment to the Constitution by the legislatures of three-fourths of the several States within seven years from the date of its submission to the States by the Congress.

Amendment XXIII [1961]

Section 1. The District constituting the seat of Government of the United States shall appoint in such manner as the Congress may direct: A number of electors of President and Vice-President equal to the whole number of Senators and Representatives in Congress to which the District would be entitled if it were a State, but in no event more than the least populous State; they shall be in addition to those appointed by the States, but they shall be considered for the purposes of the election of President and Vice-President, to be electors appointed by a State; and they shall meet in the District and perform such duties as provided by the twelfth article of amendment.

Section 2. The Congress shall have the power to enforce this article by appropriate legislation.

Amendment XXIV [1964]

Section 1. The right of citizens of the United States to vote in any primary or other election for President or Vice-President, for electors for President or Vice-President, or for Senator or Representative in Congress, shall not be denied or abridged by the United States or any State by reason of failure to pay any poll tax or other tax.

Section 2. The Congress shall have the power to enforce this article by appropriate legislation.

Amendment XXV [1967]

Section 1. In case of the removal of the President from office or of his death or resignation, the Vice-President shall become President.

Section 2. Whenever there is a vacancy in the office of the Vice-President, the President shall nominate a Vice-President who shall take office upon confirmation by a majority vote of both Houses of Congress.

Section 3. Whenever the President transmits to the President pro tempore of the Senate and the Speaker of the House of Representatives his written declaration that he is unable to discharge the powers and duties of his office, and until he transmits to them a written declaration to the contrary, such powers and duties shall be discharged by the Vice-President as Acting President.

Section 4. Whenever the Vice-President and a majority of either the principal officers of the executive departments or of such other body as Congress may by law provide, transmit to the President pro tempore of the Senate and the Speaker of the House of Representatives their written declaration that the President is unable to discharge the powers and duties of his office, the Vice-President shall immediately assume the powers and duties of the office as Acting President.

Thereafter, when the President transmits to the President pro tempore of the Senate and the Speaker of the House of Representatives his written declaration that no inability exists, he shall resume the powers and duties of his office unless the Vice-President and a majority of either the principal officers of the executive department[s] or of such other body as Congress may by law provide, transmit within four days to the President pro tempore of the Senate and the Speaker of the House of Representatives their written declaration that the President is unable to discharge the powers and duties of his office. Thereupon Congress shall decide the issue, assembling within forty-eight hours for that purpose if not in session. If the Congress, within twenty-one days after receipt of the latter written declaration, or, if Congress is not in session, within twenty-one days after Congress is required to assemble, determines by two-thirds vote of both Houses that the President is unable to discharge the powers and duties of his office, the Vice-President shall continue to discharge the same as Acting President; otherwise, the President shall resume the powers and duties of his office.

Amendment XXVI [1971]

Section 1. The right of citizens of the United States, who are eighteen years of age or older, to vote shall not be denied or abridged by the United States or by any State on account of age.

Section 2. The Congress shall have power to enforce this article by appropriate legislation.

Unratified Amendment

Equal Rights Amendment (proposed by Congress March 22, 1972; seven-year deadline for ratification extended to June 30, 1982)

Section 1. Equality of rights under the law shall not be denied or abridged by the United States or by any State on account of sex.

Section 2. The Congress shall have the power to enforce, by appropriate legislation, the provisions of this article.

Section 3. This amendment shall take effect two years after the date of ratification.

Unratified Amendment

District of Columbia Statehood Amendment (proposed by Congress August 22, 1978)

Section 1. For purposes of representation in the Congress, election of the President and Vice President, and article V of this Constitution, the District constituting the seat of government of the United States shall be treated as though it were a State.

Section 2. The exercise of the rights and powers conferred under this article shall be by the people of the District constituting the seat of government, and as shall be provided by Congress.

Section 3. The twenty-third article of amendment to the Constitution of the United States is hereby repealed.

Section 4. This article shall be inoperative, unless it shall have been ratified as an amendment to the Constitution by the legislatures of three-fourths of the several states within seven years from the date of its submission.

Amendment XXVII [1992]

No law varying the compensation for the services of the Senators and Representatives, shall take effect, until an election of Representatives shall have intervened.

Appendix

The American Nation

Admission of States into the Union

State	Date of Admission	State	Date of Admission	State	Date of Admission
1. Delaware	December 7, 1787	18. Louisiana	April 30, 1812	35. West Virginia	June 20, 1863
2. Pennsylvania	December 12, 1787	19. Indiana	December 11, 1816	36. Nevada	October 31, 1864
3. New Jersey	December 18, 1787	20. Mississippi	December 10, 1817	37. Nebraska	March 1, 1867
4. Georgia	January 2, 1788	21. Illinois	December 3, 1818	38. Colorado	August 1, 1876
5. Connecticut	January 9, 1788	22. Alabama	December 14, 1819	39. North Dakota	November 2, 1889
6. Massachusetts	February 6, 1788	23. Maine	March 15, 1820	40. South Dakota	November 2, 1889
7. Maryland	April 28, 1788	24. Missouri	August 10, 1821	41. Montana	November 8, 1889
8. South Carolina	May 23, 1788	25. Arkansas	June 15, 1836	42. Washington	November 11, 1889
9. New Hampshire	June 21, 1788	26. Michigan	January 26, 1837	43. Idaho	July 3, 1890
10. Virginia	June 25, 1788	27. Florida	March 3, 1845	44. Wyoming	July 10, 1890
11. New York	July 26, 1788	28. Texas	December 29, 1845	45. Utah	January 4, 1896
12. North Carolina	November 21, 1789	29. Iowa	December 28, 1846	46. Oklahoma	November 16, 1907
13. Rhode Island	May 29, 1790	30. Wisconsin	May 29, 1848	47. New Mexico	January 6, 1912
14. Vermont	March 4, 1791	31. California	September 9, 1850	48. Arizona	February 14, 1912
15. Kentucky	June 1, 1792	32. Minnesota	May 11, 1858	49. Alaska	January 3, 1959
16. Tennessee	June 1, 1796	33. Oregon	February 14, 1859	50. Hawaii	August 21, 1959
17. Ohio	March 1, 1803	34. Kansas	January 29, 1861		

Presidential Elections

Year	Candidates	Parties	Percentage of Popular Vote*	Electoral Vote
1789	**George Washington**	No party designations		69
	John Adams[†]			34
	Other candidates			35
1792	**George Washington**	No party designations		132
	John Adams			77
	George Clinton			50
	Other candidates			5

SOURCES: U.S. Bureau of the Census, *Historical Statistics of the United States, Colonial Times to 1970* (1975); *Statistical Abstract of the United States, 2001*; *Statistical Abstract of the United States, 2006.*

*Prior to 1824, most presidential electors were chosen by state legislators rather than by popular vote. For elections after 1824, candidates receiving less than 1.0 percent of the popular vote have been omitted from this chart. Hence the popular vote does not total 100 percent for all elections.

†Before the Twelfth Amendment was passed in 1804, the electoral college voted for two presidential candidates; the runner-up became vice president.

Year	Candidates	Parties	Percentage of Popular Vote	Electoral Vote
1796	**John Adams**	Federalist		71
	Thomas Jefferson	Democratic-Republican		68
	Thomas Pinckney	Federalist		59
	Aaron Burr	Democratic-Republican		30
	Other candidates			48
1800	**Thomas Jefferson**	Democratic-Republican		73
	Aaron Burr	Democratic-Republican		73
	John Adams	Federalist		65
	Charles C. Pinckney	Federalist		64
	John Jay	Federalist		1
1804	**Thomas Jefferson**	Democratic-Republican		162
	Charles C. Pinckney	Federalist		14
1808	**James Madison**	Democratic-Republican		122
	Charles C. Pinckney	Federalist		47
	George Clinton	Democratic-Republican		6
1812	**James Madison**	Democratic-Republican		128
	DeWitt Clinton	Federalist		89
1816	**James Monroe**	Democratic-Republican		183
	Rufus King	Federalist		34
1820	**James Monroe**	Democratic-Republican		231
	John Quincy Adams	Independent Republican		1
1824	**John Quincy Adams**	Democratic-Republican	30.5	84
	Andrew Jackson	Democratic-Republican	43.1	99
	Henry Clay	Democratic-Republican	13.2	37
	William H. Crawford	Democratic-Republican	13.1	41
1828	**Andrew Jackson**	Democratic	56.0	178
	John Quincy Adams	National Republican	44.0	83
1832	**Andrew Jackson**	Democratic	54.5	219
	Henry Clay	National Republican	37.5	49
	William Wirt	Anti-Masonic	8.0	7
	John Floyd	Democratic	‡	11
1836	**Martin Van Buren**	Democratic	50.9	170
	William H. Harrison	Whig	49.1	73
	Hugh L. White	Whig		26
	Daniel Webster	Whig		14
	W. P. Mangum	Whig		11
1840	**William H. Harrison**	Whig	53.1	234
	Martin Van Buren	Democratic	46.9	60
1844	**James K. Polk**	Democratic	49.6	170
	Henry Clay	Whig	48.1	105
	James G. Birney	Liberty	2.3	
1848	**Zachary Taylor**	Whig	47.4	163
	Lewis Cass	Democratic	42.5	127
	Martin Van Buren	Free Soil	10.1	

‡Independent Democrat John Floyd received the 11 electoral votes of South Carolina; that state's presidential electors were still chosen by its legislature, not by popular vote.

Year	Candidates	Parties	Percentage of Popular Vote	Electoral Vote
1852	**Franklin Pierce**	Democratic	50.9	254
	Winfield Scott	Whig	44.1	42
	John P. Hale	Free Soil	5.0	
1856	**James Buchanan**	Democratic	45.3	174
	John C. Frémont	Republican	33.1	114
	Millard Fillmore	American	21.6	8
1860	**Abraham Lincoln**	Republican	39.8	180
	Stephen A. Douglas	Democratic	29.5	12
	John C. Breckinridge	Democratic	18.1	72
	John Bell	Constitutional Union	12.6	39
1864	**Abraham Lincoln**	Republican	55.0	212
	George B. McClellan	Democratic	45.0	21
1868	**Ulysses S. Grant**	Republican	52.7	214
	Horatio Seymour	Democratic	47.3	80
1872	**Ulysses S. Grant**	Republican	55.6	286
	Horace Greeley	Democratic	43.9	
1876	**Rutherford B. Hayes**	Republican	48.0	185
	Samuel J. Tilden	Democratic	51.0	184
1880	**James A. Garfield**	Republican	48.5	214
	Winfield S. Hancock	Democratic	48.1	155
	James B. Weaver	Greenback-Labor	3.4	
1884	**Grover Cleveland**	Democratic	48.5	219
	James G. Blaine	Republican	48.2	182
	Benjamin F. Butler	Greenback-Labor	1.8	
	John P. St. John	Prohibition	1.5	
1888	**Benjamin Harrison**	Republican	47.9	233
	Grover Cleveland	Democratic	48.6	168
	Clinton P. Fisk	Prohibition	2.2	
	Anson J. Streeter	Union Labor	1.3	
1892	**Grover Cleveland**	Democratic	46.1	277
	Benjamin Harrison	Republican	43.0	145
	James B. Weaver	People's	8.5	22
	John Bidwell	Prohibition	2.2	
1896	**William McKinley**	Republican	51.1	271
	William J. Bryan	Democratic	47.7	176
1900	**William McKinley**	Republican	51.7	292
	William J. Bryan	Democratic; Populist	45.5	155
	John C. Wooley	Prohibition	1.5	
1904	**Theodore Roosevelt**	Republican	57.4	336
	Alton B. Parker	Democratic	37.6	140
	Eugene V. Debs	Socialist	3.0	
	Silas C. Swallow	Prohibition	1.9	
1908	**William H. Taft**	Republican	51.6	321
	William J. Bryan	Democratic	43.1	162
	Eugene V. Debs	Socialist	2.8	
	Eugene W. Chafin	Prohibition	1.7	

Year	Candidates	Parties	Percentage of Popular Vote	Electoral Vote
1912	**Woodrow Wilson**	Democratic	41.9	435
	Theodore Roosevelt	Progressive	27.4	88
	William H. Taft	Republican	23.2	8
	Eugene V. Debs	Socialist	6.0	
	Eugene W. Chafin	Prohibition	1.4	
1916	**Woodrow Wilson**	Democratic	49.4	277
	Charles E. Hughes	Republican	46.2	254
	A. L. Benson	Socialist	3.2	
	J. Frank Hanly	Prohibition	1.2	
1920	**Warren G. Harding**	Republican	60.4	404
	James M. Cox	Democratic	34.2	127
	Eugene V. Debs	Socialist	3.4	
	P. P. Christensen	Farmer-Labor	1.0	
1924	**Calvin Coolidge**	Republican	54.0	382
	John W. Davis	Democratic	28.8	136
	Robert M. La Follette	Progressive	16.6	13
1928	**Herbert C. Hoover**	Republican	58.2	444
	Alfred E. Smith	Democratic	40.9	87
1932	**Franklin D. Roosevelt**	Democratic	57.4	472
	Herbert C. Hoover	Republican	39.7	59
	Norman Thomas	Socialist	2.2	
1936	**Franklin D. Roosevelt**	Democratic	60.8	523
	Alfred M. Landon	Republican	36.5	8
	William Lemke	Union	1.9	
1940	**Franklin D. Roosevelt**	Democratic	54.8	449
	Wendell L. Willkie	Republican	44.8	82
1944	**Franklin D. Roosevelt**	Democratic	53.5	432
	Thomas E. Dewey	Republican	46.0	99
1948	**Harry S. Truman**	Democratic	49.6	303
	Thomas E. Dewey	Republican	45.1	189
	J. Strom Thurmond	States' Rights	2.4	
	Henry Wallace	Progressive	2.4	
1952	**Dwight D. Eisenhower**	Republican	55.1	442
	Adlai E. Stevenson	Democratic	44.4	89
1956	**Dwight D. Eisenhower**	Republican	57.6	457
	Adlai E. Stevenson	Democratic	42.1	73
1960	**John F. Kennedy**	Democratic	49.7	303
	Richard M. Nixon	Republican	49.5	219
1964	**Lyndon B. Johnson**	Democratic	61.1	486
	Barry M. Goldwater	Republican	38.5	52
1968	**Richard M. Nixon**	Republican	43.4	301
	Hubert H. Humphrey	Democratic	42.7	191
	George C. Wallace	American Independent	13.5	46
1972	**Richard M. Nixon**	Republican	60.7	520
	George S. McGovern	Democratic	37.5	17
	John G. Schmitz	American	1.4	

Year	Candidates	Parties	Percentage of Popular Vote	Electoral Vote
1976	**Jimmy Carter**	Democratic	50.1	297
	Gerald R. Ford	Republican	48.0	240
1980	**Ronald W. Reagan**	Republican	50.7	489
	Jimmy Carter	Democratic	41.0	49
	John B. Anderson	Independent	6.6	0
	Ed Clark	Libertarian	1.1	
1984	**Ronald W. Reagan**	Republican	58.4	525
	Walter F. Mondale	Democratic	41.6	13
1988	**George H. W. Bush**	Republican	53.4	426
	Michael Dukakis	Democratic	45.6	111*
1992	**Bill Clinton**	Democratic	43.7	370
	George H. W. Bush	Republican	38.0	168
	H. Ross Perot	Independent	19.0	0
1996	**Bill Clinton**	Democratic	49	379
	Robert J. Dole	Republican	41	159
	H. Ross Perot	Reform	8	0
2000	**George W. Bush**	Republican	47.8	271
	Albert Gore	Democratic	48.4	267
	Ralph Nader	Green	2.7	0
2004	**George W. Bush**	Republican	50.7	286
	John Kerry	Democratic	48.3	252
2008	**Barack Obama**	Democratic	52.9	365
	John McCain	Republican	45.7	173
2012	**Barack Obama**	Democratic	51	332
	Mitt Romney	Republican	47.2	206
2016	**Donald Trump**	Republican	46.4	306
	Hillary Clinton	Democratic	48.5	232

*One Dukakis elector cast a vote for Lloyd Bentsen.

Population Growth*

Year	Population	Percentage Increase	Year	Population	Percentage Increase
1610	350	—	1820	9,638,453	33.1
1620	2,300	557.1	1830	12,866,020	33.5
1630	4,600	100.0	1840	17,069,453	32.7
1640	26,600	478.3	1850	23,191,876	35.9
1650	50,400	90.8	1860	31,443,321	35.6
1660	75,100	49.0	1870	39,818,449	26.6
1670	111,900	49.0	1880	50,155,783	26.0
1680	151,500	35.4	1890	62,947,714	25.5
1690	210,400	38.9	1900	75,994,575	20.7
1700	250,900	19.2	1910	91,972,266	21.0
1710	331,700	32.2	1920	105,710,620	14.9
1720	466,200	40.5	1930	122,775,046	16.1
1730	629,400	35.0	1940	131,669,275	7.2
1740	905,600	43.9	1950	150,697,361	14.5
1750	1,170,800	29.3	1960	179,323,175	19.0
1760	1,593,600	36.1	1970	203,235,298	13.3
1770	2,148,100	34.8	1980	226,545,805	11.5
1780	2,780,400	29.4	1990	248,709,873	9.8
1790	3,929,214	41.3	2000	281,421,906	13.2
1800	5,308,483	35.1	2010	308,745,538	9.7
1810	7,239,881	36.4			

SOURCES: U.S. Bureau of the Census, *Historical Statistics of the United States, Colonial Times to 1970* (1975); *Statistical Abstract of the United States, 2010.*

*Note: Until 1890, census takers never made any effort to count the Native American people who lived outside their reserved political areas and compiled only casual and incomplete enumerations of those living within their jurisdictions. In 1890, the federal government attempted a full count of the Indian population: the Census found 125,719 Indians in 1890, compared with only 12,543 in 1870 and 33,985 in 1880.

Immigration by Decade

Year	Number	Immigrants During This Decade as a Percentage of Total Population	Year	Number	Immigrants During This Decade as a Percentage of Total Population
1821–1830	151,824	1.6	1921–1930	4,107,209	3.9
1831–1840	599,125	4.6	1931–1940	528,431	0.4
1841–1850	1,713,251	10.0	1941–1950	1,035,039	0.7
1851–1860	2,598,214	11.2	1951–1960	2,515,479	1.6
1861–1870	2,314,824	7.4	1961–1970	3,321,677	1.8
1871–1880	2,812,191	7.1	1971–1980	4,493,000	2.2
1881–1890	5,246,613	10.5	1981–1990	7,338,000	3.0
1891–1900	3,687,546	5.8	1991–2000	9,095,083	3.7
1901–1910	8,795,386	11.6	2001–2010	10,501,053	3.7
1911–1920	5,735,811	6.2	2011–2015	5,151,773	NA
Total	**33,654,785**		**Total**	**48,086,744**	
			1821–2000		
			GRAND TOTAL	**81,741,529**	

SOURCES: U.S. Bureau of the Census, *Historical Statistics of the United States, Colonial Times to 1970* (1975), part 1, 105–106; *Statistical Abstract of the United States, 2001.* U.S. Department of Homeland Security, *Yearbook of Immigration Statistics, 2015.*

Regional Origins

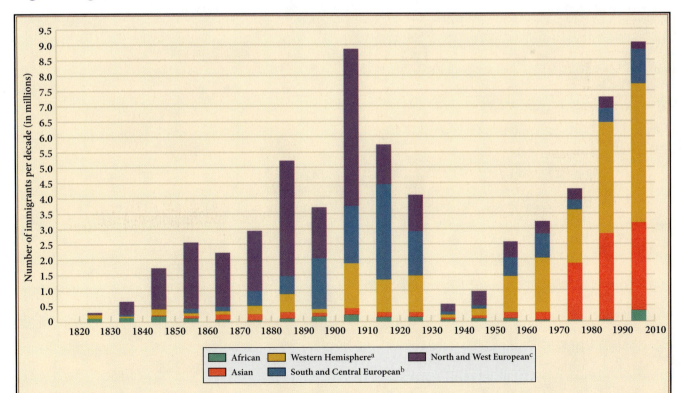

a Canada and all countries in South America and Central America.
b Italy, Spain, Portugal, Greece, Germany (Austria included, 1938–1945), Poland, Czechoslovakia (since 1920), Yugoslavia (since1920), Hungary (since 1861), Austria (since 1861, except 1938–1945), former USSR (excludes Asian USSR between 1931 and 1963), Latvia, Estonia, Lithuania, Finland, Romania, Bulgaria, Turkey (in Europe), and other European countries not classified elsewhere.
c Great Britain, Ireland, Norway, Sweden, Denmark, Iceland, Netherlands, Belgium, Luxembourg, Switzerland, and France.
SOURCES: Stephan Thernstrom, ed., *Harvard Encyclopedia of American Ethnic Groups* (1980), 480; U.S. Bureau of the Census, *Statistical Abstract of the United States, 1991*; U.S. Immigration and Naturalization Service, *Statistical Yearbook, 2010.*

Glossary

abolitionism: The social reform movement to end slavery immediately and without compensation that began in the United States in the 1830s. (p. 322)

Adams-Onís Treaty: An 1819 treaty in which John Quincy Adams persuaded Spain to cede the Florida territory to the United States. In return, the American government accepted Spain's claim to Texas and agreed to a compromise on the western boundary for the state of Louisiana. (p. 231)

African Methodist Episcopal Church: Church founded in 1816 by African Americans who were discriminated against by white Protestants. The church spread across the Northeast and Midwest and even founded a few congregations in the slave states of Missouri, Kentucky, Louisiana, and South Carolina. (p. 321)

Alamo: The 1836 defeat by the Mexican army of the Texan garrison defending the Alamo in San Antonio. Newspapers urged Americans to "Remember the Alamo," and American adventurers, lured by offers of land grants, flocked to Texas to join the rebel forces. (p. 339)

Algonquian cultures/languages: A Native American language family whose speakers were widespread in the eastern woodlands, Great Lakes, and subarctic regions of eastern North America. The Algonquian language family should not be confused with the Algonquins, who were a single nation inhabiting the St. Lawrence Valley at the time of first contact. (p. 11)

American Anti-Slavery Society: The first interracial social justice movement in the United States, which advocated the immediate, unconditional end of slavery on the basis of human rights, without compensation to slave masters. (p. 322)

American Colonization Society: Founded by Henry Clay and other prominent citizens in 1817, the society argued that slaves had to be freed and then resettled, in Africa or elsewhere. (p. 280)

American, or Know-Nothing, Party: An anti-immigrant, anti-Catholic political party formed in 1851 that arose in response to mass immigration in the 1840s, especially from Ireland and Germany. In 1854, the party gained control of the state governments of Massachusetts and Pennsylvania. (p. 384)

American Renaissance: A literary explosion during the 1840s inspired in part by Emerson's ideas on the liberation of the individual. (p. 309)

American System: The mercantilist system of national economic development advocated by Henry Clay and adopted by John Quincy Adams, with a national bank to manage the nation's financial system; protective tariffs to provide revenue and encourage industry; and a nationally funded network of roads, canals, and railroads. (p. 281)

American Woman Suffrage Association: A women's suffrage organization led by Lucy Stone, Henry Blackwell, and others who remained loyal to the Republican Party, despite its failure to include women's voting rights in the Reconstruction amendments. Stressing the urgency of voting rights for African American men, AWSA leaders held out hope that once Reconstruction had been settled, it would be women's turn. (p. 440)

Antifederalists: Opponents of ratification of the Constitution. Antifederalists feared that a powerful and distant central government would be out of touch with the needs of citizens. They also complained that it failed to guarantee individual liberties in a bill of rights. (p. 195)

Articles of Confederation: The written document defining the structure of the government from 1781 to 1788, under which the Union was a confederation of equal states, with no executive and limited powers, existing mainly to foster a common defense. (p. 187)

artisan republicanism: An ideology that celebrated small-scale producers, men and women who owned their own shops (or farms). It defined the ideal republican society as one constituted by, and dedicated to the welfare of, independent workers and citizens. (p. 261)

Bank of the United States: A bank chartered in 1790 and jointly owned by private stockholders and the national government. Alexander Hamilton argued that the bank would provide stability to the specie-starved American economy by making loans to merchants, handling government funds, and issuing bills of credit. (p. 207)

Battle of Little Big Horn: The 1876 battle begun when American cavalry under George Armstrong Custer attacked an encampment of Sioux, Arapaho, and Cheyenne Indians who were resisting removal to a reservation. Custer's force was annihilated, but with whites calling for U.S. soldiers to retaliate, the Native American military victory was short-lived. (p. 486)

Battle of Long Island (1776): First major engagement of the new Continental army, defending against 32,000 British troops outside of New York City. (p. 172)

Battle of Saratoga (1777): A multistage battle in New York ending with the surrender of British general John Burgoyne. The victory ensured the diplomatic success of American representatives in Paris, who won a military alliance with France. (p. 175)

Battle of Tippecanoe: An attack on Shawnee Indians at Prophetstown on the Tippecanoe River in 1811 by American forces headed by William Henry Harrison, Indiana's territorial governor. The governor's troops traded heavy casualties with the confederacy's warriors and then destroyed the holy village. (p. 223)

Battle of Yorktown (1781): A battle in which French and American troops and a French fleet trapped the British army under the command of General Charles Cornwallis at Yorktown, Virginia. The Franco-American victory broke the resolve of the British government. (p. 182)

Bear Flag Republic: A short-lived republic created in California by American emigrants to sponsor a rebellion against Mexican authority in 1846. The army of the Bear Flag Republic was quickly absorbed into the California Battalion of the U.S. Army under the command of John C. Frémont. (p. 360)

Beecher-Tilton scandal: A trial, triggered by revelations made by free love advocate and journalist Victoria Woodhull, that exposed unconventional sexual relationships among a leading New York abolitionist pastor and his congregants, discrediting radical Reconstruction by associating some of its advocates with alleged sexual immorality. (p. 440)

Benevolent Empire: A web of reform organizations, heavily Whig in their political orientation, built by evangelical Protestant men and women influenced by the Second Great Awakening. (p. 306)

Bill of Rights: The first ten amendments to the Constitution, officially ratified by 1791. The amendments safeguarded fundamental personal rights, including freedom of speech and religion, and mandated legal procedures, such as trial by jury. (p. 205)

Black Codes: Laws passed by southern states after the Civil War that denied ex-slaves the civil rights enjoyed by whites, punished vague crimes such as "vagrancy" or failing to have a labor contract, and tried to force African Americans back to plantation labor systems that closely mirrored those in slavery times. (p. 435)

black Protestantism: A form of Protestantism that was devised by Christian slaves in the Chesapeake and spread to the Cotton South as a result of the domestic slave trade. It emphasized the evangelical message of emotional conversion, ritual baptism, communal spirituality, and the idea that blacks were "children of God" and should be treated accordingly. (p. 342)

Burlingame Treaty: An 1868 treaty that guaranteed the rights of U.S. missionaries in China and set official terms for the emigration of Chinese laborers to work in the United States. (p. 465)

Californios: The elite Mexican ranchers in the province of California. (p. 352)

casta system: A hierarchical system of racial classification developed by colonial elites in Latin America to make sense of the complex patterns of racial mixing that developed there. (p. 41)

caucus: A meeting held by a political party to choose candidates, make policies, and enforce party discipline. (p. 277)

chain migration: A pattern by which immigrants find housing and work and learn to navigate a new environment, and then assist other immigrants from their family or home area to settle in the same location. (p. 380)

chattel principle: A system of bondage in which a slave has the legal status of property and so can be bought and sold. (p. 256)

chattel slavery: A system of bondage in which a slave has the legal status of property and so can be bought and sold like property. (p. 38)

Christianity: A religion that holds the belief that Jesus Christ was himself divine. For centuries, the Roman Catholic Church was the great unifying institution in Western Europe, and it was from Europe that Christianity spread to the Americas. (p. 21)

Church of Jesus Christ of Latter-day Saints, or Mormons: Founded by Joseph Smith in 1830. After Smith's death at the hands of an angry mob, in 1846 Brigham Young led many followers of Mormonism to lands in present-day Utah. (p. 314)

Civil Rights Act of 1866: Legislation passed by Congress that nullified the Black Codes and affirmed that African Americans should have equal benefit of the law. (p. 435)

Civil Rights Act of 1875: A law that required "full and equal" access to jury service and to transportation and public accommodations, irrespective of race. (p. 450)

Civil Rights Cases: A series of 1883 Supreme Court decisions that struck down the Civil Rights Act of 1875, rolling back key Reconstruction laws and paving the way for later decisions that sanctioned segregation. (p. 456)

classical liberalism or laissez-faire: The political ideology of individual liberty, private property, a competitive market economy, free trade, and limited government. The ideal is a *laissez faire* or "let alone" policy, in which government does the least possible, particularly in reference to economic policies such as tariffs and incentives for industrial development. Attacking corruption and defending private property, late-nineteenth-century liberals generally called for elite governance and questioned the advisability of full democratic participation. (p. 293)

coastal trade: The domestic slave trade with routes along the Atlantic coast that sent thousands of slaves to sugar plantations in Louisiana and cotton plantations in the Mississippi Valley. (p. 255)

Coercive Acts: Four British acts of 1774 meant to punish Massachusetts for the destruction of three shiploads of tea. Known in America as the Intolerable Acts, they led to open rebellion in the northern colonies. (p. 158)

Columbian Exchange: The massive global exchange of living things, including people, animals, plants, and diseases, between the Eastern and Western Hemispheres that began after the voyages of Columbus. (p. 41)

committees of correspondence: A communications network established among towns in the colonies, and among colonial assemblies, between 1772 and 1773 to provide for rapid dissemination of news about important political developments. (p. 158)

Commonwealth System: The republican system of political economy created by state governments by 1820, whereby states funneled aid to private businesses whose projects would improve the general welfare. (p. 243)

competency: The ability of a family to keep a household solvent and independent and to pass that ability on to the next generation. (p. 109)

Compromise of 1850: Laws passed in 1850 that were meant to resolve the dispute over the status of slavery in the territories. Key elements included the admission of California as a free state and a new Fugitive Slave Act. (p. 375)

Comstock Lode: A vein of silver ore discovered in Nevada in 1859, leading to one of the West's most important mining booms. The lode was so rich that a Confederate expedition tried unsuccessfully to capture it during the Civil War; its output significantly altered the ratio of silver in circulation, leading to changes in monetary policy. (p. 470)

conscience Whigs: Whig politicians who opposed the U.S.-Mexico War on moral grounds, maintaining that the purpose of the war was to expand and perpetuate control of the national government. (p. 368)

constitutional monarchy: A monarchy limited in its rule by a constitution. (p. 81)

consumer revolution: An increase in consumption in English manufactures in Britain and the British colonies fueled by the Industrial Revolution. Although the consumer revolution raised living standards, it landed many consumers — and the colonies as a whole — in debt. (p. 132)

Continental Association: An association established in 1774 by the First Continental Congress to enforce a boycott of British goods. (p. 162)

Continental Congress: September 1774 gathering of colonial delegates in Philadelphia to discuss the crisis precipitated by the Coercive Acts. The Congress produced a declaration of rights and an agreement to impose a limited boycott of trade with Britain. (p. 159)

"contrabands": Slaves who fled plantations and sought protection behind Union lines during the Civil War. (p. 406)

convict leasing: Notorious system, begun during Reconstruction, whereby southern state officials allowed private companies to hire out prisoners to labor under brutal conditions in mines and other industries. (p. 448)

corrupt bargain: A term used by Andrew Jackson's supporters for the appointment by President John Quincy Adams of Henry Clay as his secretary of state, the traditional stepping-stone to the presidency. Clay had used his influence as Speaker of the House to elect Adams rather than Jackson in the election in 1824. (p. 282)

cotton complex: The economic system that developed in the first half of the nineteenth century binding together southern cotton production with northern clothmaking, shipping, and capital. (p. 248)

Counter-Reformation: A reaction in the Catholic Church triggered by the Reformation that sought change from within and created new monastic and missionary orders, including the Jesuits (founded in 1540), who saw themselves as soldiers of Christ. (p. 23)

Covenant Chain: The alliance of the Iroquois, first with the colony of New York, then with the British Empire and its other colonies. The Covenant Chain became a model for relations between the British Empire and other Native American peoples. (p. 83)

covenant of grace: The Christian idea that God's elect are granted salvation as a pure gift of grace. This doctrine holds that nothing people do can erase their sins or earn them a place in heaven. (p. 60)

covenant of works: The Christian idea that God's elect must do good works in their earthly lives to earn their salvation. (p. 60)

coverture: A principle in English law that placed wives under the protection and authority of their husbands, so that they did not have independent legal standing. (p. 112)

Crédit Mobilier: A sham corporation set up by shareholders in the Union Pacific Railroad to secure government grants at an enormous profit. Organizers of the scheme protected it from investigation by providing gifts of its stock to powerful members of Congress. (p. 452)

"Crime of 1873": A term used by those critical of an 1873 law directing the U.S. Treasury to cease minting silver dollars, retire Civil War–era greenbacks, and replace them with notes backed by the gold standard from an expanded system of national banks. (p. 469)

Crusades: A series of wars undertaken by Christian armies between A.D. 1096 and 1291 to reverse the Muslim advance in Europe and win back the holy lands where Christ had lived. (p. 22)

currency tax: A hidden tax on the farmers and artisans who accepted Continental bills in payment for supplies and on the thousands of soldiers who took them as pay. Because of rampant inflation, Continental currency lost much of its value during the war — thus, the implicit tax on those who accepted it as payment. (p. 183)

Dawes Severalty Act: The 1887 law that gave Native Americans severalty (individual ownership of land) by dividing reservations into homesteads. The law was a disaster for Native peoples, resulting over several decades in the loss of 66 percent of lands held by Indians at the time of the law's passage. (p. 483)

Declaration of Independence: A document containing philosophical principles and a list of grievances that declared separation from Britain. Adopted by the Second Continental Congress on July 4, 1776, it ended a period of intense debate with moderates still hoping to reconcile with Britain. (p. 167)

Declaratory Act of 1766: Law issued by Parliament to assert Parliament's unassailable right to legislate for its British colonies "in all cases whatsoever," putting Americans on notice that the simultaneous repeal of the Stamp Act changed nothing in the imperial powers of Britain. (p. 150)

deism: The Enlightenment-influenced belief that the Christian God created the universe and then left it to run according to natural laws. (p. 121)

demographic transition: The sharp decline in birthrate in the United States beginning in the 1790s that was caused by changes in cultural behavior, including the use of birth control. The migration of thousands of young men to the trans-Appalachian West was also a factor in this decline. (p. 278)

domesticity: A middle-class ideal of "separate spheres" that celebrated women's special mission as homemakers, wives, and mothers who exercised a Christian influence on their families and communities; it excluded women from professional careers, politics, and civic life. (p. 325)

Dominion of New England: A royal province created by King James II in 1686 that would have absorbed Connecticut, Rhode Island, Massachusetts Bay, Plymouth, New York, and New Jersey into a single, vast colony and eliminated their assemblies and other chartered rights. James's plan was canceled by the Glorious Revolution in 1688, which removed him from the throne. (p. 80)

draft (conscription): The system for selecting individuals for conscription, or compulsory military service, first implemented during the Civil War. (p. 411)

draft riots: Violent protests against military conscription that occurred in the North, most dramatically in New York City; led by working-class men who could not buy exemption from the draft. (p. 412)

Dred Scott **decision:** The 1857 Supreme Court decision that ruled the Missouri Compromise unconstitutional. The Court ruled against slave Dred Scott, who claimed that travels with his master into free states and territories made him and his family free. The decision also denied the federal government the right to exclude slavery from the territories and declared that African Americans were not citizens. (p. 386)

Dunmore's War: A 1774 war led by Virginia's royal governor, the Earl of Dunmore, against the Ohio Shawnees, who had a long-standing claim to Kentucky as a hunting ground. The Shawnees were defeated and Dunmore and his militia forces claimed Kentucky as their own. (p. 165)

eastern woodlands: A culture area of Native Americans that extended from the Atlantic Ocean westward to the Great Plains, and from the Great Lakes to the Gulf of Mexico. The eastern woodlands could be subdivided into the southeastern and northeastern woodlands. Eastern woodlands peoples were generally semisedentary, with agriculture based on maize, beans, and squash. Most, but not all, were chiefdoms. (p. 11)

Emancipation Proclamation: President Abraham Lincoln's proclamation issued on January 1, 1863, that legally abolished slavery in all states that remained out of the Union. While the Emancipation Proclamation did not immediately free a single slave, it signaled an end to the institution of slavery. (p. 407)

Embargo Act of 1807: An act of Congress that prohibited U.S. ships from traveling to foreign ports and effectively banned overseas trade in an attempt to deter Britain from halting U.S. ships at sea. The embargo caused grave hardships for Americans engaged in overseas commerce. (p. 223)

encomienda: A grant of Indian labor in Spanish America given in the sixteenth century by the Spanish kings to prominent men. *Encomenderos* extracted tribute from these Indians in exchange for granting them protection and Christian instruction. (p. 40)

Enforcement Laws: Acts passed in Congress in 1870 and signed by President U. S. Grant that were designed to protect freedmen's rights under the Fourteenth and Fifteenth Amendments. Authorizing federal prosecutions, military intervention, and martial law to suppress terrorist activity, the Enforcement Laws largely succeeded in shutting down Klan activities. (p. 453)

English common law: The centuries-old body of legal rules and procedures that protected the lives and property of the British monarch's subjects. (p. 149)

Enlightenment: An eighteenth-century philosophical movement that emphasized the use of reason to reevaluate previously accepted doctrines and traditions and the power of reason to understand and shape the world. (p. 118)

Erie Canal: A 364-mile waterway connecting the Hudson River and Lake Erie. The Erie Canal brought prosperity to the entire Great Lakes region, and its benefits prompted civic and business leaders in Philadelphia and Baltimore to propose canals to link their cities to the Midwest. (p. 244)

Exodusters: African Americans who walked or rode out of the Deep South following the Civil War, many settling on farms in Kansas in hopes of finding peace and prosperity. (p. 473)

Federalist No. 10: An essay by James Madison in *The Federalist* (1787–1788) that challenged the view that republican governments only worked in small polities; it argued that a geographically expansive national government would better protect republican liberty. (p. 198)

Federalists: Supporters of the Constitution of 1787, which created a strong central government; their opponents, the Antifederalists, feared that a strong central government would corrupt the nation's newly won liberty. (p. 195)

Female Moral Reform Society: An organization led by middle-class Christian women who viewed prostitutes as victims of male lust and sought to expose their male customers while "rescuing" sex workers and encouraging them to pursue respectable trades. (p. 326)

Fetterman massacre: A massacre in December 1866 in which 1,500 Sioux warriors lured Captain William Fetterman and 80 soldiers from a Wyoming fort and attacked them. With the Fetterman massacre the Sioux succeeded in closing the Bozeman Trail, the main route into Montana. (p. 480)

Fifteenth Amendment: Constitutional amendment ratified in 1870 that forbade states to deny citizens the right to vote on grounds of race, color, or "previous condition of servitude." (p. 439)

"Fifty-four forty or fight!": Democratic candidate Governor James K. Polk's slogan in the election of 1844 calling for American sovereignty over the entire Oregon Country, which stretched from California to Russian-occupied Alaska and at the time was shared with Great Britain. (p. 355)

filibustering: Private paramilitary campaigns, mounted particularly by southern proslavery advocates in the 1850s, to seize additional territory in the Caribbean or Latin America in order to establish control by U.S.-born leaders, with an expectation of eventual annexation by the United States. (p. 378)

Foreign Miner's Tax: A discriminatory tax, adopted in 1850 in California Territory, that forced Chinese and Latin American immigrant miners to pay high taxes for the right to prospect for gold. The tax effectively drove these miners from the goldfields. (p. 372)

Fourierist socialism: A system of social and economic organization proposed by French thinker Charles Fourier, which was based on common ownership of goods and shared labor by members of a community. A number of nineteenth-century American utopian communities tried to put Fourierist principles into practice. (p. 312)

Fourteenth Amendment: Constitutional amendment ratified in 1868 that made all native-born or naturalized persons U.S. citizens and prohibited states from abridging the rights of national citizens, thus giving primacy to national rather than state citizenship. (p. 436)

franchise: The right to vote. Between 1820 and 1860, most states revised their constitutions to extend the vote to all adult white males. Black adult men gained the right to vote with the passage of the Fourteenth Amendment (1868). The Nineteenth Amendment (1920) granted adult women the right to vote. (p. 274)

Free African Societies: Organizations in northern free black communities that sought to help community members and work against racial discrimination, inequality, and political slavery. (p. 321)

Freedmen's Bureau: Government organization created in March 1865 to aid displaced blacks and other war refugees. Active until the early 1870s, it was the first federal agency in history that provided direct payments to assist those in poverty and to foster social welfare. (p. 435)

freeholds: Land owned in its entirety, without feudal dues or landlord obligations. Freeholders had the legal right to improve, transfer, or sell their landed property. (p. 50)

free soil movement: A political movement that opposed the expansion of slavery. In 1848 the free soilers organized the Free Soil Party, which depicted slavery as a threat to republicanism and to the Jeffersonian ideal of a freeholder society, arguments that won broad support among aspiring white farmers. (p. 370)

French Revolution: A 1789 revolution in France that was initially welcomed by most Americans because it abolished feudalism and established a constitutional monarchy, but eventually came to seem too radical to many. (p. 208)

gag rule: A procedure in the House of Representatives from 1836 to 1844 by which antislavery petitions were automatically tabled when they were received so that they could not become the subject of debate. (p. 324)

gang-labor system: A system of work discipline used on southern cotton plantations in the mid-nineteenth century in which white overseers or black drivers supervised gangs of enslaved laborers to achieve greater productivity. (p. 266)

gentility: A refined style of living and elaborate manners that came to be highly prized among well-to-do English families after 1600 and strongly influenced leading colonists after 1700. (p. 98)

Gettysburg Address: Abraham Lincoln's November 1863 speech dedicating a national cemetery at the Gettysburg battlefield. Lincoln declared the nation's founding ideal to be that "all men are created equal," and he urged listeners to dedicate themselves out of the carnage of war to a "new birth of freedom" for the United States. (p. 419)

Ghost Dance movement: Religion of the late 1880s and early 1890s that combined elements of Christianity and traditional Native American religion. It fostered Plains Indians' hope that they could, through sacred dances, resurrect the great bison herds and call up a storm to drive whites back across the Atlantic. (p. 488)

Glorious Revolution: A quick and nearly bloodless coup in 1688 in which James II of England was overthrown by William of Orange. Whig politicians forced the new King William and Queen Mary to accept the Declaration of Rights, creating a constitutional monarchy that enhanced the powers of the House of Commons at the expense of the crown. (p. 80)

gold standard: The practice of backing a country's currency with its reserves of gold. In 1873 the United States, following Great Britain and other European nations, began converting to the gold standard. (p. 469)

gradual emancipation: The practice of ending slavery in the distant future while recognizing white property rights to the slaves they owned. Generally, living slaves were not freed by gradual emancipation statutes; they applied only to slaves born after the passage of the statute, and only after they had first labored for their owners for a term of years. (p. 250)

Great American Desert: A term coined by Major Stephen H. Long in 1820 to describe the grasslands of the southern plains from the ninety-fifth meridian west to the Rocky Mountains, which he believed was "almost wholly unfit for cultivation." (p. 338)

Great Basin: An arid basin-and-range region bounded by the Rocky Mountains on the east and the Sierra Mountains on the west. All of its water drains or evaporates within the basin. A resource-scarce environment, the Great Basin was thinly populated by Native American hunter-gatherers who ranged long distances to support themselves. (p. 15)

Great Lakes: Five enormous, interconnected freshwater lakes—Ontario, Erie, Huron, Michigan, and Superior—that dominate eastern North America. In the era before long-distance overland travel, they comprised the center of the continent's transportation system. (p. 15)

Great Plains: A broad plateau region that stretches from central Texas in the south to the Canadian plains in the north, bordered on the east by the eastern woodlands and on the west by the Rocky Mountains. Averaging around 20 inches of rainfall a year, the Great Plains are primarily grasslands that support grazing but not crop agriculture. (p. 15)

greenbacks: Paper money issued by the U.S. Treasury during the Civil War to finance the war effort. (p. 409)

Gullah dialect: A Creole language that combined words from English and a variety of African languages in an African grammatical structure. Though it remained widespread in the South Carolina and Georgia lowcountry throughout the nineteenth century and is still spoken in a modified form today, Gullah did not take root in the Cotton South, where lowcountry slaves were far outnumbered. (p. 343)

habeas corpus: A legal writ forcing government authorities to justify their arrest and detention of an individual. During the Civil War, Lincoln suspended habeas corpus to stop protests against the draft and other anti-Union activities. (p. 402)

Haitian Revolution: The 1791 conflict involving diverse Haitian participants and armies from three European countries. At its end, Haiti became a free, independent nation in which former slaves were citizens. (p. 212)

hard war: The philosophy and tactics used by Union general William Tecumseh Sherman, by which he treated civilians as combatants. (p. 422)

headright system: A system of land distribution, pioneered in Virginia and used in several other colonies, that granted land—usually 50 acres—to anyone who paid the passage of a new arrival. By this means, large planters amassed huge landholdings as they imported large numbers of servants and slaves. (p. 50)

Homestead Act: The 1862 act that gave 160 acres of free western land to any applicant who occupied and improved the property. This policy led to the rapid development of the American West after the Civil War; facing arid conditions in the West, however, many homesteaders found themselves unable to live on their land. (p. 470)

household mode of production: The system of exchanging goods and labor that helped eighteenth-century New England freeholders survive on ever-shrinking farms as available land became more scarce. (p. 112)

House of Burgesses: Organ of government in colonial Virginia made up of an assembly of representatives elected by the colony's inhabitants. (p. 46)

hunters and gatherers: Societies whose members gather food by hunting, fishing, and collecting wild plants rather than relying on agriculture or animal husbandry. Because hunter-gatherers are mobile, moving seasonally through their territory to exploit resources, they have neither fixed townsites nor weighty material goods. (p. 8)

indentured servitude: System in which workers contracted for service for a specified period. In exchange for agreeing to work for four or five years (or more) without wages in the colonies, indentured workers received passage across the Atlantic, room and board, and status as a free person at the end of the contract period. (p. 50)

Indian Removal Act of 1830: Act that directed the mandatory relocation of eastern tribes to territory west of the Mississippi. Jackson insisted that his goal was to save the Indians and their culture. Indians resisted the controversial act, but in the end most were forced to comply. (p. 291)

individualism: Word coined by Alexis de Tocqueville in 1835 to describe Americans as people no longer bound by social attachments to classes, castes, associations, and families. (p. 302)

Industrial Revolution: A burst of major inventions and economic expansion based on water and steam power and the use of machine technology that transformed certain industries, such as cotton textiles and iron, between 1790 and 1860. (p. 248)

inland system: The slave trade system in the interior of the country that fed slaves to the Cotton South. (p. 255)

internal improvements: Public works such as roads and canals. (p. 282)

Iroquoian cultures/languages: A Native American language family whose speakers were concentrated in the eastern woodlands. The Iroquoian language family should not be confused with the nations of the Iroquois Confederacy, which inhabited the territory of modern-day upstate New York at the time of first contact. (p. 11)

Iroquois Confederacy: A league of five Native American nations — the Mohawks, Oneidas, Onondagas, Cayugas, and Senecas — probably formed around A.D. 1450. A sixth nation, the Tuscaroras, joined the confederacy around 1720. Condolence ceremonies introduced by a Mohawk named Hiawatha formed the basis for the league. Positioned between New France and New Netherland (later New York), the Iroquois played a central role in the era of European colonization. (p. 13)

Islam: A religion that considers Muhammad to be God's last prophet. Following the death of Muhammad in A.D. 632, the newly converted Arab peoples of North Africa used force and fervor to spread the Muslim faith into sub-Saharan Africa, India, Indonesia, Spain, and the Balkan regions of Europe. (p. 22)

Jacobins: A political faction in the French Revolution. Many Americans embraced the democratic ideology of the radical Jacobins and, like them, formed political clubs and began to address one another as "citizen." (p. 209)

Jay's Treaty: A 1795 treaty between the United States and Britain, negotiated by John Jay. The treaty accepted Britain's right to stop neutral ships. In return, it allowed Americans to submit claims for illegal seizures and required the British to remove their troops and Indian agents from the Northwest Territory. (p. 212)

joint-stock corporation: A financial organization devised by English merchants around 1550 that facilitated the colonization of North America. In these companies, a number of investors pooled their capital and received shares of stock in the enterprise in proportion to their share of the total investment. (p. 45)

Judiciary Act of 1789: Act that established a federal district court in each state and three circuit courts to hear appeals from the districts, with the Supreme Court having the final say. (p. 205)

Kansas-Nebraska Act: A controversial 1854 law that divided Indian Territory into Kansas and Nebraska, repealed the Missouri Compromise, and left the new territories to decide the issue of slavery on the basis of popular sovereignty. Far from clarifying the status of slavery in the territories, the act led to violent conflict in "Bleeding Kansas." (p. 384)

King Cotton: The Confederates' belief during the Civil War that their cotton was so important to the British and French economies that those governments would recognize the South as an independent nation and supply it with loans and arms. (p. 401)

Ku Klux Klan: Secret society that first undertook violence against African Americans in the South after the Civil War but was reborn in 1915 to fight the perceived threats posed by African Americans, immigrants, radicals, feminists, Catholics, and Jews. (p. 453)

labor theory of value: The belief that human labor produces economic value. Adherents argued that the price of a product should be determined not by the market (supply and demand) but by the amount of work required to make it, and that most of the price should be paid to the person who produced it. (p. 262)

land-grant colleges: Authorized by the Morrill Act of 1862, land-grant colleges were public universities founded to broaden educational opportunities and foster technical and scientific expertise. These universities were funded by the Morrill Act, which authorized the sale of federal lands to raise money for higher education. (p. 470)

Liberty Party: An antislavery political party that ran its first presidential candidate in 1844, controversially challenging both the Democrats and Whigs. (p. 324)

Lieber Code: Union guidelines for the laws of war, issued in April 1863. The code ruled that soldiers and prisoners must be treated equally without respect to color or race; justified a range of military actions if they were based on "necessity" that would "hasten surrender"; and outlawed use of torture. The code provided a foundation for later international agreements on the laws of war. (p. 413)

Lone Wolf v. Hitchcock: A 1903 Supreme Court ruling that Congress could make whatever Indian policies it chose, ignoring all existing treaties. (p. 483)

Louisiana Purchase: The 1803 purchase of French territory west of the Mississippi River that stretched from the Gulf of Mexico to Canada. The Louisiana Purchase nearly doubled the size of the United States and opened the way for future American expansion west. The purchase required President Thomas Jefferson to exercise powers not explicitly granted to him by the Constitution. (p. 220)

machine tools: Cutting, boring, and drilling machines used to produce standardized metal parts, which were then assembled into products such as textile looms and sewing machines. The rapid development of machine tools by American inventors in the early nineteenth century was a factor in the rapid spread of industrialization. (p. 260)

Maine Law: The nation's first state law for the prohibition of liquor manufacture and sales, passed in 1851. (p. 307)

Manifest Destiny: A term coined by John L. O'Sullivan in 1845 to express the idea that Euro-Americans were fated by God to settle the North American continent from the Atlantic to the Pacific Ocean. (p. 348)

manumission: The legal act of relinquishing property rights in slaves. Worried that a large free black population would threaten the institution of slavery, the Virginia assembly repealed Virginia's 1782 manumission law in 1792. (p. 252)

Marbury v. Madison **(1803):** A Supreme Court case that established the principle of judicial review in finding that parts of the Judiciary Act of 1789 were in conflict with the Constitution. For the first time, the Supreme Court assumed legal authority to overrule acts of other branches of the government. (p. 219)

Market Revolution: The dramatic increase between 1820 and 1850 in the exchange of goods and services in market transactions. The Market Revolution reflected the increased output of farms (including cotton plantations) and factories, the entrepreneurial activities of traders and merchants, and the creation of a transportation network of roads, canals, and railroads. (p. 246)

married women's property laws: Laws enacted between 1839 and 1860 in New York and other states that permitted married women to own, inherit, and bequeath property. (p. 327)

McCulloch v. Maryland **(1819):** A Supreme Court case that asserted the dominance of national over state statutes. (p. 230)

mechanics: A term used in the nineteenth century to refer to skilled craftsmen and inventors who built and improved machinery and machine tools for industry. (p. 248)

mercantilism: A system of political economy based on government regulation. Beginning in 1650, Britain enacted Navigation Acts that controlled colonial commerce and manufacturing for the enrichment of Britain. (p. 43)

Metacom's War: Also known as King Philip's War, it pitted a coalition of Native Americans led by the Wampanoag leader Metacom against the New England colonies in 1675–1676. A thousand colonists were killed and twelve colonial towns destroyed, but the colonies prevailed. Metacom and his allies lost some 4,500 people. (p. 66)

Mexican cession: Lands taken by the United States in the U.S.-Mexico War (1846–1848). (p. 366)

middle class: An economic group of prosperous farmers, artisans, and traders that emerged in the early nineteenth century. Its rise reflected a dramatic increase in prosperity. This surge in income, along with an abundance of inexpensive mass-produced goods, fostered a distinct middle-class urban culture. (p. 268)

Middle Passage: The brutal sea voyage from Africa to the Americas that took the lives of nearly 2 million enslaved Africans. (p. 89)

Minor v. Happersett: A Supreme Court decision in 1875 that ruled that suffrage rights were not inherent in citizenship and had not been granted by the Fourteenth Amendment, as some women's rights advocates argued. Women were citizens, the Court ruled, but state legislatures could deny women the vote if they wished. (p. 440)

minstrel shows: Popular theatrical entertainment begun around 1830, in which white actors in blackface presented comic routines that combined racist caricature and social criticism. (p. 318)

Minutemen: Colonial militiamen who stood ready to mobilize on short notice during the imperial crisis of the 1770s. These volunteers formed the core of the citizens' army that met British troops at Lexington and Concord in April 1775. (p. 165)

miscegenation: A derogatory word for interracial sexual relationships coined by Democrats in the 1864 election, as they claimed that emancipation would allow African American men to gain sexual access to white women and produce mixed-race children. (p. 424)

Mississippian culture: A Native American culture complex that flourished in the Mississippi River basin and the Southeast from around A.D. 850 to around 1700. Characterized by maize agriculture, moundbuilding, and distinctive pottery styles, Mississippian communities were complex chiefdoms usually located along the floodplains of rivers. The largest of these communities was Cahokia, in modern-day Illinois. (p. 11)

Missouri Compromise: A series of political agreements devised by Speaker of the House Henry Clay. Maine entered the Union as a free state in 1820 and Missouri followed as a slave state in 1821, preserving a balance in the Senate between North and South and setting a precedent for future admissions to the Union. Most importantly, this bargain set the northern boundary of slavery in the lands of the Louisiana Purchase at the southern boundary of Missouri, with the exception of that state. (p. 281)

mixed government: John Adams's theory from *Thoughts on Government* (1776), which called for three branches of government, each representing one function: executive, legislative, and judicial. This system of dispersed authority was devised to maintain a balance of power and ensure the legitimacy of governmental procedures. (p. 185)

Monroe Doctrine: The 1823 declaration by President James Monroe that the Western Hemisphere was closed to any further colonization or interference by European powers. In exchange, Monroe pledged that the United States would not become involved in European struggles. (p. 231)

Munn v. Illinois: An 1877 Supreme Court case that affirmed that states could regulate key businesses, such as railroads and grain elevators, if those businesses were "clothed in the public interest." (p. 467)

National Woman Suffrage Association: A suffrage group headed by Elizabeth Cady Stanton and Susan B. Anthony that stressed the need for women to lead organizations on their own behalf. The NWSA focused exclusively on women's rights — sometimes denigrating men of color in the process — and took up the battle for a federal women's suffrage amendment. (p. 440)

nativism: Opposition to immigration and to full citizenship for recent immigrants or to immigrants of a particular ethnic or national background, as expressed, for example, by anti-Irish discrimination in the 1850s and Asian exclusion laws between the 1880s and 1940s. (p. 381)

Naturalization, Alien, and Sedition Acts: Three laws passed in 1798 that limited individual rights and threatened the fledgling party system. The Naturalization Act lengthened the residency requirement for citizenship, the Alien Act authorized the deportation of foreigners, and the Sedition Act prohibited the publication of insults or malicious attacks on the president or members of Congress. (p. 214)

natural rights: The rights to life, liberty, and property. According to the English philosopher John Locke in *Two Treatises of Government* (1690), political authority was not given by God to monarchs. Instead, it derived from social compacts that people made to preserve their natural rights. (p. 120)

Navigation Acts: English laws passed, beginning in the 1650s and 1660s, requiring that certain English colonial goods be shipped through English ports on English ships manned primarily by English sailors in order to benefit English merchants, shippers, and seamen. (p. 79)

neo-Europes: Term for colonies in which colonists sought to replicate, or at least approximate, economies and social structures they knew at home. (p. 38)

neomercantilism: A system of government-assisted economic development embraced by republican state legislatures throughout the nation, especially in the Northeast. This system of activist government encouraged private entrepreneurs to seek individual opportunity and the public welfare through market exchange. (p. 240)

New Jersey Plan: Alternative to the Virginia Plan drafted by delegates from small states, retaining the confederation's single-house congress with one vote per state. It shared with the Virginia Plan enhanced congressional powers to raise revenue, control commerce, and make binding requisitions on the states. (p. 194)

New Lights: Evangelical preachers, many of them influenced by John Wesley, the founder of English Methodism, and George Whitefield, the charismatic itinerant preacher who brought his message to Britain's American colonies. They decried a Christian faith that was merely intellectual and emphasized the importance of a spiritual rebirth. (p. 124)

nonimportation movement: Colonists attempted nonimportation agreements three times: in 1766, in response to the Stamp Act; in 1768, in response to the Townshend duties; and in 1774, in response to the Coercive Acts. In each case, colonial radicals pressured merchants to stop importing British goods. In 1774 nonimportation was adopted by the First Continental Congress and enforced by the Continental Association. American women became crucial to the movement by reducing their households' consumption of imported goods and producing large quantities of homespun cloth. (p. 151)

Northwest Ordinance of 1787: A land act that provided for orderly settlement and established a process by which settled territories would become the states of Ohio, Indiana, Illinois, Michigan, and Wisconsin. It also banned slavery in the Northwest Territory. (p. 189)

notables: Northern landlords, slave-owning planters, and seaport merchants who dominated the political system of the early nineteenth century. (p. 274)

nullification: The constitutional argument advanced by John C. Calhoun that a state legislature or convention could void a law passed by Congress. (p. 286)

Old Lights: Conservative ministers opposed to the passion displayed by evangelical preachers; they preferred to emphasize the importance of cultivating a virtuous Christian life. (p. 124)

one-tenth tax: A tax adopted by the Confederacy in 1863 that required all farmers to turn over a tenth of their crops and livestock to the government for military use. The tax demonstrated the southern government's strong use of centralized power; it caused great hardship for poor families. (p. 410)

Oregon Trail: An emigrant route that originally led from Independence, Missouri, to the Willamette Valley in Oregon, a distance of some 2,000 miles. Alternate routes included the California Trail, the Mormon Trail, and the Bozeman Trail. Together they conveyed several hundred thousand migrants to the Far West in the 1840s, 1850s, and 1860s. (p. 350)

Ostend Manifesto: An 1854 manifesto that urged President Franklin Pierce to seize the slave-owning province of Cuba from Spain. Northern Democrats denounced this aggressive initiative, and the plan was scuttled. (p. 379)

Panic of 1819: First major economic crisis of the United States. Farmers and planters faced an abrupt 30 percent drop in world agricultural prices, and as farmers' income declined, they could not pay debts owed to stores and banks, many of which went bankrupt. (p. 241)

Panic of 1837: Triggered by a sharp reduction in English capital and credit flowing into the United States, the cash shortage caused a panic while the collapse of credit led to a depression — the second major economic crisis of the United States — that lasted from 1837 to 1843. (p. 296)

paternalism: The ideology held by slave owners who considered themselves committed to the welfare of their slaves. (p. 257)

patronage: The power of elected officials to grant government jobs and favors to their supporters; also the jobs and favors themselves. (p. 102)

peasants: The traditional term for farmworkers in Europe. Some peasants owned land, while others leased or rented small plots from landlords. (p. 19)

Pennsylvania constitution of 1776: A constitution that granted all taxpaying men the right to vote and hold office and created a unicameral (one-house) legislature with complete power; there was no governor to exercise a veto. Other provisions mandated a system of elementary education and protected citizens from imprisonment for debt. (p. 185)

penny papers: Sensational and popular urban newspapers that built large circulations by reporting crime and scandals. (p. 317)

personal liberty laws: Laws enacted in many northern states that guaranteed to all residents, including alleged fugitives, the right to a jury trial. (p. 377)

Philipsburg Proclamation: A 1779 proclamation that declared that any slave who deserted a rebel master would receive protection, freedom, and land from Great Britain. (p. 179)

Pietism: A Christian revival movement characterized by Bible study, the conversion experience, and the individual's personal relationship with God. It began as an effort to reform the German Lutheran Church in the mid-seventeenth century and became widely influential in Britain and its colonies in the eighteenth century. (p. 118)

Pilgrims: One of the first Protestant groups to come to America, seeking a separation from the Church of England. They founded Plymouth, the first permanent community in New England, in 1620. (p. 58)

plantation system: A system of production characterized by unfree labor producing cash crops for distant markets. The plantation complex developed in sugar-producing areas of the Mediterranean world and was transferred to the Americas, where it took hold in tropical and subtropical areas, including Brazil, the West Indies, and southeastern North America. In addition to sugar, the plantation complex was adapted to produce tobacco, rice, indigo, and cotton. (p. 35)

plural marriage: The practice of men taking multiple wives, which Mormon prophet Joseph Smith argued was biblically sanctioned and divinely ordained as a family system. (p. 315)

political machine: A highly organized group of insiders that directs a political party. As the power of notables waned in the 1820s, disciplined political parties usually run by professional politicians appeared in a number of states. (p. 276)

popular sovereignty: The principle that ultimate power lies in the hands of the electorate. Also a plan, first promoted by Democratic candidate Senator Lewis Cass as "squatter sovereignty," then revised as "popular sovereignty" by fellow Democratic presidential aspirant Stephen Douglas, under which Congress would allow settlers in each territory to determine its status as free or slave. (pp. 168, 374)

"positive good": In 1837, South Carolina Senator John C. Calhoun argued on the floor of the Senate that slavery was not a necessary evil, but a positive good, "indispensable to the peace and happiness" of blacks and whites alike. (p. 257)

Proclamation of Neutrality: A proclamation issued by President George Washington in 1793, allowing U.S. citizens to trade with all belligerents in the war between France and Great Britain. (p. 208)

proprietorship: A colony created through a grant of land from the English monarch to an individual or group, who then set up a form of government largely independent from royal control. (p. 77)

protective tariff: A tax or duty on foreign producers of goods coming into or imported into the United States; tariffs gave U.S. manufacturers a competitive advantage in America's gigantic domestic market. (p. 464)

Protestant Reformation: The reform movement that began in 1517 with Martin Luther's critiques of the Roman Catholic Church and that precipitated an enduring schism that divided Protestants from Catholics. (p. 23)

Pueblo Revolt: Also known as Popé's Rebellion, the revolt in 1680 was an uprising of 46 Native American pueblos against Spanish rule. Spaniards were driven out of New Mexico. When they returned in the 1690s, they granted more autonomy to the pueblos they claimed to rule. (p. 66)

Puritans: Dissenters from the Church of England who wanted a genuine Reformation rather than the partial Reformation sought by Henry VIII. The Puritans' religious principles emphasized the importance of an individual's relationship with God developed through Bible study, prayer, and introspection. (p. 59)

Quakers: Epithet for members of the Society of Friends. Their belief that God spoke directly to each individual through an "inner light" and that neither ministers nor the Bible was essential to discovering God's Word put them in conflict with both the Church of England and orthodox Puritans. (p. 78)

Quartering Act of 1765: A British law passed by Parliament at the request of General Thomas Gage, the British military commander in America, that required colonial governments to provide barracks and food for British troops. (p. 147)

Radical Republicans: The members of the Republican Party who were bitterly opposed to slavery and to southern slave owners since the mid-1850s. With the Confiscation Act in 1861, Radical Republicans began to use wartime legislation to destroy slavery. (p. 406)

"rain follows the plow": An unfounded theory that settlement and farming of the Great Plains caused an increase in rainfall. (p. 472)

Reconstruction Act of 1867: An act that divided the conquered South into five military districts, each under the command of a U.S. general. To reenter the Union, former Confederate states had to grant the vote to freedmen and deny it to leading ex-Confederates. (p. 437)

redemptioner: A common type of indentured servant in the Middle colonies in the eighteenth century. Unlike other indentured servants, redemptioners did not sign a contract before leaving Europe. Instead, they found employers after arriving in America. (p. 116)

Regulators: Landowning protestors who organized in North and South Carolina in the 1760s and 1770s to demand that the eastern-controlled government provide western districts with more courts, fairer taxation, and greater representation in the assembly. (p. 133)

Report on Manufactures: A proposal by treasury secretary Alexander Hamilton in 1791 calling for the federal government to urge the expansion of American manufacturing while imposing tariffs on foreign imports. (p. 207)

Report on the Public Credit: Alexander Hamilton's 1790 report recommending that the federal government should assume all state debts and fund the national debt — that is, offer interest on it rather than repaying it — at full value. Hamilton's goal was to make the new country creditworthy, not debt-free. (p. 205)

republic: A state without a monarch or prince that is governed by representatives of the people. (p. 20)

republican aristocracy: The Old South gentry that built impressive mansions, adopted the manners and values of the English landed gentry, and feared federal government interference with their slave property. (p. 335)

republican motherhood: The idea that the primary political role of American women was to instill a sense of patriotic duty and republican virtue in their children and mold them into exemplary republican citizens. (p. 278)

revival: A renewal of religious enthusiasm in a Christian congregation. In the eighteenth century, revivals were often inspired by evangelical preachers who urged their listeners to experience a rebirth. (p. 121)

Rocky Mountains: A high mountain range that spans some 3,000 miles, the Rocky Mountains are bordered by the Great Plains on the east and the Great Basin on the west. Native peoples fished, gathered roots and berries, and hunted elk, deer, and bighorn sheep there. Silver mining boomed in the Rockies in the nineteenth century. (p. 15)

romanticism: A European philosophy that rejected the ordered rationality of the eighteenth-century Enlightenment, embracing human passion, spiritual quest, and self-knowledge. Romanticism strongly influenced American transcendentalism. (p. 309)

royal colony: In the English system, a royal colony was chartered by the crown. The colony's governor was appointed by the crown and served according to the instructions of the Board of Trade. (p. 46)

salutary neglect: A term used to describe British colonial policy during the reigns of George I (r. 1714–1727) and George II (r. 1727–1760). By relaxing their supervision of internal colonial affairs, royal bureaucrats inadvertently assisted the rise of self-government in North America. (p. 102)

Sand Creek massacre: The November 29, 1864, massacre of more than a hundred peaceful Cheyennes, largely women and children, by John M. Chivington's Colorado militia. (p. 480)

Second Bank of the United States: National bank with multiple branches chartered in 1816 for twenty years. Intended to help regulate the economy, the bank became a major issue in Andrew Jackson's reelection campaign in 1832. (p. 286)

Second Continental Congress: Legislative body that governed the United States from May 1775 through the war's duration. It established an army, created its own money, and declared independence once all hope for a peaceful reconciliation with Britain was gone. (p. 165)

Second Great Awakening: A series of evangelical Protestant revivals extending from the 1790s to the 1830s that prompted thousands of conversions and widespread optimism about Americans' capacity for progress and reform. (p. 304)

Second Hundred Years' War: An era of warfare beginning with the War of the League of Augsburg in 1689 and lasting until the defeat of Napoleon at Waterloo in 1815. In that time, England fought in seven major wars; the longest era of peace lasted only twenty-six years. (p. 82)

secret ballot: Form of voting that allows the voter to enter a choice in privacy without having to submit a recognizable ballot or to voice the choice out loud to others. (p. 339)

self-made man: A nineteenth-century ideal that celebrated men who rose to wealth or social prominence from humble origins through self-discipline, hard work, and temperate habits. (p. 269)

semisedentary societies: Societies whose members combine slash-and-burn agriculture with hunting and fishing. Semisedentary societies often occupy large village sites near their fields in the summer, then disperse during the winter months into smaller hunting, fishing, and gathering camps, regathering again in spring to plant their crops. (p. 8)

Seneca Falls Convention: The first women's rights convention in the United States. Held in Seneca Falls, New York, in 1848, it resulted in a manifesto extending to women the egalitarian republican ideology of the Declaration of Independence. (p. 328)

sharecropping: The labor system by which landowners and impoverished southern farmworkers, particularly African Americans, divided the proceeds from crops harvested on the landowner's property. With local merchants providing supplies — in exchange for a lien on the crop — sharecropping pushed farmers into cash-crop production and often trapped them in long-term debt. (p. 444)

Shays's Rebellion: A 1786–1787 uprising led by dissident farmers in western Massachusetts, many of them Revolutionary War veterans, protesting the taxation policies of the eastern elites who controlled the state's government. (p. 191)

Slaughter-House Cases: A group of decisions begun in 1873 in which the Court began to undercut the power of the Fourteenth Amendment to protect African American rights. (p. 456)

"slave power" conspiracy: The political argument, made by abolitionists, free soilers, and Republicans in the pre–Civil War years, that southern slaveholders were using their unfair representative advantage under the three-fifths compromise of the Constitution, as well as their clout within the Democratic Party, to demand extreme federal proslavery policies (such as annexation of Cuba) that the majority of American voters would not support. (p. 369)

slave society: A society in which the institution of slavery affects all aspects of life. (p. 335)

Sons of Liberty: Colonists — primarily middling merchants and artisans — who banded together to protest the Stamp Act and other imperial reforms of the 1760s. The group originated in Boston in 1765 but soon spread to all the colonies. (p. 148)

South Atlantic System: A new agricultural and commercial order that produced sugar, tobacco, rice, and other tropical and subtropical products for an international market. Its plantation societies were ruled by European planter-merchants and worked by hundreds of thousands of enslaved Africans. (p. 86)

Special Field Order No. 15: An order by General William T. Sherman, later reversed by policymakers, that granted confiscated land to formerly enslaved families in Georgia and South Carolina so they could farm independently. (p. 426)

Specie Circular: An executive order in 1836 that required the Treasury Department to accept only gold and silver in payment for lands in the national domain. (p. 299)

spoils system: The widespread award of public jobs to political supporters after an electoral victory. In 1829, Andrew Jackson instituted the system on the national level, arguing that the rotation of officeholders was preferable to a permanent group of bureaucrats. (p. 277)

squatter: Someone who settles on land he or she does not own or rent. Many eighteenth-century settlers established themselves on land before it was surveyed and entered for sale, requesting the first right to purchase the land when sales began. (p. 114)

Stamp Act Congress: A congress of delegates from nine assemblies that met in New York City in October 1765 to protest the loss of American "rights and liberties," especially the right to trial by jury. The congress challenged the constitutionality of both the Stamp and Sugar Acts by declaring that only the colonists' elected representatives could tax them. (p. 148)

Stamp Act of 1765: British law imposing a tax on all paper used in the colonies. Widespread resistance to the Stamp Act prevented it from taking effect and led to its repeal in 1766. (p. 146)

states' rights: An interpretation of the Constitution that exalts the sovereignty of the states and circumscribes the authority of the national government. (p. 286)

Stono Rebellion: Slave uprising in 1739 along the Stono River in South Carolina in which a group of slaves armed themselves, plundered six plantations, and killed more than twenty colonists. Colonists quickly suppressed the rebellion. (p. 97)

Sugar Act of 1764: British law that decreased the duty on French molasses, making it more attractive for shippers to obey the law, and at the same time raised penalties for smuggling. The act enraged New England merchants, who opposed both the tax and the fact that prosecuted merchants would be tried by British-appointed judges in a vice-admiralty court. (p. 145)

Tariff of Abominations: A tariff enacted in 1828 that raised duties significantly on raw materials, textiles, and iron goods. New York senator Van Buren hoped to win the support of farmers in New York, Ohio, and Kentucky with the tariff, but it enraged the South, which had no industries that needed tariff protection and resented the higher cost of imported dutied goods. (p. 283)

task system: A system of labor common in the rice-growing regions of South Carolina in which a slave was assigned a daily task to complete and allowed to do as he wished upon its completion. (p. 346)

Tea Act of May 1773: British act that lowered the existing tax on tea and granted exemptions to the East India Company to make their tea cheaper in the colonies and entice boycotting Americans to buy it. Resistance to the Tea Act led to the passage of the Coercive Acts and imposition of military rule in Massachusetts. (p. 158)

tenancy: The rental of property. To attract tenants in New York's Hudson River Valley, Dutch and English manorial lords granted long tenancy leases, with the right to sell improvements — houses and barns, for example — to the next tenant. (p. 108)

Ten Percent Plan: A plan proposed by President Abraham Lincoln during the Civil War, but never implemented, that would have granted amnesty to most ex-Confederates and allowed each rebellious state to return to the Union as soon as 10 percent of its voters had taken a loyalty oath and the state had approved the Thirteenth Amendment. (p. 434)

toleration: The allowance of different religious practices. Lord Baltimore persuaded the Maryland assembly to enact the Toleration Act (1649), which granted all Christians the right to follow their beliefs and hold church services. The crown imposed toleration on Massachusetts Bay in its new royal charter of 1691. (p. 59)

town meeting: A system of local government in New England in which all male heads of households met regularly to elect selectmen, levy local taxes, and regulate markets, roads, and schools. (p. 65)

Townshend Act of 1767: British law that established new duties on tea, glass, lead, paper, and painters' colors imported into the colonies. The Townshend duties led to boycotts and heightened tensions between Britain and the American colonies. (p. 151)

Trail of Tears: Forced westward journey of Cherokees from their lands in Georgia to present-day Oklahoma in 1838. Nearly a quarter of the Cherokees died en route. (p. 292)

transcendentalism: A nineteenth-century American intellectual movement that posited the importance of an ideal world of mystical knowledge and harmony beyond the immediate grasp of the senses. Influenced by romanticism, transcendentalists Ralph Waldo Emerson and Henry David Thoreau called for the critical examination of society and emphasized individuality, self-reliance, and nonconformity. (p. 310)

transcontinental railroad: The railway line completed on May 10, 1869, that connected the Central Pacific and Union Pacific lines, enabling goods to move by railway from the eastern United States all the way to California. (p. 462)

Treaty of Ghent: The treaty signed on Christmas Eve 1814 that ended the War of 1812. It retained the prewar borders of the United States. (p. 228)

Treaty of Greenville: A 1795 treaty between the United States and various Indian tribes in Ohio. American negotiators acknowledged Indian ownership of the land, and, in return for various payments, the Western Confederacy ceded most of Ohio to the United States. (p. 216)

Treaty of Kanagawa: An 1854 treaty in which, after a show of military force by U.S. Commodore Matthew Perry, leaders of Japan agreed to permit American ships to refuel at two Japanese ports. (p. 378)

Treaty of Paris of 1783: The treaty that ended the Revolutionary War. In the treaty, Great Britain formally recognized American independence and relinquished its claims to lands south of the Great Lakes and east of the Mississippi River. (p. 183)

tribalization: The adaptation of stateless peoples to the demands imposed on them by neighboring states. (p. 82)

twenty-Negro rule: A law adopted by the Confederate Congress that exempted one man from military conscription for every twenty slaves owned by a family. The law showed how dependence on coerced slave labor could be a military disadvantage, and it exacerbated class resentments among nonslaveholding whites who were required to serve in the army. (p. 411)

Underground Railroad: An informal network of whites and free blacks in the South that assisted fugitive slaves to reach freedom in the North. (p. 323)

unions: Organizations of workers that began during the Industrial Revolution to bargain with employers over wages, hours, benefits, and control of the workplace. (p. 261)

U.S. Fisheries Commission: A federal bureau established in 1871 that made recommendations to stem the decline in wild fish. Its creation was an important step toward wildlife conservation and management. (p. 478)

U.S. Sanitary Commission: An organization that supported the Union war effort through professional and volunteer medical aid. (p. 414)

utopias: Communities founded by reformers and transcendentalists to help realize their spiritual and moral potential and to escape from the competition of modern industrial society. (p. 312)

Valley Forge: A military camp in which George Washington's army of 12,000 soldiers and hundreds of camp followers suffered horribly in the winter of 1777–1778. (p. 176)

vice-admiralty court: A maritime tribunal presided over by a royally appointed judge, with no jury. (p. 145)

Virginia and Kentucky Resolutions: Resolutions of 1798 condemning the Alien and Sedition Acts that were submitted to the federal government by the Virginia and Kentucky state legislatures. The resolutions tested the idea that state legislatures could judge the constitutionality of federal laws and nullify them. (p. 214)

Virginia Plan: A plan drafted by James Madison that was presented at the Philadelphia Constitutional Convention. It designed a powerful three-branch government, with representation in both houses of the congress tied to population; this plan would have eclipsed the voice of small states in the national government. (p. 193)

virtual representation: The claim made by British politicians that the interests of the American colonists were adequately represented in Parliament by merchants who traded with the colonies and by absentee landlords (mostly sugar planters) who owned estates in the West Indies. (p. 147)

Wade-Davis Bill: A bill proposed by Congress in July 1864 that required an oath of allegiance by a majority of each state's adult white men, new governments formed only by those who had never taken up arms against the Union, and permanent disenfranchisement of Confederate leaders. The plan was passed but pocket vetoed by President Abraham Lincoln. (p. 434)

Waltham-Lowell System: A system of labor using young women recruited from farm families to work in factories in Lowell, Chicopee, and other sites in Massachusetts and New Hampshire. The women lived in company boardinghouses with strict rules and curfews and were often required to attend church. (p. 249)

Whigs: The second national party, the Whig Party arose in 1834 when a group of congressmen contested Andrew Jackson's policies and conduct. The party identified itself with the pre-Revolutionary American and British parties—also called Whigs—that had opposed the arbitrary actions of British monarchs. (p. 293)

Whiskey Rebellion: A 1794 uprising by farmers in western Pennsylvania in response to enforcement of an unpopular excise tax on whiskey. (p. 209)

Wilmot Proviso: The 1846 proposal by Representative David Wilmot of Pennsylvania to ban slavery in territory acquired from the U.S.-Mexico War. (p. 368)

Woman's Loyal National League: An organization of Unionist women that worked to support the war effort, hoping the Union would recognize women's patriotism with voting rights after the war. (p. 414)

Wounded Knee: The 1890 massacre of Sioux Indians by American cavalry at Wounded Knee Creek, South Dakota. Sent to suppress the Ghost Dance, soldiers caught up with fleeing Lakotas and killed as many as three hundred. (p. 488)

XYZ Affair: A 1797 incident in which American negotiators in France were rebuffed for refusing to pay a substantial bribe. The incident led the United States into an undeclared war that curtailed American trade with the French West Indies. (p. 213)

Yellowstone National Park: Established in 1872 by Congress, Yellowstone was the United States's first national park. (p. 477)

Index

About the Authors

Rebecca Edwards is Eloise Ellery Professor of History at Vassar College, where she teaches courses on nineteenth-century politics, the Civil War, the frontier West, and women, gender, and sexuality. She is the author of, among other publications, *Angels in the Machinery: Gender in American Party Politics from the Civil War to the Progressive Era*; *New Spirits: Americans in the "Gilded Age," 1865–1905*; and the essay "Women's and Gender History" in *The New American History*. She is currently working on a book about the role of childbearing in the expansion of America's nineteenth-century empire.

Eric Hinderaker is Professor of History at the University of Utah. His research explores early modern imperialism, relations between Europeans and Native Americans, military-civilian relations in the Atlantic world, and comparative colonization. His most recent book, *Boston's Massacre*, was published in 2017. His other publications include *Elusive Empires: Constructing Colonialism in the Ohio Valley, 1673–1800*; *The Two Hendricks: Unraveling a Mohawk Mystery*, which won the Herbert H. Lehman Prize for Distinguished Scholarship in New York History from the New York Academy of History; and, with Peter C. Mancall, *At the Edge of Empire: The Backcountry in British North America*.

Robert O. Self is Mary Ann Lippitt Professor of American History at Brown University. His research focuses on urban history, American politics, and the post-1945 United States. He is the author of *American Babylon: Race and the Struggle for Postwar Oakland*, which won four professional prizes, including the James A. Rawley Prize from the Organization of American Historians, and *All in the Family: The Realignment of American Democracy Since the 1960s*. He is currently at work on a book about the centrality of houses, cars, and children to family consumption in the twentieth-century United States.

James A. Henretta is Professor Emeritus of American History at the University of Maryland, College Park. His publications include *The Evolution of American Society, 1600–1815*, *The Origins of American Capitalism*, and an edited volume, *Republicanism and Liberalism in America and the German States, 1750–1850*. His most recent publications include two long articles, "Magistrates, Common Law Lawyers, Legislators: The Three Legal Systems of British America" and "Charles Evans Hughes and the Strange Death of Liberal America," derived from his ongoing research on the liberal state in America, and in particular New York, 1820–1975.